Serbia

SINCE 1989

POLITICS AND SOCIETY UNDER MILOŠEVIĆ AND AFTER

EDITED BY SABRINA P. RAMET AND VJERAN PAVLAKOVIĆ

UNIVERSITY OF WASHINGTON PRESS • SEATTLE AND LONDON

This publication was supported in part by the Jackson School
Publications Fund, established through the generous support of the
Henry M. Jackson Foundation and other donors, in cooperation
with the Henry M. Jackson School of International Studies
and the University of Washington Press.

University of Washington Press
P.O. Box 50096, Seattle, WA 98145
www.washington.edu/uwpress

Library of Congress Cataloging-in-Publication Data
Serbia since 1989 : politics and society under Milošević and after /
edited by Sabrina P. Ramet and Vjeran Pavlakovic.
p.   cm.
Includes index.
ISBN 0-295-98538-0 (pbk. : alk. paper)
1. Serbia—History—1992–   2. Yugoslav War, 1991–1995—Serbia
and Montenegro—Serbia.   3. Milošević, Slobodan, 1941–
I. Ramet, Sabrina P., 1949–   II. Pavlakovic, Vjeran.
DR2049.S47 2005   949.7103—dc22   2005008069

TO GYÖRGY PÉTERI

AND

VERA AND IVAN PAVLAKOVIĆ

CONTENTS

PREFACE

Serbia continues to fascinate us, as few other countries have done. It remains a mysterious country—not because there are vast secrets there, but because it is the quintessential "Balkan" land if by "Balkan" we mean a land lying on the southeastern doorstep of Vienna and having a history of intrigue; because it occupies the twilight zone between democracy and authoritarianism; because it seems to be a land which hatches conspiracies and cabals; because it is a society important sectors of which are in denial: not just of the extent of Serbs' responsibility for the war and for the atrocities committed in the course of that war, not just of ordinary Serbs' complicity in the atrocities committed in Kosovo, and not just of the illegitimacy of the "Greater Serbia" project, but, for some people (as noted in chapter 10), of liberalism itself. A society in which denial is mainstream, in which nationalism still tends to be viewed as positive, in which there has been a sense of crisis in the air for most of the past century, is a society in which movement forward toward stable democracy can only be difficult.

Among the Yugoslav successor states, Serbia remains the key. The attitude of the government of Serbia will affect the future of Montenegro, Kosovo, and Bosnia-Herzegovina in obvious ways, as well as that of Croatia in less obvious ways. While Serbia may no longer have the military muscle it flexed in the early 1990s, it remains an important element for Balkan security. A stable Serbia can contribute to stability throughout the region, while continued political instability can send out ripples affecting other societies.

We are profoundly grateful to our volume contributors, for their professionalism, for their willingness to undertake revisions as needed, and for their patience during the review process. We also wish to thank Michael Duckworth, executive editor at the press, for his sensible advice; Stephen E. Hanson, director of the Russian, East European, and Central

Asian Studies Program at the University of Washington, who generously allocated funds to support a small symposium in Seattle in February 2002, at which two of the chapters published in this volume were presented; Sami Repishti for his helpful comments on an earlier draft of Frances Trix's chapter; and Christine M. Hassenstab for assisting in the copyediting of this manuscript. We are also grateful to Ozren Žunec, editor of *Polemos,* for permission to reprint chapter 5 (which appeared originally in vol. 5 of *Polemos,* nos. 1–2, December 2002); and Helge Blakkisrud, editor of *Nordisk Øst-forum,* for permission to publish a revised, English translation of Kari Osland's chapter (which appeared originally in vol. 16 of that journal [no. 2, 2002, pp. 5–18], under the title "Rettsaken mot Slobodan Milošević—et overblikk"). A portion of Dennis Reinhartz's chapter was originally published in *The South Slav Journal* (vol. 23, Spring-Summer 2002, pp. 39–45), under the title "The Roma and the Wars of Yugoslav Succession"; we are grateful to Nemanja Marčetić, editor of *South Slav Journal,* for permission to reuse this material.

SABRINA P. RAMET
Trondheim, Norway

VJERAN PAVLAKOVIĆ
Zagreb, Croatia

SERBIA SINCE 1989

INTRODUCTION

Serbia as a Dysfunctional State

VJERAN PAVLAKOVIĆ

"To live without Milošević is a feeling that spreads slowly, that enters the veins slowly, very slowly. . . . Tired, I salute the Revolution and devote myself to a bottle of 1997 Chardonnay. I officially close the chapter of my life of these thirteen years and try to begin to be normal."—PETAR LUKOVIĆ, journalist in Belgrade[1]

Since 1989, Serbia has transformed from the largest republic of Eastern Europe's most liberal country to an impoverished, barely functioning state, still in the process of disintegration and rife with numerous political, economic, and social problems. All the problems of the last thirteen years cannot be placed at the feet of one man, but the regime and political system that emerged under Slobodan Milošević can certainly be held accountable for the situation in which Serbia, one of two republics left in the Union of Serbia and Montenegro, finds itself in the beginning of the twenty-first century. The stagnation of Yugoslavia's communist system, economic crises, the political upheavals in Europe at the end of the 1980s, and resurgent nationalism throughout the six Yugoslav republics all contributed to the catastrophe which engulfed Yugoslavia in the 1990s. Rather than choosing to pursue further democratization and economic liberalization, Yugoslavia's leaders, and especially Milošević, opted for the doctrine of collective rights as strategies of political mobilization. Like his counterparts in Croatia and Bosnia-Herzegovina, Franjo Tudjman and Alija Izetbegović, Milošević used nationalism to attain, and then preserve, political power. His reign was authoritarian, yet maintained a facade of democracy. The regime retained the symbols and rhetoric of the Left but courted the extreme Right and stoked the fires of national hatred. The economic system appeared to be a chaotic mix of socialism, self-management, and capitalism, although the mafiazation of the economic sector made these terms meaningless. The chapters of this book seek to trace the transformation of Serbia (and more broadly the Yugoslav federation) from the twilight of the communist era to what it has become today: a dysfunctional state.

Each of the chapters delves into the details of what a dysfunctional state actually is. The rule of Milošević and his Serbian Socialist Party (SPS) lacked political and moral legitimacy, relying instead on the power of symbols and a seemingly endless series of conflicts to preserve his leadership. The system was also intended to maintain the power of Serbia's political and economic elite, as long as they proved useful to Milošević and his wife, Mirjana Marković. The ruling family's control over the Serbian economy led to the pauperization of society and created social problems which will continue to be felt for years to come. The dysfunctionality of the state is even more apparent in the further disintegration of the state itself, not only in the physical removal of territories from Belgrade's control (such as Kosovo) but also in the inability of the FRY's leadership to agree on the future structure of any joint state.

Chapter 2, "Serbia Transformed? Political Dynamics in the Milošević Era and After," outlines the leading political trends in Serbia from the consolidation of power by Milošević until his downfall. Despite his eventual removal by the will of the people, the Milošević regime was for the most part successful in perpetuating its control over the Serbian political establishment. Apart from the personal charismatic leadership skills of Milošević himself, the relative longevity of a government which lost four successive wars was due to the control of both symbolic (nationalist intellectuals, traditional and communist myths, the Serbian Orthodox Church) and concrete (the media, economic infrastructure, the army, regular and secret police) levers of power. As a communist apparatchik, Milošević was initially wary of the Memorandum drafted by the Serbian Academy of Sciences and Arts (SANU) in 1986, but following his experience with the Kosovo Serbs in 1987, he realized there was a significant base of support among influential Serbian intellectuals for the nationalist project. Serbian nationalist myths, from the Kosovo epic of 1389 to the Partisan victory of World War Two, were employed to realize the project of essentially creating a Greater Serbian state. Thus the symbols of the Chetniks, while not used directly by the regime, were tolerated and even co-opted as strategies of political survival, since the ideologies of both the extreme Left and Right envisioned an expanded, and centralized, Serbian state.

The Serbian Orthodox Church was likewise politicized and collaborated with the Milošević regime, as described in Sabrina P. Ramet's chapter "The Politics of the Serbian Orthodox Church." The lack of liberal voices within the Church hierarchy was the result of a number of factors, including the inherently national character of the Orthodox Church, the absence of any tradition of reform, and a greater degree of state control during the communist era, when the Church did not have access to outside resources as did the Catholic Church in other communist countries. Unlike the Catholic Church in Croatia, which criticized Tudjman's policies in Bosnia-Herzegovina, the Serbian Orthodox Church wholeheartedly supported the creation of a Greater Serbia, and as Ramet argues, actually condemned Milošević when he backed down from this endeavor in order to preserve his position of power. The chapter by Biljana Bijelić, "Nationalism, Motherhood, and the Reordering of Women's Power," details how women also became symbolic foundations of the Serbian state. Women became subjugated to the nationalist, patriarchal agenda of the Milošević regime, valued for their reproductive abilities to create soldiers for the state. As Bijelić argues in her chapter, women's reproductive and political rights gained under socialism were stripped away with the victory of the nationalist and traditionalist forces in Serbia, although their value in the economic sphere prevented a backlash in their status in the labor market.

The appropriation of nationalist symbols was only part of the Milošević political strategy; absolute control over the institutions of the state, especially the forces of repression, was essential for the survival of Milošević. Control of the armed forces is obviously vital in any modern state, but the illegitimate political system which developed in Serbia under Milošević required the state to maintain a tight grip on the media and economic assets. The ongoing conflict between the authorities and independent media reveals the importance of the free flow of ideas and information and Milošević's understanding of the danger it posed to his power. Independent radio and television stations and the Internet became bastions of opposition against Milošević. The media also played a key role in stirring up national hatreds at the beginning of the conflict in the former Yugoslavia and, throughout the 1990s, served to keep the citizens of Serbia in the dark, limiting information about political and social alternatives.

Two chapters in this volume discuss the economic impact of the Milošević years on Serbian society. "The Impact of the War on Serbia: Spoiled Appetites and Progressive Decay," by James Gow and Milena Michalski, takes a broad view of the impact of the war, discussing social desiccation, demographic outflow, and social atomization, as well as economic deterioration, while Maja Miljković and Marko Attila Hoare, in "Crime and the Economy under Milošević and His Successors," illustrate exactly how Milošević's control of Serbia's economic infrastructure enabled him to create a small elite which then became politically loyal. Throughout the 1990s, the Serbian economy became increasingly militarized and criminalized. Sanction busting, drug running, war profiteering, and the doling out of economic assets to political allies erected a completely illegitimate economic system upon the ruins of the Serbian economy. This contributed to social devastation in Serbia, which saw its best citizens flee the country for better opportunities in the West, while the remainder became politically apathetic and easily manipulated by the regime as they struggled for daily survival. The future of Serbia is its young people, and even though they played an important role in bringing down Milošević, the impact of his disastrous policies will continue to be seen in the years to come.

The war also had a psychological impact on Serbian society, as Sabrina P. Ramet shows in her chapter "Under the Holy Lime Tree: The Inculcation of Neurotic and Psychotic Syndromes as a Serbian Wartime Strategy, 1986–1995," which focuses on the themes of victimization, dehumanization of designated "others," belittlement, conspiracy, entitlement, and superhuman powers which emerged in Serbian propaganda.

Like other state institutions in the Milošević era, the legal system lost legitimacy after becoming a tool of the regime, and it will take Serbia a long time to develop the rule of law. As Eric D. Gordy argues in "Postwar Guilt and Responsibility in Serbia: The Effort to Confront It and the Effort to Avoid It," the inability (and unwillingness) of Serbian courts to address the issue of war crimes committed by Serbian forces has severe social consequences, which will further delay the pace of reforms. The manipulation of history was one of Milošević's tactics in mobilizing support, and if Serbia continues to avoid issues of accountability and responsibility, the political system will remain locked in the xenophobic and nationalist mentality of the 1990s.

Freedom of the media will be a vital aspect of a democratic Serbia, one which takes a critical look at what happened in Yugoslavia as it tore itself apart. The failure of police to stop assaults against visitors and organizers in Užice, Čačak, and Kragujevac of photographer Ron Haviv's exhibition of war photos, which graphically showed some of the crimes committed by Serbian forces, reveals that many in Serbia are still living in the darkness of Milošević's propaganda machine.[2] It is the international community and the ICTY, described in "The Trial of Slobodan Milošević," by Kari Osland, which has taken on the responsibility of investigating war crimes and punishing their perpetrators. However, cooperation with The Hague has been politically dangerous to reformers in both Serbia and Croatia, and in some cases has given fuel to nationalist forces waiting to make a comeback. In Croatia, attempts to arrest indicted General Janko Bobetko would certainly have resulted in massive street demonstrations and unrest, while in Serbia (and Republika Srpska), Ratko Mladić and Radovan Karadžić remain on the loose. The success and legitimacy of the ICTY are essential for the people of the region to avoid collective guilt and prevent the mistakes of the post-World War Two era, when the victorious communists created myths to cover up their own massacres and placed the blame solely on local "collaborators." This proved to be a formula for disaster when communism unraveled, mass graves were dug up, and the victims of World War Two became justification for a new round of communal violence. If international law is to prevail, it will require the cooperation of all the nations in the world. The unilateral policies and rejection of the new International Criminal Court (ICC) by the United States represent severe repercussions for the success of former Yugoslav states to see international law as being legitimate and functioning, in the long term, in their own best national interests.

Considering that much of Milošević's nationalism was based on the blaming of Serbia's problems on other national groups, Serbia (and, more broadly, the Union of Serbia and Montenegro) will, not surprisingly, continue to face challenges from the many ethnic groups in this very heterogeneous state. The dysfunctional nature of the FRY is made glaringly apparent in the chapters by Emil Kerenji ("Vojvodina since 1988"), Reneo Lukić ("From the Federal Republic of Yugoslavia to the Union of Serbia and Montenegro"), Dennis Reinhartz ("The Yugoslav Roma under Slobodan Milošević and After"), and Frances Trix ("Kosovar Albanians between a Rock and a Hard Place"). Since the Milošević system involved a clear rejection of the liberal project and democracy in Serbia during his reign was a farce, it is not hard to see why the constituent parts of the Yugoslav federation saw the state as illegitimate and sought to disassociate themselves from it. The Kosovar Albanians began to challenge the legitimacy of Milošević's Serbia in October 1991, when they declared a Republic of Kosova and established a parallel shadow state. After the conflict of 1998–99, NATO intervention, and the establishment of a protectorate under the control of the international community, it seems unlikely that Kosovo will ever again be subordinated to Belgrade's rule. Vojvodina, which along with Kosovo had the status of autonomous province before 1989, also resented the centralizing policies of Milošević's government.

The economic impoverishment and influx of refugees and other consequences of Milošević's rule have upset the generally good interethnic relations in this heterogeneous region, resulting in significant support for a return to autonomous status and even independence from Serbia. While Serbia's policies toward its minorities, in particular Roma, Muslims, and Albanians (in the Preševo region of southern Serbia), continue to be criticized by international and domestic human rights groups, Montenegro's bid for independence from the FRY is not ethnically based. Montenegro's president, Milo Djukanović, challenged the legitimacy of federal institutions when it became apparent that Milošević would disregard the constitution and the decisions of the parliament in order to preserve his own power. There are a number of other factors, such as political ambitions, economic interests, and a desire to distance Montenegro from the taint of war crimes, which have pushed Montenegro away from the Yugoslav federation. Overall, Milošević's political system based exclusively on collective rights made the state no longer legitimate in the eyes of a significant portion of the citizens in the FRY, thus contributing to the fragmentation of the federation and the still uncertain future of the state.

During the transition of Serbia from one illegitimate system (communism) to another illegitimate system (extreme nationalism), Serbia's opposition was unable to effectively challenge Milošević even when the regime was seemingly on the verge of collapse at several points during the 1990s. The divisions and conflicts within the opposition are detailed in "An Airplane with Eighteen Pilots: Serbia after Milošević," by Obrad Kesić, which follows the rise and fall of several coalitions before and after the events of October 2000. The personalities of the leaders of the opposition parties partly explain their inability for more than a decade to win the support of Serbia's electorate, since they squabbled among themselves and failed to offer a significant alternative to Milošević. Furthermore, in the atmosphere of Milošević's Serbia, it became impossible to realistically offer a political program which did not address the "national question," and most challengers to Milošević criticized the SPS for failing to achieve the goals of a Greater Serbia rather than criticizing the attempt to create it in the first place. Kesić analyzes how the divisions in the DOS (Democratic Opposition of Serbia) coalition, and the conflict between Zoran Djindjić and Vojislav Koštunica, hindered reforms after the honeymoon period following Milošević's downfall.

Despite the overthrow of Milošević in October 2000, Serbian politics continues to be played out in the arena created under a nationalist, authoritarian regime. In other words, symbols play more important roles than issues, and nationalist discourse remains commonplace. Vojislav Koštunica, Yugoslav president and candidate for the Serbian presidential elections of 29 September 2002, referred to Republika Srpska (one entity of the theoretically unified state of Bosnia-Herzegovina) as territory which was only "temporarily separated" from Serbia at a speech in Mali Zvornik on 7 September 2002.[3] While Koštunica later attempted to clarify his statements as merely encouraging more porous borders, others in the region and in the international community interpreted them as confirmation that the ideology of a Greater Serbia was still alive in the post-Milošević era. The Serbian press reported representatives of the European Union dismissing such comments as preelection tactics intended to gain the votes of Bosnian Serbs; nevertheless, they reveal an emphasis on the same national question manipulated by Milošević in the 1990s.[4] The candidate for the SPS, noted actor Velemir "Bata" Živojinović, stated in an interview that he would kill Boris Dvornik, a Croatian actor who had starred in some twenty films with Živojinović, if Dvornik ever came to Serbia, because "Serbs are wild men [divljaci]."[5] Extreme nationalist Vojislav Šešelj, now on trial at the ICTY for war crimes committed in Croatia, had the support of 14 percent of Serbs in preelection polls after he was endorsed by Milošević as the candidate for the Serbian Radical Party (SRS).[6] His supporters displayed a "wealth of Chetnik iconography" at a rally in Belgrade, where he promised not to forget Republika Srpska and the Serbian Krajina, the former territory held by rebel Serbs in Croatia.[7]

The presidential candidate for the parties of the DOS coalition (Grupa gradjana, Citizens' Group), Miroslav Labus, was the only leading candidate to emphasize his desire to be "the president of all citizens of Serbia,"[8] similar to the campaign goals of President Stipe Mesić in the 2000 elections in Croatia, marking a break from the nationalist policies of Tudjman. In a campaign speech in Novi Pazar, Labus declared that "Serbia is the state of Serbs, Bošnjaks [i.e., Muslims], and other citizens who need to live together to solve their economic issues and to enter into the European Union together."[9] For his antinational position, Labus was pelted with eggs in the city of Čačak by supporters of Velimir Ilić, the mayor of Čačak, who ended his own presidential bid in order to endorse Koštunica.[10]

It will be up to the new president of Serbia, and possibly new government, if early elections are called, to reconstruct Serbia as a functional and legitimate state. For this to happen, the Serbian political body needs to reject not just Milošević but also his nationalist policies. There has to be a critical and serious discussion of the Milošević era and the crimes which were perpetrated in the name of Serbia and Serbs, who in many ways ended up being the biggest losers of Yugoslavia's collapse. This was not due to the machinations of the international community, minorities, or neighboring ethnic groups, but due to the policies of their own leadership. Once those responsible for crimes against humanity are held accountable, Serbia can build a society based on tolerance, democratic principles, and moral values. This needs to take place not only in the political system but also in the economic sector, in education, in the courts, in the media, and in society in general. A rejection of the liberal project and a continuity with the Milošević era will only lead to the further collapse of the state and ongoing crises with the numerous economic and social challenges facing Serbia in the twenty-first century.

Notes

1. Institute for War and Peace Reporting, "New Serbian Dawn," *Balkan Crisis Report*, no. 183, 6 October 2000; online version at www.iwpr.net.

2. *Danas* (Belgrade), 14–15 September 2002, pp. 12–13.

3. Ibid., p. 3.

4. Ibid.

5. *Jutarnji list* (Zagreb), 20 September 2002, p. 73.

6. *Jutarnji list*, 25 September 2002, p. 15.

7. *Jutarnji list*, 27 September 2002, p. 18.

8. *Danas*, 14–15 September 2002, p. 4.

9. Ibid.

10. *Jutarnji list*, 25 September 2002, p. 15.

THE CENTER

SERBIA TRANSFORMED?

Political Dynamics in the Milošević Era and After

VJERAN PAVLAKOVIĆ

I

On 28 June 1989, Slobodan Milošević addressed a crowd of several hundred thousand Serbs at Gazimestan in Kosovo Province, near the site of the medieval battle of Kosovo Polje and the heartland of spiritual Serbdom. It was significant that Milošević chose the site of a perceived Serbian defeat (the battle in 1389 had been a military draw for both the Serbian and Ottoman forces, although in Serbian mythology it would go down as the Serbs' greatest loss) as the platform from which to address the crowd about the possibility of future battles, an ominous portent of the violence that would tear apart Yugoslavia in the 1990s.[1] Milošević was making clear parallels between the Battle of Kosovo Polje and the Yugoslav constitution of 1974, both considered to be defeats in the Serbian national consciousness. The battle in 1389 was the beginning of five hundred years of living under the Turkish yoke, while the 1974 constitution emasculated Serbia by creating two autonomous provinces and essentially transferring political power away from the center and giving it to the republics. Milošević's rise to power, beginning in 1987, was facilitated by his understanding of the dissent among Serbs regarding their status in socialist Yugoslavia. His crafty use of Serbian myths, nationalist symbols, and the media to mobilize Serbs in support of his stated goals—restoring Serbia's strength in the Yugoslav federation and reversing the decentralization of the 1974 constitution—was successfully channeled during the so-called "antibureaucratic revolution." By 1989, he had already installed allies in Vojvodina Province and Montenegro. Ethnic Serbs in Croatia, Bosnia, and Kosovo responded enthusiastically to Milošević's message, and it seemed as if Serbs would once again have the strongest position in a recentralized Yugoslavia.

However, fourteen years after his speech at the six hundredth anniversary of the Battle of Kosovo Polje, all of Milošević's promises have proven to be empty. Rather than the creation of a Greater Serbia, the Yugoslav state fragmented into several independent and semi-independent entities, while hundreds of thousands of Serbs have become refugees expelled from their ancestral homes. The independence of Croatia and Bosnia-Herzegovina was followed by the ethnic cleansing of Serbs, Croats, and Muslims, as the increasingly nationalistic leadership of all three ethnic groups strove to create ethnically homogeneous territorial units. The Serbian Republic of Krajina, set up by rebel Serbs in Croatia in 1991, was abandoned by Milošević in 1995 after they no longer proved politically useful, leading to the exodus of approximately two hundred thousand Serbs from Croatia after the Croatian army's military offensives, Operations Flash and Storm.[2] Continued repression of ethnic Albanians in the province of Kosovo led to NATO intervention in 1999, and resulted in the occupation of the territory by the international community, leaving the future status of Kosovo unclear. Even Montenegro, traditionally Serbia's strongest ally in the Yugoslav federation and the only other republic in the "Third Yugoslavia" (or Federal Republic of Yugoslavia, FRY), pushed for independence under the leadership of President Milo Djukanović.[3] Finally, Vojvodina, stripped of its autonomy by Milošević, also began demanding a return to its pre-1989 status and hinted at beginning a move toward independence, although this scenario remains highly unlikely.[4] Nevertheless, the end result of the Milošević regime was a devastated and weakened Serbia, economically enfeebled by international sanctions and lost wars, burdened by thousands of refugees, corrupt, criminalized, socially traumatized and infected by xenophobic nationalism, and considered a pariah state by most of the international community.

The end of Milošević's rule was hailed as the rebirth of a democratic Serbia and the return to normalized relations with the rest of Europe. The overthrow of Milošević in October 2000 in a "democratic revolution" and his extradition to The Hague in June 2001 seemed to clean the slate for Serbia and marked truly important changes. The role of Milošević in Serbian politics and more broadly the Yugoslav wars of the 1990s cannot be underestimated, and his removal was certainly the most important first step in the normalization of Serbian society. However, the system that Milošević built for more than a decade cannot be expected to completely collapse with the removal of one man, regardless of how much power and responsibility he had. The true level of change in Serbia remains to be seen.

This chapter will examine the nature of the Milošević regime, including the methods Milošević used to achieve and retain power. Key components of Serbian political development in the late 1980s and 1990s involved mass mobilization through fervent nationalism, the use of mythical, historical, and political symbols to prevent political change, control of media outlets, the reliance on force (including police, the Ministry of the Interior, and army) to repress opponents of the regime, the stifling of economic reform, and the creation of constant crises, often involving outside "enemies" of the state in order to keep the population loyal. While clearly an authoritarian state, Milošević's Serbia never took on the outward appearance of a full-blown dictatorship; Milošević was always careful to mask his regime with the facade of a democracy, although even this facade began to crumble in the last year of his rule. This chapter will also analyze the overthrow of Milošević in October 2000. What were the forces behind the "democratic revolution"? Was the revolution a rejection of Milošević's ideology, or a frustration with the fact that Milošević was unable to deliver on his promises? Finally, the chapter will look at the performance of the successors to the Milošević era, notably Yugoslav president Vojislav Koštunica and the late Serbian prime minister Zoran Djindjić. Koštunica has shown himself to be no less nationalistic than Milošević (which is precisely why the opposition chose him as their candidate, knowing that the Serbian body politic remained infected with nationalism), and has resisted cooperation with the West on numerous occasions. Djindjić represented the more pro-Western and reform-minded segment of Serbian politics, although he was repeatedly criticized for being too submissive to the demands of the international community, which rewarded reforms with direct economic aid. Tragically, Djindjić's increasingly bold reforms eventually cost him his life, highlighting the challenges Serbia faces in the post-Milošević era.

II

While it is clear that the dominant ideology of Serbia in the 1990s was nationalism, Milošević himself was a politician to whom nationalism was merely one facet of a strategy to achieve his goal; namely, to retain power at any cost. Serbia at the twilight of communist rule was fertile ground for the type of populist politics Milošević used to expand and consolidate his hold on the levers of power of the decaying, illegitimate Titoist system. As Yugoslavia unraveled around him, Milošević transformed the political system into something different, yet no more legitimate, shrouded in the symbols of both the Partisan struggle and older, traditional Serbian national imagery. Although the project to expand the nation-state was a dis-

astrous failure after four lost wars, it can be argued that as a politician
Milošević showed a crafty resilience and ability to stay in power, shifting
from a defender of socialist Yugoslavia to a hard-line nationalist defending Serbs everywhere, then transforming into a pragmatic negotiator with
the West when the pressure from the international community directly
threatened his power. Of course, Milošević was eventually removed from
power and is facing a war crimes tribunal in The Hague, but even there
he has shown his political savvy during his defense in front of the court,
and perhaps more importantly, in front of the Serbian public. His intense
cross-examination of witnesses from Kosovo, many of them ethnic Albanians who survived the rampage by Serb forces in the spring of 1999, offers
"an insight into the psychological pressure and deceit that he employed
both to gain and then [to] retain power in Serbia."[5] Opinion polls in Serbia reveal that most Serbs see Milošević successfully defending himself at
the court in The Hague, and that the trial is viewed as more than just a
case against Milošević, but against all of Serbia.[6]

As Milošević was rising through the ranks of the League of Communists of Serbia in the 1980s, dissent was brewing among Serbian intellectuals who blamed communism for weakening Serbia and allowing it to be
exploited by the other republics. This dissent was most pronounced in the
1986 Memorandum of the Serbian Academy of Sciences and Arts, which
was leaked to the press and revealed that among some Serbian intellectual
circles, criticism of the communist system was couched in fervently nationalistic terms. At this stage, Milošević did not respond positively to the
conclusions of the Memorandum, but there is no doubt that it revealed
to him the support which a nationalist program would enjoy among at
least a certain portion of Serbia's academics. The Serbian Orthodox
Church, at the core of Serbian ethnic identity and the preserver of Serbdom during the centuries of Ottoman rule, was another institution which
promoted Serbian nationalism in the 1980s, especially concerning issues
relating to Kosovo. Furthermore, many anticommunist dissidents, such
as Vuk Drašković, Vojislav Šešelj, and Vojislav Koštunica, likewise argued
for national rights for Serbs, often those outside of Serbia, rather than the
creation of a civil society based on citizenship and respect for individual
rights regardless of nationality. By 1989, Milošević had realized that the
atmosphere was ideal for a strong leader promising the restoration of
national rights to a historically exploited nation, and harnessed those
nationalistic forces to secure his grip on power.

As Sabrina P. Ramet notes in the conclusion, nationalism is not unique
to Serbia, but the conditions in Serbia at the end of the 1980s were nearly

ideal for the rise of a nationalist leader. Two factors which contributed to the great mobilizing potential of nationalism were "the ethnic heterogeneity of the population of Serbia (a third of which is made up of members of ethnic minorities) and long-standing tensions between ethnic groups."[7] Unlike Franjo Tudjman, the first president of Croatia whose nationalism had landed him in prison under the communists, Milošević worked within the framework of the Titoist system until he realized it could no longer serve to maintain him in power, at which point he made cosmetic changes—for example, the new political party he founded in July 1990, the Socialist Party of Serbia (SPS), retained much of the personnel and infrastructure of the League of Serbian Communists—and embraced the mantle of Serbian nationalism, to the extent that it was politically useful. Ivan Stambolić, Milošević's erstwhile mentor and friend, stated that "[Milošević] is willing to change ideology every day. He'll change his beliefs, allies as well. He'll use anyone and then throw them away."[8] Milošević was able to deftly balance the claim of continuing the socialist legacy while at the same time allowing the resurgence of nationalist forces, which were far more extreme and politically to the right, resulting in periodic coalitions with such unlikely partners as Šešelj's Serbian Radical Party (SRS) and Drašković's Serbian Renewal Movement (SPO). The structure of Serbian politics in the Milošević era reveals both the preponderance of symbols in Serbian political activity and the deep ideological divisions (communist vs. Chetnik) traceable to World War Two, two reasons nationalism wielded by a populist such as Milošević was able to sustain him in power as long as it did.

Robert Thomas argues in his comprehensive overview of Serbian politics in the 1990s that the "dominance of symbolism over politics" was a major factor in the failure to create a legitimate democratic system in Serbia after the transition from communist rule.[9] The predominance of historical and mythical symbols in political debate served to obfuscate the issues and allowed Milošević, despite bringing ruin to the Serbian state, to remain in power by casting himself as the archetypal Serbian hero resisting overwhelming odds. Belgrade scholar Ivan Čolović argues that especially in folklore form, political myths can gain legitimacy as the "voice of the people," a significant factor in a society such as Serbia's with its long tradition of folk tales.[10] The most important Serbian myth is the Kosovo epic, which emphasizes two recurrent themes in Serbian history, heroism and betrayal.[11] Since the Battle of Kosovo was interpreted as the loss of the Serbian medieval kingdom, the reconquest of that territory fueled the expansion of the independent Serbian state in the nineteenth and early twentieth centuries. Moreover, the loss at Kosovo Polje led to the migration of Serbs north, resulting in repeated attempts at uniting all Serbs in one state, which has tragically led to conflicts with other peoples of the former Yugoslavia. Between Milošević's first official visit to Kosovo in 1987 and his speech on the six hundredth anniversary of the fourteenth-century battle, he took up the cause of Serbs beyond the borders of Serbia proper, casting himself as a defender of Serbdom. After 1991, the creation of a Greater Serbia became even more explicit as the Yugoslav People's Army (JNA), cooperating with local Serbs in Croatia and Bosnia, made overt attempts at grabbing territory and expelling non-Serbs. However, when the support of Serbs across the Drina became politically costly, Milošević, not a true nationalist at heart, abandoned his erstwhile allies in the Croatian Krajina and in Republika Srpska. This is in contrast to Tudjman, for example, who stubbornly continued to finance Croats in the Herceg-Bosna para-state despite the negative impact on relations with the international community. At a time when the power of communist symbols was fading, Milošević was able to draw on symbols which were already considered legitimate by Serbs throughout Yugoslavia and had been endorsed by both the intellectual and religious establishments.

The messianic nature of the Kosovo epic, revolving around Prince Lazar's choosing the heavenly kingdom over the earthly one (leading to the defeat of the Serbian forces but securing a place in heaven), also contributed to the relative longevity of the Milošević regime. Despite repeated losses on the battlefield and international isolation, Milošević could still claim to be continuing Prince Lazar's legacy, which would find resonance among the majority of his constituents, who were for the most part from rural areas and not cosmopolitan, urban centers such as Belgrade or Novi Sad. The Kosovo epic also "casts the Serbian people as martyrs, eternally victims, and eternally sanctified by God."[12] In contrast to the image of Milošević and the SPS as the defenders of the national rights of Serbs, the opposition was consistently portrayed as betraying the Serbian cause, the contemporary incarnation of Vuk Branković, who, legend says, defected to the Ottoman side and contributed to the defeat of the Serbian forces in 1389. The common phrase *samo sloga spašava Srbe* (only unity can save the Serbs) highlights the stigma attached to the betrayal of the national interest. During periods of street protests, such as March 1991 or the winter of 1996–97, and in the aftermath of the NATO bombing, opposition groups and the student movement Otpor were often labeled as traitors, and efforts were made to draw connections between them and foreign powers, an implicit reference to the betrayal at the Battle of Kosovo. Many opposition parties were, however, even more nationalistic than Milošević, and relied on the same symbolism of Kosovo to attack the SPS. After the collapse of the Republic of Serbian Krajina in Croatia in 1995, the vice president of Koštunica's Democratic Party of Serbia (DSS), Vladan Batić, stated that "after six centuries Vuk Branković, for the first time, can sleep peacefully in his grave. A bigger traitor has now appeared and his name is Slobodan Milošević."[13]

Apart from deeply ingrained historical imagery, such as that associated with Kosovo, the legacy and divisions of World War Two also influenced the symbolic battlefield. Even though the SPS was allegedly a new party founded in 1990, it retained much of the communist legacy and symbolism, not to mention personnel.[14] The SPS remained essentially a party of the Left, and continued to uphold rituals and symbols associated with the Partisan struggle. In contrast, many of the opposition parties were anticommunist in nature, but unlike civic-based political parties in other postcommunist European countries, the ones in Serbia were based on reviving the Chetnik heritage, were pro-monarchist, and/or promoted extreme nationalism.[15] Chetnik symbols became commonplace by the late 1980s, and represented both the rebirth of Serbian nationalism and resistance to the communist system, which was reincarnated as the SPS. Drašković's SPO staged numerous public rallies at Ravna Gora, the wartime headquarters of the Chetnik leader Draža Mihailović, while Šešelj organized the paramilitary Serbian Chetnik Movement, eventually taking the title *vojvoda*, or "leader." According to Robert Thomas, the SPO's assimilation of the Ravna Gora tradition "gave to young activists a ready made and potent set of symbols in direct opposition to the communist symbols which had been embedded in Socialist state ritual."[16] Frequently, real issues became submerged as the ruling party and the opposition traded accusations of either being "communists under a different name" or fascists who wanted to create a "Chetnik Belgrade" after the victory of the opposition.[17] The overwhelming importance of political symbols made it impossible for true democratic reforms to take hold in Serbia, and enabled Milošević to appeal to common Serbs through symbols and myths already ingrained in society. Milošević was also able to mobilize support by his use of Ustasha symbolism, portraying Croats as fascists and providing justification for his project to create a Greater Serbia.[18]

A final element of Milošević's use of political symbols was his own role as a strong leader of a "national crusade." In this sense he was tapping into the Balkan tradition of strong, patriarchal leaders, which "accorded both with communist 'power relations' and with South Slav folk traditions."[19]

Military prowess and political leadership are intertwined in Serbian myths and legends, extending from the Battle of Kosovo to the resistance against Ottoman rule, and then to the heroic struggles against German aggression in the two world wars. Tito continued the tradition of a strong leader during the communist era, using force to maintain an iron grip on power and hold the country together. The weakness of the post-Tito leadership left the stage open for an ambitious man like Milošević to address Serbian grievances and reverse the alleged suppression of Serbs stemming from the hated 1974 constitution, and eventually lead Serbia on the warpath against the other Yugoslav republics.

Appropriating political symbols and using them to mobilize political support are two different things; Milošević accomplished both through his control of crucial media in Serbia from the time he made his famous appearance in Kosovo in April 1987. The most important tool for Milošević when it came to the media was Radio-Television Serbia (RTS), although a number of daily newspapers and weekly magazines contributed to the propagation of hate speech, which demonized both Serbia's ethnic enemies and the internal opposition. A study by the Helsinki Committee for Human Rights in Serbia concluded that hate speech in reference to ethnic and religious others became the essential component of the "political leadership and state agencies in Serbia, which we call *etatization of hate speech*."[20] The monopoly by the state of RTS in the early years of the Milošević regime was vital in creating the xenophobic atmosphere conducive to the sort of war-mongering Milošević and his allies were about to undertake outside Serbia's borders. This involved hate speech directed against Croats, Kosovar Albanians, and Bosnia's Muslims, often juxtaposing images of fascists from World War Two with the contemporary leadership in those republics or relying on historical comparisons stretching back to the Islamic conquest of the Balkans.[21]

Although Milošević never completely shut down independent media, he effectively, in the words of sociologist Eric D. Gordy, carried out the "destruction of alternatives."[22] The key component was of course control of RTS, which was the main source of information for most Serbs, especially as the economic catastrophe resulting from international sanctions limited the amount of money individuals could spend on newspapers and alternative media sources. Independent radio, local television stations, and opposition newspapers continued to function under Milošević, but they came under increasing pressure from the regime, often in the form of confiscation of equipment, loss of broadcasting licenses, or lawsuits which carried heavy fines. For example, in December 1996, Radio B-92 (originally established on 15 May 1989) was shut down during the massive street protests called by the opposition, and there were other times when the staff was harassed by the police, equipment was simply removed from the station, and the broadcasting signal jammed.[23] Likewise, television Studio B, under the control of Vuk Drašković, faced severe censorship and outright takeover when its programming threatened Milošević's monopoly on information. The newspaper *Borba*, which had been critical of Milošević, was effectively shut down in November 1994 following legal action by the authorities, its staff replaced by journalists willing to support the regime.[24] When Milošević was under heavy pressure, such as during the protests in the winter of 1996–97 and the NATO bombing in the spring of 1999, censorship increased to the point where there was nearly a complete information blackout. On 26 July 2000, journalist Miroslav Filipović was sentenced to seven years in prison for his reports on crimes committed by Serbian forces in Kosovo, one example of the lengths to which the Milošević regime went to silence its critics.[25] The difficulty in obtaining alternative sources of information and the constant propaganda streaming from state-controlled media stifled efforts by the opposition to mount an effective campaign against Milošević in the 1990s, and deceived the average Serb about the atrocities being committed in Croatia, Bosnia, and Kosovo by Serbian forces.

The control of information and the inability to change the political status quo were facilitated to a great extent by the economic situation, specifically three factors: the close alliance between the government and business, the pauperization of society, and the "mafiazation" of the economy. A characteristic of the Milošević regime was the control of Serbia's economic assets, inherited from the communist era and unreformed throughout the 1990s. According to Robert Thomas, "the immediate political circle surrounding [Mirjana] Marković, and through her Milošević, consisted of a clique of ultra-rich plutocrats whose business careers had been forged through the development of client-patron relationships with the state bureaucracy."[26] Thus, in return for political allegiance, Milošević handed over profitable business ventures and industries, which had been nationalized during socialist Yugoslavia, to influential members of Serbia's elite, tying their continued success to the survival of Milošević. Rather than destroying what existed of Serbia's private sector, the regime ensured that it was controlled by SPS loyalists.

In the years following the imposition of international sanctions on 30 May 1992, the Serbian economy collapsed, making it one of the poorest countries in Europe by the end of the decade. Even though the impoverishment of Serbia was a direct result of the government's policies, the economic conditions contributed to the regime's control over society. Since the average person was struggling merely to make ends meet on a day-to-day basis, there was less energy to be spent on engaging in opposition activity, in addition to less money available to get access to independent media sources.[27] This in turn produced an atmosphere of political apathy, undermining the efforts of the opposition to mobilize forces against Milošević.

Finally, the economic situation under sanctions created conditions for the emergence of a strong criminal element which had close ties to the regime. This was initially in the form of paramilitary units, which cooperated with regular JNA forces, were given varying levels of support (financial, logistical, etc.) by the Serbian government and the Interior Ministry, and were sanctioned by Milošević himself, who had personal contacts with a number of paramilitary leaders such as Željko Ražnatović "Arkan" and Vojislav Šešelj.[28] Not surprisingly, these paramilitary formations, responsible for a number of war crimes and atrocities, were manned by unsavory types with criminal records. The dual conditions of war and international sanctions turned weapon smuggling and sanctions busting into big business, creating an entire class of wealthy individuals engaged in criminal activity with links to the political, military, and economic leaderships. Because Milošević allowed this to develop unrestrained, "the entire economy of Serbia became reliant on illegal trading,"[29] not to mention the fact that rampant corruption spread through all facets of Serbian society.[30] The flagrant violations of the rule of law and the criminalization of society under Milošević greatly hindered the development of true democratic institutions in Serbia and contributed to the failure in creating a legitimate political system.

Political mobilization through the manipulation of national symbols and myths, control of the media, and alliances with economic and criminal elites were key components of the Milošević regime, but the essential factor in Milošević's tenure in power was the willingness to use force. The use of police supported by tanks to quell the protests in March 1991 revealed the methods which Milošević would use time and time again, against internal opposition as well as against external enemies. The constant crisis and atmosphere of violence served two purposes: to physically eliminate or intimidate opponents of the regime, and to perpetuate conditions which would justify the continued militarization of Serbian society. In the words of Mihaljo Marković, an SPO deputy from Kragujevac, "the lifeblood of the Serbian government is war."[31]

In the early 1990s, Milošević did not fully trust the JNA, since it had developed considerable power separate from the federal government during the communist era. In order to have a source of coercion completely loyal to him, Milošević expanded the police force, which by 1993 was heavily armed and numbered some eighty thousand men, many drawn from Croatia, Bosnia, or rural Serbia.[32] These were used effectively against the urban opposition in Belgrade, and later were involved in suppression of the Kosovo Liberation Army (KLA), which had begun to act openly against Serbian rule in the late 1990s. Another component of Milošević's tools of coercion was the secret police, which came under his control at the end of 1990. The head of the secret police (SDB), Jovica Stanišić, and Mihalj Kertes, a close ally of Milošević and an SDB agent, had numerous contacts with the criminal underground and paramilitary groups who were used extensively in the fighting in Croatia and Bosnia. The Ministry of the Interior was heavily involved in arming rebel Serbs outside of Serbia, and would eventually become complicitous in illegal activities such as weapon smuggling and drug running as the rule of law disintegrated in the former Yugoslavia.[33] Eventually the army, renamed the Army of Yugoslavia (VJ), also underwent a "professional and political weakening" following repeated purges of the officer corps, so that it became a loyal tool for Milošević to retain power.[34]

Although the previous discussion reveals the authoritarian nature of the Milošević regime, Milošević always maintained the facade of democracy to some degree, never transforming his rule into an open dictatorship. The level of repression increased when the government was directly threatened, such as the protests of March 1991 and the winter of 1996–97, during the NATO bombing in 1999, and the months leading up to Milošević's eventual overthrow in October 2000. Media blackouts, censorship, arbitrary arrests, intimidation of leading members of opposition movements, and threats to use unrestrained force became common in these periods, but opponents of the government were still able to continue their activities to some degree. Democratic elections were held periodically and a parliamentary system existed, although the elections were far from free and fair, and Milošević frequently violated the constitution as he saw fit. During the first multiparty elections in December 1990, Milošević's new SPS had the advantage of inheriting the financial assets of the defunct League of Communists of Serbia, along with almost total control of the electronic media (Milošević ally Dušan Mitević was head of RTS during this period). At this point, Milošević had genuinely developed considerable popular support for his nationalist platform, and his election to

the presidency of Serbia was not that surprising. Milošević was also politically adept enough to co-opt many of his most vocal opponents into
government coalitions, such as Šešelj's Radicals, who had criticized Milošević, represented extreme Serbian nationalism, and frequently did well
in elections. According to Nenad Čanak, president of the League of Social Democrats of Vojvodina, "Šešelj worked for the regime, he was the
striking fist in the fight against political opponents and members of national minorities."[35] In 1998, even the SPO was brought into a coalition,
which many saw as Vuk Drašković's bid for power despite many years as
a leader of the opposition. Mirjana Marković, Milošević's wife, and her
Yugoslav United Left (JUL) party were other crucial SPS allies in the federal parliament. Many analysts have suspected that she exerted considerable power behind the scenes, and was responsible for many of Milošević's
political decisions, creating a ruling family which had influence in both
legal and illegal economic activities.[36]

   As the negative aspects of the Milošević regime became more apparent later in the decade, however, the ruling party had to rely on more
authoritarian tactics to ensure victory. Control of key government institutions, the media, and police remained factors which favored the SPS.
Before federal elections in November 1996, Milošević sidestepped the
constitution and redefined Serbia's and Montenegro's electoral units, an
example of gerrymandering designed to give the ruling party victory.[37]
Subsequent evidence of ballot tampering and the refusal of the authorities to recognize the victory of the opposition in several cities throughout
Serbia, including Belgrade, sparked several months of mass rallies and
demonstrations led by opposition groups and parties.[38] Milošević eventually granted some concessions to the opposition in February 1997, but
was able to emerge from those turbulent events with his power intact. The
system had the veneer of democratic legitimacy, and Milošević was able to
keep himself in power by relying on authoritarian tactics, which included
crude propaganda and the use of force. Nevertheless, the Milošević regime
was not totalitarian, and terms such as "nationalist-authoritarian" or "soft
dictatorship" are more appropriate.

   As the violence in Kosovo in 1998–99 brought Serbia once again into
confrontation with the international community, Milošević increased the
pressure on domestic opponents. The NATO bombing appeared only to
strengthen Milošević, and once again he relied on branding members of
the opposition as traitors and stooges of the West, effectively stifling dissent. However, despite the efforts of Milošević to cling to power, his opponents survived the increased repression and were able to place enough

pressure on the authorities for new elections to be called in the fall of 2000. The events of September and October 2000 revealed that Milošević had failed to build a legitimate political system, as it had become apparent by that point that the government had neglected the vast majority of Serbia's citizens, functioning instead to ensure the wealth of the criminalized elite and maintain the ruling family in power.

III

The authoritarian nature of the Milošević regime can partly explain why it survived for as long as it did, but the inability of the opposition to find common ground or offer a viable political alternative completes the picture. The conflicting personalities and egos of the main leaders of the opposition—Zoran Djindjić, Vuk Drašković, and Vojislav Koštunica—resulted in repeated failures to build unified coalitions or even consolidate victories over Milošević, such as in the aftermath of the demonstrations in early 1997. The opposition to Milošević had tried to form blocs on several occasions to challenge the ruling party during elections; the Democratic Movement of Serbia (DEPOS) in 1992, the Democratic Alliance in December 1995, and Zajedno ("Together," formed in September 1996) had all been coalitions featuring some combination of the SPO, the DS (Democratic Party), the DSS, and the Civic Alliance of Serbia (GSS). Ideological differences and varying solutions for solving Serbia's problems prevented the formation of an effective challenge to Milošević's power, along with the fact that Milošević was willing to use coercion against domestic opponents. Moreover, most Serbs saw the opposition leaders as just another group of power-hungry individuals not much different from Milošević. The growth of Otpor, a student opposition group founded in October 1998, provided the necessary impetus for the opposition to mount a unified stand against Milošević, the first step if Serbia was ever to develop into a liberal democratic society and rejoin the international community.[39]

Instead of destroying his base of power, the NATO bombing in the spring of 1999 seemed at first to strengthen Milošević's position. He once again relied on the nationalist rhetoric and recurrent themes of Serbian victimhood—the connection was made between the NATO alliance and the Nazi bombardment of Belgrade, and films about Partisan resistance during World War Two played in a number of theaters—in an attempt to rally the Serbian nation and solidify his grip on power. Beneath the surface, however, widespread discontent at the way Milošević had handled the Kosovo crisis was a powerful psychological boost to the opposition. Milošević and other Serbian nationalists stressed the need for unity, claiming that the rest of the world was against the Serbs; after the 1990s, most of the world had turned its back on the Milošević regime, even Russia, which realized that good relations with the West were jeopardized by continued support of a government tainted by war crimes and an economy crippled by sanctions. Accusations of betrayal and collaboration with the West were slung even more fervently at opposition groups during this time period. Moreover, by early 2000 the regime began widespread takeovers of media outlets[40] and used large-scale violence to put down protests for the first time since 1991.[41] In March 2000, the government initiated legal proceedings against opposition leaders, including Vuk Obradović, Milan Protić, and Goran Svilanović, for slandering politicians during rallies in 1999,[42] and even abducted opposition deputies, such as Jan Svetlik of Vojvodina's League of Social Democrats, as part of a strategy to intimidate Milošević's opponents.[43] This shift toward greater repression indicated that the regime was facing serious challenges, not only from the opposition, which was the most vocal opponent, but from society in general and from former allies (the Serbian business elite, the army and police forces), who no longer believed Milošević could protect their interests. Rather than crush the dissent against the regime, the increased authoritarianism only served to mobilize more support for opposition groups, especially after reports that members of Otpor, who were mostly students and youths, were being arrested and abused by security forces accusing them of terrorism.

Determined to hold on to power, in July 2000 Milošević changed the Yugoslav constitution in order that he could be reelected as president of the Yugoslav federation in a popular vote, rather than being elected directly by the parliament, as had been the case in 1997.[44] These constitutional changes were followed by a call for elections on 24 September 2000, a year before Milošević's term was due to expire. The opposition was faced with a difficult decision: participate in elections which were likely to be unfair, considering the atmosphere of repression and constitutional gerrymandering, or boycott them, guaranteeing a victory for Milošević. The Democratic Opposition of Serbia (DOS), a coalition of eighteen political parties led by Djindjić's DS, agreed that challenging Milošević in the elections was the best strategy and began looking for a candidate to rally behind. Since most opposition leaders had discredited themselves in the eyes of the Serbian electorate by their petty squabbling, the DOS decided to field constitutional lawyer Vojislav Koštunica, of the DSS, as its presidential candidate. Koštunica could not be accused of being a Western stooge; nor was he tainted with collaboration with the Milošević regime. An ardent anticommunist, he did not criticize the Milošević regime for its nationalist policies, but rather charged that Milošević had failed to accomplish Serbian national goals (i.e., unification of all Serbs in one state).[45]

The fact that only another nationalist politician could stand a chance in the elections reveals the degree to which the Serbian political scene had been shaped by the chauvinistic character of the Milošević era. None of the leading candidates for the presidential election seemed ready to lead the FRY on to a liberal democratic future, regardless of who actually won. Milošević (authoritarian neocommunist) and Koštunica ("moderate" nationalist) were leaders in the polls in the months before the elections. The SPO, which had decided not to join the DOS coalition, selected Vojislav Mihajlović as its candidate, reinforcing its pro-Chetnik stance. Šešelj's SRS (right-wing extremists) nominated Tomislav Nikolić, known as the "Gravedigger" because of his former job in a cemetery, to run for the presidency, opening up the possibility of Šešelj becoming the prime minister if Nikolić won the election. In the post-Tudjman elections in Croatia, for example, Stjepan Mesić was able to win the presidency on a campaign promising greater tolerance, a rejection of the HDZ's (Croatian Democratic Community) nationalist policies, and closer cooperation with the West. Of course, Tudjman's death had cleared the political scene and had shaken up the HDZ, but it is notable that voters were given (and chose) a political option significantly different from what had dominated the 1990s. This was missing from the Yugoslav presidential elections and can help explain the slower pace of reform in Serbia.

With the United States giving some $25 million in aid for "democratization," the DOS, supported by the grassroots organization of Otpor, was able to mount an effective political campaign backed by the slogan "Gotov je!"—"He's finished!"[46] Milošević, however, still controlled the most important media outlets, leading even Vojislav Šešelj to protest against the "undemocratic propaganda methods" of the regime and the use of the army and police for political ends.[47] Koštunica embarked on a Western-style campaign, traveling throughout Serbia to shake hands and meet with the people. It was outside of the cities that Milošević drew most of his support, and thus it was vital for the opposition to make an impact in the rural areas of Serbia.

As results of the voting became available, it was clear that Milošević had miscalculated in calling for early elections. The opposition had been able to unify sufficiently to channel popular resentment toward an electoral victory, something Milošević had not anticipated based on the previous elections. According to monitors of the election, who had been trained as part of the U.S.-sponsored democratization project,[48] in the first round Koštunica won 54.66 percent of the vote, while Milošević received only 35.01 percent, a clear victory for Koštunica.[49] Voter turnout was estimated at 78 percent in Serbia, while only 25 percent voted in Montenegro, where President Milo Djukanović had called for a boycott, dismissing the elections as a show to perpetuate the "dictatorship in Belgrade."[50] Meanwhile, the Federal Elections Commission claimed that Koštunica had actually won only 48.22 percent of the vote (Milošević having allegedly received 40.23 percent), which was below the 50 percent minimum necessary for a first-round victory and would have required a second round of elections, to be held on 8 October.[51] Serbia's highest court also issued a statement that there had been voting irregularities, but the judgment was never published because events quickly spiraled out of the control of the authorities. Djindjić and other opposition leaders immediately rejected the claims of both the Federal Election Commission and the court, and called for a general strike throughout Serbia, the first one since World War Two.[52]

As Serbia ground to a halt in response to the calls for a general strike, the rest of the world waited to see if Milošević would indeed resort to unrestrained violence to hold on to power. Would the instruments of repression—the army, police, and the Ministry of the Interior—be used against the masses who gathered in the streets and streamed into Belgrade? On 29 September, miners at the important Kolubara coal mine began a strike, threatening to disrupt Serbia's power grid. As police surrounded the striking miners and as Koštunica gave a speech encouraging them to "defend their votes," the resilience of the armed forces of Serbia became tested as to whether they were willing to continue to support a leader who had lost even the facade of legitimacy.[53] The loyalty of the Yugoslav army was already questionable, since it was mostly composed of conscripts, but in the face of overwhelming popular support for Koštunica, even the police and special forces stood by as protesters mobilized, pushed aside barricades, and traveled into Belgrade in long convoys adorned with banners and flags of Otpor.

The final showdown took place in Belgrade on 5 October, as demonstrators stormed the federal parliament building, as well as the headquarters of Radio-Television Serbia, a symbol of Milošević's propaganda machine. Although police initially tried to hold back the crowd, they eventually stepped aside or even joined the opposition, which had commandeered a bulldozer and several garbage trucks, in storming the building and ransacking it. In the ensuing chaos, boxes of fake ballots were discovered and confirmed suspicions that Milošević had intended to rig the elections.[54] As the parliament building burned and tear gas wafted through the streets, Koštunica addressed "liberated Serbia" as the new president of Yugoslavia. When asked whether the events of 5 October were a revolution, he stated: "It's a democratic revolution. When I always thought of what would be the revolution in this country, it was Tocqueville and his democratic revolution. That's what I had in mind. But I suppose this is a revolutionary way of defending the will of the people."[55]

As his regime crumbled around him, Milošević remained holed up in his house in the Dedinje neighborhood of Belgrade, ordering his chief of staff Nebojša Pavković to send the army in to crush the demonstrations, which had turned into celebrations by the evening of 5 October. Pavković and the head of secret police, Rade Marković, considered a plan to retake the city, but decided the battle was already lost and that it was for the good of Serbia to concede victory to Koštunica.[56] After a one-on-one meeting with Koštunica, Milošević went on state television on 6 October to congratulate Koštunica for his victory and to state that he was going to take a short rest before working to strengthen his party for its new role as the opposition.[57] After thirteen years in power, Slobodan Milošević was overthrown by the same sort of mass mobilization which he had used to engineer his own rise in the 1980s. Although vowing to continue political activity, on 1 April 2001 he was arrested in Belgrade and transferred to The Hague on 28 June, to become the first former head of state to be tried as a war criminal.

While Otpor and other democratic NGOs did play an important role in peaceful resistance, the final push to topple Milošević was carried out by former army and paramilitary troops, especially those groups led by Velimir Ilić, the mayor of Čačak, who obviously had their own interests in removing Milošević but not necessarily in restoring the rule of law.[58] In fact, Ilić later told reporters how the final push against the parliament building not only was carried out by veterans of the wars in Croatia and Bosnia, but had been coordinated "with the most elite units of the Interior Ministry police in Belgrade."[59] Clearly the most vital elements which had supported the Milošević regime had decided to accept the inevitable and offer their services to the new leadership. Not surprisingly, the army and secret police were spared purges in the aftermath of the October events, and essentially remained unchanged under the new government. This pact with the Devil was to prove fatal to Zoran Djindjić, when he indicated that more serious action was going to be taken against the remains of Milošević's repressive regime. One scholar has noted that "Koštunica came to power in the same way as Slobodan Milošević: through a coup supported by conservative forces."[60] One of the earliest rifts between Koštunica and his DOS allies was over the issue of personnel changes in the army and secret police, with Koštunica arguing that it "would be quite irresponsible, at the moment when we are controlling things, to start experiments with the police and the secret police."[61] Furthermore, the army issued a warning on 11 October to the DOS government that any attempt to discredit the military leadership would result in "negative consequences."[62]

The DOS was successful in winning 176 out of 250 seats in the parliament after general elections on 23 December 2000, solidifying the victory of the former opposition through democratic means. However, the divisions among the members of the DOS coalition quickly came to light, as described by Obrad Kesić in chapter 4. It is undeniable that the removal of Milošević was a significant event in Serbia's attempt to build a legitimate state and political system, despite the weaknesses of the new government. The events of October 2000 were of paramount importance to the transformation of Serbia (and the FRY), even though all the details of the behind-the-scenes power deals remain unclear. The popular demonstrations culminating on 5 October were hailed as a democratic revolution around the world, and indicated the degree of resentment which had built up against Milošević. The Federal Republic of Yugoslavia had failed to create a legitimate political system, much like its socialist predecessor, and had thus descended into greater authoritarianism and semidictatorship by the end of the 1990s. However, the revolution was by no means complete, and most of the pillars of the Milošević regime remained intact. Notably, the revolution failed to remove the ideology of nationalism from the Serbian body politic, which will continue to hinder the development of liberal values (and a stable political system) in the near future.

IV

The news of Milošević's overthrow in the chaotic days of October 2000 elicited hopes throughout the West that Serbia had finally undergone the long-delayed transformation into a democratic nation ready to be reintegrated into the international community. After all, Milošević had come to embody the nationalist tyrant who ruled his country with an iron fist, and who had been especially demonized in the Western press during the NATO campaign. It was thus natural to assume that once he was removed,

Serbia would rapidly undergo normalization and shake off the legacy of his rule. Although the defeat of Milošević was absolutely vital to the project of creating a legitimate political system in Serbia, the overly optimistic predictions concerning the immediate future of Serbia have proven to be naïve, based on the first four post-Milošević years. The political infrastructure built up under Milošević could not be expected to be erased with one man's removal from power, and thus many continuities persist from the 1990s in contemporary Serbia. Furthermore, the impact on society of more than a decade of authoritarian rule, militarization, violence, rampant corruption, a xenophobic press under the control of government authorities, and a devastated economy has left a shoddy foundation upon which to build a democratic and liberal political system. Finally, the new leaders of Serbia have failed to pursue policies which diverge significantly from the nationalist goals of Milošević, resulting in the failure to address responsibility for war crimes, to cooperate with the ICTY, and to build strong relations with neighboring countries. Serbia faces many challenges ahead, and it remains to be seen whether the new authorities will make a clean break with the Milošević past, or whether they will continue to pursue the kind of politics which has led to so much tragedy in the former Yugoslavia.

One of the most important factors regarding the degree of change in Serbia was the character of Vojislav Koštunica, who was the federal president until the transformation of the FRY into Serbia and Montenegro (SiCG) in March 2003 left him without a job. First of all, Koštunica was just as much a nationalist as Milošević, which is one reason the opposition chose to rally around him and his party, the DSS, in order to appeal to a Serbian society still enthralled by the nationalist fervor whipped up by Milošević and his more than decade of rule. It has been easy in Serbia to blame all the problems on Milošević, rather than recognizing that many forces in Serbian society—the Serbian Orthodox Church, the military establishment, intellectuals, and most of the opposition—generally supported the nationalist policies of the 1990s. Serbian nationalist goals and Serbs outside of Serbia (especially in Republika Srpska and Kosovo) continued to figure prominently in Koštunica's political agenda.[63] Secondly, Koštunica, like most of the Serbian political elite, was of the generation of politicians from the era of communist control in Yugoslavia. While this is true for many of the former republics of socialist Yugoslavia, the Left in Slovenia and Croatia (for example) have shifted to more social democratic orientations such as those in Western Europe; this has not taken place in Serbia. Thirdly, Koštunica made his anti-Western position crystal clear on numerous occasions, especially relating to the NATO bombing and the issue of cooperation with the ICTY. This negative attitude toward Western Europe and the United States, which includes blaming the international community for all of Yugoslavia's woes (a tactic also commonly used by Milošević), enabled Koštunica to win an election in Serbia, but it is not an attitude that can bring about significant changes in Serbia.

Serbia's failure to cooperate with The Hague is a major stumbling block for reintegration with Europe as well as for internal democratization. Without the prosecution of individuals responsible for war crimes, responsibility and accountability for the wars resulting from the breakup of Yugoslavia will never take place, and those who are guilty will continue to remain in power if not brought to trial. Serbian society also needs to come to a realization of the crimes committed by its government in the former Yugoslavia in order for reconciliation to take place between Serbs, Croats, Albanians, and Bosnian Muslims. As noted in the chapter by Eric D. Gordy in this volume, this sort of social catharsis has not taken place in Serbia, which will continue to impede progress toward a liberal democratic order. Violence and persecution of others will continue to be seen as necessary and justifiable, whether against foreign enemies, such as other ethnic groups, or internal enemies, such as the opposition group Otpor. While Croatia and the federation half of Bosnia have cooperated with the ICTY (Croatia's president Mesić has emphasized the importance of the tribunal in avoiding the "collective guilt" of entire ethnic groups), Serbia continues to drag its feet in turning over war criminals known to be living in Belgrade and other cities, refuses to give important documents to The Hague, and has used bureaucratic and legal red tape to delay drafting laws relating to cooperation with the ICTY despite threats by the United States to cut off aid. In fact, Koštunica has on numerous occasions denounced the ICTY as a tool of the United States, and on 27 March 2002 gave a speech on television in which he claimed that he felt "sick to [his] stomach" when thinking about the war crimes tribunal.[64]

Indicted war criminals, such as Serbian president Milan Milutinović, remained in office for two years after the fall of Milošević, a clear indication that the election of Koštunica did not mark a complete overhaul of the system. The political system which was responsible for the brutal ethnic cleansing and murder of ethnic Albanians in Kosovo (not to mention the previous three wars in Slovenia, Croatia, and Bosnia) essentially remained in place. Furthermore, Otpor, the Helsinki Committee for Human Rights in Serbia, and Human Rights Watch have all issued demands for greater Serbian cooperation with the tribunal.[65] On 11 April 2002, Parliament passed a law on cooperation with the ICTY, but little has been done by Belgrade to implement the law or arrest indicted war criminals, notably Ratko Mladić who is suspected of living in Belgrade. One major loophole in this law is that it only applies to those suspected of war crimes who were indicted before the passing of the law, exempting those who may still be under secret indictment.[66] Serbia is not a liberal democratic state, and successive regimes have relied on the machinery of the police and army to suppress opposition; Koštunica's anti-Western government was no different, especially since the police, secret services, and army have seen the least change since Milošević's overthrow.

The trial of Milošević, which began on 13 February 2002, made it more than evident that much of the political and economic infrastructure of his regime remained intact. This was most apparent in Milošević's ability to gain inside information on witnesses at his trial, where he is acting as his own defense lawyer. Despite being imprisoned in the Netherlands, he was nevertheless able to access highly detailed information, through his contacts in Belgrade, on the backgrounds, activities, and relatives of witnesses, which he has used to mercilessly question them during cross-examination. Allegedly, "numerous individuals inside the army and various ministries" have been providing information to help with Milošević's defense.[67] As mentioned before, the police forces, secret services, and army are the least reformed institutions in Serbia, and most of the senior personnel from the Milošević era have remained in their positions, only now realigned behind the new leadership.[68] In some ways, it is not surprising that changes have not taken place in these institutions, since it must be remembered that they functioned for over a decade as the privileged units of a government held in power through the use of force. After Milošević fell from power in October 2000, his allies in the Interior Ministry refused to be purged from their positions. It was not until December 2000 that the head of the Interior Ministry, Rade Marković,[69] resigned, giving enough time for documents, records, and other evidence of police complicity in Milošević's repression to be destroyed.[70] In addition, this allowed much of the personnel and infrastructure to remain in place despite the alleged democratization of the political system. According to a U.S. Department of State report on human rights released on 4 March 2002, the police "continued the practice of detaining citizens at times for 'informative talks.'"[71] These were tactics used during the communist era and under Milošević's dictatorship, and did not change under Koštunica. In November 2001, members of the elite police unit the Red Berets (Crvene beretke) actually staged a mutiny, demanding the removal of Marković's successor

Dušan Mihajlović and the breaking off of cooperation with The Hague; this was, in essence, a sort of counterrevolution from a bastion of Milošević's hard-line support.[72] While Djindjić refused to accept Mihajlović's resignation and transferred the Red Beret unit to the public security department, Koštunica actually supported the mutineers and considered their concerns legitimate, once more indicating his position on responsibility for war crimes and willingness to address some of the dark legacies of the Milošević regime.[73]

Closely connected to the lack of reform in the Ministry of the Interior and the police forces is the failure to establish the rule of law in Serbia. Not only is it difficult for ordinary citizens to get fair trials in unbiased courts, but numerous high-profile murder and kidnapping cases have yet to be solved by either the Serbian judicial system or law enforcement agencies.[74] Corruption and criminality, legacies of the collapse of society during a decade of war, have become endemic throughout Serbia. One factor is that the judicial system, long under the control of Milošević, lacks "independence and authority."[75] A second factor is that many of the so-called democratic reformers, including members of Djindjić's Democratic Party, are believed to have ties to various members of the criminal underworld, which is why there was not initially a strong effort to "move against the big criminals who flourished under Milošević."[76] These conditions in Serbia led to the assassination of Djindjić in March 2003, because members of Serbian criminal organizations were able to avoid prosecution in a state where they had influence among both the judiciary and government (see below).

Both the U.S. State Department and the International Crisis Group (along with Human Rights Watch) have issued reports that the army has also seen no reform since the fall of Milošević, and is essentially out of the control of the civilian government. The International Crisis Group identified the reasons for this lack of reform as "ideological nationalism, rear guard resistance by Milošević-era cadres, and inertia,"[77] which reveals the challenge Serbia faces beyond simply removing Milošević. Hard-liners and Milošević allies continue in positions of power in the military, and the detention of a former general (Momčilo Perišić) and an American diplomat (John David Neighbor) in March 2002 poignantly illustrated the fact that antireform forces are alive and strong in Serbia.[78] Even individuals with diplomatic immunity are not immune from persecution if they are accused of being traitors or cooperating with the West.

In addition to individuals accused of war crimes staying in positions of power (such as Milutinović), Milošević's political party (SPS) and those of his close allies (Šešelj's Radicals and the Socialist People's Party [SNP] from Montenegro) comprised an antireform bloc in the federal parliament. This continuity in the political infrastructure explains the lack of change and the ongoing resistance to cooperation with the West. One of the more notorious members of the federal parliament, Šešelj, remained politically active until he voluntarily surrendered to the ICTY on 24 February 2003, three weeks before Djindjić was assassinated. Šešelj has been photographed carrying a gun into the parliament building, and has threatened members of the opposition and independent media (who he claimed were traitors to Serbia) with liquidation.[79] The fact that unsavory characters such as Šešelj, who were directly involved in the most brutal aspects of the war in the Balkans, remained active in politics was just another testament to the lack of substantial change in Serbia since Milošević's fall.

V

The dysfunctional condition of the Serbian state, one of the main legacies of the Milošević era, was made even more apparent in the period between the failure to elect a president in the fall of 2002 and the tragic assassination of Serbian prime minister Zoran Djindjić in March 2003. In the meantime, the federal Yugoslav state ceased to exist and the final status of Kosovo remained undetermined, contributing to instability in the political system and society. Despite the obvious failure of Milošević's politics to improve the lives of the majority of Serbia's citizens, chauvinism and nationalism remain entrenched in Serbian political life and appear to be supported by a significant segment of the population. Disillusioned with the slow pace of reforms and the ongoing scandals within the political establishment, Serbs may be unwilling to continue to back the politicians who are pushing the most for fulfilling the demands of the international community— in the first place, cooperation with the International Criminal Tribunal for the former Yugoslavia—and integration with the European Union. Nevertheless, after years of being international pariahs due to Serbia's role in the ethnic violence in the Balkans in the 1990s, since 2000 Serbia (and Montenegro) have renewed ties to the international community and have successfully normalized economic relations with the United States. Stabilizing the internal political situation and normalizing relations with its immediate neighbors remain important tasks for the post-Milošević Serbian leadership, which will require a tangible break with all aspects of the previous regime.

The failure to elect a president during two elections held at the end of

2002 revealed the endemic political problems facing Serbia after the fall of Milošević. On the one hand, the pro-European and reformist bloc which allegedly provided the momentum during October 2000 and which represented the new Serbia found that support for such a political option was actually lacking when Milošević was no longer in the picture: Serbs had rejected Slobodan Milošević as their leader but had not thoroughly rejected the nationalist policies of his regime. On the other hand, political apathy among the voters had reached the point that even nationalist candidates, such as Vojislav Koštunica, could not get elected, while candidates further to the right found significant support at the voting booths. As Belgrade lawyer Srdja Popović explained in an interview for the Croatian weekly *Globus*:

> Since Serbia existed, there always existed only two political parties. One was for entering into Europe, while the other was Orthodox and Balkan. Even when a single party ruled for four decades, it was divided into factions exactly along that line. In Serbia, unfortunately, the pro-European side was always beaten, as it is currently.[80]

Jevrem Brković, a leading Montenegrin literary figure, went a step further and compared the divisions in contemporary Serbia to the conflict between Serbia's two royal families in the nineteenth century: "Will the European, Obrenović Serbia, which was represented by Djindjić, be victorious, or will the scales tip in favor of the primitive, murderous, criminal Serbia of Karadjordjević and Milošević?"[81]

In the first set of presidential elections held on 29 September 2002, it was precisely the European Serbia which was soundly defeated at the polls. Miroljub Labus, the DOS's pro-reform candidate, stated that reforms should have begun immediately after the removal of Milošević, "with a declaration of a new constitution, electoral laws, and the rule of law, but no one saw any of that."[82] He added that he represented "the Serbia which wants to step forward into a European future."[83] His leading opponents— Vojislav Koštunica (DSS), Vojislav Šešelj (SRS), Vuk Drašković (SPO), and Borislav Pelević (Arkan's Party of Serbian Unity, Stranka srpskog jedinstva)—all represented various shades of the Serbian nationalism which had led to violent attempts at redrawing the territorial and ethnic borders in the Balkans. In this first round, in which 55.5 percent of the electorate participated, Koštunica received 30.9 percent of the vote, while Labus came in second with 27.4 percent, requiring a second round since no candidate had won a majority of the votes.[84] Koštunica's election performance in relation to Labus's was not surprising to political analysts following the elections; what was surprising was the 23 percent Šešelj received at the polls, indicating that the extreme-right political option had not been defeated after the "democratic revolution" of October 2000.[85]

The second round of elections between Koštunica and Labus, held on 13 October, was declared invalid because only 45.5 percent of the electorate voted, violating a Milošević-era law which stipulated that over half of the electorate needed to participate in presidential elections in order for them to be valid.[86] Even though the elections were declared invalid, Koštunica decisively defeated Labus with over 66 percent of the vote, which prompted Labus to decide not to run in another election attempt scheduled for December. Koštunica, meanwhile, blamed the Serbian parliament and Zoran Djindjić's government for the failure of the elections, even though Šešelj's call to boycott the elections had contributed to the low turnout.[87] Presidential elections were once again held on 8 December, although this time voters could choose from only three right-wing options—Koštunica, Šešelj, and Pelević—and once again they were declared invalid because of insufficient voter turnout (45.2 percent of eligible voters).[88] Thus, Koštunica, who had received 57.5 percent of the vote, had "won" the presidential elections three times but could not become president.[89] He subsequently refused to recognize the results of the elections, citing irregularities with the number of registered voters and an alleged campaign by the government against the elections.[90]

The three presidential elections in Serbia between September and December indicated two things: Serbian society had become apathetic toward the political system, which had failed to improve living conditions since the removal of Milošević, and nationalist and right-wing political parties remained strong despite the apparent victory of pro-European forces in October 2000. The president of the Serbian Helsinki Committee, Sonja Biserko, lamented that "in essence, nationalism in Serbia has not yet received a serious alternative."[91] Because the presidential elections were invalid, once Milan Milutinović's mandate expired on 5 January 2003, the president of the parliament, Nataša Mićić, was declared president of Serbia. Mićić, a young member of the ruling DOS coalition, was considered to be close to Djindjić; therefore the failure of the elections, and the defeat of Djindjić's rival Koštunica, appeared to go in favor of the Serbian reformers. However, the failure of democratic elections, which likewise occurred in Montenegro on 22 December,[92] did not bode well for future political stability and the transformation of Serbia into a "normal" country.

As Serbia emerged from its electoral debacle with its first ever female president, in early 2003 the body politic received another shock to the system with the decisive disappearance of the third Yugoslavia from the map of Europe and the transformation of the FRY into the new state of Serbia and Montenegro. Thus, the dysfunctional state of Serbia found itself in a loose federation with a de facto independent state (Montenegro), while still claiming sovereignty over a former province administered by the international community (Kosovo) and exerting political and economic influence over part of a neighboring country (Republika Srpska). The Constitutional Charter of the new state was ratified by the Serbian parliament on 27 January 2003, ten months after the so-called Belgrade Agreement, which had laid out the framework for reforming the federal structure of the FRY. One hundred and sixty-six deputies voted in favor of the new state, while forty-seven deputies—the Socialists, the Radicals, Arkan's Party of Serbian Unity, and New Serbia (NS)—were against the dismantling of the FRY.[93] Serbia and Montenegro (SiCG) officially came into existence on 4 February 2003, after its ratification by the federal parliament, but the future of this state was already put into question by a stipulation in its founding document which provided for referenda on independence three years from its inception. Some cynics already referred to SiCG as "Solania," alluding to Javier Solana, who headed the international community's determined efforts in preserving some kind of joint Serbian and Montenegrin state, despite the great degree of sovereignty already exercised by Montenegro.[94] The creation of SiCG did not only mean the conclusive end of the Yugoslav idea, first realized as a state in 1918, but also left Vojislav Koštunica, the last Yugoslav president, without a job; hence his determined efforts at becoming president of Serbia. As one Croatian journalist commented, "the new state was founded on maximum compromises and minimum ideals and goals, so it might actually have more success than the previous states on this ground."[95]

Another, more dramatic shock to Serbia's body politic was the tragic assassination of Prime Minister Zoran Djindjić on 12 March 2003, who was killed by a sniper outside his office in the center of Belgrade.[96] The murder of Djindjić was another blow to pro-West and reform forces in Serbia, and provided concrete evidence that the personnel and institutions which had represented the most repressive and authoritarian aspects of the Milošević regime were far from being eradicated in Serbia. In fact, in the weeks and months following the assassination, government investigation revealed that antireform forces with ties to the criminal underworld, paramilitary formations, intelligence services, and right-wing political parties had envisioned the murder of Djindjić as the start of a "counterrevolution" and the return of a hard-line nationalist government to power in Serbia. In the words of political theoretician Latinka Perović, Djindjić "was increasingly becoming a negative symbol for a Serbia which did not want changes, which justified war, negated our responsibility for destroying Yugoslavia, and relativized war crimes while making those who committed them into heroes."[97] A state of emergency was immediately declared, and Zoran Živković, the new prime minister, initiated a massive police operation, code named "Saber" (Sablja), against organized crime and any institutions believed to be involved in the assassination.

The primary organizer of the assassination was identified as Milorad Luković "Legija," a member of the paramilitary unit the Red Berets (Crvene beretke), who had close ties to both the criminal underworld—notably the Zemun clan—and the Serbian secret services, whose ranks were still full of Milošević-era cadres. The state of emergency quickly resulted in the arrest of thousands of suspects, from actual mafia operatives to anarchist activists. The newspapers were filled with reports and arrest warrants for a host of criminals with bizarre nicknames such as "Kum" (Godfather), "Budala" (Idiot), "Pacov" (Rat), and "Bagzi" (Bugsy). The Zemun clan faced the brunt of the assault (although by no means the only group of organized criminals in Serbia), and on 27 March the two leaders of the clan, Mile Luković "Kum" and Dušan Spasojević "Šiptar" (a derogatory term for an Albanian), were killed "resisting arrest" and their mansion quickly reduced to rubble.[98]

Subsequently the Serbian media reported that a number of politicians in the DOS ranks, including Vice Prime Ministers Čedomir Jovanović and Nebojša Čović, had been videotaped meeting Spasojević in his house, and that the liquidation of the Zemun clan leaders had been necessary to cover up ties between Djindjić's party and the mafia.[99] The media had long speculated that Zoran Djindjić had made some kind of deal with the criminal underworld in order to topple Milošević, and his assassination appeared to be prompted by his violation of that deal by initiating police actions against organized crime as well as his plans to place the army under civilian control.[100]

Operation Saber cast its net beyond just mafia thugs: newspapers which had called for the removal of Djindjić were shut down, judges who had taken bribes or released mafia members were fired from their jobs, and the Red Berets were immediately disbanded. Although tragic, the murder of Djindjić did initiate the first significant assault on the remains of the Milošević regime, and brought to light the close-knit connection between criminals, state institutions which represented the repressive arm of the Serbian nationalist system, and right-wing politicians: the degree to which Serbia had become a criminal and dysfunctional state became fully exposed. A more cynical analyst commented that "Serbia did not have its own mafia, but rather in Serbia the mafia had its own state."[101] These ties had been developed in Serbia in the 1990s because of the involvement of Serbia in the wars fought in the former Yugoslavia, as well as the economic sanctions which forced the state to rely on illegal channels to continue functioning. On 13 March, the former head of the Serbian State Security Service (SDB), Jovica Stanišić, and the former chief of the Red Berets, Franko Simatović "Frenki," were arrested for their connection to the planners of the assassination.[102] Both had been heavily involved in arming rebel Serbs in Croatia in 1990–91, organizing paramilitary units responsible for many of the most brutal war crimes in the former Yugoslavia, and maintaining contacts with the Bosnian Serb leadership.[103] The media in both Serbia and Croatia had reported on the connection between organized crime and state institutions even prior to the assassination, as well as pointing out that war crimes trials in The Hague had shown the involvement of the Serbian secret services in establishing paramilitary formations.[104] On 25 March, Zvezdan Jovanović "Zmija" (Snake), a member of the Red Berets who had fought with Arkan's forces in Croatia in 1991, was identified by the government as the assassin and arrested. After questioning, Jovanović claimed that he had committed the crime because Milorad Luković "Legija" had convinced him that the ICTY had an indictment against him and other members of the Red Berets, and only by removing Djindjić would they be able to avoid extradition to The Hague.[105] Allegedly a state coup was to have taken place following Djindjić's death, led by unnamed members of the Yugoslav army, certain politicians, organized criminals, and the Red Berets, referred to by the Serbian Interior Ministry as the "Hague Brotherhood" (Haaško bratstvo).[106] Chief prosecutor of the ICTY, Carla Del Ponte, admitted that Zoran Djindjić had told her that he would be killed because of his cooperation with the tribunal, adding that despite the assassination, there would continue to be pressure on Belgrade to hand over indicted war criminals.[107]

The arrest of Svetlana Ražnatović Ceca, widow of former warlord Željko Ražnatović "Arkan" and turbo-folk star, revealed just how deeply organized crime had permeated Serbian society. The singer, characterized in a January 2003 New York Times article as "epitomiz[ing] all that was wrong with Serbia under Slobodan Milošević," had been accused of housing known members of the Zemun clan in her house.[108] On 21 March, Milan Sarajlić, the deputy public prosecutor, admitted that he had been paid by

the Zemun clan to obstruct investigations since 5 October 2000 and reveal the names of protected witnesses.[109] In addition to Sarajlić, fifty-seven
judges were removed from their positions because of incompetence and
corruption in the course of the state of emergency. Two weeks later Vice
Prime Minister Nebojša Čović revealed that the Zemun clan had financed
Šešelj's Serbian Radical Party, which was not surprising considering the
contacts Šešelj had made with various paramilitary leaders during the war
in Croatia, and further reinforced the allegations that the mafia and war
criminals had political support from Serbia's right-wing parties.[110] Justice
Minister Vladan Batić stated that investigations were likewise taking place
into the activity of mafia-controlled media, which had apparently published over seven thousand articles until 12 March whose "satanizing,
criminalizing, and defamation had contributed to the murder of Zoran
Djindjić."[111] The one person who was not arrested was Milorad Luković
"Legija," the apparent ringleader of the assassination, who fled the country before the fatal bullet was fired.

Although Operation Saber had successfully smashed the Zemun clan
and prevented a coup, many observers criticized the government for massively violating civil rights (over eleven thousand people had been arrested
or detained by the police) and using the state of emergency to settle accounts
with its political opponents.[112] Replacing a criminal state with a police state
would not be a step forward in creating a legitimate political system; yet
this was a risk Serbia had to take. Two of Vojislav Koštunica's former
advisers, Rade Bulatović and Aco Tomić, had been arrested for having
allegedly given guarantees to the assassins that the army would not intervene in any coup attempt. Koštunica, who had likewise been implicated
in the assassination, called the arrests "something out of a Stalinist reper-
toire" and emphasized that it was the DOS government which had previously allowed the release of Zemun clan members from jail when it was
in their interest.[113]

Despite the extreme and undemocratic methods implemented after
the assassination, in retrospect they were necessary to prevent chaos and
a takeover by the "armed implementers of Milošević's politics." Zoran
Živković, a member of Djindjić's Democratic Party, was installed as prime
minister and vowed to continue the reforms initiated by his predecessor.
Minister of Defense Boris Tadić was hailed by Western observers for taking important steps aimed at reforming the army and putting it under civilian control, no simple task in light of its role during the Milošević regime.
There were even media speculations that troops from SiCG might serve
in peace-keeping operations under NATO in Afghanistan or U.S. forces

in Iraq, which is hard to believe considering that the NATO bombing is still fresh in the memories of most Serbs.[114] Investigations were reopened into a number of unresolved political murders, notably that of Ivan Stambolić, whose body was discovered after members of the Red Berets admitted to murdering him under the direct orders of Milošević, accentuating the fact that the crimes of the Milošević regime were committed not only against Serbia's neighbors but against the Serbs themselves.[115] Laura Silber, coauthor of *Yugoslavia: Death of a Nation* and friend of Zoran Djindjić, stated that Djindjić's "murder is another reminder to the Serbian people that those who committed crimes against Croats, Bosnian Muslims, and Kosovars came to roost at home. And these men could not stand the fact that Zoran was trying to wrest control of Serbia."[116]

Zoran Djindjić, who had become extremely unpopular during the course of his mandate, was transformed after his death into a heroic figure, representing the "good" Serbia. Renowned Belgrade lawyer Srdja Popović characterized Djindjić as a kind of "guerilla, who had support from the outside, but did not have the support of either the state apparatus, the police, the newly composed economic structures, or the majority of the people."[117] The Serbian government, which had been at its lowest point of popularity since 2001, was actually strengthened in the aftermath of the assassination. "With Djindjić's death, a modern myth was created in Serbia for the first time," concluded Latinka Perović, a veteran of Serbian politics. "Djindjić became a symbol of a Serbia that did not rely only on the force of a military tradition and which was not necrophiliac."[118] Ethnologist Ivan Čolović likewise agreed that Djindjić's death was being mythologized, and had "turned into a story of selfless sacrifice for the good of the nation,"[119] an interesting contrast to Milošević's own "martyrdom" in front of the tribunal at The Hague. Along with Djindjić's symbolic transformation, the death of "Serbia's Kennedy" also developed a "second shooter" myth. The head of Djindjić's personal security, Milan Veruović, who had also been wounded during the assassination, revealed to the Serbian media his theory that there was a second sniper who had actually fired the fatal bullet and who remained on the loose.[120] The assassination of Serbia's prime minister, although merely one of a number of political murders in recent Serbian history, will remain a powerful symbol of the legacy of the Milošević regime and the need for serious reforms.

In addition to trying to establish a stable political system, the Serbian leadership has grappled with two problems which have continued to hinder Serbia's development: cooperation with the ICTY and corruption. The Djindjić assassination revealed both the necessity of prosecuting war criminals and the dangers associated with government attempts at actively moving against those indicted by the tribunal. On 20 December 2002, the Serbian government initially rejected any requests by the ICTY to look at state documents and into sensitive archives, as well as refusing to arrest Milan Milutinović after the expiration of his presidential mandate.[121] However, on 30 December, Belgrade agreed to allow ICTY investigators access to some of the requested documentation, and on 20 January 2003 Milutinović voluntarily surrendered to the ICTY in The Hague. He was quickly followed on 24 February by Vojislav Šešelj, who tried to make a mockery of the court proceedings by demanding that the charges be translated into Serbian, claiming he did not understand the Croatian terminology.[122] One of the most significant indications that SiCG was increasing cooperation with The Hague was an order issued to members of the Army of Serbia and Montenegro in May to immediately report any information relating to suspected war criminals, "regardless of the rights and privileges which result from the state, political, public, or official positions of the accused individuals."[123] In late May Miroslav Radić, a former JNA officer accused of war crimes in Vukovar, voluntarily surrendered to officials in Belgrade, and on 13 June, in a spectacular police action, Veselin Šljivančanin, likewise accused of crimes at Vukovar, was arrested despite earlier threats that he would kill himself before going to The Hague. In a similar atmosphere to when Milošević was arrested in 2001, crowds gathered and chanted "Ustashe, Ustashe" and "Shame on you, what kind of Serbs are you?" at the police who had surrounded Šljivančanin's apartment, eventually engaging in sporadic street battles with them.[124] Nonetheless, Šljivančanin and Radić joined Mile Mrkšić in The Hague (forming the so-called "Vukovar trio"), where they are charged with having ordered the massacre of prisoners and civilians after Vukovar fell to Serb forces in 1991. Belgrade also promised to extradite Jovica Stanišić and Franko Simatović "Frenki," who had been in custody in Serbia following Operation Saber and who were indicted by the ICTY on 1 May 2003.

Serbia's cooperation with the ICTY, however, remains problematic on a number of levels. The most outstanding issue is the failure to capture Ratko Mladić, who has continued to evade justice somewhere in the territory of Serbia, according to the tribunal's prosecution and American diplomats. Carla Del Ponte, in reports given to the UN Security Council in early October, strongly criticized Belgrade's lack of cooperation with the ICTY, especially concerning Mladić and fellow Bosnian Serb war criminal Radovan Karadžić, who is believed to be getting support from certain elements of the Republika Srpska authorities. Furthermore, the U.S. Senate promised $113 million in economic aid on the condition that SiCG fully cooperate with the tribunal, especially concerning access to archives and a real effort to catch Mladić. The arrival of new indictments against four Serbian generals—including Sretan Lukić, who has been called "the hero of Operation Saber" by Minister of the Interior Dušan Mihajlović—on 20 October 2003 resulted in public demonstrations by Serbian police forces and heated anti-Hague rhetoric from the Serbian leadership.[125] As the arrest of Šljivančanin and the indictments against the four generals has shown, the Serbian public remains wary of the ICTY, which is perceived as an institution meant to punish only Serbs, especially those indicted based on "command responsibility" charges.[126] Considering that the nationalism of the Milošević era remains embedded in Serbian political life despite the current pro-European leadership, relations with the ICTY will continue to pose a challenge to any future Serbian government that tries to fulfill international obligations while retaining domestic support.

The second central problem facing the Serbian government is corruption, prevalent from the Milošević era onward but increasingly threatening to the stability of the government, which has been rocked by numerous publicized scandals since the murder of Djindjić. The assassination itself revealed that even the reformist government had a multitude of ties to the criminal underground, and that there were few politicians in Serbia who were not compromised by shady deals, hence the quick destruction of the Zemun clan's "fortress" and the liquidation of its leaders. In a 17 July 2003 report by the International Crisis Group, the government was criticized for remaining "excessively dependent on a Milošević-era financial oligarchy" and obstructed by "a largely unreformed state security and army sector."[127] The ICG's director of its Serbian division, James Lyon, was nearly expelled from the country in the course of preparing the report, which he argued "shows how great the influence of this financial lobby inside the state structures is—and to what extent they feel threatened by the ICG's work."[128]

The Serbian media was full of corruption scandals throughout 2003, many of which were blown out of proportion by the yellow press but nonetheless indicative of the dysfunctional state of Serbian politics. The former governor of the Serbian National Bank, Mladjan Dinkić, who was removed from his position in the summer of 2003, claimed that the "Serbian parliament was controlled by people who got rich on smuggling tobacco, drugs, and weapons," which he attributed to the fact that the "governing coalition, DOS, did not reform the police, court system, and state prosecution."[129] An analyst for the Belgrade newspaper *Kurir* alleged that the "leadership of DOS set aside 500,000 euros to buy a vote of confidence for the Serbian government," citing the figure of up to twenty thousand euros per vote, depending on the importance.[130] The very legitimacy and legality of the parliament have even been called into question by the vice president of Koštunica's DSS, who declared that in the Serbian parliament "there does not exist parliamentary life, nor does there exist true parliamentary work."[131] The scandals and allegations of corruption resulted in resignations and constant personnel shifting in the Serbian government; as of August 2003, five ministers had resigned since the government had been formed in January 2001, and there had been a total of seven prime ministers in that time period.[132] It is naïve to expect that any Serbian government in the near future is going to be immaculate, considering the dysfunctional state the country has been in for over a decade. One reason for the prevalence of corruption among government ranks is the extremely low pay for civil servants, who often need to find additional means to support their families, often through illegal channels. Nevertheless, in order to establish the rule of law and ensure a stable democratic system, the government is going to have to seriously tackle the economic elements, along with the holdover criminal and militant aspects from Milošević's Serbia.

Just as Serbia's domestic politics has highlighted the instability of the post-Milošević government, Serbia's relations with its neighbors have also indicated that not everything changed after October 2000. In a May 2003 interview for *Der Spiegel,* Prime Minister Zoran Živković firmly stated that "Kosovo is a part of Serbia," and that "Albanians were destabilizing Kosovo with the help of the international community."[133] This rhetoric was identical to that used by Milošević, who had always been inflexible on the question of Kosovo, and had used crises in that province to divert attention from domestic problems. According to the Serbian Helsinki Committee, "regarding open questions such as Kosovo, union with Montenegro, the autonomy of Vojvodina, and the question of Republika Srpska, the so-called patriotic block continues to homogenize the nation."[134] In August 2003, the murder of two Serbian youths and the wounding of five others by Albanian extremists in the Kosovo town of Goraždevac prompted the Serbian government, already embroiled in a number of corruption scandals, to suddenly draw attention once again to the situation in Kosovo. The Serbian government's chief representative for Kosovo, Nebojša Čović, flew to New York on 18 August for an emergency session at the UN Security Council, where the "terrorist activity" of individuals associated with the Kosovo Protection Force was denounced and appeals were made to allow the return of Serbian security forces into the province.[135] Čović's trip to the United States, Živković's visit to the wounded survivors in the hospital, and the burials of the murdered youths were closely covered by the print and electronic media. A series of declarations were adopted by the parliament of SiCG the following week, but Kosovar Albanians and the representatives of the international community in Kosovo dismissed them as not having real significance since only the Security Council could make decisions regarding the status of Kosovo. The Serbs of Kosovo continue to have legitimate concerns and fears, but there were also clear cases where the Serbian government was once again manipulating the Kosovo issue to draw attention away from the ongoing shake-ups within the government itself. Some initial steps were taken to begin a dialogue between Belgrade and Priština, notably a meeting held between the representatives of the Serbian and Kosovar governments in Vienna in mid-October, but the two delegations mostly defended their irreconcilable positions rather than attempting some kind of compromise. It also became evident that the international community was more interested in maintaining a status quo instead of seriously pushing some kind of final resolution of Kosovo's status, which means the Kosovo question will remain problematic for some time to come.

In contrast to the continuity with the Milošević era in policy regarding Kosovo, relations have improved with Croatia, which has long seen Serbia as the aggressor and main culprit for the wars of the 1990s. The most significant event was Croatian president Stipe Mesić's visit to Belgrade on 10 September 2003, where the president of Serbia and Montenegro, Svetozar Marović, apologized for the crimes committed by citizens of SiCG against anyone from Croatia.[136] Apparently this apology was a surprise not only to the Croatian delegation but to Marović's associates as well, and Mesić responded by likewise issuing an apology for any crimes committed by Croats. Although this was essentially a symbolic gesture issued by an official with little actual power, it was nevertheless an important step in normalizing relations between two countries that had been involved in a brutal ethnic war, whose wounds have not yet healed. Many Croats criticized Mesić for his apology, and public opinion indicated that the majority of people wanted concrete steps to be taken, such as war reparations and information about missing family members who were taken into Serbian prisoner camps, as well as having the apology take place at the site of some of the worst crimes, not distant Belgrade.[137] Mesić's visit included promises to help speed up refugee returns to Croatia (the removing of visa restrictions and resolving property rights are key elements of this endeavor) and increase economic cooperation. Although a great deal of enmity remains between the two former enemies, and several open issues, such as borders and ownership rights, continue to hinder the normalizing of relations, important symbolic steps have been taken and the leadership of SiCG has been committed to dealing with those issues through diplomacy, rather than the war-mongering of Milošević.

The transformation from an authoritarian to a democratic system cannot be expected to take place overnight, and Serbia is no different in this regard. However, the pace of change has been exceptionally slow, in part because the "bulldozer revolution" of October 2000 failed to change fundamental aspects of Serbian politics and the political system. In stark contrast to the political apathy of the 1990s, Serbia's youth has taken a more active role in bringing about change, participating in such student movements as Otpor. Organizers of the music festival EXIT, held in Novi Sad in July 2002, hoped to shake off xenophobia and encourage young people to build a more democratic and multicultural country, and reminded reporters how concerts in conjunction with street demonstrations were crucial in mobilizing support against the Milošević regime in 2000.[138]

Significantly, the events of October 2000 have created the conditions in Serbia for free and fair democratic elections to determine the political leadership. It will be up to the post-Milošević leadership, however, to lead Serbia into the twenty-first century on a course to build a legitimate and stable state. Ethnic and territorial issues continue to pose difficult challenges to Serbia (see the chapters on Montenegro, Vojvodina, Kosovo, and the Roma in this book), and it will require a rejection of the politics of nationalism to develop constructive relationships among all of Serbia's citizens and neighbors.

Notes

1. Sabrina P. Ramet, *Balkan Babel: The Disintegration of Yugoslavia from the Death of Tito to the Fall of Milošević*, 4th ed. (Boulder, Colo: Westview Press, 2002), p. 56.

2. The latest Croatian census indicates that Serbs dropped from about 12 percent of the population in 1991 to 4.54 percent, although Croatian Serb organizations claim that the data is misleading and that the actual percentage of Serbs is more than 6 percent. See *Vjesnik* (Zagreb), 19 June 2002; online at www.vjesnik.hr.

3. Under pressure from the European Union, Djukanović agreed to hold talks with Yugoslav and Serbian leaders in March 2002, yielding an agreement to cre-

ate a new joint state, Serbia and Montenegro. The viability of this new state remains to be seen, since for the last several years Montenegro has de facto already been independent, with a separate currency, market, and customs regime.

4. In February 2000, Nenad Čanak's League of Social Democrats of Vojvodina approved a document called "Vojvodina: A Republic," which called for the reorganization of Serbia into a federation of six units in order to accelerate democratization and prevent further disintegration of the Serbian state. See Radio Free Europe/Radio Liberty, *Newsline*, 28 February 2000; online at www.rferl.org.

5. *New York Times*, 28 June 2002, p. A3.

6. *New York Times*, 3 March 2002, p. A7; and *The New Yorker*, 27 May 2002, pp. 82–95.

7. Vladimir Goati, "Concluding Remarks," in *Challenges of Parliamentarism: The Case of Serbia in the Early Nineties*, ed. Vladimir Goati (Belgrade: Institute of Social Science, 1995), p. 248.

8. Quoted in Matthew Collin, *Guerrilla Radio: Rock 'n' Roll Radio and Serbia's Underground Resistance* (New York: Nation Books, 2001), p. 19.

9. Robert Thomas, *The Politics of Serbia in the 1990s* (New York: Columbia University Press, 1999), p. 9.

10. Ivan Čolović, *Politika simbola: Ogledi o političkoj antropologiji* (Belgrade: Radio B-92, 1997), p. 15.

11. Several recent studies have analyzed the Kosovo myth in detail, including Branimir Anzulovic, *Heavenly Serbia: From Myth to Genocide* (New York: New York University Press, 1999); and Olga Zirojević, "Kosovo in the Collective Memory," in *The Road to War in Serbia: Trauma and Catharsis*, ed. Nebojša Popov (Budapest: Central European University Press, 2000).

12. Stuart J. Kaufman, *Modern Hatreds: The Symbolic Politics of Ethnic War* (Ithaca, N.Y.: Cornell University Press, 2001), p. 171.

13. Thomas, *Serbia in the 1990s*, p. 239.

14. Ibid., p. 64.

15. The most notable exceptions to that generalization were Vesna Pešić's Civic Alliance of Serbia (GSS) and Zoran Djindjić's Democratic Party (DS), which focused more on economic reform and integration into Europe while downplaying the national question.

16. Thomas, *Serbia in the 1990s*, p. 214.

17. Ibid., p. 292.

18. Kaufman, *Modern Hatreds*, p. 199.

19. Thomas, *Serbia in the 1990s*, p. 48.

20. Georgije Marić, ed., *Hate Speech as Freedom of Speech* (Belgrade: Helsinki Committee for Human Rights in Serbia, 1995), p. 7.

21. For a comprehensive analysis of the role of media in the collapse of Yu-

goslavia, see Mark Thomson, *Forging War: The Media in Serbia, Croatia, and Bosnia and Herzegovina* (Luton, U.K.: University of Luton Press, 1994). While all Croats were increasingly becoming associated with the Ustasha, Kosovar Albanians and Bosniaks were referred to as "Turks," implying their supposed collaboration with Serbia's historic enemy despite the fact that many Albanians had actually fought with the Serbs against the Ottoman invasion and that Bosnia's Muslims are ethnically Slavs.

22. Eric D. Gordy, *The Culture of Power in Serbia: Nationalism and the Destruction of Alternatives* (University Park, Pa.: Penn State University Press, 1999), p. 2. Gordy argues that this destruction of alternatives applied to politics, the economy, and culture in Serbia in the 1990s.

23. Collin, *Guerrilla Radio*, p. 112.

24. Thomas, *Serbia in the 1990s*, p. 224.

25. Filipović was accused of espionage and of spreading false information. See Institute for War and Peace Reporting, "Breaking the Silence," *Balkan Crisis Report*, no. 160 (28 July 2000); online at www.iwpr.net. Filipović was released from prison after having served five months following the fall of Milošević. See *New York Times*, 11 October 2000, p. A8.

26. Thomas, *Serbia in the 1990s*, p. 230.

27. See Gordy, *Culture of Power*, pp. 166, 175.

28. Thomas, *Serbia in the 1990s*, pp. 93–106.

29. Collin, *Guerrilla Radio*, p. 73.

30. Corruption had become so prevalent in Serbia that it permeated to the school system, where students regularly (and openly) paid for good grades. See *New York Times*, 1 July 2002, p. A4.

31. Quoted in Thomas, *Serbia in the 1990s*, p. 159.

32. Ibid., p. 161.

33. See Tim Judah, *The Serbs: History, Myth, and the Destruction of Yugoslavia* (New Haven: Yale University Press, 1997), pp. 170–71. Frano Simatović "Frenki" and Radovan Stojičić "Badža" were two SDB men involved in fomenting rebellion in the Krajina.

34. James Gow, *The Serbian Project and Its Adversaries: A Strategy of War Crimes* (London: Hurst & Co., 2003), pp. 57–72; and Cohen, *Serpent in the Bosom*, p. 133.

35. Interview with Nenad Čanak in *Vjesnik*, 22 February 2003, p. 3.

36. For example, see Louis Sell, *Slobodan Milošević and the Destruction of Yugoslavia* (Durham, N.C.: Duke University Press, 2002), pp. 178–81.

37. Thomas, *Serbia in the 1990s*, p. 275.

38. For a detailed discussion of these elections and the subsequent protests, see ibid., pp. 285–316.

39. Collin, *Guerrilla Radio*, p. 175.

40. By February 2000, over sixty cases with fines totaling over US$1 million were brought against independent media based on a public information law enacted on 20 October 1998. See *New York Times*, 21 February 2000, p. A3. In May 2000, the government's takeover of Drašković's Studio B television and Radio B-92's transmitter led to numerous street demonstrations and a call for civil disobedience by Djindjić. *New York Times*, 26 May 2000; online at www.nytimes.com.

41. Eric Gordy, "Serbia's Bulldozer Revolution: Conditions and Prospects," *Southeast European Politics* 1, no. 2 (December 2000), p. 81.

42. Radio Free Europe/Radio Liberty, *Newsline*, 31 March 2000; online at www.rferl.org.

43. *Star Tribune* (Minneapolis-St. Paul), 5 April 2000; online at www.startribune .com.

44. *Los Angeles Times*, 7 July 2000; online at www.latimes.com. Other changes to the constitution, which Vuk Drašković called "legal terrorism," included the direct election of Montenegrin deputies to the federal parliament instead of being chosen by Montenegro's parliament.

45. Norman Cigar, *Vojislav Koštunica and Serbia's Future* (London: Saqi Books, 2001), p. 35.

46. *New York Times*, 20 September 2000, p. A3.

47. *New York Times*, 22 September 2000, p. A6.

48. The documentary film *Bringing Down a Dictator* (premiered 31 March 2002) shows how members of Otpor and other opposition groups met with Western advisers in Budapest and Dubrovnik for training and funding (www.pbs.org/ weta/dictator/film/). John Anelli of the International Republican Institute claimed that they had trained about 400 election monitors who returned to Serbia to train another 15,000 monitors. See *Washington Post*, 11 December 2000, p. A1.

49. *Blic* (Belgrade), 27 September 2000; online at www.blic.gates96.com. Other sources cited that Koštunica had won at least 51.33 percent of the vote, still enough to claim a first-round victory. See *New York Times*, 6 October 2000, p. A14. The biggest losers of the elections were Šelšelj and Drašković's parties; SRS candidate Nikolić won 6.5 percent of the vote, while the SPO's Mihajlović received only 3 percent. Radio Free Europe/Radio Liberty, *Newsline*, 26 September 2000; online at www.rferl.org.

50. *New York Times*, 25 September 2000, p. A12.

51. *Blic*, 27 September 2000; online at www.blic.gates96.com.

52. *New York Times*, 2 October 2000, p. A3.

53. *New York Times*, 5 October 2000, p. A6.

54. *New York Times*, 6 October 2000, p. A14.

55. Ibid.

56. Sell, *Slobodan Milošević*, pp. 349–50.

57. *Danas* (Belgrade), 7 October 2000; online at www.danas.co.yu.

58. *The Guardian* (London), 18 January 2001; online at www.guardianun limited.co.uk.

59. *New York Times*, 9 October 2000, p. A6.

60. Sonja Biserko, "Foreword," in Cigar, *Vojislav Koštunica*, p. 10.

61. *New York Times*, 16 November 2000, p. A6. The army and secret police continue to be an issue of controversy between Koštunica and Djindjić, with accusations of surveillance and misuse of police files erupting into several scandals, including the "Pavković Affair" in the summer of 2002.

62. Radio Free Europe/Radio Liberty, *Newsline*, 12 October 2000; online at www.rferl.org.

63. See Cigar, *Vojislav Koštunica*, pp. 23–47, for an overview of Koštunica's "nationalist paradigm" during his years in opposition and since he was elected president of the FRY.

64. Radio Free Europe/Radio Liberty, *Newsline*, 28 March 2002; online at www.rferl.org.

65. Radio Free Europe/Radio Liberty, *Newsline*, 21 March 2002; online at www.rferl.org.

66. See the Human Rights Watch report released 12 July 2002 for an overview of ongoing rights abuses in Serbia; online at www.hrw.org/backgrounder/eca/yugo-bcko711.htm.

67. Reported in the *New York Times*, 17 March 2002, p. A4.

68. Institute for War and Peace Reporting, *Balkan Crisis Report*, no. 264 (29 April-4 May 2002); online at www.iwpr.org.

69. Rade Marković replaced Jovica Stanišić in 1998 as head of the secret police. See Sell, *Slobodan Milošević*, p. 292.

70. See *Washington Post*, 25 February 2001, p. A20. Marković was detained by the Serbian government in February 2001 in connection with the alleged assassination attempt on Vuk Drašković. See also *New York Times*, 17 March 2002, p. A4.

71. U.S. Department of State, *Yugoslavia: Country Reports on Human Rights Practices—2001*, at www.state.gov/g/drl/rls/ hrrpt/2001/eur/, section 1.d.

72. *NIN* (Belgrade), no. 2655 (15 November 2001); online at www.nin.co.yu.

73. Radio Free Europe/Radio Liberty, *Newsline*, 16 November 2001; online at www.rferl.org.

74. International Crisis Group, "Belgrade's Lagging Reform: Cause for International Concern," *Balkan Report*, no. 126 (7 March 2002), p. 6. For example, the

political murders of Pavle Bulatović (defense minister), Radovan Stojičić (deputy minister of the interior), Žika Petrović (chairman of the national airline), and Slavko Ćuruvija (journalist) remain unsolved, along with the ongoing disappearance of former Serbian politician Ivan Stambolić.

75. Ibid.

76. *New York Times*, 24 August 2001, p. A9.

77. International Crisis Group, "Belgrade's Lagging Reform," p. 2.

78. Radio Free Europe/Radio Liberty, *Newsline* 6, no. 51, pt. 2 (18 March 2002).

79. *Los Angeles Times*, 19 February 2000, p. 11.

80. Srdja Popović in *Globus* (Zagreb), 6 December 2002, p. 60.

81. *Feral Tribune* (Split), 22 March 2003, p. 49.

82. Interview with Miroljub Labus, *Globus*, 27 September 2002, p. 62.

83. Ibid.

84. *Vreme* (Belgrade), 12 December 2002, p. 15.

85. *Jutarnji list* (Zagreb), 1 October 2002, p. 11. Vuk Drašković, once a leading opposition figure, received a paltry 4.6 percent of the votes, while Pelević received 3.8 percent.

86. *Vreme*, 12 December 2002, p. 15.

87. *Jutarnji list*, 15 October 2002, p. 10. The lowest rates of voter turnout were in Kosovo and southern Serbia (31 percent), where Šešelj's support is the strongest.

88. *Vreme*, 12 December 2002, p. 15.

89. Šešelj received 36.3 percent of the votes, while Pelević came in third place with slightly under 4 percent. Ibid.

90. *Jutarnji list*, 10 December 2002, p. 12.

91. Interview with Sonja Biserko, *Vjesnik*, 2 October 2003, p. 5.

92. Filip Vujanović was elected president of Montenegro when elections were held again on 11 May 2003, winning 64 percent of the votes. Although the opposition once again called for a boycott and voter turnout was 48 percent, the electoral law which required more than 50 percent of voter participation was changed prior to the elections. See *Vjesnik*, 13 May 2003, p. 10.

93. *Jutarnji list*, 28 January 2003, p. 11.

94. *Vjesnik*, 6 February 2003, p. 5. For an overview on the debate over sovereignty in Montenegro, see Philip Lyon, "Montenegro and Yugoslavia: Disassociation, Negotiation, Resolution?" in Vjeran Pavlaković, Sabrina P. Ramet, and Philip Lyon, "Sovereign Law vs. Sovereign Nation: The Cases of Kosovo and Montenegro," *Trondheim Studies on East European Culture and Societies*, no. 11 (October 2002). The new parliament of the joint state first met on 3 March 2003, and on 7 March they elected the new president of SiCG, Svetozar Marović, a Montenegrin deputy who ran unopposed.

95. *Vjesnik*, 6 February 2003, p. 5.

96. Numerous newspapers commented on Serbia's trend of violently removing its leaders. For example, both the *New York Times* and *Vjesnik* carried articles listing a pattern of assassinations in Serbian political life, from Aleksandar Obrenović to Željko Ražnatović "Arkan." See *New York Times*, 13 March 2003, p. A10; and *Vjesnik*, 13 March 2003, p. 3. Some Croatian media even postulated that the killing of Djindjić would speed up Croatian entry into the European Union. See *Jutarnji list*, 14 March 2003, p. 4.

97. Interview with Latinka Perović, *Vjesnik*, 16 March 2003, p. 3.

98. *Jutarnji list*, 28 March 2003, pp. 14–15.

99. *Jutarnji list*, 23 October 2003, p. 11, citing reports from *Nedeljni telegraf*.

100. *New York Times*, 13 March 2003, p. A1.

101. *Panorama* (Zagreb), 19 April 2003, p. 27.

102. *Jutarnji list*, 15 March 2003, p. 4.

103. See Gow, *The Serbian Project*, pp. 80–87.

104. For example, see the article "Criminals in the Arms of the State" in *Panorama*, 1 March 2003, p. 30.

105. *Jutarnji list*, 28 June 2003, p. 13.

106. *Jutarnji list*, 9 April 2003, p. 11. The Croatian media drew parallels with the situation in Croatia—the overlap of war criminals, right-wing political parties, and organized crime—even though Croatian criminal organizations were considered to be "incomparably more benign than those in Serbia." See *Jutarnji list*, 13 March 2003, p. 15; *Feral Tribune*, 15 March 2003, p. 9; and *Globus*, 21 March 2003, p. 46.

107. *Jutarnji list*, 19 March 2003, p. 13.

108. *New York Times*, 28 January 2003; online at www.nytimes.com/2003/01/28.

109. *Jutarnji list*, 22 March 2003, p. 15. Despite a large number of initial charges tying Sarajlić to the Zemun clan, he was eventually charged only for illegally possessing weapons.

110. *Jutarnji list*, 4 April 2003, p. 14.

111. *Jutarnji list*, 3 July 2003, p. 10.

112. *International Herald Tribune* (London), 25 August 2003, p. 4. The International Crisis Group's report on Serbia released 17 July 2003 brought attention to the fact that since March the government imposed media censorship and gave the "police sweeping powers of extrajudicial detention." See the report "Serbian Reform Stalls Again" online at www.intl-crisis-group.org.

113. Interview with Vojislav Koštunica, *Vreme*, 5 June 2003, pp. 17–18. Koštunica insinuated that the government had washed their hands of all connections to the assassins, calling them "untouchable."

114. Interview with Boris Tadić, *Globus*, 15 August 2003, p. 43.

115. Former head of the secret police Radomir Marković revealed that he had

given the task of liquidating Stambolić to Milorad Luković "Legija" and his Red Berets after Milošević ordered Stambolić removed, which was accomplished in the Fruška Gora region of Vojvodina. See *Vjesnik*, 11 September 2003, p. 28; and *Jutarnji list*, 29 March 2003, p. 4. Marković himself received seven years in prison for his role in the attempted murder of Vuk Drašković and other SPO members in 1999. *Jutarnji list*, 31 January 2003, p. 13.

116. *New York Times*, 14 March 2003, p. A27.

117. Interview with Srdja Popović, *Jutarnji list*, 17 March 2003, p. 7.

118. Interview with Latinka Perović, *Vjesnik*, 16 March 2003, p. 3.

119. *Feral Tribune*, 24 May 2003, p. 56.

120. *Jutarnji list*, 21 October 2003, p. 15.

121. *Jutarnji list*, 21 December 2002, p. 10.

122. See *Vjesnik*, 25 February 2003, p. 5; and Vjesnik, 27 February 2003, p. 2.

123. *Jutarnji list*, 2 May 2003, p. 10.

124. *Jutarnji list*, 14 June 2003, p. 5.

125. *Jutarnji list*, 25 October 2003, p. 13.

126. The Serbian public was approving of indictments based on "command responsibility" when it applied to Croatian generals, such as Ante Gotovina for his role in the Croatian military offensives of August 1995, but quickly changed its attitude when Serbian officers were indicted based on similar standards.

127. International Crisis Group, "Serbian Reform Stalls Again," online at www .intl-crisis-group.org.

128. Institute for War and Peace Reporting, *Balkan Crisis Report*, no. 442 (8 August 2003); online at www.iwpr.net.

129. *Jutarnji list*, 10 October 2003, p. 11.

130. *Jutarnji list*, 14 October 2003, p. 10.

131. *Vreme*, 5 June 2003, p. 47.

132. *Danas*, 20 August 2003, p. 4.

133. Quoted in *Jutarnji list*, 20 May 2003, p. 14.

134. Interview with Sonja Biserko, *Vjesnik*, 2 October 2003, p. 5.

135. *Danas*, 19 August 2003, p. 2.

136. *Vjesnik*, 11 September 2003, p. 1.

137. See *Vjesnik*, 11 September 2003, p. 5; and *Vjesnik*, 15 September 2003, p. 5.

138. *New York Times*, 29 July 2002, p. A4.

3

FROM THE FEDERAL REPUBLIC OF YUGOSLAVIA TO THE UNION OF SERBIA AND MONTENEGRO

RENEO LUKIĆ

"In the end, this was the only compromise that could have been reached. It was impossible to achieve more, but I would like to note that things can and should be improved in time. There are examples of such states that were loose unions at first, but have since grown stronger. The United States is one such case. After all, with the passage of time it may turn out that the existing joint powers are insufficient, and that they should be expanded."[1]

"If I were sure that we had a sufficient majority and that we could without risk obtain Montenegrin statehood, I would do just that. Unfortunately, we do not have a convincing majority, therefore it was more important to preserve the current level of Montenegrin statehood than to take the risk of losing everything if the results of the referendum were unfavourable to us."[2]

When in December 1991 the European Community announced its intention to recognize Slovenia and Croatia by 15 January of the next year, the Serbian government quickly declared (on 26 December 1991) that "a 'third Yugoslavia' had been formed with Serbia, Montenegro, and the Serbian Krajina in Croatia."[3] The territory of Krajina was seized by force from Croatia between June and December 1991, and was prepared to be annexed to the newly reemerging Yugoslavia. Serbia and Montenegro did not submit a formal request to the European Community for international recognition of this so-called "third Yugoslavia." The Republic of Serbian Krajina did submit an application for recognition, but it was turned down. The Badinter Commission decided that only the former republics of the SFRY (Croatia, Slovenia, Bosnia-Herzegovina, Serbia, Montenegro, and Macedonia) were entitled to statehood. On 12 February 1992, Serbia and Montenegro agreed to remain in the same state, which claimed continuity with the SFRY. Montenegro, one of two federal entities, then hastily organized a referendum on 1 March 1992. Of the 66 percent of the population that voted (the Montenegrin Albanian and Muslim populations refused to participate), 96 percent answered "yes" to the following question: "Do you agree that Montenegro, as a sovereign republic, should continue to exist within the common state—Yugoslavia—totally equal in rights with other republics that might wish the same?"[4] Serbia did not organize a similar referendum and none of Yugoslavia's four remaining republics ever expressed any intention to join this Yugoslavia.

The final step in forming the new state was taken on 27 April 1992, when the republican parliaments of Serbia and Montenegro and the rump Yugoslavia Federal Assembly issued a "Declaration on the Formation of the Federal Republic of Yugoslavia," which proclaimed the transformation of the SFRY into the FRY. Since then, the FRY has celebrated 27 April as a state holiday, the "Day of Statehood." The Badinter Commission, in its Opinion No. 11, also recognized 27 April 1992 as the date of succession for the FRY.

The international community rejected the Belgrade government's efforts to achieve for the FRY the same successor status vis-à-vis the SFRY as the Russian Federation achieved vis-à-vis the USSR. On 19 September 1992, UN Security Council Resolution 777 declared that the FRY could not automatically assume UN membership as the successor state to the former Socialist Federal Republic of Yugoslavia. The General Assembly was asked to require the FRY to apply for UN membership and in the meantime exclude it from the work of the General Assembly. On 16 July 1993, the Badinter Commission ruled that none of the six successor states of the SFRY (Slovenia, Croatia, Bosnia-Herzegovina, Serbia, Montenegro, and Macedonia) could claim for itself alone the membership rights previously enjoyed by the former SFRY. The Badinter Commission also decided the dates of succession for each recognized successor state of the SFRY. Slovenia and Croatia became independent on 8 October 1991, when their declarations of independence of 25 June 1991 came into effect. Macedonia became independent on 17 November 1991, when it adopted its new constitution. Bosnia-Herzegovina became independent on 6 March 1992, when the results of the 29 February-1 March 1992 referendum were officially recognized.

The four former SFRY republics—Slovenia, Croatia, Bosnia-Herzegovina, and Macedonia—decided to apply for membership in international organizations and since then have been recognized by the international community and admitted as members of the United Nations. But while President Milošević was in power, first as president of Serbia (1989–97), then as president of the FRY (1997–2000), the FRY refused to apply for membership in international organizations. The FRY considered itself the sole successor state of the SFRY, and therefore believed that it was automatically entitled to positions in international organizations previously occupied by the SFRY. The result was partial exclusion from the activities of the United Nations and suspension from other international organizations, including the CSCE (Council for Security and Cooperation in Europe), now the OSCE (Organization for Security and Cooperation in Europe).

For those eight years (1992–2000), the FRY was in legal limbo. The flag of the defunct Socialist Federal Republic of Yugoslavia continued to fly outside UN headquarters in New York since it was the last Yugoslav flag used by the UN Secretariat, but this was not the flag of the FRY. This absurd situation of perpetuating the memory of a nonexistent state had repercussions in the FRY. Between 1992 and 1997, the state holiday of the FRY was 29 November, referring to the founding day of Tito's Yugoslavia in 1943. In 1997, the FRY decided to continue to celebrate 29 November, but in reference to the year 1945, when the monarchy was abolished and replaced by the Republic.

After Milošević's ouster, the new FRY president, Vojislav Koštunica, adopted a policy aimed at integrating the FRY into international organizations and particularly into the United Nations. On 27 October 2000, Koštunica wrote to UN secretary-general Kofi Annan and formally applied for UN membership. Koštunica had been encouraged in this matter by Russia[5] and France,[6] Serbia's historic allies, who promised him support.[7] The FRY's request was processed very rapidly with no country raising any objection, and on 1 November, it became a member of the United Nations. On 23 July 2001, a European Union-FRY Consultative Task Force was inaugurated as the first step toward reaching a Stabilization and Association Agreement with the European Union.[8]

In this chapter, I shall argue that the creation of the Union of Serbia and Montenegro, the successor state of the FRY, does not guarantee the stability and longevity of this state in spite of the European Union's crucial role in its formation. My central contention is that the Union of Serbia and Montenegro is a temporary respite to the process of disintegration of

its predecessor, the FRY, which did not come to its term. The signing of
the Belgrade Agreement, on 14 March 2002, which envisaged the creation
of a new state union of "Serbia and Montenegro," and the adoption in December of the same year of the union's Constitutional Charter has not
changed the process of internal dissolution of the new federal/confederal
state. The Belgrade Agreement was rather an attempt to freeze if not the
debate then the process of disintegration of the FRY for three years (the
agreement is provisional and either party can review the arrangement after three years). It should allow all sides to buy time to find a definite settlement to the question of the statehood of Serbia, Kosovo, and Montenegro.

The Constitution of the FRY

The constitution of the FRY was adopted on 27 April 1992, together with
the "Declaration on the Formation of the Federal Republic of Yugoslavia."
According to the new constitution, the FRY was a federal state composed
of citizens and member republics. In Serbia and Montenegro, the new FRY
constitution was adopted without any public debate. Only 73 of 220
deputies from Serbia and Montenegro in the last SFRY parliament
(*savezna skupština*) voted for it. In effect, as Nebojša Čagorović, a political analyst from Montenegro, wrote, "the constitution was adopted illegally, without a quorum, by the dead legislature of a dead state."[9] As in
1918, Montenegro was once again annexed by Serbia.[10] If the new constitution was to establish legal continuity between the SFRY and the FRY,
it had to be adopted by 147 deputies of the federal chamber of the SFRY;
only in this case could the transfer of authority from the SFRY to the FRY
be considered legal.

The constitution of the FRY was adopted after the constitution of Serbia (September 1990) and before that of Montenegro (October 1992). A
cumbersome document (144 articles) with many overlapping clauses, it
attempted to reconcile two competing claims for sovereignty, one claimed
by the federal units (republics), the other by the federal state. In this regard, the FRY constitution contained the same contradictions and tensions
as had the 1974 Yugoslav constitution, oscillating between a federation and
a confederation. Despite these tensions, the FRY did function as a federal
state; the absence of clarity over the respective jurisdictions of the federal
units and the federal state was balanced until March of 1997 by the close
similarity of the interests between political elites in Serbia and Montenegro. The Montenegrin constitution (1992) was adjusted to accord with the
federal constitution, but the Serbian constitution (1990) never was. In fact,

the constitution of the FRY was an urgent response to the political vacuum created by the disintegration of the SFRY and was adopted in the aftermath of the diplomatic recognition of Slovenia and Croatia in January 1992.

Legislative power in the FRY was exercised by a bicameral parliament (Federal Assembly) representing the citizens (Chamber of Citizens) and the member republics (Chamber of Republics). According to the federal electoral law, 108 deputies to the Chamber of Citizens were elected from the Republic of Serbia. The Republic of Montenegro (with about 5 percent of the population of the FRY) safeguarded its interests through a constitutional clause (Article 80) providing it at least 30 federal deputies. The Chamber of Republics consists of 40 deputies, 20 from each republic. This power-sharing agreement was created to avoid the complete domination by Serbia of its junior partner Montenegro. In both republics, federal deputies to the Chamber of Republics were elected by the respective parliaments, taking into consideration the parliamentary representation of political parties as well as independent deputies. In reality, the political party that controlled the national parliament also controlled the federal parliament. Until the 24 September 2000 elections, the power base of former FRY president Slobodan Milošević was the Socialist Party of Serbia (SPS). Similarly, Momir Bulatović's Democratic Party of Socialists (DPS) had a majority in the national parliament of Montenegro until the May 1998 elections. Thus, the Federal Assembly reflected the balance of political forces in the national assemblies of Serbia and Montenegro. The federal deputies were delegated by the parliaments of their respective republics and were responsible to them.

Federal political power in the FRY was exercised through the relationship between the Federal Assembly and the federal government, whereby the Federal Assembly elected the federal government. The federal prime minister was the central figure in the federal government and personified it. The candidate for this post was proposed by the president of the FRY and had a free hand in selecting the members of the federal government. However, a parliamentary majority in both chambers of the Federal Assembly must approve the program of the government and the composition of the federal government.

The Role of the Presidency in the Federal Constitution

The president of the republic exercised executive power in the FRY jointly with the federal government, and the Federal Assembly elects both.

Although the constitution held that the president of the FRY and the federal prime minister should not be from the same republic (Article 97), Serbia did not always respect this rule. The first president, Dobrica Ćosić, and the first federal prime minister, Milan Panić, were both from Serbia (although Panić was an American citizen). Zoran Lilić, the president until 15 July 1997, was from Serbia, while Prime Minister Radoje Kontić was from Montenegro. Slobodan Milošević, who engineered their elections through the SPS and its Montenegrin counterpart, placed all four in power. When Ćosić and Panić went beyond the limits defined by Milošević, they were immediately deposed by the Federal Assembly, which, at that time, was controlled by the Socialist Party of Serbia and its allies. On 18 May 1998, Milošević orchestrated the dismissal of Prime Minister Radoje Kontić and the federal government, which then lost a vote of confidence in the upper house of the Yugoslav parliament. Kontić had fallen out of favor with Milošević by opposing his plan to impose a state of emergency in Montenegro as a way of blocking the inauguration of the new president, Milo Djukanović, a Milošević critic. Milošević then picked Momir Bulatović as federal prime minister. The latter had just lost the presidential elections to Milo Djukanović and was eager to work with his old ally Milošević to keep Djukanović in check.[11] During his tenure as prime minister (May 1998–October 2000), Bulatović and Milošević used all means available short of military intervention to undermine Djukanović and his government. Bulatović 's political loyalty to President Milošević did not waver throughout Milošević's presidency. In February 2000, Bulatović deemed that "President Milošević was at this moment the best choice to defend the state and national interests of the FRY. Due to the hostility of the international community toward the FRY, we have no alternative but to follow the road chosen by President Milošević."[12]

Constitutionally, the president of the FRY had rather limited state power in comparison to classical presidential political systems such as the American and the French (not to mention the Russian). Article 96 of the constitution regulated the president's prerogatives. The most important functions of the president were: representing the FRY at home and abroad; calling elections for the Federal Assembly; nominating a candidate for prime minister of the federal government; and issuing instruments of ratification for international treaties. Article 136 gave the president of the federation the power to "promote and dismiss officers of the Army of Yugoslavia." Milošević used this right very often to purge the army of allegedly disloyal high-ranking officers. Milošević conducted a spectacular purge of the federal army in 1991–92, while he was the president of Serbia. According to retired admiral Branko Mamula, himself purged by Milošević, 130 generals and high-ranking military officers were sacked from the army in 1991/92.[13] Milošević's control over the army was assured through the promotion of officers loyal to him (e.g., Generals Nebojša Pavković and Dragoljub Ojdanić) and by control over the defense budget. Milošević deliberately reduced the influence and strength of the army and built up powerful police forces (the Služba državne bezbednosti, SDB). In late 1998, Milošević dismissed Chief of Staff General Momčilo Perišić, who had opposed open confrontation with NATO during the Kosovo crisis. Personal authority, however, was the most important building block in Milošević's pyramid of power, and it rested on the formal and informal networks he had built since 1997. As Attila Agh wrote in 1998, in the FRY "the real power is concentrated in the hands of an omnipotent President without any 'checks and balances.'"[14]

It is important to bear in mind that Milošević deliberately tailored the constitution of the FRY to fit his personal needs. As long as he was the president of Serbia, he wanted the Yugoslav federation to have a constitutionally and politically weak president. A balanced relationship between the two was not in the autocratic Milošević's interest. But the situation changed after Milošević completed his second mandate as president of Serbia in June 1997 and was elected president of the FRY on 15 July 1997. Barred by the Serbian constitution from seeking a third term as president of Serbia, Milošević succeeded in getting elected by the federal parliament as president of the FRY, with a four-year mandate. The 138–member Chamber of Citizens of the federal parliament elected Milošević by 88 votes to 10; the vote in the Chamber of Republics was 29 to 2.

In preparation for assuming the position of president of the FRY, Milošević had already transferred a group of his most trusted aides from Serbian to federal institutions in spring 1997. These included Zoran Sokolović (minister of internal affairs) and Nikola Šainović (deputy prime minister). These appointments show that Milošević had already reinforced the power of federal institutions without actually changing them.

For Milošević, the Serbian and FRY presidencies became interchangeable institutions. When Milošević was elected president of the FRY, political power shifted from the Serbian presidency to the federal presidency without any institutional changes on the federal level. Milošević's proxies, directly accountable to him, controlled the Serbian presidency and deprived the parliament of its political autonomy. Thus, Milošević preserved the facade of federalism while assuming de facto dictatorial powers. Milošević's federal presidency lasted from 15 July 1997 until 6 October 2000.

Under his tenure, the FRY de facto lost Kosovo, which became a UN protectorate for an indefinite period of time when the Security Council adopted Resolution 1244 in 1999. As the president of the FRY, Milošević strained relations with Montenegro to the breaking point. By the summer of 2000, when Milošević announced his intention to seek a second term as president of the FRY, the Yugoslav federation had become completely dysfunctional. In a constitutional "coup" engineered by Milošević on 6 July 2000, the parliament hastily changed the federal constitution (Articles 97 and 98) and adopted a constitutional amendment regarding the procedure for election of the president. The Montenegrin government rejected the constitutional amendments and its parliament declared them null and void. The parliament's resolution provided the Montenegrin government with a legal base for refusing to participate in the federal presidential elections held on 24 September 2000. This is the reason the Montenegrin government did not consider Koštunica the legal president of the FRY.

Milošević opted for the election of the federal president by direct popular vote in general elections scheduled for 24 September 2000. His intention was to enhance the legitimacy and visibility of the post. A new mandate would have allowed Milošević to stay in power for another eight years. The International Criminal Tribunal for the former Yugoslavia (ICTY) in The Hague had indicted Milošević on 27 May 1999, following the campaign of ethnic cleansing in Kosovo, which he had orchestrated. Staying in power was the safest way for him to avoid extradition and trial in The Hague.

The Supreme and Constitutional Courts

Two other relevant institutions established by the federal constitution were the Supreme and Constitutional Courts. The control of the Constitutional Court by Milošević was revealed on 4 October 2000, when in an apparent attempt to keep him in power, the Court annulled parts of the contested Yugoslav elections of 24 September 2000. The Court invalidated the presidential elections and ordered new elections. Court president Milutin Srdić said, "a new election should be held before the President's mandate expires."[15] This meant that Milošević should serve out his last year in office and call a new presidential election before July 2001. The popular revolt of 5 October 2000 in Belgrade forced the Federal Electoral Commission, which had previously falsified the results of the presidential elections, to recognize Vojislav Koštunica as the winner of the elections. Thus, the decision of the Constitutional Court of 4 October 2000 became null and void.

The constitutional manipulations engineered by Milošević and his stooges demonstrated that the separation of powers between the executive, legislative, and judiciary was in fact nonexistent in the FRY.

Conflict and Cooperation between Serbia and Montenegro

Because of the ethnic, religious, and linguistic similarities between Serbs and Montenegrins, one would expect that the new federation would be more harmonious than the previous one, which included six different nations. But as Elizabeth Roberts writes, "the distinguishing feature of Montenegrin history is the way it has engendered a dual sense of identity—both Serb and Montenegrin—giving rise to bitter divisions that erupted into civil war previously this century and continue to cast their shadow today."[16] This division in Montenegro is better known as a division between the zelenaši (Greens), advocates of Montenegrin independent statehood, and the bjelaši (Whites), proponents of unilateral unification with Serbia.[17] Srdja Pavlović, a historian from Montenegro, argues that the current debate between governing and nongoverning elites in Serbia and Montenegro over the identity of Montenegrins and the future of the FRY "greatly resembles the debate that was going on in the early 1920s." He continues: "Greens and Whites are confronting each other [today] not with books but with political slogans, mass rallies, and arms."[18]

The cultural closeness between the Serbs and Montenegrins makes relations between these two political communities (federal units) very delicate. The political interests of the two are not necessarily or always compatible with their cultural and religious closeness. After World War Two, many Montenegrins moved to Serbia, particularly to Belgrade, where they assumed high positions in the federal administration. Because of its similarities with the Serbs and its complete integration into Serbian society, the Montenegrin community in Serbia (140,000 according to the census of 1991) is categorically opposed to the independence of Montenegro. The same goes for the Serbian community living in Montenegro (57,000 people according to the census of 1991). This community is also well integrated into Montenegrin society. It is the author's view that although Serbians and Montenegrins share many commonalities, they are two distinct nations like, for example, the British and American nations or the German and Austrian nations.

Milošević's family reflects well this dual identity of many Montenegrins. Milošević's father was Montenegrin, but Milošević himself was born in Serbia and he has made his entire political career in Serbia. His brother

Branislav, former FRY ambassador to Russia,[19] declared himself Montenegrin and made his diplomatic career as a cadre from Montenegro, climbing the ranks of the League of Communists of Yugoslavia (LCY).

The conflict of interests between Serbia and Montenegro was preceded by a conflict within the Montenegrin leadership. From 1988 to 1996, two politicians, Momir Bulatović and Milo Djukanović, dominated Montenegrin politics. They came to power in Montenegro by staging an internal "coup" in the League of Communists of Montenegro (LCM) in 1989. In January 1989, Milošević's supporters in Montenegro organized demonstrations against the local communist leadership, which resigned under pressure from the streets and yielded to those politicians (Bulatović and Djukanović) who supported Milošević's policy of reshaping Yugoslavia along the lines of a tightly centralized federation. Both men were associated with Milošević's "antibureaucratic revolution" and closely cooperated with the Serbian leadership during the disintegration of Yugoslavia. In 1990, the LCM changed its name to the Democratic Party of Socialists. Momir Bulatović became the chairman of the party and later the president of Montenegro. Djukanović was picked by Bulatović to be his prime minister. On 12 February 1991, at the age of twenty-nine, Djukanović became the youngest prime minister in Europe. As prime minister, Djukanović served two terms. In 1998, he became the president of Montenegro. The DPS under the leadership of Bulatović and Djukanović became a loyal satellite of the Socialist Party of Serbia, led by Milošević.

Cracks between Belgrade and Podgorica, which had been carefully hidden during the war in Croatia and Bosnia-Herzegovina, appeared in 1996. The new fragile peace in the Balkans revealed differences between the national interests of Montenegro and Serbia. With wartime solidarity gone, Montenegro realized that Serbia as ruled by Milošević remained a pariah state within the international community despite the Dayton agreement. Montenegro felt that the "outer wall" of international sanctions imposed on the FRY, banning it from membership in international financial organizations, was harming its own economy and international standing. In response, Montenegro began to display a "Slovenian syndrome"—to use an analogy from the previous Yugoslav federation—in its relations with Serbia; namely, to press for greater political autonomy from its senior partner. I would argue that the conflict between Serbia and Montenegro strongly resembles the conflict between Serbia and Slovenia between 1987 and 1991.[20] Like Slovenia and Croatia in 1990–91, Montenegro initiated a process of disassociation from the federal institutions in 1997.

The conflict between Belgrade and Podgorica is primarily political and does not have an ethnic dimension,[21] unlike the conflicts in Croatia and Bosnia-Herzegovina. Former Slovenian president Milan Kučan acknowledged the legitimacy of Montenegro's right to self-government when he declared (in late 2000) that Slovenia "will respect the democratically expressed will of Montenegro."[22] In November 2000, while receiving President Djukanović, Kučan stressed that "10 years ago Slovenia used the right to self-determination," and that Montenegro also enjoyed this same right. Kučan was one of the first statesmen in the region to insist on the positive correlation between people's right to self-determination and the establishment of a democratic polity and respect for human rights. In the case of Slovenia, independent statehood went hand in hand with membership in international organizations. President Kučan said, "Montenegro must not remain a hostage in Yugoslavia. It has the right to live democratically and become a European state."[23]

Croatia would also recognize Montenegro as an independent state if its citizens so decide in a referendum supervised by the international community. The Croatian foreign minister Tonino Picula suggested this possibility when he stated that Croatia became an independent state by urging the international community to respect its right to self-determination, which in his view is "one of the fundamental democratic rights." Picula said that Montenegrins should benefit from the same rights as Croatia had a decade before.[24]

In 1996, a pro-Western faction of the political elite within the Montenegrin ruling party, the DPS, under the leadership of Prime Minister Milo Djukanović, began openly propounding a different economic and foreign policy from that of the federal government led by the Milošević puppet Radoje Kontić. Djukanović suddenly broke politically and ideologically with Milošević and Bulatović to lead the reform-oriented wing within the Socialist Party. In contrast to Bulatović (then DPS chairman, Montenegrin president, and Milošević's closest ally), Djukanović almost overnight adopted Western values and came to lead a new generation of young technocrats. Željko Ivanović, an independent journalist from Montenegro, offered the following explanation of the sudden political transformation of Milo Djukanović:

> Thanks to his frequent contacts with foreign diplomats and officials, he [Djukanović] realized that stubborn defiance and nose-thumbing at the world powers, the trademarks of Milošević and his yes-men, amounted to

a masochistic and suicidal policy. Thus, for purely pragmatic reasons, Djukanović decided to change his tune and put an angel's mask over his tarnished face.[25]

Djukanović's prime objective was the economic development of Montenegro through cooperation with and eventually integration within Western European international organizations such as the European Union, the Council of Europe, and others. Djukanović presented Montenegro's new orientation in the following terms: "Europe is our only possible choice. This country can only have a future if it follows that road. Our place is in Europe, both geographically and historically, we belong to European civilization, and we have to remain a part of it, economically, politically and culturally."[26] While Bulatović supported Milošević's hard-line policy toward its neighbors even after the signing of the Dayton agreement, Djukanović advocated speedy normalization of diplomatic relations with former Yugoslav republics, now independent states. Between 1998 and 2000, Montenegro's government considerably improved relations with Croatia (opening the border crossing at Debeli Brijeg and establishing a Croatian Council in the town of Kotor) and also with Slovenia. The latter represented informally the interests of Montenegro at the UN Security Council. During the June 2000 Security Council session which discussed the situation in the Balkans, the Slovenian mission in the Security Council distributed to the other members a document entitled *Montenegro and the Balkan Crisis*.[27] The document was presented as a "nonpaper" (i.e., it did not have the status of an official document, but the Security Council chairman brought it to the attention of other members at the beginning of the session). In this document, the Montenegrin government denied the legitimacy of the FRY's practice of providing diplomatic representation for the interests of Montenegro in the United Nations and other international organizations.

At the end of 1996, Djukanović argued that Montenegro should distance itself from Serbia in both foreign and economic policies. In December 1996, the Serbian government, in an apparent attempt to mute the unrest caused by its cancellation of election results, decided to pay pensions, salaries, student grants, and social welfare which had been in arrears. Prime Minister Djukanović and his economic advisers feared that such payments could be made only by printing more money without the reserves to back it. This in turn could trigger a disastrous hyperinflation, as in 1993. Should hyperinflation return, Djukanović threatened, Montenegro would introduce its own national currency, the *perper*.[28] However,

Djukanović's main offense was that he dared to express open criticism of Milošević. According to Djukanović, the international image of Milošević was so bad that his election as president of the FRY could only further damage the interests of the Yugoslav federation, and thus of Montenegro. Djukanović and his economic advisers realized that Milošević's alliance with the hard-liners in Republika Srpska in Bosnia-Herzegovina, and the growing violence in Kosovo fueled by Milošević and his entourage, threatened to keep the FRY excluded from support of Western financial institutions such as the International Monetary Fund and the World Bank for the indefinite future.

The long-simmering conflict over politics and personalities between Djukanović on the one side and Bulatović and Milošević on the other came to a head in March 1997. Djukanović made this rift public after he realized that his faction within the DPS could not impose its views on Bulatović's wing, which still dominated the party's upper echelons. By going public, Djukanović took a considerable political risk. As expected, he immediately became a target of the Milošević-controlled Belgrade media. Surprisingly, he survived the first attempt by Milošević and Bulatović to eliminate him politically. During his protracted battle with Milošević and Bulatović, Djukanović won significant support within the DPS and even among the opposition Liberal Party (LSCG led by Slavko Perović) and the Popular Party of Novak Kilibarda. Djukanović's resistance was supported by independent media in Belgrade and also by the Serbian opposition organized in the Zajedno coalition. On 24 June 1997, at a meeting of the Main Board of the DPS, 56 of 97 members supported Milošević's candidacy for the presidency of the FRY, 10 abstained, and, led by Prime Minister Djukanović, 31 voted against Milošević. Although Djukanović lost this political battle with Bulatović and Milošević, he managed to retain a high profile in Montenegro. In the summer of 1997, Djukanović decided to challenge Bulatović in the presidential elections scheduled for October 1997. During the presidential campaign, Djukanović sought to build up his image as a "modernizer" and a "technocrat" who could make use of his international contacts to salvage Montenegro's sinking ship. Bulatović's campaign rhetoric drew on the symbols and traditions of Serbian nationalism, which British analyst Robert Thomas called a "strategy of national puritanism."[29] Bulatović portrayed Djukanović as a black marketeer whose wealth came from the trafficking of cigarettes.

The first round of the presidential elections in Montenegro took place on 6 October 1997. The proportion of participation was 67.38 percent. According to the official results released by the Republic Election Board, the incumbent president Momir Bulatović received the plurality of votes: 147,615, or 47.45 percent. Bulatović's challenger, Djukanović, received 143,348, or 46.72 percent. As neither candidate won an absolute majority, a second round of voting was held on 21 October. In the second round, Djukanović won 174,176 votes and Bulatović 168,864. A victory based on such a slim majority foretold a difficult presidency for Djukanović.[30]

Djukanović versus Milošević (1998–2000)

After becoming president of Montenegro, Milo Djukanović sought to consolidate his power. Between January and May 1998, his main task was to mobilize his supporters for the forthcoming parliamentary elections in Montenegro, scheduled for 31 May. Meanwhile, a split occurred within the Democratic Party of Socialists. Bulatović created the new Socialist People's Party (SNP), while Djukanović's wing retained the party name. In order to increase Bulatović's visibility and that of his new party in Montenegro, Milošević appointed Bulatović to the post of federal prime minister in May 1998. Djukanović, in preparation for the parliamentary elections, formed a coalition named "That We Might Live Better" (DZB). It was a coalition of three parties: the Democratic Party of Socialists, the People's Party (NS), and the Social Democratic Party (SDP). As the leader of this pro-reform coalition, Djukanović portrayed himself as a political alternative to the pro-Milošević coalition.

In the parliamentary elections held on 31 May, the DZB coalition won 42 of 78 seats in the National Assembly of Montenegro, while the Socialist People's Party led by Momir Bulatović won 29. Having won the parliamentary elections, the DPS candidate should have held the post of federal prime minister. Instead, as mentioned earlier, President Milošević chose the loser, Momir Bulatović, for this post, whose party, the SNP, went into opposition. The DPS considered Bulatović's appointment unconstitutional. From that moment on, the Montenegrin government and President Djukanović refused to acknowledge the legitimacy of the federal institutions; thus, the federation became dysfunctional. This was the root of the conflict between the DZB coalition and President Milošević.

Djukanović's double victory represented the most serious challenge to Milošević's rule since he had become president of the FRY. When asked what he thought about the FRY president, Djukanović stated that:

> There are two opposing concepts in Yugoslavia. There is the one that I stand for—full democratization—which undermines the other concept, that of

the charismatic leader. I stand for radical economic change and privatization, an open state toward the world. As opposed to this, Milošević's option is marked by [his] strong autocratic personality, quite counterproductive. Time is on my side.[31]

Under Djukanović's leadership, Montenegro wanted to assume important state competencies at the expense of the federal institutions. This political strategy was forced upon Montenegro by the openly hostile attitude of Milošević and the Montenegrin elite led by Bulatović. Milošević considered the federal state to be in the service of Serbian state interest. He simply ignored Montenegro's attempts to carve out separate interests, to which it was entitled as an equal member of the federation.

The "cohabitation" between Milošević and Djukanović was, thus, uneasy, particularly after the Montenegrin government submitted to the federal government a document, *The Basis for Defining the New Relationship between Montenegro and Serbia,* the aim of which was to restructure the FRY and radically transform it into an asymmetric federation with elements of confederation. This document, also called the "Platform," contained many legal provisions similar to the proposal submitted by Croatia and Slovenia in October 1990.[32] The proposal called for the creation of "two sovereign states" linked by a common currency and the exercise of some joint responsibilities in defense and foreign affairs. The sovereignty of the republics as defined in the Platform implied the exercise of internal sovereignty only. This is why the proposal envisaged the preservation of a single state, with one UN seat. The FRY, the document suggested, should be renamed the "Association of the States of Serbia and Montenegro." The Platform was presented on 5 August 1999, after NATO's occupation of Kosovo. At that moment, the FRY was in complete international isolation and the Montenegrin initiative was a desperate attempt to escape the sinking ship. The federal government and Milošević completely ignored this document and did not bother to reply.

From that moment, the Montenegrin government accentuated its strategy of disassociation with regard to the federal institutions. Learning from Croatian and Slovenian experiences, the Montenegrin government and parliament decided not to adopt a formal Declaration of Sovereignty or to proclaim outright independence, since these legal steps would have triggered open military intervention by the Army of Yugoslavia (VJ). Instead, the Montenegrin leadership opted for an indirect approach, or as some analysts have called it, "creeping independence." The aim of this strategy was the gradual buildup of an independent state.

In two years Montenegro succeeded in taking over most of the functions of the federal institutions. It also began to implement economic reforms, thus inching toward a market economy.[33] When in 2000 the newly elected president of the FRY, Vojislav Koštunica, replaced Milošević, he recognized this reality when he stated that Montenegro was, practically, not under the sovereignty of the FRY.[34] The Montenegrin government also took over the monetary and banking system, foreign trade, customs, and taxation. Montenegro did not introduce its own currency, the *per-per*, as it had threatened in 1996, but instead, on 2 November 1999, introduced the German mark (DM) as a parallel currency to the Yugoslav dinar, thus reducing the influence of the Yugoslav Central Bank on its economy. On 13 November 2000, the dinar was completely withdrawn from circulation in Montenegro, and the DM was used for all payments and transactions and thus served as the official currency. In 2002, after the euro became legal tender in the majority of EU countries, Montenegro switched to the euro. With that, a Yugoslav unified market and monetary union ceased to exist.

Other attributes of sovereign polity were taken as well, such as control of the customs regime, creation of a distinct visa regime, and internal security. In order to neutralize the intimidations coming from the federal army, the Montenegrin government built up a police and paramilitary force of some twenty thousand men to counter the fourteen thousand federal army troops based in Montenegro, along with nine hundred Milošević and Bulatović loyalists in the 7th Military Police Battalion. On 2 October 1999, the Montenegrin parliament passed a Law on Citizenship, creating a new legal category of citizenship distinct from that of the FRY. The law grants Montenegrin citizenship to individuals either on the basis of parental citizenship (*jus sanguinis*) or place of birth (*jus soli*).

To defend the acquired attributes of sovereignty under threat by the federal government, Montenegro has also relied heavily on the support of the international community (the European Union, United Nations, NATO, and the United States). In the aforementioned document *Montenegro and the Balkan Crisis,* the Montenegrin government argued that Montenegro should have access to international political and financial institutions in order that it could achieve positive change despite the existing barriers. In this way, Montenegro could represent a positive model for democratic struggle and pro-democracy forces in Serbia. When the conditions are ready, this could lead to an agreement with democratic Serbia on the shape and content of future relations, which would be most acceptable for the peoples of these two countries, for peace, stability of the region and the whole of Europe.[35]

The gradual takeover of the functions of the federal state in the territory of Montenegro created a situation of Montenegrin semi-independence, which the FRY leadership vigorously opposed. These functions are, as Montenegrin politicians used to say, the "acquis" of sovereignty that the new leadership in the FRY and in Serbia had to accept. While building a democratic polity, Montenegro has made real progress in the area of human rights, protecting the rights of minorities—both ethnic and religious—and in building a civil society. It would be fair to say that Montenegrin society, to its credit, has become since 1999 a distinct society from that of Serbia, which is, after thirteen years of Milošević's rule, at the very beginning of the process of democratization.

The Relations between Montenegro, Serbia, and the Federal Authorities after the Ouster of Milošević

President Koštunica stated on many occasions that one of his main priorities is to restructure the federal state and accommodate Montenegro. In his interview with the Serbian daily *Politika*, Koštunica said that Serbia and Montenegro should stay together because "every link that connects Serbia and Montenegro historically, spiritually and culturally, is stronger and deeper than what divides them."[36] Koštunica envisages the adoption of a new federal constitution to get rid of the current bogus federalism and, in more general terms, of Milošević's political legacy. In Koštunica's view, the new constitution should give a clean slate to the federal state and should enshrine a new federal arrangement among Montenegro, Serbia, and the federal government. According to Koštunica, the union between Serbia and Montenegro should have a single legal personality in international relations and one seat in the United Nations. The union should also have a joint federal government and president, a single army, a single currency, and a common foreign policy. These are, in Koštunica's words, "the minimal standards of a federal state." These views were expressed in the platform authored by Koštunica and Djindjić and formally approved by the Democratic Opposition of Serbia (DOS). The platform was formally proposed to the Montenegrin government on 10 January 2001, and thus represented the official view of the federal government and the Serbian government in the negotiations with Montenegro. Koštunica wanted to build a strong federal state (*Bundesstaat*), reminiscent of American or German federalism. The question is whether Montenegro, with its strong state tradition, is ready to accept this brand of federalism. Koštunica's vision of the federal state, in its ideal version, may look like Canadian federalism, with Montenegro playing the role of Quebec or British Columbia (two politically "incorrect" Canadian provinces). Koštunica asserted, and on this point he was in agreement with President Djukanović, that the "Yugoslav idea" is dead, and that it lost any meaning when two constitutive nations, the Slovenes and Croats, seceded from the "second Yugoslavia."[37] The new name of the federal state should make explicit reference to the union or commonwealth of Serbia and Montenegro.

The positions of President Djukanović and the Montenegrin government concerning a new union are quite different in content and in form from those of Koštunica and the DOS. The Montenegrin side initially favored direct negotiations between Serbia and Montenegro, thus bypassing the federal president and the federal government. The Montenegrin government wanted Serbia and Montenegro to constitute themselves into two independent sovereign states subject to international law before entering into negotiations on restructuring the federal state. In addition, Serbia and Montenegro should have two seats in the United Nations and separate memberships in international organizations. According to President Djukanović, "an independent Montenegro does not exclude the possibility of forming a union with Serbia. This initiative means a contribution to the improvement of our relationship with Serbia, and therefore an improvement of regional stability."[38] Koštunica and Djindjić received these two demands, separate statehood and a separate membership in international organizations, with hostility. In reality, Montenegro wanted a *Staatenbund* with Serbia; that is, a confederation with some elements of federation. President Djukanović wanted the new union between Serbia and Montenegro to have only three functions in common: defense, monetary policy, and foreign affairs. These demands were presented to the citizens of both federal units, by the Montenegrin government, on 28 December 2000. The new platform of the Montenegrin government, entitled *The Platform Concerning the Essence of the New Relations between Montenegro and Serbia*,[39] represented the official position of the Montenegrin government for the forthcoming negotiations with the Serbian government and the federal presidency. At the end of the negotiation process between the two federal units, Montenegro will organize a referendum to seek approval for an agreed solution, or, if the negotiations fail, to seek independence. The formal negotiations about restructuring the federal state started on 17 January 2001. The first negotiating session between Koštu-nica, Djukanović, and Djindjić was inconclusive. Both sides clung to their respective platforms.[40]

The first casualty of the new platform was the stability of the Mon-tenegrin coalition government. The People's Party, a member of the DZB coalition from its inception, left the government and joined the opposi-tion. The People's Party refused to support the platform and boycotted work on drafting new legislation for a referendum to be organized, after the agreement on constitutional restructuring of the FRY would be signed, between Belgrade and Podgorica. Dragan Šoč, the chairman of the People's Party and the former minister of justice, wanted the government to cling to the "old Platform," which was submitted to the federal government and to Milošević on 5 August 1999. With the People's Party out of the gov-ernment, the polarization of political parties in the Montenegrin parlia-ment over future ties with Serbia and the federal government was com-plete. Two parties, the People's Party and the Socialist People's Party, rejected the platform of the Montenegrin government, and now both sup-port the platform that President Koštunica and the DOS offered Monte-negro. Three political parties, the Democratic Party of Socialists, the Social Democratic Party, and the Liberal Party, all accepted the platform of the Montenegrin government as a basis for negotiations with Serbia and the federal government.

The Results of the Parliamentary Elections, 22 April 2001

Thus, holding early elections to the National Assembly of the Republic of Montenegro was the only way to break the political jam caused by the dis-integration of the ruling DZB coalition. The National Assembly was dis-solved in February 2001, followed by a call for new elections (April 2001). President Djukanović set the tone at the opening of the electoral campaign when he declared in February 2001: "The state of Serbia and the state of Montenegro are well and alive. We have to define them constitutionally, provide them with international recognition and integrate them into Europe. The Serbian nationalists will be indeed disappointed with this out-come. However, in acting so, Montenegro will finally bury the tragic idea of Greater Serbia."[41] The election campaign was characterized by a nar-row focus on the central question of Montenegro's legal status and the future of the federal state. This crucial question mobilized 82 percent of eligible voters, who took part in the elections held on 22 April 2001. The DPS and the SDP considered the elections to be a rehearsal for the referendum to follow a few weeks later.

A total of sixteen parties and coalitions registered candidate lists. The major contestants in this election were the following pro-independence and pro-federation blocs respectively: (1) the "Victory for Montenegro" coalition of the DPS and the SDP; and (2) the "Together for Yugoslavia" coalition of the NS, the Socialist People's Party, and the Serbian People's Party (SNS). Individually registered parties took a more radical stance on each side of the pro-independence/pro-federation divide, shadowing the coalitions. The Liberal Party of Montenegro was committed to unqualified independence, while the newly formed People's Socialist Party (NSS), an offshoot of the SNP representing former prime minister of the FRY Momir Bulatović, was strongly pro-federation.[42]

The pro-independence coalition "Victory for Montenegro" led by President Djukanović won the election. However, the margin of the victory was very narrow. In addition, Djukanović's coalition failed to win an outright majority. This result came as a surprise. Svetozar Marović, a vice president of the DPS, expected that the pro-Yugoslav bloc would not win more than 30 percent of the votes.[43] The real winner of this election was the pro-independence Liberal Party, which found itself in the position of a guarantor of political stability. The "Victory for Montenegro," in order to form a government, needed the support of the LSCG. The complete results of the election are shown in table 1.

According to the OSCE/ODIHR Election Observation Mission report, the election "was conducted generally in accordance with OSCE commitments for democratic elections and the Council of Europe standards."[44] Although the coalition "Together for Yugoslavia" was defeated, its leaders were satisfied with the outcome of the election. Together with President Koštunica and Prime Minister Djindjić, they submitted, in August 2001, a new platform to the coalition "Victory for Montenegro" to reform the federal state. The new platform was almost identical to that presented by Koštunica and the DOS in October 2000. On 28 August, the foreign minister of Montenegro notified his counterpart Goran Svilanović that he and his ministry, following a decision of the Montenegrin government, had cut off all contacts with the federal Ministry of Foreign Affairs.[45] The election results showed that popular support for Montenegrin statehood and independence was alive and well. This support had grown considerably from an estimated 15 percent of the population in the aftermath of the creation of the FRY in 1992 to approximately 55 percent in 2001.[46]

TABLE 1. Results of parliamentary elections, 22 April 2001

Political party or coalition	For/against independence	Votes won (%)	Seats[1]	Special constituency[2]	Total seats
Victory for Montenegro (DPS + SDP)	For	42	33	3	36
Liberal Party of Montenegro	For	7.8	6	—	6
Together for Yugoslavia (SNP + NS + SNS)	Against	40.6	33	—	33
People's Socialist Party	Against	2.9	—	—	—
Serbian Radical Party (SRP)	Against	1.2	—	—	—
Democratic Union of Albanians	For	1.2	—	1	1
Democratic League in Montenegro (ethnic-Albanian party)	For	1	—	1	1
Others	—	3.3	—	—	—
TOTAL		100	72	5	77

SOURCE: *Republic of Montenegro/Federal Republic of Yugoslavia, Parliamentary Election 22 April 2001,* OSCE/ODIHR Election Observation Mission Report, Warsaw (12 June 2001). See also "Montenegro: Resolving the Independence Deadlock," *ICG Balkans Report* no. 114 (Podgorica/Brussels).

1. The threshold to gain seats in parliament was 3 percent of the total ballots cast.
2. Special five-seat constituency covering areas where ethnic Albanians form a majority.

The International Dimension
of the Constitutional Crisis in the FRY

Until December 2000 it looked like the two-sided negotiations between Montenegro and Serbia (the Djukanović approach), or the three-sided negotiations, involving Montenegro, Serbia, and the federal government (Koštunica's approach), would decide the future of the federal state. Then a new actor emerged, namely the UN secretary-general Kofi Annan, whose main concern was how to resolve the status of Kosovo; he suggested on 21 December 2000 that a UN-sponsored conference be held in the year 2001 about the constitutional restructuring of the FRY. Annan suggested that the FRY should be transformed into a confederation, encompassing Serbia, Kosovo, and Montenegro.[47] President Koštunica and Branko Lukovac, in charge of Montenegrin diplomacy, both rejected Annan's proposal out of hand, though for different reasons. Koštunica wanted to preserve Milošević's legacy with regard to Kosovo. In 1989, Milošević had abolished Kosovo's constitutional autonomy as defined in the 1974 constitution (as will be discussed in the chapter by Frances Trix in this book). He then created a unitary Serbian state enshrined in the Serbian constitution of 1990. Koštunica did not and does not want a new federalization of Serbia. In March 2000, a few months before becoming the president of the FRY, Koštunica stated that "the idea of a Federal Serbia is a dangerous one. We have had some legal precedents, which allowed the breakdown of the federation [the SFRY]. . . . Our party [the DSS] is advocating the creation of a state composed of the regions, which should have strong elements of self-rule. Some regions may have a higher degree of self-rule than others."[48] In the same article, Koštunica lumped together the following politicians: Nenad Čanak, chairman of the Assembly of Vojvodina and the chair of the League of Social Democrats of Vojvodina, as well as the author of the document *Vojvodina Republic,* Milo Djukanović, and Slobodan Milošević, saying that "all three are interested in having maximum power on limited territory."[49] Basically, Koštunica accused them of being power hungry and harboring a political culture of medieval lords, thus encouraging the atomization of the FRY. Čanak is one of the most respected opposition leaders in Serbia and a strong supporter of the federalization of Serbia.[50] He advocates the creation of five republics in Serbia: Vojvodina, Kosovo, Sandžak, Šumadija, and Belgrade. Čanak and his party refused to support Koštunica's platform. At the meeting of the DOS held on 14 January 2001, Čanak 's party abstained from the vote on the Koštunica-Djindjić platform.

Koštunica's "Jacobin" concept of the state is at odds with constitutionally defined decentralization as advocated by Čanak and Djukanović. Koštunica seems to favor for Serbia the French administrative division of territory into "departments" and "cantons." In my view, however, this cannot be a solution for governing multiethnic Serbia. The regionalization of Serbia, if this means its "departmentalization," is not the proper answer for managing its heterogeneity. It is rather the Swiss model of decentralization that Serbia should follow. Branko Lukovac, in rejecting Annan's proposal for a three-sided confederation, wanted to disassociate Montenegro's future from that of Kosovo. The latter risks remaining a crisis spot in the region for years to come.

The Impact of Montenegro's Independence on Kosovo

Serbia, the federal government, and the international community are afraid that independence for Montenegro will open the way to independence for Kosovo. UN Security Council Resolution 1244 refers to Kosovo as part of the FRY, and not of Serbia. Thus Koštunica and Djindjić feared that international recognition of Montenegro would lead to the formal disintegration of the FRY and the subsequent loss of Kosovo. Serbian political parties in power and in opposition want to avoid at any cost a situation whereby Albanians from Kosovo could find themselves able to convince the international community to terminate the UN protectorate over Kosovo.

The Belgrade Agreement of 14 March 2002 addressed the question of Kosovo in the following way: in the event Montenegro leaves the union, Serbia will be the successor state, and explicitly so regarding the implementation of UN Security Council Resolution 1244 for Kosovo. In other words, if the union disintegrates and Montenegro becomes an independent state, Kosovo will automatically stay within Serbia. Keeping Kosovo from independence, and from Belgrade's de facto control, is also the goal of the Bush administration, which stated in July 2001 that "Kosovo is not ready for independence or for any degree of control by the new, democratic government in Belgrade."[51] The linkage between the fates of Montenegro and Kosovo is vigorously rejected by President Djukanović. In a speech at a conference in Brussels on 26 February 2000, dedicated to Montenegro, Djukanović stated that "it would be politically immoral and unjust to tie the destiny of a people, in this case the people of Montenegro, to this regional problem for which no one has a solution at this time."[52] In August 2004, the newly appointed foreign minister of Montenegro, Miodrag Vlahović, stated that "Europe is opposed to the independence of Montenegro because of the unsettled legal status of Kosovo."[53]

To accommodate Montenegro and other players in the present constitutional crisis, Miodrag Isakov, chairman of the reformist party of Vojvodina (a member of the DOS), suggested that Serbia and the federal government accept the Montenegrin platform. Isakov proposed that the constitutional changes requested by the Montenegrin government should be met by Serbia and the federal government and should be codified in the new federal constitution. However, he insisted that Montenegro should wait two to three years (with international recognition), hoping that during these years Kosovo's legal status will be sorted out. Isakov went on to say, "At this moment Serbia does not fulfill the conditions for in-

ternational recognition, because no one knows what the borders of Serbia are today, and because of the unsettled legal status of Kosovo."[54]
Isakov's observations were later taken into consideration by the European
Union and its high representative Solana when they decided to tackle the
relations between Serbia and Montenegro in December 2001. Veton Surroi, editor of the Kosovo daily *Koha Ditore,* has argued that the independence of Kosovo should be preceded by a buildup of its institutions. Surroi wrote, "I've suggested before that the final act in the disintegration of
former Yugoslavia could be played out in 'a Taiwan scenario,' in which all
three states, going through a process of internal consolidation, will necessarily focus more on the function of the state than on its international
recognition."[55] The current political strategy of mainstream Kosovo Albanian leaders such as Ibrahim Rugova is to participate actively in the buildup
of Kosovo institutions, as undertaken by the UNMIK (United Nations
Mission in Kosovo) administration. As long as the UNMIK administers
Kosovo, not a single state will recognize a unilateral declaration of independence announced by Kosovo's political parties. Albanian president Mei-
dani thinks that Kosovo could become an independent country when it
joins "the European Union together with other Balkan states."[56] It is my
view that the Union of Serbia and Montenegro was created in the first place
to give the international community time to find a permanent solution
for Kosovo, and in the second, to sort out the relations between Serbia
and Montenegro. In this respect, the Belgrade Agreement has effectively
bought time, thus the United Nations gave itself three more years to think
how to solve the Kosovo dilemma. On 14 October 2003, under the auspices of the UNMIK and in the presence of prominent representatives of
the international community (the European Union, NATO, and the
United States), Serbia and Kosovo began negotiations in Vienna to find a
modus vivendi between the two political entities. No significant progress
was made and negotiations soon collapsed.

The Attitude of the United States
toward Montenegro's Independence

Since 1997, the United States has provided Montenegro with considerable
political and economic aid. While Milošević was in power, the United
States supported Montenegro, which was seen as a democratic alternative
to the authoritarian Milošević regime. The Clinton administration urged
the unity of all opposition in Serbia and Montenegro to topple Milošević's

regime. It was Secretary of State Madeleine Albright who, though unsuccessfully, tried to convince President Djukanović and his allies to participate in the federal presidential elections in September 2000 to remove Milošević from power. According to Goran Svilanović, the first foreign minister of the FRY after the fall of Milošević, it was Albright who was the first in January 2001, a few months after the fall of Milošević, to advocate the policy of a "democratic Montenegro within a democratic Yugoslavia."[57] After Milošević was removed from power and Koštunica consolidated his hold on federal institutions, the Bush administration decided to continue with the policy of a "democratic Montenegro within a democratic Yugoslavia." Thus, the United States now opposes the independence of Montenegro. In the entourage of Javier Solana, the opinion prevails that the role of Secretary of State Colin Powell was decisive in convincing Djukanović to postpone the holding of the referendum originally scheduled for May 2002. Powell believed that the independence of Montenegro would have created further instability in the Balkans, particularly in Kosovo and Macedonia. After his meeting with Powell in February 2002, Djukanović understood that the United States would not recognize Montenegrin independence, even if the results of the referendum were favorable to the "Victory for Montenegro" coalition. During his meeting with Djukanović, Powell reiterated U.S. support for the EU policy of a "democratic Montenegro within a democratic Yugoslavia" by stating without ambiguity that Javier Solana represented the "international community" and that Montenegro should not therefore count on a division between the United States and the European Union regarding the question of independence. It is rather ironic that after Serbia voted Milošević and his cronies out of power, the international community believed that the Montenegrin "way" should end and merge with the Serbian road to a democratic polity, in order to build together a new federal state. Joseph R. Biden, a U.S. senator from Delaware (D) and chairman of the Senate Committee on Foreign Relations, disagrees with the Bush administration and the European Union on the issue of a Montenegro referendum on independence. Biden thinks that "the idea of a plebiscite, the idea of a vote on independence in Montenegro" will not be "per se an absolute, total disaster." He added, "I think we have become, as we Catholics say, more Catholic than the Pope on Montenegro."[58]

In fact, as Biden's declarations suggest, Montenegro has found some of its greatest supporters in the U.S. Congress. The Congress has earmarked or recommended substantial aid to Montenegro over the past few years:

$41 million in fiscal year (FY) 1999 and $42 million in FY 2000. For FY 2001, the estimates are that Montenegro will receive around $89 million in aid. The House Appropriations Committee, in its report about the FY 2002 foreign operations appropriations bill (passed 10 July 2001), has "strongly supported" aid to Montenegro and has recommended that the Bush administration provide $60 million worth of aid to the Republic.[59]

The Role of the European Union in the Creation of the Union of Serbia and Montenegro

After the pro-independence parties formed a government in Montene-gro following the parliamentary elections of April 2001, the dynamic pointing toward a referendum gained momentum. Between March and July, the negotiations between the leaders of Montenegro and Serbia were suspended. Meanwhile, the Liberal Party, whose support of Djukanović was crucial in order for his new-old premier Vujanović to form a gov-ernment, has energized the public debate in favor of the independence of Montenegro. A public opinion poll conducted in Montenegro by the agency DAMAR between 27 September and 4 October revealed that 55.4 percent of the population favored independence.[60] These results proba-bly encouraged the Montenegrin negotiating team to stick to its agenda during the negotiations with President Koštunica and Premier Djindjić on 26 October which ended in failure. This prompted President Koštunica to declare: "We were unable to bring our stances closer, which means only one possible route remains—and that is for the public of Montenegro to voice its view."[61] At the same time, Premier Vujanović publicly declared that the best way out of the current constitutional crisis would be the dis-solution of the FRY. Vujanović's recommendation was to repeat the Czechoslovak scenario of 1992–93, which was a consensual separation ("velvet divorce").

It was at this point that the European Union decided to step in and prevent the seemingly inevitable referendum in Montenegro. The Euro-pean Union asked its high representative, Javier Solana, to undertake a diplomatic mission whose aim was to prevent further disintegration of the FRY. Solana's task was to persuade Montenegro to reach an agreement and to preserve the federal union while creating through negotiations a new state community that would better preserve the national interest of Montenegro. The first step in the three-sided negotiations aimed at post-poning the referendum in Montenegro was scheduled for spring/summer 2002.

During his visit to the FRY in December 2001, French president Jacques Chirac clearly stated in Belgrade that the European Union might not recognize the independence of Montenegro even after a referendum. The European Union had built its argument in favor of the federal state on economic grounds. Solana warned the political leaders of Montenegro in an op-ed article published in the Montenegrin daily *Vijesti* that if their highest priority was for the Republic to join the European Union, then the idea of independence was a bad one. "My impression is that the Montenegrins need to take the new developments in Europe into account," wrote Solana. "The prosperity of the people of Montenegro will be determined by the level of inward [domestic] investments, not by a seat at the United Nations or a network of embassies. Employment and career prospects for youth will likewise depend on education and training, not on having one's own army. And the dynamism of the economy will depend on its openness and the level of regional integration, not on a separate customs service."[62] With these words, Solana sent a strong message to the Montenegrin leaders, emphasizing that the nation's economic well-being would be jeopardized if Montenegro adopted unilateral steps leading toward independence. Being the recipient of international assistance from the European Union and the United States, Montenegro could not ignore Solana's warnings. In addition, the European Union insisted that "the progress toward a Stabilisation and Association Agreement (SAA) between the EU and the FRY could be held up by the separation."[63]

The power politics practiced by Solana, who was not a neutral mediator but an advocate of a federal state, a goal shared by President Koštunica and Serbian premier Djindjić, yielded results after two months of intense diplomatic activities and arm twisting. On 14 March 2002, the political leaders of Serbia (Premier Djindjić), Montenegro (President Djukanović and Premier Filip Vujanović), and the FRY (President Koštunica and deputy prime minister of the federal government Miroljub Labus) signed an agreement in Belgrade to replace the FRY with a new state (having a single legal personality) to be called the Union of Serbia and Montenegro. The agreement bears the signatures of the legitimate leaders of Serbia, Montenegro, and of the federal institutions.

The president of Serbia, Milan Milutinović, who had been indicted by the ICTY following the campaign of ethnic cleansing and war crimes committed by the Yugoslav police and army in Kosovo in 1999, was excluded from the negotiating process supervised by Solana. Also, the federal prime minister, Dragiša Pešić, who at that time was a member of the SNP,[64] did

TABLE 2. The main political parties in Montenegro

Party	Political alignment
Democratic Party of Socialists (DPS)	Headed by President Milo Djukanović. The DPS is a communist successor party and the core of the governing coalition. It is pro-independence.
Social Democratic Party (SDP)	A pro-independence, pro-Western party, led by Ranko Krivokapić. Coalition partner of the DPS.
Liberal Party of Montenegro (LSCG)	The most consistently, radically pro-independence party, led by Miodrag Živković. Supported the DPS-SDP coalition government after the April 2001 election.
Socialist People's Party (SNP)	Biggest pro-Yugoslav Montenegrin party, opposed to independence, an offshoot of the DPS. Predrag Bulatović has headed the SNP since February 2001. Member of the "Together for Yugoslavia" coalition.
People's Party (NS)	A pro-Serbia, anti-Milošević, anti-independence party led by Dragan Šoč. Member of the "Together for Yugoslavia" coalition.
Serbian People's Party (SNS)	A pro-Serbia, anti-independence party led by Božidar Bojović; an offshoot of the NS. Member of the "Together for Yugoslavia" coalition.
People's Socialist Party (NSS)	Pro-Yugoslav party that split with the SNP in February 2001 after the SNP forced former leader Momir Bulatović to resign.

SOURCE: International Crisis Group, "Still Buying Time: Montenegro, Serbia and the European Union," *Balkans Report* no. 129, Podgorica/Belgrade/Brussels (7 May 2002), p. 19.

not sign the document. It was his deputy, Labus, who signed it, an apparent concession to Montenegrin president Djukanović.

The Belgrade Agreement comprised the elements of three platforms, two presented by Montenegro in 1999 and 2001, and one presented by Koštunica and his allies from Montenegro in 2001–2. The agreement is a compromise between two opposing political projects which were on the negotiating table between January and March 2002: one was an independent statehood for Montenegro and the other was a "new" federal state. It is important to bear in mind that the Belgrade Agreement was reached only after massive horse-trading, supervised by Javier Solana, had taken place. In my view, this agreement will last only as long as the European Union is unambiguously behind it.

The creation of the new state was the direct outcome of the work of the international community (the European Union and the United States in the first place) and was backed by all major international organizations, the United Nations, OSCE, and the Council of Europe. The primary objective of the agreement was to stop the process of disintegration of the FRY which, at the end of October 2001, seemed to be unstoppable.

The Belgrade Agreement is a short document which gives very little detail or guidance as to how the new state would work in practice. The principal provisions of the agreement can be summarized as follows:[65]

1. The agreement will be in force for three years. After this period, the member states will be allowed to reconsider their allegiance to the union. If Montenegro should leave the union after three years, Serbia will be considered the successor state, specifically concerning the provisions of UN Security Council Resolution 1244 on Kosovo. Serbia will also, in this case, inherit the membership in international organizations (the IMF, World Bank, United Nations, etc.).

2. The union will have a unicameral parliament in which the Montenegrin representatives will benefit from positive discrimination measures, a Council of Ministers with duties that shall be specified at a later date, and a court with constitutional and administrative functions. A president will also be elected by the parliament. The agreement allows the Constitutional Charter to decide the mode of selection for the MPs who will sit in the union's new parliament: by delegation from the national parliaments or by direct elections in each republic (state).

3. The president will be in charge of proposing the composition of the Council of Ministers. The Council of Ministers will comprise five departments: foreign affairs, defense, international economic relations, internal economic relations, and the protection of minority and human rights.

4. The presidents of the union, of Serbia, and of Montenegro will form a Supreme Defense Council, which will have control over the army and military affairs. The conscripts will have the right to serve in their home republic.

5. The functions of ministers and deputy ministers will be allocated under a system of rotation of offices, in which representatives of each mem-

ber state will occupy these functions in turn. A provision for rotation will also be established for the representation in international organizations such as the United Nations, the OSCE, or the Council of Europe.

6. Some federal institutions will be located in Podgorica, the capital city of Montenegro.

7. Even if the agreement does not deal extensively with the economic sphere, some details indicate that Montenegro should be able to retain the economic independence attained over the last three years. However, the agreement calls for the establishment of a common market between Serbia and Montenegro. The customs policies of the two states will also be harmonized in line with the policies of the European Union.

8. The European Union will be responsible for the implementation of the agreement. It will also be bound to take into account the complaints of either of the member states if one of them feels that the other one is not following the agreement, notably on the matters concerning the development of a common market or the harmonization of the customs policies.

The signatory parties to the Belgrade Agreement decided that the next step toward implementation of the process of creating a new state should be to draft a new Constitutional Charter, a legal foundation for the common state. An ambitious agenda was set in March 2002, providing that by the end of June 2002, a Constitutional Commission delegated by the parliaments of the FRY, Serbia, and Montenegro (twenty-seven members, nine from each parliament) should finish a draft of the Constitutional Charter for the new union. Soon after, the Constitutional Charter should be adopted by the parliaments of Serbia and Montenegro and submitted to the FRY parliament. The Constitutional Charter was finalized in December 2002. On 4 February 2003, the new state of Serbia and Montenegro was proclaimed after its Constitutional Charter had been approved by the lower house of parliament of the old Federal Republic of Yugoslavia.

Reactions to the Belgrade Agreement in Montenegro and Serbia

Then president Djukanović made a considerable personal effort to justify the Belgrade Agreement. He emphasized the positive sides of the agreement, arguing that it was the maximum Montenegro was able to achieve at that particular moment. It seems that the hostility of the international community toward the independence of Montenegro was essential in forcing Djukanović and Vujanović to sign the agreement. All things considered, Montenegrin public opinion has favorably received the Belgrade

Agreement. One month after the signing, 61.6 percent of citizens of Montenegro supported the agreement, and President Djukanović was, as of April 2002, by far the most popular leader in Montenegro.[66]

Among the critics of the Belgrade Agreement, the Liberal Party has most strongly rejected it. The leaders of the Liberal Party, Vesna Perović, Miodrag Vicković, and Miodrag Živković, accused Djukanović of treason. In the view of the Liberal Party, Djukanović betrayed the national interest of Montenegro and the agreement between the DPS and the Liberal Party providing that the latter will support the government if it continues to work for independence. To demonstrate its dissatisfaction with the Belgrade Agreement, the Liberal Party's members of parliament withdrew support of the government coalition and provoked its fall, in spite of the efforts of Javier Solana and Djukanović to convince them to continue to back it. President Djukanović was thus obliged to schedule new parliamentary elections for 6 October 2002. The Liberal Party was determined to inflict maximum political damage on Djukanović and the DPS. Liberals entered into the coalition with the SNP in several municipalities, which they now govern together, to the dismay of their former allies, the DPS and the SDP.

President Koštunica was satisfied with the Belgrade Agreement because it "did stop the disintegration of the country."[67] In his address to the Federal Assembly, Koštunica stated, in a manner reminiscent of Milošević, that the Belgrade Agreement had defeated the partisans of the independence of Montenegro, such as Latinka Perović and Ivo Banac, respectively a Serbian and a Croatian American historian, as well as Sonja Biserko, a human rights activist from Belgrade.[68] Koštunica believes in the future of the Union of Serbia and Montenegro because, as he said, "the European Union actively supports the take-off of this state."[69] However, Koštunica, who in early 2004 would reemerge as prime minister of Serbia, also envisages that after three years, Montenegro may walk away from the common state. If this happens, Koštunica underlines, "Serbia and Montenegro will go for a velvet divorce, as the Czechs and Slovaks did in 1992."[70]

In Serbia, among those who expressed reservations regarding the agreement, the Democratic Christian Party of Serbia (DHSS) and its chairman Vladan Batić voiced opposition to the new state of Serbia and Montenegro. Batić and his party rejected the common state on the ground that it does not advance the national interest of Serbia. Batić argues that Serbia and Montenegro need to be independent states before engaging in a new cooperative model, most likely confederal. Such a confederation has to be based on an international treaty between the two states, both having a legal personality in international organizations and separate seats in the United Nations. In promotion of this political project, the DHSS collected four hundred thousand signatures in Serbia and in July 2002 presented them to the Serbian parliament.[71] The DHSS insisted that the citizens of Serbia have to decide for themselves about the independence of their state and advocated organizing a referendum on the question.

The Links of President Djukanović to Organized Crime

Ottavio del Turco, former Italian finance minister, was one of the first among Western leaders to accuse Montenegrin politicians of having links with organized crime controlling the black marketing of cigarettes in the Balkans. Branko Perović, former foreign minister of Montenegro, resigned after del Turco made his accusation public. In the spring of 2002 the public prosecutor of the city of Bari, Giusseppe Scelsi, initiated an investigation into the alleged involvement of President Djukanović in the traffic of cigarettes. In July 2002, Scelsi invited the editor of the Croatian weekly *Nacional*, Ivo Pukanić, to give a deposition concerning the activities of the "tobacco mafia" in the Balkans.[72] *Nacional* had published in 2001–2 several articles on the subject, claiming that President Djukanović was directly involved in the illegal traffic of cigarettes and that he had made millions of dollars by providing a legal cover for money laundering and other activities. Following the publication of the articles in *Nacional*, the Montenegrin assembly (parliament) established a commission to verify the allegations.

President Djukanović has always denied any involvement in the traffic of cigarettes. He himself proposed to the Montenegrin parliament the creation of the commission to clear his name. Vesna Perović, the chairwoman of the parliament and a political opponent of Djukanović, has accused the latter of trying to obstruct the work of the commission in its investigations.[73] On 25 July 2002, the report of the commission was adopted by the Montenegrin parliament, although without the votes of the MPs from the DPS, who walked out during the vote. The report confirmed that Montenegro was a hub for the traffic of cigarettes. However, it stopped short of accusing President Djukanović of involvement in criminal activities.[74] The charges in the report were serious enough to prompt the aforementioned prosecutor, Scelsi, to invite the chairman of the commission, Vuksan Simonović, to testify in Bari on 7 August 2002 and to present the evidence the commission had gathered during the investigation. It does not seem that President Djukanović has been politically weakened by the recent scandals brought against him and the Montenegrin government in different European capitals. In the parliamentary elections held in 2002, Djukanović's coalition won an absolute majority. Djukanović became the new prime minister, while Filip Vujanović, the former prime minister, was elected president in the 2003 presidential elections.

Conclusion

The roots of the constitutional crisis between Serbia and Montenegro go back to the years 1996–97, when the consensus between the two national elites who created the FRY was broken. The conflict of interests between Serbia and Montenegro, and the conflict of personalities (Milošević versus Djukanović), are the main causes of the present crisis. I have emphasized the primacy of conflicting interests because the conflict between the two federal units continues even after the ouster of Milošević. The rhetoric in Serbia among the political establishment and media with regard to the Montenegrin drive toward independence is hostile, as it was during the 1980s when Slovenia began its drive toward independence. For the Serbian media, the main culprit responsible for the bad state of Serbian-Montenegrin relations is a "secessionist leadership in Podgorica," led by Prime Minister Djukanović. This negative image of the Montenegrin leadership in Serbia did not change considerably even after Milošević's departure from political life. Only after Koštunica resigned in 2003, and Svetozar Marović, a Montenegrin, became the first president of the new Union of Serbia and Montenegro, did the tone and rhetoric slightly change in Serbia with regard to Djukanović and the pro-independence bloc.

From 1997 on Montenegro has chosen, like Slovenia ten years before, the road to Europe as its economic future. Serbia, by contrast, has been in conflict with the Atlantic community since 1991, and its exclusion from Europe, after the indictment of Milošević by the ICTY, became definitive. For Montenegro's long-term interests, this position became untenable and a possible future stumbling block.

The future of the Union of Serbia and Montenegro is on the negotiating table, and the Serbian and Montenegrin political elites are discussing it passionately. Vojislav Koštunica and Milo Djukanović, the respective prime ministers of Serbia and Montenegro, have both publicly asserted that the state created on 14 March 2002 may be just another temporary solution for Montenegro and Serbia as was the FRY, which lasted ten years. Unlike Milošević, who possessed a near absolute determination to use force to preserve the communist federation, Koštunica has promised a democratic and peaceful solution to the present constitutional crisis between Serbia and Montenegro over the common state's future. In his endeavor to salvage the common state, Koštunica has received unconditional backing from the European Union, the United States, and international organizations. Svetozar Marović, Koštunica's replacement, wishes to carry out the Belgrade Agreement and promised to actively support the institutions of the new state. At the same time, Marović declared to the Montenegrin press on 17 March 2004, "I was born in Montenegro and I feel like a Montenegrin. I see the future in Montenegro's right to independently choose its own path."[75]

The persistence of differences between Serbia and Montenegro after the fall of Milošević stems from the structural differences between the two federal units and their size,[76] though one should not underestimate the determination of the Montenegrin elites to defend the present de facto status of an independent state which Montenegro enjoys. The Montenegrin elite, which today governs the country, began to realize after 1997 that the federal state cannot be built only upon the temporary consensus of the political elites, as was the case in 1992. When in 1997–98 the consensus was definitively lost, the Montenegrin government and president found themselves in the extremely vulnerable position of being at the mercy of Milošević and the federal army. Now the Montenegrin political elites have an adamant desire to build a nation-state, which they consider to be the most effective instrument for protecting the established political order in Montenegro from the illiberal Serbian alliance which is still alive and well in Serbia. The latter, together with the remaining supporters of Milošević and the Serbian Radical Party, occupy 103 seats out of 250 in the Serbian parliament, elected in 2003.

If there is no explicit and firm commitment by the Serbs and Montenegrins to live in one state, then the Union of Serbia and Montenegro cannot become a viable federal state. As Vojtech Mastny has convincingly demonstrated, federalism in East Central Europe in the nineteenth and twentieth centuries was a monumental failure.[77] The signing into creation of the Union of Serbia and Montenegro in 2002 has extended the lease of the federal/confederal state for three more years. It seems that it is only in 2005 that Serbs and Montenegrins will decide whether they will live in a single state or in two states.

Notes

I would like to thank Professor Sabrina Ramet for her comments on earlier drafts of this chapter. Jean-François Morel, a graduate student from Laval University (Quebec City, Canada) was my research assistant for this chapter, and I thank him for the valuable help he provided. I would also like to thank NATO for the generous support I received for this research during my tenure as a NATO Fellow (2000–2002). The views expressed in this chapter do not reflect the position or policy of NATO and are strictly personal.

1. Vojislav Koštunica, "Yugoslav President's Address to the Federal Assembly," 18 April 2002, online at www.predsednik.gov.yu/press/tekst.php?id=551&strana= naslovna.

2. Milo Djukanović, *Vijesti* (Podgorica), 15 March 2002, online at www.vijesti .cg.yu.

3. International Crisis Group, "Current Legal Status of the Federal Republic of Yugoslavia (FRY) and of Serbia and Montenegro," *Balkan Report* (Washington/ Brussels), no. 101 (19 September 2000), p. 6; online at www.crisisweb.org.

4. Ibid., p. 8.

5. For Russia, Serbia remains, before and after the ouster of Slobodan Milošević, the last outpost in Europe, after the Soviet Union lost its sphere of influence in East/Central Europe following the disintegration of the international communist system. Serbia welcomed the Russian military presence in Kosovo (KFOR) and in Bosnia-Herzegovina (SFOR). In contrast, the Russian military presence in Moldova is strongly challenged not only by the host country but also by the overwhelming majority of the OSCE states. In fact, Russia refused to reduce, and ultimately withdrew, its forces from Moldova, although it had announced to do so at the Istanbul summit of the OSCE states in Turkey in 1999. See "OSCE and Russia Fall Out over Chechnya," *BBC News*, 28 November 2000, online at news .bbc.co.uk.

6. For France's very ambiguous attitude toward Serbia and the FRY during a decade of Yugoslav wars (1991–99), see my previous work "The US, Europe and the Balkans Wars," in *Rethinking the International Conflict in Communist and Post-Communist States: Essays in Honor of Miklos Molnar,* ed. Reneo Lukić (Aldershot, U.K.: Ashgate, 1998), pp. 101–39. See also Reneo Lukić, "l'Antiamericanisme des opposants a la participation française a la guerre contre la Republic federale yougoslave," *Etudes internationales* (Canada) 31, no. 1 (March 2000), pp. 135–64. In his book *Crimes de guerre a l'OTAN,* Pierre-Henry Bunel, former French intelligence officer, condemned by the French authorities for spying on behalf of

the FRY, described not only his personal sympathy for the Serbs, historical ally of France, but also for his colleagues, most of them, like Bunel, graduates of the prestigious military academy Saint-Cyr. Pierre-Henry Bunel, *Crimes de guerre a l'OTAN* (Paris: Editions Première, 2000).

7. Interview with Vojislav Koštunica, "Koštunica: Uspravili smo se kao država i vratili u svet" (We rose as a state and returned to the world), in the daily *Politika* (Belgrade), 12 November 2000, p. 1.

8. International Crisis Group, *Balkans Report* (Podgorica/Brussels), no. 114 (1 August 2001), p. 1.

9. Nebojša Čagorović, "Conflicting Constitutions in Serbia and Montenegro," *Transition* (Prague) 3, no. 4 (7 March 1997), p. 28.

10. Srdja Pavlović, "The Podgorica Assembly in 1918: Notes on the Yugoslav Historiography (1919–1970) about the Unification of Montenegro and Serbia," *Canadian Slavonic Papers* 41, no. 2 (June 1999), pp. 157–76. See also Dimitrije Vujović, *Ujedinjenje Crne Gore i Srbije* (The unification of Montenegro and Serbia) (Titograd: Istorijski Institut Crne Gore, 1962), p. 325; and Barbara Jelavich and Charles Jelavich, *The Establishment of the Balkan National States, 1804–1920* (Seattle: University of Washington Press, 1977).

11. On 14 and 15 January 1998, on the eve of President Djukanović's inauguration, Momir Bulatović organized and led the demonstrations in Podgorica. The demonstrations led to violence between the supporters of Bulatović and the police. Bulatović accused Djukanović of electoral fraud in the presidential elections.

12. Interview with Momir Bulatović, "Djukanović je naivan momak" (Djukanović is a naïve guy), *NIN* (Belgrade), no. 2565 (24 February 2000), p. 17.

13. Branko Mamula, "Poslije Miloševićevog sloma" (After Milošević's downfall), *Monitor* (Podgorica), no. 525 (10 November 2000); online at www.monitor .cg.yu.

14. Attila Agh, *Emerging Democracies in East Central Europe* (Glos., U.K.: Edward Elgar, 1998), p. 202.

15. Philippa Flether, "Serbians Appear to Unseat Milošević in Popular Revolt," *Reuters,* 5 October 2000.

16. Elizabeth Roberts, "Montenegro," *The South Slav Journal* 20, nos. 1–2 (Spring-Summer 1999), p. 9.

17. Ivo Banac, *The National Question in Yugoslavia: Origins, History, Politics* (Ithaca, N.Y.: Cornell University Press, 1984), pp. 270–91.

18. Pavlović, "The Podgorica Assembly," p. 170.

19. Branislav Milošević was recalled from Moscow in December 2000, after the downfall of Slobodan Milošević.

20. Fundamental differences developed which the SFRY could not resolve between Slovenia and Serbia regarding their national interests in the late 1980s.

Slovenia, at that time, was aiming to join European international organizations, a symbol of economic prosperity, while Serbia opted for strengthening its ethnic nation-state (Greater Serbia) through wars and ethnic cleansing. See Reneo Lukić and Allen Lynch, *Europe from the Balkans to the Urals: The Disintegration of Yugoslavia and the Soviet Union* (Oxford: Oxford University Press, 1996), pp. 144–94.

21. Ethnic conflict breaks out when there is a denial of collective rights and identity by one group over another, while political conflict concerns the distribution of power and resources among two or more competing political elites.

22. Quoted by Esad Kočan, "Slovenija na jugu" (Slovenia in the south), *Monitor*, no. 527 (24 November 2000); online at www.monitor.cg.yu.

23. Quoted in the *New York Times*, 12 August 2000; online at nytimes.com/library/opinion.

24. Quoted by *Vijesti*, 3 February 2001, online at www.vijesti.cg.yu.

25. Željko Ivanović, "Reform as Expediency," *Transition* 5, no. 3 (March 1998), p. 56.

26. Milo Djukanović, "Strategic Initiatives of the Federal Republic of Yugoslavia—Fundamentals for a New Beginning," *Document* (Podgorica), 3 April 1998, online at www.montenet.org/mnews/osnoveeng.htm.

27. "Montenegro and the Balkan Crisis" online at www.mnews.net.

28. Lukić, *Rethinking the International Conflict*, p. 146.

29. Robert Thomas, *The Politics of Serbia in the 1990s* (New York: Columbia University Press, 1999), p. 379.

30. "Elections in Montenegro," *Review of International Affairs* (Belgrade), no. 1061 (15 October 1997), p. 40.

31. Interview with Milo Djukanović, "Leader May Begin New Wave in Balkan," *The Globe and Mail* (Toronto), 24 October 1997, p. A15.

32. Lukić and Lynch, *Europe from the Balkans to the Urals*, pp. 169–73.

33. *Vijesti*, 22 November 2000, at www.vijesti.cg.yu.

34. Interview with Vojislav Koštunica, "Neču završiti kao Gorbačov" (I will not end up like Gorbachev), Vreme (Belgrade), no. 519 (14 December 2000); online at www.vreme.com/519.

35. "Montenegro and the Balkan Crisis" online at www.mnnews.net.

36. Interview with Vojislav Koštunica, "Država po volji naroda" (The state according to the will of the people), *Politika*, 30 December 2000, p. 1.

37. Interview with Vojislav Koštunica, "U novi vek s uredjenom državom," (In a new century with a well-settled state), *Glas javnosti* (Belgrade), 7 December 2000; online at www.glas-javnosti.co.yu.

38. "Montenegro's Djukanović Digs in Heels on Independence Despite US Opposition," *AFP*, 6 February 2001; online at sg.dailynews.yahoo.com.

39. *Vijesti*, 29 December 2000; online at www.vijesti.cg.yu.

40. *New York Times*, 18 January 2001, p. A8.

41. Milo Djukanović, *Vijesti*, 2 February 2001; online at www.vijesti.cg.yu.

42. Republic of Montenegro/Federal Republic of Yugoslavia, Parliamentary Elections 22 April 2001, OSCE/ODIHR Election Observation Mission Report Warsaw, 12 June 2001.

43. Interview with Svetozar Marović, *Monitor*, no. 548 (20 April 2001); online at www.monitor.cg.yu.

44. Republic of Montenegro/Federal Republic of Yugoslavia, Parliamentary Elections, 22 April 2001.

45. *Vijesti*, 28 August 2001; online at www.vijesti.cg.yu.

46. Janusz Bugajski, "The Case for Montenegro Independence," online at www.csis.org.

47. *Glas javnosti*, 21 December 2000, online at www.glas-javnosti.co.yu.

48. Batić Bačević, "Severna liga" (Northern league), *NIN*, no. 2566 (2 March 2000), p. 22.

49. Ibid.

50. On 20 August 2001, representatives of the leading political parties and NGOs in Vojvodina adopted a "platform" to facilitate the restructuring of relations between Vojvodina and Serbia. The platform calls for the adoption of the new constitution of Serbia, in which Vojvodina will enjoy a high level of political autonomy, similar to that which it had in the 1974 constitution of the SFRY. See *Pobjeda* (Podgorica), 21 August 2001, online at www.pobjeda.co.yu.

51. *New York Times*, 25 July 2001, p. A1.

52. Quoted by the International Crisis Group, "Montenegro: Settling for Independence?" *Balkans Report* (Podgorica/Brussels), no. 107 (28 March 2001), p. 19; online at www.intl-crisis-group.org.

53. "Europa zbog Kosova neće referendum u Crnoj Gori," in *Danas* (Belgrade), 18 August 2004, on line at www.danas.co.yu.

54. *Vijesti*, 9 January 2001, online at www.vijesti.cg.yu.

55. Veton Surroi, "Kosova Priorities," Institute for War and Peace Reporting, *Balkan Crisis Report*, no. 209 (15 January 2001); online at www.iwpr.net.

56. "Kosovo če postati nezavisno u procesu integracije u EU" (Kosovo will become independent through the process of integration into the EU), *Vijesti*, 22 August 2001, online at www.vijesti.cg.yu.

57. Interview with Goran Svilanović by Sonja Drobac, *Monitor*, no. 574 (19 October 2001); online at www.monitor.cg.yu.

58. U.S. Congress, Senate, *The Crisis in Macedonia and U.S. Engagement in the Balkans: Hearing before the Committee on Foreign Relations*, 107th Cong., 13 June 2001, p. 44; available online at www.access.gpo.gov/congress/senate.

59. Steven Woehrel, "Montenegro and U.S. Policy," *CSIS U.S.-Montenegrin Policy Forum—Eastern Europe Program*, 20 July 2001, online at www.csis.org.

60. *Vijesti*, 23 October 2001, online at www.vijesti.cg.yu.

61. International Crisis Group, "Still Buying Time: Montenegro, Serbia and the European Union," *Balkans Report* (Podgorica/Belgrade/Brussels), no. 129 (7 May 2002), p. 5.

62. Javier Solana, "The Fastest Way to Full European Integration," *Vijesti*, 22 February 2002. The English version of this article is available on the European Union Internet Web site at ue.eu.int/pressdata/EN/articles/69522.pdf.

63. International Crisis Group, "Still Buying Time," p. 8.

64. The Socialist People's Party is the largest pro-Yugoslav party in Montenegro and a leading member of the coalition "Together for Yugoslavia," which was opposed in the parliamentary elections (2001) to the coalition "Victory for Montenegro," led by President Djukanović. The SNP was a main political ally of Milošević in Montenegro up to his fall in October 2000.

65. The following paragraphs are based on International Crisis Group, "Still Buying Time," pp. 11–12.

66. *Vijesti*, 19 April 2002, online at www.vijesti.cg.yu.

67. "Yugoslav President's Letter to Federal Assembly Representatives," 31 May 2002, online at www.predsjednik.gov.yu.

68. "Yugoslav President's Address to the Federal Assembly," 18 April 2002, online at www.predsednik.gov.yu.

69. Interview with Vojislav Koštunica by Von Michael Martens, "Den Haag ist voreingenommen, Ein Gespräch mit Kostunica," *Frankfurter Allgemeine Zeitung*, 1 August 2002, online at www.faz.net.

70. Ibid.

71. "Serbija če biti samostalna" (Serbia will be independent), *Glas javnosti*, 29 July 2002, online at www.glas-javnosti.co.yu.

72. *Vjesnik*, Zagreb, 20 July 2002, online at www.vjesnik.com.

73. Interview with Vesna Perović, *Nacional* (Zagreb), no. 348 (17 July 2002), online at www.nacional.hr.

74. Komisija Skupštine Republike Crne Gore, Izviještaj o radu (Podgorica), 28 July 2002. The report of the commission of the Montenegrin parliament was posted on the Web site of the Croatian weekly Nacional at www.nacional.com.

75. Quoted by Dragana Nikolić-Solomon, "Serbia and Montenegro: An Unhappy Marriage," Institute for War and Peace Reporting, *Balkan Crisis Report*, no. 493 (22 April 2004), online at www.iwpr.net.

76. Serbia and Montenegro are disproportionately different in size. Serbia is in terms of population seventeen times bigger than Montenegro.

77. "Obstacles to federalism in East Central Europe, aggravated by the forty

years of communism, were rooted in the long historical experience of its people. Little in that experience made the idea attractive or even interesting. Federal structure of any kind had been exceptional and federalist thinking at best marginal in the part of Europe whose modern history had been so prominently shaped by an ethnic quest for self-assertion within national states. The notion of a citizen's legitimate allegiance to more than a single state entity had been alien there." Vojtech Mastny, "The Historical Experience of Federalism in East Central Europe," *East European Politics and Society* 14, no. 1 (Winter 2000), p. 94.

4

AN AIRPLANE WITH EIGHTEEN PILOTS

Serbia after Milošević

OBRAD KESIĆ

On 12 March 2003 Serbian prime minister Zoran Djindjić was assassinated in front of his government offices. His death was both a tragedy for the people of Serbia, desperately wanting to live in a normal country, and a wake-up call for politicians in the country who had squandered opportunities in order to pursue narrow agendas of personal interests and opportunism. Following Milošević's ouster from power, Serbian politics had degenerated into bitter bickering between the two main personalities of the victorious Democratic Opposition of Serbia (DOS), Zoran Djindjić and Vojislav Koštunica. Important public support for needed reforms was squandered as the feuding political parties lurched from scandal to scandal. As the democratic forces in Serbia fragmented and many of the leading figures of the DOS became entangled in corruption and allegations of links to organized crime, reform stalled and Djindjić and his allies within the DOS increasingly consolidated power outside government institutions and within Djindjić's cabinet and the DOS presidency. Vojislav Koštunica, who had headed the DOS's successful election ticket, could not translate popularity and moral authority into effective leadership and quickly found himself a figurehead and bystander.

The DOS rode a roller coaster from crisis to crisis. At first, most of Serbia's citizens gave the DOS the benefit of the doubt, maintaining their patience while waiting for everyday life to improve, for a much longer time than most observers thought possible. However, by August 2002, it was clear, even to the most naïve follower of Serbian politics, that things had gone past the point of no return in the DOS internal conflict. Most of Serbia's citizens either joined the ranks of the apathetic or accepted that their hopes for a complete and quick break with both the Milošević past and the Yugoslav communist past would not be realized under the rule of the DOS.

There are many reasons for the DOS's success in toppling Milošević and for its subsequent failure to provide effective and stable leadership. Some of the reasons for the DOS's failure are to be found in the nature of the coalition itself, and others can be found in the political baggage the Serbian opposition accumulated as it fought Milošević for over a decade. All this came on top of the legacy Milošević left behind—a dysfunctional state with disintegrating institutions ruled by one man, his family, and a quasi-mafia political elite—and proved to be too much for the DOS's leaders to overcome. The relationship with the international community, especially with the United States, also had a negative impact on the DOS's ability to govern and strengthened the forces that tore the DOS apart. Finally, one must also look closely at the political personalities within Serbia—Koštunica, Djindjić, and others, whose differing visions, hubris, and desire for power have created the engine driving Serbia's continuing chain of crises.

Zoran Djindjić's death not only shocked Serbia but also abruptly changed the political landscape and created a leadership void that will present Serbia with major challenges and possible instability for the foreseeable future. This chapter is an attempt to explain how the DOS fell apart and how Serbia has found itself in an extended period of crisis with little prospect of a quick solution. In order to try to understand where Serbia is going, one first needs to examine where it has been and focus especially on why the DOS has failed to transform Serbia into the stable democratic, and normal, state most of its citizens so desperately desire.[1] Here I look at all of the factors that contributed to this failure and have organized my analysis into three major sections: "The Milošević Era," "The DOS in Charge," and "The DOS's Legacy to Serbia's Future."

The Milošević Era

Much has been written about Slobodan Milošević, his rise to power, and how he ruled Serbia.[2] Much less has been written about how the experiences of the Milošević era affected Serbia's former opposition political parties and their leaders. The DOS's inability to provide effective and honest leadership is very much a part of Milošević's legacy, and the lingering psychological and emotional wounds that were suffered during this period.

The perceptions of Serbia's political opposition, both in the country and abroad, were that it was weak, ineffective, egotistical, fragmented, and corrupt.[3] Most of these characterizations were of course accurate, but they were rather superficial. There is much more to it. In spite of the major role Serbia's opposition parties played in ending Milošević's rule, it is hard to avoid concluding that this major success cannot wipe away the image of Serbia's opposition as a group of incompetent, bickering adolescents.

While part of this perception is based on fact, there are also a number of factors which contributed to the opposition's negative image that were beyond their control. First, Milošević was a master of manipulation. As an opportunist, driven by the desire for absolute power and, once he achieved it, the desire to remain in power, regardless of the cost to Serbia and its peoples, he was not constrained by ideology. In 1989–91, he took away the ideal platform for the opposition by·camouflaging himself as a reformer, thus narrowing the possibilities for a mobilization of people around an anticommunist movement. By enthusiastically embracing populist nationalism, Milošević further narrowed the opposition's field of maneuver.

The spontaneous street demonstration of 9 March 1991 led by opposition leader Vuk Drašković rattled Milošević's confidence; this protest was the first serious challenge to Milošević's rule.[4] As Milošević ordered the police and army into the streets, Serbia seemed to have crossed a threshold and was catching up to the street demonstrations which had brought down the communist governments from East Germany to Hungary. Unfortunately for Serbia, the opening that was created that day was not exploited as Drašković and the student leaders settled for the resignations of Radmilo Bogdanović, Serbia's interior minister, and Dušan Mitević, the director of the state television network. The Serbian opposition lacked the vision and determination to follow through with a death blow to the regime.[5] Milošević, on the other hand, quickly recovered from his initial shock and moved to drain energy from the demonstrations. He bought time with the resignation of his officials and then used the conflict over the future of Yugoslavia and the fear of a looming war to convince Serbia's citizens that any challenge to his government was tantamount to treason because any instability within Serbia would harm Serb national interests.

From this point on, Milošević no longer enjoyed the popular mandate he had won by reinventing himself as a populist and a nationalist. Instead, he had to rely on his ability to fully exploit Serbia's political system, which gave his ruling Socialist Party disproportionate power, on his ability to use war(s) to curb any opposition, and on his propaganda machine, which portrayed him as the only real choice to govern Serbia during those times of conflict and crisis. Very early on, Milošević and his advisers concluded that the best formula for maintaining power in Serbia was to stuff ballot boxes, portray Milošević as a committed defender of Serbia's interests and people, and, more importantly, portray him as a moderate and rational choice between two extremes. These were, on the one hand, the failed communist experiment of Tito's Yugoslavia as represented by the political and intellectual leftist elite in Belgrade (which he had first co-opted and then defeated in Serbia's League of Communists [LCS]) and, on the other hand, the caricature of the Serbian nationalist opposition his media created that portrayed most of the opposition parties as being a collection of motley and primitive monarchists and chauvinists led either by raving mad men (Vojislav Šešelj and Vuk Drašković) or by out of touch intellectuals (Dragoljub Mićunović).

The opposition for its part played right into Milošević's hands. Instead of unifying their forces, opposition leaders bickered among themselves and fought parochial battles. Instead of mobilizing Serbs over Milošević's economic mismanagement and corruption, pointing out how these hurt ordinary citizens, the opposition leaders tried to portray themselves as greater patriots and better defenders of the Serbian nation. This allowed Milošević to paint them both within Serbia and internationally as radical nationalists, who, if they came to power, would be even more uncompromising in their defense of Serbs in Croatia and Bosnia. Within Serbia, Milošević portrayed himself as the only moderate choice and real leader able to pull Serbia (intact) from conflict and crisis. To the outside world, Milošević tried to portray the opposition as being both irrelevant and indistinct. He wanted the international community to accept that it was "better to deal with the devil you know than the one you don't know." In this, he was greatly helped by American and Serbian NGOs and human rights activists, who lumped the opposition together with Milošević as "anti-Western Serbian nationalists." For example, one of the more vocal human rights activists in Serbia, Sonja Biserko, the president of the Helsinki Committee for Human Rights in Serbia, in her public comments continually stressed that there were no real differences between the Milošević regime and the opposition when it came to nationalism and democracy. On the eve of presidential elections in Serbia, Biserko, in an interview published by the Network of Independent Journalists, stated:

> For 15 years there has been one system that has been going on without any new impulses. New alternatives are just emerging, but they haven't enough room and [the] four main election candidates for the Yugoslav President show that Serbian citizens in fact have no choice.[6]

Serbian opposition leaders found themselves in a position where, instead of concentrating their resources and efforts on exposing Milošević's destructive and failed policies, they had to defend themselves from charges that they were at best a little different from him. Of course, this served Milošević's interests of maintaining his hold on power very well.

Opposition frustrations with an international community which, in the view of opposition leaders, totally ignored them and in some perverted way preferred Milošević to them, were founded on some kernels of truth, but they themselves contributed to this development. The lack of unity within the opposition, coupled with the inability of opposition leaders to define themselves or their policies in a way that would allow no room for doubt that they were indeed pro-Western reformers who favored negotiations to end the wars in Croatia and Bosnia, allowed Milošević to emerge as the only credible peacemaker in Serbia. A vicious cycle developed where Milošević used his credibility as peacemaker before an international community desperate for peace in Bosnia to maintain his legitimacy within Serbia.

Over time, as missed opportunities to rid Serbia of Milošević piled up, the Serbian opposition leaders lost confidence in themselves, in the Serbian people, and in the international community. Following March 1991, there were at least two major opportunities to topple Milošević: the first the presidential elections of December 1992, missed because the opposition candidate, Milan Panić, did not get the support he needed from the international community, especially from the United States, and because Milošević's apparatus railroaded the counting of ballots; and the mass demonstrations of 1996–97, which failed because of the infighting among Serbian opposition leaders and because once again the support needed from the international community was too little, too late.

In 1992 the opposition united behind a single candidate, Milan Panić, and almost pulled off a miracle even with the blatant irregularities and outright theft of votes that accompanied the election. The complete absence of support from the United States and the relative indifference shown by the international community crushed the spirit of Serbia's opposition movement. For the next several years, the opposition put up a more passive resistance to Milošević, almost resigning itself to the idea that he could only be toppled either by a popular uprising or by outside intervention, neither of which appeared imminent.

By the time Milošević established himself, with the great help of American negotiator Richard Holbrooke, as a pillar of the Dayton Peace Accords for Bosnia, Serbia's opposition leaders had all but disappeared from Serbia's political landscape.[7] Many had embraced the popular notion prevalent throughout Serbia that the West actually wanted Milošević in power. All kinds of conspiracy theories were floated in Belgrade's oppo-

sition circles, and whereas a sense of relief prevailed at the conclusion of
the bloody war in Bosnia and at the lifting of most international economic
sanctions against Serbia, nonetheless most members of Serbia's opposition could not escape the conclusion that all of this was accomplished at
the expense of the indefinite postponement of needed political change and
democratization.

Because of the prevailing atmosphere of gloom and pessimism following municipal elections in the winter of 1996–97, the leaders of the opposition coalition Zajedno [Together] (Zoran Djindjić, Vesna Pešić, and Vuk
Drašković) found themselves surprised and unprepared for the spontaneous mass demonstrations which exploded in most of Serbia's cities following Milošević's blatant attempt to change the catastrophic defeat of his
Socialist Party of Serbia (SPS) in most urban municipalities.[8] The Zajedno
leaders quickly moved to harness the energy of this mass discontent in Serbia's cities. They gave structure and organization to what had started as
spontaneous rallies. It took seventy-eight days of continuous protest in Serbia's main municipalities and pressure from a special EU delegation led by
former Spanish prime minister Felipe González before Milošević conceded
defeat and reversed his election theft in most, but not all, disputed municipalities. Once again, Milošević had dodged a bullet, this time mostly
thanks to the bitter rivalry between Djindjić and Drašković. As heads of
the two, at that time, best organized and largest opposition parties, Drašković's Serbian Renewal Movement (SPO) and Djindjić's Democratic Party
(DS), each viewed himself as the principal opposition leader and viewed
the other as a backstabbing, ambitious rival bent on securing ultimate and
total power. Neither man was able to overcome the animosity which he felt
toward the other and instead each wasted precious energy and resources
trying to discredit his Zajedno partner. Later it came to light that, during
this time, both had conducted secret negotiations with Milošević. The
international community compounded the problems within Zajedno
through lukewarm support for the protests and by applying no pressure
on the Zajedno leaders to maintain their unity. Instead, individual European states seemed indirectly to endorse their own favorites: France stood
behind Drašković while it was clear Djindjić had Germany's confidence. In
the end, one of the main factors that led the Zajedno leaders to end demonstrations and take the deal offered by Milošević was the advice given to them
by European and American diplomats.[9]

The demonstrations of the winter of 1996–97 marked both a high and
low point for Serbia's opposition. Milošević had had to admit his first electoral setback to an opposition he didn't take seriously, but at the same time

the fight between Djindjić and Drašković had all but discredited the opposition in the eyes of both Serbia's citizens and the international community. Drašković and Djindjić would never make up and in some strange way each replaced Milošević as the main enemy in the eyes of the other. From 1997 until the start of NATO's bombing of Serbia in March 1999, it appeared that Serbia's opposition parties spent more time fighting among themselves than they did in trying to oust Milošević. Lenard J. Cohen does a good job in capturing the essence of the flaws within Serbia's opposition:

> The political deficits of the opposition parties in Serbia have also proved highly beneficial to Milošević. For example, because of their constant personal squabbling and political differences among non-ruling party rulers and elites, the opposition parties proved unable to maintain a coherent electoral alliance for any sustained period of time. . . . More often than not, the divided nature of the opposition was due to personal jealousies among leaders, each wanting to control the inter-party alliances and to ensure a future position for [himself] in an eventual government. The highly personalized control of leadership within most of the opposition parties tended to reinforce such power seeking and power struggles.[10]

In particular, the personalized control of power became the principal characteristic of Serbia's political parties. As if in imitation of the Titoist style of governance, in which Tito had embodied the party and in which the party's whole meaning had been defined by his personality, both Milošević and the opposition leaders distinguished and differentiated themselves from each other, not by program but rather on the basis of the personality of each leader. Each of these leaders in turn sought to consolidate his hold on power within his own party by maintaining all of the levers of power (the presidency, finances, and even the role of spokesperson) and by discouraging internal opposition. Instead of nurturing potential new generations of leaders within their parties, the leaders used and discarded individuals based almost exclusively on loyalty to themselves.

This type of personality-driven politics left little room for a democratic culture to be established within Serbia's opposition. Tolerance and compromise were seen as signs of weakness, while ruthlessness and rigidity were worn like badges of honor. Confrontation was the lifeblood of opposition political life. As Cohen has documented:

> Opposition leaders were also obsessed with holding power, even if they only controlled a minor non-ruling party organization, and maintained the hope

of acquiring more power once the incumbent ruler was unseated. Compromise and cooperation [were] of secondary value to power maintenance. Indeed, the word "compromise" was considered as highly negative, both in [c]ommunist jargon and in traditional Serbian political discourse. Such unbridled ambition to become "the leader" is also captured by the Serbian term *liderstvo,* which denotes both blind ambition to get to the top of the greasy pole, and also a willingness to engage in a broad array of political machinations necessary to remain there.[11]

Within their political parties themselves, opposition leaders displayed a noticeable lack of democratic behavior; dissident views were quickly silenced and potential rivals were summarily expelled. The degree to which this type of behavior had become a part of the prevailing political culture can best be seen in the way the DOS governed after seizing power from Milošević in October 2000.

The DOS in Charge

Milošević's fall on 5 October 2000, following his loss to Vojislav Koštunica, was sudden and dramatic. Although many observers had predicted that his corrupt regime would implode once he lost an election, few actually expected to see him leave office without bloodshed. While many observers also knew that Milošević would lose the actual election to the DOS's candidate, Vojislav Koštunica, few expected that Koštunica's victory would be a landslide and even fewer believed that Milošević would ever acknowledge defeat. What made the victory even sweeter for the opposition leaders was the fact that they had all but vindicated themselves by achieving what had been thought to be unachievable: the defeat of Milošević through unity and a well-organized election campaign.

In the wake of Milošević's defeat, leaders of the Serbian opposition and Washington political figures began boasting and claiming the lion's share of credit in the victory. The leaders of the eighteen opposition parties which had created the DOS coalition played up their own roles and downplayed the roles of their colleagues in the victory. On the surface, the euphoria over Milošević's fall created an illusion of a harmonious and cohesive DOS, but behind the scenes the conflicts within the DOS were as petty and prevalent as ever. One of the main triggers of the behind-the-scenes squabbles was jealousy. The DOS's individual leaders were jealous of how much credit for Milošević's fall Koštunica and Djindjić were being given, and they also bickered over the division of the spoils. Each DOS leader laid claim to a specific government ministry and to board directorships in state and quasi-state companies. As Milošević's ministers and government officials resigned, the DOS replaced them in a manner previously agreed upon within the coalition, but never fully defined, which was based on a party key, according to which each party leader of the DOS was guaranteed a certain percentage of power in government and in state companies.

The massive street demonstrations and the mob takeovers of the federal parliament and Radio-Television Serbia (RTS) headquarters on 5 October gave a revolutionary feel to the DOS's victory. Many of the DOS's leaders wanted to exploit this atmosphere and move quickly using revolutionary justice to dismantle Milošević's regime and replace his cadres with their own loyalists. This created major tension within the DOS as, on the one hand, most of its leaders were for a decisive and quick distribution of power, while, on the other hand, the coalition's victorious presidential candidate and Yugoslavia's new president, Koštunica, insisted on a more controlled and deliberate dismantling of the regime, all to be done under the law and with respect for the integrity of government institutions. Koštunica's stubborn insistence on this issue grated on his DOS colleagues' nerves. They believed he was only indulging in "legalism" because he was in the driver's seat and personified the DOS's victory over Milošević. Many of his colleagues envied the attention and international acclaim Koštunica was receiving, especially because most of the DOS leaders felt it was undeserved and given at the expense of their own sacrifices. They believed that Koštunica, as the head of the Democratic Party of Serbia (DSS), would never have won the election without the DOS's organization and leadership. His DSS was, in their eyes, more a "debate club" or a "religious cult" than a political party, and what really irritated many DOS leaders was that Koštunica himself was opposed to the type of street violence which had forced Milošević to concede defeat. In fact, on 5 October, Koštunica was at home and took no part in that day's events. In addition to all of these reasons for resentment, some of the other DOS leaders really believed that Koštunica was making a major mistake in not pursuing revolutionary justice with members of the previous regime. They believed that Milošević would see every gesture of legality as a sign of weakness and would exploit any weakness to undermine the DOS's attempts to consolidate power. Velimir Ilić, the president of New Serbia (NS) and mayor of Čačak, explained why he was unhappy with the pace of change: "I would immediately and in a radical way solve some problems. Milošević would be in jail, so that we would once and for all clear up if he is guilty or not guilty."[12]

For his part, Koštunica was growing more and more uncomfortable with his DOS colleagues' revolutionary brand of justice and governance. He had four basic objections to the type of change his DOS partners desired:

1. He believed that the law and state institutions needed to be respected in order to be the nucleus of democratic reform and in order to avoid chaos and conflict on the streets.

2. He also felt that reforms which were too radical and too quick would hurt many ordinary people.

3. As he already viewed most of his DOS partners as being corrupt, he believed that the "revolution" would be used as a cover for even greater corruption.

4. Finally, as a determined anticommunist, he saw the DOS's revolutionary justice as being closely related to the mentality of Tito's victorious communist forces in 1945.

Koštunica's views on these issues bear closer scrutiny as they are essential to understanding why there was little chance for compromise and cooperation between him and the majority of the other DOS leaders. Koštunica himself realized that his differences with the other leaders were deep and substantive. Early on in his presidency, he described the situation in these terms:

> I would never orient myself negatively toward the other members of DOS, even toward the Democratic Party of Zoran Djindjić. I would rather speak about these things upon which I insist. And that was expressed in the conditions I set upon accepting that my name be put at the head of DOS's election slate. That is firstly a state based on laws. To be more precise, first the state and then a state based on laws. That is my obsession.[13]

Koštunica was unwilling to compromise on this issue of preserving the state and his insistence on the rule of law through establishing credibility of state institutions. Any deviance from this path, he held, would be embracing the methods of Tito and Milošević, and this would ensure that Serbia would never become a normal democratic state. He explained:

> The state question is very important, but not just any kind of state, but a democratic one based on law. Sometimes in these changes, we only think of democratic change, democratic institutions, and the state in this story is

forgotten and bypassed, even though there is no democracy without the state. It is the atmosphere under which democratic institutions are realized. In the last half of a century we have experienced a party-state, which is the property of one man and party, never of the people. We also experienced the phenomenon, which is gathering greater attention in this region—that is a mafia-state. So we have had a party-state and following that a combination of a party-state and a mafia-state, we are now on the path to create a normal democratic state, a state of law, without these prior characteristics.[14]

Added to Koštunica's strong belief that preserving the state was essential to any democratic change was his passionate anticommunism. The majority of his professional life was marked by his rejection of communism. He was uncompromising in this. Where some of his colleagues compromised in order to keep jobs or gain promotions, Koštunica did not. He spent his time writing about multiparty democracy and providing legal assistance to dissidents and political prisoners. He was suspicious of the other DOS leaders because he viewed most of them as being products of Tito's communist mentality; and some of them, such as Nebojša Čović, the former mayor of Belgrade and an SPS member, and Dušan Mihajlović, the president of New Democracy and former Milošević coalition partner, he saw as being products of Milošević's regime. Koštunica viewed any compromise on his basic belief on the state and democracy as being a victory for the Titoist/Miloševist mentalities. As he explained in December 2001:

It is a fact that I and some other people in DOS come from different worlds. Some maybe belong to that which may be called "Partisan excess" [partizanstinom], something has remained in them. My family was a victim of that, but a victim who does not [seek] revenge and does not want to exchange one "Partisan excess" for another.[15]

This latter observation by Koštunica is important because it touches on the deep divisions still existing within Serbian society which have their roots in the World War Two division between Partisans and Chetniks. More importantly, these divisions figure as psychological barriers hindering reform, fueling confrontation, and often preventing compromise. The Milošević era served to deepen and compound these divisions. The gap between the leftist and rightist political blocs in Serbia is rarely discussed, even as it is one of the greatest obstacles to democratic reform. There is little tolerance between these two political poles. Each is rigid and uncompromising in its belief that its way is the right way and the only way. Each views its opponents as discredited and dire threats to the country.

The Left views the Right as being primitive in its embrace of the monarchy, the Church, the Chetniks, and traditional Serbian folk culture. More importantly the Left blames the Right for the wars, isolation, and suffering endured over the last decade. It even blames the Right for Milošević's rise to power. For the Left, the greatest sin of the Right is the primitive nationalism it associates with right-wing ideology. Like many activists and analysts in the United States, the Left views nationalism as being destructive and negative. Within the Left, there are at least four major groups: the "Eighth Session Veterans," a significant group of former members of the League of Communists of Serbia, who were purged by Milošević at or shortly following the Eighth Session of the Central Committee of the LCS; the Partisan veterans and pensioners, who were a pillar of Milošević's support; a third group called "the Disciples," whose members were a part of Milošević's regime but whose ideological beliefs are confused and not very deep; and the "Activists," mostly human rights and nongovernmental organization (NGO) activists who are few in number but extremely vocal.

The Right has an equally negative view of the Left and is equally rigid and intolerant in its confrontation with its opponents. The Right views the Left as being corrupt, insensitive to ordinary Serbs, and ruthless in its thirst for power. In addition, the Right holds the Left and its Titoist legacy primarily responsible for Milošević's rise to power and for the wars and suffering during the decade of Yugoslavia's disintegration. Rightists also see leftists as hypocrites, as many leftist political leaders and activists now portray themselves as defenders of democracy and human rights, even though, in Tito's Yugoslavia, they were silent beneficiaries of a one-party system which had incarcerated large numbers of political prisoners.

Each group views the other as being out of touch with the rest of the world and especially out of touch with mainstream democratic values. Each views the other as an enemy and each views the potential victory of the other as an unmitigated disaster for Serbia. The conflict within the DOS and especially that between Koštunica and Djindjić have further added to the divisions between these two groups of society, with the Left reluctantly rallying around Djindjić and the Right around Koštunica.

KOŠTUNICA VERSUS DJINDJIĆ

The conflict between Koštunica and Djindjić was much deeper and more complex than a simple battle over power. It represented the clash of two mutually exclusive visions of reform; it was also an extension of the conflict between the Left and Right factions of Serbia's society and elites. Early on, in the first few months of the DOS's rise to power, it appeared that the two men could cooperate with one another and that the two Serbias they came to symbolize could peacefully coexist. Djindjić himself seemed to acknowledge this: "To everyone it is clear that Koštunica is necessary as a bridge between traditional and reform oriented Serbia. Without him we would be a nation divided into two uncompromising blocs, as in Montenegro. None of us need this."[16] Despite the public tolerance pledged by both Djindjić and Koštunica initially, behind the scenes they were barely speaking to each other. Most outside observers oversimplified these differences. In a rare exception, Timothy Garton Ash described the two protagonists as: "[Koštunica] the Girondin, always wanting to use peaceful, legal, constitutional means, demonstratively starting as he intends to go on; Djindjić, the Jacobin, more inclined to take direct action."[17] Others thought the conflict was between the more "pro-Western" and "pragmatic" Djindjić and the more "nationalist" and "deliberate" Koštunica. Some even went so far as to describe the conflict as between the "reformist" Djindjić and the "antireformist" Koštunica.[18] Besides being overly simplistic, such analyses misidentified the causes behind the conflict and what was actually at stake in the conflict's outcome.

First, both Koštunica and Djindjić shared the same overall goals, and these were to see Serbia fully integrated into Europe and established as a modern democratic state. Where these two leaders differed was over their views as to what path was best to take in order to reach these goals. Koštunica favored slower, more "humane" reform based on the rule of law and the integrity of state institutions. Djindjić, on the other hand, favored rapid reforms by any means necessary, even if they were illegal, unconstitutional, or even unethical. For Djindjić, the greater good demanded uncompromising change, while Koštunica had little sympathy for this view because to him it resembled too closely the Marxist principle that "the ends justify the means." Second, each man's inflexibility in dealing with the other allowed other shortcomings in the DOS to become even greater problems and even greater barriers to real reform.

Among the most disturbing problems in the DOS were: corruption, a perceived insensitivity to the plight of average citizens, a desire to build democracy through undemocratic and antidemocratic means, and a deep hubris among DOS leaders. Another problem, which intensified these other problems, was the way that the DOS parties decided to divide power among themselves and how the DOS presidency became, in a throwback to the communist legacy, a quasi Central Committee. The egos of the individual DOS party leaders demanded that each receive a prominent seat in the Republic government.[19] Ministerial seats in Serbian prime minister Djindjić's government, with the exception of the economic ministries, went to the heads of the DOS's political parties.[20] This made it extremely difficult to govern, as each political leader treated his ministry as his own personal fiefdom. It also made it difficult to achieve comprehensive reform quickly as each DOS minister had his own reform plan based on his desire to consolidate his own base of power. For many ministers this meant co-opting Milošević's administrators and bureaucrats and having very little commitment to democratic reform. Miodrag Perišić, Yugoslavia's late ambassador to Canada and a former vice president of Djindjić's Democratic Party, in an interview with *Blic* described the DOS's division of power and the problems it created, arguing that "we should have completely changed the model of political functioning. Instead . . . there was neither strategic agreement nor planning."[21]

Prime Minister Djindjić could not simply remove incompetent ministers as this would have jeopardized his government, because each DOS leader could order his parliamentary delegates to vote with Koštunica's DSS and the opposition. A lust for power drove cooperation within Djindjić's government and unity was maintained by the animosity of the DOS's individual leaders toward Koštunica and the fear that any crack in the DOS rump would lead to new elections and a loss of power. This division of power among the DOS's political leaders created a system of political governance which barely functioned and which gave disproportionate power to leaders, whose credibility in the eyes of Serbian voters was suspect and whose tiny political parties, in most cases, could not win enough votes on their own to pass the threshold for entry into parliament. This produced a ridiculous situation in which the Yugoslav and Serbian governments did not have a single coherent policy on any significant issue. Whether discussion turned to Kosovo or to economic reform, there were eighteen policies and eighteen points of view which battled with one another for dominance. The conflict between Koštunica and the remainder of the DOS further complicated this situation because Djindjić's government could not push anything through Serbia's parliament, which was paralyzed by the DOS's infighting. In response to this, Djindjić and the rump DOS coalition simply bypassed parliament and instead relied on extragovernmental institutions and on decrees to govern. Later, they simply decided to reengineer the composition of parliament by throwing out the DSS deputies and by manipulating decisions as to who really had mandates in fractured parties such as the SPS. The DOS presidency came to serve in the capacity of an unofficial, but powerful, combination of executive and legislative branches of the country's government. As confrontation within the DOS grew, power increasingly shifted outside of government institutions and into the hands of the rump DOS presidency and Prime Minister Zoran Djindjić. Even within the rump DOS, this caused concern that the DOS was simply re-creating a new version of Milošević's way of governing. Dragoljub Mićunović, the president of the Democratic Center, is one of the few leaders to have expressed this concern publicly.[22]

A consequence of this circumventing of state institutions has also been that the perception of corruption came to taint both the Djindjić government and the rump DOS leaders. Nepotism and cronyism became characteristics of the DOS's leadership. Recognizing that the perception of corruption was becoming a problem for his government, Djindjić formed a Council for the Fight against Corruption under the authority of Serbia's government. But even this council found that any attempts to eliminate the perception of corruption were often blocked by DOS leaders bent on fully benefiting from their, even limited, time in power. Among its first decisions, the council called for the adoption of a law that would define conflict of interest and ban ministers and other high government officials from conducting private businesses while in office.[23] This call was at first ignored and later, as members of the council made their disappointment known publicly, some members of the DOS accused them of nurturing an "ambition to delegitimize the entire government and reform."[24]

This response represented the main line of defense and revealed the mind-set of most DOS leaders. This mind-set went along these lines: We are the best that Serbia has. We are the only ones committed to carrying out reform. If we fail, the reforms will fail and Serbia will be doomed. So, any attack on us or on our leadership is a direct attack on the reforms and on Serbia.

Whoever disagreed with the DOS leaders was branded as being "antireform" or "anti-Western." They were characterized as being equivalent to either Milošević's Socialists or Vojislav Šešelj's Radicals. It is difficult to escape the conclusion that the "DOS revolution" had already fallen prey to the illness associated with most revolutionary leaderships: hubris and a lust for power corrupting the very values the revolution had sought to install. This hubris can be seen in Prime Minister Djindjić's response to the charge that a perception of ethical lapses was created by his use of a private airplane said to belong to an underworld figure and his privately funded 2002 New Year's Eve celebration in the United Arab Emirates. At first Djindjić's office denied both charges only to have to admit later that they were accurate.[25] Djindjić himself seemed to be outraged that this would be perceived as being inappropriate, boldly stating: "That [the allegation] is stupid. Even Clinton spent his vacation at the expense of some man, as his guest and of course he did not pay."[26] Djindjić's self-righteous attitude thus not only generated a new definition for conflict of interest and corruption, but also classified anyone who did not agree with this definition as being out of touch with normal practices in the West and even out of touch with Western values.

It is little wonder that support for Djindjić, the DOS, and reforms steadily declined among Serbia's voters; even within the rump DOS parties there was revulsion at the blatant attempt to hide corruption behind a transparent defense of the need for better laws. As Branko Pavlović, Social Democratic Party (SDP) vice president and a member of the Serbian parliament's Security Committee, explained:

> The law can give results only when the influence of organized crime here is reduced to the level that the mafia has in Italy. Here this influence is significantly greater and no procedure can help. . . . That which is now being done is for some future time, when the people who undertake this [writing laws against corruption and organized crime] will have confidence in the entire state structure which will be used in the fight against organized crime, and that for sure is not this government.[27]

Pavlović reflected a mainstream perception within Serbia that the DOS and the Djindjić government lacked the determination to effectively deal with Serbia's enormous problems of corruption and organized crime. For his outspokenness on this issue and on other issues on which he disagreed with the DOS presidency, Pavlović was isolated within his party by Žarko Korać, SDP president and one of Djindjić's deputy prime ministers. Korać even tried to prevent Serbia's media, by intimidation, from airing Pavlović's opinions.[28]

All of this was bad enough, but the insensitivity to the plight of ordinary citizens further undermined support for the DOS, Djindjić, and their reforms. When Serbia's citizens complained about rapidly rising electrical prices, Ljubomir Gerić, the director of the Electric Industry of Serbia (EPS) suggested that "citizens borrow money from their neighbors" to pay their electricity bills,[29] or, better yet, "It would be ideal if Serbian housewives would change their habits and start cooking at night."[30] Serbia's new minister of energy, Kori Udovički, had more practical advice on this subject. She advised that the most logical solution would be that "pensioners who cannot pay their electrical bills should sell their big apartments."[31] Serbia's pensioners, workers, and peasants were incredulous at Serbia's government's arrogance and stupidity. After all, everyone was familiar with the fact that political figures such as Deputy Prime Minister Nebojša Čović and Minister of Interior Dušan Mihajlović both owned businesses they had acquired while in Milošević's government and that both of them had thrived during their tenure as part of the DOS's government. All of this made it unlikely that the DOS's efforts at reform were completely genuine and highly unlikely that they would maintain enough popular support to be successful. The DOS honeymoon period with the Serbian voters was over, but the honeymoon period with the international community continued.

OUTSIDE FACTORS

The international community rushed to shore up the DOS governments (federal and Republic) through normalization of relations, debt forgiveness, direct loans, and financial assistance. They continually ignored the DOS's bickering and shortcomings for fear that the remnants of Milošević's regime could make a comeback. A DOS government with all its flaws was better than some Milošević resurgence or a nationalist government. The Europeans were especially quick to support the DOS. The United States, on the other hand, although supportive of the changes in Serbia, found itself at odds with both its European partners and the DOS leaders. The arrival of a new president, George W. Bush, and a new administration brought a fresh perspective on the Balkans. The Bush administration sought to disengage itself from the large involvement and commitments undertaken by President Bill Clinton. Serbia, simply put, did not represent a vital American interest, in the view of the Bush administration. As a result, it was not important enough to warrant a fight with Congress over conditions that the Senate was placing on U.S. assistance to Serbia. These conditions, which tied assistance to Serbia's cooperation with the International Criminal Tribunal for the former Yugoslavia in The Hague, implementation of the Dayton agreement, and release of Albanian prisoners, were often at odds with Bush's other foreign policy priorities. For example, at the same time that the Bush administration supported the Senate's pressure on Serbia to extradite those of its citizens who had been indicted for war crimes to The Hague tribunal, it was locked in a bitter fight to protect Americans from the new International Criminal Court and pressured Serbia and other countries to sign a bilateral agreement which would protect Americans from extradition.

The desire to disengage in Washington, D.C., created a policy void toward Serbia. As a result, DOS leaders were left to their own devices to try to sort out what the Americans really wanted, and U.S. Ambassador William Montgomery, a carryover from the Clinton administration's heavy-handed involvement in internal Balkan politics, was allowed to continue his very deep involvement in Serbia's internal politics. This accomplished three things: it made Montgomery one of the three most influential figures in Serbia's politics; it allowed Djindjić and the rump DOS to manipulate perceptions of American support for their own parochial purposes; and it deepened the divisions between Koštunica and Djindjić. It was no secret that Koštunica's relationship with Montgomery was extremely rocky. Koštunica at the time of the normalization of relations with America had indirectly indicated his preference for a new person as ambassador, someone who had not been associated with Clinton's covert efforts to topple Milošević. For his part, Montgomery was much more comfortable with Djindjić and the other DOS officials with whom he had established working relationships and to whom he had funneled U.S. money used to finance the DOS's battle against Milošević. Furthermore, Montgomery seemed to prefer the more animated and better packaged DOS leaders, such as Djindjić and Čović, to the more deliberate and "boring" Koštunica. All of this created a situation in which America's pressure hindered reform and fueled the DOS's internal conflicts. As Djindjić admitted to the BBC's Tim Sebastian, America's pressure to arrest and extradite Milošević to the Hague tribunal compounded the DOS's problems because "we split the ruling coalition and we postponed reforms."[32] The perception that Ambassador Montgomery supported one faction over the other and that he was a patron of individual DOS leaders such as Čović and presidential candidate Miroljub Labus put the United States in a position of once again being at odds with the majority of Serbs. American support of personalities over processes contributed to the conditions for the DOS's failure to provide effective leadership.

ASSASSINATION AND THE DOS'S LEADERSHIP CRISIS

Despite the loss of popular support among Serbia's citizens, Zoran Djindjić's consolidation of power seemed to be complete, especially after he was able to orchestrate two failed presidential elections at the end of 2002 which left

Koštunica looking weaker and Serbia without a president. This was followed in early 2003 by an agreement largely negotiated between Djindjić and Milo Djukanović and facilitated by the European Union that preserved a joint state between Serbia and Montenegro. This new state not only closed the chapter on the violent life and death of Yugoslavia (in all its forms), it also ended Koštunica's term as Yugoslav president, effectively leaving him without a job and a base of power. Things had never seemed better for Djindjić and his DOS allies. Finally, they could concentrate on pushing through the political and economic legislation they had prepared to legitimate their hold on all levers of power (for example, the DOS leaders announced that parliament would appoint Serbia's president.)

Djindjić himself now turned his attention to ridding himself of a few of his shadier friends whom he had used in overthrowing Milošević and in consolidating his hold on power. In early January 2003, he confided to journalists and other DOS leaders that the "Americans were applying pressure" in an effort to force him to arrest a few of the mafia clan leaders and the volatile former leader of the special police forces, Milorad Luković "Legija."[33] In order to redirect attention from the DOS's shortcomings, he turned to a proven technique: he used populism and nationalism. He embraced the issue of Kosovo, he criticized the United States for the conditions being attached to American assistance, and he promised a crackdown on crime. In January 2003, he reasserted Serbia's claim to Kosovo and boldly stated that if Kosovo were given independence, then Serbia would "demand a new Dayton Conference to redraw borders in the Balkans."[34] He went on to state that even if the U.S. government cut assistance to Serbia because it did not fully cooperate with the international war crimes tribunal, it would not be "a tragedy."[35]

In the meantime, there were warning signs that it was becoming more difficult for Djindjić to juggle numerous issues and to manipulate his way out of tough situations. In January 2003, in local elections in five districts, the DOS was able to win only one mayoral seat; the others went to Koštunica's DSS and coalitions of Milošević's SPS with local independent candidates. Djindjić thought that he could control this latest development by provoking crises in local governments and then simply have the Serbian government appoint emergency governments. He also concentrated on fragmenting Milošević's Socialists and on co-opting the faction led by Branislav Ivković. Nonetheless, these moves left the DOS even more unpopular throughout Serbia, and it undermined the DOS's claims that it was committed to completely dismantling every structure of Milošević's regime.

In addition to his political problems, Djindjić was facing growing media scrutiny over his alleged ties to Serbia's mafia clan leaders. A series of public letters, allegedly written by Ljiljana Buha, the wife of Surčin clan mafia leader Ljubiša Buha "Čume," accused Djindjić and several of his key allies of having social and business ties with the Surčin clan. Then in January 2003, Buha himself, in an interview with TV B-92, dropped a public bombshell with accusations against rival Zemun clan leader Dušan Spasojević "Šiptar" and Legija. Among other things, he accused them of having kidnapped his wife, of having attempted to murder him, of having organized the uprising of the Red Berets (special police forces) the previous autumn, of the kidnappings of at least eight businessmen, and of more than thirty murders, including that of Ivan Stambolić, the former president of Serbia and once mentor and later rival of Slobodan Milošević.[36] Buha also accused several members of the police and the prosecutor's office of being on their payroll.[37] Buha followed this interview with a public letter to the state prosecutor, Rade Terzić, in which he repeated his allegations and implied that Terzić and his assistant were in league with Spasojević and Legija. Not to be outdone, Legija published his own public letter in response to Buha's accusations. In this letter, Legija directly attacked the DOS government, accusing the DOS leaders of "squandering the opportunities" promised by 5 October, of undermining the dignity of the country by selling its citizens to The Hague tribunal, and of "lacking the will" to deal with crime and the "few fragmented bands" that it was labeling a mafia.[38]

These public accusations and counteraccusations further frustrated average citizens, who were tired of gangland slayings in their streets, of the arrogance of the clan leaders who hid behind patriotic slogans, and of the apparent inability or lack of will on the part of the DOS leaders to deal with this problem. While most people saw the situation as being bad, no one could imagine that it was so bad that it would soon claim the life of the country's prime minister.

Djindjić's death came as a brutal wake-up call for the country. The other DOS leaders came out of their shock with a declaration of a state of emergency in the country and chose a new prime minister, Zoran Živković, who launched the anticrime offensive Operation Saber, already described in chapter 2. The state of emergency would last until 22 April 2003. During this time the Serbian police rounded up more than 11,600 suspects; of these, 2,697 were ordered to be held, in most cases without contact with attorneys or family.[39] During this state of emergency, the DOS leadership also pushed through laws on the judiciary and on criminal investigations.

They fired judges and prosecutors. Many of these leaders also saw it as an opportunity to make political points and to attack their political enemies. Average people, for the most part, were very supportive of the crackdown. Hundreds of thousands of them had turned out for Djindjić's funeral to pay their last respects, but also to show their determination to win the fight against the forces that would transform Serbia into a lawless land ruled by the gun. Support for the government skyrocketed. Once again a revolutionary atmosphere prevailed in Serbia.

This enthusiasm soon waned and gave way to cynicism and disillusionment. There were several reasons for this shift in public support for the government's crackdown. Among the most important were indications that members of the government were connected to organized crime figures, continuous scandals involving various ministers, and taking the crackdown too far by increasingly politicizing Djindjić's murder and by radical infringement of individual rights. The government's botched handling of the investigation of Djindjić's death (for example, two of the three main suspects were gunned down by the police and a reconstruction of the crime was never conducted) also greatly hurt its credibility and led to the perception that someone within the government may have been involved in the assassination. The allegations made by members of the DOS government that Koštunica and his party were somehow involved in the assassination plot never gained public acceptance and allowed Koštunica to win public sympathy effectively. The arrest of his former national security adviser Rade Bulatović, who was respected by Western diplomats, also undermined international support for Operation Saber.

The major damage to DOS credibility and authority was inflicted by a series of scandals which began during the first week of the state of emergency. For example, when Deputy Prime Minister Nebojša Čović accused unnamed members of the government of having ties with the Zemun clan, this soon led to a very public polemic with Čedomir Jovanović, another deputy prime minister. Following this ugly public argument, another high-ranking DOS official, Nenad Čanak, admitted to a friendship with a convicted drug seller and mafia figure. This was followed by an unfortunate accident in which a pedestrian was killed by the speeding car of the minister of agriculture, Dragan Veselinov. His arrogant response to public criticism and his refusal to take responsibility for the recklessness of his driver created a major public backlash which eventually led to his bitter resignation. Throughout all of these events the new Živković government appeared confused and disorganized, while the new prime minister lacked the charisma and the political skills of his predecessor.

All this hurt the DOS, but the two key events which would bring about its downfall were the overzealous attempts by the shadowy spinmaster Vladimir Beba Popović to manage and intimidate Serbia's independent media and exploit the ugly split of the DOS's core economic reformers. Popović targeted the popular TV B-92 and several very popular independent journalists. He berated them over the telephone with profanity and outright threats. Once this was revealed, support for the DOS's crackdown both within Serbia and internationally began to fall. This was one of the factors which led to EU pressure on the government to lift the state of emergency; it also led to the first public dispute between the DOS and U.S. Ambassador William Montgomery. The split between the core economic team started in May with the announcement that the government had decided to replace Miroljub Labus and two other members of the Bank Regulatory Agency. Labus, the president of the G17, the DOS's presidential candidate in the 2002 elections, and one of the architects of the economic reforms, was very respected both within Serbia and abroad. This move to fire him set off a very public and ugly argument between the G17 leadership (Labus and Mladjan Dinkić, the governor of the National Bank) and the DOS-led Serbian government. This conflict dragged out over six months and ended with the firing of Dinkić and major accusations of corruption of DOS leaders made by Dinkić in a spectacular press conference in which evidence was presented to support his claims.

By October 2003, the DOS was on life support. Public support for the Serbian government had vanished, and there were almost daily protests which, by November, would turn violent. Dragoljub Mićunović's major defeat at the hands of Šešelj's protégé, Tomislav Nikolić, in the failed November 2003 presidential election showed the level of public dissatisfaction with the DOS. By November 2003, it was also clear that the DOS would lose a vote of confidence in the Serbian parliament; rather than allowing this final humiliation, Prime Minister Živković dissolved parliament and new elections were called for 28 December 2003.

The DOS's Legacy to the Future of Serbia

The parliamentary elections held in Serbia on 28 December 2003 were the final chapter in the story of the DOS, and even though they signified progress in Serbia's democratic tradition, the country is still a long way from the stability it desperately needs. The most disturbing trend has been the considerable number of voters who have supported the extreme nationalist Serbian Radical Party (SRS), led by Tomislav Nikolić since Šešelj's departure for The Hague, in both the parliamentary elections and the pres-idential elections held in the summer of 2004. The SRS won the single greatest number of votes of any party (27.7 percent), but because of pres-sure from the West, their only coalition partner was the SPS, which had garnered 7.4 percent of the vote.[40] Koštunica, whose DSS won 18 percent of the vote, was able to cobble together a minority coalition, after squab-bles with the DS threatened to force another round of elections, which many analysts predicted would give even more votes to the SRS. On 2 March 2004, Koštunica became prime minister of a government that included members of the DSS, G17, SPO, NS, and Social Democratic Party (SDP). Initially, this coalition relied on the support of Milosevic's SPS in order to form the minority government.[41] Later, the DS, under the leadership of former defense minister Boris Tadić, also threw its support behind the coalition but refused to join the government.

Nikolić, the SRS candidate for the presidential elections held on 13 June 2004, once again received the greatest number of votes (30.1 percent), but since he did not get a majority, a run-off election against the Democratic Party's candidate, Boris Tadić (who received 27.3 percent of the votes), was held two weeks later.[42] One of the first legislative acts of the new govern-ment was to abolish the Milošević-era law stipulating a voter turnout of more than 50 percent, which had invalidated previous presidential elec-tions; so even though less than half of the electorate went to the polls for both rounds (47.7 and 48.7 percent, respectively), Serbia was going to get a president. Despite the animosity between the DS and DSS, which had characterized the DOS era and had nearly scuttled attempts to form a gov-ernment in early 2004, Tadić was able to rally Serbia's democratic forces with a promise of a Serbia oriented to the West. He narrowly defeated Nikolić in the 27 June election, receiving 53.7 percent of the votes. The strong showing of the SRS in both the parliamentary and presidential elec-tions indicates that the populist option cloaked in. nationalistic rhetoric and a socialist program represented by the Radicals is still appealing to large numbers of Serbs, despite the disastrous legacy of the Milošević era. The Radicals tried to tone down their anti-Western statements during the campaign and used pro-European integration slogans to modify their im-age, but at the same time their platform also included promises to "liber-ate" lost Serbian lands (notably the Krajina region in Croatia), discontinue all cooperation with the ICTY, scale back privatization and other eco-nomic reforms championed by the DOS government, and pursue an un-compromising policy to keep Kosovo part of Serbia.[43] Another factor which helps explain the surprisingly strong SRS electoral results is the degree to which Serbs had become frustrated with and angered by the constant infighting, scandals, and inefficiency of the DOS government, especially after the high hopes following Milošević's ouster.

With Djindjić's death, the remainder of the DOS government, because of its crackdown on organized crime, rode a new wave of public confidence and support unseen in Serbia since the early euphoria following Milošević's ouster. This was short-lived and the DOS suffered a rapid and undignified end by December 2003, less than nine months after Djindjić's own untimely death. The unprecedented popular support and confidence which the DOS had enjoyed after toppling Milošević had been squandered. With it went the opportunity to transform Serbia from an autocratic, quasi-mafia state to a modern multiparty democracy. Everywhere the remnants of the Milošević and Titoist systems remained and the personality-driven politics they represented became the preferred model of governance for the DOS's leadership.

All of the DOS's leaders proved to be poor leaders and less than capable managers. Koštunica's passivity, slow deliberation, and inability to express his vision to the Serbian nation helped ensure that Djindjić's circumvention of Serbia's laws and institutions would be an irreversible blow to Serbia's democratization. Serbia will continue to struggle to realize the promise of being a normal European country and against the reality of being a normal Balkan country—poor, characterized by corruption and organized crime, plagued by fears of new wars, ruled by a weak coalition government with weak government institutions, and with a political culture characterized by hubris, intolerance, and undemocratic tendencies. While Serbia will probably never fully return to Milošević's brand of autocracy, it will, however, probably continue to hover in the mediocrity that characterized both Milošević's and the subsequent DOS governments. Meanwhile, Serbia's citizens will suffer the consequences of poor leaders and leadership. A sense of hopelessness and a resignation that things will not improve dramatically for the foreseeable future now prevails in the country. Most Serbs have lapsed into apathy, many will continue to leave the country, and all are bound to be disappointed. As popular singer Djordje Balašević stated when asked to express how he felt after the DOS's first year of power: "My whole life I have waited for our guys to come to power; now I have realized that they are not our guys."[44] Serbia's transition to democracy, started with Milošević's downfall, will have to wait for a new generation of leaders, who will not have the baggage of the Titoist and Miloševist legacies, and who will have a better understanding of democracy and a greater commitment to democratic values.

Notes

1. Koštunica used the imagery of a normal and boring state to appeal to Serbian voters who were fatigued by a decade of war, political conflict, and economic ruin.

2. Among the more interesting are Slavoljub Djukić's books *Kako se dogodijo vodja: Borba za vlast u Srbiji posle Josipa Broza* (Belgrade: Filip Višnjić, 1992), *Izmedju slave i anateme: Politička biografija Slobodana Miloševića* (Belgrade: Filip Višnjić, 1994), *On, Ona i Mi* (Belgrade: Radio B-92, 1997), and *Kraj Srpske Bajke* (Belgrade: Samizdat/Free B-92, 1999). For a more scholarly approach, see Lenard J. Cohen's *Serpent in the Bosom: The Rise and Fall of Slobodan Milošević* (Boulder, Colo.: Westview Press, 2001).

3. For example, in his book *The Culture of Power in Serbia: Nationalism and the Destruction of Alternatives* (University Park, Pa.: Penn State University Press, 1999), Eric D. Gordy chronicles well how most Serbs viewed the opposition as being discredited and a failure. In particular, see pages 55–56, 59, 200–202, and 208.

4. For good accounts of the March demonstrations, see Gordy, *The Culture of Power in Serbia,* pp. 34–43; and Misha Glenny, *The Fall of Yugoslavia: The Third Balkan War* (New York: Penguin Books, 1993), pp. 51–58.

5. In conversations with opposition leaders in the years following the demonstration of 9 March 1991, including conversations with Vuk Drašković, it was clear to the author that they were also surprised by the sheer size of the crowd on that day and by the passionate determination and courage of the mostly young students, who fought Milošević's police. It was as if they had unleashed a powerful and dangerous energy no one knew existed, and once unleashed it sought direction, but no one had thought through what to do with it. Also, with war looming in Croatia, and Yugoslavia on the edge of disintegration, the opposition leaders were leery of undermining Serb unity at a time when most Serbs thought there was an imminent danger to the nation. Recently, in reminiscing about this time, Drašković told the author that he had no support among the other opposition leaders nor within his own party, the Serbian Renewal Movement, to pursue a violent overthrow of the government.

6. Sanja Vukčević, "The Regime and Opposition Balanced in Mutual Helplessness," *Network of Independent Journalists Weekly Service,* no. 187 (24 August 2000); online at www.indee.org/nis187.html.

7. For a more complete description of how Dayton benefited Milošević, see Obrad Kesić, "Defeating 'Greater Serbia,' Building Greater Milošević," in *Crises in the Balkans: Views from the Participants,* ed. Constantine P. Danopoulos and Kostas G. Messas (Boulder, Colo.: Westview Press, 1997), pp. 47–73.

8. Going into the elections, most opposition leaders believed that Zajedno would not do well at the polls because tensions between Drašković and Djindjić were already showing and because key leaders like Vojislav Koštunica reluctantly "joined" Zajedno almost on the eve of the elections.

9. All three leaders, Drašković, Pešić, and Djindjić, at different times have expressed to the author their belief that the demonstrations were losing steam and that the West was encouraging them to declare victory and end the demonstrations.

10. Cohen, *Serpent in the Bosom*, pp. 126–27.

11. Ibid., p. 127.

12. *Reporter,* no. 190 (13 December 2001), p. 15.

13. *Vreme* (Belgrade), no. 571 (13 December 2001), p. 19.

14. Ibid., p. 20.

15. Ibid. The word *partizanstinom* is a blend of meanings that combines the notion of Partisan excess with a lust for power and revenge. Its historic meaning is directly tied to the excess and crimes committed by Tito's Partisan forces as they consolidated power in 1945.

16. *NIN* (Belgrade), no. 2610 (4 July 2001), p. 16.

17. Timothy Garton Ash, "The Last Revolution," *The New York Review of Books,* 16 November 2000, p. 9.

18. See the International Crisis Group's reports on Serbia, such as "Belgrade's Lagging Reform: Cause for International Concern," *Balkan Report,* no. 126 (7 March 2002), p. 19.

19. They sent secondary figures from their parties to the federal ministries, the only exceptions being Goran Svilanović, the head of the Civic Alliance of Serbia, who became federal foreign minister, and Dragoljub Mićunović, mentor to both Koštunica and Djindjić, the head of the Democratic Center, who became speaker of the federal parliament.

20. Djindjić insisted that the economic ministries go to experts whom he would select. This underlined his belief that the economy was the main engine for all reforms and the real base of power in Serbia.

21. *Blic Newspaper Online,* 23 April 2002, online at www.blic.co.yu.

22. *Reporter,* no. 126 (5 June 2002), p. 20.

23. *NIN,* no. 2665 (24 January 2002), p. 11.

24. Ibid.

25. *Nacional* (Zagreb), 21 March 2002, p. 5.

26. *NIN,* no. 2665 (24 January 2002), p. 12.

27. *Reporter* (Belgrade), no. 221 (6 July 2002), pp. 16–17.

28. As told to the author by editors at Beta and B-92 TV.

29. *NIN,* no. 2665 (4 January 2002), p. 5.

30. *NIN,* no. 2688 (14 July 2002), p. 3.

31. *NIN*, no. 2687 (7 June 2002), p. 4.

32. *BBC Hardtalk*, 26 April 2002.

33. As told to the author by two Belgrade journalists and a leader of the DOS's presidency.

34. Radio B-92 News Bulletin, 1 January 2003, online at www.b92.net.

35. Ibid., 22 January 2003.

36. Ibid., 24 January 2003.

37. Ibid.

38. Ibid., 27 January 2003.

39. Ibid., 17 May 2003.

40. For complete election results, see the Centar za slobodne izbore i demokratiju (CeSID) Web site at www.cedis.org. Voter turnout was 59.7 percent, a high number considering that for two years Serbia had been without a president because of invalid elections due to low voter turnout.

41. See *Vreme* (4 March 2004), pp. 12–18; and Radio Free Europe Feature Article (2 March 2004) online at www.rferl.org.

42. For all statistics related to the elections, see www.cedis.org.

43. *Nacional* (6 January 2004), pp. 32–35.

44. *NIN*, no. 2684 (6 June 2002), p. 12.

THE LEGACY OF THE WAR

5

UNDER THE HOLY LIME TREE

The Inculcation of Neurotic and
Psychotic Syndromes as a Serbian
Wartime Strategy, 1986–95

SABRINA P. RAMET

The 1991–95 War of Yugoslav Succession affected Serbian society in multifarious ways, including also the psychological health of Serbian society. This chapter looks at some of the recurrent themes in Serbian propaganda 1986–95, examining their operation in inculcating collective neurotic and psychotic syndromes and noting the relevance of those syndromes for the war against Croatia and Bosnia, 1991–95. Six pivotal themes in Serbian propaganda are examined:

1. Victimization, in which Serbs were constructed as collective victims first of the NDH (Nezavisna Država Hrvatska, or Independent State of Croatia), then of Tito's Yugoslavia, and more specifically of Croats, Albanians, Bosniaks, and other non-Serbs.

2. Dehumanization of designated "others," in which Croats were depicted as "genocidal" and as "Ustashe," Bosniaks were portrayed as "fanatical fundamentalists," and Albanians were represented as not fully human. These processes of dehumanization effectively removed these designated "others" from the moral field, sanctifying their murder or expulsion.

3. Belittlement, in which Serbia's enemies were represented as beneath contempt.

4. Conspiracy, in which Croats, Slovenes, Albanians, the Vatican, Germany, Austria, and sometimes also the Bosniaks as well as the United States and other foreign states, were seen as united in a conspiracy to break up the SFRY (Socialist Federated Republic of Yugoslavia) and hurt Serbia.

In this way, the Belgrade regime's obstinate disregard for the fundamental standards of international law was dressed up as heroic defiance of an anti-Serb conspiracy.

5. Entitlement, in which the Serbs were constructed as "entitled" to create a Greater Serbian state to which parts of Croatia and Bosnia would be attached, under the motto "All Serbs should live in one state."

6. Superhuman powers and divine sanction. The Serbs were told that they were, in some sense, "super." They were the best fighters on the planet, they could stand up to the entire world, they were sanctioned by God himself, because of Tsar Lazar and the fact that Lazar had chosen the heavenly kingdom. Moreover, since Lazar had chosen the heavenly kingdom, the Serbs, encouraged to view themselves as Lazar's heirs, were entitled to the earthly kingdom which Lazar had repudiated, as their patrimony.

Introduction

Were we to construct a psychological profile of an individual who viewed himself as a perennial victim of various contemptible "others" who had sought to overcome their inferiority by uniting in a conspiracy against him, who considered himself "entitled" to vastly more than was his lot, and who was determined to punish the conspirators and take their possessions, we would say that the person in question was a paranoid schizophrenic with neurotic or psychotic delusions. We would also conclude that he could be dangerous to those coming into contact with him. Where individuals are concerned, aggressive behavior is generally dysfunctional, but for nations going to war, heightened aggressiveness may be all too functional. It is for this reason that nations setting out on premeditated wars of conquest—and what wars of conquest are not premeditated?—are apt to adopt a calculated policy of inculcating mass paranoid schizophrenia in the public. The media can readily be used to make paranoia mainstream, and as paranoia becomes mainstream, it becomes ever harder for citizens to resist its snares, temptations, and oversimplifications.

A further conclusion may also be inferred, viz., that if one can define collective syndromes which reveal a society's lapses into mental illness, then one can define what characteristics are constitutive of a society's good mental health and outline at least the rudiments of such policies and structures as are conducive to such health.

A Theory of Libidinal Politics

I find myself intrigued by the possibility of placing Max Weber's ideal types of legitimate authority alongside Sigmund Freud's theory of the human psyche. I shall take it for granted that my readers are familiar with these respective theories and shall not waste any space explaining what should be common knowledge. Rather, on the basis of this assumed acquaintance, I wish to suggest that one might posit three sets of pairs: traditional authority + the superego (understanding that both appeal to sacred and/or bequeathed moral codes), bureaucratic authority + the ego (viewing this as the "secular" domain, in which the bureaucracy, like the ego, replicates patterns it has established over time), and charismatic authority + the id/libido (viewing both charisma and the libido as reservoirs of transrational energy, and independent motivation, which may unleash creative and destructive drives alike). In the case of an individual, psychological health entails a balance among these three facets; when balance is lost, psychological health suffers. A parallel claim may be registered in terms of sources of authority in a modern state, which is to say that, in a modern state, there must be a balance among traditional authority, the secular state, and libidinal values, with the former two working to keep the latter in check, without, however, extinguishing them. The particular power of a charismatic leader or a leader appealing to charismatic/libidinal values (such as national expansionism) is to tap into the collective libido, pushing society into an excited state. This is the realm of pain and pleasure, in which the pains of the past are the most keenly felt and in which fantasies of national "salvation" and triumph—those two being often equated—are the most pleasurable. When a society is at the height of libidinal fever, it is like a man driven wild with sexual frenzy: rational judgment is suspended, cost-benefit analysis is held in contempt if it is regarded at all, and all that remains is the collective lust for satisfaction.

But the more the libido is fed, the larger it grows in proportion to the ego and the superego, until the latter two are either subverted or reduced to marginality—or both. The charismatic leader, thus, serves up a libidinal fare and enjoys what might, alternatively, be called "libidinal authority." Because his authority is libidinal, rather than based on sacred or secular-bureaucratic legitimation, it is more dependent upon producing sensations of pleasure (triumph, expansion, defiance of stronger powers, the infliction of suffering on "enemy" nations and groups, etc.). When a libidinal leader ceases to be able to serve up the promised pleasures, his power crumbles. The speed with which it crumbles is, of course, a contingent fact, which depends on various factors, including the level of economic deterioration of the society, the magnitude of his gamble (and hence of his failure), and the loyalty of the army and police forces. The last mentioned factor cannot be underestimated; indeed, as long as the army and police are loyal, a libidinal leader can weather many storms (Libya's Qaddafi, for example, survived the missile attack on his palace authorized by U.S. president Reagan in the mid-1980s and even cut back on his support to international terrorism after that, without losing his grip on power). But a libidinal leader unable to pleasure his society is a leader utterly without authority of any kind.

What should be stressed is that a society which has been mobilized along libidinal lines develops symptoms of collective neurosis or collective psychosis. This concept is well known in psychoanalytic and psychological literature. Quite apart from Freud's use of the concept of collective neurosis in *The Future of an Illusion,* one can also point to theories about collective psychosis developed by Robert Waelder[1] and to the work on collective paranoia carried out by Roderick Kramer and David Messick.[2] For that matter, collective mental states were also elaborated by Emile Durkheim.[3] Societies, like individuals, do not develop psychoses or paranoias spontaneously; there are always histories, situations, triggers, and the like. In the case of societies, the role of intellectuals[4] and political leaders cannot be ignored.

What occurred in Serbia in the years 1981–87 could be described as a massive tectonic shift in which perceptions, values, and expectations changed dramatically, preparing the way for Slobodan Milošević's seizure of power within the Serbian party apparatus and his launching of his abortive "antibureacratic revolution." Even the terminology here is significant: a libidinal leader inevitably finds himself at war with the quasi rationalism of bureaucracies. But the 1980s were also years in which Serbs increasingly revisited the past, raising questions about the prison camps at Goli Otok and Lepoglava, about Tito's establishment of Kosovo as an autonomous province, about the removal of factories from Serbia to the highlands in Slovenia and Croatia at the height of the Stalin-Tito conflict, and about the denigration of Draža Mihailović and his Chetniks by Tito-era historiography, and parading the bones of Tsar Dušan (in 1968) and Tsar Lazar (in 1989) in macabre clerical demonstrations of national commitment. Particularly poisonous was Vasilije Krestić's 1986 article "On the Origin of the Genocide of Serbs in the Independent State of Croatia," which argued that the "genocide against the Serbs in [Ustasha] Croatia is a specific phenomenon in our [Serbian] centuries-old common life with the Croats. The protracted development of the genocidal idea in certain centers of Croatian society . . . [which] did not necessarily have some narrow—but rather a broad—base, took deep roots in the consciousness of many generations [of Croats]."[5] Where Tito-era historiography had vilified both the Ustashe and the Chetniks, Serbian historiography after 1983 increasingly sought to rehabilitate the Chetniks, while ignoring the roles played by Ljotić and Nedić and exaggerating the numbers of Serbs dying during World War Two.[6] The result was that the Croatian fascists took on ever darker hues in the thinking of both Serbian intellectuals and the Serbian public at this time, while corresponding Serbian renegades either were whitewashed or disappeared from view. This phenomenon is known to psychologists as *dysphoric rumination,* which is defined as "the tendency for individuals to unhappily reimagine, rethink, and relive pleasant or unpleasant events . . . [resulting in an] increase [in] negative thinking about those events and contribut[ing] to a pessimistic explanatory style when trying to explain them."[7] Dysphoric rumination is considered a contributory factor to paranoid cognition.

It was also in the mid-1980s that Vladimir Dedijer and others began to ruminate about a Vatican-Comintern conspiracy, to which various other states were said to have subscribed. This increasing tendency to treat the Vatican, Germany, Austria, and other states as enemies, even before the breakup of 1991, culminated in Milošević's claim in a public speech in November 1988—astounding some of his listeners—that "Serbia's enemies outside the country are plotting against it, along with those in[side] the country."[8] To the extent that such claims became part of the public discourse of Serbian society in the late 1980s, one may say that Serbia was increasingly given to exaggerated perceptions of conspiracy. As Kramer and Messick note, this tendency involves the overestimation of "the extent to which [the group's] perceived outgroup enemies or adversaries are engaged in coordinated and concerted hostile or malevolent actions against them."[9] This does not imply that out-group enemies are not in fact engaged in hostile actions; this is only to suggest that overestimation of the extent of hostile actions may be a sign of a troubled mind (or a troubled society).

In the latter half of the 1980s, Serbs were also repeatedly hearing (and believing) reports of Albanian rapes of Serbian women, the revival of an Ustasha mentality among Croats, and the like, with not only Croats and Kosovar Albanians but also the Hungarians of Vojvodina and the Muslims of Bosnia-Herzegovina cast as villains in rumors. What interests me here is not the question of the extent to which one or another rumor had

some truth to it, but rather the composite character of the deluge of rumors which—seemingly uniformly—attributed ill intentions to the non-
Serbs of Yugoslavia. This syndrome, known as sinister attribution error,
involves the "tendency. . . to overattribute hostile intentions and malevolent motives to others."[10]

And, given the foregoing, Serbs increasingly felt the need to be vigilant
about their coethnics in Kosovo and Croatia especially. These concerns
were effusively articulated in the infamous Memorandum drafted by
members of the Serbian Academy of Sciences and Arts (SANU, mentioned in chapter 2) and leaked to the press in September 1986; according
to the Memorandum, the federal system had been designed by Tito
specifically to weaken Serbia, neither Bosnia-Herzegovina nor Montenegro had any legitimate claim to republic status, and the threat then posed
to the Serbs of Croatia by their Croatian neighbors (in what was still com-
munist-ruled Croatia) could only be compared to the fascist depredations
of the NDH! The Serbian Writers' Association on the Francuska ulica in
Belgrade began to host weekly meetings to discuss the tribulations of the
Serbs, and books and special issues of magazines were published detailing the situation of Serbs in Kosovo. Serbia, thus, slid into a habit of hypervigilant social information processing, a dangerous habit in which every
move taken by Croats, Albanians, and Muslims was subjected to scrutiny
and given potentially enormous significance.

One more element is needed in the equation: the belief in a just world.
This belief, hypothesized by M. J. Lerner,[11] involves people's need to believe that the world is basically just and that people get what they deserve.
In the late 1980s, this belief fueled nationalist Serbs' confidence that they
would get what they thought they deserved—a Greater Serbia, in which
few non-Serbs would remain. As the nationalist discourse became dominant, justice was increasingly understood in terms of the national program.

The aforementioned reactions—dysphoric rumination, exaggerated
perceptions of conspiracy, sinister attribution error, and hypervigilant social information processing—are associated, according to Kramer and
Messick, with collective paranoia, manifested in social alienation, heightened antagonism toward others, and an attitude of hostility toward the
outside world.[12] To the extent that Serbian society already manifested these
symptoms by the late 1980s, it was already susceptible to the themes of Serbian war propaganda and vulnerable to manipulation. Fearful of the gathering conspiracies which it fancied were being concocted by its enemies
and ever more troubled by the evolving memories of the national past,
and perhaps especially of the sufferings associated with World War Two,

Serbian society was receptive to a libidinal leader who would lift the weight from their shoulders and give Serbs what they "justly" deserved.[13] Perhaps Serbs might even experience the fulfillment of their historical aspirations, once associated, by Serb followers of Slovak Ljudevit Štúr and Czech Jan Kollár, with the unification of Slavs "under the holy Slav lime-tree."[14]

Redesigning the Ego

How does a nation view itself and its place in the world? To the extent that one may speak of a national "ego" or self-identity of the nation, that ego may become the subject of conscious manipulation, aiming at the redefinition and redesigning of the national ego itself. Insofar as the national ego, the self-identity of a nation, includes concepts of its relationship to other nations and its attitude toward those living within its territory, any redesign of the national ego will have consequences for issues of democracy vs. authoritarianism.

In the course of the 1980s and 1990s, Serbia's mythmakers, whether literary figures such as Dobrica Ćosić or ordinary propagandists, painted Serbia in ever grander hues. Here was a Serbia existing beyond time and space,[15] a Serbia simultaneously non-European and the most European of all,[16] a Serbia standing guard over the most important spiritual values against the shallow materialism "of the extortionist-atheistic and demonic international community,"[17] a Serbia which, in its dreams of "complete separation" from this decadent world, went into orbit as the tenth planet of the solar system, "the Serbian planet."[18] As Ivan Čolović has recounted in a brilliant work first published in 1997, the Serbian national political myth— which is to say, the set of propositions in wide circulation in Serbia— holds that Serbia is the oldest nation in the world, the nation from which all other nations developed, so that, as Relja Novaković has urged, the peoples inhabiting states "from Great Britain to India" may ultimately trace their national origin back to the Serbian *Urvolk*.[19] Serbs were wont to boast about their martial prowess and about their fierceness in battle,[20] but also claimed some special advantage in the sexual realm as well. As Danilo Kiš put it, in a gloss on a poem written by Jan Kollár, "[O]ther peoples have good fortune, tradition, erudition, history, ratio, but genitals are ours alone."[21] And hence, the Serbian Insurrectionary War offered the prospect of the dawn of a new age for all of Europe, if not for the entire world. Serbia, compared variously (in the pages of *Pravoslavlje* and *Književne novine*) to Job, to the Jewish people, even to Christ himself, offered itself as the new savior. And just as Christ had to die on the cross, in order to rise again after three days to claim his place in the Kingdom of Heaven, so too Serbia, whose tsar, Lazar, had renounced the earthly kingdom for a heavenly one in 1389, had to wait for six centuries before rising again to claim its earthly kingdom, earned through long suffering.

This grandiose redesign of the national ego was, at the same time, libidinal in nature in that it began the process of unleashing the energies of the libido and bringing about the conquest of the national ego by the nationalist libido. The claim that "all Serbs should live in one state" was, moreover, not universalizable, because it was premised on the notion that lands with mixed populations (Serbs and non-Serbs) should be assigned to the Serbian national state rather than to the national state of one or another non-Serb nation. This claim was, thus, a claim to unique entitlement, a claim which could be registered only in the realm of the libido.

As the national myth gained in strength, Serbian society became convinced of its unique role in history, its special suffering, and its entitlement to realize "heavenly Serbia" on earth. As Lerner noted in 1987, this entitlement "is experienced affectively and motivationally as an imperative, a sense of requiredness between the actor's perceived outcomes and the person's attributes or acts."[22] Or, to put it another way, as the 1980s wore on, Serbia was reaching the point that Raskolnikov reached in Dostoyevsky's *Crime and Punishment* as he reflected on whether he occupied some unique niche in the moral universe. But for Serbia, as for Raskolnikov, there were moments of hesitation before making the fateful breach with the moral order, expressed by the Serbian students who bravely marched on the streets of Belgrade on 9 March 1991 or by the antiwar protestors led by Patriarch Pavle on 14 June 1992 who demanded that Milošević resign. But these reservations, though significant, did not carry the day. The superego would be stilled, and the ego would be redesigned.

The Stilling of the Superego

The processes of instilling in Serbs feelings of victimization and of entitlement to grandeur, and of their uniqueness, and of fears of various sorts of conspiracies against them were not all orchestrated. Neither the Serbian Church's "Appeal on Behalf of the Serbian Residents of Kosovo and Their Holy Shrines" (of 1982) nor the SANU Memorandum (of 1986) was part of a strategy orchestrated by the political establishment; the former came on the initiative of some of the priests in the Church, while the latter was the result of the autonomous decision taken by the Serbian Academy of Sciences and Arts at a time when the ruling party of Serbia (a branch of the League of Communists of Yugoslavia) was still holding to the line that "every nationalism is (potentially) dangerous." But after Milošević's seizure of power in the Serbian party in late 1987, that party quickly took up the tasks dictated by that Memorandum and at that point, the continuation of these processes of "neuroticization" or even "psychoticization" of the Serbian public became a matter of official policy. Not only were the Serbs unique among the peoples of the planet, even constituting in some extraspatial sense their own planet, but they also enjoyed the special favor of God. In talking of "heavenly Serbia," the clerics of the Serbian Orthodox Church laid claim to divine sanction for the program of Serbian territorial expansionism[23] and, in the pages of *Pravoslavlje,* offered historical arguments for Serbian annexation of portions of eastern Slavonia. Later, it would even be claimed that God had specifically bequeathed Bosnia to the Serbs.[24] Karadžić himself claimed to be doing God's work and was, in turn, described by Dragan Nedeljković as "one of the heroes of this end of the twentieth century."[25]

But in spite of these changes to the national ego, which—as is well known—came at a time of shrinking economic capacities and general economic crisis, the collective "superego" remained, as already mentioned, an obstacle even though, by early 1990, if not before, Milošević had decided on war against Croatia and perhaps also other republics.[26] To convert an already fearful population into soldiers prepared to fight against their former neighbors and friends (often in a literal sense), they had to be released from moral constraints and infused with hatred for the target peoples. As Ćosić noted in a widely read work of fiction, "[D]riven by hatred, all men will fight . . . ; hatred is the force which gathers and unites all energies."[27] Moral disengagement, as Albert Bandura, a widely respected expert on the subject, noted in a 1999 article, can be achieved through a combination of displacement of responsibility (with, in this case, the Milošević government assuming moral responsibility for the war), diffusion of responsibility (so that harm can always be attributed to the agency of others or to peer pressure), distortion of the consequences (aptly represented by the Bosnian Serb newspaper *Javnost*'s representation of the massacre at Srebrenica as the "cleansing of a blot on the map"), and, perhaps above all, dehumanization and demonization.[28] In Serbian war propaganda, as is well known, Croats were routinely described as fascistic and genocidal by nature, referred to as "Ustashe," and accused of wanting to revive the NDH (a charge which was true of some Croats, to be sure, but not of the majority of Croats). In the eyes of Serb propagandists, all Bosnian Muslims were "Islamic fundamentalists" and all Albanians were "rapists" and secessionists. Demonization specifically makes it possible for perpetrators of atrocities to maintain a positive self-image even while victimizing innocent civilians—on the argument that "no one is innocent."[29]

Thus, paradoxically, Serb nationalists engaged in the war typically upheld two contradictory theses: that they themselves were innocent victims of Croats, Albanians, Bosnian Muslims, et al., and that all sides were guilty and no one innocent! Since they never uttered these sentences sequentially, the blatant absurdity of this belief system was never, as far as I am aware, exposed by the media of any nation. Even the demonization of Germany for its alleged responsibility in plotting the dismantlement of socialist Yugoslavia and for its alleged culpability in starting the war in the first place through its advocacy of the recognition of Slovenia and Croatia (after the outbreak of hostilities) played a useful role in Serbian war propaganda.[30] As Voltaire once said, "Those who can make you believe absurdities can make you commit atrocities."[31]

We know that the process of moral disengagement was still far from complete at the time the war broke out (it was, in fact, never complete as such), because many of the JNA (Yugoslav People's Army) soldiers expressed confusion as to why they were suddenly fighting their fellow "Yugoslavs," while many others went AWOL, even fleeing the country, rather than serve in the subsequent war against the Croats. But several processes contributed to further stilling the stirrings of the superego. First, as the violence continued, it became part of the daily routine, it became unsurprising, and many people ceased to be as shocked and outraged as they were when the fighting first broke out. Second, the role of some of the hierarchy of the Serbian Orthodox Church in sanctioning the violence first in Croatia and later in Bosnia-Herzegovina made a significant contribution toward moral desensitization. After all, if some of the official guardians of spirituality and morality have no qualms about supporting the war, why should ordinary Serbs worry about it? Moreover, insofar as the Church placed itself, thus, in alliance first with the Milošević regime and then with Bosnian Serb leader Radovan Karadžić, the classic syndrome of the agentic state came into play. Experiments conducted by S. Milgram more than thirty years ago demonstrated that the desire of individuals to obey and please authorities is often sufficient to override moral reservations, even in the absence of any feelings of having been victimized by those on whom the experimental subject was prepared to inflict harm.[32] In the agentic state, individuals do not abandon their moral principles. Rather, they engage in moral rationalization, thereby convincing themselves that their actions are, in spite of appearances to the contrary, consistent with their core moral standards.

Other processes used to dull the moral sense include(d) the use of eu-
phemistic language (in which mass murder and the forcible expulsion of
non-Serbs were prettified by the term "ethnic cleansing"); advantageous
comparison (in which Muslims and Croats were said to have behaved far
worse than the Serbs: for example, Patriarch Pavle joined Karadžić in
claiming that there had been no rape camps operated by Serbs and no systematic rapes carried out by Serbs, even while accusing Croats and Muslims of having done precisely those things); diffusion or displacement of
responsibility; and instances of blaming the victim. The last-mentioned
tactic was employed not only in the obvious sense of claiming that, for
example, Tudjman's firing of Serbs from positions in the police justified
an insurrection against Zagreb, but also in the more brazen sense of actually blaming the victims for the atrocities which they suffered. Thus, in
Serbian propaganda, it was the Croats themselves who had rocketed Tudjman's presidential palace in 1991, it was the Croats themselves who had
laid siege to the port city of Dubrovnik and were shelling the Croatian sea-
side town of Šibenik, it was the Muslims themselves who had fired upon
their own coethnics in the Pirkala marketplace in 1994, and it was the Muslims themselves who had carried out the massacre at Srebrenica with the
help of German and American operatives.[33] The Serbs even had an explanation for the alleged, consistent idiocy of their antagonists: they did
these things in order to make the Serbs look bad.[34]

These various methods of moral rationalization and disengagement had
some unintended side effects. The first was that the habituation to violence led to an escalation of violence within the family, with husbands beating wives and fathers beating children.[35] Second, moral disengagement
made it impossible to return to the behaviors and patterns of the pre-war
days. As Jo-Ann Tsang explains in an article published in the *Review of
General Psychology*, "the commission of immoral behavior makes it more
costly [in terms of self-image] to act morally in the future, increasing the
likelihood of further evil."[36] After all, to take pride in subscribing to an
ethic of, let us say, nonviolence is virtually impossible for someone who
has established a persona based on killing large numbers of "enemies of
the nation."

Unleashing the Libido

If modern warfare may be thought of as a libidinal state, then mobilizing
people for war requires more than redesigning the national ego and stilling the superego. It also involves and requires an unleashing of the ener-

gies of the libido in the service of the national fantasy. As I have already noted, the process of unleashing the libido began simultaneously with the redesigning of the national ego, indeed was, from the beginning, an essential part of the Serb nationalist strategy of transforming the mood, values, expectations, hopes, ambitions, and thinking of ordinary Serbs. Sometimes the libidinal character of Serbian war propaganda was implicit, for example when Vuk Drašković said of the Serbian army, "This is an army with the soul of a girl, the behavior of a priest, and the heart of Obilić."[37] At other times, sexuality was made explicit, whether through the use of highly attractive young women dressed in uniform to beguile young men into associating war with sex or by explicitly advising young men that soldiers were sexually attractive to young women or through the sublimation of sexuality into the fetish of weapons, as in the refrain, "My companion is my rifle, . . . My bride is now my cartridge belt."[38]

But, as Freud knew, the libido embraces much more than just sexuality, and war finds its libidinal character not just in sex but in violence itself. Richard Morrock notes how "in lynch mobs . . . [t]he killers do not look like people forced to take unpleasant measures in order to protect their communities from criminals—their own rationalizations for their sadistic acts. Instead, they look like they are having a good time."[39] The positive pleasure experienced in violence is reinforced by moral inversion (in which the Serbs imagined themselves as "remnants of a slaughtered people," as Serbian writer Matija Bečković put it) and by the belittlement of one's *antagonists*. Again this results in paradox: if one's enemies are threatening demons, how can they be fools? Or if they are fools, how can they be taken seriously as demons? But propaganda does not have to be consistent to be effective. On the contrary, by playing on contradictory themes, propaganda may actually be more effective than if it were entirely consistent.

Here the psychiatrists of both Belgrade and Zagreb played their part in creating belittling national stereotypes. Zagreb psychiatrists E. Klein and M. Jakovljević both portrayed Serbs as suffering from a collective inferiority complex, with the latter attributing patterns of "pathological possessiveness" to the Serbs as a nation.[40] Belgrade psychiatrist J. Marić, for his part, found (in a work published in 1998) that Serbs were well meaning and pacifist and had "never resorted to bad-mouthing or vilifying other peoples," while Croats were allegedly "egoistic" and were "not keen on giving themselves to other human beings" having been "enslaved by objects" (unlike the Serbs).[41] Jovan Rašković, at one time professor of psychiatry at the University of Belgrade and the later cofounder of the Serbian Democratic Party in Croatia, famously discovered that Croats were, as a people, suffering from a castration complex, living in fear that "something terrible" was going to happen to them and irrationally "afraid of being deceived." Judging that Serbs had "aggressive oedipal traits," Rašković concluded that "people who have a castration type of personality structure are obsessed by a fear of those who have aggressive oedipal traits."[42]

But belittlement need not be confined to national groups, as proven by the Serbian propaganda machine's charge that Tudjman had tried to kill himself "in order to spite Serbia."[43] Of course, this portrayed Tudjman simultaneously as self-destructive and as a bungler unable even to kill himself; in combination, this suggested that Tudjman was an unworthy adversary. Moreover, it is well known that in rape situations, it is common for the rapist to insult and disparage his victim, thereby communicating to her that she "deserved" to be raped.

Nationalism does not have to assume a libidinal form, perhaps not even in war. But in order to conduct an offensive war, it is a huge advantage if those engaged in it first, actively, even passionately, deny the fact of the war's being offensive, and second, succumb to a libidinal fever in which the murder of one's adversaries becomes both pleasurable and the object of cult worship. One need only think of the cult which grew up around Serbian war "hero" Željko Ražnatović "Arkan" to see the point. And yet, this embrace of Thanatos and Libido—death instinct and life instinct—at one and the same time banishes the nation to a "spectral" world occupying the twilight between life and death. Indeed, in the species of "eroticism," if that is the word, represented by a well-known (to Serbs) poem by Desanka Maksimović,

> Love exists only if it is deprived of touch, only in some sentimental, trashy suffering, from a distance, which is, however, the condition of [the] possibility of love, since [the] very closeness, every touch, deadens love; the body is the death of the life of love, the other is loved only as apparition, only as the spectre that is held at a distance: "Oh no, do not approach, I want from [a] distance to love and kiss these two eyes of yours"; in fact, we are not bodies at all, we are not alive either, we are somehow un-dead (to say nothing about the fact that the dead themselves can also approach us) . . . [O]ur bodies are not alive, or [rather], they are living graves; they are not in any way a source of enjoyment, and that is why the love relation should be spectral, un-dead.[44]

Conclusion

Serbian society began to stray down the path to war more or less unwittingly. Already in the years 1981–86, long before the other republics experienced anything like a "national awakening," Serbia (and here one may include Kosovo too) was already sliding into a syndrome in which myths, threats, the allure of victory, and belligerent rhetoric filled the public discourse, giving Serbs a sense of common destiny but also separating them, psychologically, from the other peoples of socialist Yugoslavia. That this was an unhealthy state of collective mind is clear from the prominence of the themes of victimization, conspiracy, national entitlement, and divine sanction of the Serbian national project, as well as from the insistent campaigns of dehumanization, demonization, and belittlement of Croats, Bosnian Muslims, and Albanians, as well as other peoples and states, which began at this time. This syndrome, in an individual, would be considered psychotic; to the extent that it permeated much of Serbian society, perhaps especially in the countryside, one may speak of Serbia having been sucked into a kind of collective psychosis. And to the extent that Serbian war propaganda aimed at reinforcing and stimulating this state of mind, we may say that it aimed at inculcating and reinforcing neurotic and psychotic syndromes in Serbian society. This psychosis had its cultic saints—portraits of Milošević and Chetnik leader Draža Mihailović were often displayed alongside those of saints canonized by the Church—had its bards (such as Simonida Stanković and Ceca Ražnatović), and even had its official music, "turbo-folk," a pop mixture of folk-ethnic style with a rhythmic pounding beat. Moreover, this psychosis could even transport those infected to a state of consciousness which they mistook for a better world. Milošević, for example, arriving dramatically at Kosovo Polje in a helicopter on 28 June 1989, told those gathered for the six hundredth anniversary of Serbia's mythic confrontation with its national destiny that in that fourteenth-century battle, Serbia had defended not just herself but all of European culture and civilization. Fine oratory might even be called the elixir of national psychosis. Here, one may recall what Socrates said to Menexenus on the subject:

> O Menexenus! Death in battle is certainly in many respects a noble thing. The dead man gets a fine and costly funeral, although he may have been poor, and an elaborate speech is made over him by a wise man who has long ago prepared what he has to say. . . . The speakers praise him for what he has done and for what he has not done . . . and they steal away our souls

with their embellished words. In every conceivable form they praise the city, and they praise those who died in war, and all our ancestors who went before us, and they praise ourselves also who are still alive, until I feel quite elevated by their laudations, and I stand listening to their words, Menexenus, and become enchanted by them, and all in a moment I imagine myself to have become a greater and nobler and finer man than I was before. And if, as often happens, there are any foreigners who accompany me to the speech, I become suddenly conscious of having [the experience of] a sort of triumph over them, and they seem to experience a corresponding feeling of admiration at me, and at the greatness of the city, which appears to them, when they are under the influence of the speaker, more wonderful than ever. This consciousness of dignity lasts me more than three days, and not until the fourth or fifth day do I come to my senses and know where I am—in the meantime, I have been living in the Islands of the Blessed.[45]

Or, one might say, under the holy lime tree.

Notes

This chapter was originally published in *Polemos* (Zagreb) 5, nos. 1–2 (January–December 2002): pp. 83—97.

1. Samuel A. Guttman, "Robert Waelder and the Application of Psychoanalytic Principles to Social and Political Phenomena," *Journal of the American Psychoanalytic Association* 34, no. 4 (1986), pp. 835—62.

2. Roderick M. Kramer and David M. Messick, "Getting By with a Little Help from Our Enemies: Collective Paranoia and Its Role in Intergroup Relations," in *Intergroup Cognition and Intergroup Behavior,* ed. Constantine Sedikides, John Schopler, and Chester A. Insko (Mahwah, N.J.: Lawrence Erlbaum Associates, 1998), pp. 233–55.

3. Emile Durkheim, *The Rules of the Sociological Method* (New York: The Free Press, 1964), as cited in William W. Bostock, "South Africa's Language Policy: Controlled Status Enhancement and Reduction," *Mots pluriels,* no. 13 (April 2000), online at www.arts.uwa.edu.au/MotsPluriels/MP1300wban.html (accessed 13 May 2002).

4. See, for example, Nicholas J. Miller, "The Nonconformists: Dobrica Ćosić and Mica Popović Envision Serbia," *Slavic Review* 58, no. 3 (Fall 1999), pp. 515–36.

5. Quoted in Ivo Banac, "The Dissolution of Yugoslav Historiography," in *Beyond Yugoslavia: Politics, Economics, and Culture in a Shattered Community,* ed.

Sabrina Petra Ramet and Ljubiša S. Adamovich (Boulder, Colo.: Westview Press, 1995), pp. 55–56.

6. On the exaggerations of casualties, see Vladimir Žerjavić, *Population Losses in Yugoslavia 1941–1945* (Zagreb: Dom i svijet and Hrvatski Institut za Povijest, 1997), pp. 53–113.

7. Kramer and Messick, "Getting By with a Little Help," p. 246.

8. Belgrade Domestic Service, 19 November 1988, trans. in Foreign Broadcast Information Service (FBIS), *Daily Report* (Eastern Europe), 21 November 1988, pp. 72–73.

9. Kramer and Messick, "Getting By with a Little Help," p. 247.

10. Ibid., p. 246.

11. M. J. Lerner, *The Belief in a Just World: A Fundamental Delusion* (New York: Plenum Press, 1980).

12. Kramer and Messick, "Getting By with a Little Help," pp. 245–48; and John Mirowsky and Catherine E. Ross, "Paranoia and the Structure of Powerlessness," *American Sociological Review* 48, no. 2 (April 1983), p. 236.

13. See N. T. Feather, "Deservingness, Entitlement, and Reactions to Outcomes," and John H. Ellard, Christina D. Miller, Terri-Lynne Baumle, and James M. Olson, "Just World Processes in Demonizing," both in *The Justice Motive in Everyday Life*, ed. Michael Ross and Dale T. Miller (Cambridge: Cambridge University Press, 2002).

14. Ivan Čolović, *The Politics of Symbol in Serbia: Essays in Political Anthropology*, trans. from Serbian by Celia Hawkesworth (London: Hurst and Co., 2002), p. 91.

15. Ibid., pp. 14–15.

16. Ibid., p. 41.

17. Ibid., p. 9; see also p. 8.

18. Ibid., p. 66.

19. Ibid., pp. 7, 67–68.

20. A boast not without some foundation, judging by the terror which Serb forces fighting for Austrian Empress Maria Theresa struck into the hearts of their adversaries.

21. Quoted in Čolović, *Politics of Symbol*, p. 92n.

22. M. J. Lerner, "Integrating Societal and Psychological Rules of Entitlement: The Basic Task of Each Social Actor and Fundamental Problem for the Social Sciences," in *Social Justice Research* 1 (1987), as quoted in Feather, "Deservingness, Entitlement," p. 335.

23. Milorad Tomanić, *Srpska crkva u ratu i ratovi u njoj* (Belgrade: Medijska knjižara krug, 2001), p. 73.

24. Čolović, *Politics of Symbol*, p. 31.

25. Quoted in ibid., p. 19.

26. Borisav Jović, *Poslednji dani SFRJ. Izvodi iz dnevnika* (Belgrade: Politika, 1995), p. 131 (entry for 26 March 1990). However, the demonization of Croats began in earnest in mid-summer 1989, at a time when Ivica Račan was generally expected to remain in power. The later Serbian claim that the tensions between Croats and Croatian Serbs began only after the election of Franjo Tudjman to the Croatian presidency is therefore contrary to fact.

27. Dobrica Ćosić, *South to Destiny*, vol. 4 of *This Land, This Time* (the English title provided for the translation of *Vreme smrti*), trans. from Serbian by Muriel Heppell (New York: Harcourt Brace Jovanovich, 1981), p. 145.

28. Albert Bandura, "Moral Disengagement in the Perpetuation of Inhumanities," in *Personality and Social Psychology Review* 3, no. 3 (1999), pp. 196–200; and *Javnost* (22 July 1995), as quoted in Čolovič, *Politics of Symbol*, p. 42. See also Herbert C. Kelman, "Violence without Moral Restraint: Reflections on the Dehumanization of Victims and Victimizers," *Journal of Social Issues* 29, no. 4 (1973), pp. 25–61; and David M. Bersoff, "Why Good People Sometimes Do Bad Things: Motivated Reasoning and Unethical Behavior," *Personality and Social Psychology Bulletin* 25, no. 1 (January 1999), pp. 28–39.

29. Ellard, Miller, Baumle, and Olson, "Just World Processes," p. 352; and Carolyn L. Hafer, "Why We Reject Innocent Victims," in Ross and Miller, *Justice Motive*, esp. pp. 109–110, 113, 116.

30. For a corrective, see Sabrina P. Ramet and Letty Coffin, "German Foreign Policy Toward the Yugoslav Successor States, 1991–1999," *Problems of Post-Communism* 48, no. 1 (January-February 2001), pp. 48–64.

31. Quoted in Bandura, "Moral Disengagement," p. 195.

32. S. Milgram, *Obedience to Authority* (New York: Harper and Row, 1974), as summarized in Jo-Ann Tsang, "Moral Rationalization and the Integration of Situational Factors and Psychological Processes in Immoral Behavior," in *Review of General Psychology* 6, no. 1 (March 2002), pp. 27–28.

33. See Zdravko Tomac, *The Struggle for the Croatian State . . . through Hell to Democracy,* trans. Profikon (Zagreb: Profikon, 1993), pp. 417–18; and Mark Thompson, *Forging War: The Media in Serbia, Croatia, Bosnia and Herzegovina,* revised and expanded ed. (Luton: University of Luton Press, 1999), passim.

34. The displacement of responsibility is scarcely unique to Serbs. In Kosovo in 1986, local Albanians blamed a local Serb for the fact that a glass bottle ended up inserted into his anus. See the detailed discussion in Julie A. Mertus, *Kosovo: How Myths and Truths Started a War* (Berkeley and Los Angeles: University of California Press, 1999), passim.

35. Lepa Mladjenović, "Beyond War Hierarchies: Belgrade Feminists' Experience Working with Female Survivors of War," in *Women and Therapy* 22, no. 1 (1999), pp. 84–85.

36. Tsang, "Moral Rationalization," p. 44.

37. Quoted in Čolović, *Politics of Symbol*, p. 51. Miloš Obilić is traditionally credited, in Serbian epic poems, with having sacrificed his own life in 1389 in order to stab the Ottoman sultan Murad.

38. Quoted in Čolović, *Politics of Symbol*, p. 53.

39. Richard Morrock, "The Genocidal Impulse: Why Nations Kill Other Nations," *Journal of Psychohistory* 27, no. 2 (Fall 1999), p. 159.

40. Extracts quoted in Dušan Kecmanović, "Psychiatrists in Times of Ethnonationalism," *Australian and New Zealand Journal of Psychiatry* 33, no. 3 (June 1999), p. 310.

41. Extracts quoted in ibid., p. 311.

42. Jovan Rašković, *Crazy Country* (Belgrade: Acquarius, 1990), as quoted in Kecmanović, "Psychiatrists in Times of Ethnonationalism," p. 312.

43. Tomac, *Struggle for the Croatian State*, p. 418.

44. Branka Arsić, "On the Dark Side of the Twilight," *Social Identities* 7, no. 4 (December 2001), p. 562.

45. Plato, *Menexenus*, trans. from ancient Greek by Benjamin Jowett, 235 B-C, in Plato, *The Collected Dialogues*, edited by Edith Hamilton and Huntington Cairns, Bollingen Series LXXI (Princeton, N.J.: Princeton University Press, 1961), p. 187.

6

THE IMPACT OF THE WAR ON SERBIA

Spoiled Appetites and Progressive Decay

JAMES GOW AND MILENA MICHALSKI

Belgrade, the capital of Serbia, is spotted with destroyed, burned-out buildings, the mementos of the 1999 U.S.-led NATO air campaign. On the surface, this evidence can be introduced to answer the question posed to one of us, originally, and addressed by both of us in this chapter: what was the impact of the war on Serbia?[1] In short, this bomb damage in Belgrade, as well as that elsewhere in Serbia, is the impact of the war on Serbia. To this the burned-out villages in Kosovo and the graves across the country might be added. These features represent the impact of the war on Serbia, but they are by no means sufficient. Indeed, the surface might be most relevant only for that which it signifies as lying beneath it.

The buildings destroyed by the NATO bombing were those at the heart of Serbian statehood and power, for the most part carefully selected to mark a difference between the Serbian political leadership at the time and the Serbian people more generally. Those wrecked buildings are the pockmarks of the political disease that blighted Serbia for over ten years. The continuing failure to begin to renovate any of them is perhaps not only a scar of that period but also a sign that the disease has not been wholly eradicated from the Serbian body politic. The failure to renovate can be taken as signaling that, as well as other understandable priorities, there are those who seek to cultivate the scars, to preserve them as wounds (if possible), and to maintain a victim syndrome. This does not apply to the whole of Serbia; nor do those who perhaps seek to incubate the remnants of the disease represent the whole of the Serbian people. But, whatever the rough balance between malign forces and neutral or benign elements, the absence of reconstruction marks the impact of the war on Serbia, superficially and symbolically. Those who encourage sickness continue to cast their shadow because of the general debilitation caused by years of misrule and war.

To explore this situation, we approach the question in three ways. One of these is more obvious and involves empirical assessment of the economic and political consequences of the war. The third, which delivers the core message, is a diversion into the cinema of one director, Srdjan Dragojević, whose films through the 1990s perhaps offer a clearer and more imaginative vehicle for assessing the impact of the war on Serbia. The first stage, however, is to explore the question itself, ostensibly naïve, but replete with complexity.

The Question

What was the impact of the war on Serbia? This superficially simple question immediately taxes the enquiring mind in at least three ways. Almost before the question is posed, the subordinate question springs into action: is it possible to differentiate the impact of the war from that of Slobodan Milošević's rule, the leader who propelled Serbia through thirteen years of decline and war? Not far after that is the question of which war, especially when asking individuals from Serbia, who tend more to think of "the war" as referring to NATO's aerial action to stop Milošević's strategy of ethnic cleansing in the southern Serbian province of Kosovo in 1999, rather than the earlier phase of his belligerence during the 1990s. And not far behind these questions there comes the more philosophical question of how to judge impact when the basic parameters are quite different at the start and finish of the period in question; Serbia's status at the end of a decade of armed conflict and political change was not what it had been when war began.

Taking these questions in reverse order, how should we understand "Serbia"? It began the 1990s as one state among six embraced by the Socialist Federative Republic of Yugoslavia (SFRY), with two formally autonomous provinces (Vojvodina and Kosovo), but ended as a de facto independent polity, yet de facto and de jure deprived of one of the provinces, Kosovo, in all but one respect, the status of borders. The word *federative* is crucial in this context, and its significance is widely ignored in the literature, which generally uses the description "federal" in its stead. The use of "federal," including in international official documentation, however, fails to capture the nature of the beast. The by now infamous 1974 constitution of the SFRY recognized the sovereign statehood of its component parts, as well as the right to self-determination, including the right to secession. It was the confirmation of political arrangements that emerged to handle a situation in which the SFRY's existence had been threatened by fissiparous tensions. The new arrangements consolidated communist rule, but did so at the level of the member states, not the federation. That confirmed power at the state level, nicely captured by Stevan Pavlowitch as "socialist feudalism."[2] To accompany this, there was an important lexical shift in the 1974 constitution from the Serbian *federalna*—federal—used in earlier constitutions, to *federativna,* federative. This semantic nuance is important for recognizing that real authority lay with the member states.

Within that federative framework, Serbia's position was distinct from that of any other state. First, it was the only state to have two autonomous provinces, each of which was an acknowledged part of the federal structure, albeit still subject to the devolved exercise of sovereign rights pertaining to Serbia. This, as has been well recognized, was a source of political discontent in Serbia. Secondly, the various versions of Yugoslavia that had come and gone since 1918 had satisfied the nineteenth-century Serbian nationalist ambition to have all those regarded as Serbs (by themselves, or by others) live in one state. While technically the post-1945 communist constitutions had not quite achieved that formally, they had done so to all intents and appearances. The 1974 constitution was a step away from that situation, confirming as it did the authority of the member states. In doing so, it also confirmed that ethnic Serbs in Croatia and in Bosnia-Herzegovina were not part of the same state as Serbs in Serbia.

There were pressures on the SFRY during the 1980s, which required further constitutional adjustment. Those pressures and the inability to negotiate a way around them generated the conditions for war in the following decade. However, the conditions for armed conflict do not in themselves make armed conflict inevitable, although there might come a point where individual actors are trapped by circumstances to such a degree that they can no longer avert it. The key difference between war and its avoidance is human agency, however much those agents are sometimes bound by structure. Thus, it is possible to imagine that until some point—it is not necessary precisely to define it, though it might well have been as late as June 1991—war might have been avoided. The same is also true for the dissolution of the SFRY, which had ceased to function and had ceased to serve the needs of its members—or at least some of them—by the time the breakup came, but which might, theoretically, have been reconfigured to restore legitimacy.[3]

Gauging the loss of Yugoslavia for Serbia is difficult. But it is clear that, on one level, Serbia lost what it had gained with the formation of Yugoslavia and the First and Second World Wars—a framework in which "all Serbs" lived in one state. If Serbia perhaps had the least genuine commitment to the Yugoslav idea as Royal Yugoslavia formed after the end of global hostilities in 1918, as Stevan Pavlowitch notes, it nonetheless came to invest the most emotionally in the conglomerate polity, and Serbs came most to see their Serb and Yugoslav identities as interchangeable.[4] In the end, it would be exceptionally hard to disagree with Pavlowitch's wise assessment that, although Yugoslavia was not their idea, Serbia and the Serbs, from a mixture of realism and idealism, probably invested most and committed most to that idea throughout the history of the joint enterprise. Yet, they did so never realizing quite how others involved felt differently and certainly shared neither the Serbian sense of what Yugoslavia was nor Serbian self-images.[5] This imagination of common purpose and sacrifice for that cause, however out of touch with the realities of the time, meant that the loss of the Yugoslav federation through war was more than physical; it was also the loss of emotional investment. And, just as with marriages that break down with one partner at least having a completely delusory notion of his or her positive role, the loss and the sense of loss are no less real because one side of the relationship had been based on misguided mental constructs. Nor, as might also happen in the domestic context, is the impact lessened because, largely unwittingly and unreflexively, just as Serbia had perhaps contributed most to making Yugoslavia a reality, it also clearly contributed most to its demise and to the accompanying inhumanity. The impact of the war on Serbia was therefore not only loss of what it had achieved through the formation of Yugoslavia: it was also a loss of belief.

In the case of the de facto loss of Kosovo, the political-territorial loss also includes what it had achieved in its rise prior to the shared South Slav state. The armed conflict over Kosovo in 1999 is what people in Serbia, albeit with a little uncertainty and hesitation, might regard as "the war"—certainly most respondents to our question on the impact of the war assumed this, or asked, "Which war?" The focus on the Kosovo clash is easily explained. This was the relatively short phase of the war where, in a dramatic but still limited sense, the war came home: NATO bombs fell on Belgrade and other Serbian towns. This contrasts with the years of war in Croatia and in Bosnia-Herzegovina, as well as the earlier parts even of the Kosovo conflict, where the destruction for which the Serbian authorities were primarily responsible was elsewhere, while the people of Serbia could see these conflicts as someone else's affair. The inflow of ethnic Serb refugees from Croatia and from Bosnia-Herzegovina, as well as the deprivations attributable to Serbia's international ostracism, meant that the people could not be wholly unaware of the war. But it also meant that they could believe that it was not their affair, that the Serbs of the neighboring states to the west were defending themselves, and that the world, by imposing sanctions, was against them (and unfairly, too, given that the dominant Serbian version of events had all the actors bearing equal responsibility for the bloody mayhem). U.S.-led air action meant that, whatever the understanding of the motivations involved, there could be no avoiding recognition of Belgrade's involvement.

Belgrade's involvement is at the core of the understanding here that there was one war, conducted in different theaters, over about ten years.[6] There is a temptation to see several discrete wars, spanning the decade, especially if viewed from the perspective of one geographical focus—Slovenia, Croatia, Bosnia-Herzegovina, or Kosovo. However, this is to miss the essence of Serbia's political-territorial aims in the war: the creation of new borders in the west and the consolidation of existing borders in the south, and in both cases strategically ensuring that there would be a more or less ethnically homogeneous and, above all, reliable population within those borders. Hence the Serbian strategy of ethnic cleansing was applied. A good number of authors write about or refer to individual wars in particular places (and most at least make a distinction between the war to create new borders in the west, where armed action ended in 1995, and destructive engagement to secure existing borders in the south, which reached its height in 1999). Yet, this is to miss the integrity of Milošević's belligerence in the region. The same may be said of World War Two, which comprised different theaters of war around the world and within regions, such as Europe (the war in Poland, for example, is not treated as a wholly discrete conflict, but as part of the whole). In addition, the engagement of international actors beyond the Yugoslav region is continuous and linked throughout the decade of war—in one sense there is a ten-year war between Milošević and the West. This is the perspective in which we have conducted research and writing for the present purpose.[7]

The last problematic issue in posing our apparently simple question is linked to the understanding that there was one war and that, while it takes two to tango and several more to square dance, Belgrade led the dance of death and destruction. Second-guessing and counterfactually investigating "what might have been" is a potentially treacherous exercise. It is not one that we propose to undertake significantly here. However, it is hard to imagine that events would have taken the same course as they did in the 1990s had Milošević not been the Serbian leader.[8] Of course, there would have been problems, which might have included violent unrest and even armed conflict at some level in the region. Indeed, hypothetically, it is even admissible that things might have been worse, though few would wish to explore this avenue too deeply. The reality is that Milošević was the author of war and that the Yugoslav war and consequently its impact on Serbia are a product of his rule.

In most respects, it is all but impossible to divorce the impact of the war from the impact of Milošević's rule; it is merely one facet of that disagreeable reign. However, there is one crucial way in which the war might be said to have had a clear impact on Serbia: prolonging the Milošević era.[9] As already stated, there can be no way of surely knowing what might have been. But, it does seem reasonable to suppose that the reinforcing effect of war meant that Milošević went rotten by staying in office long after his use-by date. Initially successful, he might well have lasted into the mid-1990s as a dominant political force, in normal circumstances. The shifts in governmental composition in other Central and East European countries making the transition from communism to some kind of democracy might confirm this. Those who were popular and held office at the outset, from whichever part of the political spectrum, had been replaced by the end of 1996 as the breathing-in-and-out process of competitive electoral democracy animated them.[10] Thus, it is reasonable to infer that without war—and even taking into account the deliberate debasing and atomizing of political and social alternatives that ensured his rule[11]—Milošević would not have lasted so long in power.

In seeking to gauge the impact of the war on Serbia in the remainder of this study, we are working with the three assumptions established in this section, each of which is wrapped in the problems of knowledge. First, Serbia is taken to be the state that formed part of and formally survived the Yugoslav federation, but it is taken to be an uncertain and traumatized polity in terms of political community. Secondly, the impact of the war is taken to mean the overall effect of the whole war over a ten-year period, rather than any part of it. And finally any assessment of the impact of the war is necessarily also an evaluation of the impact of Milošević's rule, with the reflexive caveat that the war for which he had prime responsibility also served to extend his hold on power. In the following sections, we will turn to the impact of the war on Serbia, understood in these terms, on the economy, politics, and society, and, through one example from the cultural sphere, its impact morally.

Economics, Politics, and Society

While separating the impact of the war and that of Milošević is almost impossible for the most part, it is possible to identify one clear impact of the war alone: its role in quite probably prolonging Milošević's hold on power. With war all around, it was never likely that the Serbian political elite, let alone the Serbian people, would turn on their leader as swiftly as they might have done had his performance been solely a matter of failing to deliver political or economic goods. The effect of corrupt leadership and war was to spoil Serbia's appetite for economic (other than minority criminal activity[12]), political, and social engagement. The sum was progressive decay.

The war had a major impact on the structure of the economy.[13] A big factor in changing the shape of the economy was the imposition of general economic sanctions by the UN Security Council. As a result of this, there were significant losses of markets. For example, the pharmaceuticals firm ICN Galenika had US$37 million of business in Russia prior to the war. This was wiped out. So too was Zastava's successful venture into the U.S. automobile market—and with it, just about, Zastava itself. The production and export of cigarettes and gas were significantly transformed, with gas almost disappearing as an important economic factor, while trade in cigarettes shifted to the black market, one of the ways in which the regime used organized criminal activity to keep itself afloat and to line the pockets of some of its leaders. In terms of agriculture, export markets were lost, and with that loss also came a loss of development. As a result, for example, where there had once been a burgeoning export of meat to EU countries, in 2003 only three slaughterhouses in Serbia were of a suitable standard to be allowed to export to the European Union. Not only had significant agricultural trade and markets been lost at the time, but also any possibility of a significant return was constrained by not keeping up with contemporary developments and upholding EU standards.

A company such as Eniš, engaged in electronics, lost the capability to do anything more than provide spare parts, at best, for equipment it had previously produced. But over ten years, it had lost its status, having no positive image or place in the market. And worse, it had received no investment and had demonstrated no innovation for ten years. This was a recipe for terminal decline in a sphere where the pace of change, refinement, and invention seemed to get ever faster. It was also part of an overall pattern of decline in manufacturing, which saw output fall to 44 percent of its 1990 level by 2001.[14]

Along with these other developments, there was a significant loss of jobs. While no reliable statistics exist, for the most part this is a clear product of the war years. Although a few new businesses emerged and created new employment—mostly in domestic food production offsetting the impact of sanctions to a very limited extent—the general trend was toward rising unemployment, which stood at 923,000 in 2002, around 40 percent of the available workforce, excluding Kosovo.[15]

The combined effects of war, international sanctions, and misrule on Serbia's infrastructure could be seen by reference to the train service. Where in the early 1990s, long, full trains would run regularly from Belgrade to, say, Užice, by 2003 the service was more limited and such trains would have only three carriages. Only on the Belgrade to Bar route did "good trains" still run. Rolling stock and rails were in poor condition.

The same was also true of Serbia's potentially important waterways communication, where the Rivers Danube and Sava in particular played an important part. However, these were made impassable by the destruction of five bridges on the former and two on the latter during the NATO air campaign of 1999; as with the shells of bombed-out buildings mentioned above, there appeared to be little interest initially on the part of the Belgrade government in repairing the damage.

The communications infrastructure was also heavily hit by fuel shortages, particularly of petrol for motor vehicles; one of the abiding memories for anyone visiting Belgrade in the mid-1990s had to be the long queues of vehicles waiting for days in case fuel should become available. Those who could manage to do so did not wait in queues but preferred to use the black market; for those who could get through Montenegro or Kosovo to Albania, only half a mile inside the border there were roadside sellers of petrol in portable canisters. Those who were inclined to do so would take such fuel not only for their own immediate use but also for profit on the black market. In addition to this small-time smuggling, of course, there was larger scale activity with the connivance of the ruling elite (which took a share of the profits one way or another). All this was part of the political and social corruption of Serbia throughout the years of war.

In many ways, the worst part of this sorry tale of political, social, and especially economic decline is that the impositions could conceivably have offered an opportunity and a rationale for fundamental economic reform. Ironically, the isolation created by sanctions could be seen as a potential benefit: root and branch reform was possible precisely because links to the outside world, which might otherwise have imposed constraints, were simply not there. Thus, there would have been complete freedom to turn adversity to achievement. But, because the regime was not interested in the welfare of the Serbian economy or its people—indeed, it benefited from decline, decay, and dissipation—this was an opportunity never likely to be taken.

Even after the fall of Milošević, reform remained patchy. While transparency in government budgeting began to be introduced and privatization grew,[16] internal disputes in the democratic government meant that the pace of change was variable. While reformist prime minister Zoran Djindjić sought rapid change, others, such as Vojislav Koštunica, were more conservative and cautious. It was perhaps the greatest blow to Serbia's post-Milošević development that Djindjić, Serbia's best hope, was assassinated in March 2003. Djindjić understood the country's needs and was the most able political figure on the scene. However, his popularity was limited, in part, because like most other prominent opposition politicians during the war years, such as Vuk Drašković, leader of the popular Serbian Renewal Movement, or Dobrica Ćosić and Milan Panić (who were respectively Federal Republic of Yugoslavia president and prime minister in the early 1990s), the leader of the Democratic Party at one point had been sucked into Milošević's manipulative force field. This was symptomatic of a trend in Serbian politics where most figures at some point believed that they could do business with the Serbian leader, or that they would be the ones who could make the difference, who could change Milošević and his policies by working from within, or with the grain. Perhaps, in some cases, politicians were simply being lured by the chance of apparent power.[17] This was all part of the decay in Serbian politics. Djindjić extricated himself from these temptations earlier than most and, having been bitten, was shy of offering himself again. His life threatened, he moved to Montenegro during the war over Kosovo in 1999. This, coupled with his having been implicated in political dealings with Milošević, meant that, whilst undoubtedly being the best person to lead Serbia, he was distrusted and not liked at the popular level. In contrast, it was precisely the fact that Vojislav Koštunica, leader of the Democratic Party of Serbia, was the only prominent political figure not to have dirtied his hands with Milošević that made him the only credible and electable candidate to run against the Belgrade bully in the 2000 elections. It was to Djindjić's credit that he realized this and worked as part of a unified opposition front.

In a murky plot involving members of the security forces, the criminal underworld, and the secret club of war crimes suspects, against all of whom the prime minister was boldly moving, Djindjić was shot entering a government building. This violence, including its poisonous admixture of politics, special forces' and intelligence agents' action outside the law, and assassination is, in some ways, part of the dark side of Serbian political culture, as the assassination of monarchs, both belonging to Belgrade and to other countries, might confirm. In particular, the record of agencies from within the security apparatus is dim—whether the "Black Hand" prior to World War One; the KOS (military counterintelligence) during and after Tito's Yugoslavia; or the JSO, a special forces unit run by the Serbian Security Service (SDB) to spearhead inter alia ethnic cleansing.[18] Elements from these secret bodies appear to act traditionally as states within states. This was compounded by political competition in which various security services not only competed against each other, but were also used by politicians against their opponents; for example, Djindjić, although undoubtedly on the side of the angels, made use of the SDB, while Koštunica relied on KOS.

The initial response of the frightened government was robust, ironically invoking emergency laws designed by Milošević to protect his regime in order to arrest thousands of opponents for thirty- or sixty-day periods of detention without charge, to take control of the situation. However, once the immediate position was stabilized and forty-four of those suspected of direct involvement in the murder plot had been arrested, the government lifted the state of emergency and released most of those detained, in part responding to understandable but unfortunate pressure from Western governments. After the initial fear of a violent overthrow or potential civil war had passed, the government under new prime minister Zoran Živković was prey to internal division and drift, failing to keep momentum.

The growing impotence of the government reflected the dismal political conditions in which Serbia had twice failed to elect a president because less than 50 percent of the electorate bothered to turn out to vote (a level required to make the vote valid). It was only the strong showing of the Serbian Radical Party (SRS) that offered any prospect of motivating the democratic forces to discipline themselves and work together. This discipline was needed, with the SRS the single largest party in the parliament, led by Vojislav Šešelj from his prison cell in The Hague, where he was facing trial for his role in crimes against humanity during the war. The prospects of a solid coalition that could regain momentum were limited. With the conservative Koštunica being prince-maker or likely prime minister, the prospects of anything more than uneven progress were not great, as others of more radical persuasions would have to work with him. It was almost inevitable that whichever coalition emerged, it would be uncertain and unstable, however long it managed to hold together.

The electoral outcome was an indication of two layers in Serbia's political-social strata. The first was the degree to which a dangerous brand of nationalism could mobilize support in Serbia—for this was essentially the platform of the SRS as it gained over one-third of the seats in the 240–member parliament. The other was the sense of disillusionment broadly among the Serbian electorate. This was not just a result of the Djindjić-Živković period of government, nor was it only a product of the years of Milošević's rule. The latter certainly played its part, having almost mortified Serbia socially. The former, especially in its last months, marked by internal bickering and often credible accusations of corruption and criminality against some of its members, such as Čedo Jovanović, one of the deputy prime ministers, also did little to give people confidence. This was particularly damaging, as it revealed little prospect of reviving morale or morality in Serbia swiftly or completely, even though some things were clearly better.

Even where there had been signs of morale and morality, for example, as the NATO air campaign began in 1999, these quickly slipped away to be replaced by apathy and asocial qualities. At the beginning of the bombing, there was one moment where a man gave half a loaf of bread to one of our respondents when she asked where he had got the bread he was carrying, doing so because he knew that there was no more.[19] However, sparks such as this were quickly lost. By the end of the bombing, at which point it seemed to those on the ground as though it would go on forever, boredom had set in. People would sit out, playing cards (or something similar), listlessly waiting for the raids.[20]

Social desiccation was compounded by demographic change. Loss of morale translated into loss of some parts of the population. There was a major loss of educated people, mostly among the younger elements in the population. While no one has an exact figure, it is estimated that the number who left during the war years is around 200,000 (the influx of over 700,000 refugees and 330,000 internally displaced people [from Kosovo] was an additional burden that offered nothing to offset this loss). This is a significant chunk of a total population of around 7.6 million people (that is, Serbia excluding Kosovo).[21] A large part of the middle class was lost. So too were the benefits of education. And so too was the future. One way or another, whether they left the country (although there were exceptions here) or stayed, a generation lost the best years of their lives, while the prospects for the coming generations were poor, given the degraded social, educational, and spiritual fabric in Serbia.

The effect of factors such as the demographic outflow of younger, more intellectually capable people on political life was significant. Aside from anything else, the most important aspect of this was the loss of renewal. No new generation has emerged on the political scene, in any of the parties. While some of the more able figures in the movement which deposed Milošević and formed governments after the democratic forces came to power surfaced largely in response to the situation—notably Goran Svilan-ović, who became Belgrade's foreign minister—for the most part, there were no new faces and there was no new blood. The same people had been developing political careers, on whichever side of the fence, since the war began. There was set to be a continuing generational problem. The compound effect of no new political figures, no confidence in any politicians or political processes, and the complete breakdown of morale and morality was that few, if any, of the younger people who had stayed in Serbia throughout the war and who had some appropriate qualities had any reason to hold political ambition.

The impact on social cohesion and standards was devastating. While atomization was a direct product of Milošević's style of rule,[22] other aspects of change were by-products of war and his rule. One of these was the cult of dealers and smugglers—captured in the film *Rane* (discussed below)—where even schoolchildren saw this as the model. In this world, parents and teachers struggled to persuade children of the value of study. After all, in the view of the youngsters attracted to heroes of crime, there could be little point in working hard and getting good marks at school and staying on in education to become well qualified.[23] For the children of this generation, there was no point: they could look at parents who had studied and worked and who sought to be responsible parents earning 30 DM a month, at best (and if they actually got paid), while the dealers and smugglers were gathering remarkable wealth relatively easily, it seemed. Thus, there was a considerable—and very damaging—shift in values.

The most significant, if by no means the only, test of Serbia's loss of morality concerned the legacy of war crimes. Throughout the war years, there appeared to be a broad tendency to believe that, as far as atrocities were committed in the Western theaters, these were committed by all sides and were part of a historical pattern of violence in the region—and as far as ethnic Serbs might be responsible, this was not Serbia's responsibility. This form of denial continued to some extent during the Kosovo phase of the war. More troubling was the degree to which there was still a tendency in a sizeable chunk of the population to reject any suggestion of culpability—more or less the third of those who supported Šešelj's party in 2003. This was the case even after the Serbian government had begun to cooperate, albeit less than perfectly at times, with the International Tribunal in The Hague, and even after it had publicly produced evidence of some of Milošević's attempts to cover up mass murder in Kosovo.

For the most part, those who did not actively reject accusations of crimes against humanity preferred not so much to accept Serbia's responsibility openly as quietly to forget the issue, as far as possible, and pragmatically to do what was necessary to remove the topic from the international agenda for relations with Belgrade. Facing up to the war crimes issue was of course a necessary component of practical politics with the rest of the world. But, responding at this level was not in itself likely to be enough. Serbia's loss of moral integrity and genuine honor required a new approach. This had to be one in which war crimes suspects, such as the most notorious of them all, General Ratko Mladić, were not regarded either as heroes (as was the case by many who voted for the SRS, it might be supposed) or as an embarrassment to be protected or at least quietly left alone out of loyalty. This would require a new element in Serbian political discourse. The dominant theme would become the understanding that, if the general were indeed an honorable Serb, then he would surrender to The Hague, rather than see Serbia's international progress blocked because of him; and conversely that, if he did not surrender, then he must be presumed not to be an honest and honorable Serbian citizen.

Embedded, corrupted political discourse was a major product of Milošević and his war. Discourse about politics, according to Ivan Čolović, "is largely confined to story telling," even though there is not necessarily a full narrative form to sketches of stories that overlap and interact but constitute a "series of more or less connected plots, concerned with the Serbian nation, the Serbian state, the Serbian land and other important national themes."[24] It is these "plots" that provide what passes for the knowledge basis regarding political life—even where empirical evidence, or alternative ideas, enter the frame, these are shaped by the network of plots that made the fabric of Serbian politics during the last two decades of the twentieth century, at least.

These plots and the overall narrative they approximated have been well reviewed and summarized by various authors, revealing common themes. Čolović has provided perhaps the most developed appraisal of this narrative and its component parts.[25] Sabrina P. Ramet has provided a more condensed version of the narrative elements elsewhere in this volume.[26] Her account is interestingly used to explore Serbian identity and politics in the last part of the twentieth century in both sociological (Weberian) and psychological (Freudian) terms. The most cogent summary of the ideas that dominated Serbian politics before, during, and (to a considerably lesser degree) after the war is offered by Stevan Pavlowitch, who insightfully also addresses the place of Yugoslavia and its demise clearly: "At one level Serbs still identified with Yugoslavia, which they had thought worth fighting for. At another, they came to view the creation of Yugoslavia as a great historical mistake that had robbed them of their identity and broken their back."[27] The contradictory notions thus juxtaposed could nonetheless be complementary to each other in the simultaneously self-inflating and self-pitying Serbian collective psyche which epitomizes the bivalent pattern of Serbian narratives.

After the fall of Milošević and the arrival of Vojislav Koštunica as president of the Federal Republic of Yugoslavia, there were elements of a new style. The latter was inaugurated in a simple ceremony; as has been observed, it was more akin to a formal civil wedding than a marriage of leader and people, surrounded by pomp and circumstance.[28] The modesty of the ceremony was the first phrase of a new story, one that might begin to counter those which had dominated the previous two decades. It is hard not to share the prayer of Stevan Pavlowitch for a new story to supplant Serbia's traditional self-pitying and incompletely understood reliance on St. Vitus (also known as St. Guy, or St. Vid),[29] founded on the legend of heroic loss in the Battle of Kosovo Polje on Vidovdan, St. Vitus' Day, 28 June 1389. His suggestion of invoking St. Jonah, on whose day—5 October—in 2000 Serbia was finally delivered from the belly of Milošević's whale, might well be a good starting point symbolically, even if it might equally not be strong enough in itself to deliver those refusing to recognize the reality of the 1990s, struggling to return fully to that belly. The question was whether the strong showing for nationalist forces in parliamentary elections and the failure to complete presidential elections represented attachment to St. Vid and the whale, or simply the absence of moral strength to forge a brave new Serbia.

The biggest impact of all on Serbia was on morale and morality. The combination of war and misrule created conditions in which optimism was almost absent. Electoral failure—both falling short of the 50 percent mark in presidential elections and the dismal outcome of the parliamentary elections—was a manifestation of absent morale, of there being no belief or confidence in politics or, indeed, the future. This was the cumulative negative sum of democratic dissipation, de-communization, the impact of the war and Milošević, where "everything was destroyed,"[30] and there was a "complete loss of morals."[31] In perhaps the best description, society had been "pulverized."[32] This was a development that could be grasped darkly through familiarity with the country, or through a survey of disparate statistics and events. But, it is most cogently read by viewing and having an appreciation of three films by one director and the way in which they reflect the impact of the war on Serbia, as well as on the director himself, Srdjan Dragojević.

Spoiling the Appetite:
Guns, Progressive Decay, and the Cinema of Srdjan Dragojević

A cinema of war and suffering, if not yet true heroism, emerged in response to, or reflecting, the Yugoslav war of the 1990s.[33] However, in the case of Serbian director Srdjan Dragojević, responsible for three box-office successes in Serbia and critical successes in the outside world, the attempt to deal with the war went beyond the war itself and captured the decay in Serbian society and culture. Of course, in writing about these three films and how they reveal the impact of the war on the director and the country, we can offer only a weak reflection of the real effect they have when viewed. At some moments, only a few minutes of the films evoke something that no end of descriptive text could ever match. There is no satisfactory substitute for viewing the films, we therefore recognize. However, there is purpose in reviewing here the trajectory they follow, both in terms of the director himself and the depiction of Serbia's twisted transformation. The mutation of Serbian society Dragojević depicts reflects his own transition from purveyor of lively youth comedy, with social underpinning, to preeminent figure in Serbia's cinema of devastation.[34]

The challenge, if Dragojević's mission statement is taken to provide the guideline, is to remind the wider world of the effects of the Yugoslav war and, in doing so, to put comfortable Westerners off their food and generally to make them uneasy. It was equally a mission to show the way in which Serbia and its people had lost direction and integrity—and how Serbian appetites for fun, honesty, and Western democracy had been thoroughly spoiled. This personal mission, with implications for other films of the 1990s, was stated in relation to the second of Dragojević's three completed films to date, *Lepa sela, lepo gore* (Pretty village, pretty flame) of 1996:

> Many people would tell a charming, heartbreaking story about this war that you would go to see with your loved one, comfortably seated in the movie theater, and afterwards you would discuss in some fine restaurant over a good steak, and an even better bottle of wine, how this world could be better than all the other ones, if we could only be a little more tolerant and behave a little better towards each other. . . . I'll admit that my wish is to make that steak, wine and easy conversation miserable for you. Because somewhere, at a safe distance from your fine, civilized restaurant happens to exist

a country where people have lost everything, where everything has been taken away from them, their houses, their years, all those nice restaurants, good food, fun and art, hope and pride, and even their lives.[35]

With this comment, Dragojević explicitly and implicitly opens a number of questions regarding film and the Yugoslav war, and regarding the relationship between artistic creation, individual expression, cultural resonance, and cross-cultural, metacultural, or universal significance. On one level, he is explicitly throwing down two simultaneous challenges for the filmmaker: to capture the pain of the Yugoslav experience in the 1990s and offer an interpretation of it, and to avoid apparently easy routes into exploration and interpretation of that experience. This is a more or less direct challenge to the work of other directors in the same context. On another, less visible level, his challenge poses the awkward, perennial question of how to approach and engage a potential audience for the work while confronting that audience with disquieting glimpses of harsh truth. Finally, and implicitly, Dragojević therefore highlights the discrete but often overlapping needs of creative and creating individuals to satisfy themselves and to offer that personal understanding to others, both in the original culture from which the artists and the artistic creations emerge, and to a wider audience beyond that culture. While great works of art may transcend parochial cultural boundaries, they must be, first and foremost, finely accomplished, individual expressions of the best to be found within those boundaries. Culture is the essence that makes any given society distinctive, and the ultimate hallmarks of that culture, going beyond the learned behavior patterns and symbols of communication for mastering material needs and companionship, is the quest for inherent refinement, refinement for its own sake. As will be argued below, Dragojević and his films of provocation, while important and accomplished, are less successful and less relevant as treatments of the Yugoslav war for universal understanding than for their reflection and depiction of the decomposition of Yugoslav, or rather more particularly, Serbian, society in the 1990s.

Violence is uncompromising in *Lepa sela, lepo gore,* one of the internationally better-known films of the Yugoslav war. Yet, in many senses, the violence in this film is tempered a little by the context of soldiers at war. This is a contrast to the director's later film, *Rane* (Wounds), which moves away from the scene of battle and the way in which unsuspecting Serbs could be dragged into a conflict and turned into demonic fork wielders. Instead, it depicts the early loss of any innocence by two Belgrade teenagers, who become caught up in the world of organized crime, drug abuse, and gun wielding that characterize the demoralized and atomized Serbian people at the end of the twentieth century. Just as Milan is transformed from the laid-back friend of Halil the Muslim to a maniacal murderer of Muslims, so the boys are transformed from gauche early adolescence to destructive and fatal gangster life, with no sense of redemption, only bitter and futile loss. This hollowed-out society and its complete decomposition mark the end of a transition both for the director and society through the 1990s. The teenage wasteland of the two friends' culminating round of deliberate honor shooting at the end of *Rane* is a step further into hopelessness and irresponsible cultural dissolution than the defilement of Serbdom represented by Milan's transformation in *Lepa sela, lepo gore*. Both, however, are in the most marked contrast to Dragojević's first film, *Mi nismo andjeli* (We are no angels) a colorful, playful, and light take on aspects of Serbian culture, notably the irresponsibility of the male and the potential for maturation and acceptance of fatherhood. To read the three films chronologically is to witness the transformation of both the director and the culture. From the irresponsibility of candy floss carelessness in love and sex, hosted by an angel and a devil, there is a descent into hell and the abandon of Belgrade dereliction and self-destruction.

The progression of Dragojević's films confirms the simultaneous transformation of the director and society in the 1990s. The bare horror of devastated youth in the last of the three films follows the depiction of individuals sucked into the quicksand of an unwanted war, as depicted in the second film. Both reflect the shadows created by a decade of conflict and are a world away from the timelessness of the first film, in which the issue is not the devastation of youth by war but the harnessing of wild, immature male youth to commitment and fatherhood. One indicator of this transformation is the presence and use of guns in the three films.

The first of the Dragojević films was *Mi nismo andjeli*, from 1992. This is a popcorn pink, orange, and blue extravaganza of one young man's sexual and social irresponsibility and his coming to maturity. In the tradition of films that take part of their spirit from the early 1960s, it also nods to the 1980s of directors such as Jean-Jacques Beneix and Luc Besson in its blending of rock 'n' roll, punk, and opera, along with references to Wenders and Powell and Pressburger in its use of fantasy and spirits from other worlds. The film opens and closes with an angel and a devil, who are seen competing for the character of Nikola, the wilful bachelor at large on whom the film focuses. At times, the two appear together to perform quasi-diegetic punk-pop-cum-Seattle-grunge numbers. In the meantime, Nikola, a Don Juan of downtown Belgrade, is finally brought to responsibility and marriage by Marina, the somewhat homely fashion student he has made pregnant on an utterly forgotten (and, implicitly, forgettable) one-night stand, but only after a playful sequence of ruses to win his attention, heart, and hand. While the predominantly easy diner pop soundtrack and color scheme are redolent of *Grease* and other treatments of teenage heartache and humor, and leave the viewer well entertained, the film also captures the character of bright young Belgrade, careless and carefree, unknowingly on the eve of a spiritual destruction beyond even the prescient grasp of Dragojević's otherworld hosts.

In this world of young love and lust (a pairing explicitly disputed by the angel and the devil as they open the curtains on Belgrade with a Ping-Pong exchange of "making love," "no—fucking" exchanges), violence is all but absent. There is only one appearance of a gun in this film. This is the starting pistol fired to set a pram race in motion, as Nikola's subconscious tussles with the notion of fatherhood. Rather than the appearance of a gun paving the way to scenes as bloody as the uncooked steaks Dragojević would later want to prevent viewers from feeling well enough to eat, it is the precursor to a wayward and poor performance at the helm of a pram in an absurd fantasy race, worthy of Monty Python.

The presence of guns is very different in *Lepa sela, lepo gore*. There is apparently sadistic brutality, committed both by Serbs—resulting in Milan's shooting two Chetniks—and by the Muslims who taunt the platoon in the tunnel. There is also a clear link between sex and violence, as Velja, an apparent womanizer (played again by Nikola Kojo, who played Nikola in *Mi nismo andjeli*), places a pistol against his head, then asks the American journalist who has joined the Serbian platoon and has lost some of her initial hostility toward them as she has shared their experience in the tunnel, for a kiss. At the moment it seems the kiss might have stopped him from committing suicide, he declares, "Just kidding," and pulls the trigger. This is a scene of necessary horror from a tunnel, if not a heart, of darkness, reinforced by the mixed texture created by the use of video-camera monochrome as well as celluloid color.

Dragojević's last film, *Rane*, presents a very strong example of the impact of the war on society. A complement to his earlier *Lepa sela, lepo gore*, *Rane* is a gripping, brutal depiction of the way in which the Milošević war has corrupted Serbian society. Such is the film's salience that RTS (Radio-Television Serbia), the state-run main broadcaster in Serbia—which had partly financed *Lepa sela, lepo gore*—refused to run advertisements for the film, which was nonetheless the most successful film in Serbia that year (exceeding the total audience for *Titanic,* the second most popular film of the year, in its first week alone[36]). The war is never immediately present; it is always in the background. However, it is the catalyst for social change in which the guiding forces of innocent boys are transformed from initial hero worship of opportunist-looter-black-marketeer Kure, returning with booty from the front, to nihilism and violence as they become thugs involved in an underworld. The corruption of these boys (Pinki, Diabola, and Švaba), against the background of the war and sanctions, represents the corruption of society, even while the boys meet in a car, sometime after one has shot the other, against the backdrop of the pro-democracy protests in Belgrade during late 1996.

Gun culture and gratuitous violence are prevalent (including a scene in which Kure's girlfriend lands a sturdy kitchen knife in his shoulder, which he takes, like a bull spiked by the toreador, and from which he finds an erotic stimulus). The acceptance of violence is most overtly exposed at the end of the film, where Pinki and Švaba sit against gravestones in the darkness, with a dilapidated car in the background, as the latter willingly takes deliberate gunshots from the former. This is an act of honor, because Švaba has earlier been responsible for the shooting of Pinki, his friend and comrade in crime. Five shots are to be administered for the five shots Pinki received. The scene is played with deliberate slowness, intensifying the empty, soulless brutality of the situation. Its gnawing, awful tension is broken only by the appearance of the third boy, Diabola, hysterically distraught and ready for revenge murder. Švaba and Pinki have both been involved with Diabola's mother, a TV presenter who flirts on and off screen with the best of Belgrade's gangsters and hoodlums. (Her TV program in the film *Puls asfalta* (Pulse of the asphalt) is based on a real program, *Crni biseri* (Black pearls), hosted by Vanja Bulić.) Švaba killed her at the same time he wounded Pinki out of jealousy. As the disciplined punishment shooting is coming to its formal end, a final finish is put to all three boys as the deranged Diabola opens fire on the other two, beginning an exchange that ends with all three dead.

The lust and lust for life, coupled with the wit and positive emotional exchange in *Mi nismo andjeli*, has been lost. Ingenuity and creative communication within the film are the hallmarks of a sociable but undisciplined society. The only place for a gun in this world of frivolity and promise is as a starting pistol in a fantasy pram race. While some of these elements are retained in *Lepa sela, lepo gore*, a transition takes place and the darker side enters in. Guns become instruments of desperation, symptomatic of a misled and twisted collective psyche in which guns complement conversation and kisses. By the time Dragojević has reached the grim world of *Rane,* social interaction has been debased entirely to a dialogue of gun barrels, underpinning the hollow soul of a people rendered hopeless and otherwise voiceless.

Conclusion

While taking aim at the comfortable middle classes of the West and seeking to prick their collective conscience and lead them to a new understanding—and if not understanding, then gloom—Dragojević accomplished more than this. Not only did he produce an individual perspective but, through his three films, all made in the 1990s, he also captured the essence of Serbian culture and its ruin in the 1990s. This is seen most clearly if his first film *Mi nismo andjeli* is taken into account. In the end, his better-known, later films are not so much missives to the West, or indeed to anywhere, about the war, as they are distressing and saddening reflections of cultural decay, captured, ironically, through supreme cultural expression. The transformation of Serbian society in the films is paralleled by the director's own journey from the vibrant colors and light humor of his first film to the dark mood and ashen cast of his latest. Having so deeply mined his specific cultural surroundings, but having made an international mark in doing so, it is almost no surprise that Dragojević, after taking his appetite-spoiling style to Hollywood, more or less disappeared from the radar screen. It was likely to be only when he returned to his native idiom that Dragojević would create again. And that might only be possible when Serbian politics, society, and culture have begun to be restored.

Serbian society and culture in the 1990s was debased and atomized. The manipulative rule of Slobodan Milošević was predicated on politically proclaiming to uphold what was Serbian, while practically stripping Serbia and most Serbs of dignity and common values. This rule was founded on destroying the possibility of alternatives, whether political, cultural, social, or economic. It thrived in an atmosphere where the need for weary spirits to expend all energy on coping with the day to day meant no time or strength to oppose what had happened, politically, morally, culturally, or economically. While some may have enthusiastically, if misguidedly, supported Milošević's war to begin with, only the barons of a venal and false society based on murder and Mafia business blended with the spinal cord of communist power mechanisms benefited. The impact of the war on Serbia generally was a loss of integrity, both physically, and more significantly, morally. While this Serbian loss cannot be directly compared to the physical loss and psychological nightmare of those who suffered the

Serbian leader's war in Bosnia-Herzegovina or Kosovo, it is nonetheless a case of social ravaging.

Notes

1. This was the question specifically posed by Sabrina Ramet to James Gow in August 2003. Its apparent simplicity instantly became a complex challenge that could not be resisted, but which was almost impossible to tackle successfully. It should be noted that the question and all its terms are assumed at this stage, but will be explored later in this piece. While we have attempted to engage with this question in different ways, it became clear that, at the more straightforward level, it had been answered as well as it could be in the elegant essay that is the last chapter of Stevan Pavlowitch's *Serbia: The History Behind the Name* (London: Hurst & Co., 2002). (The only question mark against Pavlowitch's assessment is the approach to Montenegro, which overlooks issues of Montenegrin identity, for example, at the time of Yugoslavia's proclamation, but even here, the tone and approach are still most reasonable.) Because this treatment could not be significantly bettered, we draw on it extensively at relevant points.

2. Pavlowitch, *Serbia*, p. 231.

3. It is arguable that the interests of Bosnia-Herzegovina were best served by the continuation of any kind of federation. While this is arguable and was surely the case in the immediate circumstances of 1991, it did not necessarily have to be the case; to say so would be to assume that violence and nationalist passions are inherently linked, as well as to assume that there can be no negotiation and moderation of ideological impulses, which is patently not the case, given the history of many polities and communities around the world which have reached modi vivendi.

4. Pavlowitch, *Serbia*, p. 231.

5. Ibid., p. 229.

6. This is an argument made more fully in James Gow, *The Serbian Project and Its Adversaries: A Strategy of War Crimes* (London: Hurst & Co., 2003).

7. On a methodological note, having asked the question baldly and naïvely, initially, the follow-up was always to explain the researcher's understanding of this issue.

8. Only very belatedly at the end of Milošević's leadership did biographical studies begin to appear in English. Of the titles that appeared in English editions, Duško Doder and Louise Branson's *Milošević: Portrait of a Tyrant* (New York: The Free Press, 1999), despite the misjudgment of its title ("tyrant" was not really applicable), made a good start, drawing on long experience, and revealing good

detail clearly from well-placed sources at times. The best of the books is Louis Sell's commanding work not so much on the man himself, though he is well treated, but on his role in events, *Slobodan Milošević and the Destruction of Yugoslavia* (Durham, N.C.: Duke University Press, 2002), where pretty much every key judgment can be relied on. By contrast, *Serpent in the Bosom: The Rise and Fall of Slobodan Milošević* (Boulder, Colo.: Westview Press, 2001), by Lenard Cohen, although the work of a noted scholar in the field, is a disappointment and reveals doubtful judgment at a number of points, for example, the treatment of the much misunderstood military annex to the draft Rambouillet Agreement (p. 267); cf. Gow, *The Serbian Project and Its Adversaries* [note 6], pp. 284–85.

9. This point was made initially in an interview with Miroslav Rebić, retail banking manager, Société Générale Yugoslav Bank Headquarters, Belgrade, October 2003. The point was otherwise reinforced by strongly affirmative responses when put to other respondents.

10. Romania was the tardiest of these countries, only witnessing its first real change of government at the end of 1996. It should be noted that a similar "war effect" meant that there were pressures prolonging the longevity of particular governments in other Yugoslav states, notably Croatia, where elections were held, and Bosnia and Herzegovina, where they were not.

11. For an excellent study of this, see Eric D. Gordy, *The Culture of Power in Serbia: Nationalism and the Destruction of Alternatives* (University Park, Pa.: Penn State University Press, 1999).

12. See chapter 8 in this volume.

13. The present analysis draws notably on the knowledge, understanding, and insight of Miroslav Rebić, to whom we express our gratitude. Data mentioned in the main text were provided by him, unless otherwise stated.

14. Economist's Intelligence Unit, *Country Profile 2003: Serbia and Montenegro* (London: EIU, 2003), p. 38.

15. Federal Statistical Office, *Statistical Pocketbook,* Belgrade 2003, cited in EIU, *Country Profile 2003,* p. 51.

16. The 2001 budget was the first to include expenditure on social security and pensions and the first not to have an extrabudgetary balance. The budget was supported by privatization, in some cases through corruption to keep the regime afloat under Milošević, but also, following careful and lengthy planning, by the democratic government, with the result that by September 2003, Serbia had sold 843 companies and was on track to have completed 60 percent of its privatization process by the end of the year. EIU, *Country Profile,* pp. 35–36.

17. Robert Thomas, *Serbia under Milošević* (London: Hurst & Co., 1999), offers a detailed account of the intricacies and maneuvering in Serbian politics during the 1990s.

18. See Gow, *The Serbian Project and Its Adversaries*, pp. 86–89.

19. Author's interview with Zorana Lukač, branch assistant, Société Générale Yugoslav Bank, Belgrade, October 2003.

20. Author's interview with Veselin Poznić, Security Office, British Embassy, Belgrade.

21. EIU, *Country Report*, p. 22.

22. Gordy, *Culture of Power*.

23. Author's interview with Miroslav Rebić.

24. Ivan Čolović, *The Politics of Symbol in Serbia: Essays in Political Anthropology*, trans. from Serbian by Celia Hawkesworth (London: Hurst & Co., 2002), p. 7.

25. Ibid., pp. 7–9.

26. See chapter 5, this volume.

27. Pavlowitch, *Serbia*, p. 232.

28. Čolović, *Politics of Symbol*, p. 305.

29. Pavlowitch, *Serbia*, p. 236.

30. Author's interview with Venja Janićević, hairdresser from Belgrade, December 2003.

31. Author's interview with Zorana Lukač.

32. Pavlowitch, *Serbia*, p. 233.

33. This cinema was dominated by films with a primary connection to Serbia, and films emerged both from Bosnia and Herzegovina, and from outside the region, although in the context of the late-twentieth-century film industry, international finance and cooperation were just about always present. Dina Iordanova, *Cinema of Flames: Balkan Film, Culture and the Media* (London: BFI, 2001); Daniel J. Goulding, *Liberated Cinema: The Yugoslav Experience, 1945–2001*, rev. ed. (Bloomington, Ind.: Indiana University Press, 2002); and James Gow and Milena Michalski, *Viewing Contemporary Conflict after September 11* (London: Hurst & Co., forthcoming).

34. We focus on the work of Dragojević because of the parallel development of director and content. However, we might have focused on only the outcome and described the effects of Milošević and the war, rather than conveying "before," "transition," and "after." Had we taken this other course, Dragojević's *Rane* would have had a central place, alongside Goran Paškaljević's *Bure Baruta* (also known as *Cabaret Balkan*) and Dušan Kovačević's *Profesionalac*.

35. Quotation by the director for the Premiers Plans: Festival d'Angers 1997, at which the film shared the Grand Prix du Jury. See online at www.anjou.com/premiersplans/us-lm10.html, 21 October 1999.

36. *Film Français*, 21 August 1998, p. 5.

7

POSTWAR GUILT AND RESPONSIBILITY IN SERBIA

The Effort to Confront It and the Effort to Avoid It

ERIC D. GORDY

Y ou must always have in mind that maybe tomorrow your friend will be your enemy," a survivor of the siege of Sarajevo told psychiatrist Stevan M. Weine.[1] The respondent "meant the remark as a way of explaining the experience of "ethnic cleansing,"[2] and how this changed relationships and values during the period of war. And what may a friend be after the war? More to the point, after the war, what may a friend be to herself or himself? These are the issues at stake in what is probably the most delicate part of Serbia's transition to democracy, and its return to peaceful relationships in the region, after the fall of Slobodan Milošević and his regime in October 2000. In the long term, the greatest implications of the process are on the level of self-perception and identity, and have a bearing on the question of whether the political transformation of Serbia will lead to a social transformation as well. But in the shorter term, these large questions are displaced onto smaller practical questions of law and politics, where the conflict over guilt and responsibility is actually played out.[3] This chapter will inquire how it is played out in domestic law, in domestic political relations, in terms of the relationship between Serbia-Montenegro and the International Criminal Tribunal for the Former Yugoslavia (ICTY), and in cultural efforts to approach the question.

Domestic Prosecutions and Issues

The categories of crimes contained in the ICTY statute are not the only crimes which Serbia needs to address in order to achieve its transition. The legal burden of the new regime is further complicated by the fact that all of the crimes which the ICTY may prosecute are also crimes under domestic law, and the Serbian and federal governments have a positive obligation to prosecute them.

So far, the record of prosecuting violations of international humanitarian law has been dismal, and the record of prosecuting violations of domestic law spotty. The issue of enforcing domestic law is, of course, a matter of greater domestic than international concern. Some of the issues at stake are largely of domestic political importance, such as the continued conflict over who has rights to the property which formerly belonged to the League of Communists of Yugoslavia and the League of Communists of Serbia, the ongoing revelations of ways in which former officials in the Milošević regime used public offices for private gain or political promotion, and various instances of political and media repression. Among the most frequent targets of state action have also been individuals and companies which realized extraordinary profit during the period of Milošević's rule, but all indicators are that this set of issues will be resolved by liquidation of the assets of the most egregious offenders and punitive taxes for the rest. There is at least a potential connection between the corruption cases and the cases related to the conduct of the war, to the degree that offshore banks and underground transactions were used to finance paramilitary organizations.[4] With regard to acts of domestic political violence, the ICTY has claimed no oversight for these cases, and law enforcement agencies have resolved none of them.[5]

Violations of international law have had, and continue to have, greater repercussions globally, and for the treatment of Serbia by international institutions. One of the principal reasons that the ICTY exists at all is that military and paramilitary forces systematically failed to record, prevent, and punish violations; another reason is that domestic courts in the states of the former Yugoslavia systematically failed to investigate and prosecute them. This is in spite of the fact that all parties to the conflicts explicitly and openly recognized their obligations under the Hague and Geneva Conventions when the war first began. For example, in October 1991, the Yugoslav army issued a declaration detailing its recognition of the obligations imposed by the Hague and Geneva Conventions, including obligations of collecting information and of preventing and punishing violations.[6] A joint declaration of the warring parties in the Croatian conflict and the International Committee of the Red Cross in 1991 detailed obligations under the two conventions, and the three warring parties in Bosnia-Herzegovina signed a similar joint declaration in 1992.[7] Combatants demonstrated their recognition of the authority of international law in more indirect ways as well: one discharged paramilitary fighter in the Bosnian war was issued a document declaring that he had "participated in the struggles for the liberation of the Serbian territory of Zvornik and did not participate in any criminal activities."[8]

Obviously these agreements and declarations cannot be said to have achieved much in terms of actually preventing violations. On the contrary, a tremendous abyss between the public rhetoric of political leaders and the actual behavior of their administrative and military forces was apparent throughout the wars. What the declarations show, however, is of crucial importance: at no time during the wars could the leaders of any state or entity claim that they were unaware of or did not recognize their obligations under international law. These obligations were not imposed by imperial masters, but derived from domestic law, from agreements voluntarily signed by the combatants, and from declarations made openly by the combatants. Among the obligations were the duty to prevent violations, and to record and punish violations which occurred. If one factor contributed more than others to the internationalization of the wars of Yugoslav succession—the involvement of international organizations and the United Nations—it was the failure of the warring parties to meet the obligations they had recognized under international law.

Acting on evidence both of the commission of violations of international law and of the failure of legal bodies, the Security Council of the United Nations adopted a series of resolutions in 1991 and 1992 (Resolutions 721, 752, and 764) declaring the conduct of the wars to be a matter of international concern. In Resolution 771 (1992), the Security Council enumerated violations of international humanitarian law and demanded that all sides cease committing them. The international conference on Yugoslavia held in London in 1992 adopted an instruction to governments and international organizations to inform the United Nations about the observance of Resolution 771, and this instruction was formalized in Resolution 780 (1992), which established a commission of experts to report on violations of international humanitarian law. On the basis of the commission's report, which was presented in February 1993, the Security Council adopted Resolution 808 (1993), which called for the establishment of an international court and called on the secretary-general of the United Nations to prepare the ground for the court's statute. The secretary-general's report was adopted in Resolution 827 (1993) as the statute of the ICTY.

On some level this series of events can be interpreted as meaning that at least one major factor which led to the establishment of the ICTY, the first international criminal tribunal to be set up by the United Nations, and hence to some degree the first assertion of the right of international governance in humanitarian matters, was the failure of domestic courts in the former SFRY (Socialist Federated Republic of Yugoslavia) to do their job. Mark Ellis argues:

> Although the Tribunal has primacy over national courts, which defer to its competence, it still has recognized the right of national courts to conduct war-crimes trials. In creating the Tribunal, the United Nations made clear that its intention was to encourage states to prosecute war criminals. It was not interested in depriving national courts of their jurisdiction over such . . . crimes. However, so long as national judicial systems are viewed as partial, ineffective, and incapable of diligently undertaking prosecutions, the Tribunal will rightfully retain its primacy over those selected criminal proceedings that are taking place in the national courts.[9]

The position was put in simpler form by a prominent ICTY defense attorney. Michail Wladimiroff, who led the defense of Dušan Tadić in the first ICTY trial, and acted for a time as one of Milošević's "friend-of-the-court" defenders by the ICTY,[10] remarked that "if the states of the former Yugoslavia would properly prosecute their own perpetrators of war crimes and crimes against humanity and do so with the same quality of fair trial, there would be no need for the International Tribunal for the Former Yugoslavia."[11]

Now that the regimes whose behavior contributed to the establishment of the ICTY have gone out of power, it may be increasingly important to ask not how many people can be tried by the international tribunal, but how well domestic courts can take up the burden and under what conditions and in which circumstances that may be appropriate. There is some evidence that the political will exists to prosecute suspects for violations of humanitarian law domestically. Public opinion surveys consistently demonstrate an overwhelming preference for this option,[12] and it seems to be the preference of most leading politicians as well (excepting those who continue to deny that any violations occurred). It is also clear that both the capacity and the continued existence of the ICTY are limited, and that domestic courts and prosecutors will have to be heavily involved if any significant number of offenders is to be prosecuted at all. The ICTY prosecutors are aware of this, and have already begun to defer to UNMIK-organized courts in Kosovo, and to Croatian courts in the case of the "Gospić five," by way of testing the capacity of other sites of prosecution and trial. From the point of view of political transition, there are also several compelling reasons to encourage domestic prosecution: domestic courts enjoy, in principle, greater legitimacy in public perception and the documentary record they produce would be likely to enjoy greater credibility. At the same time, energetic prosecution and fair trials for the people most responsible for planning and organizing gross violations of human rights would allow legal institutions to establish convincing evidence for their competence and independence.

But the Serbian and federal courts are in no condition to take on the task. In the first place, the issue of legitimacy is not perfectly clear, since surveys have shown for some time that Serbian courts do not enjoy high levels of public trust. These low levels of trust exist for good reason: the independence of the courts from administrative bodies of the state was highly questionable in the communist period, and worsened rather than improved during the period of nationalist authoritarianism. Both judicial personnel and judicial processes were subject to political instrumentalization. In fact, the production of judicial decisions was among the Milošević regime's favorite weapons during the 1990s: the independent newspaper *Borba* was shut down, the results of the 1996 and 2000 elections were overturned, and political opponents were harassed and intimidated through the use of the courts. Judges who proved unwilling to allow their courts to be used for such purposes were often fired.[13] In consequence, judicial institutions in Serbia receive consistently low measures of public confidence in surveys. A 1996 survey found 57 percent of respondents declaring a lack of trust in judicial institutions, with 37 percent expressing trust.[14] This is less than the level of distrust displayed toward representative institutions such as the federal parliament (62 percent), the federal government (61 percent), the Serbian parliament (62 percent), the Serbian government (60 percent), and political parties (71 percent). However, among law enforcement, administrative, and civic institutions, only the Serbian police (57 percent) and state-owned media (65 percent) received equal or higher ratings of distrust.[15] This puts the judicial system on a level of public esteem comparable to that of some of the most despised and reviled institutions in Serbia.

There is every reason to expect levels of trust to be lower still with regard to the ability of courts to try cases related to humanitarian law, considering the record the Serbian judiciary has compiled to date. This is particularly likely with regard to crimes involving the Albanian population, as the decade of the 1990s saw a large number of dubious convictions on charges of terrorism.[16] The most widely publicized of these was the conviction of 143 ethnic Albanians from the town of Djakovica on charges of terrorism, despite a lack of evidence connecting any single one of them to any terrorist acts or attempts. The presiding judge in the case, Goran Petronijević, admitted that there was no evidence of guilt, but justified the verdict with an interesting innovation in legal theory: "It was not possible to demonstrate individual guilt, but for the essence of the crime of terrorism that is not necessary."[17] The precedent established by this case presents an obstacle to efforts on the part of legal authorities to argue for their principled rejection of concepts of collective guilt.

The task of enabling judicial organs to function independently and capably remains a large one, about which the new authorities have so far done little. Various types of pressure from the executive on the judicial authorities, from ordering verdicts to altering personnel, have left a deep effect. The material situation of the courts also represents a long-term challenge, as their budgets for office and trial space, investigation, and salaries of judges and other officials remain below levels in other parts of government, one consequence being that for capable attorneys, the financial compensation for judicial work cannot compete with the potential rewards of private practice.[18] Shortly after being named to preside over the Supreme Court of Serbia (Vrhovni sud Srbije), Leposava Karamarković described the situation in an address to the Society of Judges of Serbia (Društvo sudija Srbije):

> For decades in this country the principle of utilitarianism *(svrsishodnost)* dominated, instead of the principle of legality, and it reached its shameful height at the time of the previous regime. Legal pragmatism occupied the place of the legal system. In pursuing its goals, the oligarchy did not want its hands to be tied by any formal or abstract rules or norms. So it expressed contempt for the law and for legal form, and recognized it only to the extent that it was useful.
>
> That led to the worst possible consequence for the legal system of any country—the legal system collapsed, fell apart, and life went on in spite of it and outside of it. And so a schizophrenic reality developed in which everybody was (declaratively) in favor of legality, while everybody knew that real life was in another category, in which interests are realized, while the existing legal system simply postulated some idealistic and unattainable relationships.
>
> The masters of manipulation brought fear into the courtroom, ordering

up not only trials but sentences as well. Judges were reduced to minimal
pay and to a humiliating position, probably because it was believed that it
is easier to direct and rule poor people without interference.

Few judges in the legal system managed to remain upright and to oppose
such methods, and when somebody did do that, and suffered because of it,
and eventually lost her or his job, most of the other judges remained silent
and acted as if it was not their problem. That indicates that some of the responsibility for their current state is borne by the judges themselves, who
did not react when in the dissolution of Yugoslavia, cities were destroyed,
people were killed, and shocking ethnic cleansing was carried out.

If more judges had resisted the influence and demands of the executive
branch, the results might have been different.[19]

The present administrators of the judicial system realize themselves, and
do not hide this realization, that the system will require extensive reform,
new personnel, and internal accounts of responsibility before it can take
up the obligations of a credible and independent judiciary.

The Development of New Political Coalitions

One of the axes along which new political alignments seem to be developing is the issue of cooperation with the ICTY. The DOS (Democratic
Opposition of Serbia) coalition was a shaky construction from the beginning, bringing together liberal, nationalist, regional autonomist, and
social democratic parties under a single umbrella for the purpose of presenting a united front against Milošević. The parties have little in common programmatically. The coalition was formally led by Koštunica in
the 2000 elections, but he and his party passed definitively into opposition by 2002. During his tenure as president of the FRY (Federal Republic of Yugoslavia), Koštunica was probably constrained by the fact that he
was permitted to take power in October 2000 mainly through the acqui-
escence of the police and army, who refused to intervene against the mass
anti-Milošević protests in Belgrade. This may have, at least implicitly,
indebted the incoming government, creating an obligation to protect
high-ranking officers from prosecution for past deeds.[20]

The surrender of Milošević to the ICTY provoked the first major crisis in the DOS, and brought to light conflicts over the legal status of war
criminals which remain unresolved. Koštunica had been arguing since
January of 2001 that the government could not respond to demands for
cooperation with the ICTY without a federal law regulating this cooper-

ation. His cabinet was said to be preparing, and continually delayed the introduction of, this law for several months. Eventually a draft emerged which would have established a process for receiving and complying with requests for extradition and information, which would have involved the Ministry of Justice and domestic courts in any decision. It became clear, however, that the draft law would not pass in the federal parliament, principally because of the refusal of the Montenegrin parties to support it.[21]

Faced with deadlines from the international community to show evidence of cooperation or forfeit financial assistance, the Serbian government decided to act unilaterally. In June 2001, the federal government (with Koštunica absent) quickly took up another mechanism of cooperation, adopting the proposed law on cooperation as a decree.[22] The Federal Constitutional Court (Savezni Ustavni Sud) immediately suspended the decree, however. Then the republican government of Serbia maneuvered to shortcut the conflict, adopting the ICTY statute as domestic law and immediately transferring Milošević to the custody of the tribunal.

Koštunica claimed at the time that he had not been informed of the action, and argued that the Serbian prime minister Zoran Djindjić had acted without authority and provoked a constitutional crisis. Legally, Djindjić seemed to have the upper hand in the disagreement, though this was largely due to the failure of the new government to pass a new constitution—the current constitution, declared under Milošević by single-party legislatures in 1990 on the republican level and 1992 on the federal level, is an artifact of the period in which Serbia and Slovenia fought over rights to secession among other issues, and reserves for republics the right of primacy over federal law.[23] The conflict over the authority to extradite suspects remained active, however, with Koštunica continuing to argue that a federal law was needed while doing nothing to bring one about, and Djindjić continuing to argue that suspects must be extradited as a legal obligation of the government while doing so only under immediate threat.[24] The conflict seemed to be coming to a head when, after being ordered to offer technical assistance to the police in arresting two ICTY suspects in November 2001, members of a special operations unit (the Red Berets) went on strike and organized a series of threatening public protests. Among the demands of the members of the unit was the passage of a law regulating cooperation with the ICTY and the replacement of the minister of the interior. Koštunica publicly defended the provocative actions of the Red Berets and Djindjić went to visit them at their base, but the conflict eventually fizzled and no law was immediately passed.[25]

Much of the internal disagreement in the governing DOS coalition was related to the fact that Serbia's multiparty system is still in development, and in the absence of a viable opposition outside the government, the expectation was that in the near future both the governing coalition and the opposition would develop out of the DOS. Here the competition broke down between the blocs led by the DSS (Democratic Party of Serbia) and the DS (Democratic Party), with the small social democratic parties and the various regional and ethnic parties forming a potential third bloc. The DS generally demonstrated its strong influence over more of the DOS parties, and when the coalition collapsed in 2002, most of these parties aligned themselves with the DS. The support of the DSS is based principally on Koštunica's personal popularity, which remains high but not high enough to allow his party to present a broad-based challenge to the DS-led bloc. As a result, the DSS has moved steadily to the right, allying itself on some issues with the formerly pro-Milošević parties (these are the formerly ruling Socialist Party of Serbia [SPS]; its erstwhile coalition partner, the Serbian Radical Party [SRS]; and the marginal right-wing Party of Serbian Unity [SSJ]), for which the questions of prosecutions of humanitarian violations and cooperation with the ICTY provide an opportune platform. The larger context has to do with competition for the votes of the supporters of the former regime, with one side calculating that votes are more likely to go to the party which is more successful at establishing international relationships and bringing economic security, and the other side calculating that they will go to the party which does the most to prevent radical changes and displacements in replacing the old system.

Milošević and Relations with the ICTY

The very low level of sympathy for the former populist leader is remarkable. Although advance knowledge of his April 2001 arrest was widespread, he managed to gather only a few hundred mostly elderly protesters to try to block the police, and the only resistance was offered by a poorly organized force led by the marginal "red duke" Siniša Vučinić[26] and, eventually, a few random gunshots from Milošević's intoxicated and distraught daughter Marija.[27] No serious protests followed his transfer to the ICTY, and even in the week before the beginning of his trial, an anti-Hague protest in the center of Belgrade attracted no more than five thousand people to hear speeches by SPS leaders and the obscurantist right-wing painter Dragoš Kalajić. Surveys at the time indicated that a broad majority of people wanted to see Milošević prosecuted, although the majority would have liked to see him prosecuted for domestic violations rather than for violations of international law. Even though a majority continues to regard the decision to send him to The Hague as mistaken, it is hardly an overwhelming majority. Ljiljana Bačević, director of the Center for Political and Public Opinion Research of the Institute for Social Sciences in Belgrade, summarized the findings of public opinion research in the first half of 2001 as follows:

> The extradition of Milošević to The Hague did not especially disturb public opinion in Serbia. Three-quarters of the citizens of Serbia consider that the people accused of war crimes, including Mr. Milošević, should be tried, and when they say tried they usually mean they should be convicted as well, which means that people are persuaded of that guilt. The results of public opinion research demonstrate the complete apathy of a convincing majority of the public toward Milošević, and the only thing that is controversial for them is whether he should be tried in The Hague rather than in Serbia. A large majority of people believe that the trial should be held in Serbia, and a large majority of citizens believes that Milošević, even before the trial has begun, is guilty of everything The Hague tribunal accuses him of, and also that he is guilty of political killings and embezzlement.[28]

To the degree that Milošević's defense before the ICTY has enjoyed some sympathy in domestic public opinion, much of this can probably be attributed to the perception that the tribunal is selective in its prosecution.

Even out of power and in The Hague, however, Milošević remains capable of doing considerable damage to Serbia. While at the time of this writing, he has yet to present his defense, most indications from his statements at arraignment and his cross-examinations suggest that he intends to relativize his guilt by pointing to the complicity of domestic and international actors.

The stakes of Milošević's trial were dramatically raised in 2001 with the release of two new indictments against him. The initial indictment, filed by prosecutor Louise Arbour in 1999, charged Milošević and four other individuals with personal and command responsibility for war crimes and crimes against humanity committed in Kosovo. Two more indictments were filed by Arbour's successor, Carla Del Ponte, in 2001. The Croatia indictment, released in October, names other individuals as part of the "joint criminal enterprise" and adds the charge of grave breaches of the Geneva Conventions. In November, a third indictment related to Bosnia-Herzegovina was released, and here the charge of genocide was added.

Milošević is charged with genocide, as with the other crimes, as an individual. Although the 1948 Convention on the Prevention and Punishment of the Crime of Genocide is clear that guilt for genocide may apply to "constitutionally responsible rulers, public officials or private individuals" (Article 4), meaning that an individual may be prosecuted for genocide, the portion of the definition of genocide requiring "intent" (Article 2) implies that a policy to commit genocide must exist. This suggests that while individuals can be held criminally accountable, ultimate responsibility for genocide lies with states rather than exclusively with individuals. The responsibility of a state survives the regime which committed the criminal acts: the present German government continues to pay reparations to victims of the Holocaust, and the present Turkish government continues to deny charges that the Ottoman Empire committed genocide against the Armenian population. If Milošević is convicted of genocide, this would impose obligations on future governments in Serbia, a prospect which has raised concerns even among people who regard Milošević and the "Greater Serbia" project with the greatest distaste.

Cultural Iterations of Responsibility

There is no certainty that the political powers will do any more than economically powerful governments explicitly require of them, if even that. In particular, however much the Serbian government might respond to pressure to establish the guilt of organizers and perpetrators, it is likely that the new rulers feel far less incentive to approach the issue of the responsibility of the society at large, or to encourage strategies of confronting that responsibility. This may not be a task which governments are well positioned to carry out in any case. The most important initiatives for confronting the question have come from groups not associated with the state, especially from independent (and generally small) groups of intellectuals. Among these certainly have to be counted the ongoing "Another Serbia" (Druga Srbija) campaign of the Belgrade Circle of Independent Intellectuals (Beogradski krug nezavisnih intelektualaca), the ongoing documentation efforts of the Belgrade Center for Human Rights (Beogradski centar za ljudska prava), and the Fund for Humanitarian Law (Fond za humanitarno pravo), and perhaps most effectively, the conference "Istina, odgovornost, pomirenje," (Truth, Responsibility, Reconciliation) held in Ulcinj in the spring of 2000. Ongoing efforts have been a part of many civic initiatives throughout Serbia, and have become a fixture in the presentations of the Center for Cultural Decontamination, which has become a major cultural destination in Belgrade.[29] Some other contributions were made in publications such as *Republika* and *Helsinska povelja,* associated with the Yugoslav Helsinki Committee. The independent radio station B-92 also maintained energetic efforts to inform the debate, translating and publishing books of analysis and documentation about the wars,[30] featuring discussions of the issue and documentaries in its broadcast programs, and dedicating special issues of the magazine *Reč* associated with the station to the theme. However, the debate could not reach a wide audience as long as Milošević was in power, partly because most major media were controlled by a regime which had a concrete interest in suppressing the question, and partly because the fresh experience of war (combined with mostly one-sided information about the war) did not prepare many members of the public for an honest discussion.

Often this meant that discussion which could not be carried out through political channels was guided through cultural ones. One way of looking at this is to examine the various diaries and autobiographical works of literature which were produced in Serbia during the war period. A number of writers produced "war diaries" which examined the events they had experienced or witnessed, and explored their own responses to them. There is no way of knowing how many people shared the impressions offered in these works, most of which were consciously presented as an alternative to official "patriotic" propaganda, but enough of them were produced that they might be considered a significant subgenre of contemporary Balkan literature.[31]

First, writers displayed a keen consciousness of the way in which Serbs were perceived in the world as the primary perpetrators of atrocities in the wars of succession. Mileta Prodanović tells of meeting an old and internationally prominent East European writer at a conference. "I shook hands with the old man (who was the only Nobel laureate I had ever met personally), told him where I was from, and at once noticed a change in his blue Slavic eyes."[32] Discomfited by the writer's gaze,

I understood. The old man was disappointed. The questions which he really, undoubtedly, wanted to ask me could be, for example: "And how many unfortunate Bosnian children did you slaughter with your own hands? Did you participate in mass rapes? Are you a relative of one of the leaders of the paramilitary formations, or maybe just one of the 'weekend warriors'?" I ran to my hotel room, ripped off the top of the plastic container of red ink for my "Rotring" pen with my teeth, spread the ink over my shirt and rubbed it on my hands. When I returned to the lecture room, I could see the relief on the face of the old poet. It seemed to me that he even nodded his head a little bit.[33]

Other writers tried responding to what they knew was the negative global reputation of Serbs, rather than taking refuge in bitter humor. Vladimir Arsenijević quotes an e-mail message he wrote to an Albanian friend:

My compassion really and naturally belongs only to people, regardless of their nationality and/or religion. I know that everything we have been going through in this country for the past decade or so is simply a long chain of consequences of our President's irresponsible and highly destructive behavior. You say that people are suffering here just for the fact that "they are Albanians" and I totally agree with you—they do—but you should also know that what you are concerned with is just one part of the big problem. Because many more people than just those of Albanian nationality have been going through enormous problems here, for a very long time now. It is a kind of inverted nationalism to think that only those citizens who are of non-Serbian nationality suffer here. There is no favouritism in this society, you can be sure of that. Everybody is Albanian here, and this is not just an apt, if shabby, analogy. . . .

And as for us, Bashkim, people like you and me, Serbs as well as Albanians, those who suffered a lot although they never caused any of this to happen, well—we are just flesh, valueless bodies for both parties to play with. That seems to be our most common ground. I'm sorry to say that. Because this is what our region has given us, such a hideous legacy. We are Nothings. We can easily be killed, and hardly anyone would blink, but many would cheer, because—we are Those Who Are Easily Killed. And, even if we manage to escape the borders of our misguided, stupid, sad countries, we are still not in a position to shake off that negative identity. Our countries, small and miserable as they are, nevertheless remain stronger than us.[34]

Regardless of the way in which they approached the problem, all of these writers needed in some way or another to confront the perception of collective guilt which the events of the wars had caused many people in the world to have about Serbs. Sometimes this took the form of satirizing the imposition of an unwelcome identity, sometimes it took the form of attempting to find a specific social location for blame, and sometimes it took the form of skepticism toward Serbian identity itself.

However, the stereotypes which other people developed about Serbs were not the only burden which Serbian writers faced. They also had to develop an approach toward the kind of patriotic models of identity which were offered up constantly in state-sponsored media. At the same time that media in other parts of the world were developing the image of Serbs-as-war-criminals, another mythology was developing in state-sponsored nationalist media of Serbs-as-Übermenschen, the oldest,[35] most virtuous, most democratic, and altogether finest people. Goran Marković offers an account of one Dr. Jovan E. Deretić,[36] one of the "historians" presented on TV Palma:

> He was speaking about some Serbon Makeridov, a conqueror who lived long before Alexander the Great and conquered much more territory than he. . . . That Serbon, the father of all nations, was a Serb. That is to say, all of his descendants, or rather all known peoples, have a Serbian origin. Contemporary Serbs, in fact, are just some of the many Serbs who, over time, became Greeks and Celts and so on. Serbs, according to this lively old fellow, are not a nation but a race. In fact, why hide it, all Indo-European peoples have Serbian origins.
>
> Even that lesser conqueror than Serbon, Alexander, was named Aleksandar Karanović and he was of Serbian origin too. He conquered the world with an army that was recruited from areas settled by Serbs, our ancestors were so brave. And the most beautiful girls, who can be seen on ancient Greek vases, were also Serbs, there is indisputable evidence for that. . . .
>
> About this doctor. Of course, Deretić has the right to assert whatever he likes, just like the audience has the right to believe it or, like me, simply to ignore it. But [here] something else is in question: the context of the story. It was disgusting, and at the same time typical. The host of the program, a Serb primitive who is delighted by every Serbian heraldic symbol, even completely nebulous ones, in archaeological digs, and who triumphally grins over every bit of "evidence," even the most suspicious, of the Serbian origin of everyone and everything, and his interlocutor . . . were perfect partners in this pig's race of nationalism. It was a real orgy of stupidity in the service of deceiving exhausted people, a last effort to inject hungry and scared people with the feeling that they still have a reason to live. I am not against nationalism a priori. I do not think that love for one's people is negative by definition. What makes me angry is not even the falsehood or artificiality of what those two people were claiming. I am ashamed because my feeling of belonging to a nation has been made into something crude, used for dirty purposes, because my personal feelings are being sold publicly by TV Palma, like prostitutes on Gavrilo Princip street.[37]

Similar themes are apparent in several diaries of the period, in which a falsified collective pride, widely publicized, is perceived by the writers as an attack on individual pride, and massively promoted nationalist feeling makes national identity impossible.

A similar response is offered to the discourse of victimization. Arsenijević responds to the efforts of state television to promote a feeling of victimization with what seems to be insensitive rationality. Describing an interview with people in a bomb shelter, he tries to place the rhetoric and its motivation in perspective:

> "He is completely hysterical!" a young mother said in a shaky voice into the microphones of the state television news, squinting from the bright lights which were pointed right into her eyes as if she were at a police interrogation. In her arms she was holding a baby who did not seem the least bit hysterical.
>
> "How does he behave?" asked the invisible interviewer, with pathos.
>
> "Sometimes he laughs. Sometimes he cries," the young mother answered.
>
> But isn't that what babies generally do? Sometimes they laugh. Sometimes they cry. All the time, even in the shelters when you are bombing them. But I don't think the problem is with the baby. What is worse, it's not with the mother either.[38]

Here the writers face an unusual rhetorical challenge. At once, they are materially and genuinely faced with the danger and other difficulties associated with the bombing campaign, while at the same time they feel compelled to resist messages from official media telling them that they are victims and should feel angry and helpless. At some level, this requires dismissing some real troubles, or explaining away some real situations.

On the other hand, there is a distinct consciousness that, in spite of the inflated claims made for the importance of nationalist wars in terms of "maintaining threatened identity" or "resisting the New World Order," the countries offering these images of themselves are in fact small, remote, and of little economic or political consequence. Prodanović offers an ironic self-location which begins with an interrupted story:

> . . . organizations for the protection of animals began a campaign for the permanent protection of the striped-neck swan. These until-recently little-known birds have their habitat in . . . Well, after all, it is not important where their habitat is—the average resident of the civilized world cannot pro-

nounce the name of that country. The most important things are principles and the determination to sacrifice oneself completely for the sake of
an idea.

These are just a few additional reasons why we, East Europeans, even
after the fall of the Berlin Wall and the arrival of perfect democracy to our
small and lost-in-East-European-space homelands, even when it is now possible to buy at our kiosks condoms in thousands of shapes, colors, flavors
and fragrances, and not just the Czechoslovakian "Tigar" brand like in the
time of the single-party dictatorship, still try to emigrate to one of those
states where so much attention is paid not just to the rights of people but
also various types of animals, to one of those countries where order, peace
and mutual respect reign, where even in times of senseless racial violence
one can sense an unusually high degree of political correctness.

The governments of the great democracies of the West, of course,
would be faced with insurmountable problems if they tried to cram masses
of morally, materially, and mentally neglected people from Eastern Europe
into their clean cities, into cities with well-maintained facades and rows of
well watered flowers, if they let these lazybugs into the hives where every
worker bee knows its place. To prevent this undesirable migration, invisi-
ble barriers have been placed in the form of visas. People of the East, it is
known, fear two things—drafts and bureaucratic procedures. About the
East European fear of drafts, those murderous currents of air in rooms,
about the awful diseases one can get by exposure to drafts, entire tracts have
been written—the fear of bureaucratic procedure is less well researched,
but no smaller. This fear is well known to great and small strategists in the
West, and so in order to receive a visa, aside from the rigid conditions, barriers have been established in the form of numerous questionnaires, which
people, who wish to feel the enchantment of orderly countries or even to
settle in these countries, must fill out in the unpleasant waiting rooms of
embassies and consulates, after long waits in line.[39]

In the sense apparent in this passage from Prodanović, the antipatrio-
tism of these writers did not function as substitution. The transparent lies
and overwrought nationalist rhetoric of the regime did not force many
people to believe that the regime's external opponents (whether these
are considered as other national groups from the former SFRY or as the
NATO alliance or an abstractly conceived "West")[40] or even internal opponents (especially those epitomized by the political party leaders) were
necessarily any better.

Instead, there seems to develop on the one hand an ambivalent attitude among the Serbian writers toward their own identity as Serbs. This is accompanied not by the advocacy of some other type of nationally structured alternative, but by taking refuge in various aspects of individuality. Arsenijević explains, in part, his friendly relationship with the Albanian writer from Kosovo Xhevdet Bajraj by the fact that neither was nationally inclined, and both liked the same kind of music. Marković talks about his inspiration by (and eventual disillusionment with) organizers of protests around Serbia after the end of the bombing campaign, but, by the end, the most probable vision of the future he can generate is:

> When the moment of liberation comes, the most important assistance we can get will be—psychiatric. We will need a whole lot of good doctors who will have the will and the knowledge to wrestle with the effects that the last decade or more has left us.
>
> And in that awakening of mental health it will be most necessary to establish a basic criterion: what is normal and what is not. I know that is not easy and that these things change, depending on the society and culture in question, but this will really be a special case, worthy of the deepest observation. This country will be an Eldorado for future scientists, something like a laboratory with live people instead of white mice.[41]

Under such conditions, in which some people have maintained enough of an equilibrium that they feel prepared, like the writers discussed here, to offer some kind of more or less moral stories to their readers, but many more are certain that they have gone through a period of madness which may or may not have ended, it is easy to understand why "public opinion" may not be so apparently solid. The discourse of responsibility is complex and by no means assured of success in the endeavor to come to terms with the events in question, of people's experience of these events, and of people's experience of themselves. None of these things are stable.

Denial and Displacement

The position that no crimes worth accounting for were committed, or that any crimes which were committed were justified, does exist in Serbian public opinion and in political discourse. For the most part, this is a marginal position, restricted to exponents of the extreme right and people who have a material interest in denial. Far more common are the several rhetorical means by which responsibility for violations is diffused, displaced, or relativized. One of these is contained in the mandate of the ill-starred investigatory commission appointed by Koštunica in 2001, which aside from responsibility for violations of international humanitarian law was charged with assessing responsibility for the dissolution of the SFRY. Another is implicit in the argument that accounting for crimes requires accounting for all crimes, including those committed by other forces during the wars, those permitted or encouraged by international intervention, and those committed in earlier periods including World War Two and the repressions carried out during the Ottoman Empire. In all of these currents, the tendency to argue in favor of a dispensation for crimes committed in the context of self-defense is apparent.

There is a marked tendency in public opinion to displace responsibility onto more distant actors. In an extensive survey on the subject of responsibility by Strategic Marketing in 2001, for example, respondents were asked to name the most important reason for NATO intervention against the Federal Republic of Yugoslavia in 1999. Some 29.8 percent named "the policy of the Milošević regime," while 55.2 percent identified either the political or the economic "interest of the West."[42] The factor of distance applies on comparative scales as well. Asked to choose between two options for "guilt for misfortune," respondents named Slovenes (45.3 percent) more than Serbs (10.8 percent), the United States (27.3 percent) more than NATO (25.2 percent), the "international community" (44.8 percent) more than "all the peoples of the former Yugoslavia" (20.5 percent), Milošević (42 percent) more than "the people who elected him" (17.6 percent), and the interests of international business (53.7 percent) more than the interests of domestic business (11.2 percent).

A legitimate complaint can be added to the list of obstacles to confrontation with responsibility: that is the responsibility of others. In the conflicts which followed the breakup of the SFRY, while few informed observers would deny that the vast majority of crimes were committed by ethnic Serbs with the vast majority of victims being people of different nationalities, this does not account for all of the crimes committed. People in Serbia are acutely aware, for example, of the large-scale targeting of civilian objects[43] during the NATO bombing campaign in 1999, the massive exodus of Serbs from Croatia in 1995 and Kosovo since 1999, and the imprisonments and forced migrations of Serbs in Bosnia-Herzegovina. The perception that these crimes have not been prosecuted or publicized as energetically as others is widespread.

An issue of priority is also raised frequently. Even among people who agree that leading figures from the Milošević regime ought to be prosecuted for crimes against people of other nationalities, there is a feeling that energetic prosecution of these crimes by an international tribunal removes suspects from the jurisdiction of domestic courts, and so precludes energetic prosecution of crimes committed by the regime in Serbia against Serbs. Sometimes this is expressed in the general sense, that political leaders need to be called to account for the collapse of the state and the destruction of the economy. At other times, the concerns are more specific, particularly in relation to the extensive corruption of the Milošević era, especially the distribution of state property in the form of luxurious houses and apartments, manipulation of the banking system and the system of currency exchange, and possible extortion or bribery in connection with the sale and privatization of state-owned corporations. This concern is also frequently applied to conspiracies to falsify the results of elections, particularly the elections of November 1996 and September 2000.

In addition to these concerns, some worry that an exclusive concentration on violations of international law will eclipse the possibility for the prosecution of several widely publicized acts of political violence in Serbia, including the murder of newspaper editor Slavko Ćuruvija in 1999, the attempted murder of politician Vuk Drašković (four people were killed in the attempt) in 1999, the murder of organized-crime figure Željko Ražnatović "Arkan" in 2000, and the disappearance of former president Ivan Stambolić in 2000. Several acts of ethnic violence committed or organized within the borders of Serbia could also remain uninvestigated or unpunished: for example, the kidnapping and murder of nineteen ethnic Muslim passengers from the Belgrade-Bar railway at Strpci in 1993, the intimidation and expulsion of ethnic Croatian residents of the village of Hrtkovci in 1992, and the kidnapping and murder of seventeen ethnic Muslim passengers from a bus in the village of Sjeverin in 1992. While domestic prosecutions have been carried out in the Sjeverin and Strpci cases, these have concentrated on the immediate perpetrators of the crimes, leaving untouched the people who most likely ordered their commission, who are in any case beyond the reach of domestic prosecutors in ICTY custody.

Why It Matters

The Yugoslav project for unity of the South Slavic peoples, founded as it was on romantic nationalist ideas and relations of power in the Ottoman and Habsburg empires, is certainly finished as a political goal. But there can be little doubt that the future of all of the states in the region lies in more middle-range projects of integration between political communities which have economic, cultural, and developmental goals in common. The legacy of the wars of Yugoslav succession presents the most serious obstacle to such efforts. This was certainly on the mind of Croatian foreign minister Tonino Picula when discussing the improvement of bilateral relations between Zagreb and Belgrade. After enumerating several benefits he expected for the Croatian economy as a result of trade, transport, and exchange agreements with its former Yugoslav neighbors, he enumerated the topics of discussion for an upcoming meeting with his Belgrade counterpart, Goran Svilanović: "the issues of missing persons, refugees, return of property, tenancy rights, arrests of returnees who have been indicted, [and] problems with borders and border policies."[44] The *Vreme* magazine writer Dejan Anastasijević referred, in a memorable essay, to the greatest problems facing the new government as "the poisoned apples that Milošević left on the table."[45] In many cases, little can be accomplished until they are cleared away.

An effort to build a culture of responsibility probably does more to challenge authoritarian legacies and lay a groundwork for a democratic future than any other kind of intervention in political culture. The twentieth century in Serbia saw decades of royal authoritarianism followed by fascist occupation, communist monopoly followed by bloody nationalist kleptocracy. One of the things which made this tolerable for a great many citizens was the lasting conviction that all of these social and political orders were imposed—and were therefore somebody else's fault. An ethic of passivity and powerlessness developed which combined ongoing practical frustration with supreme moral comfort.

At the same time, a bit of context is probably worth considering. From the perspective of one version of contemporary morality (a version which I, for the most part, share), which places human rights high on the hierarchy of values and argues that a serious confrontation with the recent past is a necessary precondition for a relatively free move toward the future, the process of coming to terms with questions of guilt and responsibility appears to be a clear necessity. But this is not the way the issue has been regarded in most places during most of human history, which offers precious few instances of a far-reaching confrontation (post–World War Two Germany may be the only example), and no instances of a quick one. If the state and society in Serbia do in fact rise to the challenge, it will be a rare achievement. That there is some significant degree of resistance to the effort should not be especially surprising.

Notes

The research for this chapter was supported by a fellowship at the Institute for Advanced Study, Collegium Budapest.

1. Stevan M. Weine, "Redefining *Merhamet* after a Historical Nightmare," in *Neighbors at War: Anthropological Perspectives on Yugoslav Ethnicity, Culture, and History,* ed. Joel M. Halpern and David A. Kideckel (University Park, Pa.: Penn State University Press, 2000), p. 406.

2. "Ethnic cleansing" is the term used by Weine, and has come to be so commonly used in reference to the conduct of the wars of Yugoslav succession, especially on the part of Bosnian and Croatian Serb forces, that it might be considered as having acquired all of the attributes of a popular neologism, and even possibly as having entered everyday usage. I object to the term strongly, only partly because of its possible functions either as euphemism or as epithet, and principally because it describes nothing concrete. For a list of actual crimes recognized under international law which are often subsumed under the category of "ethnic cleansing," I refer readers to the Rome Statute of the International Criminal Court, particularly Article 7 ("Crimes Against Humanity") and Article 8 ("War Crimes").

3. In the present essay, the term *guilt* is used to refer to the criminal guilt of a person convicted of violations of law, or the potential criminal guilt of a person accused. The term *responsibility* is used in the sense suggested by Karl Jaspers in *The Question of German Guilt,* trans. E. B. Ashton (New York: Fordham University Press, 2002), where he distinguished criminal guilt from political, moral, and metaphysical guilt. For the sake of clarity, the first of these is referred to here as *guilt,* and the latter three as *responsibility.*

4. A selection of the evidence regarding this charge was presented by Isabel Vincent, "Milosevic and the 14bn 'Theft of the Century,'" *The Daily Telegraph* (London), 9 February 2002, online at news.telegraph.co.uk/news/main.jhtml ?xml=%2Fnews%2F2002%2F02%2F09%2Fwmil009.xml.

5. Prosecutions have taken place with regard to the attempted murder of politician Vuk Drašković in the "Ibar Highway" case, but they have been accompanied by complaints of a lack of thoroughness, not least from Drašković himself. One result of "Operation Saber" in 2003 was the discovery of the fate of former Serbian president Ivan Stambolić, who was kidnapped and murdered in 2000, though the case has yet to be tried. No progress has been made in the case of newspaper editor Slavko Ćuruvija, murdered in 1999.

6. The declaration was published in the army journal *Narodna armija* on 19 October 1991 and is reproduced in detail in Vladan A. Vasiljević, *Zločin i odgovornost* (Belgrade: Prometej, 1995), pp. 118–19.

7. Ibid., pp. 120–21.

8. Ibid., p. 116.

9. Paper presented at the International Conference on War Crimes Trials, Belgrade, November 1998, published in Lazar Stojanović, ed., *Spotlight on War Crimes Trials,* trans. Djurdja Stanimirović (Belgrade: Humanitarian Law Center, 2000), p. 170.

10. Wladimiroff was dismissed by the ICTY on 10 October 2002 after giving a media interview in which he offered his assessment that Milošević was unlikely to avoid conviction.

11. In Stojanović, *Spotlight,* pp. 214–15. The arguments offered by Ellis and Wladimiroff may of course be wrong, but it will not be possible to tell until domestic courts build a record of prosecution for violations of international humanitarian law.

12. The survey agency which has followed this question most closely has been the Belgrade-based Strategic Marketing Agency, which issued its most thorough report in SMMRI, "Vidjenje istine u Srbiji," May 2001. The principal findings are available online in either PDF or PowerPoint format at www.b92.net/doc/sm/.

13. For several examples, see Vojin Dimitrijević, ed., *Ljudska prava u Jugoslaviji 1999* (Belgrade: Beogradski centar za ljudska prava, 2000), pp. 77–91, 207–15.

14. Institut društvenih nauka, *Jugoslovensko javno mnjenje 1996,* cited in Ognjen Pribićević, "Da li je minimalistički koncept demokratije još uvek validan? Slučaj Srbije," 1998. The article is available online at www.komunikacija.org.yu/komunikacija/casopisi/sociologija/XLč3/Clo3/document.

15. Stjepan Gredelj, "Vrednosno utemeljenje blokirane transformacije srpskog društva," in *Rački hod: Srbija u transformacijskim procesima,* ed. Mladen Lazić (Belgrade: Filip Višnjić, 2000), p. 228, table 18.

16. For several examples, see Humanitarian Law Center, "Trials of Kosovo Albanians," a selection of press releases from the HLC in relation to current cases. The documents are available online at www.hlc.org.yu/english/toka.htm.

17. See Zoran Kosanović, "Sudjenje djakovičkim Albancima u Nišu: Za 143 Albanca kazna 1632 godine," *AIM,* 29 May 2001. The article is available online at www.aimpress.org/dyn/pubs/archive/data/200005/00528–003–pubs-pod.htm. Goran Petronijević was one of the attorneys retained as counsel by Veselin Sljivančanin after his arrest and transfer to the ICTY, but the tribunal refused to accredit him to represent Sljivančanin, partly because his decision in the Djakovica case reflected poorly on his legal capacity.

18. A detailed description of the material state of the Belgrade district court is provided by presiding judge Gordana Mihajlović in her interview with Zlatoje Martinov, "Sa Gordanom Mihajlović, predsednicom II opštinskog suda," in *Republika,* no. 263 (16–30 June 2001).

19. The text of the address is reproduced in "Kraj agonije pravosudja: Reč Leposave Karamarković, predsednice Vrhovnog suda Srbije, na skupštini Društva sudija Srbije, održanoj 7. aprila u Palati pravde u Beogradu," *Republika,* no. 262 (1–15 June 2001). Leposava Karamarković was compelled to resign her judicial position as a result of political pressure in 2003.

20. For an early narrative which focuses on relations between the political parties and military and police forces in October 2000, see Ivan Radovanović and Dragan Bujosević, *5. oktobar: 24 sata prevrata* (Belgrade: Media Centar, 2001).

21. This fact cannot necessarily be taken as a representation of public opinion in Montenegro. After the 2000 elections, only the parties formerly allied with the Milošević regime were represented in the federal parliament, as the ruling coalition boycotted the federal elections of September 2000. While the Montenegrin parties represented in the federal parliament wielded considerable political power due to their ability to control the composition of the federal government, the level of support they had among their constituencies was at best uncertain.

22. The text of the law, as it was adopted by the federal government in the form of a decree on 23 June 2001, is reproduced in "Uredba o saradnji sa haškim tribunalom: Sudska procedura kao u krivičnom postupku," *Danas* (Belgrade), 25 June 2001.

23. The legal foundation for the decision is in Article 16 of the 1992 federal constitution, which declares all international conventions and agreements to be a part of domestic law, and Article 135 of the 1990 Serbian constitution, which grants Serbia the right to ignore decisions of the federal government which it regards as being contrary to the national interest. See Miloš Vasić, "Slobodan Milošević pred Haškim sudom: Pritvorenik broj 039," *Vreme* (Belgrade), no. 548 (5 July 2001), pp. 11–12.

24. Faced by another deadline from the United States, a version of the law was passed in a rush in April 2002.

25. The Red Berets later became well known internationally as the group principally suspected in the assassination of Zoran Djindjić in March 2003.

26. Siniša Vučinić is one of a group of seven deputies of the Serbian Radical Party which broke with the party in 1994 to provide a majority for Milošević's SPS, which did not have one at the time. Later, as Vučinić became closer to the Milošević family and Mirjana Marković's Yugoslav United Left (JUL), he renamed his group "The Radical Party of the Left-Nikola Pašić" (RSL-NP). The party did not retain its representation in parliament, but Vučinić became a part of the circle of individuals concentrated around the regime.

27. The gun fired by Marija Milošević was received by her as a gift from General Nebojša Pavković, the military chief of staff during the last period of Milošević's rule who retained the same position until 2002. It was engraved with his signature.

28. Quoted in Ivan Djordjević, "Miloševićev problem," *Free Serbia,* 7 June 2001. The article can be found in a reproduced version online at www.srpskadijaspora .info/komentar/milosevic/0607.asp. More detail is provided in a survey by the Center for the Study of Alternatives (Centar za proučavanje alternativa), reported in *Nezavisna svetlost* in March 2001 ("Sudeti Miloševiću," *Nezavisna svetlost,* no. 287 (31 March 2001), www.svetlost.co.yu/orhiva/2001/287/287-6.htm.) The survey reported that 82 percent of respondents agreed that Milošević should be tried for "war crimes, corruption, electoral fraud, and abuse of power," while only 4 percent agreed that he should be tried only for war crimes. On the question of whether Milošević should be sent to The Hague (the survey was carried out before his arrest), 56 percent of people with higher education said yes, as did 45 percent of those with the equivalent of a high school education or less. Sixteen percent of those with higher education, and 24 percent of those without, were opposed to sending Milošević to The Hague. The results are summarized in "Suditi Miloševiću," *Nezavisna svetlost,* no. 287 (24–31 March 2001), online at www.svetlost.co .yu/arhiva/2001/287/287-6.htm. An interesting finding, although there is no assurance whatsoever of a random sample, can be found in the informal poll on the Web site of the weekly magazine *NIN,* www.nin.co.yu. *NIN* has been asking visitors to vote "yes" or "no" on the question, "Should Milošević have been delivered to The Hague tribunal?" since the week he was delivered, with the results generally hovering between 35–40 percent in favor and 60–65 percent opposed since June 2001. A check of the site after the beginning of Milošević's trial, however, indicated a change. On 14 February 2002, the continuous informal poll showed 45.5 percent voting "yes" and 54.5 percent voting "no." These results should probably be taken with some reservation, however, as a number of factors other than shifts in public opinion could easily influence this sort of survey.

29. The center opened in 1995 and featured in its first year an exhibit dedicated to the experience of siege in Sarajevo. A frequent site for academic panels and book promotions, among its recent offerings has been Slobodan Snajder's play *Snake Skin* (Zmijin svlak), a drama dealing with the experiences of rape victims in Bosnia.

30. In the interest of full disclosure, it ought to be noted that one of these books was a translation by Biljana Lukić of my *Culture of Power in Serbia: Nationalism and the Destruction of Alternatives* (University Park, Pa.: Penn State University Press, 1999), which was released as *Kultura vlasti u Srbiji* (Belgrade: Samizdat B-92, 2001).

31. A methodological note here: I do not want to make ambitious claims that the perspectives outlined in these literary works are either constitutive of national identities, as Andrew Wachtel (*Making a Nation, Breaking a Nation* [Stanford: Stanford University Press, 1998]) argues, or that they represent untapped or secretly

mystic populist reserves, as Branimir Anzulović (*Heavenly Serbia* [N.Y.: New York University Press, 1999]) argues. In fact, I do not know how widely read either "patriotic" literature or the literature I am discussing is (neither do they: statistics of this type in Serbia are notoriously unreliable), or how widely shared the ideas presented in these books (or any books) are. Of the writers whose work I discuss in this section, none are of the "best-selling" range, with the exception of Vladimir Arsenijević. But here I think it is sufficient to avoid excessive claims for the effects of literature and simply to observe that this genre of literature makes available a set of perspectives which developed around the events discussed, and represents one of the ways that some writers tried to intervene in the process of popular understanding.

32. Mileta Prodanović, *Ovo bi mogao biti Vaš srećan dan* (Belgrade: Stubovi kulture, 2000), p. 10.

33. Ibid., p. 11.

34. Vladimir Arsenijević, *Meksiko: Ratni dnevnik* (Belgrade: Rende, 2000), pp. 94–95, 96. The passage is in English in the original.

35. Various theses about the origins of all world civilizations with Serbs were promoted during the war period. For examples, see Olga Luković-Pjanović, *Srbi: Narod najstariji* (Belgrade: AIZ Dosije, 1990), and Draško Scekić, *Sorabi: Istoropis* (Belgrade and Podgorica: Sfairos and Timor, 1994). The rhetoric of ancient historical greatness was designed to add insult to the injury offered by the rhetoric of nation-as-victim pathetics.

36. As Goran Marković himself points out (p. 159), and as the historian Predrag J. Marković (who is no relation to Goran) made certain I understood, the charlatan discussed in the passage quoted here is one Jovan E. Deretić, and is not to be confused with the Jovan Deretić with no middle "E.," who was a perfectly respectable professor of literature and author of several authoritative texts on Serbian literary history. Goran Marković, *Godina dana* (Belgrade: Forum pisaca, 2000), p. 159.

37. Ibid., pp. 157, 158–59.

38. Arsenijević, *Meksiko*, pp. 62–63.

39. Prodanović, *Ovo bi mogao biti*, pp. 26–27.

40. Unsurprisingly, no writer had anything positive to say about the propaganda leaflets which NATO airplanes delivered together with explosives in 1999. Arsenijević and Rakezić both reproduce them in their books, certain that the foolishness of the propaganda speaks for itself (Sasa Rakezic [aka Aleksandar Zograf], *Bulletins from Serbia: E-mails and Cartoon Strips from Beyond the Front Line* [New York: Slab-o-Concrete Publications, 1999]). Marković, *Godina dana* [note 36], p. 45, comments: "The content of those leaflets was one of the big surprises of this war for me. I have not seen anything so stupid and illiterate for a long time. Like

somebody is joking. Aside from the grammatical and stylistic errors, the whole concept of this propaganda material was based on Serbian nationalism!!! Someone who is sending the message, and NATO is in the signature, is whining because of the loss of Serb territory in Croatia, in Bosnia, because of the loss of Sarajevo!? Milošević is responsible for everything and if it were not for him, Serbia would stretch all the way to Tokyo, says this clever propagandist. Either the propagandist is stupid, or he has complete contempt for the readers of the leaflets. Or maybe both are true: that it was thought up by an idiot and that his strategy is perfect for the public here."

41. Marković, *Godina dana,* p. 151.

42. SMMRI, "Vidjenje istine u Srbiji," May 2001, p. 15.

43. Among the civilian objects targeted were roads and bridges, as well as the more well-known examples of the state Radio-Television Serbia broadcasting headquarters and the embassy of the People's Republic of China. The use of cluster bombs is also, arguably, a violation of the 1977 Protocols to the Geneva Conventions. Several civilian objects, including homes and businesses, were also hit by mistake, which is a matter of controversy but most likely not a violation of the laws and customs of war.

44. Radio Free Europe/Radio Liberty, *Newsline,* 6 February 2002, online at www.rferl.com.

45. Dejan Anastasijević, "Srbija i Crna Gora: Platforma za razlaz," *Vreme,* no. 522, 4 January 2001, p. 12.

8

CRIME AND THE ECONOMY UNDER MILOŠEVIĆ AND HIS SUCCESSORS

MAJA MILJKOVIĆ AND MARKO ATTILA HOARE

The Serbian regime of Slobodan Milošević is usually associated in Western minds with Greater Serbian nationalism and expansionism. Yet there was another side to the coin: the Milošević regime was neocommunist and represented the negative flowering of a half century of communist rule. As such, Serbia under Milošević followed the pattern of the Soviet Union under Stalin and China under Mao: a communist regime brings into being a new elite, one that—to use Marxist-Leninist terminology—lacks the cohesiveness or "class consciousness" of a genuine "bourgeoisie"; the new elite then implodes, inflicting massive damage on its own people, their state, and economy. The violence and destruction inflicted by the Milošević regime on its own people, although not on the scale of Stalin's Great Purges or Mao's Cultural Revolution, nevertheless bear some similarities. They succeeded in transforming Serbia from one of the richest countries of communist Europe into one of the poorest of postcommunist Europe within the space of less than fifteen years. The total control over the Serbian economy exercised by the ruling Socialist Party of Serbia (SPS) and the Yugoslav United Left (JUL)—Serbia's twin neocommunist parties—was a means by which members of the Serbian elite could enrich themselves through a systematic plunder of the state, in what amounted to one of the biggest asset-stripping operations in history. Among other relevant factors, the prevailing impoverishment of the Serbian people under Milošević produced a rising discontent at both the popular and the elite levels that culminated in the revolution of October 2000. Yet it was only with the assassination of Prime Minister Zoran Djindjić on 12 March 2003 that the reformist, post-Milošević regime finally moved against the Serbian criminal elite, hopefully paving the way for a future economic recovery. A year after the Djindjić assassination, the future prospects for Serbia are uncertain. Serbia has lost its main pro-reform engine. Right-wing politicians are rising again and the overall atmosphere in Belgrade is more depressive than ever. Life is increasingly difficult for ordinary people, and the high hopes for the future are definitely lost.

Part I: The Destruction of the Serbian Economy
(Maja Miljković)

The destruction of the Serbian economy by the Serbian political elite under Milošević began with the defeat of Ante Marković, the last prime minister of the Socialist Federated Republic of Yugoslavia (SFRY). Marković was one of the last politicians on the Yugoslav political scene to endeavor to safeguard the SFRY and to enact essential social and economic reforms, and his name still commands wide respect in Serbia today. In the consciousness of ordinary people in Serbia the "golden age of Ante Marković" represents the last days of Atlantis. After Marković's fall began the worst period in Serbia's history since World War Two. Marković's main policy, one that accorded with the wishes of millions of Serbian citizens and Yugoslavs generally, was to reform the old political and economic system while safeguarding the Yugoslav federation. His ultimate goal was the introduction of a Western-style democracy. However, every sober analyst at the time rated the chance of Marković's reforms succeeding as very low. The Yugoslav state was absolutely bureaucratized and the Yugoslav public was accustomed to an authoritarian and two-dimensional ruling ideology, while the process of disintegration of the federation had already reached the point of no return. The political elites of Serbia, Croatia, Slovenia, and Montenegro had ceased to support a united Yugoslavia and looked unfavorably on the reform program of Marković, who consequently played the historical role of the last "Yugoslav" politician. Marković's reforms centered on the building of market institutions, the development of a market economy, the opening of the country to the world market, the establishment of a legal state, the broadening of civic and human rights, and the abolition of the League of Communists' monopoly on power and introduction of a multiparty system. His failure was part and parcel of the collapse of Yugoslavia into fratricidal war. The destruction of the Serbian economy was one aspect of this collapse.

Under the Milošević regime the Serbian political elite succeeded in destroying the basis of the identity of the Serbian nation: its democratic structure, economy, and culture. An important part of the Serbian identity was based on relatively good relations with the West, but in the period of the recent wars the positive image of Serbia and the Serbs has been absolutely destroyed. Thanks to the political decisions of Milošević's elite, the Serbs have received an epithet that will for decades remain in the consciousness of the citizens of the world: that of a genocidal nation guilty of systematic murder and rape in Bosnia-Herzegovina and in Kosovo; of the "ethnic cleansing" of Muslims, Croats, and Albanians; of the destruction of Sarajevo and Vukovar and the massacres of Srebrenica and Račak. The efforts of the International Criminal Tribunal for the former Yugoslavia (ICTY) to demonstrate individual rather than collective responsibility for these crimes are unlikely to change this. Nevertheless, the proof that it was the Serbian political elite rather than the Serbian people that was guilty of the destruction can best be found in the suffering of the Serbs themselves under a regime for which nothing was holy. Serbian traditions, the Serbian Orthodox religion, the ideology of Yugoslavism, the ideology of communism—all were manipulated and abused just as the lives of millions of Yugoslavs—Serbs and non-Serbs—were destroyed physically, spiritually, and materially. One expression of this is the phenomenon of Serbian depopulation, the disappearance of the Serbs from Serbia itself.

During the 1990s, six hundred thousand Serbs left Serbia as refugees to seek a better life abroad and are today to be found everywhere from London to Tokyo.[1] In addition, according to the statistics of the new Serbian government, four hundred thousand Serbs from Serbia are working outside Serbia as economic migrants without any widespread desire to ever return to their homeland. Serbia today has both absolutely and relatively a smaller population than it had in 1991, despite the influx of large numbers of refugees following every one of Milošević's military defeats in Slovenia, Croatia, Bosnia-Herzegovina, and Kosovo. The refugees fled to Serbia to escape death or discrimination under the new non-Serbian regimes, while the native Serbs of Serbia themselves sought to leave their native land to escape military conscription and poverty.[2]

The generation of young Serbs who reached adulthood in 1990 is today on the verge of complete destitution. They have spent weeks, months, even years participating in demonstrations, freezing, suppressing tears, and receiving beatings from the police. The freedom that came on 6 October arrived late for the young people who had brought the change about; they were too tired and disillusioned and the ideal of the normal life that their parents had once enjoyed appeared as a bitter joke. This generation lived for ten years in acute poverty, hounded by the authorities to serve in the army and arrested and beaten for "antistate" activities, in other words for their free thinking and desire for a democratic society. In their newly attained maturity they have lost their strength and optimism.

The future of Serbia is brought into question by the massive criminalization of all state structures, from which the virus of corruption spread into all the cells of the Serbian body. The greatest damage lies in the destruction of traditional morals and rules of social conduct. This corruption has spread into the judicial system; legality lost its respect and authority as the number of unpunished acts of embezzlement spiraled out of control; the courts were wholly deprived of any power to punish the guilty members of the elite. Instead, they became a pliable tool in the hands of those with the most political influence. Judges and lawyers had no choice but to toe the line or lose their jobs and possibly their lives. The long list of "disobedient" judges who "disappeared" is testimony to this.

The Milošević regime succeeded also in bringing about the collapse of both public health care and education. Serbia's health service, once among the best in Europe, has been plundered mercilessly; expensive medical equipment such as ultrasound scanners and X-rays was systematically removed from hospitals and sold on the black market by members of the hospital staff and management. Hospitals were frequently left unable to treat patients unless the latter brought all the necessary medical equipment with them, from needles, hypodermics, and bandages to alcohol and drugs. Schools and universities, the sources of the young opponents of the regime, were similarly devastated, with the impoverished teaching staff providing children with the most glaring proof that it was impossible to earn a living through one's education and learning. An entire generation of youthful gangsters and their molls was spawned by Milošević's school system. Criminality and prostitution became the way of life for a large section of Serbian youth.

THE SERBIAN ELITE UNDER MILOŠEVIĆ

The quest for power, privilege, and money motivated a host of politicians to participate in policies that resulted in the economic destruction of Serbia. Yet it is not immediately apparent who formed the most immediate circle of power around Milošević. During Milošević's first years in power, a small but extremely powerful political and economic elite formed around him that was drawn from three different social categories: (1) high-ranking members of the communist authorities; (2) directors of the state firms and banks; and (3) the owners of formally private but in fact para-state economic enterprises.[3] This narrow social layer succeeded in achieving enormous wealth in Milošević's Serbia. Economic success was not due to any particular entrepreneurial talent but to various forms of monopoly, which included the printing and distribution of money, the import and sale of certain goods, the granting of important positions in state or social institutions, and the control of and access to the media. They enjoyed also a privileged status with regard to their own financial and fiscal obligations toward the state.[4] The Milošević regime guaranteed the monopoly position of the Serbian economic elite, receiving in return a share of the material spoils. This partnership resulted, on the one hand, in a politically stable regime for most of the 1990s, but on the other in an economic free fall.[5] Milorad Savičević, manager of the Genex and Zastava corporations, comments on the Serbian economy under Milošević: "We had low production, no investment and lots of corruption. The result is a nation with 4 million really poor people and 10,000 really rich people."[6]

The secret of Milošević's survival in office for so long was his absolute control over the centers of financial power, something that was possible in a system not governed by genuine private ownership of property. For this reason, Milošević never carried out a genuine program of privatization of socially owned economic assets because he did not wish to lose the power that he enjoyed thanks to his ability to appoint and control the managers of state firms and banks. Those directors of firms and banks who were politically loyal to the regime could carry out financial manipulations and embezzlements and illegally enrich themselves at the expense of their enterprises without fear, so long as they enjoyed the blessing of their presidential protector. Conversely, the directors owed their positions not to any economic expertise but solely to regime patronage; none could afford to exercise any real autonomy or defy the will of their political master. Meanwhile there was no chance of private capital entering the country contrary to the will and outside the control of the political establishment.

Independent capital, uncontrolled by the political elite, could have brought about the fall of the regime. That was one of the fundamental reasons why Milošević, right up to the end, maintained a diktat over all aspects of state finance and over the economy of the country as a whole. He effectively adopted the proven system by which communist and quasi-socialist regimes maintained themselves in power: control over state economic assets and the defense of economic autarky.[7] Strong private capital and a developed market and market institutions would only have reduced Milošević's power. In 1998, only 37 percent of economic output was produced by private-sector firms. The constant lack of transparency of the slow and postponed process of privatization, the frequent changes in legislation and reversals in announced policies, the ambiguous property rights, and the corrupt political and economic practice together resulted in the enrichment of a small number of individuals while the majority of the population lived and continue to live in poverty. The Milošević regime has stimulated corruption and criminal activities linked to the informal and black market economy. Meanwhile those strong and viable firms that did exist but whose managements were politically opposed to the regime were destroyed or taken over, regardless of the economic cost. After ten years of Milošević's reign, in 1998 the GDP was only 35 percent of the GDP level of 1989. From 1997 to 2000, more than half a million working people lost their jobs. On the eve of Milošević's fall, over a third of Serbia's work-force had neither steady employment nor reliable incomes.

This phenomenon of state-sponsored plunder of the citizenry is most graphically illustrated by the collapse of the so-called "pyramid banks" of Jezdimir Vasiljević and Dafina Milanović, whom Milošević used quite lit-erally to rob Serbia's citizens of their foreign-currency earnings. Vasiljević ("Jezda the Boss") founded the Jugoskandik Bank in 1990 in Milošević's home town of Požarevac. Its activities began in January 1991 and it regis-tered as the Jugoskandik Bank in March 1992. During the local elections of that year, Vasiljević donated 200,000 to the SPS campaign. He also do-nated 7 million DM for the equipping of paramilitary forces. A classic pyramid bank, Jugoskandik collapsed in March 1993 and Vasiljević fled the country.

Along the same lines, Dafina Milanović founded the Dafiment Bank on 9 October 1991. Its investments were concentrated in the SPS heart-land of southern Serbia. Prior to the December 1991 elections, Milanović contributed 7 billion dinars to the state pension funds in order to secure votes for the SPS. In July 1992, Milomir Minić, director of Belgrade's rail-ways and subsequently general secretary of the SPS, and Milutin Mrkonjić, director of the CIP engineering and construction institute, demanded that Dafiment invest money in the construction of the Belgrade metro. Forty million DM were subsequently removed from the Dafiment Bank by the police and Serbian National Bank officials, but none of the money reached the metro. In the spring of 1993, Dafiment collapsed. The collapse of Ju-goskandik and Dafiment left many Serbian families destitute, but they served the financial interests of the regime while they lasted.[8]

The phenomenon of Milošević's economic elite can be approached by looking at the careers of its typical representatives. One of these was Mirko Marjanović, who served as president of the assembly of the Cham-ber of Commerce of Belgrade, vice president of the Soccer Federation of Yugoslavia, and president of Belgrade's Partizan soccer club. His career underwent its greatest rise after the crucial 8th Session of the League of

Communists of Serbia in 1987, when Milošević assumed domination over the Serbian communist regime. Until that time, he had been the general manager of the Progres export and import company. A member of the Executive Committee of the SPS, he was later closely linked with Mirjana Marković's JUL. Thanks to Milošević's patronage, he was elected prime minister of Serbia in March 1994. At that time, the financially astute Dragoslav Avramović, head of the Yugoslav National Bank, was appointed minister of finance with the task of curbing the country's galloping inflation, which during the 1993 economic crisis had reached a monthly rate of over 200 percent in February, 1,880 percent in August, 20,190 percent in November, and 313,563,558 percent in December/January. However, Avramović's economic reforms went much further than the regime wanted. Avramović's program was intended to consolidate the economy and enable rapid reforms and a painless period of transition, but Milošević had no interest in such a course of events, and Marjanović was his key agent in the sabotaging of Avramović's program, something that guaranteed the Serbian economy would decline to the level in which it is today. While formally advocating full implementation of Avramović's program, Marjanović in practice did everything to undermine its success. Two years later, Avramović openly accused the governments of Serbia and of the Yugoslav federation of preventing the implementation of the program, but to no avail.

Marjanović's government was called the "government of the managers" because many of the ministerial positions were given to the directors of large state-run companies. Marjanović himself remained the director general of Progres, which concluded business agreements with Russia at this time. Djindjić accused Marjanović in 1995 of misusing his official position in a business transaction concerning the export of Russian gas to Yugoslavia. Djindjić also claimed he had diverted company money to private bank accounts in Cyprus. Djindjić, then leader of the Democratic Party, was consequently accused in turn of tarnishing the reputation of the Republic of Serbia and sentenced to four months in prison in September 1996, receiving in addition a two-year suspended sentence. The judges of Belgrade's district court said that they had been under pressure from Marjanović's office during the trial. They were supposed to end the trial as soon as possible and rule in favor of the premier. At the same time, the state-run media put heavy pressure on judges and the judiciary in general. At the beginning of February 1998, Marjanović took an active role in a campaign carried out by part of the state-run media which accused the independent media of destabilizing the national currency and undermining the country's economic resources. He said that the independent media was responsible for "serious disturbances on the market, damaging the standard of living and increasing anxiety among the population." Thanks to his connections in Moscow and the possibility of securing Russian gas for Yugoslavia, Marjanović was mandated to form a new Serbian government in 1998.

A second typical representative of Milošević's economic elite was Nikola Šainović. He was a deputy prime minister who also rose to the top of the Serbian hierarchy in the early 1990s and remained there until 5 October 2002. Well-informed sources said that he was "the man Milošević trusted most." From the post of vice president of the Bor Mining Group in 1989 he was appointed to the Serbian government as secretary for industry, energy, and civil engineering. After that his political career went from strength to strength: deputy prime minister of Serbia in 1991, minister of finance in 1992, prime minister of Serbia in 1993, and deputy prime minister of the FRY in 1994. Šainović was also a member of the executive board of the SPS. During the Bosnian war, he was Milošević's key intermediary for coordinating with the Bosnian Serb leadership in Pale. In June 1996, along with Jovica Stanišić, the then head of state security, Šainović arranged on Milošević's behalf the removal of Radovan Karadžić, president of the Serb Republic. The independent press claimed that Šainović had played a special role in eliminating the Niš leadership of the SPS in December 1996, after the latter had lost the local elections in the city, which had been an SPS stronghold. The protests began in Niš and spread to all cities in Serbia. According to Nebojša Čović, Šainović was a "major actor in the rigging of the election results." Šainović was a member of the state delegation that unsuccessfully attempted to negotiate a solution to the Kosovo crisis with representatives of the Kosovo Albanians. He participated in talks to identify a solution to the Kosovo issue held in France in February and March 1999. He was one of the five top-ranking Serbian leaders to be indicted for war crimes in Kosovo by the ICTY in 1999.[9]

Dragan Tomić, speaker of the Serbian parliament and senior official in the SPS, is a third example. His character is best illustrated in one of the many congratulatory messages that Tomić, always eager to be the first, sent to Milošević shortly after he was dismissed from the prestigious position of Belgrade SPS chief by the will of the latter himself: "Dear President, we can promise you that we will never allow our country, our Serbia and our Yugoslavia to be conquered. With you at the helm of our party and our state, there is no obligation to peace and [the] development of our people and all the world that we will not fulfill." At the time of the 8th

Session in September 1987, Tomić supported Milošević's political rival Ivan Stambolić, then Serbian president. However, after he realized that Stambolić was losing the power struggle, Tomić swiftly changed sides and joined Milošević in his ascent. Afterward, Tomić played a very important role in fortifying Milošević's position, organizing a huge rally in Belgrade in his support, and was rewarded for his efforts with several profitable positions. He was appointed general manager of the largest national oil company, Jugopetrol, and remained there throughout Milošević's reign. Also, Tomić was chairman of the management board of the powerful pro-government media house Politika. Forever loyal to Milošević and always in the circle of his closest associates, Tomić accepted his sacrifice as a good "soldier of the party"—obediently and silently. Indeed, he thereafter continued to advocate the regime's policy even more fervently.[10]

Zoran Andjelković came from a small town in the interior and, with a limited worldview, never enjoyed the reputation of a serious politician but rather only of a provincial apparatchik with close links to those more powerful than himself. Yet this image was deceptive. Andjelković started his career as a sales clerk in a department store in a small town, and his political rise began at the end of the 1980s when he became executive secretary of the Central Committee of the League of Communists of Serbia. During the 1990s, he served as an SPS party whip. Thanks to his political activities, he was appointed to the position of general manager of Genex Systems, the most powerful Serbian firm which the Milošević regime was undermining. Working at Genex, Andjelković did not work in the interest of the firm but, instead, functioned as the loyal executor of Milošević's orders. Andjelković then served as president of the Provisional Executive Council of Kosovo-Metohija, where his propaganda served to prepare the Serbian public for the assault on the ethnic Albanian population.[11]

No member of Milošević's circle played a more important role than Mihalj Kertes, the organizer of the "Yogurt Revolution," by which Milošević had seized control of Vojvodina in October 1988. As security chief of the Dafiment Bank, Kertes oversaw its plunder and collapse. Kertes served variously as president of the Serbian parliament, deputy federal interior minister, and, most importantly, director of the federal customs administration from 1994, where he siphoned off huge sums—possibly as much as US$4 billion by 2000—on Milošević's behalf. At least part of these sums went to finance Serb forces in Bosnia. Kertes's hometown of Bačka Palanka, near the Croatian border in Vojvodina, prospered through Kertes's patronage; Kertes was known to dole out confiscated goods to the children at local kindergartens. On 4 October 2000, two days before Milošević's fall,

Kertes gave the latter's wife, Mira Marković, a receipt for 2 million DM. When Kertes was arrested following the revolution, police found a trove of US$1.3 million in deutschmarks and dinars in his office, along with fifteen sniper rifles, ten luxury bulletproof cars, and seven kilos of high-grade heroin.[12] Of mixed Hungarian-Croat ethnic background, Kertes was also typical of many prominent non-Serbs in Serbia who had no place in the postcommunist parties of traditional Serb nationalism but who could play an important role in the SPS regime, which had inherited a multi-ethnic membership from the former League of Communists. Others in a similar position included Simatović, the ethnic Croat leader of the JSO (Units for Special Operations), Marta Strukharik, Milošević's ethnic Slo-vak legal expert in the manipulation of election results, and Sejdo Ba-jramović, Milošević's ethnic Albanian puppet representative for Kosovo on the Yugoslav presidency. In the eyes of members of Milošević's elite, their "nation" was not the Serb nation but consisted of the Yugoslav state, the ruling parties (SPS and JUL), and all Milošević's servants in all branches of society and the economy.

Milošević's wife, Mirjana Marković, played an absolutely central role both in politics and in the economy; after her husband, she was the most powerful individual in the FRY. She was the principal force behind the founding of a new left-wing party, the JUL, an absolutely elitist organi-zation in terms of its membership and structure. It was possible to join the JUL only through personal connections with figures at the head of the party. From its foundation in 1994, the JUL gradually took control over important financial operations in the country and had an immense influence on government and the state, including on the police and State Security Service. Marković's personal influence was enormous, and she was able to bring about the dismissal of those members of the regime whom she disliked, such as the powerful chief of the State Security Ser-vice Jovica Stanišić and the Yugoslav army chief of staff Momčilo Perišić. The JUL slowly and systematically squeezed out the SPS and took con-trol of all levels of power. That caused considerable discontent among the SPS elite and occasionally internal showdowns within the circles of power. Hidden conflicts between the two ruling parties—the SPS and the JUL—ended in murders and only in rare instances in arrests. Though the two parties were coalition partners, there was a permanent suppressed rivalry between them for control over the state and economy.

The JUL secretary general Zoran Todorović "Kundak" was assassinated on 24 October 1997 by a professional assassin. He was killed in a public place, in front of Beopetrol, of which he was the manager at the time. Several months before Todorović was killed, on 10 April, unknown gunmen assassinated the deputy interior minister of Serbia, Radovan Stojičić "Badža," a former Milošević loyalist. Vlada Kovačević "Tref," owner of an export-import company and a business associate of Milošević's son Marko, was killed on 20 February. All three assassinations happened in public places and were the work of professional assassins who disappeared without a trace. The fact that none of them were ever caught clearly indicates that those who contracted the liquidations must have been powerful enough to have prevented the investigations from succeeding. There were two theories concerning the Todorović assassination. According to the first, it had exclusively to do with "business interests," but according to the second, Todorović had started to make political difficulties for the circles gathered around Milošević and his interference could not be eliminated in any other way than through his murder.

Obviously money, politics, and crime were closely connected in the period of extreme social, political, and economic turmoil that marked Milošević's rule. Politicians and businessmen were deeply involved in illegal deals and with organized crime. The assassinations served as a true indicator that the struggle over power was not being waged in the parliament and in so-called public institutions but behind the scenes, among the power centers of which the public was hardly aware. Todorović was in charge of strengthening the economic basis of the JUL. He succeeded in taking over Beopetrol, the second largest oil firm in the country. The independent press in Serbia (the daily *Naša borba*) claimed that there was a plan according to which Todorović was to squeeze out the senior SPS official Dragan Tomić and concentrate in his hands all the most profitable and monopolistic oil contracts.

Todorović was considered an extremely ruthless man, and there were many of those who would have been more than glad to see him eliminated. During the war in the former Yugoslavia and at a time when the international sanctions against the FRY were still in effect, Todorović was one of the key persons in ATL, which used to carry out major domestic and foreign financial transactions on behalf of the state. Subsequently he left ATL and founded the T&M Trade Company. Shortly afterward, the ATL manager for Yugoslavia Siniša Djukić committed suicide, followed by the company's general manager Milenko Isakov. Todorović had been successful in combining his political and business ambitions. He was one of the shareholders of the protection agency Komet, whose seat was in the former premises of the Central Committee of the League of Communists of Yugoslavia. Owing to good political connections, Todorović managed to get a loan on very favorable terms to purchase a huge bankrupt farm in Voj-vodina at an extremely low price. At the same time, his T&M Trade Com-pany purchased lots and buildings in the prestigious Belgrade suburb of Dedinje. Todorović was killed at a time when his protector, Mira Marković, was on an official trip to India. Unofficial sources claim that Marković's trip was paid for by an Indian pharmaceutical dealer, Ramgobal, who was a Belgrade representative of the Madras-based company Hardgate In-vestment. The assassination may have been linked to quarrels within the elite related to these business activities on the part of the JUL leadership.

In the late 1990s, Nenad Djordjević, another high-ranking JUL official, left the political scene. Djordjević spent eight years working in the State Security Service of the former Yugoslavia in the counterintelligence sec-tor. He subsequently became a professor at the Serbian police college and remained there for seventeen years. He was dismissed from the post of director of the Serbian Health Insurance Fund, but the reasons for the dismissal were not disclosed. At that time Beta News Agency's sources claimed that Djordjević had opposed the import of pharmaceuticals from India, arousing the anger of Mira Marković and the Serbian health minis-ter, Leposava Miličević, who were "sponsors" of the import deal. The dis-missal was a clear sign of Djordjević's pending downfall.

Djordjević was considered to be one of the wealthiest persons in the FRY during the 1990s, but he became a successful businessman solely due to his connections with the Milošević elite. In 1992, he established ties with the Komet company (Todorović was one of the shareholders), which was financed by the Alliance of the League of Communists/Movement for Yu-goslavia, the precursor to the JUL. Djordjević was one of the most promi-nent activists of this party, which took over all the assets of the former communist organization of the Yugoslav People's Army. Subsequently, Djordjević became the owner of the company Belgrade Trade Center (BTC). This company was founded with capital Djordjević had obtained by selling a ship that had belonged to the late president Tito. Thanks to his connections with the elite, the ship was proclaimed "private property." Djordjević proceeded with his successful business activities and soon opened a series of stores, ice cream parlors, and bakeries, built office build-ings in Belgrade, and eventually established a company in Cyprus. Djord-jević became so rich that he bought the island of St. Nikola in the Adri-atic Sea near the Montenegrin coast. The first official announcement of Djordjević's arrest said that he was apprehended as a suspect in the em-bezzlement of the Health Insurance Fund and that he had accrued legal charges of over US$10 million. The Belgrade daily *Večernje novosti* stressed in its reports that Djordjević was one of the founders of the J U L and listed his business deals made on behalf of the party. The paper published a photograph of the impressive J U L building in the center of Belgrade, noting that it was Djordjević's "gift to the J U L." The previous owner of the building was Genex Systems. Djordjević's arrest came as a surprise only to the wider public. The J U L leadership had obviously quickly grasped what was going on and the party members simply abandoned their benefactor and comrade. Political observers pointed out that Djordjević was arrested only a day after Serbian president Milan Milutinović appointed Mirko Marjanović as the new Serbian prime minister designate. Well-informed circles commented that the J U L was opposed to Marjanović's appointment and that the latter was made only with Milošević's assistance.

Thus, members of the regime considered "disobedient" or whose activities angered other, more powerful factions within the same regime were purged. Economic politics were governed above all by this struggle between rival factions for exploitation of the country's economic assets. All these factions were ultimately headed by Milošević and Marković, for whose favor they competed and who periodically took action against those who displeased them. This mafia-like struggle inevitably had a deleterious effect on the economy and only compounded the problems caused by war, sanctions, inflation, an antiquated communist economic system, and general mismanagement. In this period, Yugoslav exports were 7.5 times lower than Hungarian exports and 11 times lower than Czech exports. The unemployment rate in Yugoslavia was 2.5 times higher than in the Czech Republic. The corruption index in Yugoslavia stood at 7.4, with a possible maximum of 9. The same index for Albania was 5.7, for Macedonia 5.4, for Croatia 4, for Hungary 1.2, and for Slovenia 0.7.[13]

With the consolidation of Milošević's hold on power, the dissolution of the Yugoslav federation, and the start of the wars, conditions were created in which many native organized criminals, who had until then based their activities primarily in Western Europe, could now relocate back home to Serbia. The start of the wars represented for them a "golden age." On the one hand, the regime needed such gangsters, who were ready to do whatever was required of them and who were ready to perform the dirtiest jobs that the Yugoslav military was unwilling to do. On the other, Milošević's media and propaganda machine created the myth of the warrior-heroes and linked it to these figures, trumpeted as hard young men and fierce patriots. The true picture gradually emerged into public view thanks to a series of murders that took place among the leading ranks of this section of the "elite." Almost all those murdered had been definitely linked to the secret police before the war, and all had become extremely wealthy as a result of their subsequent activities. Yet as soon as they showed an inclination toward independent action or came into conflict with anyone from Milošević's immediate circle, for example with Milošević's son Marko, who at this time took control over the narcotics trade in Serbia, they would be eliminated.

One of the figures who characterized the 1990s in Serbia was Željko Ražnatović "Arkan." At the time of his assassination, he was the most powerful and the most influential underground chief in Serbia, on whose services both the Serbian and the Yugoslav authorities had relied. Ražnatović began his career as a local criminal while he was still a teenager in Belgrade. In the 1970s and 1980s, he was several times arrested, in Sweden, Belgium, and the Netherlands, for his involvement in bank robberies, but he managed to escape from prison twice. He made no secret of his ties either with the former Yugoslav state security or with its successor, the State Security Service in Serbia. His ascent from an ordinary robber and killer to a great and uncontested mafia boss was closely linked with the military operations Belgrade conducted in Bosnia and Croatia. Skillful enough to use the fact that authorities needed him and unscrupulous enough to eliminate anyone in his way, Ražnatović managed to build a whole empire over the years in which enormous sums of money circulated. Ražnatović's biography was interwoven with numerous links with the Italian mafia, business and political connections he built and consolidated over the years. At the beginning of the war in Croatia, as the leader of the fans of the Red Star football club, he recruited young people and formed the paramilitary Serb Volunteer Guard, whose members were known as the Tigers. Arkan's Tigers most often acted as the advance party to the VJ (Army of Yugoslavia) in the war zones in Croatia and Bosnia. His military success mainly consisted of "clearing the ground before army attacks." Arkan knew how to charge for his services. He organized a well-developed network of people in the "liberated territories," where they were in charge of transporting stolen cars and goods to Serbia.

Different underworld sources, as well as those close to the authorities, claim that the immediate reason for the assassination of Ražnatović on 15 January 2000 was his decision to take control of the import of oil and oil products in Yugoslavia. This upset leaders of the state-owned oil companies of Jugopetrol and Beopetrol. In his bid to take control of the oil market, Arkan appears to have caused particular annoyance to the JUL, which allegedly exerted significant influence on the profitable trade in oil and gasoline.

The long series of spectacular assassinations of prominent members of the elite included among its victims Miroslav Bižić "Biža," a JUL supporter, criminal, and former police chief, on 21 May 1996; Yugoslav defense minister Pavle Bulatović on 8 February 2000; Žika Petrović, director general of the JAT (Yugoslav Air Transport) airline and a JUL member and close friend of the Milošević family, on 25 April 2000; and Boško Perošević, president of the Executive Council of Vojvodina and chairman of the Novi Sad Committee of the SPS, on 13 May 2000. Theories on the reasons for Petrović's murder include that he knew too much about the regime's money-laundering operations, in which the JAT was heavily implicated. According to another theory, he was murdered for favoring the privatization of the JAT.[14] Several of those murdered, like Ražnatović and Stojičić, had been closely involved in organizing Serb paramilitary groups in Croatia and Bosnia or in organizing the "war economy."

The Vojvodinan gangster Branislav Lainović "Dugi" was murdered on 20 March 2000. Nenad Čanak, the leader of the League of Vojvodina Social Democrats, a party that Lainović is believed to have occasionally financed, assessed that "the regime is liquidating people who had any ties to the war operations in Croatia and Bosnia, people who could give inopportune testimony regarding the events at the time." Lainović became known at the beginning of 1991 when he established the paramilitary group "Serbian Guard" together with Djordje Božović "Giška" and Branislav Matić "Beli." The Serbian Guard was connected with the SPO (Serbian Renewal Movement), and that was the main reason it was disbanded in 1992. Both Božović and Matić were subsequently killed by professional assassins. After 1992, Lainović devoted himself to business and in a short time had built up an empire worth several dozen million marks. He was the owner of the Paradiso Club in Novi Sad, which with 1,400 square meters of floor space, is believed to be the largest in the Balkans. He also owned several large houses, a number of apartments and business premises, about forty shops and a dozen kiosks, an Adidas sports equipment retail outlet, and two smaller hotels in Spain and the Netherlands. In the mid-1990s, he began publicly to advocate the autonomy of Vojvodina and to support regionally oriented parties. At the end of 1999, Lainović gave several political statements calling on "anyone with any sentiments for Vojvodina and Serbia to join the struggle against the authorities," but also pointed the finger at corruption and treason within the opposition ranks, stating that "those opposition people enabled the regime to remain in power the entire time." However, Jezdimir Vasiljević accused Lainović in 1993, after the collapse of his bank and flight abroad, of organizing the kidnapping of his (Vasiljević's) family in Italy, something that was never proven. The Swiss-based *Wochenzeitung* at one time claimed that Lainović was mixed up in selling arms to the Bosnian Serbs and that Radovan Karadžić had made a great deal of money from the dealings. He was killed at the moment when he was making final preparations to start a local newspaper and radio and television stations, a few months after the Ražnatović assassination.

The way in which Milošević's economic elite wrecked the Serbian economy is best illustrated by the case of the Genex firm. "Genex was the first casualty in the economic policy of those who led this country to collapse and moral destruction," observed Milorad Savičević, the director of Genex in the firm's heyday. Genex was founded in 1952, but its heyday was during the 1980s under Savičević. The strength of the firm was such that foreign countries preferred to take guarantees from Genex rather than from the National Bank of Yugoslavia. In 1989, Genex accounted for 13 percent of Yugoslavia's entire economy and 27 percent of Serbia's; its annual turnover was US$6 billion, and it employed over 6,500 workers in sixty subsidiary companies. Genex had subsidiaries in all continents, of which the most successful were Centroprodukt in Milan and Paris, Kombik in Frankfurt, BSE in London, and IMPEX in New York, though its office in the Soviet Union had the greatest economic impact of all. In Yugoslavia itself the most profitable subsidiary was Yugotours, which up to the early 1990s brought 800,000 foreign tourists to Yugoslavia annually. Genex's airline Aviogenex carried 600,000 travelers annually. The most prestigious hotels on the territory of the SFRY, the Intercontinental apartments on Kopaonik, were part of the Genex chain. The managers of Genex were the first to succeed in what in other East European countries had been impossible: the opening of McDonald's and Deli France restaurants in their capital city. The Belgrade branches of the McDonald's chain earned more than the European and American averages.[15]

The transfer of Genex to the patronage of Milošević's regime quickly brought about its collapse. At the start of the 1990s, Andrija Dozet, someone who had never been a business manager of note but who was a member of the JUL, was placed at the head of Genex. After ten years, there was practically nothing left of Genex. Yugotours was sold to the Greek company Spiros Hambas for only a quarter of a million deutschmarks. At the time of the sale, a Swiss firm had offered 2 million DM for Yugotours, but this offer was rejected in favor of Spiros Hambas on account of the latter's close links with the SPS.[16] The McDonald's branches were likewise sold at well below their true market value. Milorad Savičević, who had already lost his post as director of Genex, commented that the sale of these restaurants was "an insane action devoid of any healthy logic or reason, which perhaps Director Dozet is carrying out deliberately, because it is otherwise difficult to believe that anyone would kill the hen that lays the golden egg."[17] The Aviogenex airplanes were also sold. The plunder of this firm went so far that the above-mentioned Nenad Djordjević was able to acquire from Genex and at no cost to himself an elite villa in the center of Belgrade in order that he might give it as a present to the leadership of the JUL. During the various transfers of money that this plunder involved, US$20 million "disappeared" in transit between London and the Bahamas.

A decisive role in the destruction of Genex was played by Dozet, its director general until 1997 and a member of the JUL. His position was then assumed by Danilo Todorović, who took the decision to "liquidate" Genex's subsidiary, the firm Centroprodukt in Milan and Paris, despite its sound financial condition. While Borislav Vučković was a member of the Executive Council of Genex—as well as being a member of the directorship of the JUL and federal minister for foreign trade—US$100 million "disappeared" from Kombik's account in Frankfurt. The massive "disappearance" of money may be partly explained through the presence in the Administrative Council of Genex of Borka Vučić, Milošević's close ally, who at all times controlled the flow of currency between foreign accounts both during and after the period of sanctions. Zoran Andjelković was also one of the general directors of Genex, as was Radoman Božović, who earned in the process the nickname "Robberman."[18] Thanks to their "successful" management, Serbia's once-richest firm had action taken against it by the Belgrade Court of Commerce in 1998, at the request of the Yugoslav National Bank, because its account had been blocked for longer than sixty days and because of its debts of 18 million DM.

In the opinion of many analysts, the replacement of Milorad Savičević as general director marked a definite turning point. Until 1990, Genex epitomized the highly successful Yugoslav firm for which everyone wanted to work. One of the greatest assets of this firm lay in its huge concentration of skilled cadres. More than two hundred managers worked in the Genex offices across the world, from Europe, through China, India, the Near East, America, and North Africa. Genex's internal organization was far superior to the regional average. By the end of the 1980s, Genex held sixteenth place among the top six hundred firms in the developing countries. The value of Genex lay above all in its modern spirit of management and business ethos, which were fully equivalent to those of private companies in the West. The Milošević regime naturally wished to impose its control on a firm of this caliber. The first step was the direct demand on the part of Milošević that Savičević appoint as his deputy Zoran Todorović. Savičević at first refused but was quickly forced to accept. He quickly came into conflict with his new deputy and, after the latter had behaved rudely and aggressively toward him at their first meeting, threw him out of his office. Several days later, Milošević personally informed Savičević, in the presence of Dušan Mitević, the director of Radio-Television Serbia, and Živorad Mišović, the director of the Politika media company, that Savičević's career at Genex was over.[19] In attempting to explain his conflict with Milošević, Savičević noted that this was not only a conflict between individuals but between fundamental economic and political concepts. Savičević represented the principle of the open economy, while Milošević endeavored to take control over all branches of the economy so as to harness them to his political goals.

Following Savičević's departure, the most competent people left the firm to establish their own companies, which gradually took over the business and markets of Genex. The most prominent example of this was Delta, the firm of Miroslav Mišković, a former Serbian government minister who successfully copied the internal organization of Genex and its system of management. The departure of Savičević from the head of Genex coincided with another occurrence of crucial importance for the fate of this firm, the collapse of the Soviet Union. A large part of Genex's success was due to the fact that the Soviet Union traded with the world on the basis of barter and every year drew up lists of goods such as oil, gas, and ores which it offered in exchange for other commodities. Genex located the requested goods both in Yugoslavia and on the world market and was paid in goods that could be sold anywhere in the world for hard currency. Owing to the chaos which occurred following Savičević's departure, Genex was wholly unprepared for the changes in the market brought about by the collapse of the former Soviet Union. Its fate was sealed by the policies of the Milošević regime and the sanctions that, in fact, affected only some firms and not others. While Genex gradually died, losing market after market, the firm Progres, under Mirko Marjanović, took over its former business in Russia, thanks to the monopoly given him by Milošević.

The incompetence and irresponsibility of the management of Genex under Milošević do not in themselves explain the "Titanic-style" policies that they pursued. The role that Milošević imposed on practically all the big firms in Serbia meant that they had to accept unequivocally his diktat and include his people in their management, otherwise they would be gradually squeezed to death. In the majority of cases, the story would end with

Milošević's people taking control of firms that had already been thoroughly plundered and brought to the verge of complete collapse. Their assets were then sold at minimal prices and their directors, having embezzled all they could, would then blame the catastrophe on the war and sanctions.

Another major Serbian firm to be sacrificed to the interests of Milošević's regime was Telecom Serbia. This was the first large Serbian firm to be privatized in 1997. The principal reason for its sale to foreign companies was the extremely unfavorable political situation in which Milošević found himself at the time. In the second round of the local elections held on 17 November 1996, a coalition of opposition parties called "Zajedno" managed to win a majority in fourteen out of the fifteen largest cities in Serbia, including Belgrade. The authorities overturned the election results, sparking protests in Belgrade, Niš, Novi Sad, and other cities. These protests spread throughout Serbia and lasted for more than three months. Zajedno gradually broke up in the months that followed, failing as its leaders did to reach an agreement on joint participation in the presidential and parliamentary elections in Serbia to be held in September 1997. The Democratic Party and the Civic Alliance of Serbia believed that the electoral conditions were unfair and refused to participate, as did most other opposition parties, but the SPO agreed to take part nonetheless. The opposition accused the SPO of giving undue credibility to the elections by its participation and of therefore having "sold itself" to the regime. Fearing for his political survival, Milošević decided to arrange an injection of foreign capital into the country. Following extensive negotiations with possible buyers, in which an important role was played by Douglas Hurd, Pauline Neville-Jones, and Lamberto Dini, an agreement was reached in July 1996 for the sale of Telecom for about 1.5 billion DM. Italy's Telecom Italia was to purchase a 29 percent share and Greece's OTE a 20 percent share in Telecom Serbia. The buyers paid the money into an account in a Cypriot bank, while for its part NatWest Markets received a commission of 30 million DM from the Italian and Greek buyers. The sales contract itself remained a strict state secret for the rest of Milošević's term in office. Not even the ministers of telecommunications were allowed to see it.

Very little of the proceeds of the sale of this firm, which employed about twelve thousand, found its way into the firm's own account. According to Telecom, the money ended up distributed among private bank accounts all over the world. The transfer of the money from Cyprus was organized primarily by Borka Vučić. In the opinion of some analysts and according to documents published subsequently by the media, at least part of the money was used to buy "civic peace" in Serbia, in other words to pay pensions directly before the elections of 1997, as well as to buy weapons for covert use in Kosovo. However, the fate of the largest proportion of the money remains unknown; 78 million DM paid by the foreign purchasers simply "disappeared." Italy's Commission of Forty, formed by Prime Minister Berlusconi to investigate the Telecom Serbia scandal and composed of twenty senators and twenty judges, demonstrated that the Italian side paid significantly more for Telecom Serbia than its true value. The money raised from the sale enabled Milošević to survive another three years in power.[20]

Following the fall of the Milošević regime, the new government endeavored to introduce rules for economic management that had been wholly disregarded during the previous decade. At a conference on British investment in the FRY held 10–11 May 2001 in London, Minister for Privatization Aleksandar Vlahović stated that on the subject of the further privatization of Serbia's telecommunications, there would be no direct negotiations with any company. Only when the legal and proprietorial questions left open since the Milošević period had been resolved, in other words when the true structure of ownership and the fate of state capital had been determined would the Serbian government tender the privatization of the state's share of the telephone network. British Vodaphone was very welcome to apply, as were all interested firms, but the sale would be made to the highest bidder on the basis of a fair auction. Djindjić thus hoped to avoid any one firm monopolizing the buying process and dictating its terms, as had been the case with the sale of Telecom Serbia. The strong business connections that existed between Milošević's regime and certain British companies were reason enough for Djindjić to tread carefully in his own dealings with the latter and to insist on the principle that the final deal would not be made on the basis of personal connections.

As the Milošević regime neared its collapse, Leposava Miličević, the JUL parliamentary representative and former minister of health, attempted in parliament to blame its economic failures on external causes, claiming that "this country has already lived for ten years with an economy in chains [from sanctions]. . . . Perhaps Europe doesn't know this and perhaps most of the world doesn't know this."[21] Miličević, a close friend and collaborator of Mira Marković's, was herself an active participant in the regime's state-sanctioned robbery. As minister of health, she engineered in February 1999 the illegal nationalization of the Zemun drug factory ICN Yugoslavia (Galenika)—the FRY's largest drug manufacturer—in which the U.S. company ICN Pharmaceuticals had owned a majority stake, by transferring majority ownership of the Zemun drug factory to the regime-controlled Galenika Holding Company. In this way, the regime simply expropriated property belonging to a foreign company. To do this, Živorad Tešić, acting director of the Board for Evaluation of Capital, on behalf of the Ministry for Privatization, justified his decision on the basis of a law that was no longer valid but backdated the board's decision by three months, to November 1998, when the law was apparently still valid. The change in ownership was forcibly carried out by the illegal nomination of Deputy Health Minister Marija Krstajić as the new director of ICN Yugoslavia, who arrived at the factory escorted by armed police officers. Milan Panić, president of the management board of ICN Pharmaceuticals, commented: "The attempt of the government of Serbia to forcibly take over ownership and control of ICN Yugoslavia is utterly illegal. This is violence which has nothing to do with law. The decision on possible change of ownership relations can be reached only by international arbitration in Paris, and not by the authorities of the Serbian state."[22] Miličević was one of the former ministers against whom Minister of Finance Djelić announced criminal charges in November 2001.

Part II: Crime and the Economy in Serbia after Milošević
(Marko Attila Hoare)

Following the change of regime in October 2000, the new government reversed the economic policies of the Milošević era, adopting a program of economic reform and seeking to integrate the Serbian economy with the European Union. Within two years, trade and prices were liberalized, new fiscal and monetary policies had substantially reduced inflationary pressure, the exchange rate was stabilized, foreign currency reserves accumulated, transparency in budgetary matters improved, relations with international creditors largely normalized, banking sector reform strongly advanced—with the four largest banks (Beogradska Banka, Beobanka, Investbanka, and Jugobanka) closed as insolvent—and foreign investment began to be welcomed. Comprehensive privatization legislation was passed: in July 2001 a new law permitted state enterprises to be sold off without prior restructuring, through a tendering and auction process. The FRY rejoined the International Monetary Fund in December 2000, followed by the World Bank and the European Bank for Reconstruction and Development. In November 2001, an international agreement rescheduled the FRY's US$4.5 billion Paris Club government debts, writing off two-thirds of the latter. Both the European Union and the United States lifted economic sanctions and provided small quantities of aid. The economy grew by about 6 percent per year during 2000 and 2001. Symbolic of the progress made in economic reform is the fact that Jovan Ranković, Yugoslav finance minister and a member of Koštunica's antireformist Democratic Party of Serbia, resigned in January 2002 in protest at the bank closures.[23]

Structural weaknesses have nevertheless remained: a fragile budget, strained by the costs of enterprise restructuring and maintenance of a social safety net; high taxation discouraging entrepreneurship; an overblown state bureaucracy; heavy foreign debt; weak domestic industry; and an increasing rate of imports combined with continuing weak exports. Wages and household imports have grown but have been more than counterbalanced by a rise in prices of food, consumer goods, and utilities.[24] By mid-2001, inflation was still running at 40 percent annually.[25] In November 2001, a year after Milošević's fall, the Federal Republic of Yugoslavia's foreign debt stood at US$11.4 billion—equal to 140 percent of GDP—Serbia's domestic GDP was 60 percent of its 1991 level, and average wages were a mere US$40 per month.[26] This amounts in part to a hangover from the losses sustained during the Milošević era. Governor of the Yugoslav National Bank Mladjan Dinkić estimated that Milošević's circle during its reign took altogether over US$10 billion out of the country, a loss of astronomical proportions that will take a long time to recover. Furthermore, the change of regime in October 2000 does not appear to have lessened the emigratory pressures. An opinion poll commissioned by the Organization for Security and Cooperation in Europe in November 2002 revealed that 30 percent of the Serbian population would consider emigrating, while more than 50 percent of young people positively wanted to do so.[27]

In such circumstances, Serbia's economic recovery was and remains dependent upon Western assistance. Yet such assistance has come with strings attached, the most significant of which has been the Western insistence that Serbia cooperate with the International Criminal Tribunal for the former Yugoslavia (ICTY).[28] In this way the interlinking of the war and economic ruin under Milošević was posed most starkly: the same clique of individuals, from the overlapping political and criminal elites, was responsible both for the waging of war and the atrocities involved and for the plunder of Serbia. Yet these individuals were very often the ones whose abandonment of Milošević in the autumn of 2000 had made possible the bloodless October revolution, and the regime of President Vojislav Koštunica, who, as heir to the nationalist mantle, remained dependent upon their support. Franko Simatović, former chief of the Special Operations Units (JSO—Jedinice za specijalne operacije, or "Red Berets"), Aco Tomić, chief

of the Yugoslav army Security Department, Nebojša Pavković, chief of staff
of the Yugoslav army, and others were deeply implicated in the crimes of
the Milošević era, yet became pillars of the fledgling Koštunica regime. In
this way the battle was opened between the reformist wing of the post-
Milošević elite under Djindjić and the technocrats of "Group 17+," which
sought friendly relations with the West, and the nationalist wing under
Koštunica, which aimed to continue to pursue Milošević's goals by other
means.

Initially, the reformists proceeded cautiously and were generally unwilling to purge the Serbian state of Milošević's former followers, who were
treated with excessive leniency. This was highlighted shortly after midnight
on 15 October 2000 when Borka Vučić, general manager of the Belgrade
Bank until two days previously, broke into the bank's premises with the
aid of an armed retinue, overpowered the security guards, and stole a collection of sensitive documents. Through the Belgrade Bank, Vučić had
allegedly controlled two-thirds of the FRY's financial markets, while the
remaining third was controlled by other agents of Milošević through other
banks. In the view of Milko Štimac, a leading Serbian economist, the Yugoslav National Bank was "turned into a passive administrator of the national
oligarchy."[29] As Milošević's top banking official, Vučić masterminded the
transfer of vast sums of money out of Serbia via Cyprus to private bank
accounts, in various foreign countries. These accounts were controlled by
Milošević and his circle.[30] Following her act of bank robbery, she was nevertheless reemployed as a financial consultant by the post-Milošević government in an effort to restore order into the state finances.

One official who was removed, though only belatedly, was Radomir
Marković, chief of state security under Milošević, who remained in his
post until January 2001 before being arrested in February and eventually
sentenced to seven years in prison for the attempted assassination of opposition leader Vuk Drašković of the Serbian Renewal Movement and the
killing of four other members of his party on 3 October 1999. While still
serving the new government, Marković took advantage of its inexperience
and of the widespread confusion to systematically destroy incriminating
State Security Service documents in archives throughout Serbia. Furthermore, he appears to have been involved in manufacturing two serious
crises that engulfed Serbia immediately following the revolution: the wave
of prison revolts that broke out across the country in November 2000 and
the Albanian uprising in south Serbia in the same month. Both revolts
served to increase the regime's dependency on the State Security Service.[31]
Meanwhile, even as notorious an embezzler as Jezdimir Vasiljević, once

infamous as "Jezda the Boss" of the Jugoskandik pyramid bank scandal, was treated with kid gloves. Vasiljević, widely hated as the man guilty of robbing the Serbian citizenry of their meager savings during the 1990s, was arrested in February 2001 but released on bail six months later by the Okrug Court of Belgrade so that he could "defend himself from a position of freedom." Dinkić, one of the few members of the present establishment genuinely concerned with bringing the financial criminals to justice, commented bitterly on Vasiljević's release, saying that "until we have strict and adequate punishments for criminal acts there will be nothing of reform in this sector," pointing out that in behaving in this manner, the judicial organs were casting doubt on the ability of the new government either to punish the profiteers or to reform the economy. Milošević himself was arrested only on 1 April 2001, six months after the revolution.

The failure of the Koštunica-Djindjić regime to punish high-ranking economic criminals was not through want of suspects. Minister of Finance Božidar Djelić in November 2001 finally announced thirty-four criminal charges for abuse of office and illegal use of money from the Republican budget against a group of Milošević's former ministers.[32] Ten former ministers alone are said to have embezzled 315,384,506 dinars (10.5 million euros). The first on the list of successful embezzlers was Jovan Pejić, a former director of the Pension and Invalids Fund. While Serbia's pensioners fought with stray cats over rubbish bins for scraps of food or committed suicide out of desperation, Pejić succeeded in embezzling 4.23 million euros. Second on this list was Borislav Miličić, a former minister of finance, who embezzled 2.38 million euros. Others included Jovan Babović, the former minister of the economy, who embezzled 1.128 million euros, Zoran Andjelković, who embezzled 340,000 euros, and Tomislav Milenković, a former minister of labor, who embezzled 243,000 euros. The list includes many others.[33]

Moreover, these figures, as well as the individuals cited, represent only the tip of the iceberg. Djelić issued the criminal charges only on the basis of the documents that he had succeeded in finding from the moment when he took over the Ministry of Finance. The true extent of the corruption is many times worse. Yet, given the systematic destruction of documents by the State Security Service and other branches of the state apparatus, the new government was faced on the one hand with enormous public pressure for the prosecution of those who plundered the country under Milošević and on the other, a general absence of incriminating evidence. At the end of May 2002, all of those among Milošević's circle who were responsible for the legal and financial chaos arising from the sale of Telecom Serbia in 1997 were finally brought before the courts. They appeared only as witnesses in their own respective cases and not as witnesses against one another. Bribery and corruption were the principal issues for which former Serbia Telecom director Milorad Jakšić was called to account, as were also former director of the Serbian post-office network Aleksa Jokić, former Serbian minister for privatization Milan Beko, former head of the Belgrade Bank Borka Vučić, former deputy prime minister Nikola Šainović, the sitting president of Serbia Milan Milutinović, and the former foreign minister Vladislav Jovanović.

The fall of Milošević on 6 October 2000 did not end the series of assassinations among members of the Serbian criminal-political elite, who continued in a bloody fashion to settle old scores and to silence witnesses to their former activities. Vladimir Bokan, a Serb multimillionaire with Greek citizenship and based in Greece, had earned his riches by smuggling in violation of the embargo on the FRY. Bokan was involved in fuel and arms smuggling on behalf of Milošević with the complicity of the Greek Mitsotakis government, and his own bank accounts in Greece and other countries were regularly used by Milošević. Bokan reinvested his huge wealth in Serbia, and his assets included chains of kiosks and clothing stores in Belgrade and Vojvodina as well as a real-estate company and a shipyard on the Danube. He was assassinated on 7 October, the day after Milošević's fall, possibly with the complicity of the Greek authorities.[34] On 6 February 2001, Zoran Sokolović, former Yugoslav interior minister under Milošević, was found dead in his car at his native village of Knjazevac in eastern Serbia. Although the police attributed Sokolović's death to suicide, his mother and others cast doubt on this interpretation.[35] Klara Mandić, president of the Serbian-Jewish Friendship Society, was murdered on 10 May 2001. Mandić had been a close ally of Milošević and his intermediary in dealings with semilegal business enterprises on whose support he drew. She had also been engaged in propaganda activities in Serb-controlled Bosnia and was a close associate of both Ražnatović "Arkan" and Radovan Karadžić.[36]

A turning point in the struggle to break the stranglehold of officials of the old regime over the new appeared to have been reached when Milošević was deported to The Hague on 28 June 2001 in a move engineered by Djindjić. Milošević's deportation was expected to enable Serbia to qualify for an expected US$1.28 billion promised by Western nations at the subsequent international donors' conference in Belgium.[37] The deportation immediately provoked the resignation of Yugoslav prime minister Zoran Žižić of the formerly pro-Milošević Socialist People's Party. Yet although the deportation netted a pledge of the expected US$1.28 billion, these funds were only provided gradually, at a rate insufficient to complete the planned economic transition to a free-market economy.[38] This was followed belatedly the following April by the surrender to the ICTY of former Yugoslav deputy prime minister Nikola Šainović and former Yugoslav chief of staff Dragoljub Ojdanić, both indicted for war crimes in Kosovo, while a third indictee, former interior minister Vlajko Stojiljković, committed suicide to avoid deportation. Mile Mrkšić, a Yugoslav general indicted for war crimes at Vukovar, surrendered to the ICTY in May 2002.

Yet, in this period representatives of the ancien régime struck back repeatedly. On 9 April 2001, the businessman Miroslav Mišković, owner of Delta Holdings, was kidnapped and released only after a ransom of 7 million DM was paid. Part of the ransom money went to finance the fugitive Radovan Karadžić's personal security. Several individuals arrested in connection with the kidnapping, who nevertheless succeeded in avoiding justice on this occasion, were subsequently involved in the Djindjić assassination. These included Dušan Spasojević and Mileta Luković.[39] On 3 August 2001, Momir Gavrilović, a high-ranking official of the State Security Service, was assassinated after he approached Koštunica with documents concerning the relations of members of the government to organized crime.[40] In November 2001, members of the JSO staged a successful revolt in protest at the government's cooperation with the ICTY. The revolt, which Koštunica himself described as "justified," brought about the dismissal of the reformist State Security chief Goran Petrović and his deputy Zoran Mijatović.[41] On 10 June 2002, Major-General Boško Buha, deputy chief of the Public Security Department of the Serbian Interior Ministry, was assassinated in Zemun; on 27 October of that year, two people, one of them a member of the JSO, were arrested in connection with the murder.[42]

Cooperation with the ICTY, slow and reluctant though it was, went hand in hand with continued economic reforms. In July 2002, Serbia left the euro zone, in an effort to compel citizens to do business exclusively in the national currency, thereby stabilizing the latter and making money-laundering operations more difficult. Taxes were liberalized to encourage further investment.[43] The Serbian economy grew by about 3.5–4 percent during 2002, and its foreign trade reached nearly US$5 billion, with growth in exports estimated at 20.6 percent. Foreign investment reached US$550 million in 2002.[44] By the end of December, Djindjić had emerged victorious in his power struggle with Koštunica after the latter had failed to win Serbia's presidential election. Nataša Mićić, a member of the Civic

Alliance and president of the Serbian parliament, acceded to the Serbian presidency by default, so that for the first time since the October revolution, the Serbian head of state as well as the prime minister was a reformist. In January 2003, the Serbian minister of privatization Aleksandar Vlahović announced that 1,200 smaller and medium enterprises, amounting to 60 percent of Serbia's economy, were to be privatized by September. At the same time, Bell Corporation, the world's leading beverage can producer, announced that it would open a 75 million euro plant in the Zemun municipality of Belgrade that would create 300 new jobs and produce 600 million cans, 80 percent of which would be exported.[45] In February 2003, on the basis of an agreement reached in March of the previous year, the FRY became the Union of Serbia and Montenegro, belatedly consigning the discredited Yugoslav name to the dustbin of history. It was in this context that Djindjić was assassinated, as a last, desperate attempt by remnants of the Milošević regime to derail the reform process and cooperation with the ICTY.

Operation Saber, already discussed by Vjeran Pavlaković in chapter 2 in this volume, has had a similarly ambiguous legacy so far as economic reform and the fight against organized crime are concerned. Engineered by Acting President Nataša Mićić, Interior Minister Dušan Vasiljević, Deputy Interior Minister Nenad Milić, Justice Minister Vladan Batić, and Deputy Prime Minister Nebojša Čović, it was the reformist regime's counterstroke to the Djindjić assassination. An assault upon organized crime and former Milošević henchmen within the state apparatus, it involved a declaration of a state of emergency and the arrest of over 10,000 people, of whom at least 4,000 were detained. The operation brought about a more profound upheaval within the ranks of the Serbian elite than the overthrow of the dictator a year and a half before. The principal thrust of Operation Saber was against the "Zemun clan" of the Belgrade state-sponsored mafia, which had instigated the assassination and which had been deeply involved in Milošević's crimes against his domestic opponents, as well as in war crimes. The Zemun clan's chief, Milorad Ulemek Luković "Legija," was the former chief of the JSO. The JSO had been involved in military operations in Croatia and Bosnia-Herzegovina during the war of 1991–95 and in organizing and training Serb paramilitary forces there. These included the Tigers of Željko Ražnatović "Arkan," the most powerful state-sponsored gangster, who was himself assassinated on 15 January 2000. The JSO was subsequently involved in atrocities against Albanians in Kosovo in 1998–99 and in hiding Albanian corpses. They were also behind the attempted assassination of Drašković. Djindjić's assassin, Zvezdan Jovanović, was himself a member of the JSO and a former Milošević bodyguard. Yet the JSO became a pillar of the Koštunica regime and was, under Luković "Legija's" leadership, involved in the arrest of Milošević on 1 April 2001. Nevertheless, with Operation Saber the JSO was belatedly disbanded and its former chief Franko Simatović arrested and deported to the ICTY, along with Jovica Stanišić, former chief of the State Security Service. On 27 March, police special forces shot dead two leaders of the Zemun clan, Dušan Spasojević "Šiptar" and Mile Luković "Kum."[46]

The body of another JSO victim, former Serbian president Ivan Stambolić, who had disappeared in August 2000, was discovered at this time. As a longtime director of the Yugoslav Bank for International Economic Cooperation, the post he kept for ten full years after he left politics, Stambolić was no doubt well informed about many financial operations, and it is likely that he knew about the secret monetary transfers executed by the Milošević regime. According to sources close to the Yugoslav army, one of the reasons for Stambolić's disappearance was the fact that he had taken the position of director of the Jubmes bank, which had been founded collectively by all the Yugoslav republics prior to the SFRY's demise. During the wars in Croatia and Bosnia, the Yugoslav army, according to these sources, sold weapons to its Croatian and Bosnian enemies via a third party and received payment in its account at Jubmes. Given Stambolić's full knowledge of these scandalous transactions, he had become a potentially dangerous witness at a time when Milošević's hold on power was increasingly shaky.[47]

The backlash against the Djindjić assassination did not affect only members of the JSO and mafia, but many senior figures of the Milošević and Koštunica regimes. One week after the assassination, the Serbian parliament cleared the way for Operation Saber by voting to dismiss thirty-five judges, including seven supreme court justices, in a purge of the judiciary that had shielded the mafia. Milan Sarajlić, deputy Serbian public prosecutor, was arrested as an accomplice of the Zemun clan.[48] Two nationalist Belgrade newspapers linked to Radovan Karadžić and Milorad Luković "Legija," *Nacional* and *Identitet,* were closed down. Former deputy police chief Milorad Bračanović was arrested in connection with the attempt on Drašković's life. A warrant was issued for the arrest of Milošević's wife, Mira Marković, who fled to Russia. Former Yugoslav army chief of staff Nebojša Pavković was arrested in connection with the attempted assassination of Drašković. Ražnatović "Arkan"'s widow, Svetlana, was also arrested in connection with the Djindjić assassination. Dragoljub Milanović, director of Radio-Television Serbia under Milošević, was arrested in Montenegro, where he had fled with the aid of the Zemun clan to avoid a ten-year prison sentence, imposed upon him for complicity in the deaths of sixteen of his employees during the Kosovo war.[49] Vojislav Šešelj, the leader of the Serbian Radical Party in custody at The Hague, was implicated by Dušan Mihajlović in the Djindjić assassination.[50]

The sweep encompassed close allies of former president Koštunica, including former military intelligence chief Aco Tomić and Koštunica's former security adviser Rade Bulatović, both of whom were arrested in April.[51] These arrests highlighted the fact that Koštunica had inherited the support of Milošević's circle within the state apparatus, many of them with blood on their hands. Although many of the arrested individuals were subsequently released, including Tomić, Bulatović, and Svetlana Ražnatović, the members of the Serbian elite responsible for the wars in Croatia, Bosnia-Herzegovina, and Kosovo and for the criminalization of Serbian society were finally placed on the defensive. The Serbian police arrested Captain Miroslav Radić in May, followed by Colonel Veselin Šljivančanin in June—both indicted by the ICTY for war crimes at Vukovar—in time to meet a U.S. Congressional deadline that made the provision of financial assistance dependent on cooperation with the tribunal. Both Radić and Šljivančanin were promptly deported to The Hague. Finally, the absent Milošević himself was indicted by the Serbian special prosecutor in September 2003 for having ordered the assassinations of Drašković and Stambolić.[52]

Tragic as the assassination was, it had acted as a spur to the purging of the Serbian body politic, without which no genuine democratization or economic liberalization was possible. As Madžid Dušan Pajić, Serbian assistant minister of finance, stated in an interview in August: "There is some truth to the belief that the assassination has in the short term increased the difficulties in the economy, but paradoxically, Operation Saber and the struggle against organized criminals will bring us benefits in the future, which we could not perhaps have counted on before."[53] By breaking the power of the mafia, Operation Saber created the conditions for the suppression of a large part of the black market that had dominated the Serbian economy. Dragan Šutanovac, president of the Council for Security of the Serbian parliament, claimed in an interview in May: "After 5 October 2000 we succeeded in suppressing the illegal trade in people, weapons, tobacco, automobiles, counterfeit money and pirate goods. We have reduced them to a tolerable security level, equivalent to, for example, that in many European states." Nevertheless, he noted also that the post-Milošević regime had obstructed the passage of legislation to deal with organized crime, pointing the finger in particular at Koštunica's Democratic Party of Serbia: "I don't know if this was just some political intrigue on the part of our former coalition partners at the federal level, or whether they charged Milošević's functionaries for the protection that allowed them to maintain their representative immunity."[54] Operation Saber was quickly followed by the passage of new economic laws. The Law on a Guarantee Fund makes it easier for Serbian companies to get access to foreign currency for trading purposes. In addition, an excise bill makes privatization of the state-owned petrol station chain Beopetrol viable, and the Law on Concessions provides a legal base for Serbia to undertake a series of long-needed and ambitious public infrastructure projects.[55]

Nevertheless, Operation Saber did not amount to a complete break with the past. It involved the police arresting many criminals whose activities had been known to them before Djindjić's assassination but for whose arrest the political will had been lacking. And, as one Serbian newspaper reported in July, "What is most worrying is that the government has, since the lifting of the state of emergency on 22 April 2003, completely abandoned the struggle against corruption and economic criminals."[56] The forces of reform had won a decisive battle but lacked the motivation to win the war. Ultimately, the very state structures that implemented Operation Saber were themselves compromised by association with organized crime and war crimes. The Security and Information Agency, formerly the State Security Service, was not targeted during Operation Saber, even though it had been centrally involved in the Djindjić assassination.

Economic reforms have continued to be hampered by the corruption and lack of funds of the state's financial structures. In March 2003, the European Union suspended imports of domestically manufactured sugar from Serbia and Montenegro companies after several of them were revealed to have repeatedly resold large quantities of sugar of non-Serbian origin, with the assistance of corrupt Serbian customs and tax officials. When Vladan Begović, director of Serbian customs, announced he would take action against the companies involved, he was dismissed by the government.[57] In August, justice minister Batić demanded a commission be set up to investigate the activities of the Belgrade Commercial Court, citing increasing irregularities in its work, especially with regard to privatization and liquidation.[58] The Agency for Tobacco, set up to combat the role of tobacco smuggling in organized crime, has remained a toothless, underfunded body, according to its own director, the former customs director Vladan Begović.[59] The oligarchy of businessmen and companies that previously financed the Milošević regime and depended upon its patronage continues to exert significant control over the current government of Zoran Živković. Political parties belonging to the ruling DOS (Democratic Opposition of Serbia) coalition as well as to the opposition are financed by members of this semicriminal oligarchy. For example, the Milošević-era oligarch Bogoljub Karić finances the League of Social Democrats of Vojvodina, the Social Democrats, Christian Democratic Party of Serbia, Socialist People's Party, and the Party of Serbian Unity, according to Dinkić, who claims that, through the influence this gives him, Karić has been able to avoid paying back taxes on his Milošević-era profits and to stave off the closure of his Astra Bank, which has consistently violated Serbian banking regulations.[60]

The government decided to dismiss Dinkić himself on 9 June in response to his efforts to maintain the independence of the National Bank and to resist the government's plunder of the bank's foreign-currency reserves to finance companies belonging to the oligarchy.[61] The hastily passed National Bank Law of July effectively subordinated the National Bank to government control and paves the way for increased public spending, aimed at shoring up the government's falling popular support and handing out loans to members of the oligarchy.[62] Dinkić attributed the Law on the National Bank to an effort of the government to control the bank dating back to the Milošević era: "The Law on the National Bank of Yugoslavia is Milošević's."[63] In response, Dinkić published documents implicating Zoran Janjušević, security adviser to both Djindjić and Živković and a former member of the Bosnian Serb secret police, and Nemanja Kolesar, executive director of the government's Bank Reconstruction Agency, of large-scale money laundering.[64] With the resignation of G17+'s Tomislav Milosavljević as minister of health in August and of Rodoljub Šabić as deputy prime minister, and the expected resignation of Božidar Djelić as minister of finance, the government is on the verge of losing all vestiges of its reformist credibility.[65] The struggle between reformists on the one hand and ancien régime elements on the other implicated in corruption, war crimes, and organized crime is yet to be resolved.

Conclusion

The reform of the Serbian economy in the post-Djindjić period is a painful ongoing process. Major steps have been taken to introduce a genuine free-market economy based upon the rule of law, yet Serbia is still burdened by a criminal-bureaucratic infrastructure inherited from the Milošević regime, and this slows the pace of reform. The politicians of the new Serbian elite remain torn between their desire for reform and their own links with the old elite. Yet every revolution preserves as much as it changes. As important as the rooting out of Milošević-era criminals is, the gradual adoption of a new ruling ethos, based upon participation in European and Atlantic political, economic, and military structures is also important. However half-hearted the Serbian politicians' collaboration with the ICTY, however superficial the resulting sense of catharsis, and however desirous they may be of regaining Kosovo and strengthening links with the Serb Republic in Bosnia-Herzegovina, these changes are still important. Just as with the early medieval pagans converting to Christianity, it may be that respect for the form of government will gradually begin to change its content. Symbolic of how the post-Djindjić Serbian political elite combines its desire to reform with its desire to accommodate the old order is the Živković government's offer to the United States to supply a battalion of 250 Serbian military personnel for service in Afghanistan. The proposed commander of the battalion is Colonel-General of Police Goran Radosavljević-Guri, a man implicated in war crimes in Kosovo for whom Afghanistan may seem preferable to The Hague. Furthermore, the battalion would include former JSO members who would thereby be removed from the Serbian scene.[66] Thus, Serbia's first tentative step as an ally of the United States is at once another move in the accommodation of the ancien régime.

Notes

This article was written while Marko Attila Hoare was in receipt of a British Academy Postdoctoral Fellowship. He would like to thank the British Academy for its support.

1. The figure includes those Serbs who were native to Croatia or Bosnia-Herzegovina and traveled first to Serbia before emigrating further.

2. Research on the consequences of the trauma experienced by people as a result of the war is just beginning to appear. One of the pioneer works is Nataša Ljubimirović, "The Psychological Consequences of War-Related Stress among Adolescents," *Gledišta*, no. 1–2, pp. 143–59, which shows the majority of teenage refugees suffers from serious psychological problems such as anxiety, depression, insomnia, lack of attention, as well as behavioral problems in relation to society. For all the young people encompassed by the research, being a refugee represented the greatest trauma; the abandonment of the home was deeply seared into their

memories. These problems were frequently linked to alcohol abuse, sexual promiscuity, truancy from schools, and aggressive behavior.

3. See Mladen Lazić, ed., *Razaranje društva* (Belgrade: Filip Visnić, 1994).

4. Mladjan Dinkić, *Ekonomija destrukcije: Velika pljačka naroda* (Belgrade: Stubovi kulture, 2000), pp. 234–35.

5. Ibid., p. 257.

6. R. Jeffrey Smith and Peter Finn, "Depth of Corruption," *Washington Post*, October 22, 2000.

7. Dinkić, *Ekonomija destrukcije*, p. 257.

8. See Robert Thomas, *Serbia under Milošević* (London: Hurst & Co., 1999).

9. International Criminal Tribunal for the former Yugoslavia, indictment of Slobodan Milošević, Milan Milutinović, Nikola Sainović, Dragoljub Ojdanić, Vlajko Stojiljković, 22 May 1999.

10. Nenad Lj. Stefanović, "Dragan Tomić, the speaker," *Vreme News Digest Agency* (Belgrade), no. 124 (7 February 1994).

11. "Fear and Loathing in Belgrade: What the Serbian State Media Say about Albanians," International Crisis Group Yugoslavia Briefing, 26 January 1999.

12. *Time Europe*, 15 September 2002.

13. *The Economist*, February 2002.

14. AIM Press (Podgorica), 1 May 2000.

15. *Borba* (Belgrade), 12 October 2000.

16. *Svedok* (Belgrade), 9 March 1999.

17. *Nedeljni telegraf* (Belgrade), 19 November 1997.

18. *Nedeljni telegraf,* 22 April 1998; and *Borba,* 12 December 2000.

19. *Politika* (Belgrade), 11 October 2000.

20. Misa Brkić, "Provizija, mito i tajni računi," *Vreme* (Belgrade), no. 665 (2 October 2003); online at www.vreme.co.yu.

21. "The Serbian Parliament, July 2000, extraordinary session at which were adopted several economic laws," *B-92 vesti,* 13 July 2000, pp. 18, 21.

22. Veselin Kovačević, "Državni lopovluk na delu," AIM Press, 9 February 1999; online at www.aimpress.ch.

23. "Yugoslav Finance Minister Steps Down," Reuters, 5 January 2002.

24. "Federal Republic of Yugoslavia: Economic Assessment 2002," Organisation for Economic Cooperation and Development economic survey, 12 November 2002.

25. "2003 Index of Economic Freedom: Yugoslavia, Federal Republic of (Serbia-Montenegro)," The Heritage Foundation, Washington, D.C., 2002.

26. Jeffrey Donovan, "Yugoslavia: Serbian Prime Minister Seeks Greater Economic Assistance," *Radio Free Europe,* 6 November 2001, online at www.rferl.org.

27. Cited in "Serbia after Djindjić," in International Crisis Group, *Balkan Report* (Belgrade/Brussels), no. 141 (18 March 2003), p. 7.

28. Harry Cohen, *The Serbian Economy: Reconstruction and Transition Challenge—Draft Interim Report,* NATO Parliamentary Assembly, Sub-Committee on East-West Economic Cooperation and Convergence, 18 April 2001.

29. *Washington Post,* 22 October 2000, online at www.washingtonpost.com.

30. *The Guardian* (London), 29 March 2001, online at www.guardian.co.uk.

31. Dejan Anastasijević, "Večni plamen," *Vreme,* no. 666 (9 October 2003), online at www.vreme.co.yu.

32. "Podnete krivične prijave protiv bivših funkcionera," *Tanjug* (Belgrade), 1 November 2001.

33. D. Milinković, "Afere prepuštene novinarima: Vlast i dalje ćuti!" *Nedeljni telegraf,* online at www.nedeljnitelegraf.co.yu.

34. AIM Press (Athens), 26 October 2000.

35. "Sokolović pronadjen mrtav: Nelogičnosti u slučaju Sokolović," *Nezavisne novine,* 9 February 2001.

36. AIM Press (Belgrade), 21 May 2001; and Associated Press, 12 May 2001.

37. "Belgrade Awaits Donors Money with Top Priorities," *Agence France-Presse,* 1 July 2001.

38. Donovan, "Yugoslavia" [see note 26].

39. Milan Milošević, "10 afere koje su potresli Srbiju," *Vreme,* no. 660 (28 August 2003), online at www.vreme.co.yu.

40. "Gavrilović Dossier," *Serbiainfo: Home News,* 10 August 2001.

41. *The [London] Daily Telegraph* 18 November 2001; and Miloš Vasić, "Special Murders Unit" (in English), *Vreme,* no. 638 (27 March 2003), online at www.vreme.co.yu.

42. "Znaju se atentatori na Buha," *Danas* (Belgrade), no. 1858 (30 October 2002).

43. Christopher Deliso, "Serbian Banking Reform," United Press International, 15 July 2002.

44. Global Trade and Technology Network, Field Office Information, Market Research, Europe and Eurasia Finance, 2002.

45. "FR Yugoslavia: Economic Bulletin," Eteba S.A.: FRY R.O., 13–17 January 2003.

46. A. Roknić, "Otkriveni zahvaljujuci Bagziju," *Danas* (29–30 March 2003); V. Z. Cvijić, "Od Krajine, preko Ibarske magstrale i Kosova do atentata na Đinđića," *Danas* (29–30 March 2003); and International Criminal Tribunal for the former Yugoslavia, indictment of Jovica Stanišić and Franko Simatović, 1 May 2003.

47. *Sunday Times* (London), 15 April 2001.

48. *The Guardian,* 20 March 2003, online at www.guardian.co.uk.

49. Nenad M. Stevanović, "Puna mreća 'krupnih riba,'" *Patriot*, no. 61 (4 April 2003).

50. "Bulatović, Tomić and Šešelj Also Accused," *Blic Online*, 30 April–2 May 2003, online at www.blic.co.yu.

51. *The Guardian*, 9 April 2003, online at www.guardian.co.uk.

52. "Milošević Indicted for Ordering Political Murders," *Southeast European Times*, from RFE/RL, Bloomberg, Tanjug, 24 September 2003; AFP, Reuters, BBC, UPI, Radio B-92, 23 September 2003.

53. Madžid Dušan Pajić, "Koliko košta novac?" *Ekonomist online*, 12 August 2003.

54. Dragan Šutanovac, "Legija nije uhapšen, ne nalazi se u CZ i nije tačno da ga je Pauel odveo u Hag," *Nedeljni telegraf*, no. 368 (14 May 2003), online at www .nedeljnitelegraf.co.yu.

55. International Crisis Group, "Serbian Reform Stalls Again," *Balkans Report* (Belgrade/Brussels), no. 145 (17 July 2003), p. 8.

56. "Kriminalci dozvoljeno da deluju nekažnjeno," *Danas*, 21 July 2003.

57. International Crisis Group, "Serbian Reform Stalls Again" [see note 55], pp. 18–19.

58. *Beta* (Belgrade), 26 August 2003.

59. International Crisis Group, "Serbian Reform Stalls Again" [see note 55], p. 9.

60. Ibid., pp. 17–20.

61. Ibid., pp. 23–24.

62. "Serbia: Government Asserts Control over the Central Bank," *Civilitas Research*, 28 July 2003.

63. Mladjan Dinkić, "Narodna Banka neće bit nezavisna," *Vreme*, no. 654 (17 July 2003), online at www.vreme.co.yu.

64. Željko Cvijanović, "Serbia Rocked by Seychelles Affair," Institute for War and Peace Reporting, *Balkan Crisis Report*, no. 448 (30 July 2003).

65. Željko Cvijanović, "Serbia: Government Crisis Deepens," Institute for War and Peace Reporting, *Balkan Crisis Report*, no. 456 (29 August 2003).

66. Dejan Anastasijević, "Srpski žandari pod američkom komandom," *Vreme*, no. 664 (25 September 2003), online at www.vreme.co.yu.

9

THE TRIAL OF SLOBODAN MILOŠEVIĆ

KARI M. OSLAND

On 12 February 2002 a historic trial began proceedings in The Hague against Slobodan Milošević. He is the first head of state ever to be tried before an international war crimes tribunal.[1] The trial is important for several reasons: First, because this is the person whom the Office of the Prosecutor (OTP) of the International Criminal Tribunal for the former Yugoslavia (ICTY) sees as one of the chief architects behind the atrocities committed on the territory of the former Yugoslavia since 1991, and who therefore has a main responsibility vis-à-vis the many victims and their families.[2] Second, this trial can assist in removing the feeling of collective guilt many Serbs feel has been applied to them. Third, the ICTY will to a great degree be judged on the basis of how this case is handled. This case is not only about trying Milošević; it is also about testing the capacity and legitimacy of international judicial institutions as instruments of policy. However, whether it is perceived as legitimate is not purely a legal question. It can be argued that it is the level of perceived legitimacy in public opinion that ultimately will decide whether the ICTY will prove to be successful. This is crucial, first and foremost because if the verdict and eventual sentence are considered to be convincing and legitimate, the basis and credibility of the newly established International Criminal Court (ICC) will be strengthened.

The Arrest and Time Frame

On 27 May 1999, the ICTY indicted Milošević (and four other top Yugoslav and Serbian officials) for crimes against humanity and war crimes committed in the conflict in Kosovo. Although this decision was expected and welcomed by many, the timing of making it public was not. The reason for this was that the indictment was issued when the NATO-led war against Yugoslavia was in its sixty-third day and the Russian special en-

voy, Viktor Chernomyrdin, and former Finnish president, Martti Ahtisaari, were in the middle of negotiations with Milošević on a possible
peace deal. A crucial question arose, namely whether it would be possible to negotiate with an indicted war criminal. Although Western leaders had threatened Balkan leaders with war crimes trials several times
during the 1990s, they had been careful to avoid blaming President
Milošević directly, knowing that they would probably have to deal with
him at the conference table again.[3] Louise Arbour, the then chief war
crimes prosecutor of the ICTY, said in an interview with CNN on 27 May
that same year that the indictment was unlikely to affect the ongoing negotiations, but added that "the evidence upon which this indictment was
confirmed raises serious questions about their [i.e., the indictees'] suit-
ability to be the guarantors of any deal, let alone a peace agreement."[4]
However, as the news of the indictment broke, Clinton administration
officials insisted that they could still work with the Serbian leader. And
this proved to be the case. Chernomyrdin and Ahtisaari managed to agree
to a peace deal with Milošević, and some days later, the NATO war
against Yugoslavia (Operation Allied Force) ended, after seventy-eight
days.

   In April 2001, Milošević was arrested in his home in Belgrade. He was
first taken to Belgrade's main prison, where he was charged with mis-
appropriation of state funds and abuse of his official position. At the
same time, the U.S. Congress demanded that in order for Yugoslavia to
qualify for financial assistance, it had to fulfill the criteria for cooperation. These included ending the financing of the Bosnian Serb army, re-
leasing all ethnic Albanian prisoners, and extraditing further named suspects to The Hague. By the deadline on 31 March, all the demands apart
from the latter had been met. On 28 June 2001, St. Vitus' Day, the Serbian prime minister Zoran Djindjić overruled the Constitutional Court
and extradited Milošević to the ICTY in The Hague.[5] In February 2002,
the trial began in The Hague. The hearing of the OTP lasted approximately
two years (it has been delayed several times due to the ill health of the
accused).

   Milošević has the right to the same court time as the prosecutors and
to call the same number of witnesses; the prosecutors have used approximately three hundred days and called in around three hundred witnesses.[6]
On 2 September 2003, Milošević called for a two-year break in order for
him to work on his tribunal defense. A ruling that was issued on 17 September granted Milošević three months so that he could prepare his defense.[7] Milošević was supposed to begin his defense on 8 June 2004,[8] but

because of his bad health it was delayed until 31 August. What are the charges against Milošević?[9]

"Medieval savagery and a calculated cruelty"

These were the words used by chief UN prosecutor Carla Del Ponte in her opening statement in February 2002 to characterize the atrocities committed in the former Yugoslavia. In more legalistic language, Milošević is accused of grave breaches of the 1949 Geneva Conventions, violations on the laws or customs of war, crimes against humanity, and genocide. The jurisdiction of the ICTY concerns individual responsibility according to the same breaches of law.[10] On this point, the Nuremberg court established the precedent for later courts.[11]

More specifically, Slobodan Milošević is accused of war crimes committed in Croatia (in the period between at least 1 August 1991 and August 1992), in Bosnia-Herzegovina (BiH) (from 1 March 1992 to 31 December 1995), and in Kosovo (from 1 January to 20 June 1999). The indictment also includes genocide committed in BiH in the mentioned time span.[12] The prosecution asserts that Milošević participated in a joint criminal enterprise that aimed to exterminate and expel all non-Serbs as part of a systematic plan to create an ethnically pure Greater Serbia.[13] Milošević has refused to enter a plea. The presiding judge has, therefore, as the rules of the tribunal require, recorded a "not guilty" plea to all the charges on his behalf.

The first phase of the hearing of the OTP (from 12 February until 11 September 2002) focused on Kosovo and the killing of about 900 individually identified ethnic Albanians and the deportation of 800,000 Kosovars by Serb security forces. Milošević is one of five defendants facing charges related to events in Kosovo. The second phase lasted from 26 September 2002 until 25 February 2004 and focused on BiH and Croatia. The charges relating to Croatia center on Milošević's alleged responsibility for the murders of hundreds of civilians and the expulsion of 170,000 non-Serbs from their hometowns. The indictment in connection with BiH states that Milošević was responsible for the killing of thousands of Bosnian Muslims and Bosnian Croats and the deportation or imprisonment of more than 250,000 people. These two phases differed in that there were fewer crime-based witnesses who testified in court in the second phase compared to the first. The reason for this is partly that a large number of the crimes have been established in other trials before the ICTY and partly that the prosecution relied more on documents, intercepts, and transcripts from other trials in the second phase.[14] Furthermore, time pressures may also have contributed to this.

The fact that Bosnia-Herzegovina, Croatia, and Kosovo are handled as one case can be seen to have both advantages and disadvantages, depending on whether you see it from the prosecutor's perspective or from the point of view of the accused.[15] The prosecutors want to prove that the atrocities in the different countries were not isolated happenings, but rather that they were part of an overall strategy. Technically, it is easier and more cost-effective to handle the cases as one when it comes to the hearing of witnesses because they will have to testify only once. The accused will consider it to be a disadvantage because it may be difficult for the judges not to look at the three cases as one: connecting the cases may create more clear-cut conclusions from the start than if the cases had been handled separately. But what are the more legalistic characteristics of these breaches?

Crimes of War and Genocide

Article 2 in the statutes of the ICTY defines grave breaches of the Geneva Conventions. These imply acts committed against persons or property protected under the relevant convention. Examples range from murder and torture to destruction of property that cannot be legitimated as a military target.[16] Breaches of the customs of war are defined in Article 3. Without being restricted to the following, they include among other things the use of poison gas and other types of weapons that inflict unnecessary suffering, attack on defenseless settlements, destruction of areas that cannot be legitimated militarily, and the destruction of historic monuments.[17]

Articles 2 and 3 refer to the "classic" war crimes that have taken place under armed conflict. Crimes against humanity are defined in Article 5. They include murder, extermination, slavery, deportation, imprisonment, torture and rape, political, racial, and religious persecution, and other inhumane actions.[18] The statutes of the ICTY specify that this is valid only during armed conflict. This restriction has been removed in the statutes of the ICC.

The most serious of the four main indictments is genocide. Article 4 of the statutes of the tribunal gives the following definition: "Genocide means any of the following acts committed with intent to destroy, in whole or in part, a national, ethnic, racial or religious group, as such."[19] The acts referred to here involve killing members of a group, seriously harming—physically or mentally—members of a group, committing actions with the intent to prevent members of the group from giving birth, etc.[20] It is underlined in the article that it is punishable not only to commit genocide, but also to attempt to commit or to be complicit in the crime of genocide.[21]

Among the aforementioned violations of law, it is only in the case of genocide that the prosecutors must prove that the perpetrator had a specific intent to exterminate a group of people.[22] This is extremely difficult to prove. It is not enough to find written evidence of such a plan because the plan may not have been put into action. Therefore, the prosecutors will most probably focus on the process leading up to the killings and try to find evidence of this specific intent. It is likely that this is the strategy behind the prosecutors' wish to try to prove that Milošević was part of a "joint criminal enterprise" with the aim of removing and exterminating all non-Serbs in order to create a Greater Serbia. However, this focus on intent may draw attention away from the carnage and suffering to the reasons the killings were committed. If specific intent cannot be proven, crimes against humanity can be applied.

Furthermore, the indictment for genocide separates itself from the other charges in that it does not matter whether it took place during times of war or peace; it is also applicable in times of peace. It is somewhat unclear how the Hague tribunal will deal with the atrocities against non-Albanians in Kosovo after the war in June 1999, when the forced expulsion of Serbs started.[23] It is not likely that the genocide article will be applied here. The question is, therefore, how to prosecute atrocities that were committed against the Serbian population in Kosovo. After the end of NATO's bombing campaign, a peace agreement was signed (the Military Technical Agreement). The war had, therefore, formally ended. If one succeeds in defining what followed as an armed conflict, the prosecutors may use Article 5 in the statutes, namely crimes against humanity. If not, the UN Security Council may have to change the statutes of the ICTY and remove the criterion of armed conflict.

The genocide convention was established in 1949. So far, eight persons have been found guilty of this serious crime in the International Criminal Tribunal for Rwanda (ICTR), while one, Radislav Krstić, has been convicted in the ICTY. Krstić assumed command of the Drina Corps during the Bosnian Serb massacre at Srebrenica in 1995. He was convicted in 2001 and sentenced to prison for forty-six years.[24] Although Chamber I has established that genocide occurred in Srebrenica in 1995, the trial chamber of Milošević (Chamber III) is not bound to follow this decision (trial chambers are only bound to follow legal rulings of the Appellate Chamber). So far, it does not seem that the trial chamber has managed to establish that Milošević had an intent to destroy, in whole or in part, any of the

other ethnic groups. It is obviously difficult to have a totally informed opinion about this, especially because, although the case is extremely transparent, some of the evidence has been presented in closed sessions and is
not available to the public. However, several of the witnesses have testified
along lines showing that Milošević was de facto in power over the Bosnian Serbs and that he knew that those who led the campaign in Srebrenica
(primarily Radovan Karadžić and Ratko Mladić, the Bosnian Serb political and military leaders, respectively) had an intent to destroy the Bosnian Muslims. If the judges are convinced that Milošević both knew this
and contributed to its implementation, they may convict him for complicity to genocide. However, on 5 March 2004, the amici curiae filed a
ninety-five-page motion requesting that the genocide charges be dropped.[25]
The prosecution must respond to this and the judges must issue their ruling before Milošević starts his defense.

Jurisdiction, Defense, and the Prosecution

The ICTY is divided into three separate entities: the Registry, the Chambers, and the Office of the Prosecutor. The Registry is responsible for the
administration and judicial support services of the tribunal. It runs the
legal-aid program by which most defendants get legal counsel, has responsibility for the welfare of the detainees, and administers most aspects of
the tribunal's relations with witnesses, such as protection measures and
travel.[26]

The Chambers consists of sixteen permanent judges and a maximum
of eight *ad litem* judges at any time.[27] The judges are divided among three
trial chambers and one appeals chamber. Trial Chamber III has responsibility for the Milošević case. A panel of three judges was appointed to
administer the trial and will make the ultimate determination of Milošević's guilt or innocence: Richard May from the United Kingdom was
the presiding judge, and his associate judges were Patrick Robinson from
Jamaica and O-Gon Kwon from South Korea. On 22 February 2004, the
ICTY announced that Judge May would resign due to ill health, effective
from 31 May 2004.[28] Shortly after, it was decided that Judge Robinson would
become presiding judge and that Iain Bonomy of the United Kingdom
would fill his position.[29] The new judge had to become familiar with
around 30,000 pages of court transcripts and 600,000 pages in the prosecution case.

The prosecution consists of UN chief prosecutor Carla Del Ponte from
Switzerland, Geoffrey Nice from Great Britain, Hildegard Uertz-Retzlaff

from Germany, Dirk Ryneveld from the Netherlands, and Dermot Groome from the United States.[30] Their task is to prove that Milošević gave the order to commit encroachment, or knew about atrocities committed by subordinates without preventing them from taking place. As for de jure command responsibility, this is most easily proven in Kosovo, because Milošević was president of Yugoslavia at the time (and therefore also commander in chief of the Serbian security forces in the province). When the atrocities took place in BiH and Croatia, these countries had declared independence and had also been recognized as independent by the European Union and later also by the United Nations. According to the indictment, Milošević did not have de jure but rather de facto responsibility for what the Yugoslav People's Army (JNA) units, local Territorial Defense (TO) units and TO units from Serbia and Montenegro, local and Serbian Ministry of Internal Affairs (MUP) police units and paramilitary units did in Croatia, and both de jure and de facto responsibility for what similar units, as well as the Bosnian Serb army, did in BiH.[31]

Milošević does not recognize the tribunal. Hence, he does not want a defense lawyer and therefore defends himself. It is on this basis that the trial chamber has appointed three so-called "friends of the court" (amici curiae), whose role it is to help Milošević secure a fair trial. The three "friends" are Steven Kay from England, Branislav Tapušković from Serbia, and Timothy McCormack from Australia.[32] They cannot take instructions from Milošević but are entitled to cross-examine witnesses and draw attention to any evidence that may indicate Milošević's innocence. Nevertheless, Milošević has a number of legal experts he can draw on in Belgrade.

Milošević is a lawyer by training but has never worked as such. This, combined with the fact that Milošević does not have a regular defense, may explain why Judge May allowed Milošević a broader scope for cross-examination, which has taken up time allotted to the prosecution to outline its evidence: Milošević used one day more than the prosecution for his opening procedures; he has been given more time to cross-examine the witnesses than the prosecution; and he has been allowed to use more aggressive tactics. Among journalists following the trial, the question is no longer whether Milošević will get a fair trial but rather to what extent the prosecution will be treated "fairly."[33] Milošević has been very well prepared in his cross-examinations, at least if judged by the level of details with which he has confronted the witnesses, independent of whether a farmer from a tiny village, a Western diplomat, or a former colleague. However, it is a balancing game in that Milošević on the one hand regards the

ICTY as illegitimate and therefore uses every opportunity to make his political case and on the other, follows to a certain extent the rules and procedures of the court. Judge May, due to his expertise in the rules of procedure and evidence, tackled this well. There have been many clashes between Milošević and Judge May, and a typical one in this regard is the following from the Status Conference on 30 August 2001:

> *Milošević:* Well, I would like to know, first of all, can I speak or are you going to turn off my microphone like first time?
> *Judge May:* Mr. Milošević, if you follow the rules, you will be able to speak. If you deal with relevant matters, of course you will be able to speak.[34]

Two and a half years later, on 15 January 2004, not much seems to have changed:

> *Milošević:* So the fact that the constitution says . . .
> *Judge May:* The witness must have the chance to answer these points.
> *Milošević:* Please, Mr. May. Would you refrain from switching off my microphone before my sentence is over, because . . .
> *Judge May:* No. I shall cut off your microphone at any occasion when you abuse it, in particular by these over-lengthy questions which are not allowing the witnesses to answer. The witness must have the opportunity to answer your question. You are simply to ask questions, not make speeches.[35]

Although these two extracts from the transcripts give an impression of disrespect between Judge May and Milošević, many other incidents show how Judge May managed to balance the rights of the accused and efficient trial management. In these instances, even Milošević seems to have accorded him some respect.

Sentence and Imprisonment

Each of the sixty-six counts against Milošević carries a maximum sentence of life imprisonment. Milošević was born on 20 August 1941. This means that he may have to live his last years in jail in one of the ten countries which so far have agreed to take in convicted war criminals: Norway, Sweden, Denmark, Finland, France, Spain, Italy, Austria, Germany, and the United Kingdom.[36] A few of these countries have limitations requiring that they cannot imprison a person longer than the maximum term of imprisonment in their own country.[37] None of the Scandinavian countries have made such a reservation, but should the ICTY come with such an inquiry, the mentioned countries would have to specifically consider it.[38]

To take an example, if Milošević is found guilty and, for instance, sent to Norway to serve his sentence, it is difficult to imagine that he would be imprisoned for longer than would be possible had he been tried in a Norwegian court (where the maximum term of imprisonment is twenty-one years). There are, however, other possible solutions: after having served twenty-one years, he could be transferred to preventive custodial supervision. One must also consider that he may be released after serving two-thirds of the twenty-one years, which is normal in Norway if the prisoner's behavior is good. And everything indicates that this would be the case: according to the prison guards at the detention center in Scheveningen, Milošević's behavior has proven exemplary. In anticipation of the trial in The Hague, Milošević used his time to read Ernest Hemingway and listen to Frank Sinatra and Céline Dion. The prison guards have also spread a rumor that Milošević listens to Sinatra's "My Way" at least once a day! Nevertheless, having said this, taking into consideration the sentences given to so-called "smaller fish" than Milošević so far, it seems to be unrealistic to expect him to receive less than a life sentence and that this will have to be fulfilled in one way or the other—in order for justice to prevail.

When the new prime minister in Serbia, Vojislav Koštunica, presented his minority government to the parliament on 2 March 2004, he argued that people who have received their sentence in the ICTY and who are from Serbia should be entitled to serve the sentence in Serbia. Although this probably is preferable for many due to closeness to family, for instance, the standards of the prisons are better in most of the countries that have made the agreement with the ICTY. The latter fact may be considered unfair by the victims and their families. The general public may also perceive it as unfair that the "smaller fish" will serve their sentences under worse conditions than the "bigger fish."

The ICTY

UN Security Council Resolution 827 established the Hague tribunal, or the ICTY, in May 1993. This was the first international court of its kind since the Nuremberg and Tokyo tribunals. A year later, the International Criminal Tribunal for Rwanda was established.[39] In the years since, ad hoc war tribunals have been set up for East Timor, Sierra Leone, and Cambodia. Since the ICTY was established under Chapter VII of the UN Charter, all countries are obliged to cooperate with the tribunal.[40] The tribunal has jurisdiction to convict individuals responsible for war crimes and genocide committed in the territory of the former Yugoslavia since 1991. It has created precedence on the interpretation of rape as a form of torture and as a crime against humanity. Furthermore, the ICTY has contributed to further develop the doctrine on responsibility of command, and to clarify the application of the Geneva Conventions.

What importance does the work of the Hague tribunal have? First and foremost, it is important that the people responsible for the atrocities committed are convicted, so that justice prevails. This is of crucial importance both for the victims and their dependents' hope of moral compensation and to improve the chances of a successful process of reconciliation. Secondly, the trials can contribute to removing the feeling of collective guilt and placing it where it belongs, namely with the individuals who were directly responsible. Thirdly, it is to be hoped that this kind of case will have a preventive effect when it comes to other, future war criminals. And finally, it is expected to contribute to the restoration of peace by promoting reconciliation in the former Yugoslavia.

Many have compared the Hague tribunal with Nuremberg, and with reason because of the similarities between them.

1. Both tribunals are so-called ad hoc, temporary law courts established to convict people who have committed grave crimes within a specific territory and within a specific time frame.

2. When the Hague tribunal was established, the same structure as that used during the Tokyo and Nuremberg tribunals was chosen, with a panel of three judges. The advantage with three judges is that one gets a thorough argument for the sentence. On the other hand, if the panel had consisted of a jury or an increased number of judges, its critics might have considered the trial fairer. However, given the complexity of the case, the number of witnesses, and the relatively untried areas of law, a panel of jurors may not really have been an option.

3. Many assert that the ICTY, as was the case with the Nuremberg tribunal, represents a "victor's justice" since both were established by the victors. There is no doubt that the victors established the Nuremberg court after World War Two, but it is not so clear-cut when it comes to the ICTY. The ICTY was established by the UN Security Council. Although the Council is supposed to represent all members of the United Nations and therefore cannot be considered to represent only the victors, in reality countries that participated in the bombing of the Federal Republic of Yugo-

slavia in 1999, such as Great Britain, France, and the United States, are permanent veto members with enormously more influence than most other countries.

On the other hand, while the judges in Nuremberg were from the victorious powers, the ICTY has drawn its judges also from nations that were not involved in the NATO war against Yugoslavia. However, as of 23 January 2004, among the twenty-nine "top people" in the ICTY, thirteen come from NATO-member countries.[41] A fourth point concerns the legal procedure: while Nazi Germany documented much of what it did in written text, little such material is said to exist with the prosecutors in The Hague, either because the orders were given orally and/or because much of the written material that existed has been destroyed. This means that the prosecutors depend to a large extent on testimonies as well as military intelligence information, the latter being difficult to reexamine. Fifth, and finally, while the Nuremberg court was a military court, the ICTY is not.

The Role of the West

Around three hundred witnesses were called in by the OTP.[42] Among these, many Western politicians and diplomats have given witness, for instance former British MP Paddy Ashdown; former chairman of the Organization for Security and Cooperation in Europe (OSCE) Knut Vollebæk; and former head of the Kosovo Verification Mission (KVM) William Walker. Also, Milošević has said that he wants to summon many former and present leaders in the West, among them American ex-president Bill Clinton, the prime minister of Great Britain, Tony Blair, UN secretary-general Kofi Annan, French president Jacques Chirac, former German chancellor Helmut Kohl, former U.S. negotiator Richard Holbrooke, and former U.S. secretary of state Madeleine Albright. It is up to the trial chamber to decide whether these witnesses are relevant for the trial and therefore whether they shall be subpoenaed. Milošević probably wants these people to testify because he hopes to show that compromises and agreements were made, proving that Western leaders saw him as a stabilizing factor in the Balkans in the 1990s—the guardian of peace in the Balkans. There is no doubt that Milošević did play an important role in for instance the Dayton agreement on BiH in 1995.[43] And even though the purpose of the West was to prevent more loss of human life, it will be interesting to bring to light what the different peace negotiators knew and silently accepted. Besides, Milošević probably wants to accuse the witnesses of responsibility for "NATO's war against the Serbs," which is his way of denouncing NATO's bomb campaign against Yugoslavia, and accuse them of contributing to the dissolution of the former Yugoslavia.

Many people believe that the role of NATO should be examined and that Western leaders should be held responsible for the bombing of civilians during the Kosovo war in 1999. It is not likely that a new court of justice will be established in order to examine the role of NATO alone. One could therefore ask when such an examination should take place, if not now. One argument against this is that it would remove the focus from Milošević. Another argument is that it is not very likely that one would manage to put NATO as such on trial. If this happened, it would have to be leaders who to a greater extent than others were directly involved in the decisions taken for the bombing.

However, the prosecution team in The Hague has already examined whether NATO did commit war crimes and their conclusion is that this was not the case, that the bombing of civilian targets was not the purpose but rather a side effect or so-called collateral damage. If one accepts this conclusion when it comes to whether NATO actually committed war crimes, there are still several controversial issues that remain unanswered when looking at the intervention as such. Although NATO legitimated its intervention on humanitarian grounds, one could argue that this was a mere pretext.[44] For many Western countries, the Kosovo war implicitly concerned NATO's position in the security-political landscape, as well as represented an opportunity to weaken Milošević, who was no longer considered a stabilizing factor.[45] Furthermore, the world has witnessed many atrocities before and after those in Kosovo, without claims for intervention on the part of any NATO countries.[46]

From Villain to Hero: The Martyrdom of Milošević

According to Mirko Klarin, Milošević has played to both the domestic and the international gallery, switching between Serbian and English in his addresses.[47] In the beginning, he tried to attract a global audience by presenting himself as a martyr for the antiglobalization movement. After 11 September, he emphasized his long-lasting war against terrorism. At the start of the trial on 12 February, he began focusing on his domestic audience by concentrating on how Serbia, its people, history, and traditions are on trial, rather than himself. This has fueled many Serbs' feelings that they are being victimized and fostered the perception of Milošević as a living martyr.

Many Serbs believe that Milošević is innocent. This is not only because he has consistently tried to present himself in a favorable light in the court, but also because the media in Serbia to a great extent has presented the ICTY as a political rather than a legal institution.[48] Milošević presents himself, and the whole Serbian nation, as NATO's victim. During his thirteen years in power, he learned how the media could be used in order to make the people follow him. In the words of Susan Woodward, "to win against public opinion, nationalist leaders had to engage in psychological warfare" both through the use of the media and symbolic actions.[49] However, the ICTY has also helped Milošević increase the suspicion some feel toward the tribunal: the fact that the trial started with the last of the three wars in which crimes were committed has assisted Milošević in exploiting many Serbs' negative feelings toward NATO.[50] Besides, if you follow the trial, either from the live Webcast on the Internet or from the visitors' gallery of Courtroom One, you get the impression of "professionals . . . routinely going about their jobs," which easily makes one forget what the trial really is about, namely the thousands of citizens who lost their lives, the millions who lost their home and property, and the hundreds of thousands who were forcibly displaced.[51]

According to Srdjan Bobosavljević, director of the Strategic Marketing Agency (SMRI), who conducted opinion-poll research in Serbia in 2002 based on 2,200 interviews, four-fifths of the population believe that the ICTY is biased.[52] Many people in Serbia have followed only the trial against Milošević and are unaware that the tribunal has convicted people from all ethnic groups in other trials. The survey in Serbia formed part of a regional survey, conducted in January and February 2002. The figures show that the trust ratings for the Hague tribunal are highest in Kosovo (83 percent) and the Bosnian Federation (51 percent) and lowest in Serbia (7.6 percent) and Republika Srpska (4 percent).[53] Significantly, the most trusted public figures in Republika Sprska are ICTY indictees Ratko Mladić (53 percent) and Radovan Karadžić (47 percent). In Serbia, Milošević received a rating of 14 percent, although 17 percent indicated that they did not wish to answer such questions about their former leader.[54] This latter point is quite understandable because people for years thought that Milošević was the one and only leader, while they now are told that they should be against him.

At the same time, Bobosavljević reveals that while around 40 percent were against any cooperation with the Hague tribunal in February 2001, this number has halved according to the latest opinion polls. This development may be due to the fact that many people are tired of politics and just want to get on with a normal life. However, since then, the perception seems to have changed somewhat. In the parliamentary elections in

December 2003, four Serbian political parties had tribunal indictees on their election tickets, including Milošević and Vojislav Šešelj. Furthermore, the new government has declared that it will not extradite any more indicted war criminals to the ICTY. Hence, their negative stand toward the ICTY has increased people's negative perception of the tribunal.

The common perception is that the economic aid the country receives from the West depends on cooperation with the court. This is very much the case: As mentioned above, the arrest by Serb authorities in April 2001 came on the eve of a deadline by the U.S. Congress for giving financial aid, and the extradition of Milošević to The Hague on 28 June that same year preceded an international donors conference. Again in 2004, the United States announced that if the Serbian government did not show satisfactory cooperation with the ICTY and extradite Ratko Mladić by 31 March, US$100 million would be withheld. The problem with this kind of conditionality is that it gives the impression that cooperation with the ICTY is a necessary evil which has to be met so that Serbia can gain financially and/or politically. The result of this is that the moral component becomes devalued. This has undoubtedly served to further decrease the perceived legitimacy of the ICTY.

Many seem to think that it would have been better if Milošević had been put on trial in his home country because he would have received a fair trial. This, of course, would not be seen as just by the victims of the Milošević regime. Some of the people who are of the opinion that Milošević should have been put on trial in Belgrade do not necessarily think of the war crimes he has committed but rather of the crimes he is suspected of having committed in his own country. In Yugoslavia, Milošević is accused of corruption, misuse of power, and embezzlement of state funds. Nevertheless, it is important to remember that many Serbs feel they are also victims of the very crimes for which Milošević is being held responsible in The Hague, because Milošević brought them into a war where many Serbian lives were lost, because he and his associates successfully brainwashed many to believe that other groups, especially the Muslims and Albanians, were unworthy and represented a threat to the Serbs, and because many Serbs carry a feeling of collective guilt. If Milošević continues his strategy in the court of fighting to preserve the honor of his people and country—against the rest of the world—and parts of the media in Serbia continue to transmit exclusively what Milošević has to say and very little of what the prosecution team and its witnesses present, the impression may take hold that this is the little man's fight against the system, and therefore his stamp of martyrdom will also grow stronger. As Goran Svilanović, then foreign minister of Yugoslavia, said in 2002: "It is important that Serbs recognize that this is all about the responsibility of Milošević and other individuals, and has nothing to do with the collective guilt of the Serbs, which is the way Milošević tries to present the case. Every individual must be responsible to seek the truth so that it does not happen again."[55]

The Court's Progress

As of 24 August 2004, of the seventy-nine indictees, fifty-eight indictees are in custody at the detention unit and five have been provisionally released. Twenty-one remain at large.[56] Two of the persons who have received the most attention recently belong to this latter category, Radovan Karadžić and Ratko Mladić. They are charged with responsibility for the Srebrenica massacre which took place in July 1995, when more than seven thousand men and boys were killed. The North Atlantic Council has given the Stabilization Force (SFOR) the mandate to arrest people accused of war crimes and hand them over to The Hague.[57] This has, however, not proven to be easy for the SFOR, as their mandate only allows the arrest of such persons if and when they accidentally come in contact with them while they are serving their daily duties. The SFOR has tried several times to arrest Karadžić but failed. On one such occasion, between 28 February and 1 March 2003, rumors hold that Karadžić and his security personnel were tipped off about impending action by somebody within the NATO system. For the same reasons as the trial against Milošević is important, it is also crucial that Karadžić, Mladić, and other indicted war criminals be arrested and brought to justice. Earlier, there was a concern that too much pressure on the Serbian and Bosnian governments in this matter (when it comes to the extradition of Mladić and Karadžić, respectively) may weaken the fragile democracies that are in the making. This argument is not valid any longer, first and foremost because the reform processes have come so far that there is little risk of a setback. Besides, given the time frame of the closure of the ICTY, and the importance for the OTP to strengthen the case against Milošević, the attempts to arrest people like Karadžić and Mladić will most probably intensify during 2004.

Of the fifty-eight persons currently in custody at the detention unit, twenty were arrested by national police forces (in Serbia, BiH, Croatia, Slovenia, and Germany); seventeen were apprehended by international forces (SFOR and KFOR); and twenty-one surrendered voluntarily.[58] So far, thirty-five cases have been completed; among these, twenty-one were withdrawn, while fourteen of the accused died, including five after the commencement of the proceedings. A total of one hundred and three persons have appeared in proceedings before the tribunal.

From the ICTY to the ICC

According to chief prosecutor Carla Del Ponte, the trial against Milošević marks the beginning of the end of the work of the ICTY. The International Criminal Court, which is also to be seated in The Hague, shall replace it. Since the end of the Cold War, work to establish an international criminal court has been intensified. After a suggestion from Trinidad and Tobago, the idea of establishing such a court was relaunched in the United Nations in 1989. The General Assembly asked the International Law Commission to make a draft, which was presented in 1994.[59] When the ICTY and the ICTR were established in 1993 and 1994, respectively, this contributed to speeding up the process of establishing the ICC. Hundreds of hours of lobbying culminated in a Conference of Plenipotentiaries in Rome 15–17 July 1998, where the Convention on the Establishment of an International Criminal Court was adopted.[60] Some 120 countries voted for, 7 against, and 21 abstained. The United States was among the countries that voted against, fearing that the court would charge American citizens with crimes.[61]

Sixty countries had to ratify the treaty to make it valid. On 1 July 2002, the ICC was formally established.[62] Contrary to the ad hoc tribunals, the ICC is complementary to national courts rather than superior: the court is to be activated when national will or ability to prosecute is not present (naturally, in most cases it will not be the lack of ability but the lack of will that makes the intervention of the ICC necessary). Moreover, the ICC will not be limited in time and space, as the temporary tribunals have been, and will therefore be able to react more quickly when necessary. Furthermore, for the court to be able to take on a case, either the crime must have been committed in a country that has ratified the treaty, or a national of a country that has ratified the treaty must have committed the crime. The Security Council can also refer a matter to the court. All this implies that criminal law administration will become a permanent part of international relations in a completely different degree from ever before.

The Important Continuation

The trial against Slobodan Milošević raises many dilemmas that have barely been mentioned in this chapter. For instance, is it problematic that the international community most probably made compromises with Milošević in order to settle the Dayton agreement and then later filed charges against him?[63] Such a process offers few incentives to state leaders in similar situations when it comes to a willingness to negotiate. Another problem is that Milošević seems to have become a martyr in the eyes of many Serbs. This will neither ease access of the Hague tribunal to crucial witnesses nor make it easier to start the much-needed reconciliation process among the people who fought against each other during the 1990s. So far, nothing seems to indicate that the trial has contributed to a positive development toward reconciliation among different ethnic groups in the Balkans.

If the ICTY is to have legitimacy and contribute in the development of the permanent International Criminal Court, and thereby also move international law in a direction where political leaders have more personal responsibility to respect human rights, the presentation of evidence must be total and the court must be seen as independent from political interests. Securing independence in international criminal law administration is more important than making sure that some of the actors involved in Yugoslavia's destruction do not lose face. The trial is, and will continue to be, followed very closely. Despite what many see as Milošević's demonization in the West, he is still innocent until proven guilty. According to the European Convention on Human Rights, one of the key tests is not just the impartiality of a judge but the perception that he or she is impartial. The tribunal itself is as much on trial as the man in the dock. Despite certain reservations, however, there is reason to believe that the ICTY and the trial against Milošević mark the beginning of a new era for international law, where it is no longer possible, not even for heads of states, to commit atrocities against their own population. Furthermore, international justice can only be universally legitimate when all war crimes, committed by any country, come under the jurisdiction of the same international legal framework. It is therefore important that, in the near future, the countries that have still not signed and ratified the treaty of the ICC do so.

According to Security Council Resolution 1503 of August 2003, the Hague tribunal is supposed to complete its trials by the end of 2008, and appeals by 2010. The main reason for this schedule is the lack of funding. Most people believe, however, that this time frame is impossible due to the number of cases that have not yet started and the number of those already in process. The ICTY has started preparing for a handover of cases to nations of the former Yugoslavia by contributing to establishing national war crimes courts. This work has already started in BiH, Croatia, and Serbia, but much more is needed in order to strengthen indigenous capacity. The ICTY must continue, through its so-called Outreach Program, to conduct workshops for judges, prosecutors, attorneys, and police investigators from these states. Funding must be ensured as well as witness-protection measures. The few domestic war crimes trials that have been conducted so far have received poor reviews, due to accusations against judges of being ethnically biased, lack of witness protection, and lack of cooperation between states concerning extradition and evidentiary matters. The devolution of trials to local courts may, however, bring several advantages: it may be considered more legitimate by the public, it may start the long-needed reconciliation process, and it will probably speed up the process of reforming the judiciary system in these countries.

Last, but not least, it is also crucial that the ICTY and its trials are perceived as legitimate by the public. And here, more than legal means are required.

Notes

This is a revised version of an article that was originally printed in *Nordisk Øst-forum*. Kari M. Osland, "Rettsaken mot Slobodan Milošević: et overblikk" in *Nordisk Øst-forum* 16 (2002), no. 1, pp. 5–18. Thanks to Sabrina Ramet and two anonymous referees for comments. Needless to say, only the author is to be blamed for the contentions and errors found in this chapter.

1. Jean Kambanda, prime minister in Rwanda during the genocide in 1994, was sentenced to life imprisonment in September 1998 by the International Criminal Tribunal for Rwanda (ICTR). He was found guilty of genocide and crimes against humanity. Under the constitution of 10 June 1991, the president of the republic exercises executive power. Kambanda was therefore the first head of government, but not head of state, to face the reckoning of an international war crimes tribunal. Furthermore, Kambanda is the first suspect an international court has sentenced for the crime of genocide.

2. For updated information from the ICTY, see UN ICTY (2003) *Official Internet Site for the International Criminal Tribunal for the Former Yugoslavia*, online at www.un.org/icty.

3. As they did in 1995 when Milošević was invited to Dayton, Ohio, to participate in the U.S.-led peace talks that ultimately brought an end to the war in Bosnia and Herzegovina.

4. See article "Milošević Indictment Makes History," online at www.edition .cnn.com/WORLD/europe/9905/27/kosovo.milosevic.04.

5. St. Vitus' Day, or Vidovdan in Serbo-Croatian, has a particular place in Serbian history. It was the day on which the independence of the medieval Serbian empire ended; it was the day when Gavrilo Princip, a young Serb, assassinated Austrian Archduke Franz Ferdinand in Sarajevo in 1914, an event that triggered the First World War; it was the day when the first constitution of the new Yugoslav state was adopted in 1921; and it was the day in 1948 when Stalin expelled the Socialist Federal Republic of Yugoslavia (SFRY) from the Cominform and terminated trade and economic assistance to Yugoslavia. For more on this, see Louis Sells, *Slobodan Milošević and the Destruction of Yugoslavia* (Durham, N.C.: Duke University Press, 2002), pp. 354–55.

6. ICTY press briefing, 12 February 2004, online at www.un.org/icty/briefing/ 2004/PB010212.htm.

According to the "Order Rescheduling and Setting the Time Available to Present the Defence Case," dated 25 February 2004, "the Prosecution spent approximately 360 hours presenting its case in chief, or approximately 90 sitting days, which will be the amount of time for the Accused to present his case in chief." To that "is added two-thirds of that time for cross-examination of Defence witnesses and administrative matters, which amounts to approximately 240 hours, or 60 sitting days; and therefore, the Accused shall have 150 sitting days in which to present his case, which shall be subject to adjustment depending on the time taken in cross-examination and administrative matters." Pp. 2–3; see online at www.un.org/icty/ milosevic/crialc/order-e/040225.htm.

7. In response to Trial Chamber III's order of 17 September, the Registry has provided facilities and logistical support for Milošević to prepare his defense. These include two offices where Milošević can meet with witnesses and make phone calls, and the appointment of liaison officers who will provide assistance to Milošević and liaise between Milošević and the Victims and Witnesses Section (VWS). For more information, see "ICTY Weekly Press Briefing," 3 March 2004, online at www.un.org/icty/briefing/2004/PB040404.htm.

8. According to ICTY's press release dated 25 August 2004, with reference no. JP/PIS/886e. See online at www.iwpr.net.

9. In addition to the indictments by the Hague tribunal, Milošević was indicted in Serbia in September 2003 on charges of having ordered the murder and attempted murder of two political opponents, Ivan Stambolić and Vuk Drašković, respectively, in 2000.

10. Article 7, paragraph 1, says that "a person who planned, instigated, ordered, committed or otherwise aided and abetted in the planning, preparation or execution of a crime referred to in Articles 2 to 5 of the present Statute, shall be in-

dividually responsible for the crime." See online at www.un.org/icty/basic/
statut/stat2000.htm#1.

11. Leo Kuper, *International Action against Genocide* (London: Minority Rights
Group, 1984); and Agrell and Alcalá, *Den Rättsliga Interventionen* (Stockholm:
Norstedts Juridik, 1997), p. 49.

12. More precisely, Milošević is charged for breaches of the laws of war and
crimes against humanity in Croatia, those already mentioned plus grave breaches
against the Geneva Conventions in Kosovo, and breaches of the laws of war, crimes
against humanity, grave breaches against the Geneva Conventions as well as genocide in BiH. See online at www.un.org/icty/glance/index.htm.

13. According to the indictment, the joint criminal enterprise was in existence
by 1 August 1991 and continued until at least 31 December 1995. Apart from Slobodan Milošević, the individuals participating in this enterprise included, among
other known and unknown participants, Radovan Karadžić, Momčilo Krajišnik,
Biljana Plavšić, General Ratko Mladić, Borisav Jović, Branko Kostić, Veljko
Kadijević, Blagoje Adžić, Milan Martić, Jovica Stanišić, Franko Simatović (also
known as "Frenki"), Radovan Stojičić (also known as "Badža"), Vojislav Šešelj,
and Željko Ražnatović (also known as "Arkan"). See online at www.un.org/icty/
latest/index.htm.

14. Coalition for International Justice, "Prosecution Does Creditable Job in
Croatia and Bosnia Cases against Milošević," 18 February 2004, online at www.cij
.org/index.cfm?fuseaction=viewReport&reportID=522&tribunalID=1.

15. This was ordered by the Appeals Chamber on 1 February 2002.

16. More precisely, this includes "(a) willful killing; (b) torture or inhuman
treatment, including biological experiments; (c) wilfully causing great suffering
or serious injury to body or health; (d) extensive destruction and appropriation
of property, not justified by military necessity and carried out unlawfully and wan-
tonly; (e) compelling a prisoner of war or a civilian to serve in the forces of a hostile power; (f) wilfully depriving a prisoner of war or a civilian of the rights of fair
and regular trial; (g) unlawful deportation or transfer or unlawful confinement
of a civilian; and (h) taking civilians as hostages." See online at www.un.org/
icty/legaldoc/index.htm.

17. This implies "(a) employment of poisonous weapons or other weapons calculated to cause unnecessary suffering; (b) wanton destruction of cities, towns or
villages, or devastation not justified by military necessity; (c) attack or bombardment, by whatever means, of undefended towns, villages, dwellings, or buildings;
(d) seizure of, destruction or willful damage done to institutions dedicated to religion, charity and education, the arts and sciences, historic monuments and works
of art and science; and (e) plunder of public or private property." Ibid.

18. The original text uses the following words: "(a) murder; (b) extermination;

(c) enslavement; (d) deportation; (e) imprisonment; (f) torture; (g) rape; (h) persecutions on political, racial, and religious grounds; and (i) other inhumane acts." Ibid.

19. This is taken directly from the United Nations Genocide Convention (UNGC) of 1948, Articles 2 and 3. See online at www.unhchr.ch/html/menu3/b/ p-genoci.htm.

20. The wording of the UNGC is as follows: "(a) killing members of the group; (b) causing serious bodily or mental harm to members of the group; (c) deliberately inflicting on the group conditions of life calculated to bring about its physical destruction in whole or in part; (d) imposing measures intended to prevent births within the group; and (e) forcibly transferring children of the group to another group." Ibid.

21. More precisely this includes: "(a) genocide; (b) conspiracy to commit genocide; (c) direct and public incitement to commit genocide; (d) attempt to commit genocide; and (e) complicity in genocide." Ibid.

22. Agrell and Alcalá, *Den Rättsliga Interventionen*, p. 91.

23. During the Kosovo war, the Serbs committed "ethnic cleansing" against Kosovo Albanians. After the war, Kosovo Albanians committed reverse ethnic cleansing against non-Albanians. While genocide implies the extermination of a group of people, ethnic cleansing implies the expulsion of a group of people from a given territory. For a discussion of the concept of ethnic cleansing see Agrell and Alcalá, *Den Rättsliga Interventionen*, pp. 95ff. See also Kari Osland, *A Process-Theoretical Approach to Genocide: Applied on the Cases of Bosnia and Herzegovina and Rwanda* (Bergen: University of Bergen, 2000), pp. 25–26.

24. According to the judgment on 2 August 2001, the Drina Corps of the Bosnian Serb Army (VRS) shelled the Srebrenica "safe areas" and attacked Dutch-manned UN observations posts that were located there. Furthermore, by 18 July 1995, those forces either expelled or killed most of the members of the Bosnian Muslim population of the Srebrenica enclave. See "Prosecutor vs. Krstić," case no. IT-98–33, online at www.un.org/icty/krstic/TrialC1/judgement/index.htm.

25. See online at www.un.org/icty/milosevic/motion/040305.pdf.

26. Since 1 January 2001, Hans Holthuis from the Netherlands has served as registrar while David Tolbert from the United States has served as deputy registrar since 20 August 2003.

27. Since February 2003, Theodor Meron from the United States has been serving as president of the Chambers and, hence, also of the ICTY.

28. Judge May died on 1 July 2004 at the age of sixty-five, after having served at the ICTY for more than six years, from 1997 to 2004.

29. As of 22 August 2004. See online at www.un.org/icty/milosevic/trialc/ order-e/040226.htm.

30. As of 22 August 2004. They all work in the Office of the Prosecutor, which operates independently of any state or international organization, the Security Council, and other organs of the ICTY.

31. For more about this, see the indictment online at www.un.org/icty/latest/index.htm.

32. Steven Kay, Branislav Tapušković, and Professor Michail Wladimiroff (from the Netherlands) were appointed by Hans Holthuis, the registrar of the Tribunal, on 6 September and 7 and 27 November 2001, in the three cases. On 10 October 2002, the Trial Chamber instructed the registrar to revoke the designation of Professor Wladimiroff as amicus curiae. Timothy McCormack was designated to act as amicus curiae on 22 November 2002. For more information, see online at www.un.org/icty/glance/milosevic.htm.

33. Mirko Klarin, "Milošević Mishandling Defence," Institute for War and Peace Reporting, Tribunal Update no. 256, 2 March 2002, online at www.iwpr.net/index.pl?archive/tri/tri_256_1_eng.txt.

34. See transcript of the Milošević case (IT-02–54), p. 19, online at www.un.org/icty/transe54/010830SC.htm.

35. This happened during Milošević's cross-examination of Ante Marković, pp. 30,837–38. See online at www.un.org/icty/transe54/040115ED.htm.

36. As of 11 March 2004.

37. For instance, according to the agreement between the United Nations and Spain, Article 3, paragraph 2: "Spain will only consider the enforcement of sentences pronounced by the International Tribunal where the duration of the sentence imposed by the International Tribunal does not exceed the highest maximum sentence for any crime under Spanish law." See the agreement online at www.un.org/icty/legaldoc/index.htm.

38. For instance, according to the agreement between the United Nations and Norway on the enforcement of sentences of the ICTY, Article 3, paragraph 1: "In enforcing the sentence pronounced by the International Tribunal, the competent national authorities of the requested State shall be bound by the duration of the sentence." Ibid.

39. The ICTR was established by UN Security Council Resolution 955 on 8 November 1994. The aim was to prosecute people responsible for genocide and other serious breaches of international humanitarian law committed in Rwanda between 1 January and 31 December 1994. For more information, see UN ICTR (2002) *Official Internet Site for the International Criminal Tribunal for Rwanda*, online at www.un.org/ictr/ and www.ictr.org. Although it is true that we have had only two international war crimes tribunals, there are important developments under way in this regard: First, on 16 January 2002, the government of Sierra Leone and the United Nations decided to establish a Special Court for Sierra Leone. This

Special Court is to prosecute war crimes committed during the war. This will neither be a UN body along the lines of the ICTY and ICTR nor a domestic tribunal. Rather, it will be a hybrid court, jointly administered by the United Nations and the Sierra Leone government. For more information, see online at www.un .org/Depts/dpko/unamsil/spcourt.htm.

Second, on 17 March 2003, the United Nations reached a draft agreement with the Cambodian government for an international criminal tribunal to try former Khmer Rouge members. Also, this tribunal is more domestic than the ICTY and ICTR. For instance, will the majority of judges be Cambodians? For more information, see, e.g., Yale's Cambodian Genocide Program online at www.yale.edu/ cgp/news.html.

Third, the United Nation's International Commission of Inquiry recommended in January 2000 that an international tribunal be created for East Timor. No such tribunal was created and the Special Panels for Serious Crimes established in the Dili District Court and the Ad Hoc Human Rights Court in Jakarta have tried to fill that void. For more information, see, e.g., online at www.hrw.org/ doc/?t+asia&c+eastti.

40. All members of the UN are *ipso facto* bound to the statutes of the ICTY since the tribunal was established by Chapter VII of the UN Charter concerning efforts to maintain or restore international peace and security.

41. They being the president, vice president, presiding judges, judges, *ad litem* judges, chief- and deputy prosecutors, and chief- and deputy registrars.

42. According to a press release from the ICTY dated 2 December 2003, no. CC/P.I.S./805–e, from 1 January 1998 to the present day, more than 2,330 witnesses have testified before a Trial Chamber of the ICTY. Of this number, approximately 58% were called by the OTP, 40% by the Defence Council and 2% by the Trial Chambers themselves. Furthermore, 60% testified openly without any protective measures, 59% were resident in BiH, and 19% were female witnesses; while 30% were aged over 51 years, 6% were younger than 30 years. See online at www.un.org/ icty/latest/index.htm.

43. Richard Holbrooke, *To End a War* (New York: Random House, 1998); Misha Glenny, *The Balkans: Nationalism, War and the Great Powers* (London: Granta Publications, 1999), pp. 649–51; David Owen, *Balkan Odyssey* (London: Indigo, 1996); and Noel Malcolm, *Bosnia: A Short History,* rev. ed. (Basingstoke/ Oxford: Macmillan, 1996).

44. Glenny, *The Balkans,* p. 660.

45. After the Cold War, NATO redefined its role from having been primarily a defense alliance to becoming a supporter of peace. During the Kosovo war, NATO established its new strategic concept (23–24 April 1999). It therefore became even more important to show in reality that the alliance could play a new

role. This came in addition to the fact that during the negotiations with Milošević, NATO made threats about bombing. It soon became clear that if NATO did not follow through on these threats, the organization would lose its legitimacy (see, e.g., Glenny, *The Balkans,* p. 657). As for Milošević, the international community never really considered him a credible partner for peace in the Balkans. The problem was basically that there were not so many other people that had the power to ensure that the agreements, at least to a certain degree, could or would be fulfilled.

46. For a discussion on humanitarian intervention, see Anne Julie Semb, "Suverenitet i støpeskjeen: Intervensjoner," *Norsk Statsvitenskapelig Tidsskrift* 17 (2001), no. 2, pp. 179–95; Michael Walzer, *Just and Unjust Wars: A Moral Argument with Historical Illustrations* (New York: Basic Books, 1977); Hedley Bull, *The Anarchical Society: A Study of Order in World Politics* (London: Macmillan Press, 1995); and Espen Barth Eide, "Intervening without the UN: A Rejoinder," in *Security Dialogue* 30 (1999), no. 1, pp. 91–94.

47. Mirko Klarin, "Milošević Hague Anniversary," Institute for War and Peace Reporting, Tribunal Update no. 272, 24 June 2002, online at www.iwpr.net/ index.pl?archive/tri/tri_272_1_eng.txt.

48. For more on this, see Biljana Kovačević-Vuco, "Comment: Milošević on Trial—the Serb View," Institute for War and Peace Reporting, Tribunal Update no. 348, 15 March 2004; online at www.iwpr.net/index.pl2archive/tri/tri_348_4.eng.txt.

49. Susan L. Woodward, *Balkan Tragedy: Chaos and Dissolution after the Cold War* (Washington, D.C.: The Brookings Institution, 1995), p. 228. See also Osland, *A Process-Theoretical Approach,* p. 94.

50. Klarin, "Milošević Hague Anniversary."

51. Quoted from Guy Lesser, "War Crime and Punishment: What the United States Could Learn from the Milosevic Trial," *Harper's Magazine* (January 2004); see online at www.findarticles.com/cf_dls/m1111/1844_308/112905950/print.jhtml.

52. Bojan Tončić, "Milošević Trial Grips Nation," Institute for War and Peace Reporting, Balkan Crisis Report no. 318, 15 February 2002; see online at www.iwpr.net/index.pl?archive/bcr2/bcr2_20020215_1_eng.txt.

53. The survey was released by South East Europe Democracy Support (SEEDS), a network of regional survey organizations and think tanks supported by the International Institute for Democracy and Electoral Assistance (International IDEA). The whole survey involved around ten thousand face-to-face interviews conducted in Serbia, Montenegro, Kosovo, BiH (with one survey for the Federation and one for Republika Srpska), Croatia, Macedonia, Bulgaria, and Romania. For more information, see online at www.idea.int/balkans.

54. Ibid.

55. Seminar entitled "A New Yugoslav Foreign Policy: Priorities, Challenges,

and Achievements," held at the Norwegian Institute of International Affairs (NUPI), Oslo, 27 February 2002.

56. For an update, see online at www.un.org/icty/glance/index.htm. In addition to this official list, the ICTY also operates with an unofficial list.

57. Den norske Atlanterhavskomité (1998), *NATO-Håndboken. 50–årsutgave. NATO 1949–1999.* See online at www.atlanterhavskomiteen.no/publikasjoner/ andre/haandbok/5.htm.

58. For an update, see case information sheets online at www.un.org/icty/ glance/index.htm.

59. See the background of the establishment of the International Criminal Court online at www.un.org/law/icc/general/overview.htm.

60. Gunnar M. Karlsen, "En permanent internasjonal straffedomstol," *Aftenposten* (Oslo), 13 May 1998; online at www.tux1.aftenposten.no/bakgr/980513/ kronikk.htm.

61. The Bush administration has gone even further in its opposition. On 7 December 2001, the Senate passed the American Servicemen Protection Act (ASPA), also called the "Hague invasion clause." The ASPA empowers the American president to use all necessary means appropriate to free any American detained by the ICC. It also prohibits cooperation of any kind with the court.

62. As of 25 February 2004, there were 139 signatories while 92 countries had ratified the treaty. See the Web site of the ICC at www.icc-cpi.int/php/index.php. See also Coalition of the ICC (2004): *Coalition for the ICC Home Page on the International Criminal Court,* online at www.iccnow.org/.

63. Ironically, Milošević ended up in The Hague thanks to a stipulation in the Dayton Peace Accords, which committed all parties to cooperate with the tribunal.

CULTURE AND VALUES

10

THE POLITICS OF THE SERBIAN
ORTHODOX CHURCH

SABRINA P. RAMET

I t has often been observed that the Serbian Orthodox Church is a political organization first and foremost and a religious organization only sec-
ondarily. Whether this statement is true or not depends, above all, on
what one understands by the terms "political organization" and "religious
organization." If we define "political organization" to mean an organization striving for power on earth and seeking to advance a policy agenda
affecting laws, notions of rights, school curricula, and values, then most,
if not all, religious organizations would qualify as political organizations.
Indeed, can one even imagine a religious organization which would not
also be political? Could we imagine a religious organization which would
not seek to promote specific social values (especially concerning sexuality, but also concerning social mores more generally), which would not
have strong views about school curricula, literature, and the limits of individual rights, and which would not seek to use the laws to advance and
safeguard its interests and agenda?

The politicization of religion is, thus, not merely a phenomenon of Or-
thodox religion. On the contrary, examples of this phenomenon abound,
whether one looks at the United States, Russia, Egypt, Mexico, Israel, Spain,
Iran, Germany, Croatia, Bosnia, or any of a multitude of other national
contexts. Yet Orthodoxy is not interchangeable with any other religion.
What is distinct to Orthodoxy, as opposed to, let us say, Catholicism or
Islam or Buddhism, is its shying away from universalism. The Orthodox
Churches, like the ancient religions, are the Churches of their respective
nations, their myths being the myths of their respective nations. The Battle of Kosovo, for example, is consecrated as an event with religious significance,[1] but it is only the Serbian Church which is interested in this myth
in the first place. For the Russian Orthodox Church, for example, it is not
even on the horizon.

Serbian Orthodoxy, Democracy, and War

If one wanted to portray the Serbian Orthodox Church as a pro-demo-cratic institution, one might, perhaps, note Patriarch Pavle's demand in June 1992 and again in July–August 1999 that Slobodan Milošević resign from office, backing calls for fresh elections. If one wanted to portray the Serbian Orthodox Church as, let us say, "internationalist," then one might perhaps point to Pavle's collaboration with Catholic archbishop Franjo Cardinal Kuharić in September 1992 in calling for peace, and Pavle's statement later that year that "the war benefits only one common enemy—the devil!"[2]

But these characterizations should strike us as artificial. Far from be-ing oriented to the give-and-take of democracy, prominent figures in the Serbian Orthodox Church have repeatedly seen theirs as a world apart, a better world, potentially even a celestial kingdom. In this spirit, for ex-ample, Svetozar Dušanić, in an article for *Pravoslavlje* (1 October 1987), conjured up notions of cultural incompatibility in a way which seemed to call into question the future of Serb-Croat cohabitation:

> The world which developed under 'Byzantine influence' . . . differs from the
> world which evolved under the 'Western-Roman influence,' not only in its
> religion, but also in its culture, historical development, ethics, psychology,
> and mentality. The Byzantine world cannot envision a common survival
> in the same state with the members of the Western-Roman tradition, par-
> ticularly not after the Second World War.[3]

Nor can one forget that during 1990 and 1991, the Serbian Church's news organ, *Pravoslavlje*, stoked the flames of nationalist resentment by pub-lishing article after article on the allegedly Serbian heritage of eastern Slavo-nia (then under siege), including Osijek, and on the sufferings of the Ser-bian people (only) during World War Two. Already in September 1989, when the air in Belgrade was thick with nationalism, the Serbian Church recalled that there had been eighty-six Orthodox priests and 134 churches in the Orthodox eparchy of Slavonia in 1937, vs. forty-two priests and 94 churches as of 1989.[4] The Church did not mention anything about changes in the size of the Orthodox population over the course of the fifty years, or the fact that the Serbian Church had been able to restore 64 churches, 2 monasteries, 15 residential buildings, and 9 chapels in Croatia in the years 1945–85, and to build 25 new churches alongside 4 chapels and 16 new res-idential buildings (some of them in Slavonia).

Again, in January 1991, even as ethnic tensions in both Croatia and Bosnia were escalating, the Orthodox Church began to conduct funeral services at locations across the latter republic, to commemorate the fiftieth anniversary of the establishment of the Independent State of Croatia, with symbolic funeral services conducted in Žitomislić, Prebilovci, Ljubinje, Trebinje, Majevica, Banja Luka, and other locations.[5] Curiously, the Church did not want to wait until April, when the fiftieth anniversary actually would occur.

In fact, the Serbian Orthodox Church was animated by dreams of finally realizing the earthly kingdom allegedly spurned by Tsar Lazar six hundred years earlier, an earthly kingdom of God, but an earthly kingdom all the same. Hence, when, in March 1991, Mihajlo Marković, Dobrica Ćosić, and Matija Bečković, among others, created an initiative committee to establish a Serbian National Council (Srpski nacionalni savet, or SNS), which would "represent the interests of all Serbs without regard to where they live"[6]—a committee which was inspired, thus, by expansionist and irredentist fantasies—the Serbian Orthodox Church lent its support. The SNS was short-lived, but not so the Greater Serbian pretensions of the Serbian Church. On the contrary, as Milorad Tomanić notes, the Serbian Orthodox Church's territorial pretensions vis-à-vis Croatia "were almost identical with the demands of certain Serbian political figures such as, for example, Vojislav Šešelj and Vuk Draškovic."[7]

The Serbian Orthodox Church constantly stirred up memories of World War Two, but always in a way which cast the Serbs as victims and the Croats (not merely the Ustashe) as perpetrators. For example, the Serbian Church demanded on three occasions (May 1990, December 1990, and May 1991) that the responsible state organs authorize the disinterment of the last remains of persons hurled into caves during World War Two, so that their skeletal remains might be reinterred with proper ceremony.[8] Given the escalation in nationalist rhetoric and violent incidents at the time, the Serbian Church may be held responsible for fueling the nationalist frenzy which prepared the peoples of the SFRY (Socialist Federated Republic of Yugoslavia) for war. Then, in May 1991, Patriarch Pavle chose to conduct the opening ceremonies for the regular meeting of the Sabor (normally held in Belgrade), not in Belgrade but at Jasenovac (site of an infamous wartime concentration camp), with a holy liturgy commemorating the fiftieth anniversary of the "crucifixion" of the Serbs. Among Croats, this ill-timed act of symbolic politics was seen as opening new wounds.[9] That same month, in an eerie sign of the sacralization of that moment in Serbian history, the last remains of Nikolaj Velimirović, bishop of Žička, were brought back (from America) to the country of his birth.

After the antiwar demonstrations of 9 March 1991 on the streets of Belgrade, one might have expected a statement for peace from the patriarchate, and perhaps some estrangement between the Church and the regime. Instead, relations between the Milošević regime and the Church actually improved, because the bishops saw in Milošević the promise of the realization of their fantasies about a Greater Serbian (and Orthodox) state. The Church remained consistently pro-war throughout the campaign in Croatia (June–December 1991), and after Serbian insurgents, backed by the JNA (Yugoslav People's Army), expelled Croats from eastern Slavonia, the Serbian Church hastened to establish a new diocese in the occupied territory, constructing new churches in some cases in villages which had been populated entirely by Croats.[10]

Later, in January 1992, as interethnic tensions were heating up in Bosnia-Herzegovina, the Orthodox bishops held a synod at which they issued a warning that Bosnia's Serbs were living "under the threat that genocide will again be visited upon them."[11] In spite of the antiregime demonstration of 14 June 1992, in which Patriarch Pavle played a signal role, the Serbian Church gave full support to the expansionist plans being pursued by Karadžić's forces. The Church's partisanship was aptly illustrated by the statement issued by the Orthodox prelates at the end of 1992, "categorically denying that Serbs [had] organized rapes and challenging anyone to name a single concentration camp where such rapes [had] occurred, while simultaneously charging that many Serbian women had been raped by Muslims and Croats."[12] Further, the Church remained committed to the idea of a Greater Serbia throughout the war, both before the Vance-Owen plan over which Karadžić and Milošević split, and after. Their split had roots in personality differences and in an underlying rivalry, but broke into the open in April 1993 when Karadžić defied Milošević by refusing to accept the proffered peace plan. Patriarch Pavle and Metropolitan Amfilohije declared their opposition to the Vance-Owen plan for the same reason that Karadžić did: they hoped to see even more lands annexed by the Serbian side. Throughout the war, Patriarch Pavle and the Holy Synod repeatedly denied the existence of Serb-run concentration camps in Bosnia, and in 1994, the Serbian Church denounced the "Contact Group" plan, which proposed to award 49 percent of Bosnian land to the Serbs, who had made up only 32 percent of the population of Bosnia in the 1991 census; the Church did so on the grounds that the plan was "unfair" to Serbs.[13] Not surprisingly, after the signing of the Dayton Accords in 1995, the Serbian Church denounced what it called "the Dayton diktat."[14] There were two problems with the Dayton Accords, from the Church's viewpoint: first, they appeared to codify Belgrade's abandonment of the Greater Serbian project; second, they established a framework within which Serbs from Croatia and parts of Bosnia-Herzegovina, who had managed to hold on to their homes during the four years of warfare, abandoned their domiciles and fled to Serbia or to Republika Srpska. The Church responded with appeals to the international authorities to ensure the safety of those Serbs who might choose to stay in the Bosniak-ruled part of Sarajevo and in Croatia, and to the Serbs themselves "not to leave their ancestral homes." The Holy Synod called on its bishops to return to their sees in Bosnia and Croatia,[15] while Patriarch Pavle and Bishop Atanasije called on Belgrade to refuse to cooperate with the International Criminal Tribunal in The Hague.[16]

The war left a bitter legacy for all the peoples concerned and for their religious organizations. Aside from the tally of the dead, the wounded, the displaced, and of those who had lost loved ones, there was the massive destruction to infrastructure, the complete disruption of the patterns of life which had been established in the decades since the end of World War Two, and the dispersal of populations which had lived together since Ottoman times. The destruction also extended to cultural objects, such as churches and holy shrines. Where the Serbian Orthodox Church was concerned, an estimated 438 religious edifices had been destroyed or damaged in the war in Croatia and Bosnia already by March 1994.[17] Moreover, quite apart from such further church facilities as were destroyed later, there was the fact that in recapturing the Krajina, Croatian authorities took many of the Serbian Orthodox churches standing there and turned them over to the Catholic Church, to replace the facilities lost by the Catholics.

Three and a half years after Dayton, Patriarch Pavle paid a visit to Zagreb, as the guest of Zagreb's archbishop, Josip Bozanić. The patriarch came in peace and joined his Croatian Catholic counterpart in calling for tolerance and peaceful coexistence. But memories of the war and of the Orthodox Church's contribution to it were still fresh, and several Croatian parties—specifically, the Croatian Christian-Democratic Union, the Croatian Party of Right, the Croatian Pure Party of Right, and Dobroslav Paraga's Croatian Party of Right 1861—protested the Orthodox prelate's visit. Paraga pointed out, for example, that "the patriarch [has] never admitted his great sin of fomenting wartime hatreds and his calls for Serbian conquest. In the worst tradition of the notorious Chetnik movement, this bellicose and chauvinistic patriarch called for a bloody revision of the state borders and brought nothing but pain and suffering to the Croats. A man who even today does not renounce the Great Serbian program of 1844 cannot be welcome in Croatia."[18]

Aside from the war in Croatia and Bosnia, one can speak of the Serbian Orthodox Church as having been engaged in three other "fronts": Kosovo, Montenegro, and Serbia itself.

The Church and Kosovo

During much of the 1990s, the Serbian Church worked hand in glove with the Milošević regime in Kosovo, in a combined effort to shore up the Serbian demographic and symbolic presence in the province. In December 1992, for example, the Serbian Church laid the foundation stone for a new Church of Christ the Savior on the spot where, allegedly, a church by the same name had been demolished by the Ottomans after the famous battle in 1389.[19] But the site was in the middle of the University of Priština complex and had already been allocated for the construction of a new facility for the Faculty of Arts. In response, the League of Democrats of Kosova presidency issued a statement declaring that "the consequences of this act may be very grave and incurable."[20] A decade later—in January 2003—the local administration, now under Albanian control, ordered the destruction of the unfinished facility.[21] In the 1990s, however, this was only one of a number of Serbian Church building projects under construction or renovation; others included a reconstruction of the Church of Djakova, and the erection of new churches in Gure e Kocit and Poterc i Eperm.[22] For the Church, the construction of facilities was a way of claiming Kosovo for its earthly kingdom: the Albanians understood the construction projects in these terms, and would act on this formula after June 1999.

Even when the Serbian Church spoke out for Albanian interests, its statements were colored by nationalism. For example, in early January 1998, Patriarch Pavle sent a public letter to the students' union of the University of Priština, condemning Serbian police brutality against a group of Albanian students who had been demonstrating peacefully on 30 December; but in spite of this, Pavle referred in his letter to the Albanians as "Šiptari," rather than "Albanci"[23]; although the word "Šiptari" is closely related to the Albanian name for Albanians, its use by Serbs is generally intended to be derogatory and is understood by Albanians to be a slur, much in the way that Russians do not appreciate it when Americans call them "ruskies." Or again, in June 1998, when the Serbian Orthodox

Church criticized the "totalitarian" regime in Belgrade for the worsening situation in Kosovo, it nonetheless included "the fanaticism of the ethnic Albanian community" in its condemnation.[24] But the Serbian Church has always been conscious of its chosen role as champion of the Serbian nation. It was in this spirit that Metropolitan Artemije Radosavljević of Raška-Prizren requested in early February 1999 that representatives of the Serbian Church be allowed to take part in the Rambouillet conference on Kosovo being held in order to find a negotiated solution to the growing conflict in the province.[25]

During the seventy-eight-day air campaign conducted by NATO against the FRY (Federal Republic of Yugoslavia) in an effort to end Belgrade's repression in Kosovo, leading representatives of the Church condemned what they called "barbaric aggression, which above all affects innocent civilians."[26] On 9 April, Bishop Artemije sarcastically "congratulated" NATO for "truly glittering results" in having destroyed "many factories and residential districts, blasted many bridges and radio towers, [and for having] caused much death and suffering."[27] Members of the Serbian Orthodox Church and even officials of the Belgrade government accused NATO of deliberately targeting and destroying Serbian monasteries of great historic and aesthetic value, posting these charges, for example, on the Web site of the Belgrade government's Institute for the Protection of Cultural Monuments of Serbia.[28] No evidence of such destruction was provided either then or later. Subsequently, after the NATO air campaign had ended, much of the Church hierarchy remained unrepentant. But Luka Novaković, deacon at the patriarchal library in Belgrade, declared, in a public statement, "We have learned that some Serbs did terrible things in Kosovo, and admitting that is the first step in changing things for the better. . . . It is important for a country to know the truth. It has to know; otherwise it will just continue on without confessing."[29]

The NATO air campaign was a watershed for Serbia, the point at which Serbs realized that the strategy of opposing the entire world could not work. In the first three months after the end of the campaign and the deployment of the KFOR (Kosovo International Security Force) peacekeeping force, more than 160,000 Kosovar Serbs were said to have been expelled from the province, while around seventy Orthodox shrines were destroyed, according to Serb sources.[30] By the end of the year, according to Serbian Orthodox Church sources, the number of Serbs to have fled Kosovo exceeded 250,000.[31] In Priština alone, the number of Serbs plummeted rapidly from 20,000 before the NATO aerial campaign to just 2,000 by mid-July 1999.[32] This was in spite of the fact that Patriarch Pavle had

hurried to Kosovo in mid-June to urge local Serbs to remain in the province.[33] The dynamiting of Serbian holy places was nothing less than a direct Albanian assault on the ecclesiastical markers of the Belgrade patriarchate's would-be "earthly kingdom" in Kosovo. The arson was motivated
by national rivalry over land, rather than by religious intolerance, as illustrated by the dynamiting of a statue of the fourteenth-century Serbian
tsar, Dušan the Mighty, in downtown Prizren in July 1999.[34] With the Serbian "Jerusalem" being patrolled by international peacekeepers and local
Albanians talking of establishing an independent Republic of Kosova
under Albanian control, the Holy Synod called on Yugoslav president
Milošević to resign. Metropolitan Artemije even nurtured the hope that
the removal of Milošević from office would put a stop to Western support
for an independent Kosovo and save the province for Serbia.[35]

Meanwhile, the Albanians continued to blow up Serbian religious objects across the province, setting off a bomb in the new Serbian Orthodox
cathedral in Priština at the beginning of August.[36] Among those monasteries damaged by Albanian arsonists were those at Dečani, Sopočani, Peć,
Kuršumlija, Hopovo, Sisatovac, Zdrebaonik, and Dajbabe (not far from
Podgorica). In the first few months after the end of the air campaign, more
than a hundred Serbian Orthodox churches and monasteries were said to
have been destroyed by vengeful Albanians; thirty-three of these cases involved pre-sixteenth-century churches.[37] In this context, it seems rather
striking to find Fr. Sava Janjić, hieromonk of the Dečani Monastery and
a leading spokesperson for the Church in Kosovo, expressing "his regret
for [the] violence perpetrated by Serbs against the province's ethnic Albanian community" in November 1999. "I am taking this opportunity once
again," he told UN Radio in Priština, "to express my greatest regret for
everything which was done by members of the Serbian people and special forces against the Albanian civilians, which is a very serious crime."[38]

On 29 November 1999, just a few months after he had demanded that
Milošević resign from office, Patriarch Pavle took part in the Republic Day
celebration hosted by Milošević. Angered by this move, which might be
interpreted as ostensible reconfirmation of Church support for the regime,
Metropolitan Artemije sent an open letter to the patriarch, telling him
that he was "turning his back on his own people and, with his attendance
at the 29th November ceremony, . . . shoring up the rickety chair of the
Destroyer of the Serbian nation."[39] As Biserka Matić has pointed out,
Artemije's letter brought before the public eye the depth of dissension
among the Serbian Orthodox clergy concerning the attitude to be taken
toward the Milošević regime.[40]

Gradually, during the period 1999–2001, the number of violent crimes being committed by Albanians against Serbs declined. Meanwhile, in Kosovo, Serbs were being pushed into certain fixed regions, mostly in the north, while new potentially independent political institutions were being set up under KFOR supervision. Father Sava tried, in a March 2002 interview, to put all of this in perspective. "The Western media very frequently state that the number of murders, thefts, and other crimes against Serbs has gone down," he stated.

> However, they forget that this is not the result of an improvement in the political situation but of the absolute ghettoization of the Serbs who are increasingly hermetically separated from the Albanians for security reasons. . . . Unfortunately, I must say that Kosovo is not free for all its residents and that the policy of discrimination and ethnic repression, especially against Serbs and Roma, is still continuing despite the presence of the UN and KFOR.[41]

Then, in late 2002, the Church of St. Basil of Ostrog in the village of Ljubovo was completely destroyed by vandals and the Church of All Serbian Saints in the village of Djurakovac was damaged by three consecutive explosions.[42] The UNMIK's (United Nations Mission in Kosovo) chief of mission, Michael Steiner, ordered repairs to the latter facility, provoking protests from the Diocese of Raška and Prizren of the Serbian Orthodox Church, whose bishop, Artemije, wanted prior consultations before repairs were carried out.[43] Individual acts of vandalism have continued,[44] provoking Patriarch Pavle to appeal to domestic and international authorities in August 2003 to put an end to the violence and vandalism in Kosovo.[45]

The violence is, among other things, a symptom of Albanian determination to end Serbian control of the province. But the Church remains adamant that Kosovo must remain under Belgrade's control. Thus, in July 2003, the Holy Synod declared its support for Serbian deputy premier Nebojša Čović, who has been heading the State Coordinating Center for Kosovo-Metohija, and whose position is that "no one in Serbia ha[s] the right to give up Kosovo and Metohija."[46] Bishop Ignatije of Braničevo spoke for all Serbian bishops when he offered that "if there is an awareness among the Serb people that Kosovo is ours and that it should remain so, not because it is a piece of land, but because of an identity which is precisely linked with it, I think that the necessary strength will be found [to keep it]."[47]

Ecclesiastical Dissension in Montenegro

In Montenegro, an autocephalous Montenegrin Orthodox Church was proclaimed in January 1991, enthroning Mirać Dedajić as Metropolitan Mihajlo on 31 October 1998. This came a little over a year after Ecumenical Patriarch Bartolomeios, acting in agreement with the Belgrade patriarchate, had excommunicated Dedajić from the Church.[48] The Serbian Orthodox Church quickly branded the new Church "schismatic" and as local believers voted to join the Montenegrin Church organization, Serbian Church spokespersons denounced what they called the "theft" of Serbian Church property. But, in fact, the Montenegrin Orthodox Church had been functioning autonomously until 1920, when Crown Prince Aleksandar, regent of the Kingdom of Serbs, Croats, and Slovenes, quashed its autonomy and turned its properties over to the Belgrade patriarchate.[49]

But Montenegrin ecclesiastical politics is, in fact, an epiphenomenon of Montenegrin politics more generally, and as the cause of Montenegrin independence has waxed, so too has the cause of Montenegrin ecclesiastical autocephaly. By 1999, if not before, the Montenegrin Church had reached the point of no return, as violence escalated between the two Church communities. Not surprisingly, Yugoslav prime minister Momir Bulatović, Milošević's man in Podgorica, condemned the Montenegrin government's recognition of the Montenegrin Church as "an invitation to conflict" in Montenegro.[50] Independence-minded Montenegrin president (later prime minister) Milo Djukanović, by contrast, has given the Montenegrin Orthodox Church his solid support.

Tensions between the two Churches escalated sharply in October 1998, as preparations got under way for the enthronement of Metropolitan Mihajlo. Significantly, the enthronement was held in the traditional Montenegrin capital of Cetinje, rather than in Podgorica; several thousand adherents attended the ceremony, held outside King Nikola's palace.[51] On the event of the enthronement, however, Slobodan Tomović, the Montenegrin minister of religious affairs and a member of the Social Democratic Party, issued a statement alleging that the Montenegrin government endorsed the Serbian Orthodox Church, rather than the restorationist Montenegrin Church, a statement which proved to be inaccurate but which, in the short run, contributed to inflaming passions.[52] Violent incidents between adherents of the two Churches quickly became routine,[53] but Montenegrin Church adherents were determined to reclaim what they felt had been taken from them in 1920. Serbian Church adherents were just as determined to prevent the Montenegrin autocephalists from doing so. The disagreements over property only contributed to the violence. In March 1999, a group of twelve Montenegrin and Serbian attorneys announced that they would be filing charges against the Serbian Orthodox Church for the "usurpation" of sacred buildings rightfully belonging to the Montenegrin Orthodox Church.[54]

The rival Montenegrin ecclesiastical leader, representing the Belgrade patriarchate, was Metropolitan Amfilohije Radović, regarded by members of a group calling itself the Montenegrin Homeland Club as "an exponent of Slobodan Milošević's policy" who had been "installed" in his position in order to play a role "within the Greater Serbian project."[55]

Since the Serbian Orthodox Church has famously taken the position that Montenegrins are not nationally distinct from Serbs,[56] the ecclesiastical dispute inescapably had a nationalist character from the beginning. At one point, the FRY minister without portfolio Nebojša Veličković accused the Montenegrin authorities of seeking to promote divisions among the people of Montenegro and specifically of supporting the Montenegrin Church "so as to facilitate the achievement of their sinister goals."[57] As the violence continued, Metropolitan Amfilohije of Montenegro and the Littoral, loyal to the Belgrade patriarchate, issued a statement condemning "blasphemous attacks on priests discharging their official duties by people who falsely represent themselves and sow hatred and discord among the people, undermining basic religious and human rights."[58]

But the Montenegrin authorities were prepared to use threats to get their way, advising Amfilohije, who had been demanding the introduction of religious instruction into Montenegrin state schools, that that would happen only after the autocephaly of the Montenegrin Orthodox Church was recognized.[59] In fact, the Montenegrin Church was officially registered by Montenegrin state authorities in mid-January 2000, but ecumenical recognition of that Church's autocephaly was still—and is still—lacking. The Holy Synod of the Belgrade patriarchate replied by condemning the Montenegrin autocephalists as "atheists."[60] Disputes over property, mutual insults, and violent incidents continued during 2000, with Metropolitan Mihajlo demanding the return of some six hundred places of worship used by the Serbian Orthodox Church since the subordination of the Montenegrin Church to the reestablished Belgrade patriarchate eighty years earlier.[61]

Montenegrin deputy prime minister Novak Kilibarda seemed to be sounding a call for mutual tolerance in late January 2000 when he called on the two Churches to coexist.[62] But scarcely three weeks later, the legal council of the Montenegrin-Littoral diocese (loyal to the Belgrade patriarchate) issued a statement asserting that it was the only canonical Church body functioning in Montenegro[63]—a statement which was literally true but not without political intentions. The same council subsequently declared that baptisms and other religious rites carried out by the "non-existing" Montenegrin Orthodox Church were "null and void" and, therefore, inefficacious.[64]

In May 2000, the ecumenical patriarch, Bartolomeios of Constantinople, sent a public letter to President Djukanović criticizing Metropolitan Mihajlo, who, said Bartolomeios, was "passing himself off to be a priest in violation of every law and is thereby upsetting the Orthodox people in Montenegro," adding that a Church which "functions through a defrocked person is not recognized by any Orthodox Church."[65] He closed by asking Djukanović to distance himself from Mihajlo.

If anyone imagined that either Montenegrin separatism or the movement for Montenegrin ecclesiastical autocephaly would disappear with the fall of Milošević, s/he would have been in for a surprise. On the contrary, violent incidents seemed, if anything, to escalate in the weeks following 5 October 2000. Toward the end of the year, there were even allegations that paramilitary forces loyal to Podgorica were being used to support the Montenegrin Church's efforts to take back property from the Serbian Church.[66]

As the dispute continued, the patriarch of Moscow, Aleksii II, intervened to give his support to the Belgrade patriarchate and to remind everyone that requests for the recognition of "newly formed" Churches had to await certain established procedures.[67] Whether the suppression of Montenegrin autonomy had been canonically recognized through established procedures he did not say; but no autocephalist would accept Aleksii's characterization of the restored Montenegrin Church as a "newly formed" institution.

And so the dispute has continued, with tensions and violence continuing. For example, on Orthodox Christmas Eve (6 January 2002), some thirty members of the Montenegrin Church gathered at a public place to light a Yule log. Soon some two thousand members of the Serbian Church, led by the local mayor and several priests, charged the Montenegrin Church adherents with axes and automatic weapons, shouting all the while the names of Milošević and Karadžić.[68] Back in Cetinje, Metropolitan Mihajlo offered an olive branch of sorts, declaring, "We must extend a hand of friendship to our enemies, to save them from themselves and from their uncontrollable evil that has shaken the entire Montenegro."[69]

But relations between the ecclesiastical rivals remain acrimonious. In January 2002, for example, Metropolitan Antonije of Ravenna and All Italy visited Cetinje as the guest of the Montenegrin Orthodox Church, and, in an interview with the Podgorica weekly magazine *Monitor*, affirmed, almost matter-of-factly, that Montenegro had always had an autocephalous Church and that this could not be denied by reasonable persons. Urging that "Serbian priests from Montenegro who do not accept the autocephaly of the Montenegrin Church should go to Serbia," he noted that Metropolitan Amfilohije had associated himself with such persons as Karadžić and the infamous "Arkan," adding that it was "certain" that Amfilohije was an atheist.[70] The following month, Metropolitan Amfilohije gave an interview to the Belgrade daily newspaper *Glas javnosti*, in which he described the Montenegrin Church as a "so-called Church" and a "pseudo-Church," alleging that it reflected processes of "de-Christianization."[71]

Champions of Montenegrin autocephaly claim that in opposing autocephaly, the Belgrade patriarchate is motivated, among other things, by the denial that Montenegrins are distinct from Serbs and by the desire to assimilate Montenegro into Serbia.[72] The metropolitanate, in turn, replies that the autocephalists are "false priests," that the government in Podgorica, insofar as it is supporting autocephaly, is following in the footsteps of Pontius Pilate, and that the result of these activities is lawlessness in the ecclesiastical realm.[73]

Then came the shooting of Serbian prime minister Zoran Djindjić in mid-March 2003. In life, Djindjić had been highly controversial. But in death he came to be viewed as a kind of saint, and was freely compared to U.S. president John F. Kennedy, who had been assassinated some forty years earlier. Metropolitan Amfilohije created a storm of controversy with his eulogy at Djindjić's funeral, at which he compared Djindjić to fourteenth-century Serbian tsar Lazar, declared it "impossible" to say whether the assassination of the prime minister or the killing of a little girl named Milica Rajić in the course of the NATO air campaign in 1999 was the greater tragedy for Serbia, and described Djindjić's "grievous wound" as "the most precious aspect of his being and his most precious possession."[74] The Helsinki Committee for Human Rights in Serbia condemned the homily as a species of "political extremism,"[75] while the Serbian government characterized Amfilohije's thoughts as "a political tirade . . . [which] offended the family and friends."[76] The autocephalous Montenegrin Orthodox Church also criticized Amfilohije, claiming that his homily "once again confirmed his unreserved loyalty and devotion to everything which opposes peace, goodness, and progress, which is also contradictory to universal values and ideas of an emancipated society."[77] The homily may have been embarrassing, but no one expected it to have any impact on the strength of the resistance put up by the Belgrade patriarchate to Montenegrin autocephaly. On the contrary, the dispute has continued unabated.[78]

The Macedonian Schism

The Macedonian Church's credentials would appear, on the face of it, to be excellent. The archbishopric of Ohrid was originally established in 1019 and lasted for eight centuries before being abolished in 1767. In 1891, Metropolitan Teodor of Skopje first raised the demand for a revival of an independent Macedonian Church, but after World War One, ecclesiastical jurisdiction in Macedonia was entrusted to the Belgrade patriarchate. The rivalry between Macedonian and Serbian bishops simmered until March 1945, when "a council of local clergy and laity met in Partisan-held Skopje and adopted a resolution proclaiming the right of the Macedonian nation to a national Church."[79] The demand was ignored, but in 1957, permission was granted for the use of the Macedonian language in diocesan administration in Macedonia. The following year, in a bold move, Macedonian clergy declared the reestablishment of the archbishopric of Ohrid, electing Bishop Dositej Stojković archbishop of Ohrid and metropolitan of Macedonia. These moves were supported by the government of the Socialist Republic of Macedonia. In autumn 1966, shortly after the fall of Aleksandar Ranković from power (he had been vice president and chief of the secret police), the Macedonian bishops handed the patriarch of Belgrade an ultimatum: either he would recognize Macedonian autocephaly or the Macedonians would act unilaterally. The Belgrade patriarchate suggested autonomy as a compromise, but the Macedonians were not interested and, in mid-July 1967, unilaterally declared autocephaly. The socialist government supported Macedonian ecclesiastical autocephaly as part of its strategy of supporting Macedonian culture and nationality. Although the Belgrade patriarchate was powerless to quash the Macedonian Church, the Macedonians in turn were unable to win ecumenical recognition of their organization, which continued to be treated as a schismatic Church in the Orthodox community.

But with the breakup of the Yugoslav federation, the Serbian Orthodox Church revived the pressure. In 1992, a proposal for joint liturgy and canonical unity between the Macedonian and Serbian Orthodox Churches was drafted and adopted by commissions from the two bodies, but it was later vetoed by the Holy Synod of the Serbian Orthodox Church.[80] A decade later, there was another agreement on the table, abolishing the autocephalous status of the Macedonian Church and setting it up as an autonomous entity within the Serbian Church. The agreement was confirmed on the Serbian side, and found supporters on the Macedonian side, sowing division in the ranks of that Church. Specifically, Bishops Timotej of Ohrid and Kičevo, Naum of Strumica, Jovan of Veles Povardarie, and Petar of Australia and New Zealand supported the proposal for autonomy. On the other side stood Bishops Kiril of Polog and Kumanovo (the last surviving signatory of the 1967 proclamation of autocephaly), Agatangel of Bregalnica, and Goražd of Western Europe, who continued to insist on Macedonian autocephaly. Archbishop Stefan of Ohrid, head of the Macedonian Church, declared himself neutral, though there is every reason to believe that he favored autocephaly.[81] When the agreement fell through, all the autonomists accepted that result with one exception. The exception was Metropolitan Jovan, who was unable to reconcile himself to that result and accepted an invitation from Patriarch Pavle to recognize the Belgrade patriarchate. Interestingly enough, Bishop Jovan was said to be working on a Ph.D. dissertation about the question of autonomous vs. autocephalous status in the Orthodox Church.[82] The Synod of the Macedonian Orthodox Church met urgently on 5 July 2002 and voted unanimously to relieve Jovan of his episcopal authority and to order him to transfer to the Monastery of Martyr Gorgi near the town of Negotin. Instead of removing to the monastery, however, now-ex-Metropolitan Jovan reportedly fled to Greece.[83] The following month, some seventy thousand people attended a dedication ceremony for a new sixty-six-meter-high cross erected by the Macedonian Church on Mount Vodno, fifteen kilometers outside Skopje. Although the Catholics and Muslims of Macedonia interpreted the cross as directed against them, it was more likely an assertion of Macedonia's millennium of autocephaly, directed against the Serbian Church.

On 24 May 2003, the Serbian Orthodox patriarchate issued an ultimatum to the Macedonian Church, demanding that the latter recognize the authority of the Belgrade patriarchate by 1 September or see the demotion of its metropolitans. Jovan, who had in the interim been appointed exarch in Macedonia on behalf of the Serbian Orthodox Church, was by now acting as spokesperson for Belgrade's reunification program. Only at this point did the Holy Synod of the Macedonian Orthodox Church vote to strip Jovan of his rank as bishop and defrock him, declaring that he should henceforth be known by his civilian name, Zoran Vraniskovski. It was also claimed now that he was suspected of having embezzled funds from the Church while serving as metropolitan of Bregalnica and Veles.[84] In the wake of a dispute relating to the Prohor Pčinski monastery (a monastery of great importance to Orthodox Macedonians, situated in Serbia), the Macedonian government issued a regulation requiring that Serbian Orthodox clerics wishing to enter Macedonian territory in clerical attire should present either an official invitation from the Macedonian Church or documentation showing that they were merely transiting through the country. Then, when Jovan/Zoran entered the country without such paperwork, he was incarcerated for five days, provoking howls of protest from Belgrade.[85] As the dispute escalated, the Serbian Ministry of Religious Affairs protested to the Macedonian embassy in Belgrade, intimating that Jovan/Zoran's arrest could impact Serb-Macedonian relations negatively,[86] while the Macedonian community in Serbia and Montenegro sent a letter of support to the Holy Synod of the Macedonian Church, declaring that it was "familiar with the aggressiveness of the Serbian Orthodox Church."[87] In a second letter, sent three days later, the Macedonian community rejected the Belgrade patriarchate's claim that the dispute was rooted in religious questions and alluded, vaguely, to wider interests.[88] There were dark suggestions, in some circles, that the Greek government and Greek Church were encouraging the Serbs to stir up disputes with the Macedonian Church. By this point, the patriarchate had also declared that it would not allow Macedonian clergy to enter the monastery at Prohor Pčinski. In late July, Dragoljub Mičunović, Federal Assembly speaker, entered the fray, reproving both Churches and demanding that they cease their pressure on their respective governments.[89]

In the course of 2003, the conflict escalated when Patriarch Pavle named Metropolitan Jovan to head the "autonomous archbishopric of Ohrid," which would be subordinate to Belgrade. Then, in his traditional Christmas sermon in January 2004, Pavle invited Orthodox believers in Macedonia to leave their Church and affiliate with the "autonomous archbishopric" which he controlled[90]; it was an open provocation. A few days later, Metropolitan Jovan—defrocked by the Macedonian Church but elevated by the Serbian Church—came to Bitola, Macedonia, to announce that he had succeeded in winning over three Macedonian monasteries to "canonical unity" with the Belgrade patriarchate.[91] Macedonian authorities immediately had the wayward cleric arrested and put him in prison for the second time in two years, accusing him of spreading "national, religious, and racial hatred."[92] Serbian bishop Irinej (Bulović) of Bačka, whose

Church had spent much of the quarter century since Tito's death trying to undermine the Macedonian Church and ensuring its ostracism within the Orthodox community of Churches, reacted by claiming that the Serbian Church had shown "huge patience over all these decades" since the proclamation of Macedonian ecclesiastical autocephaly in 1967 and by repudiating the traditional Orthodox canon, according to which an independent state of a distinct nation is entitled to its own autocephalous Church.[93] In response, the Holy Synod of the Macedonian Orthodox Church issued a statement on 13 January accusing Patriarch Pavle of sowing "unrest" in its ranks and "meddling" in another Church's internal affairs, and charging the Serbian bishops collectively with being "lackeys of [Serbian] . . . national chauvinism and of Greater Serbian ideas."[94]

The Home Front

Within Serbia itself, the Serbian Orthodox Church has looked to the past, insistently fighting internationalization, globalization, secularization, tolerance, and, for the most part, any admission that many Serbs might bear some responsibility for the atrocities perpetrated in the years 1989–2000. The Church has not only dismissed the International Criminal Tribunal in The Hague as prejudiced against Serbs, but it has also done its best to fan hysteria about the Rotary Club, the Optimists Society, and the Pen Club, and achieved a "success" for its agenda in autumn 2001, when the Serbian government agreed to introduce catechism classes in the regular curriculum in elementary and secondary public schools.[95] This last measure provoked jubilation in Church circles, which took pleasure in the thought that it would "lead to a return to traditional values" in Serbia,[96] but controversy in Vojvodina, in spite of the fact that, in recognition of the religious diversity of the province, it was decided to authorize catechism for six different religions in Vojvodina's schools. An association called "Forum juris," based in Novi Sad, challenged the constitutionality of the ordinance, taking the case before the Constitutional Court of the FRY. The group's spokespersons alleged that the ordinance would create conditions which would discriminate in favor of the "traditional" religious associations.[97] With some thirty-nine distinct religious associations registered in the province, there was room to fear that at least some of the thirty-three religions not included in access to the classroom would find the measure discriminatory. An additional problem cited by foes of the ordinance was that it would inevitably entail segregating children by religious creed for the catechism class, thereby building up psychological distance between children of different faiths. The irrepressible Nenad Čanak, president of Vojvodina's assembly, warned that

> the Taliban surrounding Koštunica are bent on making an Orthodox Jamahiriya, a purely religious state. . . . This is exactly what is going on at the moment, combined with growing fascist tendencies. What we are dealing with here is not fascism spread by means of state repression, but a sort of fascism permeating every single pore of the social tissue, motivating and mobilizing the needy and the social psychopaths to, say, brutally beat protesting homosexuals today, only to switch to those who bathe much too often in view of the local hygienic tradition tomorrow—up to whacking anyone and everyone daring to distance himself even slightly from the pervading milieu of hopelessness and terror. No economic boom will do the job. What is needed is a thorough and complex process of denazification, accompanied by a steady recovery of the economy and incessant questioning of the results achieved.[98]

Zoran Djindjić tried to mollify critics on the liberal left by offering that pupils could sign up for a class in citizenship (actually, the class would be called "the basics of democracy") in place of religion, but this only poured oil on the fire, by suggesting that religion might be a substitute for knowledge about the workings of democracy, or vice versa. Djordje Subotić, a high official in the Reform Party of Vojvodina and a deputy in the provincial assembly, concluded that "in a roundabout way, state religion is being introduced into our society."[99] The state co-minister of education, Vigor Majić, even resigned his office in protest over the ordinance. But for the Serbian Orthodox Church the introduction of religious instruction in state schools was an important victory. For many religious associations, the opportunity to disseminate their teachings to a captive audience is one of the most important goals to be achieved.

The Serbian Orthodox Church is, of course, not a monolithic body, as the discussion about dissent between Patriarch Pavle and Metropolitan Artemije already made clear. The Church's "liberal" faction is probably best represented by Artemije himself, who is "liberal" in the sense of having promoted Serb-Albanian tolerance and dialogue for a number of years. But there is also a reactionary fringe associated, inter alia, with the St. Justin the Philosopher Association of Students and the editorial council of the journal *Dveri srpske*. These groups joined the Church choir of the Shrine of St. Alexander Nevsky in staging, on 6 December 2001, the "first assembly of Orthodox-national Serbian youth at the University of Belgrade since 1944," that is, since the era of Serbian fascism. Held at the Filosofski fakultet, this meeting saw the championing of "Orthodoxy, nationalism, monarchism, anticommunism, [and] antiglobalism," calls for the establishment of a Greater Serbia uniting all Serbs, and condemnations of gays and lesbians, feminists, and advocates of secularization.[100] Participants at this meeting complained that, thanks to communist rule, the University of Belgrade had become "a spiritually dead building, the ideological hatch of atheism and anti-Serbianism," and claimed that it was not "a Serbian national university." For the organizers, George Soros, founder of the Open Society network to promote liberal values, seemed to be "the most odious enemy," while the introduction of religious instruction into the state schools was essential "because without spiritual renewal there can be neither political nor state renewal."[101] Professor Bora Kuzmanović, a central figure in this event, offered his diagnosis that Serbian society was experiencing a spiritual crisis, urging that "re-traditionalization . . . is one answer to the social crisis and crisis of values."[102] What might Kuzmanović have in mind by "re-traditionalization"? The journal *Dveri srpske* offered the following observation about at least one "tradition" which it wanted to encourage:

> Male rule is a great alleviation for women. This view is not arbitrary and it is not without support. It is endorsed over and over in the Old and New Testament. The apostle Paul, for example, says in one place: "Women should submit to their husbands as to the Lord, because a husband is a woman's head, much as Christ is the head of the Church."[103]

Intolerance has grown enormously in Serbia in the years since Milošević took power, thanks to the war, to the xenophobic agitation of Vojislav Šešelj and other radical right extremists, and the growing conviction among many Serbs that much of the world is against their country. Continued violent expressions of anti-Semitism as well as other forms of racism,[104] the thrashing meted out to would-be participants in what was intended to be Serbia's first Gay Pride parade (in July 2001),[105] the Orthodox Church's stubborn condemnation of homosexuality,[106] repeated assaults on the members of various Protestant communities on the grounds that they "damage [the] physical and psychological development of [Serbian] children,"[107] the Church's inability to see in a papal visit to Bosnia anything but a "provocation,"[108] and hostile public reaction in Belgrade, Užice, and Čačak to an exhibition of photographs documenting events in the recent war[109] are all symptoms of a generalized phobia of everyone and everything different, whether that be religiously, nationally, sexually, or culturally. In this context, it comes as little surprise that the Holy Synod, acting unanimously at a session on 19 May 2003, declared the canonization of Bishop Nikolaj Velimirović (1881–1956), the infamous Europhobic supporter of the chauvinistic Chetnik movement, who deplored European washing habits and condemned democracy, tolerance, pacifism, and Jews.[110] What is troubling, however, is that recent polls show that the Serbian Orthodox Church is the most trusted institution in Serbia today. In a poll conducted among 1,100 adults in thirty-seven districts in summer 2003, 68 percent of respondents said that they trusted the Church, with 61 percent expressing trust in the army. These figures compared with 48 percent who trust the police, 44 percent who trust the National Bank, 39 percent who trust the government, and 38 percent who trust the judiciary. On the other hand, 22 percent of respondents said that they had no trust in the Serbian Orthodox Church.[111]

The Social Agenda of the Orthodox Church

If one were to survey also the Orthodox Church establishments in neighboring Romania and Bulgaria, one would note, where Romania is concerned, that the Orthodox Church in that country has had some rather obvious problems adapting to pluralist conditions. Like the Serbian Orthodox Church, it is infected by nationalism, religious chauvinism, and sexual phobias. The last of these has been manifested in efforts on the part of hierarchs of the Romanian Orthodox Church to block the legalization of gay and lesbian rights, to prevent transsexuals from being able to obtain therapy and surgery, or even appropriate pharmaceutical products, and to restore the highly unpopular ban on abortions which had been enforced in the Ceaușescu era.[112] The nationalist engagement has been manifested, inter alia, in "a fever of construction of Orthodox churches in almost entirely Hungarian areas," according to the head of the Office for Hungarian Minorities Abroad.[113] The Bulgarian Orthodox Church, paralyzed in the years 1991–98 by a schism, with two patriarchs vying for leadership,[114] has more recently engaged in battles for the control of cultural products, pressuring the state television to cancel the planned broadcast of the film *The Last Temptation of Christ* in January 2002 and condemning the Harry Potter books in March 2002, alleging that the books "diminish readers' [ability] to react against black magic and make them interested in evil deeds."[115]

If one were to draw up a "social creed" to which the Orthodox Churches, including the Serbian, could be said to subscribe, it might include the following:

1. Divine law is higher than positive law, and therefore the Orthodox Church has the right and duty to declare which laws and proposed laws are sinful, and to fight to see divine law (as understood by the Orthodox Church) reflected in positive law.

2. Tolerance is a vice: the guidelines of the Church are clear and nothing which departs from those guidelines is deserving of tolerance. Sexual tolerance is the "worst" form of tolerance.

3. The traditional family (including patriarchal predominance) is an institution made sacred by God's will and any efforts on behalf of gender equality are to be deplored; any alternatives to heterosexuality are anathema.

4. The nation is the Church and the Church must tend to the interests, needs, and goals of the nation; the nation has a right to live together in one state, with one Church.

5. It is legitimate to harm those who have sinned against the Church (or prevented the nation from realizing its objectives).

6. It is the duty of the state to protect its Church and to advance its agenda.

7. There can be no equal rights for rival religious organizations, and their agendas should not be considered by lawmakers, except to the extent that they are compatible with the Orthodox agenda (e.g., religious instruction for Catholics and Lutherans alongside Orthodox in state schools).

In all of these ways, however, the Orthodox Church sets itself against the liberal project, defending, at best, a nationalist, uncivic concept of democracy. The Serbian Orthodox Church, specifically, represents an obstruction, thus, to the development of liberal democracy in Serbia, and to the extent that liberal democracy may be able to develop in Serbia, the Church will be increasingly marginalized. I would add, further, that the Orthodox Church has become a factor—though obviously not the only one—for continued instability in Serbia.

In making these assertions, I do not wish to rule out the possibility as such that the Church might change, only to suggest that I consider the prospects for significant change on the part of the Church to be remote. Unlike the Catholic Church, the Orthodox Church never went through the challenge of anything like the Reformation, never had to mount anything like a Counter-Reformation. Moreover, unlike the Catholic and Lutheran Churches, the Orthodox Church has no real liberal wing, no experience with sexual tolerance, no tradition of ecumenism. Moreover, in confronting decades of communist rule, the Orthodox Church had distinctly fewer resources (especially fewer resources lying outside the communist world) than the Catholic Church, and, much more than the Catholic Church, the Orthodox Church found itself trapped in a situation where its only weapon against the communists (and here I am thinking of Serbia specifically) was to hold on to a nationalist ideology, in which, as Thomas Fitzgerald has put it, "[s]alvation is not simply personal but also communal."[116]

In endeavoring to trace the origins of the (Serbian) Orthodox outlook, one could adopt a cultural approach (what is it about Orthodoxy or about Orthodoxy in the region which results in this set of attitudes?), a functionalist approach (what manifest and latent functions are served by the Church's social agenda?), a contextualist approach (what is it in the given set of circumstances which is conducive to this result?), or a geneticist approach (what are the patterns which have been established over time, how and when were they established, and how have they changed over time, and why? In what ways are we seeing the continuation of past patterns? To what extent are present patterns rooted in institutions, structures, and procedures established at some point in the past?). One might, indeed, adopt a combination of the foregoing approaches, keeping in mind at all points that some patterns might be universal to religious associations functioning within identifiable political conditions (such as the praetorian syndrome described by Huntington in a 1968 work[117]).

Given the Serbian Church's embrace of nationalism, it is scarcely surprising that the hierarchy turned against Milošević at those points when the Serbian/Yugoslav president compromised on the vital Greater Serbian project (Vance-Owen, Dayton), and abandoned him altogether, calling upon him to resign after the NATO aerial campaign of spring 1999 which was, for Serbia, a complete and unadulterated disaster. On 15 June, 8 July, and again on 11 August 1999, Serbian Church elders called on Milošević to step down from office.[118] Patriarch Pavle himself, speaking on the six hundred tenth anniversary of the Battle of Kosovo, seemed to abandon the Greater Serbian project, telling his listeners, "If the only way to create a greater Serbia is by crime, then I do not accept that, and let that Serbia disappear. And also, if a lesser Serbia can only survive by crime, let it too disappear."[119] What the Orthodox patriarch has wanted is no less than that the Serbs might be collectively absolved of their sins, inviting them, in his Christmas message in January 2002, to return to a path of peace, thereby restoring the unity and spiritual strength of the Serbian people and suggesting that they could, in so doing, become "as pure as children."[120]

But it would be a great error to conclude, as a *Newsday* headline-writer did in composing a misleading headline for an article from my pen, that the "Serbian Church Isn't a Promoter of Aggression."[121] Certainly, Serbian Orthodox prelates must accept responsibility for their Church's past links with Serbian fascists in the 1930s and 1940s,[122] for its endorsement of the Greater Serbian project, for having contributed to an atmosphere of confrontation in Kosovo with vague warnings about the "Islamic menace,"[123] for having fostered a collective sense of victimhood, in which Serbia is portrayed as a crucified nation,[124] and for having adopted a hostile attitude toward non-Orthodox neighbors in general. Archimandrite Dr. Justin Popović, one of the two most important Serbian Orthodox theologians of the twentieth century, spoke with authority when, in 1974, he denounced the Catholic Church's Second Vatican Council as "a renaissance of all European humanisms, a renaissance of corpses,"[125] denouncing the Catholic and Lutheran Churches in fierce and uncompromising terms.[126] Nor is it without significance that, in mid-March 1999, as tensions in Kosovo were running high, the Serbian Church chose not to celebrate the feast of Easter, as it had traditionally done, as a feast day of reconciliation, but as a commemorative celebration of the resurrection of the Serbian spirit.[127] As long as the Serbian Church emphasizes its national character, spurns ecumenism, and, in essence, repudiates the story of "the good Samaritan," its culture will be one of hatred, not of reconciliation.

Notes

1. See Branislav Anzulović, *Heavenly Serbia: From Myth to Genocide* (London: Hurst and Co., 1999), pp. 122–24. See also Christos Mylonas, *Serbian Orthodox Fundamentals: The Quest for an Eternal Identity* (Budapest: Central European University Press, 2003), esp. chaps. 1–2.

2. Quoted in *Church Bulletin* of St. George Orthodox Church (Schererville), December 1992–January 1993.

3. Quoted in Radmila Radić, "The Church and the 'Serbian Question,'" in

The Road to War in Serbia: Trauma and Catharsis, ed. Nebojša Popov, English version by Drinka Gojković (Budapest: Central European University Press, 2000), p. 253.

4. See discussion in Sabrina Petra Ramet, "The Serbian Church and the Serbian Nation," in *Render Unto Caesar: The Religious Sphere in World Politics,* ed. Sabrina Petra Ramet and Donald W. Treadgold (Washington, D.C.: American University Press, 1995), pp. 313–15.

5. Radić, "The Church and the 'Serbian Question,'" p. 260.

6. Quoted in Milorad Tomanić, *Sprska crkva u ratu i ratovi u njoj* (Belgrade: Medijska knjižara krug, 2001), p. 39.

7. Ibid., p. 73.

8. Ibid., p. 40.

9. Ibid., p. 43.

10. *Croatia Weekly* (Zagreb), 25 March 1999, p. 3.

11. Synodal statement, quoted in Norman Cigar, *Genocide in Bosnia: The Policy of "Ethnic Cleansing"* (College Station, Tex.: Texas A&M University Press, 1995), p. 78.

12. Paul Mojzes, "The Role of the Religious Communities in the War in Former Yugoslavia," *Religion in Eastern Europe* 13, no. 3 (June 1993), pp. 23–24.

13. Michael Sells, "Patriarch Pavle and the Bosnia Genocide" (6/12/96), online at www.haverford.edu/relg/sells/postings/patriarch_pavle.html.

14. SRNA (Bijeljina), 25 May 1996, trans. in FBIS, *Daily Report* (Eastern Europe), 28 May 1996, p. 85. Regarding the Church's support for Karadžić, see Jože Pirjevec, *Le guerre jugoslave 1991–1999* (Torino: Giulio Einaudi editore, 2001), pp. 396–97; and Tomanić, *Srpska crkva u ratu,* passim.

15. SRNA, 23 December 1995, trans. in FBIS, *Daily Report* (Eastern Europe), 26 December 1995, p. 21.

16. Sells, "Patriarch Pavle" [note 13], p. 1.

17. Ejub Štitkovac, "Demolition of Places of Worship in the War," *AIM Press* (Paris), 21 March 1994, p. 2, online at www.aimpress.org/dyn/trae/archive/data/199403/40321–004–trae-beo.htm.

18. Quoted in *Croatia Weekly,* 25 March 1999, p. 3.

19. Yugoslav News Agency, 6 December 1992, in *BBC Summary of World Broadcasts,* 8 December 1992, in *Lexis-Nexis Academic Universe* (hereafter, LNAU).

20. Albanian Radio, 8 December 1992, trans. in *BBC Summary of World Broadcasts,* 11 December 1992, in LNAU.

21. FoNet news agency (Belgrade), 20 January 2003, trans. in *BBC Monitoring Europe: Political,* in LNAU.

22. ATA (Tirana), 16 March 1993, in *BBC Summary of World Broadcasts,* 17 March 1993, in LNAU.

23. *Kosova Daily Report* (Priština), 5 January 1998, in *BBC Summary of World Broadcasts*, 9 January 1998, in LNAU.

24. Radio B-92 (Belgrade), 12 June 1998, trans. in *BBC Summary of World Broadcasts*, 15 June 1998, in LNAU.

25. Beta news agency (Belgrade), 3 February 1999, trans. in *BBC Summary of World Broadcasts*, 5 February 1999, in LNAU.

26. Quoted in Klaus Buchenau, "Verspätete Ernüchterung: Die Serbische Orthodoxe Kirche im Kosovokonflikt 1960–1999," in Klaus Buchenau and Stefan Troebst, *Die Serbische Orthodoxe Kirche im Kosovokonflikt. Krieg auf dem Balkan*, Arbeitspapiere des Osteuropa-Instituts, no. 2 (Freie Universität Berlin, 1999), p. 37.

27. Quoted in ibid., p. 37.

28. Michael Sells, "How Serbs Used Monasteries to Entice Ethnic Hatred," posted online at www.ess.uwe.ac.uk/Kosovo/Kosovo-Current_News233.htm, p. 1.

29. Quoted in *The Guardian* (London), 25 June 1999, p. 13, in LNAU.

30. SRNA (Bijeljina), 16 September 1999, trans. in *BBC Summary of World Broadcasts*, 18 September 1999, in LNAU.

31. "Memorandum on Kosovo and Metohija: Summary," *Novosti, Informativna služba Srpske Pravoslavne Crkve*, 7 August 2003, p. 6.

32. Pravoslavlje Press Web site (Belgrade), 13 July 1999, in *BBC Summary of World Broadcasts*, 16 July 1999, in LNAU.

33. Agence France-Presse (Paris), 17 June 1999, in LNAU.

34. Agence France-Presse, 5 July 1999, in LNAU.

35. Beta news agency, 9 August 1999, trans. in *BBC Summary of World Broadcasts*, 9 August 1999, in LNAU; and SRNA, 16 September 1999, trans. in *BBC Summary of World Broadcasts*, 18 September 1999, in LNAU.

36. *The Scotsman*, 2 August 1999, p. 7, in LNAU.

37. "Memorandum on Kosovo and Metohija," p. 6; confirmed in Geraldine Fagan and Branko Bjelejac, "The 'Last Anchor' of Serb Presence: Serbian Orthodox Sites in Kosovo," *Frontier*, no. 1 (2002), pp. 6–7.

38. Agence France-Presse, 9 November 1999, in LNAU.

39. Quoted in Beta news agency, 7 December 1999, trans. in *BBC Summary of World Broadcasts*, 9 December 1999, in LNAU.

40. Biserka Matić, "Divisions in the Serbian Orthodox Church," *AIM Press*, 21 December 1999, p. 2, online at www.aimpress.org/dyn/trae/archive/data/199912/91221–015–trae-pod.htm.

41. "The Interview for the Herald of Kosovo and Metohija, Hieromonk Sava Janjić, Dečani Monastery, 15 March 2002," *News from Kosovo*, online at www.decani.yunet.com/glaskim_int.html.

42. Agence France-Presse, 17 November 2002, in LNAU; FoNet news agency,

17 November 2002, trans. in *BBC Monitoring Europe: Political,* 17 November 2002, in LNAU; and Kosovapress news agency Web site (Prishtina), 18 November 2002, trans. in *BBC Monitoring Europe: Political,* 19 November 2002, in LNAU.

43. *Global News Wire,* 21 November 2002, in *Financial Times Information,* in LNAU.

44. For documentation, see: Tanjug news agency (Belgrade), 29 November 2002, in *BBC Monitoring International Reports,* 29 November 2002, in LNAU; FoNet news agency, 27 January 2003, trans. in *BBC Monitoring Europe: Political,* 27 January 2003, in LNAU; Beta news agency, 11 May 2003, trans. in *BBC Monitoring Europe: Political,* 11 May 2003, in LNAU; "Diocese of Raška and Prizren Most Strongly Condemns Stoning of St. Nicholas Church in Priština," *Novosti* (Belgrade), 11 May 2003, online at www.spc.org.yu; and Branko Bjelajac, "Continuing Destruction of Our Churches," *Forum 18 News Service,* 10 July 2003, republished in *Orthodox News* 5, no. 30, online 14 July 2003 at www.orthodoxnews.netfirms .com, p. 1.

45. Clive Leviev-Sawyer, "Serbian Orthodox Church Leader Calls for End to Violence in Kosovo," *Ecumenical News International Daily News Service,* 14 August 2003, republished in *Orthodox News* 5, no. 34; online 14 August 2003 at www .orthodoxnews.netfirms.com, p. 1.

46. Tanjug news agency, 19 July 2003, in *BBC Monitoring International Reports,* 20 July 2003, in LNAU.

47. Bishop Ignatije, as heard on BKTV (Belgrade), 28 April 2003, trans. in *BBC Monitoring Europe: Political,* 28 April 2003, in LNAU.

48. Web site of Montenegrin Orthodox Church, "Archbishop of Cetinje and Montenegrin Metropolitan Mihajlo," pp. 2–3, online at www.moc-cpc.org/ustrojstvo /mitropolit_e.htm.

49. See "Crnogorska pravoslavna crkva. Mir u Mircu," *Monitor* (Podgorica), no. 604 (17 May 2002), online at www.monitor.cg.yu, p. 2.

50. Quoted in Tanjug news agency, 25 January 2000, trans. in *BBC Summary of World Broadcasts,* 27 January 2000, in LNAU.

51. Beta news agency, 31 October 1998, trans. in *BBC Summary of World Broadcasts,* 3 November 1998, in LNAU.

52. Montena-fax agency (Podgorica), 31 October 1998, trans. in *BBC Summary of World Broadcasts,* 1 November 1998, in LNAU.

53. Serb Radio Sarajevo (Lukavica), 23 November 1998, trans. in *BBC Summary of World Broadcasts,* 25 November 1998, in LNAU.

54. Radio Montenegro (Podgorica), 4 March 1999, trans. in *BBC Summary of World Broadcasts,* 6 March 1999, in LNAU.

55. Montena-fax agency, 24 November 1999, trans. in *BBC Summary of World Broadcasts,* 26 November 1999, in LNAU. See also Dragoljub Vuković, "Amfilo-

THE POLITICS OF THE SERBIAN ORTHODOX CHURCH

hije protiv Djukanovića," *Monitor,* no. 498 (2000), online at www.monitor.cg.yu/
a_498_05.html.

56. See, for example, the Montenegrin Information Ministry Web site (Podgorica), 29 June 1999, in *BBC Summary of World Broadcasts,* 1 July 1999, in LNAU.

57. Beta news agency, 12 October 1999, trans. in *BBC Summary of World Broadcasts,* 15 October 1999, in LNAU.

58. Quoted in SRNA, 11 December 1999, trans. in *BBC Monitoring Europe:
Political,* 11 December 1999, in LNAU.

59. Beta news agency, 20 December 1999, trans. in *BBC Summary of World
Broadcasts,* 22 December 1999, in LNAU.

60. See "Osudjeno anticrkveno delovanje bezbožnicke grupe u Crnoj Gori,"
Politika (Belgrade), 27 May 2000, online at www.politika.co.yu. This charge was
repeated by the metropolitanate of Montenegro and the Littoral two months later.
See "Public Statement of the Orthodox Metropolitanate of Montenegro and the
Littoral Regarding Violence Against [the] Orthodox Church," at the Metropolitanate of Montenegro and the Littoral Web site, Cetinje, 10 July 2000, at www
.mitropolija.cg.yu.

61. Montena-fax agency, 3 May 2000, trans. in *BBC Monitoring Europe: Political,* 3 May 2000, in LNAU.

62. Beta news agency, 31 January 2000, trans. in *BBC Summary of World Broadcasts,* 2 February 2000, in LNAU.

63. SRNA, 19 February 2000, trans. in *BBC Summary of World Broadcasts,* 22
February 2000, in LNAU.

64. Montena-fax agency, 13 March 2000, trans. in *BBC Summary of World
Broadcasts,* 15 March 2000, in LNAU.

65. Quoted in Montena-fax agency, 3 May 2000, trans. in *BBC Summary of
World Broadcasts,* 6 May 2000, in LNAU.

66. SRNA, 18 December 2000, trans. in *BBC Summary of World Broadcasts,* 20
December 2000, in LNAU.

67. TASS (Moscow), 19 April 2001, in LNAU.

68. Milka Tadić, "Montenegro: Church Divisions Deepen," Institute for War
and Peace Reporting (hereafter IWPR), *Balkan Crisis Report,* no. 309 (17 January
2002), online at www.iwpr.net.

69. Quoted in "Montenegrin Churches Mark Christmas," *Washington Post,* 6
January 2002, online at www.washingtonpost.com.

70. Veseljko Koprivica, "Intervju: Antonije, Mitropolit Italijanske Pravoslavne
Crkve—Amfilohije ne vjeruju u Boga," *Monitor,* 18 January 2002, online at www
.monitor.cg.yu/broj/str_04.html.

71. *Glas javnosti* (Belgrade), 3 February 2002, online at www.arhiva.glas-javnosti
.co.yu.

72. Mina news agency (Podgorica), 4 November 2002, trans. in *BBC Monitoring Europe: Political,* 4 November 2002, in LNAU; Mina news agency, 25 August 2003, trans. in *BBC Monitoring International Reports,* 26 August 2003, in LNAU; ONASA news agency, 27 August 2003, in LNAU; and Radio Montenegro, 27 August 2003, trans. in *BBC Monitoring International Reports,* 27 August 2003, in LNAU.

73. "Public Statement" [note 60], p. 2; and RTS SAT TV (Belgrade), 27 April 2003, trans. in *BBC Monitoring International Reports,* 20 June 2003, in LNAU. See also Rajko Cerović, "Crna Gora i Srpska Pravoslavna Crkva: Povratak u srednji vijek," *Monitor,* no. 603 (10 May 2002), online at www.monitor.cg.yu.

74. From the full text, "Homily of His Eminence Metropolitan Amfilohije of Montenegro and the Littoral at the Funeral of Dr. Zoran Djindjić, Given in the Church of Saint Sava in Belgrade," *Novosti,* 15 March 2003, online at www.spc.org.yu.

75. *Glas javnosti,* 18 March 2003, online at www.glas-javnosti.co.yu.

76. Beta news agency, 19 March 2003, trans. in *BBC Monitoring International Reports,* 19 March 2003, in LNAU.

77. Quoted in Mina news agency, 17 March 2003, trans. in *BBC Monitoring Europe: Political,* 17 March 2003, in LNAU.

78. See, for example, Mina news agency, 18 August 2003, trans. in *BBC Monitoring International Reports,* 18 August 2003, in LNAU. Earlier in the year, controversy had erupted over the army's sale of property in Cetinje to the Serbian Orthodox Church for a nominal sum. On this point, see "Montenegrin Social Democrats Protest Army's Sale of Land to Church," *Radio Free Europe,* 12 February 2003, republished in *Orthodox News* 5, no. 9, posted online 6 March 2003 at www.orthodoxnews.netfirms.com; and Mina news agency, 19 February 2003, trans. in *BBC Monitoring International Reports,* 19 February 2003.

79. Sabrina P. Ramet, *Nihil Obstat: Religion, Politics, and Social Change in East-Central Europe and Russia* (Durham, N.C.: Duke University Press, 1998), pp. 163–64.

80. "Announcement from the Archpriest Synod of the MOC," in *Macedonian Information Agency* (Skopje), 28 June 2002, online at www.mia.com.mk.

81. Zoran Bojarovski, "Macedonia: Church Deal Bishops Accused of Treason," IWPR, *Balkan Crisis Report,* no. 341 (7 June 2002), online at www.iwpr.net, p. 1; and Nada Andrejević, "Crkva kao cirkus," *NIN* (Belgrade), no. 2744 (31 July 2003), online at www.nin.co.yu.

82. Zoran Bojarovski, "Macedonia: A Holy Row," IWPR, *Balkan Crisis Report,* no. 347 (3 July 2002), online at www.iwpr.net. See also Živica Tucić, "Zaokret u Makedoniji," *NIN,* no. 2687 (27 June 2002), online at www.nin.co.yu; and Živica

Tucić, "Pištoljem do pokajanja," *NIN*, no. 2689 (11 July 2002), online at www.nin .co.yu.

83. HINA news agency (Zagreb), 7 July 2002, in *BBC Monitoring International Reports*, 7 July 2002, in LNAU; and "Makedonski vjernici protjerali 'raskolničkog' vladiku Jovana," *Vijesti on-line* (Podgorica), 22 July 2002, online at www.vijesti.cg.yu.

84. MIA news agency (Skopje), 10 July 2003, in *BBC Monitoring International Reports*, 10 July 2003, in LNAU.

85. Regarding Prohor Pčinski, see Zoran Bojarovski, "Macedonia: Religious Dispute Escalates," IWPR, *Balkan Crisis Report*, no. 448 (30 July 2003), online at www.iwpr.net; and MIA news agency, 18 July 2003, in *BBC Monitoring Europe: Political*, 18 July 2003 in LNAU. Regarding the arrest of Jovan/Zoran, see MIA news agency, 21 July 2003, in *BBC Monitoring International Reports*, 21 July 2003, in LNAU; and Branko Bjelajac, "Serbian Bishop Sentenced to Solitary Confinement," *F18 News*, 24 July 2003, republished in *Orthodox News* 5, no. 33 (11 August 2003), online at www.orthodoxnews.netfirms.com.

86. MIA news agency, 25 July 2003, in *BBC Monitoring Europe: Political*, 25 July 2003, in LNAU.

87. Quoted in MIA news agency, 28 July 2003, in *BBC Monitoring Europe: Political*, in LNAU.

88. MIA news agency, 31 July 2003, in *BBC Monitoring Europe: Political*, in LNAU.

89. Radio B-92, 31 July 2003, trans. in *BBC Monitoring Europe: Political*, 31 July 2003, in LNAU.

90. *Vjesnik* (Zagreb), 8 January 2004, p. 7.

91. *B-92 News* (Belgrade), 12 January 2004, online at www.b92.net/.

92. *Glas javnosti*, 14 January 2004, online at www.glas-javnosti.co.yu.

93. Mirjana Kuburović, "Kanoni ne podležu pritisku," *Politika*, 20 January 2004, online at www.politika.co.yu. The same claim of "huge patience" was also registered by Metropolitan Amfilohije (Radović), member of the SOC Holy Synod. See *Glas javnosti*, 14 January 2004, online at www.glas-javnosti.co.yu.

94. Quoted in Radio Free Europe/Radio Liberty, *Newsline* (Prague), 13 January 2004, online at www.rferl.org/newsline/.

95. ICTY, SRNA, 25 May 1996, trans. in FBIS, *Daily Report* (Eastern Europe), 28 May 1996, p. 85; Rotary et al., "Masonerija i satanizam," *Serbian Life*, 22 June 2000, online at www.beograd.com/Serbianlife/masoni/masoni.html; on religious instruction, see *Glas javnosti*, 19 September 2001, online at arhiva.glas-javnosti .co-yu. For an update on the status of religious instruction, see the detailed report in *Glas javnosti*, 18 January 2004, online at www.glas-javnosti.co.yu.

96. *Inter Press Service*, 1 August 2001, in LNAU.

97. *Glas javnosti,* 11 October 2001, online at www.glas-javnosti.co.yu.

98. Quoted in Milena Putnik, "Vojvodina: Catechism in Schools," *AIM Press,* 7 August 2001, online at www.aimpress.ch.

99. Quoted in ibid.

100. Marijana Milosavljević, "Pravoslavni protiv Madone," *NIN,* no. 2659 (13 December 2001), online at www.nin.co.yu.

101. Ibid.

102. Quoted in ibid.

103. Quoted in ibid.

104. *Glas javnosti,* 7 January 2003, trans. in *BBC Monitoring Europe: Political,* 7 January 2003, in LNAU. In February 2002, the Holy Synod of the Serbian Orthodox Church issued an unambiguous condemnation of anti-Semitism. See Associated Press Worldstream, 5 February 2002, in LNAU.

105. Ana Simo, "Violence Stops Yugoslavia Gay Pride," theGully.com, 5 July 2001, online at www.thegully.com/essays/gaymundo/010705gay_yugoslavia.html; and "Federal Republic of Yugoslavia: Lesbian and Gay Rights are Human Rights," *Amnesty International,* 13 July 2001, online at www.amnesty.org/library/print/ ENGEUR700162001.

106. Documented in Sabrina P. Ramet, "The Way We Were: And Should Be Again? European Orthodox Churches and the 'Idyllic Past,'" in a book being edited by Timothy Byrnes and Peter Katzenstein (accepted for publication by Cambridge University Press).

107. Zoran Luković, a police inspector in Serbia, as quoted in Branko Bjelajac, "Evangelical Churches Stoned, Vandalized," in *Christianity Today* (Carol Stream, Ill.), posted online 20 July 2001 at www.christianitytoday.com.

108. "Papina posjeta Srpskoj je provokacija," *Pravoslavlje,* 4 June 2003, online at www.trebinje.com.

109. Želimir Bojović, "Serb Extremists Block Atrocities Exhibition," 6 September 2002, online at www.genocidewatch.org/serbdenial.htm.

110. Bosnian Institute, *Bosnia Report,* new series nos. 32–34 (December 2002– July 2003), p. 43.

111. A. R. Popović, "They Trust the Church and the Army," *Global News Wire,* 14 August 2003, in LNAU.

112. *Reuter News Service,* 19 April 1995, in LNAU; Agence France-Presse, 28 June 1995, in LNAU; *The Guardian,* 4 March 1994, p. 11; and "Romanian Orthodox Oppose Legalization of Homosexual Acts," *Catholic World News,* 13 September 2000, online at www.cwnews.com/Browse/2000/09/13805.htm.

113. Joszef Baliant-Pataki, as quoted in the *Washington Post,* 11 February 2000, p. A30, online at www.transylvanianet.com/orthodox_crusade.

114. Details in Ramet, *Nihil Obstat,* pp. 282–85; Janice Broun, "The Schism in

the Bulgarian Orthodox Church," *Religion, State and Society: The Keston Journal* 21, no. 2 (1993).

115. Quoted in Reuters, 1 March 2002, online at www.reuters.co.uk.

116. Thomas E. Fitzgerald, *The Orthodox Church* (Westport, Conn.: Greenwood Press, 1995), p. 11.

117. Samuel P. Huntington, *Political Order in Changing Societies* (New Haven, Conn.: Yale University Press, 1968).

118. *Frankfurter Allgemeine Zeitung,* 16 June 1999, p. 2; *Die Welt* (Berlin), 16 June 1999, online at www.welt.de; *Die Welt,* 9 July 1999, online at www.welt.de; *The Star Tribune* (Minneapolis-St. Paul), 11 August 1999, online at www.startribune .com; *Die Welt,* 11 August 1999, online at www.diewelt.de/meldungen; and *The Baltimore Sun,* 12 August 1999, online at www.baltimoresun.com.

119. Quoted in *New York Times,* 29 June 1999, p. A9.

120. *Glas javnosti,* 6–7 January 2002, online at www.glas-javnosti.co.yu.

121. *Newsday* (New York), 5 August 1999, p. A16. Portions of my text mysteriously disappeared from the final version as published in the newspaper, with the unfortunate result that my meaning was seriously distorted.

122. Patriarch Gavrilo Dožić, a prelate of great integrity, staunchly opposed Yugoslavia's adherence to the Tripartite Pact on 25 March 1941 and was openly anti-Nazi; he spent much of the war in internment in several places, among them Dachau. On the other hand, Nikolaj Velimirović, bishop of Žica, though anti-Nazi, was sympathetic to the Serbian fascist "Zbor" movement led by Dimitrije Ljotić. During the war years, with Patriarch Gavrilo interned, the Serbian Church was led by Metropolitan Josif, who, together with the Holy Synod, collaborated with both the quisling Nedić regime and, up to a point, with the German occupation army, according to Tomašević. See Jozo Tomašević, *War and Revolution in Yugoslavia, 1941–1945: Occupation and Collaboration* (Stanford, Calif.: Stanford University Press, 2001), pp. 512–14. See also Ljubica Stefan, *Srpska pravoslavna crkva i fašizam* (Zagreb: Nakladni zavod Globus, 1996); and Philip J. Cohen, *Serbia's Secret War: Propaganda and the Deceit of History* (College Station, Tex.: Texas A&M University Press, 1996), passim.

123. *The Star Tribune,* 29 June 1999, online at www.startribune.com.

124. See discussion in Ramet, "The Serbian Church and the Serbian Nation," especially pp. 308–10; and Anzulović, *Heavenly Serbia,* pp. 122–24.

125. Justin Popović, *Pravoslavna crkva i ekumenizam* (Solun: Izdanje manastira Hilandara, 1974), p. 184.

126. Ibid., p. 202.

127. *OÖNachrichten,* 14 April 1999, online at www1.oon.at.

11

NATIONALISM, MOTHERHOOD, AND THE
REORDERING OF WOMEN'S POWER

BILJANA BIJELIĆ

W hat would be the answer to the question as to what character-ized the relationship of the Milošević regime toward women beyond the, nowadays somewhat obvious, conclusion of au-thoritarian systems being inherently misogynist? Is there a way to under-stand the nature of the regime by observing the way it treated women? The status of women in Serbia at the beginning of the 1990s was charac-terized by a general backlash in rights and political status, which also char-acterized the rest of the postcommunist countries. In observing the sta-tus of women in any of these countries, one usually finds two typical extremes in the distribution of power, the marked absence of women from the public and political spheres and "their overwhelming presence in the private sphere."[1]

There are also many specificities in the Serbian case: while in the other postcommunist countries, patriarchy was revitalized as a part of a project of re-traditionalization of the society, brought about by nationalism as a total ideological reaction to communism/socialism and its values, Serbia in 1989 did not pass through an anticommunist revolution. Instead, Milošević's Socialist Party of Serbia was widely accepted as if it had arisen in opposition to the old communist regime and despite the fact that its nationalism did not attack the communist/socialist ideological heritage. In many ways, Milošević's Socialist Party of Serbia was a new-old politi-cal party, with most of its members and infrastructure inherited from the League of Communists of Serbia, after the party membership had been purified of nonnationalists. Its ideological hybridity was reflected primarily in the combination of a language of social justice and gender equality with the nationalist rhetoric, which was the liveliest engine which preserved the Milošević regime in power for a whole decade. The rhetoric of nationalist populism, fostered by the ruling Socialists but also by the opposition parties as well, constantly promoted nationalism as an ideology of every-day life which very soon turned out to involve (in one of its segments) the traditionalization of gender roles. In addition to the nationalist ideology, militarism also promoted an image of women serving a political purpose as reproductive vehicles. After Milošević's rise to power, women repre-sented a rich source for maintaining social, economic, and demographic stability in the circumstances of a social, political, and economic crisis and chaos. Serbian anthropologist Žarana Papić summarizes this situation:

> The insecurity in the production and reproduction of life and everyday ex-istence, endless time and energy consumption, and the return to old tech-niques and technologies of domestic labor, strengthened women's patri-archal self-denial and orientation toward others and their needs but, at the same time, gave them new power and control over others through their dependency in crisis as a form of "self-sacrificing micro-matriarchy."[2]

To a great extent, the relationship of the regime toward women explains the nature of the Milošević regime and reflects its deep indifference toward people who were instrumentalized and convinced through na-tionalist indoctrination. The result was "nation-building" projects in combination with leftist rhetoric employed in order to present an image of concern for social justice and equality with the single purpose of pre-serving Slobodan Milošević and his ruling clique in power.

In order to preserve the mass support of women, the regime strategi-cally manipulated the two presumptions of patriarchal order: on the one hand, women's passivity and withdrawal into the private sphere and, on the other, motherhood as the highest vocation for women and women's "hidden" power within traditional family relations. This was mirrored in Croatian mainstream politics in 1990, where a nationalistic and conser-vative ideology understood motherhood as the primary form of female political agency and even proclaimed "mother-nurturer" (a mother of three or more children) as a profession. Nationalistic conservative ideol-ogy applied its popular mythology to motivate women to sacrifice for the fatherland and give birth to potential soldiers, while during the times of economic crisis when the regime had to rely on women's capacities to con-tribute to the state's economy with their paid and unpaid labor, calling upon the leftist and socialist ideological strategies to remind women of their strength and economic competence.

I aim to expose the use of this chameleonic ideology to convince women to remain obedient supporters of the regime and to readily sacrifice for the prosperity of the nation. Furthermore, I want to discuss three issues which illustrate the double-sidedness and ambivalence of the regime toward women and their clear treatment as objects and not subjects of politics. This double-sidedness and ambivalence appeared most clearly around women's status in the labor market, women's reproductive rights, and political participation. In the cases of women's reproductive rights and women's political participation, there is a clear departure from the legitimacy of the socialist system and an overwhelming victory of the nationalistic and traditionalist sphere of political influence. In the case of women and labor, although women suffered consequences of economic crisis and escalating poverty, the regime turned toward women, displaying the other side of its Janus face (the quasi-socialist one), and even though there is no room to speak about the "affirmation of women's power," women's status in the labor market at least did not suffer a backlash. An economically pragmatic answer to this phenomenon is that despite their expulsion from the sphere of decision making, women preserved their relatively high representation in the labor force because the country's devastated economy certainly needed women's professional, low-paid, and unpaid labor in order to survive.

I want to trace the sociopolitical conditions which made these paradoxes possible: inefficiencies in maintaining gender policies established in the socialist era, preservation of the patriarchal tradition, and the militarization of society. Finally, I want to present the reverse situation: women who articulate ambivalence toward the nationalistic politics, militarization, and re-traditionalization of Serbian society. At the time of the re-traditionalization of Serbian society, the "mother-hero"[3] was positioned as a conserver and renovator of patriarchal traditions, but she also figured as a rebel against the same patriarchal traditions. Serbian women continued to pursue political goals no matter how conservative the politics became, and therefore did not fit into the role which the regime had wanted women to play—silence and passivity, presence in the private arena, and absence from the public sphere. The mother-hero paradoxically opposes the feminine ideal, although her ideological worldview of nationalism helps in the instrumentalization of this feminine ideal. The mother-hero is, of course, only one of the identity strategies which Serbian women adopted: as opposed to the political implications of motherhood employed to legitimate aggressive nationalism, women in antiwar and feminist civil initiatives were among the most vocal voices of resistance to xenophobia and political oppression. The case of the mother-hero is examined not only because it symmetrically mirrors back the regime's ambivalences, but also because of the present debate on responsibility and guilt of individuals and complicity of ordinary people and society at large.

In addition to trying to explain the nature of the Milošević regime through the regime's treatment of the status of women, I shall explain the tragedy of Serbia under Milošević by explaining the system's weak ideological content. The regime's viciousness was proven to lie not in its systematic ideological commitment but rather in its ambiguity epitomized in its position halfway between the nationalist and socialist ideology.

Women's Human Rights:
Backlashes vs. "Affirmation" of Women's Power

Serbian women in the 1990s faced gender-specific hardships within the already difficult circumstances faced by society as a whole. Nationalism, built upon the rhetoric of kinship and family, found fertile ground in a patriarchal culture only partially camouflaged by the political practices of socialism. The result was a specific ideological hybrid which wondrously reconciled the conservative politics of pushing women out of the public sphere while at the same time exploiting their material and intellectual resources to sustain power. The exclusion of women from political life and decision-making bodies, and the assignment of women's roles as mothers and keepers of the nation's demographic good standing contrasted with their experience in the economic realm, where women did not suddenly suffer discrimination as they did in other fields of public life.

The economic status of women in the 1990s was significantly influenced by increasing poverty as a result of the hyperinflation and growth of the black market. Economic sanctions introduced by the UN Security Council, as a consequence of the Serbian military involvement in the war in Bosnia-Herzegovina, affected the economic situation of Serbia and economic position of Serbian women profoundly. Official data did not reveal significant discriminatory practices in the employment rate—women made up over 40 percent of all employees as of 1998, and women's employment has been increasing since 1990 in both the private and public sectors.[4] When these numbers are compared with the percentages of women in the work force in Serbia throughout the previous decades, there is notable progress (21 percent in 1952; 25 percent in 1960; 29 percent in 1970; 34 percent in 1980; 39 percent in 1988).[5]

Nevertheless, it would be an exaggeration to state that women's economic life is devoid of gender-based discriminatory practices. Despite the fact that the Serbian constitution guarantees equal opportunities and equal rights to employment, women often face discrimination in the form of lower wages.[6] This is partly a consequence of women being employed in the professions which are less well paid: trade, administration, social work. When these professions are protected by the state administration, they enjoy the higher security of employment but offer lower wages. Women are those family members who most often accept positions with less pay but more security.[7]

In the private sector, women have faced a larger economic backlash. Furthermore, higher rates of women's unemployment could be treated as indicators of sex-based discrimination against women with regard to employment rights.[8] This practice is related to the gaps in equal access to higher paying professional positions and women's occupancy of the professions which traditionally pay less (the textile and food industries, for example). And, of course, available statistics relate only to the legal labor market, which, according to the *Report on the Status of Women in the FRY*, has employed one-quarter of the total work force. The hidden or black economy in 1992 accounted for approximately 40 percent of the GDP. While approximately 1.2 million people work in the hidden labor market, women comprise about one-third of that number. Throughout the period of hardship caused by the war economy, the widespread theft by the Milošević regime, and economic sanctions imposed on the FRY (Federal Republic of Yugoslavia) by the United Nations from 1992 to 1995, women were carrying most of the burden through their paid and unpaid labor.

In the circumstances of extreme poverty in which Serbian society has been functioning throughout the last decade, women have assumed the lion's share of the burden in helping the fragile economy by producing food, preserving energy, and providing alternative ways for their households' survival. In the words of Žarana Papić, "[b]y activating their 'natural' survival potentials, women actually bore Serbia's heaviest burden during the social and economic crisis in the period of the UN sanctions, and therefore, willingly or not, actually played the part of Milošević's faithful allies."[9] However, the fact that women reactivated their potential and creativity in the time of crisis only reflects women's hidden, often perceived as subversive, power over the private sphere, in exchange for the real power in political decision-making bodies.

After the first multiparty elections in 1990, political participation decreased significantly, and the realm of politics is probably the most obvious zone of a backlash against women when compared to the socialist era. Such a decline in women's participation in decision-making bodies marked all of the transitions from communism in Eastern Europe. Under socialism, women's participation in the Central Committee of the League of Communists of Serbia was 17.8 percent, while women's party membership in the League of Communists of Serbia stood at 27.5 percent.[10] One should also keep in mind that the socialist parliament was not a democratically elected institution and that such a percentage of women in parliament is not actually an outcome of a democratic decision-making process. In the period 1990–93, the percentage of women in the Serbian parliament was as small as 1.6 percent, while in spring 2000, women still comprised only 2.08 percent of people's representatives in the Serbian parliament.[11]

However, the virtual absence of women in formal power positions did not empower men as such. On the contrary, as Žarana Papić has suggested, Milošević as despotic patriarch disempowered men almost to the same degree as women. As she wrote toward the end of the Milošević era, Serbian men "have invested, delegated, and transferred all aspects of their own public power to the mysterious, unpredictable, and uncontrolled power of One Man."[12] In spite of the fact that there were so few women in parliament, several women were remarkably visible in politics and in the public life of Serbia throughout the 1990s. The most striking among these women was certainly Milošević's wife, Mirjana ("Mira") Marković, head of the Yugoslav United Left party, which, in coalition with the Socialist Party of Serbia and sometimes in coalition with Šešelj's Radical Party (the notorious Red-Black coalition), created a formula for tyranny and ruthless rule wrapped up in nationalistic ideology and occasionally combined with leftist and feminist phraseology: as a columnist in the Serbian weekly *Duga*, Mira Marković very openly critiqued nationalism and any other form of discrimination from a "communist-feminist" standpoint. Nevertheless, Marković will probably be remembered for her contributions to the dissolution of morally responsible politics and the centralization of power which she very often used as a deadly weapon against her political opponents.

For Milošević, the displacement of women from the public sphere was a necessity to maintain the nationalistic and militaristic agenda which he had used to install himself in power and to maintain his political position. Ironically, the willingness with which he shared power with his wife seems like a symbolic affirmation of full gender equality, with the tyrannical rule of one man being replaced with the rule of one couple. Despite the fact that a significant decrease in women's representation in parliament is typical for postcommunist countries, the specific characteristic of the Milošević regime was that his Socialist Party of Serbia was made up of reformed communists and therefore by definition ideologically concerned with the issues of women's rights and gender equality. However, Milošević's Socialist Party was, in different stages of his rule, in coalition with political parties, with the result that a consistent political program was hardly possible. In the initial phases of his rule, he created a coalition with the radical right Serbian Radical Party headed by Vojislav Šešelj, as well as with his wife's Yugoslav United Left. Neither political consistency nor moral integrity seemed to be an issue of great concern for the regime.

In October 2000, major political changes occurred with the electoral victory of the Democratic Opposition of Serbia, the revolutionary overthrow of Milošević, and the beginning of a new era of Serbian politics. With the onset of the new government, there were high expectations for the improvement of women's rights. This is because NGOs for women's human rights had been among the most prominent and vocal critics of the Milošević regime. The Women's Political Network, an organization of women in politics established in the initial phase of the preelection campaign, lobbied opposition political parties to implement a 30 percent quota for female candidates on electoral lists, however without success.[13] The still insufficient degree of women's participation in decision-making bodies in post-Milošević Serbia is a sign of the unfulfilled promise of the now ruling coalition of the Democratic Opposition of Serbia. Currently, 11 percent of parliamentary deputies in the Serbian parliament are women, 5 percent of deputies in the federal parliament are women, and between 2 percent and 10 percent of deputies in the local parliaments are women. If the revolutionary atmosphere of the October elections was a litmus test for the way the civic nationalist parties of the ruling coalition have been treating the issue of women's political participation, the next decade will not be short of challenges and struggles for women's nongovernmental organizations and women's sections within political parties which represent the main political forces concerned with empowering women politically. According to Brankica Grupković, leader of the Women's Political Network, the problem lies not only in the small number of women parliamentarians, but also in the relative powerlessness of the women's lobby in parliament, caused by women's dispersion in different sectors, which prevents them from forming a powerful women's lobby in parliament. Nevertheless, Grupković articulates an optimistic attitude and cites research figures of 62.5 percent of women and 47.6 percent of men favoring more women in politics.[14] On the other hand, research by the Media Index polling agency found that Serbian women generally do not see the lack of women in decision-making bodies as the most burning issue.[15] Rather, according to the researchers, women believe that powerful female politicians end up neglecting the most important issues for women, such as poverty, health care, and domestic violence, in the same manner as male politicians.

Violence against women has been on a steady increase in a society brutalized by war, poverty, and political oppression. Research conducted by Media Index in October 2001 showed that violence is so overwhelmingly present in Serbia that every third woman is exposed to some sort of violence. An even more significant finding of this research is that if they are not the victims, more than 50 percent of interviewed women experience fear of violence.[16] The fear is especially widespread among women with less education. Unfortunately, there is a good basis for fear of violence against women, since legal mechanisms are still not effectively protecting women who are victims of violence, by not recognizing violence against women as a specific form of violence.[17] Around 30 percent of court cases of violent crimes involve domestic violence.[18] The majority of the cases of domestic violence pass by unreported because of the mistrust in police and the judicial system, which usually blame the victim. Victims of violence are severely disadvantaged because of their often limited education, unemployment, and material dependence on husbands. Police inefficacy in the cases of domestic violence is notorious, as is the case with other patriarchal societies which treat domestic violence at best as a private issue between wife and husband and at worst as women's shame. These are perhaps only some of the reasons why violence against women is among the criminal acts for which there still do not exist official statistics or state-sponsored institutions to help victims of violence. This vacuum is filled by the material and psychological help provided by women's NGOs, which number around thirty in Serbia and Montenegro; however, their ability to help is very limited due to shortages of space for victims of violence (there are only two shelters for the whole of Serbia).[19]

Family values never ceased to represent high social and cultural values during the socialist era, but, in conditions of extreme poverty, nationalist and conservative ideology provided the justification for state intervention into private life and its promotion of a revival of traditional and conservative values. The atmosphere of continuous moral, political, and economic breakdown tightened family ties more than ever. According to the *Investigation into the Status of Women's Rights in Central and South-Eastern Europe and the Newly Independent States,* in the Federal Republic of Yugoslavia, the divorce rate significantly decreased during the 1990s.[20] Conservative forces, whose main goal of limiting a woman's right to an abortion was con-

nected with the demographic-xenophobic paranoia that the Serbian nation was being overwhelmed by Albanians and Muslims with their "traditionally" and "naturally" high birth rates, intervened by proposing a law
which limited the time for requesting legal abortion to ten weeks of preg-
nancy. This came after several drafts, including some extremely conservative drafts, had been defeated. Among them was a bill which would not even
have recognized rape as one of the legitimate reasons for an abortion.[21]
Žarana Papić correctly concluded that through such measures of promoting demographic growth in which women were turned into reproductive
vehicles, the Serbian regime of Slobodan Milošević adopted the very same
behavior which it had labeled "demographic genocide" in the case of Albanians and Muslims—interpreting their high birth rate as a political agenda
serving the goal of overwhelming the Serbian nation. The political changes
since 2000 have resulted in a reduction in xenophobic-demographic politics. However, the fear that Christianity and Orthodoxy are threatened
by the high birth rate among the Muslim population is still painfully observ-
able in the media.[22] Typically, the emancipation of Serbian women is
blamed for the lower birth rates, which, according to catastrophic demographic predictions, will keep on dropping.

After the dissolution of the Milošević regime, some advancements in
politics appeared as the beginning of a radical break with the past. In spite
of the continuing marginalization of women's issues, two events represented an advancement in the incorporation of women's issues into mainstream politics. Both cases provided further affirmation of women's right
to live free from any form of violence. The first came in May 2001, when
Vuk Obradović, Serbian deputy prime minister and head of the governmental commission to fight corruption, was accused of sexual harassment
of his colleagues in the Social Democratic Party, the government, and the
media. Obradović was dismissed from his posts, in a move which signaled
that sexual harassment was being taken seriously. Obradović's supporters, however, offered a wide range of conspiracy theories in order to shift
attention from violence against women, treating the accusations as instruments of Obradović's political enemies opposed to his decisiveness in
prosecuting economic crime and corruption.[23] Then, in November 2002,
the Montenegrin and Serbian public were astonished when it was announced that Montenegro's deputy public prosecutor, Zoran Piperović,
was among four men who had been implicated in the trafficking of
women.[24] Although trafficking in women and children had been a problem throughout the Balkans since about 1990, this was the first time that
a highly placed politician had been arrested for involvement in so serious

a crime against women. The arrest came after a nineteen-year-old Moldovan woman escaped from her captors to a women's safe house in Podgorica and testified about her ordeal to activists there, who revealed the story to the public and asked for Piperović's arrest and for the resignation of public attorney Božidar Vukčević.[25]

Both these events bear witness not only to the persistently widespread patriarchal worldview, moral corruption, and criminal activities among the political elite, but also to the decisiveness of the public to ostracize such behavior and penalize the perpetrators. Such public decisiveness is a direct product of the systematic campaigning and consciousness-raising by women's groups, which earned credibility during the gloomy decade of the 1990s by standing up to the regime and speaking out against war and patriarchy alike.

Sociocultural Preconditions for Gender Inequality

The ambivalent relationship of the regime to women was embodied in the appeal to "save" the nation, although the nation was to be saved every time in a different fashion: on the first occasion, by evoking national pride, and on another, by evoking a sense of social justice through the preservation of egalitarian concepts, in which gender equality and the emancipation of women were taken over from the former Communist Party's program. By reconciling socialist and nationalistic ideology, the ruling party was appealing to the two main bases upon which it formulated its legitimacy. This legitimacy was, for Serbian political scientist Marija Obradović, anchored in preserving the status quo (through keeping state ownership as the basis of socioeconomic relations) and in a sociopolitical mobilization around the Serbian national question. What both ideological poles have in common is their collectivist and traditionalist characteristics, which persuaded large numbers of traditionally minded Serbian people that by voting for Milošević and his party, the goal of national liberation would be achieved without losing the benefits of "socialism with a human face," that is, social security, social equality, and preservation of the Yugoslav federation. The happy marriage between the "egalitarian-communist" and "traditional-nationalist" ideology was possible due to the fact that the leadership had chosen "repression in the name of unity."[26] A minor difference is, as Obradović suggests, that the communists achieved ideological purity through political purges, while the nationalists aspired to effect homogenization through "ethnic cleansing." Despite its continuous failures in almost all fields of the state's management—political (military aggression in Croatia and Bosnia, international isolation) and economic (UN sanctions, hyperinflation, and extreme pauperization)—the regime largely succeeded in maintaining its relative popularity until spring 1999, when protests calling on Milošević to resign spread across northern and central Serbia.

Sociologist Josip Županov explains this phenomenon as the "coalition of the societal top and bottom," meaning that the lowest social strata never stopped believing in the fulfillment of promises of national and economic prosperity which the Socialist Party of Serbia had been giving since 1990. Nor did they ever suspend their belief that Milošević and his regime were genuinely concerned about the lives of the people who had catapulted him into political orbit through the mass populist meetings throughout the 1980s. Typically, Milošević's supporters were recruited from among the socially insecure and low-income strata, from the ranks of the elderly, who opposed the great upheaval since Tito's death in 1980, the rural population, and the population with only a lower education, if any at all; among Milošević's supporters, women constituted a significant number due to their high number in those socially fragile and economically disadvantaged groups.[27] In Serbia, as in the rest of the postcommunist world, the patriarchal family maintained and affirmed its status throughout the communist period, in spite of the radical discourse on gender equality. Patriarchal social relations survived due to: (1) the inability of the socialist system to fulfill its promises and achieve gender equality in all spheres of public and private life; (2) the preservation of traditional values and patriarchal family relations; and (3) the militarization of society with its radicalization of discrimination against women through the reduction of women's role to their reproductive function.

Inefficient Socialist Gender Policy

The question I now wish to address is, Why were women so eager to embrace the limited power of the private sphere? Reducing women to the private sphere has been shown to be a powerful weapon for reproducing patriarchal values, which limit women's choices in their professional and personal lives and, in the given context, exclude women from political power. One of the answers lies in the overestimation of the status of women in socialist Yugoslavia and gender equality during the socialist era. In a work published in 1999, Sabrina Ramet analyzed the gender policy of the League of Communists of Yugoslavia in the Tito and early post-Tito eras, and found that the LCY continually refused to recognize the autonomy of the issue of "gender relations"; consequently, it was not "considered legitimate to organize autonomous bodies or activities to promote gender equality."[28] Women's participation in the main leadership bodies—for example, the Central Committees and Provincial Committees of the LCY—was rising steadily after 1945, but even in the 1980s, the proportion of women in even the most modernized republics (Slovenia, Croatia) did not exceed 22 percent.[29] In addition, for the generation of Yugoslav men and women growing up after World War Two, communist propaganda became the object of ridicule and disavowal as the system fell into decay. The place where messages on gender equality could probably make a positive difference would be the elementary and secondary schools, as Ramet has noted. However, gender issues never became a serious part of the educational system; moreover, a study conducted in the late 1970s showed that elementary school textbooks promoted rather sexist perceptions of the world.[30]

Patriarchy and the Traditional Family

The inefficacy of the socialist regime in challenging the "bastions of patriarchy" enabled the patriarchal tradition to persist in society as a coherent social order during and especially after the fall of communism. The ideal socialist "superwoman" embodied emancipation, education, and employment, but never at the expense of her family. Milošević's regime correctly estimated women's willingness to sacrifice for the "public good," withdraw from politics, and instead devote themselves to their families' well-being. Since in the nationalistic discourse, the nation is all about kinship, family, and common love and solidarity (directed as a weapon against other nations), it was not hard to convince women that sacrificing themselves for the nation was merely the continuation of their natural mission in the patriarchal family. Like every story of victimhood, women did not simply give up the power of the public sphere, they rather "exchanged" it for the hidden power of the private sphere. For the great majority of Serbian women, the renewed push of women into the private sphere was not a backlash, but rather an affirmation of power. Andrei Simić characterized women's position within the traditional Yugoslav family under the term "cryptomatriarchy." The term defines family relations according to which the central role and power position in the family belong to the mother. In the patriarchal family, women's power is conditioned by the subordination of other women (the mother of the family exercising power over her daughter-in-law). In this way, "women legitimate their status within their husbands' kinship groups by giving birth to sons and through the influence they exert over their children."[31] In such a constellation of family power dynamics where women earn higher status in the family through exercising their power over their children and, more importantly, over the new, young, and disempowered woman in the family, the exercise of women's power over the less powerful has the logic of any oppressive system, where *power over the less powerful amortizes the sense of one's own oppression.*

Militarism and Women

Although the regime's engagement in the war(s) of Yugoslav succession has not been a secret, officials never tired of stressing that "the country was never at war," and as a core of Serbian nationhood, the country embraced the image of a mother-nurturer who fed and sheltered Serbian refugees from Croatia and Bosnia. But even more often, the country was gendered as a powerless object which needed protection, serving to legitimate militarization and military aggression into other states' territory. Because such militarization was clearly expansionist, it gendered the roles of the savior-warrior (the leader) as a male and the nation as a female object which is to be saved and protected. The dynamics of the private sphere in which the male leader subordinates to his power the feminized nation is a macro preview behind which the revival and celebration of patriarchal values takes place at the micro level. Julie Mostov explains this dynamic: "The heroic warrior images provide the core notions of masculinity for nationalist rhetoric even during peacetime. Sacrifices and sacred spaces marked by fallen warriors provide the stuff of national mythology and models of virility, sexual conduct, and patriarchal values."[32]

The militarization of society contributed to the disappearance of women from the public sphere and their almost exclusive appearance in the roles of the old patriarchal dichotomies: mothers/nurturers and women for entertainment. Women from both categories at the time of the conflict are fulfilling the various functions of serving through comforting and caressing wounded soldiers. The moral purity of the mother symbolizes the holiness of the war for the motherland's freedom. Mothers as actual or potential victims (for the victim is always innocent) are providing the perfect legitimation of the fight for justice.

Case Study: The Mother-Hero

The response of women to re-traditionalization can be traced in three general directions: feminist resistance, passive compliance with the rules of re-traditionalization, and the somewhat hybrid position of what I term the mother-hero. At the beginning of the 1990s, nationalist populism opposed the ideas of self-management socialism and gender equality and radically changed the shape of gender politics. The return to "ancient" values included the renewal of the old dichotomies through delegating the private sphere (such as house, kitchen, church) to "honest women," while the public sphere was reserved for entertainers and show-business stars. In such a constellation of identity politics, the mother-hero occupied an ambivalent position, accepting nationalist politics, yet politicizing her maternal identity into the public sphere, which the same nationalistic politics had reserved for men and freed from women. Refusing to limit her identity as mother only to its biological (reproductive) dimension, the mother-hero demanded to be the moral and educational guardian of her children (actual or symbolic). She rejected the position of feminine identity (constructed and viewed as such through the patriarchal lenses) as one of fragility, weakness, and powerlessness, affirming herself as a political actor, only leaving uncertain how autonomous her political action could be. Her involvement in politics was conditioned by her suspicion of the capacities of the politicians in power. But her suspicion of the male authorities only at first glance suggested that she was a rebel against masculine politics. Although it was the exclusion of women from political life which was responsible for the plight of people for whose well-being she was concerned, the mother-hero's political critique was not feminist, nor was the aim of her political activism the general emancipation of women. She aimed only at her own individual emancipation from "women's destiny": suffering in silence and obedient acceptance of injustices. The fact that the majority of women remained in the second-class category of this "women's destiny" is a measure of her success in the "male world" of politics. Silence, passivity, and bitterness in the time of historical missions and heroic deeds seemed trivial and prosaic to the mother-hero. The survival strategies of ordinary women such as gossip and patient endurance were fetters to be rejected with indignation.

Zorica Mitić, a physician and frontline volunteer, witness to the war in Croatia, is a good example of the figure of the mother-hero. In Mitić's words, "I do not have many friends among women. I get tired of complaining about husbands and mothers-in-law. I have a completely different approach which I have validated in my life. I do not complain, but when I am fed up I move on and change everything."[33]

The mother-hero affirms her motherhood by politicizing its characteristics. Motherhood and victimhood in silence are confronted with

heroic motherhood and suffering inspired by political purpose. It is note-
worthy that conservative politicians also politicized motherhood. But the
mother-hero is doing something different. Her fashion of politicization
of motherhood opposes the conservative aim to politicize motherhood
by keeping mothers away from the sphere of political influence. On the
contrary, the mother-hero is taking her "destiny" into her own hands and
tries to involve herself in politics.

This phenomenon brings us to the perspective against which American political theorist Iris Young has warned: the group identified as other
(usually oppressed or discriminated against) incorporates itself into the
societal system of universal values by seeking to transcend and disavow
the qualities which define its otherness. The mother-hero accepts the
equation of femininity with weakness and passivity, but refuses to identify herself with that category. Just as Croats, according to anthropologist Marko Živković, pass the stigma of Balkanism further south in order
to exorcise their own Balkanness, the mother-hero assimilates herself
to the dominant norms of gender, passing the stigma of femininity on
to the rest of women.[34] The result of such a neglect of one's own difference leads to the maintenance of the status quo. This is why, for Iris
Young, assimilation means the invitation to a game after the game has already started and after the major roles in the power share have already
been assigned.[35] One of the outcomes of such assimilation is strikingly
present in the mother-hero phenomenon: a tendency to see oneself through
the eyes of the oppressor. For women with the aspiration to become included in the patriarchal standards, that would mean to reject crying, fragile, faceless femininity and to embrace the new one created according to
patriarchal perception of masculinity. Women whose motherhood possesses a political-historical mission affirm themselves as mother-heroes
of patriarchal society, strong and competent enough to estimate the current political situation and try to correct it. At the same time, they are
encouraging the continuation of maternal victimization among other
women because it is their exclusive position as an exceptional woman
in a male club that makes their mission so heroic. The position of the
mother-hero in the patriarchal society is an exception that proves the rule
even when her public involvement is garnished with the phrases of
women's emancipation. It does not advocate the general emancipation
of women, because her occupation of this niche in the patriarchal system only confirms and maintains patriarchal criteria.

Insofar as the mother-hero is an assimilated insider of the patriarchal
system in which she earns legitimacy by imitating the patriarchal stereo-

typing of women, one would assume that her obedience to the political regime would evaporate at the point when the escalation of violence threatens to kill her children. The belief that pacifism naturally grows out of motherly behavior offers a simple formula: a mother as a nurturer of children, caretaker of their integrity and security, ought to oppose war as an ultimate threat to the security of her children, family, and home. However, the mother-hero is not as reliably pacifist as might be expected. Although resistance to the militarist politics is the main cause of her political action, ironically her pacifism is instrumentalized by the nationalistic regime in order to purify its political purpose from its militaristic characteristics. Thus, while the tendency to identify motherhood with pacifism is used sometimes by the feminist and peace movements as a women's politics of resistance, it is also used by the nationalistic ideology as a smoke screen for its militaristic ambitions.

As a physician and a mother-hero, Zorica Mitić cries over the wounded girl who happens to be an ethnic Croat in the chapter "Croatian Child, Nevertheless a Child,"[36] thereby repudiating ethnic difference and discrimination, which were generators of the war, and refusing to let them affect the two fundamental determinants of her identity: motherly love and medical ethics. Mitić writes, "At the time when I felt lonely in my room, far from everyone, I was crying, and crying because of her and other children suffering in this war. Powerless and with a misery greater than myself, I prayed to God to help children from this insane war, all children, who are supposed to live with or without the borders, but to live."[37] However, maternal feelings toward children of all ethnic origins, as well as her medical ethics to help the soldiers of the enemy's army, are, in her case, the means to an end completely different from the universal humanism that both motherly love and medical ethics embody. The function of this misuse of universal humanism is to beatify the nationalism of "our side" in the conflict. The unconditional love of the mother-hero who saves enemies' children and even enemy soldiers is nothing but mere proof of the just cause where the supposed war crimes perpetrated by our side exist as a lie created and promoted by the enemy side or as a hallucination of posttraumatic soldiers. In one place in her war diary, Mitić notes her encounter with a young Serbian soldier torn with memories from the front line and worried that he may have committed a war crime. Her comforting words are as follows:

> You, my little one, you found yourself torn between the ignorance and cowardice of others. The one who is a soldier in the army is just doing his job.

Therefore, if the soldier kills—especially if he does that in self-defense—that one is not a murderer. The blond young man stares at me with tears in his eyes: "Am I really not a murderer? I was defending myself, I didn't even know if I killed someone." You, young man, are the honest, good and normal man. Only people like that have a dilemma. You didn't make the war.[38]

The sympathies which mother-heroes feel toward nationalism in spite of their antimilitaristic attitudes induced in their motherhood can be easily instrumentalized and used by the same nationalistic politics to justify its end: national liberation through militaristic means being beatified by the presence of a mother-hero, an unquestionable pacifist. The motherly comfort of the nation, her symbolic child, is prevented from ever waking up from the dream of victimhood and the politics of irresponsibility.

Conclusion

Both the mother-hero and the Milošević regime shared an ambivalent relationship to the issue of women's status in society. Both sent mixed messages: the mother-hero stepped into the masculine public sphere while preserving a stigmatized femininity from which she alone has escaped. The Milošević regime's combination of nationalism and leftist rhetoric excluded women from political participation and reduced their social role to reproduction, while using their labor power to maintain everyday life amidst sanctions and economic hardship. The exclusion of women from the political sphere brought about further re-traditionalization of society. The fall of communism and the reinvocation of nationalism only strengthened the patriarchy, sexism, and misogyny that had existed all along, covered by the formal pronunciation of the equality of women and their inclusion in politics and the decision-making bodies. The socialist goal of the inclusion of women was only partially fulfilled, leaving women's issues always as of second-rate political interest. As the political sphere of the Serbian League of Communists was slowly filling with female party cadres, the resentment against the communist regime was proportionally rising. The abandonment of the ideological values constituted by the communist regime caused women's emancipation to be identified with the fading ideology of socialism and consequently to be replaced with a nationalism and traditionalization of gender roles. If one of the characteristics of the Milošević regime was ambivalence toward women's rights, epitomized through its need to instrumentalize women in order to maintain legitimacy, then the mother-hero represents the only logical response, where nationalist rhetoric is instrumentalized by the mother-hero in order to reclaim some small measure of political power within the limited political space radically purged of women.

The intellectual patrons of the new Serbia struggle to disentangle the country from nationalism based on ethnic and kinship ties and to develop a civic "nationalism," finding its transformative engine in the rehabilitation of the autonomous individual and responsible citizen. This approach, while ultimately promising democratic changes (as functionalist evolutionary theory is trying to convince us), carries, however, the possibility of neglecting the realm of cultural influences from which the project of individual responsibility tries to distance itself. Serbian nationalism from the 1990s used the primordial idea of national character as ingrained in the culture and traditions which consequently formed the nationalistic politics. While the argument of cultural essentialism deserves critique, the opposite extreme of neglecting the power of cultural influence of the political context, particularly of gender dynamics, presents another hazard. The present context of gender relations in Serbia is to a great extent a product of particular power relations in the family, which constitute ambivalent power positions of women that in turn encourage their power over the private sphere in place of actual political power. While it is undeniably important to renounce the idea that cultural practices predetermine reality, the underestimation of the influence of such practices is the main obstacle to their deconstruction.

Notes

1. Marina Blagojević, "Discrimination, Unpaid, Underpaid and Underestimated," in *Women's Rights and Social Transition in FR Yugoslavia,* ed. Vesna Nikolić-Ristanović (Belgrade: Center for Women's Studies, Research, and Communication, 1997), p. 23.

2. Žarana Papić, "Women in Serbia: Post-Communism, War, and Nationalist Mutations," in *Gender Politics in the Western Balkans: Women and Society in Yugoslavia and the Yugoslav Successor States,* ed. Sabrina P. Ramet (University Park, Pa.: Penn State University Press, 1999), p. 167.

3. I use the expression "mother-hero" in this chapter rather than "mother-heroine" because this best captures the spirit of the Serbian *majka-heroj,* with its intimation of masculinity. "Mother-hero" also reflects perfectly the way in which socialist-realist poetry portrayed mothers giving birth to future soldiers for the

Fatherland. At the same time, there is a hint in the expression that women, as "mother-heroes," can register a claim to a share in patriarchal power.

4. According to "Federal Republic of Yugoslavia (Kosovo and Serbia)," in *Women 2000: An Investigation into the Status of Women's Rights in Central and South-Eastern Europe and the Newly Independent States* (Vienna: International Helsinki Federation for Human Rights, 2000), p. 522.

5. *Jugoslavija 1918–1988 Statistički Godišnjak,* as cited in Obrad Kesić, "Women and Revolution in Yugoslavia," in *Women and Revolution in Africa, Asia, and the New World,* ed. Mary Ann Tetreault (Columbia: University of North Carolina Press, 1994), p. 245.

6. According to the results of the Survey on the Work Force from 1997, women's average wage was 11 percent lower than the average men's wage and 7 percent lower than the overall average wage; in "Federal Republic of Yugoslavia" [note 4], p. 523.

7. Ibid., p. 522.

8. Ibid., p. 524.

9. Papić, "Women in Serbia" [note 2], p. 167.

10. Jasna A. Petrović, "Žene u SK danas," *Žena* 44, no. 4 (1986), p. 7, as cited in Sabrina P. Ramet, "In Tito's Time," in Ramet, *Gender Politics in the Western Balkans* [note 2], p. 102.

11. "Federal Republic of Yugoslavia" [note 4], p. 529.

12. Papić, "Women in Serbia" [note 2], p. 167.

13. Cited in "Žene hoće svoj deo" (2001), online at www.pub18.ezboard.com/ fbalkansfrm14.showMessage?topicID=44.topic.

14. Despite this discouragement, in the following period the Women's Political Network is going to lobby Serbian political parties for 50 percent women's quota; in "Žene hoće svoj deo" [note 13].

15. Marijan Milosavljević, "Žene na sve spremne," *NIN* (Belgrade), no 2655 (15 November 2001), pp. 33–35.

16. Data cited in ibid., pp. 33–35.

17. "Federal Republic of Yugoslavia" [note 4], p. 531.

18. Ibid., p. 531.

19. Ibid., p. 532.

20. Ibid., p. 526.

21. Papić, "Women in Serbia" [note 2], p. 163.

22. See, for instance, Olivera Stajić, "Demografska tranzicija: Tata na porodiljskom," *AIM Press* (Paris), January 2002, online at www.aimpress.ch/dyn/ pubs/archive/dta/200201/20123–005–pubs-be.

23. See, for example, "Slučaj Obradovića: Seksualna afera u Srbiji," *Monitor* (Podgorica), 18 May 2001, online at www.medijaklub.cg.yu/zanimljivi/zanimljivi.

24. "Montenegro: Authorities Arrest Deputy Prosecutor, Crack Down on Trafficking in Women," Radio Free Europe/Radio Liberty, 3 December 2002, online at www.rferl.org.

25. Ibid.

26. Marija Obradović, "Vladajuća stranka: Ideologije i tehnologija dominacije," in *Srpska strana rata: Trauma i katarza u istorijskom pamćenju*, ed. Nebojša Popov (Belgrade: BIGZ, 1996), p. 499.

27. Žarana Papić explains this by the women's being seduced by Milošević's political power.

28. Ramet, "In Tito's Time" [note 10], p. 92.

29. Ibid., p. 102.

30. Ibid., p. 104.

31. Andrei Simić, "Machismo and Cryptomatriarchy: Power, Affect, and Authority in the Traditional Yugoslav Family," in Ramet, *Gender Politics in the Western Balkans*, pp. 11–29.

32. Julie Mostov, "Women and the Radical Right: Ethnocracy and Body Politics," in *The Radical Right in Central and Eastern Europe since 1989*, ed. Sabrina P. Ramet (University Park, Pa.: Penn State University Press, 1999), pp. 49–63.

33. Zorica Mitić, *Iz Krajine koje više nema: Dnevnik lekarke dobrovoljca 1991–1995* (Belgrade: Filip Višnjić, 1997), p. 112.

34. Marko Živković, "The Stories Serbs Tell Themselves (and Others) about Themselves" (Ph.D. diss., University of Chicago, 2001).

35. Iris Marion Young, *Justice and the Politics of Difference* (Princeton, N.J.: Princeton University Press, 1990) p. 165.

36. Mitić, *Iz Krajine*, p. 20

37. Ibid., p. 22.

38. Ibid., pp. 41–45

PERIPHERIES

12

KOSOVAR ALBANIANS BETWEEN A ROCK AND A HARD PLACE

FRANCES TRIX

Through various machinations, Slobodan Milošević was able to rescind the autonomous province status of Kosova (Kosovo)[1] in 1989. Within two years he had reduced Kosova to a police state run largely by Serbs, while the population itself remained over 90 percent Albanian. The response of the Kosovar Albanians was unexpected. Instead of acquiescing, exiting in massive numbers, or rebelling in armed conflict, the Kosovar Albanians agreed on a constitution (1990), held a referendum (1991) and elections (1992), and established parallel administrative, educational, medical, and safety-net institutions in place of those closed to them by the Serbian police regime. With Ibrahim Rugova as president and Bujar Bukoshi as prime minister, the self-proclaimed Republic of Kosova declared a policy of nonviolence which they maintained, despite continual and intense harassment and provocation, until well after the Dayton Peace Accords.

In this chapter on Kosova under Milošević and after, I focus on the quandary of the Kosovar Albanians, caught between Milošević's policies aimed at making life unlivable for Albanians in Kosova, and the lack of interest of Western nations in "interfering in a sovereign state," no matter the human rights abuses. In particular, I focus on Kosova in 1997, a year largely ignored by the international press but one in which tensions between the Kosovar Albanians and Milošević's police state accelerated, as did the tensions between Rugova's LDK (Lidhja Demokratike e Kosovës, the Democratic League of Kosova) and other political groups, including the Independent Student Union that sought a more activist response. My focus, thus, will be on the post-Dayton period, and the Dayton Peace Accords (1995) with their nonreference to Kosova, despite promises to consider Kosova after Bosnia. This epitomizes the "hard place" in which the Kosovar Albanians found themselves, hoping for outside recognition and support. It was in this context that the UÇK (Ushtria çlirimtare e Kosovës), the Kosova Liberation Army, slowly grew. The end of the outright Bosnian conflict also freed up the Serbian paramilitaries for action in Kosova. And it brought Serbian refugees from the Krajina in Croatia to Kosova, where they were forcibly settled and given jobs and resources, thus impinging upon both Albanian and Serb Kosovars.

There are multiple studies which provide valuable perspectives on Kosova, including overviews by Biberaj (1993),[2] Malcolm (1998),[3] and Vickers (1998);[4] more focused studies on human rights by Booth (2001)[5] and O'Neill (2002),[6] and civil resistance by Clark (2000);[7] and political analyses by Ramet (1999),[8] Ramet and Lyon (2002),[9] and Maliqi (1998).[10] This study draws from these and others, as well as from document anthologies like Krieger's (2001) on international law,[11] the archives of the Kosova Information Agency (LDK-sponsored Qendra për Informim e Kosovës), Albanian newspapers of the times (*Koha Ditore, Bujku,* and *Illyria*), reports issued by human rights organizations (particularly Human Rights Watch), and my extended study of Albanians and Albanian, including study at the University of Prishtina (Priština) in 1987–88, and work with Kosovar refugees from 1999 to the present. By focusing on a particular year, I want to emphasize the exigencies of weekly life, something that can be lost in academic studies but which is crucial for understanding events and the motivations of people. Further, where possible I include events from areas in Kosova that were less well covered by the international press, especially the strategic western third of Kosova with its cities of Peja (Peć) and Gjakova (Djakovica).

In the broader historical picture, Kosova has long been a contested region. It possesses the main mineral wealth in southeast Europe and is located along north-south trade routes. Nationalist claims from the nineteenth century to the present, principally Serbian and Albanian, but also Montenegrin and Bulgarian, have clashed over the region. In 1912–13, Serbia expanded militarily into Kosova, then part of the Ottoman Empire. Despite the fact that the majority of the population was Albanian and opposed to Serbian rule, the Great Powers acquiesced in Serbia's conquest. Albanian diplomats fought this decision internationally, while Albanian guerrilla groups fought Serbian domination well into the 1920s. Belgrade countered with systematic oppression of Albanians and campaigns of Serbian colonization of Kosova in 1922–29 and 1933–38. In the early years of World War Two, the tables turned and it was the Serbian colonists who were pushed out of Kosova by Albanians, for whom entry of the Italians and the Germans brought respite from Belgrade policies. After World War

Two, there was another period of intense harassment of Albanians in Kosova by Serbian authorities that tapered off with the fall of Interior Minister Aleksandar Ranković in 1966. The decentralization policies of the late 1960s in Yugoslavia led to greater status for both Kosova in the south and Vojvodina in the north as autonomous provinces of Serbia that also had federal participation. The growth of the University of Prishtina in the early 1970s and the 1974 constitution in which the autonomous regions were allowed their own constitutions represented a high point for Albanians under Serb rule. The death of Tito in 1980, the severe response to the demonstrations in Kosova in 1981, the declining economic situation in Europe, and the growth of Serbian nationalism in the 1980s that was championed by Milošević all led to a decline in the status, security, and living conditions of Kosovar Albanians. The following decade of Milošević's rule of the 1990s are the immediate context of this study.

To orient the study, I begin with the powerful symbols of naming and language policy. Then, as legitimacy is a central issue of the conflict and a major concern of this book, I consider how Milošević abolished the autonomy of Kosova, as well as how Kosovar Albanians responded. Overall, Milošević's policies toward Kosova from 1989 to the spring of 1999 can be seen as forms of bureaucratic expulsion. Both immediate actions, including the dismissal of Albanians from state employment in 1990 and the closing of secondary and higher education to Albanians in 1991, and the more gradual actions, such the revision of the law of inheritance in 1995 to prohibit the passing on of property to people who had not fulfilled the duties of citizenship, that is, served in the Yugoslav military,[12] were cloaked in a veneer of bureaucratic process. The goal, however, was the expulsion of Albanians from Kosova. From any understanding of legitimacy that includes consideration of the people affected by government action, these were grossly illegitimate actions. As for the self-proclaimed Republic of Kosova, its institutions sought legitimacy within Kosova, as well as externally in international recognition and support. Over time, the efficacy of the policies of the self-proclaimed republic and the democracy of its ruling party were called into question, but never its post-1991 goal of independence. Externally, it was only recognized by Albania, for in spite of the war in Bosnia, the international community remained more interested in the maintenance of borders than in the expulsion of people. Thus, with questions of political and moral legitimacy in mind, I examine the Kosovar Albanians under Milošević—their strategies for survival, and the evolution of their identity and institutions, with specific examples drawn from the pivotal year of 1997.

Background in 1989:
Serbianizing the Landscape and Loss of Autonomy

One of the signs of Milošević's policy toward Kosova was the change of official reference from "Kosovo" back to the earlier Serbian formulation of "Kosovo and Metohija." Serbian nationalists in the 1980s, including Vuk Drašković,[13] and the 1986 petition by Serbian intellectuals,[14] had used this formulation, as had the earlier Kingdom of Serbs, Croats, and Slovenes, and Yugoslavia until 1968. But its use had long irritated the Albanians. The name "Metohija," from the Greek *metoh*, meaning "an estate owned by the Church," referred to the western third of Kosova, which in the four-teenth century, had been made up largely of estates of Serbian Orthodox monasteries. However, much had changed since that time. And while the monastery of Dečani and that of the patriarchate of Peć still stood, the overwhelming majority of landowners and people living in this region were Albanian. Indeed, this western third of Kosova was known to Albanians as *Rrafsh i Dukagjinit*, the plateau of Dukagjin. This name resonated with Albanians as the name of an important Albanian feudal family and a com-patriot of the fifteenth-century Albanian national hero Skenderbeg, that is, Lek Dukagjin, to whom is ascribed the main assembled customary law of Albanians, the Kanun of Lek Dukagjin. As a concession after the Alba-nian demonstrations of 1968, "Metohija" was dropped, and the official appellation of the province in Yugoslavia became simply "Kosovo." In the crucially important constitution of 1974, the province is referred to as "Kosovo." Thus Milošević's use of "Kosovo and Metohija" is seen as a sign of undoing the earlier reforms, and of linguistically lording over the Albanians.

During the time of Milošević, Serbianization in naming practices, that is substituting Serbian names for Albanian ones, became a policy of the state. This affected street, boulevard, and community center names. It is politically interesting because, while the law for use of language and names was promulgated 27 July 1991, such changes could be initiated at the mu-nicipal level and, in fact, were, several years earlier. An incident during the time of transition in the western city of Peja (Peć) is most telling in this regard.

On 17 November 1989, a festive day of commemoration of the libera-tion of Peja, its communal assembly adopted an initiative, proposed by the chairman of the Communal Committee, Dr. Miladin Ivanović, to change the names of city streets. In particular, the street theretofore known as "The League of Prizren" would be called "Kosovski Junaci"; the street

"Haxhi Zeka"[15] would be known as "Dušan Labović"; the street "Bajram Curri" would be known as "Musa Muhadzeri"; the street "The Frashëri Brothers" would be known as "Braća Jugović"; the street "Luigj Gurakuqi" would be known as "Liman Kaba"; and the street "Hasan Prishtina" would be known as "Jug Bogdani."[16] Clearly the changes were all of streets named after an Albanian patriotic organization and Albanian patriots to the names of Serbs, their heroes in the Battle of Kosovo (1389), or others who had fought with the Serbs.

What was equally galling to Albanians was the procedure through which they were approved. Two days before the actual adoption, the presidency of the Communal Committee of the League of Communists of Peja had discussed a proposal of that committee on changing street names. Without consultation with members and without offering justification, the committee approved the changes and suggested that they should be presented to the communal assembly at the commemorative meeting on 17 November, where there could be no discussion. At that meeting, when members did try to debate the changes, they were interrupted and the proposal pushed through "by acclamation," without a full vote of the chamber of the assembly.[17]

There followed letters of protest to officials from Albanian Kosovar academics[18] and citizens, printed in *Alternativa*, a journal published in Ljubljana. The protest from the citizens of Peja was signed by over seven hundred workers of the Ramiz Sadiku enterprise, the Leather and Footwear Combine, the Alcohol Factory, the Sugar Factory, the Union of Joint Services Workers, employees of the communal assembly, instructors in a regional school, and 3,480 citizens of local communities. This citizens' protest made seven points: (1) that the procedure of adopting name changes was suspect and illegal; (2) that the Albanian figures and league named were central to their liberation struggle so that their negation was a negation of their identity and history; (3) that the Albanian figures were also important in Albanian literature; (4) that the names to be deleted were not those of anti-Yugoslavs; (5) that the citizens respected and admired the figures of the new names which should however be given to new streets; (6) that the current decision to adopt the new names should be annulled; and (7) that the decision was hasty and did not contribute to the stabilization of the political situation about which they were concerned.[19]

The political situation to which they referred was indeed most tense. As Milošević had sought to consolidate his power, he had deposed the leadership of the Communist Party in Montenegro, Vojvodina, and Kosova,

and replaced it with people loyal to him. This went quickly in Montenegro and Vojvodina, but Milošević's dismissal of the Kosovar leaders, Azem
Vllasi and Kaqusha Jashari, had led to the Miners' March to Prishtina with
large demonstrations of three hundred thousand people in solidarity in
November 1988. Then in February 1989, the Serb national assembly passed
amendments to Serbia's constitution to give Belgrade broader powers over
Kosova, amendments that according to the 1974 constitution needed to
be approved by the Kosova assembly. Still in February, when Milošević
refused to dismiss the party loyalists he had appointed for Kosova, the miners went on strike. There was even a support rally for the Kosovar miners
in Slovenia. However, martial law was declared in Kosova, federal troops
were called in, and Vllasi was arrested and charged with "counterrevolu-
tionary endangering of the social order."

The Kosova assembly met on 23 March 1989. Albanians refer to this as
the "Constitution of the Tanks," for tanks surrounded the meeting place,
and there were members of the Serbian state police inside the building as
well. Members of the assembly had been threatened by these police in preceding days, and on the day of the vote, no roll call was taken. Discussion
was disorderly, particularly regarding Amendment 47 to repeal the veto
power of the Kosova assembly over amendments to the Serbian constitution pertaining to Kosova. The floor was crowded with 400 people, many
of whom were Communist Party functionaries and unelected officials.
Only 150 were voting members of the 184-member assembly. Opponents
of the amendment decided to abstain, since the amendment required a
two-thirds majority. During the voting, many voted for the amendment
who did not have the right to vote, while most of the Albanian delegates
abstained, although 10 voted outright against the amendment. The Serbian president of the Kosova assembly, Jokanović, counted only the negative votes and on this basis declared the amendment passed.[20] On 28
March, when the constitutional amendments passed the Serbian assembly, giving Serbia control over Kosova's police, courts, educational policy,
economic policy, and even official language, with all elected municipal
bodies and communal authorities in Kosova henceforth suspended, there
were massive demonstrations in Kosova, with an official death toll of
twenty-four, but an unofficial one of two hundred.[21] Milošević held his
famous rally on 28 June 1989, on the field of the Battle of Kosovo, and called
for "a return of Serbs to Kosovo." There were major demonstrations again
in October when Vllasi's trial was to be held. This, then, was the context
of the change of street names in Peja in November 1989.

The changing of street names and names of other public places took place throughout Kosova. In the capital city of Prishtina, for example, "Hajdar Dushi Street" was renamed "Vojvode Stepe," and "Nexhmedin Mustafa Street" was renamed "Vase Carapica."[22] By the end of 1992, it was reported that in Prishtina, this changing of names and replacing those which referred in any way to Albanians was largely complete. Still, in 1997 in Prishtina, there was an incident over the changing of the name of an elementary school. In May 1997, Serbian security officers removed a board with the name "Zenel Hajdini" from in front of an elementary school in Prishtina, which six Serb policemen replaced with a board bearing the name of the Serb writer "Aleksa Santić." This was done under orders of the Serb-installed principal, Nada Milosavljević. As a rule, schools that had classes for Serbian and Albanian children had both a Serbian and an Albanian name; however, this school had only Albanian students and had never had any Serbian students. The following week, the Albanian school management, teachers, and the students of the school organized a protest meeting to express exasperation over the change of the school name.[23]

Such a protest meeting was in line with a new level of organizational activism that had grown among Kosovar Albanians, beginning in December 1989, although some trace it earlier to the moving and memorable Miners' March and Miners' Strike.[24] Specifically, in December of 1989, two important organizations were formed. First, the Council for the Defense of Human Rights and Freedoms was founded by academics on 14 December 1989. It set about documenting police abuse, human rights violations, and mistreatment of Albanians in the Yugoslav army. In 1991, Adem Demaçi, who had spent twenty-eight years in Serbian prisons for alleged political offenses, was elected president. Initially former political prisoners like Demaçi were the core of its province-wide network, but by the mid-1990s, there were subbranches in every community of Kosova. Over two thousand volunteers would visit scenes of incidents as soon as possible, carefully note the human rights violations, and pass the information on to the council in Prishtina so it could be made known internationally. Documenting and naming the violence was to have a transformative effect, "at best converting an attitude of resentful submission into a durable resistance."[25] The second organization, the Democratic League of Kosova, the LDK, was founded on 23 December 1989 as a national party of Albanians in Kosova. It drew its leader from the Writers' Association of Kosova, whose president was Ibrahim Rugova. People were drawn to the LDK as a way of responding to repression. Within five weeks of its founding, there were claimed to be over two hundred thousand members. This would become the main political party for the next eight years.

Meanwhile, the Serbianizing of the public landscape was not just a change of language but also involved a change of script. In the past, both Serbian and Albanian names of public places had been written in the Latin alphabet in Kosova. But with Milošević in power, the Cyrillic alphabet was used for public place names throughout Kosova. The obvious Serbian and Orthodox cultural associations were designed to assert the Serbian character of Kosova, even at the expense of alienating those used to the former names and especially those who could not read the script. One wonders how all of this figured in the programming of Belgrade television, for Kosova served as a convenient backyard theater whenever Milošević had need of distracting his constituents. Also for colonists, the Serbian names and script were meant to show how "Serbian" Kosova really was. However, the Serbian refugees from Croatia were not used to the Cyrillic alphabet on public signs either. Graffiti too was often in Cyrillic, especially the Serbian slogan of the four "s's," "only unity can save the Serbs," also known as the Serbian swastika, that was scrawled on walls, mosques, homes, and even cut into Albanians' bodies.[26] Undoubtedly there was graffiti in Albanian, too, but the risks were much greater, for sentences of five years in prison had been handed down to Albanians in the early 1980s for writing the "hostile slogan *Kosova—Republikë*."[27] But it was not just public places that required Cyrillic script. Prescriptions for medicine could not be filled unless they were written in Cyrillic[28]—yet another way to make daily life difficult for Albanians.

And not just the written language, but also the realm of the spoken language was changed in that Albanian was no longer an official language in Kosova. This meant that all official meetings were held in Serbian. And court cases were conducted in Serbian, with translation only of the questions and responses when a defendant did not know Serbo-Croatian, but not of comments of the judge or other participants. Throughout the 1990s, many of the police sent to Kosova from regions in inner Serbia spoke only Serbian. In 1997, incidents of beatings of young Albanians were reported whose initiating offense, besides that of being Albanian, was that they hadn't been able to answer the police's questions in Serbian and so were seen to give offense.[29] Certainly one of the outcomes of having closed all the state secondary schools to Albanians since 1991 was that young Albanians no longer learned Serbo-Croatian.

Survival in an Apartheid Society:
Economic, Medical, Human Rights, and Judicial Aspects

Belgrade's control of Kosova's state institutions and enterprises included control of state employment. In the first year of this control, 1990, there were massive dismissals of workers and professionals, from 115,000 to 120,000 Albanians, allegedly on separatist and other manufactured grounds. In early 1990, the Union of Independent Trade Unions of Kosova (*Bashkimi i sindikatave të pavarura të Kosovës*) was founded to try to protect Albanian workers from unjust dismissal, but it soon became rather an association for the welfare of dismissed workers. That year, Albanian police were fired and 2,500 Serbian police were brought in to take the place of the fired Albanians. Albanians who worked for the media, the courts, state enterprises, sports, and health-care clinics were also fired, and Serbs or Montenegrins installed in their places. In 1991, Albanian teachers, university professors, and most remaining doctors were fired. The question was how to survive economically.

People coped by cultivating gardens and by drawing on funds from family members overseas, contributions from the Albanian Diaspora, aid from Kosova organizations like the Mother Teresa Association, the LDK Solidarity Fund, and the union, minimal salaries from the 3 percent tax which Kosovar Albanians levied on themselves for teachers and medical workers, and from newly started small trading businesses. The small traders of Kosova contrasted sharply with the corrupt, crime-ridden, and mismanaged economy of Serbia of this time. By 1995, there were over eighteen thousand small firms registered in Kosova, compared to seventeen hundred in 1987. With their contacts in Macedonia, Albanian traders were renowned. But there was no overall plan to better use resources,[30] and there was much hardship. By mid-1995, half a million Albanians, out of a population of close to 2 million, faced food shortages.[31]

By mid-1997, a representative of the Economic Institute in Prishtina noted that the Serbian occupation had resulted in 70 percent unemployment with 60 percent of the Albanian people of Kosova living in conditions of extreme poverty.[32] There was reported weekly plundering of the small businesses and food vendors in marketplaces by police, along with "fiscal police," sometimes known as "inspectors." For example, in June 1997, Serbian police with fiscal police raided the marketplace in Malisheva, in central Kosova, seizing merchandise from twenty-five Albanian vendors, and taking it away in three trucks.[33] On 1 August 1997, forty Serbian market inspectors along with Serbian police looted the marketplace in Prishtina. Fines of several hundred DM were levied against vendors who did not have the requisite permissions for selling goods. The vendors noted that they had tried on numerous occasions to obtain these permissions but had been refused.[34] Serbian agricultural inspectors also continued to destroy cows and sheep owned by Albanians on the pretext they had contagious diseases. The previous year, 1996, these inspectors, along with the police, had killed four thousand farm animals belonging to Albanians on the pretext that they had hoof-and-mouth disease. Research showed no evidence of such disease.[35] Meanwhile Albanians were charged higher administrative taxes than Serbs. For example, in Vushtrri, where Albanians were an absolute majority, they had to pay up to 400 dinars for a car license, whereas Serbs in nearby Zubin Potok paid only 15 dinars for the license.[36]

On a larger scale, there was looting of resources of Kosova. For example, the National Bank of Kosova, which had been a force for development and the guarantor of loans, had its assets transferred to Belgrade banks on 5 December 1990. The foreign currency savings accounts of 66,000 individuals, worth an estimated US$98 million, were confiscated by the state-owned Jugobanka in Belgrade.[37] In April of 1997, the giro accounts of the National Bank of Kosova were transferred from Prishtina to Belgrade.[38] On 5 May 1997, Belgrade signed a five-year US$519 million contract with the Greek Mytilineos Holding Company in Athens for mining of lead and zinc from the Trepça mines in Kosova.[39] Clearly the beneficiaries of this were Belgrade and Mytilineos Holdings at the expense of the people of Kosova, who should have had some benefit from their natural resources, or at the very least, employment in their extraction.

Along with economic deprivation and abuse, there were also significant health concerns. Despite being largely rural, Kosova was the most densely populated region in Yugoslavia, and the second-most densely populated area in Europe. Its sewage and water systems were not well developed, and contagious disease had been a problem before 1990. But conditions had gotten much worse. For example, in 1994, infant mortality was 17 percent, the highest in Europe, and three times higher than it had been in the early 1980s.[40] Doctors who had been dismissed set up private practice, but medicines were in short supply. The Kosovar Albanians set up the Mother Teresa Association (named after the most famous Albanian of the twentieth century, whose mother was from Prizren) in 1990 to distribute food and aid. In 1992, it set up its first clinic, and by the end of 1997, there were ninety-one clinics and 7,000 volunteers. The aid was given free of charge, and in the first years was supported totally by local businesspeople, with staff who donated their services.[41] Later, European humanitarian groups contributed, and even some Serbs came for treatment. But in the difficult conditions, there was fear of epidemics, as many of the rural children had not been vaccinated. In December of 1997, the Serb-installed director of the Peja Clinic of Chronic Diseases, Joco Stankov, noted that thirty-five hundred people in Kosovo had tuberculosis, over 20 percent of them children, and that while the disease was not under the control of health organizations, the Serbian Ministry of Health had not shown much interest in preventing its spread.[42]

Along with health concerns, there were also continuing human rights abuses. Human Rights Watch documented such abuses in 1993, in 1998, and during and after the bombing in 1999.[43] But for the first half of 1997, from January to July, the Kosovar Center for the Defense of Human Rights and Freedoms (CDHRF) documented the following abuses.[44] Serbian police had searched the homes of 501 families on the pretext of seeking arms; in 90 percent of the cases, they had found no weapons. (Such searches were a main instrument of terror. They were usually conducted in the early morning and involved the beating of young men, destruction of furniture, intimidation of women and the aged, and traumatizing of children.) The police had detained 466 people, of whom 333 reported having been subjected to torture while in custody. The police had summoned 420 people to police stations for interrogation. Eighteen Albanian families were forcefully evicted from their apartments and Serbian families settled in them in their stead. Serbian police ill-treated 206 political, humanitarian, and sports activists and journalists in Kosova, largely through summoning them for "information conversations" in Serbian security centers, where they were subjected to various forms of ill-treatment. Twenty-five people had died violent deaths,[45] including 2 who died of torture in Serbian custody, 5 who were killed by Serbian police, and 2 who committed suicide after being called for questioning by the police multiple times. "Being severely harassed by authorities had become a way of life for Kosova Albanians: it was estimated that between 1981 and 1995 more than half of the Albanian population of Kosova was subjected to police harassment in some form, with such cases becoming more frequent in the 1990s."[46] The Center for the Defense of Human Rights and Freedoms also noted the staged political trial in May, in which 20 Albanians were sentenced to many years in prison.

Indeed, 1997 was a year for staged political trials in Kosova. There were three during that year, in May, June–July, and October–December. And while there had been several instances of violence from a slowly emerging UÇK, directed against Serb police and Albanian informants, the political trials in 1997 seemed largely directed at an international audience to discredit the policy of peaceful resistance of the Kosovar Albanians. For example, the European Union approved autonomous trade measures for rump Yugoslavia and easing of international sanctions 29 April 1997. The first of the large political trials began soon after in Prishtina on 19 May, although the defendants had been in custody since January. Building on this message of Albanian "terrorism," the second trial was held from 3 June to 15 July. Then in October and November of that year, there was growing concern among international groups over the nonimplementation of the 1996 Education Agreement, and the undue force used by Serb police against the peaceful student protest in Prishtina, 1 October 1997. The third trial began 27 October and ended 15 December 1997.

Such political trials were not new to Kosova. There had been the famous Prizren Trial in 1956, in which high-level Kosovar Albanian communists, as well as three dervish sheiks, had been convicted of spying for Albania, although their convictions were overturned twelve years later.[47] More recently there had been a staged trial of former army officers in Kosova in 1994, and a trial of former police officers in Kosova in 1995.

In the May 1997 trial, twenty young Albanians, including two women, most of whom had been taken into custody in January 1997, were charged with suspected affiliation and planning with a terrorist organization, but not with violent activity. At the actual trial, there were only seventeen defendants in the court, as two were tried in absentia, and one had died in custody in February. They were sentenced to a total of 107 years in prison. The June–July trial involved fifteen people, charged in the autumn of 1996 with terrorism in killing four people and attempting to kill sixteen others. Twelve were being charged in absentia; only three were in court. As a group, they were sentenced to 264 years in prison. The October–December trial involved twenty-one people initially; however, two had fled, one had been shot by a Serbian policeman, and one had died in custody, so there were only seventeen in court. They had been picked up in the spring of 1997 and were charged with affiliation with a terrorist organization and alleged involvement in terrorist activities. All but one were convicted; they were sentenced to 186 years in prison. The one who was set free, a twenty-two-year-old medical student from Prishtina, Alban Neziri, was then able to describe his eleven months in detention, the different forms of torture he experienced, and how he had held off signing the false confession until he heard his father's voice through the wall in the torture room of the prison.[48]

These trials are especially useful for considering the legitimacy of the judicial process in Kosova at this time, as there were outside witnesses who made public their evaluations of the proceedings. These witnesses include: Elisabeth Rehn, the Special Rapporteur of the United Nations High Commission on Human Rights; Human Rights Watch; John Dinger, a USIS information officer; and the Humanitarian Law Center in Belgrade. The most thorough report is that of Rehn on the first two trials. She noted that "both trials failed to meet minimum guarantees for fair trial provided in UN standards, notably the International Covenant on Civil and Political Rights and the Convention against Torture, which the Federal Republic of Yugoslavia was bound to uphold."[49] She also noted that procedural requirements of Yugoslav law were not met regarding evidence, and that there was an absence of credible material evidence linking the accused to the crimes they allegedly committed. She noted that there were serious doubts, on the basis of the evidence presented and the illegal manner in which many statements were extracted, whether the accused should have been found guilty. She concluded that the accused had been denied a fair trial.[50] With regard to the third trial, the Belgrade-based Humanitarian Law Center noted that the only evidence the court used in sentencing was statements made in pretrial proceedings, and that the court authorities did nothing to investigate the claims of defendants that they had been tortured and forced to make incriminating confessions, something a court is obliged to investigate under the UN Convention. The Humanitarian Law Center also noted that witnesses in the courtroom could not claim they had seen the defendants at the scene of the crime, and that the rights of both detainees and lawyers had been violated in that the former were subjected to brutal torture while the latter were denied access to their clients during the investigative proceedings.[51]

The international witnesses' accounts coincided with those in Albanian newspapers to a great extent. Both sources noted that the presiding judge in the May trial, Dragolub Zdravković, had also been the presiding judge for the large trials of former Kosovar Albanian army officers in 1994, and former Kosovar Albanian police in 1995. UN Special Rapporteur Elisabeth Rehn noted that "the appearance of impartiality and independence of judicial and prosecution officials involved in trying political prisoners would be strengthened if these cases were heard by rotating benches."[52] But the Albanian newspapers carried as well the comments of one of the defending attorneys, Nekibe Kelmendi, that Presiding Judge Zdravković, besides committing infringements, had also used offensive language during the trial proceedings. He had used the word Šiptar, a Serbian derogatory term for Albanians,[53] instead of *Albanci*, the more neutral term. This is akin to having a white judge in the United States refer to black defendants as "niggers" in the courtroom in the course of their trial.

The Evolving Identity and Institutions
of Kosovar Albanians toward Nonviolence

One of the reasons Albanians had felt like second-class citizens in Yugoslavia was that they had not been accorded their own republic, despite being more numerous than the Montenegrins. They were also from the poorer southern regions of Yugoslavia, and on the whole less educated, although Serbia's prohibiting of schooling in Albanian or even their attendance at state schools before World War Two had contributed to this situation. But the particular disregard for Albanians increased in the 1980s as the Serbian-controlled press broke with Tito's injunction not to criticize other ethnic groups. The slurs on Albanians increased, especially after the Serbian intellectuals' petition of 1986, in which Kosovar Albanians had been accused of desecrating Serbian graves and raping Serbian nuns. These accusations had no basis in fact. In the late 1980s, Milošević's "Rallies of Truth" were often occasions for disparaging Albanians. There they were referred to as murderers, rapists, arsonists, primitive and violent people, and even different species of animals, a derogatory way to allude to their much higher birthrate. Indeed, Kosovar Albanians did have the highest birthrate in Europe. But their largely rural and often problematic economic situation certainly contributed to this fact. At base, Kosovar Serb fears and complaints about their minority status in Kosova were being used to stoke the Serbian nationalist fire. The disparagement and dehumanization of Albanians fed into this phenomenon. Through the 1990s, this disparagement got worse, for as Hannah Arendt noted, violence always needs justification, so escalation in violence may bring about a truly racist ideology to justify it.[54]

From an Albanian perspective, Albanians had traditionally valued honor, bravery in war, and freedom. The Albanian national hero Gjergj Kastrioti Skenderbeg (1405–68) had stood up against Ottoman military might for twenty-five years. In line with this, there were many Albanians in 1989 who wanted revenge against Serbian usurpation. But then suddenly, in 1990 and 1991, as political philosopher Shkëlzen Maliqi put it, "warriors went out of fashion over night. . . . The strategy of nonviolence was somehow self-imposed."[55] Some saw nonviolence as a pragmatic response to the overwhelming Serb military strength. Rugova often explained it that way: "There is no choice but self-control when facing terror."[56] But Maliqi offered a more anthropological analysis, suggesting that the Kosovar Albanians were "asserting themselves by emphasizing their differences from the Serbs." That is, "they were restructuring their identity in contrast to the Other, here the ruined enemy nation."[57] This self-defining of an oppressed group in contradistinction to the oppressor, that is, "we are what they are not," is well documented in ethnographic research.[58] Thus, where Serbs were warlike and nondemocratic, the Albanians would be peaceful and democratic. And the Serbs had no idea how to respond to the Albanians' nonviolent movement, which was the first organized mass response in Kosova's history.[59] Further, the Kosovar Albanians' espousal of democracy and nonviolence in 1990 was well in tune with the ideological shift to democracy that Eastern Europe had been undergoing since the late 1980s.

Maliqi traces the first political articulation of this change to the Miners' March in November 1988, which maintained strict nonviolence, nonvandalism, and dignified order in their almost sixty-kilometer march from the Trepça mines south to Prishtina. They avoided any insulting slogans, even shouting, "Long live the brave Serbian people," in an attempt to distinguish the Serbian people from the regime.[60] And as with their hunger strike the following February, their central focus was to maintain the constitution of 1974. At the very least these actions flew in the face of the all-too-pervasive Serbian defamation of Albanians.

What makes the change in Albanian identity more remarkable is that it occurred in the winter and spring of 1990 at the height of the Serbian regime's hate campaign against Albanians. As a manifestation of this change, Albanians worked to root out violence in their own customs, in particular the blood feud. The Center for the Defense of Human Rights and Freedoms asked a member of their board, Dr. Anton Çetta, professor emeritus of folklore, to lead a campaign to resolve blood feuds. Dr. Çetta, along with five hundred volunteers, including many students, traveled all over Kosova for the next two years, resolving blood feuds. "Paqjet e gjaqeve," "appeasing blood," was a slogan of the times.[61] By the end of the campaign, over one thousand families in public ceremony had "put forth their hand and forgiven in the name of the people, youth, and the flag."[62] In the course of these travels in villages and towns of Kosova, the volunteers became aware of the desperate needs of the people for food and services. Some see the founding of the Mother Teresa Association in May 1990 as a response to meet these needs. Indeed, Dr. Çetta was the first president of the Mother Teresa Association.

With their evolving identity, a new political and social activism blossomed. This was embodied in the organization and activities of the Council for the Defense of Human Rights and Freedoms, founded in 1989; the Mother Teresa Association, founded in 1990; Motrat Qiriazi, founded in 1991 by Igo Rugova and others to work for rural women's literacy; and the Center for the Protection of Women and Children, founded in 1993 by Drs. Vjosa Dobruna and Sevide Ahmeti for medical care. (In the Albanian Diaspora as well there was new unity of purpose in organizations like the New York branch of the LDK[63] and the National Albanian American Council [NAAC], founded in 1996 to lobby the American government.) These volunteer organizations in Kosova continued to flourish, thanks to "an unprecedented sense of community and a new social unity in the struggle for economic and political survival that served to replace the familialism of the past."[64] And these organizations nurtured leadership and organizational skills among those who worked in them. For example, in 1997, Nazlie Bala, who had worked for five years as a field coordinator for the Center for the Defense of Human Rights and Freedoms, founded an organization, Elena, to monitor violations against women.

The Albanian media in Kosova also became an arena for the growth of leaders, as well as the continued participation of non-LDK leaders. Not surprisingly, it was an early target of the Serb police regime. In 1990, the main Albanian publishing house was taken over, its main newspaper, *Rilindja* (the Renaissance), closed, and 290 employees were fired. To fill its place, the agricultural weekly *Bujku* (the Farmer), took on added dimensions, and the former youth magazine *Zëri* (the Voice), became a political weekly under editor Blerim Shala. The new weekly *Koha Ditore* (the Daily Times), first founded in 1990, evolved into the main independent newspaper under editor Veton Surroi, and became a daily in 1997. This was a dangerous profession, however, as journalists and editors were routinely picked up by the Serbian police and many were beaten. Indeed, between 1991 and 1992, every editor served prison time.[65] In the related field of book publishing, the excellent Dukagjin Press in Peja was expanded.[66] The electronic media were more easily controlled by Belgrade. All thirteen hundred Albanian employees of radio and television were fired, and the only broadcasts retained in Albanian were direct translations of the Serbian news. At first, Radio Zagreb's ten-minute daily Albanian bulletins provided an alternative, but later, the 6:30 evening news of Albanian television from Tirana was dedicated to issues affecting Kosova. The Kosova Information Center was also an important source of news. However, it should be noted that *Bujku*, the Tirana broadcasts, and the Kosova Information Center were all controlled by Rugova's LDK.

To the international community, Ibrahim Rugova, head of the LDK since 1989, and president of the self-proclaimed Republic of Kosova since the 1992 election, represented Kosova. But within Kosova, the situation was more nuanced. Indeed, one of the results of the growth in activism was the growth of multiple leaders. The West had little appreciation, for example, that twenty-four political organizations had taken part in the April 1992 elections that first elected Rugova and the LDK. Yet the more severe the oppression by the police regime, the more difficult it was for parties other than the LDK to maneuver. Maliqi has gone so far as to say that even in 1993, there were no real parties, merely pluralized elements of a national liberation movement whose overriding goal was the establishment of an independent Kosova.[67]

The LDK, as represented by President Rugova and vice president and party ideologist Fehmi Agani, did not waver from their goal of an independent Kosova, although it was sometimes phrased as a protectorate under UN auspices. They based this on the results of the September 1991 referendum in which the people had overwhelmingly voted for an independent and neutral state. The LDK's problem was that the international community was not interested in considering a change of borders; the Western states and Russia saw Kosova as an internal problem of Yugoslavia. However, Kosovar Albanians had never considered themselves a minority.[68] Rather they saw Kosova as a compact, largely Albanian settled region that had been erroneously awarded to Serbia in 1912 through Great Power rivalry with no regard for the local population. They had protested against this annexation immediately and repeatedly. Some argued that, in agreeing to the 1974 constitution, they had accepted Yugoslav sovereignty. But as the 1974 constitution had been abrogated, this was moot. An additional problem of the LDK was that the international community was also not particularly interested in human rights abuses against Albanians in Kosova. But the LDK was still hopeful that if only the international community could be made to see how Albanians were being treated in Kosova, they could be brought around. Thus, their refrain from 1990 to 1999 was for more international involvement in Kosova.

Accomplishments of the LDK included building an international network of branches that sent funds to Kosova, levying a 3 percent tax on Kosovar Albanians to support the parallel school system and medical clinics, and coordinating news services, like the Kosova Information Center, to keep people informed of the slightest interest of the international community in Kosova, to document abuses, and to pass on words and observations of their leaders. A main need was to keep up morale in a situation of constant emergency and siege. Yet the most crucial accomplishment of the LDK, with much help from other community leaders, was the effective maintenance for many years of a nonviolent response to Serb police occupation and aggression. The importance of this cannot be underestimated. There are many who hold that Serbia intended to provoke violence in Kosova and then to use this pretext to expel the Albanians, preferably while the world was distracted with the first Gulf War. There are others who hold that Croatia also tried to provoke such violence in Kosova so that Serbia would have to fight on two fronts in 1991.

People have disputed Rugova's role in these accomplishments as well as his political acumen, particularly after Dayton. But they do not dispute that he served well as a symbol of Albanians' new identity: European, reasoned, and nonviolent. In contrast to the traditional Albanian model and the later UÇK image, Rugova was not a warrior in experience or demeanor. He symbolized the moral legitimacy of the Kosovar Albanians' movement. Further, what does not come across in newspaper photographs is the deep resonance of his voice, his authority, and his diplomatic abilities. Rugova was able to steer a course, or preside over one, which allowed for survival and which fostered community and social volunteerism. What refugee after refugee told me in 1999 was that Rugova gave them hope.

A main success of Rugova's early administration was the organizing and fostering of the parallel school system. All Albanian faculty and students at the secondary school and university level had been forced out of the state educational system and facilities, and at the elementary level, Belgrade had refused to pay Albanian teachers and staff. This occurred over 1990 and 1991. First, in 1990, all Serbian and Montenegrin teachers in Kosova were given salary raises, two and three times their usual salary, so that their salaries would be commensurate with those in Belgrade. In the winter of 1991, the Albanian teachers were not paid at all. The following summer, Albanian teachers were told to sign loyalty oaths to the regime and informed they must teach the Serbian language curriculum and teach in Serbian. When they refused, they were fired. In the fall of 1991, Albanian students were blocked from entering the schools. At the same time, all the 1,000 Albanian staff and 27,000 Albanian students at the University of Prishtina were expelled. Serbian staff and students took over the university. The Albanological Institute was closed. The main reading rooms in the National Library in Prishtina were given to a Serbian Orthodox school, and non-Serbs were refused entry to the library. (Later, the empty Albanian secondary schools would be used to house the Serbian refugees from Croatia.) The dismissed Albanian teachers and professors began teaching largely in private homes, garages, and storerooms. This was the start of the parallel school system which provided for significant numbers of Kosova's 400,000 students.

In 1995, the parallel school system reportedly served about 312,000 elementary school students, 56,920 secondary students, and twenty faculties and colleges of 12,200 students at the post-secondary level. It had an Institute for the Publication of Textbooks and teachers' unions.[69] The system was funded largely from the 3 percent tax levied by Kosovar Albanians on themselves, with 30 percent from contributions from overseas. The facilities often were cold, lacked sufficient furniture and light, and in the first two years, the Albanian Teachers Association reported that 3,300 teachers were detained and interrogated by the police, with two directors of primary schools killed.[70] Nonetheless, the school system was a remarkable achievement. Its establishment and survival were put forth as evidence for the legitimacy of the self-proclaimed republic. Some even suggested that Rugova should more correctly be called "President of the Parallel Schools of Kosova," rather than "President of the Republic of Kosova."[71]

In the mid-1990s, however, there was growing frustration with the difficult learning conditions, and there were declining numbers of students. Teachers were being paid less regularly as the economy in Kosova continued to be exploited by the police state, and it was proving harder to get funds safely into Kosova from overseas. Then two blows were dealt Kosova and Rugova. First, the Dayton Peace Accords of December 1995 rewarded violence as the Bosnian Serbs got Republika Srpska, while the Kosovars, with their remarkable fortitude, forbearance, and nonviolence, were not even mentioned. Then, on 1 September 1996, the Vatican St. Egidio Community brokered the Education Agreement, signed separately by Milošević and Rugova, to provide for the return of Albanian students and teachers to the state schools.[72] This offered a short spate of hope for improvement in educational facilities. But it was not implemented. This greatly increased people's frustration, and Rugova was seen as unwise to have trusted that Milošević would follow through on anything that mattered to the Albanians. Throughout 1997, the nonimplementation of the St. Egidio Education Agreement festered, giving fuel to the cynics and the extremists. If there could be no agreement on something as basic as school buildings, how could there ever be trust for larger issues?

Challenges to Kosova in 1997

Rugova began his first news conference in 1997 by stating that the year would be a significant one for the realization of Kosova's freedom and in-

dependence, an independence that would be achieved through an organized and civilized resistance.[73] Unfortunately this was not to be, nor would
there be much attention accorded Kosova until the last months of the year.
Rather, other parts of the Balkans captured world attention.

In particular, in the first half of the year, the Serbian opposition coalition, Zajedno [Together], was in the limelight. Although it had won significant numbers of municipalities in the November 1996 elections, Milošević had tried to prevent its elected candidates from taking office. The
ongoing popular demonstrations in the streets of Serbia, despite the cold
winter, showed the hope of the people for change. In February, Djindjić
and others were finally allowed to take office. Not just the Serbian people
but also international leaders hoped this would lead to real change in
Serbia. Journalists asked the Kosovar Albanians how this change would
affect them. Earlier, veteran Kosovar political prisoner and activist
Adem Demaçi had sent a message of support to the protesting Serbian
people in December 1996,[74] but more representative was the response of
Hydajet Hyseni, the third in power in the LDK after Rugova and Agani.
When asked in an interview in Geneva in February 1997 if the LDK placed
much hope in the Serbian opposition movement, he responded, "We support the democratization of the regime in Belgrade, but we remain dis-
trustful of the coalition 'Together.' Its leaders are as chauvinistic as
Milošević. We have no illusion that from that side will come any resolution of our problems."[75]

By April, the coalition had effectively fallen apart. As Milošević could
not run for a third term himself, he engineered his election to the hith-
erto largely ceremonial post of president of Yugoslavia on 15 July 1997. But
it was clear Milošević was still the power broker within Serbia, and outside Serbia, the title of "President of Yugoslavia" carried weight as that of
the major ruler. The fall elections in Serbia, held 21 September, 5 October,
and 7 December, became a struggle between Šešelj's Radicals and Milošević's chosen candidates, with the opposition, apart from Drašković, boy-
cotting the elections. The Kosovar Albanians also boycotted the election
as they had all previous elections from Belgrade since 1990. For them to
have voted in such an election would have been to accept the illegal constitutional changes to their status, enacted by the Serbian assembly in 1989,
and the illegal dissolution of their assembly. However, in the December
election, Šešelj's Radicals complained of voter fraud in that the numbers
of votes for Milošević's candidate from Kosova polling stations far exceeded the numbers of Serbs registered to vote there.

In contrast to the divisiveness of political campaigns were the polio vaccination campaigns, conducted in Kosova in the spring of 1997, and earlier in the fall of 1996. During these campaigns, 455,565 children were vaccinated, both Albanian and Serb, through a joint venture of the Mother Teresa Association and the state health system, in cooperation with the World Health Organization and the United Nations Children's Fund. The teams of medical workers were designed to reflect the ethnic balance of the targeted communities, and the police did not interfere. Such cooperation was most remarkable, especially at this time of heightened tension.

Europe's contribution to the situation in Kosova in 1997 was shortsighted and increased the tension. In April 1997, the European Union granted Yugoslavia preferential trade status. (Six months earlier, in October 1996, the United Nations had suspended sanctions against Yugoslavia.) The stated objective of the EU action was to support the Serbian opposition, and not Milošević. But by then the opposition had already fallen apart. Then, on 15 May 1997, the European Commission approved an aid package for Yugoslavia worth US$112 million. Neither of these rewards had any conditions attached. The plight of the Kosovars was being totally ignored by Europe. To add insult to injury, Switzerland concluded an agreement with Belgrade on 4 July 1997 to return to Yugoslavia refugees whose asylum requests had been declined. This included 12,000 Kosovar Albanians. This agreement was based on the agreement that the German government had previously made with Belgrade in October 1996 to repatriate 120,000 unsuccessful asylum seekers, of whom 100,000 were Kosovar Albanians. A similar agreement between Sweden and Belgrade was in the offing as well. The forced repatriation of Kosovar Albanians most certainly resulted in the deterioration of an already strained political and social situation. Rugova responded that the return of the refugees "could lead to a social collapse," as there were no jobs or food for them. And Special Rapporteur Elisabeth Rehn noted that "tensions in Kosovo have reached unprecedented levels and could deteriorate into civil war at any moment."[76] It was not until 29 December 1997 that the European Union recognized that the preferential trade status to Yugoslavia was unwarranted and put sanctions back in place.

Within Kosova, 1997 was a year in which there was growing dissatisfaction with Rugova and the LDK. Parliamentary elections, which were to have taken place in March 1996, were now to be held 24 March 1997. However, in March, Rugova put these off until 27 December, saying that he had done this in consultation with the other political parties. The other political parties denied this. It turned out that the Americans had exerted pressure against holding the elections in the spring of 1997, naïvely hoping that the Kosovars would take part in the Serbian election in the fall. Then, in December, Rugova put off the scheduled elections until 22 March 1998. Elections were an exercise in political legitimacy, and polls of Kosova's two major cities showed that the LDK would have won the March 1997 election with a two-thirds majority. Here was a case of affirmation of internal legitimacy being sacrificed in the hope of external support.

Then in June 1997, Serbia proposed a law for local self-government in Kosova whereby bicameral assemblies would be created for the twenty-eight municipalities of ethnically mixed areas (Serbia had already increased by seven the number of municipalities in areas of Serb population) such that one chamber would be made up of representatives of Serb and Montenegrin people, with veto rights, while the other chamber would be for "national minorities and ethnic groups." This would be in keeping with former deputy prime minister Ratko Marković's understanding that "while the Serbs in Kosovo are a minority in quantity, they are a majority in quality; while the Albanians, though a majority in quantity, are a minority in quality."[77] Even the U.S. State Department noted that such a law was unlikely to further reconciliation.[78]

Meanwhile, three Kosovar groups challenged Rugova and the policies of the LDK in different ways throughout 1997, for there was a general feeling that Rugova's policies were going nowhere. The first was the Parliamentary Party of Kosova (PKK), which, since January, had been led by former political prisoner Adem Demaçi, who remained as well the head of the Center for the Defense of Human Rights and Freedoms. Demaçi was the only one in Kosova with the stature to compete with Rugova. He called for a move from passive nonviolence to active nonviolence, something people inside and outside the LDK had been requesting for several years. Earlier, in 1996, Demaçi had put forth a proposal for Kosova to be one of three republics in what he called "Balkania." But this idea had not caught on among Kosovars, or anyone else. In November 1997, Demaçi's party had tried to organize a democratic forum of political parties, but had not been successful. Then, in December, after the UÇK had appeared publicly at a funeral, Demaçi requested from them a three-month ceasefire to give politicians a last chance to try to reach a peaceful settlement. By the following August, Demaçi had become spokesperson for the UÇK (Kosovo Liberation Army), after he had publicly given up his "Balkania" proposal.

The second group to challenge Rugova in 1997 was the UÇK. The incidences of attacks on Serb police and Albanians who were seen to collaborate had increased in 1996, but it was not clear if they were isolated acts of revenge or represented a larger organized effort. Rugova continued to label such incidences as provocative acts by Serbs or unknown terrorists. However, in the spring of 1997, those in Kosova who sought armed resistance against the Serbs received an unexpected gift. Berisha's government in Albania fell in March 1997, and the subsequent looting of army and police depots made available a source of cheap weapons in close proximity to Kosova. Funds that had been sent to Kosova from the emigrant communities in Germany and Switzerland for the parallel school and social safety-net were now diverted to Albania to purchase weapons. In September 1997, there were assaults on ten police stations in Kosova which showed careful organization.

On 2 December 1997, the UÇK made its first public appearance in Kosova at a funeral for an Albanian teacher who had been killed in crossfire by Serb police. Three masked armed members of the Kosova Liberation Army attended and publicly announced that the Kosova Liberation Army was "the only force fighting for the freedom of Kosova."[79] It has been argued that the UÇK never had the full support of Albanian intellectuals or the leaders of large families, but rather drew its members from former political prisoners, returned refugees from Europe who didn't understand the situation in Kosova, and young villagers caught in the melee.[80] The results of the municipal elections in October 2000 in which the UÇK was resoundingly defeated support these observations. But in late 1997, there was encouragement for a new response, and, after the Serb killing of Adem Jashari and forty members of his family in March 1998, greater support for the UÇK. Still, it was observed that when the UÇK engaged in actions, it was unable to protect the surrounding people.

Finally, the third group that challenged Rugova in 1997 was the Independent Student Union of the University of Prishtina (UPSUP). Like Demaçi, the student union called for more active nonviolence, and like the UÇK, it was not afraid of confrontation. Union leaders consulted with the LDK and other political parties, but resolved to go their own way and called for a demonstration for the first day of university classes, on 1 October 1997, to demonstrate for their members' basic right to study. In mid-September, the LDK had supported the proposed protest, but the week before it was to take place, Rugova asked the students not to demonstrate. Apparently there was concern from international parties that the protest could provoke bloodshed. The students went ahead anyhow, to the shock of the LDK. The students were well organized, with protests planned in six cities in Kosova, to take place starting at 11 A.M. Only university students and faculty, dressed in white, were to take part in the procession,

and a strict code of nonviolence was promulgated, and participants ad-
hered to that code. The police also prepared and put up barriers where
the protest was scheduled to pass. Indeed the police blocked the procession, and for an hour, there was no movement. Then the police attacked
with batons, tear-gas grenades, and armored vehicles, breaking up the
demonstration and beating and arresting leaders.

As would happen in the time of the expulsion in 1999, the most violently repressed demonstrations were in the western part of Kosova in Peja
and Gjakova.[81] The combination of the peaceful demonstration by the students and the brutal disruption of it by the police brought international
support. The students held protests 29 October and 30 December 1997 as
well. But before the last one, they had been upstaged by the UÇK, and
their active nonviolence took a back seat to increasingly violent confrontations in 1998, culminating in the expulsions of 1999.

In his New Year message at the end of 1997, Rugova acknowledged that
it had been a difficult year, but that its end saw "the persistence of the young
Kosovar generation to actively participate in the society in an organized
way. Kosova is steadily becoming an international subject," he declared.[82]

Escalation and Denouement

Indeed, Rugova was right and Kosova did become an international subject in 1998, only not in the way he had hoped. Rather, it was a combination of increasing UÇK skirmishes, overkill reaction by Serbian forces,
and ambiguous responses of the international community that led to an
escalation of violence. In speeches in Prishtina and Belgrade in late February 1998, U.S. ambassador Gelbard branded the UÇK as terrorists. Within
the week, a Serb police action began in villages in Drenica, a central region
of Kosova long known for resistance to Serbs. There was a large Albanian
demonstration in Prishtina to protest this police action on 2 March. Yet,
three days later, on 5 March 1998, the Serb police killing of all members
of the Jashari family, except for one eleven-year-old girl, along with
neighbors—in all eighty-three killed, including twenty-four women and
children—was a turning point for Albanians. The Serb police had sought
Adem Jashari, a known UÇK leader. But their massive overkill of him
and his entire extended family, along with others in the village, made him
a martyr and led many Kosovars who had held firm for nonviolent resistance for eight years to support the UÇK.

Serbia began an offensive in the western part of Kosova in May, just
after Rugova had been persuaded to meet with Milošević in Belgrade. This

further undercut Rugova's authority. The fighting in Kosova continued throughout the summer, until by September 1998, there were an estimated three hundred thousand internal refugees. Ambassador Holbrooke brokered a cease-fire agreement in October with Milošević that called for OSCE (Organization for Security and Cooperation in Europe) verifiers,[83] but the verifiers had no enforcement mechanism and did not include the UÇK. For Milošević, the presence of the verifiers was a guarantee that there would be no air-based military action against him then, and so he continued military buildup and actions in Kosova.

Yet early the following year, the Serb police massacre of forty-five villagers in Raçak on 15 January 1999 was a turning point for the West, just as the killing of the Jashari family had been a turning point for Kosovar Albanians the previous winter. U.S. ambassador William Walker, who was head of the OSCE mission of verifiers, called this incident to world attention. From 6 February to 22 February 1999, there were negotiations designed to establish a political solution for Kosova at Rambouillet outside Paris. As a sign of growing UÇK power, Hashim Thaçi, head of the UÇK, was elected head of the Albanian delegation, clearly another blow to Rugova's authority. In the end, the FRY (Federal Republic of Yugoslavia) never signed the Rambouillet Agreement; only the Albanians signed, under duress, and with the understanding that there could be no bombing of the Serbs if the Albanians did not sign.[84]

Nevertheless, the Rambouillet Agreement is important for its influence on later events. It was during the negotiations at Rambouillet that the NATO sectors for the five NATO powers were designated. Kosova's northern sector of Mitrovica was clearly the most sensitive for it bordered Serbia and included the mineral-rich Trepça mines. American general Wesley Clark, then Supreme Allied Commander, Europe, had hoped the United States would take this sector as it had taken the most sensitive sector in Bosnia. But the Pentagon refused and rather took the southeast sector that largely bordered Macedonia, which appeared to be the easiest sector from which the Americans could "withdraw early" and leave it to the Europeans.[85] Britain requested and received the sector with the capital city of Prishtina. The Germans wanted the sector with the least Serbs, as World War Two weighed on them, and so were given the sector of Prizren in the south. The Italians took the western sector. And the French, traditional allies of the Serbs, took the northern sector of Mitrovica. Indeed, a French NATO official had given main parts of the NATO operational plans to Belgrade in October of 1998. The way the French later handled this sector allowed the "ethnic cleansing" of Albanians there in

1999 after the end of the war, as well as ongoing conflict and de facto partition.

Further, an analysis of gender in the United Nations Mission in Kosovo (UNMIK) cites the influence of Rambouillet with its Interim Administrative Council of Hashim Thaçi, Ibrahim Rugova, and Rexhep Qosja (all male) and the virtual absence of women in these peace negotiations as "having perpetuated and institutionalized the marginalization of women in the political process after the conflict."[86] The role of the UÇK at Rambouillet also led Western nations to overestimate its influence in Kosovar society, and further ignore the nonviolent movement, its leaders, and institutions, which were more pervasive and had persisted over a much longer period than the UÇK.

Not only did the FRY not sign the Rambouillet Agreement, but Milošević used the time of the negotiations for further military buildup and arming of Serb civilians in Kosova. The OSCE verifiers were withdrawn 20 March, Serbia started its Operation Horseshoe to expel Albanians that same day, and the NATO air campaign began 24 March 1999. NATO described the change from negotiations to an air-based bombing campaign as a movement from "diplomacy backed by threat" to "diplomacy backed by force."[87] Clearly the reputation of NATO was at stake. But the coordination and cohesion of fifteen member nations over the eleven weeks of the bombing campaign, including the United States with its inflexible Pentagon and politically polarized Congress, were most remarkable. However, what the NATO air forces were least able to do was protect Kosovar Albanians on the ground from the state-sponsored violence unleashed upon them.

This violence was a "coordinated and systematic campaign to terrorize, kill, and expel Albanians, organized by the highest level of Serb and Yugoslav government at the time."[88] This was carried out through close cooperation of military, police, and paramilitary. Five hundred villages were destroyed, an estimated 10,500 people killed, with 3,525 people missing.[89] There was killing to facilitate the forced expulsions, targeted killing of human rights lawyers such as Bajram Kelmendi of Prishtina and his two sons, doctors such as Dr. Izet Hima of Gjakova, activists, especially those who had aided the OSCE verifiers, and revenge killings, like the 300 murdered in the small Albanian Catholic village of Meja on 27 April, reportedly for the death of five Serb police. At the same time, there was a deliberate attempt to destroy evidence and remove bodies,[90] as documented in the five mass graves of Kosovar Albanians found later in Serbia. Over 40 percent of residential homes were heavily damaged or destroyed, and 60 percent of the schools were destroyed. The organization of the expulsions and killings was evident in the coordination of the large-scale forcible deportations of Albanians from cities like Peja and Prishtina, and the systematic nature of the three waves of executions in Gjakova. Fully 90 percent of Kosovar Albanians were displaced from their homes, with 850,000 expelled from Kosova.[91]

Milošević worked to split the NATO alliance and destabilize the region by sending massive numbers of refugees to Macedonia. General Wesley Clark saw the forced expulsions of Kosovar Albanians from Prishtina to Macedonia as a blunder on the part of Milošević, for the television images of these refugees further galvanized support for the campaign at a time when Europeans were concerned about the civilian casualties in Serbia. One of the main reasons many European countries supported the NATO campaign was their fear of 1.5 million Kosovar refugees should the campaign fail. This is supported by the European Union's stand that the Kosovar refugees should be kept "in the region of origin,"[92] that is in neighboring countries in the Balkans. The Bosnian refugee experience was fresh in their minds, particularly that of Germany, which had taken in many Bosnian refugees at great expense.

Indeed, there were similarities in the Bosnian and Kosovar experiences, but one difference was that the Kosovars had ethnic kin in neighboring and nearby countries. Of the 460,000 refugees taken in by Albania—the poorest country in Europe—fully 260,000 were taken in by private families who received no international aid supplies. In Macedonia, of the 300,000 refugees who fled there, Albanian-Macedonian households took in 138,000 refugees. In Montenegro, of the 60,000 refugees who fled there, 30,000 were taken in by Albanian-Montenegrin households. And in Turkey, which took in a total of about 24,000 refugees, 9,000 were taken in by private households, many of which consisted of people who themselves had been expelled from Kosova in one of the three earlier mass expulsions by Serbs (1912–15, 100,000 Kosovars to Turkey; inter-war period, 120,000 Kosovars to Turkey; postwar period, 100,000 Kosovars to Turkey).[93] In contrast, 91,000 refugees were airlifted to the West from Macedonia, with the United States accepting 9,198. And the subsequent rapid return of most refugees, seen as the largest spontaneous movement of refugees since World War Two, is explained partly by the large numbers in private households who were most aware of the burden they placed on their hosts.

The Military Technical Agreement that the FRY and the Republic of Serbia signed with NATO on 9 June 1999 called for a total withdrawal of Serb and Yugoslav forces within eleven days. On 10 June 1999, the United

Nations passed Resolution 1244, creating the United Nations Mission in Kosovo, such that Kosova essentially became a UN protectorate, with NATO forces providing security as the Serb and FRY forces departed, but where the sovereignty of the Federal Republic of Yugoslavia continued to be acknowledged. The document was initially based on the Dayton Peace Accords and the Rambouillet Agreement, but there were many drafts. An earlier version included a provision requiring the Serbs to account for and release Albanian missing persons and prisoners. This provision was most injudiciously dropped by the Pentagon on 5 June in order to make the document more acceptable to the Serbs.[94]

Milošević capitalized on the omission of a provision on prisoners by transferring over 2,000 Albanians held in prisons in Kosova to prisons in inner Serbia on 10 June 1999. Most of these prisoners were civilians arrested illegally by Serbian police during the war. Their trials continued throughout 1999 and 2000 in Serbia to the utter frustration and anger of the Kosovars. As with the trials conducted in 1997, there were forced confessions after torture and grave violations of due process. Dr. Flora Brovina, pediatrician and head of the League of Albanian Women, had been arrested in April 1999 and transferred to Požarevac prison in inner Serbia 10 June. She was tried by a Niš court, convicted of antistate activities, and sentenced to twelve years in prison in December 1999, only to be released in November 2000. Another high-profile case was that of Albin Kurti, who had been a major leader of the nonviolent student demonstrations in the fall of 1997, and who later worked as a translator for Adem Demaçi. He was arrested in April 1999 and imprisoned and tortured first in Kosova, and then moved to prison in Serbia 10 June. He was tried and sentenced to fifteen years in prison in March 2000 but was released from the Niš prison 7 December 2001. The last Albanian prisoners were finally released in March 2002. But there remain more than 3,000 missing persons: 2,752 Albanians, 549 Serbs, 144 Roma, and 57 Montenegrins, whom the UNMIK in 2002 advised people to consider dead.[95]

The postwar situation in Kosova was characterized by lack of civic order, despite the presence of NATO KFOR (Kosovo International Security Force) troops. (One would have hoped that this experience would have helped planners for the occupation of Iraq in 2003.) The slowness of the United Nations in appointing administrators and finding international civilian police allowed the UÇK to fill the power vacuum. After twelve months, there were barely half the number of authorized international civilian police. There was revenge against local Serbs, and both Albanian and Serb communities tolerated extremists, who tended to further polarize them. The KFOR and the UNMIK lacked the political will to control these extremists.[96] There was no functioning judiciary; there was even argument about what law applied there. Without such a judiciary, it was hard to control violence, or threat of violence, and at least one hundred fifty thousand minorities left Kosova for Serbia and Montenegro, mostly in the first six weeks after the entry of KFOR troops.[97] There was also internal displacement, with Serbs moving into the northern sector and Albanians being pushed out of that sector. But in all fairness, the transition from war and a police state posed massive problems. And the lack of clarity about the final political situation of Kosova gave further clout to extremists of both sides. Finally, in spite of all the work of NATO to prevent the partition of Kosova, the French KFOR allowed this to happen along the Ibar River through the middle of the city of Mitrovica.[98]

Still people reconstructed homes and businesses, and postwar conditions for Albanians were somewhat improved, although this was not generally the case for Serbs there. A positive accomplishment was the police school, set up in Vushtrri in September 1999 by the OSCE to train members of the civilian Kosova Police Service. As of March 2002, over 4,000 people had graduated from the school, 84 percent of whom were Albanians, 9 percent Serbs, and 19 percent of whom were women.[99] Over a year later, by June 2003, there were 5,878 graduates of the OSCE police service school. The relative percentages of the graduating class in June 2003 were higher for minorities but lower for women; namely 65 percent of the graduates of this class were Kosovar Albanian, 27 percent were from minority communities (Serb and Roma), while only 7 percent were women.[100]

Another accomplishment was the successful holding of three major elections in Kosova since the war. The OSCE has overseen these elections, with the overall plan to shift main responsibility for elections to local authorities in time for the assembly elections of 2004. The first of these elections were municipal ones, held in October 2000, in which there was a 79 percent voter turnout. The LDK, the party of Rugova, won 58 percent of the vote, while the PDK (Democratic Party of Kosova), the party of UÇK leader Thaçi, won only 27 percent of the vote. This was a clear-cut victory for the LDK and Rugova, which showed the disenchantment of many people with the UÇK after the war and the extent to which the UÇK did not represent the broader society. The third party by popular vote was the Alliance for the Future of Kosova (AAK), which won 8 percent of the vote. The Serbs in Kosova, however, did not vote in this election.

The second elections, held in October 2001, were for seats in the 120-member Kosova assembly. Here there was a 65 percent voter turnout.

Again the LDK of Rugova won the most votes, with 46 percent, and was allotted forty-seven seats. The PDK of Thaçi won 26 percent of the votes, the equivalent of twenty-six seats. While the next largest number of votes, 11 percent, was won by the Serbian Povratak [Return] Coalition, it was with the special understanding that it was allotted twenty-two seats. The voting of Serbs in this election was a distinct accomplishment, although some of those north of the Ibar River were intimidated from participating. But what drew attention away from the success of this election was the month-long deadlock between the two main parties in allocating the two top positions. LDK leaders had been killed by the UÇK since the war, and Rugova would not accept Thaçi as prime minister. Finally there was a compromise, and on 4 March 2002, Rugova of the LDK was elected president of Kosova with Bajram Rexhepi of the PDK as its prime minister. The assembly, however, was forbidden from taking action to decide the final political status of Kosova, and the Special Representative of the Secretary-General of the United Nations retained major powers.

The third elections, held in October 2002, were municipal elections, with a 54 percent voter turnout. The decrease in voter turnout appears to reflect disillusionment in the ability of local authorities to affect significant change.[101] International personnel continue to exert interference and have veto power at all levels of authority over locally elected people. This reportedly has had a chilling effect on local initiative. As for the election results, among Kosovar Albanians, they were similar to previous elections, with Rugova's LDK winning the greatest number of votes, followed by the PDK and the AAK. However, the PDK and the AAK had increased percentages, while the LDK had decreased percentages relative to earlier elections. Unfortunately, the Serbs in Kosova did not come together; their participation was less than in the previous election.

An interesting feature of this third election was the increase in the percentage of women elected as municipal deputies. In the first municipal elections in 2000, only 8 percent of the municipal deputies were women, while in the 2002 election, 28 percent were women.[102] This reflects the Central Election Commission's electoral rule of August 2002 that required political entities to include a female candidate in each group of three candidates in the first two-thirds of the candidate list of every participating party. Behind this rule, however, is the influence of leaders of the Kosova Women's Network. By the winter of 1999, Kosovar Albanian women leaders had already become disenchanted with how both the United Nations and the OSCE were marginalizing women and ignoring the self-organizing work that Albanians had done throughout the 1990s. In January 2000, they founded the Kosova Women's Network, representing over thirty-two women's groups, and worked for measures to include women in meaningful ways in political areas and not just in "soft issues."

Meanwhile, the relation of Montenegro and Serbia had been in question since 1999, with Djukanović favoring independence for Montenegro. In March 2002, the Solana plan was announced, through which Serbia and Montenegro agreed to establish a loose confederation, to be known as Serbia and Montenegro. Thus the Federal Republic of Yugoslavia no longer existed. This immediately raised the question of the status of Kosova, for the Military Technical Agreement had left Kosova under the sovereignty of the Federal Republic of Yugoslavia, not Serbia. But Solana himself announced that the change would have no effect on the status of Kosova, which remained under the United Nations.[103] In the Solana plan, it is clearly stated that what was accorded to the FRY would devolve to Serbia in this case. Further, the commander of the French KFOR stated in a radio interview that, as both Solana and the new prime minister of Kosova, Dr. Bajram Rexhepi, had stated, the new understanding between Serbia and Montenegro would not affect Kosova.[104] The fear was that if Montenegro were permitted to declare its own independence, this would encourage Kosova also to declare its independence.

Not surprisingly, the commission to draft a new constitution for Serbia that began work in April 2003 considered Kosova as part of Serbia. As members of the Kosova assembly refused to take part, the commission asked for participation by a member of the Kosovar Serbian party Povratak. The mention of Kosova as part of Serbia in the prologue of the earlier constitution of Serbia-Montenegro angered the Kosovar Albanians, as did the 2003 Kosovo Declaration in the Serbian parliament that declares Kosova to be part of the Serbia-Montenegrin union. Serbs see the rewriting of their constitution as undoing the work of "Milošević's constitution" that took away the autonomous status of Kosovo and the Vojvodina and led to conflict in the region.[105] It is as if the only problem were Milošević and that constitution, while the broader responsibility of the Serbian people who consistently elected Milošević and who took part in the decade of oppression, expulsions, and killing in Kosova do not figure.[106]

Conclusion

In this chapter, I have highlighted the nonviolent policies and institution building of the self-declared Republic of Kosova from 1990 until 1997, and the challenges and stresses it confronted. Although I included the last section on the increasing violence of 1998, and the war of 1999 and its after-math, I do not want this to overshadow the earlier nonviolent period which has been largely unrecognized by the international agencies and forces that control postwar Kosova. In the UN protectorate, an independent com-mission noted a lingering attitude of imperial condescension by some members of the international administration as regards the Kosovars' ca-pacity for self-rule.[107] Indeed, the international administration and NGOs did not build on the organizations of civil society the Kosovars had so painstakingly crafted throughout the 1990s.

The main criticism of international authorities, however, is that they still cannot bring themselves to acknowledge that Kosovar Albanians will not be governed by Belgrade, and so Kosova is still in limbo, albeit no longer a Serbian police state. The experience of Kosova should lead to se-rious discussion in international law toward defining standards for the abrogation of sovereignty based most likely on UN principles support-ing decolonization,[108] or on Chapter VII of the UN Charter regarding threats to peace,[109] or the Genocide Convention.[110] Ramet's discussion of state sovereignty should be basic to this discussion.[111]

As for Rugova's LDK administration before the 1999 war, it did become more authoritarian toward other Albanian political parties; it acted more like a one-party state after the 1992 election, allowing the Council of Political Parties to languish, stifling debate, and putting off scheduled elections, although it eventually held them in 1998 and won handily. Nonetheless, overall its policies retained the approval of the people. Even after Dayton, the basic policy of nonviolent resistance was largely supported, only a more active nonviolence was sought, one less constrained by fears of international second secretaries and confronta-tion. The LDK's main challenge in means and personnel, but not goal, was the Kosova Liberation Army, which gained support but never mass par-ticipation, and which has been criticized by Albanians for its behavior after 10 June 1999, and relegated in the following elections to secondary status despite its move for control after the war. Thus, Rugova's earlier administration could be considered politically and morally legitimate, if not fully democratic.

The same cannot be said for the Serbian regime. Milošević's dismissal and arrest of the Kosovar party officers, his strong-arming to push the vote through the Kosova assembly in 1989, and his dissolution of that assem-bly in 1990 were clearly illegal. The subsequent administration of Kosova, including the dismissal of Albanians from state jobs, the closing of state schools to Albanian students, the regular and pervasive abuse of human rights, and the use of the courts as a weapon of the police were all grossly illegitimate policies, as was the proposed distortion of democratic principles in structuring local government, and the unleashing of the paramilitary and military on a civilian population, the expulsion of half that population, and the destruction of their identity papers. As for Serbia under Koštunica, what is most disconcerting is that the structure and personnel of the military and police of the former regime are still in place. The Serbian government transferred Milošević to The Hague largely for economic reasons, and Serbian nationalism, with its grassroots extremism and Kosova as a central symbol, has not been repudiated. Koštunica himself is a traditional right-wing nationalist whose connections with Serb paramilitary leaders in postwar Mitrovica, his speech there in December 1999, his denial of systematic war crimes,[112] and his obstruction of the International Criminal Tribunal do not suggest movement from an all too familiar Serbian nationalism.

At The Hague, the first part of Milošević's trial, in which he was accused of planning, instigating, ordering, committing, or otherwise aiding and abetting a deliberate and widespread or systematic campaign of terror and violence directed at Kosovar Albanian civilians living in Kosova in the FRY, lasted from February to September 2002. Milošević's strategy during this time was to discredit NATO and insist on his and the Serbs' victimhood. The broadcast of the trial and Serbian media coverage did not appear to lead to reflection or discussion of broader responsibility. At most, Milošević was scapegoated, as if his possible guilt absolved anyone else. It was only with the roundup of his supporters after the assassination of Zoran Djindjić in March 2003 that those who had been intimidating witnesses were apprehended.[113] Indeed, the problem may be with the Serbian people,[114] as well as the Serbian regime. For I detect no change in Serbs' attitude toward Albanians, no acknowledgment of wrongs, no apology, no movement from the cultural autism and the culture of lies[115] that have so affected this people.

The question remains, Why did the West ignore Kosova, with its adherence to democratic nonviolence in the face of pervasive human rights abuses, even after it knew Milošević and his record in Bosnia? Kosova was the most obvious place of conflict in the former Yugoslavia. And thanks to the restraint of the Kosovar Albanians, it was "the war that the international community had the greatest opportunity to prevent."[116] And yet, other concerns always seemed to take precedence, supported by blindness and arrogance. General Clark noted that during the summer and fall of 1998, the United States seemed more concerned with Saddam Hussein's violations of the UN sanctions in Iraq than the potential for another crisis in the former Yugoslavia.[117] Overall, the West's responses to Milošević's actions during 1998 were ambivalent and showed no clear threat.[118] Even earlier, when Rugova presented his vision for an independent and neutral Kosova to Lord Owen, the fact that, unlike Milošević's regime, Rugova had not dehumanized the Serbs and had reserved seats for them in the parliament, made no impact on Owen whatsoever. Rather, "Owen saw Rugova simply as a 'nationalist leader,' the moral equivalent of Milošević."[119] Scholars continue to argue the legality and legitimacy of the NATO action in 1999, with some seeing the action as illegal by UN rules but morally justifiable.[120] But it is the lack of timely, concerted action by the international community in the ten preceding years that I find most damning.

As for the Kosovar Albanians, I would hope that they will be entrusted with conditional independence, as recommended by the International Independent Commission on Kosovo in their report and follow-up,[121] for UN Security Council Resolution 1244 by itself is no solution. Under Milošević, the Kosovar Albanians changed, as is now expressed in the names of their streets, boulevards, and centers. The main street in Prishtina, formerly "Marshal Tito Boulevard," was renamed in 1992 during the period of nonviolence "Mother Teresa Boulevard." But the community center in Gjakova (Djakovica) that was formerly known as "United Brotherhood" was renamed in 1999, after the war, the "Adem Jashari Center."

Regrettably, more than six years after the 1999 war, things appear stalled in Kosova. The economy is not good, there is still no reliable electric power, important privatization has not occurred, Mitrovica is still a divided city, with the northern French KFOR section run by Serbs connected with Belgrade, there has been an increase in organized crime, the return of Kosovar Serbs has been promoted but is still limited, and despite the freely elected Kosovar officials, international personnel have held on to most meaningful authority. The main problem in all this is the lack of even a timetable for discussion of final status. This limbo stunts both economic and political programs at all levels, for who will invest under such conditions, and who will work to build relationships when there is still fear of Belgrade trying to reassert authority? The failure of the international community to move toward a final status discussion undermines political stability,[122] leaving the Kosovar Albanians yet again between a rock and a hard place.

Notes

1. In pronunciation, Serbs stress the first syllable (KO-sovo), while Albanians stress the second syllable and lengthen its vowel (Ko-SO-va). The final vowel varies with "o" for the Serbian form, "ë" for the indefinite Albanian form, and "a" for the definite Albanian form. As this article focuses on the Kosovar Albanians, I will use their definite form as standard reference.

2. Elez Biberaj, *Kosova: The Balkan Power Keg* (London: Institute for the Study of Conflict and Terrorism, 1993).

3. Noel Malcolm, *Kosovo: A Short History* (New York: New York University Press, 1998).

4. Miranda Vickers, *Between Serb and Albanian: A History of Kosovo* (New York: Columbia University Press, 1998).

5. Ken Booth, ed., *The Kosovo Tragedy: The Human Rights Dimensions* (Portland, Ore.: Frank Cass, 2001).

6. William G. O'Neill, *Kosovo: An Unfinished Peace* (Boulder, Colo.: Lynne Rienner, 2002).

7. Howard Clark, *Civil Resistance in Kosovo* (London: Pluto Press, 2000).

8. Sabrina P. Ramet, "Kosovo: A Liberal Approach," in *Society* 36, no. 6 (September–October 1999), pp. 62–69.

9. Sabrina P. Ramet and Philip W. Lyon, "Discord, Denial, Dysfunction: The Serbia-Montenegro-Kosovo Triangle," in *Problems of Post-Communism* 49, no. 5 (September–October 2002), pp. 3–19.

10. Shkëlzen Maliqi, *Kosova: Separate Worlds* (Peja: MM Society & Dukagjini, 1998); see also Maliqi, *Nyja e Kosovës: As Vllasi, as Millosheviqi* (Ljubljana: Knjižna zbirka KRT, 1998).

11. Heike Krieger, *The Kosovo Conflict and International Law: An Analytical Documentation, 1974–1999* (Cambridge: Cambridge University Press, 2001).

12. Hugh Poulton and Miranda Vickers, "The Kosovo Albanians: Ethnic Confrontation with the Slav State," in *Muslim Identity and the Balkan State*, ed. Hugh Poulton and Suha Taji-Farouki (London: Hurst & Co., 1997), pp. 139–69.

13. Alex Bellamy, "Human Wrongs in Kosovo, 1974–99," in Booth, *The Kosovo Tragedy*, p. 111.

14. Branka Magaš, *The Destruction of Yugoslavia: Tracking the Break-up, 1980–1992* (London: Verso Press, 1993), pp. 49–52.

15. The loss of this name would have especially offended Albanians in Peja for Haxhi Zeka had been the head of Besa-Besë, the Albanian patriotic organization of Peja in 1898.

16. *Rilindja* (Prishtina), 16 November 1989, cited in Harillaq Kekezi and

Rexhep Hida, eds., *What the Kosovars Say and Demand*, vol. 2 (Tirana: 8 Nëntori, 1996), p. 335.

17. Ibid., pp. 332, 336–37, 347–48.

18. Ibid., pp. 332–34.

19. Ibid., pp. 335–39.

20. This remarkable description of the 23 March 1989 Kosova assembly was brought to my attention by Dr. Sami Repishti, who graciously provided me with a copy of the reference in the article by Michael Galligan, Deborah Jacobs, Morris Panner, and Warren Stern, "The Kosovo Crisis and Human Rights in Yugoslavia: A Report of the Committee on International Human Rights," *The Record of the Association of the Bar of the City of New York* 46, no. 3 (April 1991), pp. 228–30.

21. Christine von Kohl and Wolfgang Libal, "Kosovo, the Gordian Knot of the Balkans," in *Kosovo in the Heart of the Powder Keg*, ed. Robert Elsie (Boulder, Colo.: East European Monographs, 1997), p. 84.

22. Sabrina P. Ramet, *Social Currents in Eastern Europe: The Sources and Consequences of the Great Transformation*, 2d ed. (Durham, N.C.: Duke University Press, 1995), p. 423.

23. *Qendra për Informim e Kosovës* (Prishtina), 17 May 1997.

24. Jelena Lovris, "Trepça on Strike," as cited in Magaš, *The Destruction of Yugoslavia*, pp. 179–80.

25. Clark, *Civil Resistance*, p. 59.

26. Bellamy, "Human Wrongs in Kosovo," p. 118.

27. Ibid., p. 110.

28. Ibid., p. 117.

29. *Koha Ditore*, cited in *Qendra për Informim e Kosovës*, 24 July 1997.

30. Clark, *Civil Resistance*, pp. 113–14.

31. Advocacy Project, "Repression," online at www.advocacynet.org/kosovo _repression_3_41.

32. *Bujku* (Prishtina), as cited in *Qendra për Informim e Kosovës*, 10 July 1997.

33. *Qendra për Informim e Kosovës*, 4 June 1997.

34. *Qendra për Informim e Kosovës*, 1 August 1997.

35. *Qendra për Informim e Kosovës*, 10 June 1997.

36. *Bujku* (Prishtina), as cited in *Qendra për Informim e Kosovës*, 15 May 1997.

37. Vickers, *Between Serb and Albanian*, p. 249.

38. *Qendra për Informim e Kosovës*, 22 April 1997.

39. "Dje në Athinë u nënshkrua një marrëveshje mes një firme greke e Trepçës," *Illyria* (New York), 7–9 May 1997, p. 13.

40. Sabrina P. Ramet, *Whose Democracy? Nationalism, Religion, and the Doctrine of Collective Rights in Post-1989 Eastern Europe* (Lanham, Md. and Oxford: Rowman & Littlefield, 1997), p. 149.

41. Clark, *Civil Resistance*, p. 107.

42. *Blic* (Belgrade), as cited in *Qendra për Informim e Kosovës*, 17 December 1997.

43. Julie Mertus and Vlatka Mihelić, *Open Wounds: Human Rights Abuses in Kosova* (New York: Human Rights Watch, 1993); *Humanitarian Law Violations in Kosovo* (New York: Human Rights Watch, 1998); and *Under Orders: War Crimes in Kosovo* (New York: Human Rights Watch, 2001).

44. *Qendra për Informim e Kosovës*, 17 July 1997.

45. In contrast, in the first half of 1998, according to the CDHRF, 416 people were killed in Kosova, while in the first half of 1999, it is estimated that 9,000 people were killed.

46. Poulton and Vickers, "The Kosovo Albanians," p. 159.

47. Malcolm, *Kosovo*, pp. 321–22.

48. *Qendra për Informim e Kosovës*, 18 December 1997.

49. Krieger, *The Kosovo Conflict and International Law*, p. 36.

50. Ibid., p. 37.

51. *Naša Borba* (Belgrade), as cited in *Qendra për Informim e Kosovës*, 17 December 1997.

52. Krieger, *The Kosovo Conflict and International Law*, p. 32.

53. *Bujku*, as cited in *Qendra për Informim e Kosovës*, 22 May 1997.

54. Hannah Arendt, *On Violence* (New York: Harcourt, Brace & World, 1970), p. 77.

55. Maliqi, "Self-Understanding of the Albanians in Non-Violence," in *Kosova*, p. 62.

56. The fuller quotation by Rugova is: "Our movement was born out of necessity as well as choice. People understand that in the long term one can win—and at the same time, there is no choice but self-control when facing terror." Ibrahim Rugova, *La question de Kosovo* (Paris: Fayard, 1994), p. 3.

57. Maliqi, "Self-Understanding of the Albanians," p. 62.

58. Keith Basso, *Portraits of "The White Man": Linguistic Play and Cultural Symbols among the Western Apache* (New York: Cambridge University Press, 1979), p. 64.

59. Personal communication from Dr. Sami Repishti, September 2003.

60. Maliqi, "Self-Understanding of the Albanians," p. 64.

61. Another form of this is "pajtimet e gjaqeve," or "reconciling blood."

62. Clark, *Civil Resistance*, p. 62.

63. Artur Kopani and Naim Dedushaj, *LDK në SHBA: Historia e një Lëvizjeje* (New York: Albanian Yellow Pages, Inc., 2000).

64. Janet Reineck, "The Past as Refuge: Gender, Migration, and Ideology among the Kosova Albanians" (Ph.D. diss., University of California at Berkeley, 1991), p. 201.

65. Clark, *Civil Resistance*, p. 108.

66. Frances Trix, "Publishing in Kosova: Focus on Kosovar Albanians," *Slavic and East European Information Resources* 1, no. 2/3 (2000), p. 164.

67. Maliqi, "The Albanian Movement in Kosova," in *Kosova*, p. 23.

68. Independent intellectual Rexhep Qosja, who favored union with Albania, saw Albanians not as a minority but as a divided nation, with those in Kosova caught in a colonial situation. See Elsie, *Kosovo in the Heart of the Powder Keg*, pp. 209–11.

69. Maliqi, "The School of Resistance," in *Kosova*, p. 69.

70. Masha Gessen, "The Parallel University: A Journey through Kosovo's Secret Classrooms," *Lingua Franca*, vol. 5, no. 1 (November–December 1994), p. 32.

71. Denisa Kostovicova, "Albanian Schooling in Kosovo 1992–1998," in *Kosovo: The Politics of Delusion*, ed. Michael Waller, Kyril Drezov, and Bulent Gokay (Portland, Ore.: Frank Cass, 2001), p. 15.

72. Krieger, *The Kosovo Conflict and International Law*, p. 11.

73. *Qendra për Informim e Kosovës*, 10 January 1997.

74. Robert Thomas, *Serbia under Milošević: Politics in the 1990s* (London: Hurst & Co., 1999), p. 297.

75. "En Kosove, toute autorité serbe est condamnée à être dictatoriale," 1 February, 1997, online at euconflict@euconflict.org.

76. "Refugee Repatriations Will Raise Tensions in Kosovo," *Wall Street Journal Europe* (online journal), 2 May 1997, WSJE9712200019.

77. *Jedinstvo* (Prishtina), cited in *Qendra për Informim e Kosovës*, 13 June 1997.

78. *Qendra për Informim e Kosovës*, 24 June 1997. The blatant social discrimination, evident in the proposed law and Marković's explanation, was for Albanians the main source of friction. Later in 2000, in a meeting with Ambassador Holbrooke and Ambassador Dobbins, Dr. Repishti, as representative of the National Albanian American Council, presented a memo stating just that—that social discrimination was the main source of friction—to which Dobbins heartily agreed; personal communication with Dr. Repishti, September 2003.

79. Vickers, *Between Serb and Albanian*, p. 313.

80. Clark, *Civil Resistance*, p. 177.

81. Ibid., 151–57 (an excellent description of the student protests).

82. *Qendra për Informim e Kosovës*, 31 December 1997.

83. The importance of the OSCE verifiers, according to Ambassador Holbrooke, was that they set a precedent for international involvement in Kosova; personal communication from Dr. Repishti, respected Albanian academic and president of the NAAC, who met with Holbrooke, along with the rest of the Board of the NAAC who participated in sessions of the NAAC.

84. Secretary Albright informed the Albanian delegation of this at Rambouillet, leading to a major shift in their position.

85. General Wesley Clark, *Waging Modern War: Bosnia, Kosovo, and the Future of Combat* (New York: Public Affairs, 2001), p. 163.

86. Annette Lyth, ed., *Getting It Right? A Gender Approach to UNMIK Administration in Kosovo* (Stockholm: Kvinna till Kvinna Foundation, 2001), p. 8.

87. Clark, *Waging Modern War*, p. 254.

88. Human Rights Watch, *Under Orders*, p. 3.

89. Ibid., pp. 121–25.

90. Ibid., p. 122.

91. Ibid., p. 4.

92. Joanne van Selm, *Kosovo's Refugees in the European Union* (London: Pinter, 2000), p. 6.

93. Frances Trix, "Reframing the Forced Migration and Rapid Return of Kosovar Albanians," in *Rethinking Refuge and Displacement: Selected Papers on Refugees and Immigrants*, ed. Elzbieta Gozdziak and Dianna Shandy, vol. VIII (Arlington, Va: American Anthropological Association, 2000), p. 264.

94. Clark, *Waging Modern War*, pp. 361, 370.

95. "Almost All Missing Are Dead, UNMIK Official Says," *Illyria* 12, no. 1129 (9–11 April 2002), p. 2.

96. O'Neill, *Kosovo: An Unfinished Peace*, p. 18.

97. Human Rights Watch, *Under Orders*, p. 454.

98. For a hypothetical view of partition, voiced during the 1999 war, see Sami Repishti, "The Difficult Road to Independence," *Illyria* (5 April 1999).

99. "New Graduates Join Police Force," *Illyria* 12, no. 1127 (2–4 April 2002), p. 5.

100. "Nearly 6,000 Police Cadets Trained by OSCE in Kosovo," 27 June 2003, online at www.osce.org.

101. Louis Sell, *Kosovo: Time to Negotiate Final Status, A Field Report* (Public International Law and Policy Group, January 2003), p. 12.

102. "Stronger Representation for Kosovo Women in New Assemblies," 4 November 2002, online at www.osce.org/Kosovo/elections.

103. "Havier Solana thotë se Kosova do të mbetet të udhëhiqet nga Kombet e Bashkuara" (Brussels), 4 March 2002, online at www.kosova.com.

104. "M. Valenten: Marrëveshja midis Serbisë dhe Malit të Zi nuk do të refektojë kurrfarë efekti në sigurinë e Kosovës" (Mitrovice), 18 March 2002, online at www.kosova.com.

105. Dušan Kosanović, "Deadline for Passing the New Serbian Constitution Expires in August," *Southeast European Times* (Belgrade), 22 May 2003.

106. Sabrina P. Ramet, "The Kingdom of God or the Kingdom of Ends: Kosovo in Serbian Perception," in *Kosovo: Perceptions of War and Its Aftermath*, ed. Mary Buckley and Sally N. Cummings (London: Continuum, 2001), pp. 30–45.

107. Richard Goldstone and Carl Tham, eds., *Why Conditional Independence? The Follow-up of the Kosovo Report* (Solna, Sweden: Independent International Commission on Kosovo, 2001), p. 20.

108. "Although the international system has disfavored secessionist claims, the system's own justificatory principles suggest that secession not be excluded as a solution where an existing political community's configuration durably subjects a minority to a predatory majority, provided that the subjugated minority is so geographically concentrated as to be identified with a defined territory. The principles supporting decolonization, expressed abstractly in General Assembly Resolution 1541, arguably have application to territories such as Kosovo and Chechnya, which are no better represented in Belgrade and Moscow than Angola was in Lisbon." From Brad R. Roth, "'Peoples' as Political Communities," *Proceedings of the American Society of International Law* 93 (1999), p. 56.

109. Julie Mertus, "Beyond Borders: The Human Rights Imperative for Intervention in Kosovo," *Human Rights Review* 1, no. 2 (January–March 2000), p. 80.

110. James Gow, "Law, War, and Kosovo: Further Loosening the Bands of Wickedness," *Human Rights Review* 1, no. 2 (January–March 2000), p. 99.

111. See Sabrina Ramet, "Evil and the Obsolescence of State Sovereignty," *Human Rights Review* 1, no. 2 (January–March 2000), pp. 129–33. A related earlier reference, suggested by Dr. Sami Repishti, is that of Secretary of State Kissinger, who three weeks after the signing of the Helsinki Act in 1975 noted, "At Helsinki, for the first time in the postwar period, human rights and fundamental freedoms became recognized subjects of East-West discourse and negotiations. The conference put forward . . . standards of humane conduct, which have been—and still are—a beacon of hope to millions," Rep. Christopher H. Smith of New Jersey, "Calling the President to Issue a Proclamation Recognizing the 25th Anniversary of the Helsinki Final Act," *Congressional Record* 146 (25 September 2000).

112. Norman Cigar, *Vojislav Koštunica and Serbia's Future* (London: Saqi Books, 2002), pp. 72–73.

113. Chris Stephen, "Milošević Faces New Wartime Evidence," *The Observer* (London), 11 May 2003, p. 1.

114. Stacy Sullivan, "Milošević's Willing Executioners," *The New Republic* (Washington, D.C.), 10 May 1999, pp. 26–29, 30, 35.

115. Dubravka Ugrešić, *The Culture of Lies: Antipolitical Essays* (University Park, Pa.: Pennsylvania State University Press, 1998), p. 162.

116. Clark, *Civil Resistance*, p. 158.

117. Clark, *Waging Modern War*, p. 447.

118. Ibid., p. 419.
119. Bellamy, "Human Wrongs in Kosovo," p. 122.
120. Goldstone and Tham, *Why Conditional Independence?*, p. 10.
121. Ibid., pp. 25–28.
122. Sell, "Kosovo: Time to Negotiate Final Status," pp. 5–7.

13

VOJVODINA SINCE 1988

EMIL KERENJI

The decade of the 1990s in Vojvodina really began in 1988, with the so-called "Yogurt Revolution" and the subjugation of the province by Slobodan Milošević, then the leader of the League of Communists of Serbia. In the twelve years between Milošević's overthrow of the Vojvodinan leadership and his own fall, the province went through one of the most turbulent periods in its history. The Milošević years left a permanent mark on the relations among Vojvodina's ethnic groups and on its overall ethnic structure. The 1990s were also the years of the beginnings of the struggle for autonomy of the province. After the effective end of political autonomy in 1990, and the marginalization of the autonomist movement, much of the political history of Vojvodina has been a story of the inability of the autonomist camp to present a viable alternative to the regime. After 5 October 2000, when the Milošević regime crumbled, the Vojvodinan institutions asserted demands that the province's autonomy be restored. Even though some important steps toward the return of political autonomy to the province have been taken, different visions of autonomy and old rivalries among the Vojvodinan parties have prevented the formation of a unified political bloc that would press the urgency of this particular issue, among the myriad of difficult issues which confronted the new reform government of Zoran Djindjić. After Djindjić's murder on 12 March 2003, however, the issue of Vojvodina faded away from serious political discussion in Serbia; it seems that, after the parliamentary elections of 28 December 2003, which were held according to the law from the Milošević era that disfavors minority and regional representation, the Vojvodinan political issues will be shelved for quite some time.

The "Yogurt Revolution": Milošević Comes to Vojvodina

The late 1980s saw the rise of revisionist Serbian nationalism both in official and unofficial circles in Belgrade. It was in that period that the foundations of federated communist Yugoslavia were irreversibly shaken.[1] In the

1980s, the stage was set for the series of bloody wars that were to commence several years later. Between 24 April 1987, when Milošević made his fateful visit to Kosovo Polje, and the 8th Session of the Central Committee of the League of Communists of Serbia in September of that same year, Slobodan Milošević underwent a fundamental transformation from a faceless party apparatchik into the leader of the Serbian communists.[2] His rise would have been impossible without the existence of the strong nationalist currents which had come to dominate the political and literary discourse in Serbia in the 1980s. After the fall of 1987, when Milošević fortified his position in Serbia by formally becoming the president of the League of Communists of Serbia, it seemed that some kind of revision in the Yugoslav federation was inevitable; the question was whether it was going to be peaceful or not. Milošević's way of dealing with his political enemies suggested that the latter would be the case.[3]

Less than a year after the victory of Milošević's wing in the Serbian Communist Party organization, Vojvodina became a playground for what then seemed to be a demonstration of popular discontent with the pace and methods of solving the problem of Kosovo, but which, in fact, was the beginning of the process of *Gleichschaltung* in Vojvodina orchestrated by Milošević and his associates. On 9 July 1988, around five hundred Serbs and Montenegrins from Kosovo arrived in Novi Sad, in an attempt, as one of their leaders put it, "to familiarize the citizens and the leadership of Vojvodina with the situation in Kosovo" and "seek support for constitutional reforms in the Socialist Republic of Serbia."[4] Interestingly enough, the Serbian Party leadership was initially skeptical about the potential of such a visit of the Kosovo Serbs and Montenegrins to Vojvodina, and proposed that the trip be delayed until the fall; however, Milomir Minić, Milošević's envoy, was not allowed to speak at the meeting organized on 24 June 1988 in Kosovo Polje by the Committee for the Preparation for the Departure to Novi Sad, and the hard-line circle around Miroslav Šolević carried the day.[5] Once off the train in Novi Sad, surrounded by the police, Šolević demagogically demanded from the Vojvodinan leadership that the whole group of people be invited for talks, which was quickly refused. Inexperienced in functioning in this new world of politics spilling over into the streets, later so masterfully employed by Milošević, the Vojvodinan leadership made several mistakes, refusing, for example, to provide loudspeakers and drinking water to the delegation from Kosovo, refusals which were later cited in denouncing the provincial leadership's alleged "bureaucratic" and "inhumane" character.[6] After a protest walk around Novi Sad, the delegation left the city in the afternoon, without having spoken to a single Vojvodinan official.

In the days following 9 July, all political structures in Vojvodina, together with some federal ones, denounced the protest visit as a provocation and a dangerous play of nationalist cards, which could result in disaster. Boško Krunić, a member of the presidency of the Central Committee of the League of Communists of Yugoslavia from Vojvodina, condemned it as a "hunt after people and institutions in Vojvodina."[7] Various levels of the Vojvodinan communist hierarchy reacted against the rally in Novi Sad, which was seen as an "attack on Vojvodina and its leadership," a "manipulation with the ills of the people," and an "attempt at destabilizing Vojvodina."[8] The tone of the official statements became increasingly sharper, explicitly denouncing the *srbovanje* (which can be roughly translated as "Serbing around") of the protesters, and stressing condescendingly that "Vojvodina [was] nobody's *pashalik*."[9] The culmination of the campaign of denunciations which had spread over the communist infrastructure in Vojvodina was the qualification of the rally by the Provincial Conference of the League of Communists of Vojvodina as "the fiercest assault on the political being of the Socialist Autonomous Province of Vojvodina and its leadership since their existence."[10] It seemed that, at least in the world of Vojvodinan political institutions, a consensus had been reached that the rally was counterproductive and did not contribute to the solution of the situation in Kosovo.

However, this was just the beginning. In the three months following the first rally in Novi Sad, Šolević's Committee for the Organization of Protest Rallies, which succeeded the one for the "departure for Novi Sad," organized thirty-two rallies in twenty-eight towns and cities across Vojvodina.[11] It is interesting that all but three of those—Novi Sad, Sremska Mitrovica, and Čurug—were towns and cities in which the majority of the population was colonist.[12] In other words, the majority of the population in those towns and cities were first- or second-generation colonists who had been resettled in Vojvodina in the years immediately following the end of World War Two, from Bosnia-Herzegovina, Montenegro, and other "passive" regions of Yugoslavia. According to Dimitrije Boarov, from the passing of the Law on Agricultural Reform and Colonization on 23 August 1945 until 15 July 1947, 225,696 people were resettled in Vojvodina, around 90 percent of whom were Serbs and Montenegrins.[13] With the local Germans and significant numbers of Hungarians gone (in various ways) after the liberation, the number of colonists de facto changed the ethnic structure of Vojvodina. This presented a possibility—which later became a reality—that Serbs would constitute the majority of the population in the province. This was a new development with far-reaching consequences.[14]

Deliberate or not, the abrupt change of demographic structure in Vojvodina in the late 1940s created long-term rifts along various axes, and among different populations; by no means were those rifts restricted to ethnic lines. Usually dormant, but nevertheless looming in the background, and periodically reconstructed as relevant or even crucial, the divisions between Serbs and non-Serbs as well as between "new" and "old" Serbs, "highlanders" and "people from the plains," or "people from the city" and "people from the village," have persisted in Vojvodina to this day. When planning their rallies, Šolević and his group were either very perceptive of this fact, or could only muster significant support in predominantly colonist areas, but the fact remains that the rallies served to reinforce that divisive potential. This, of course, is not to imply that the rallies were less authentically "Vojvodinan" because of the structure of their participants, or that the colonists served as some kind of a "fifth column" paving the way for the inauguration of Milošević's rule in Vojvodina. The point, rather, is that Šolević and his comrades, deliberately or not, de facto furthered Milošević's interests by playing politics by his rules, reinventing divisions, preferring confrontation to dialogue, and inspiring distrust.

The series of protest rallies in Vojvodina over the summer and early fall of 1988 has subsequently been referred to as the "antibureaucratic revolution" by its proponents and supporters; on the eve of the fall of the Berlin Wall, however, the "antibureaucratic revolution" was, rather than the first instance of political pluralism in Central and Eastern Europe, as some commentators have termed it, the first glimpse of life under Milošević in Serbia.[15] Instead of instituting democratic procedures and processes and a multiparty system, and returning politics from institutions of the party to the institutions of the state, as would be demanded in the streets and squares of Central and Eastern Europe the following year, the rallies in Vojvodina called for homogenization, exclusion, suspicion, and intolerance, relying on the force of extra-institutional action. Although Milošević later called the rallies "the escalation of brotherhood, anger, and Yugoslavism," there was very little brotherhood and Yugoslavism in the air.[16] The speakers at the rallies, as well as the chants, songs, and slogans of the crowds, revealed an atmosphere that was far from "pluralist" in nature. The slogans at the rallies ranged from ordinary vulgar ones to out-of-place communist classics to outright racist and murderous ones; even though Belgrade propaganda portrayed the rallies as peaceful, democratic, and nonnationalist, the atmosphere at the rallies was quite different.[17] As the summer drew to a close, the pace of rallying across Vojvodina intensified.

On 25 September 1988, another rally was organized in Novi Sad. This time, however, rather than being sealed off by police, the rally was attended by significant numbers of citizens of Novi Sad, as well as workers from some factories and companies from Novi Sad and elsewhere in Vojvodina. Gaining momentum from the benefits of orchestrated propaganda of the Belgrade media controlled by Milošević, as well as (by this point) logistical support from his security police, the wave of rallies seemed unstoppable, and it was only a question of time before it would sweep away the Vojvodinan leadership.[18] On 2 October, a rally in Bačka Palanka, a town some forty kilometers west of Novi Sad, was attended by some twenty thousand people; Mihalj Kertes and Radovan Pankov, both local party officials, directly invited the crowd—in an atmosphere dominated by aggressive Serbian nationalist slogans—to overthrow the Vojvodinan establishment.[19] When, the following day, the Vojvodinan party and government structures announced that Kertes and Pankov were to face the consequences of their actions, the two led a march-on-Rome-style demonstration from Bačka Palanka to Novi Sad on 5 October.[20] An unprecedented (in the history of communist Yugoslavia) crowd of people gathered in the city to demand political change; Kertes and Pankov had organized workers from the factories in Bačka Palanka, who were later joined by their comrades from Novi Sad. The march was well organized, and numbers of people from local factories, hospitals, schools, and other institutions joined the massive rally.[21] As tensions rose, and as tens of thousands of protesters (estimates put the number of participants between sixty thousand and one hundred thousand) became impatient—pelting the Vojvodinan party headquarters in the center of Novi Sad with stones and yogurt which the local milk-producing plant distributed to the demonstrators, and which gave its name to those events, immortalizing them as the "Yogurt Revolution"—the Vojvodinan politicians asked the presidency of Yugoslavia to authorize intervention by the federal army. This was routinely blocked by the member of the presidency from Serbia, whose consent was necessary according to the constitution, since the unrest was taking place on Serbian territory.[22] That same evening, a delegation of the besieged Vojvodinan leaders was dispatched to Belgrade, where they met Milošević and asked him to appeal to the protesters and calm them down.[23] He flatly refused to do that; the only way left to escape lynching by the angry mob in front of the party building was to offer a collective resignation. This is exactly what the president of the Provincial Conference of the League of Communists of Vojvodina, Milovan Šogorov, and the other members did in the early hours of 6 October.[24] Later that day, some two hundred thousand people gathered to listen to victorious speeches by Zoran Sokolović and Borisav Jović, Milošević's veterans from the 8th Session, who vowed not to "let anyone partition Yugoslavia."[25]

In the following days and months, the party structures across Vojvodina were thoroughly cleansed of "autonomists"; this label became an omnipresent threat bearing on every Vojvodinan politician's career. Mihalj Kertes, a pioneer of the revolution, who rhetorically asked why "Serbs [should] fear Serbia" when he, as a Hungarian, "is not afraid," was particularly on a hunt for "autonomists."[26] His loyalty to Milošević during the days of the "Yogurt Revolution" was later repaid by the lucrative post of director of the Yugoslav customs. Although there are no official statistics, according to some estimates, around forty thousand political appointees, civil servants, judges, police chiefs, managers of TV and radio stations, newspaper editors, and directors of cultural institutions, as well as various other decision makers, were replaced in Vojvodina in the wake of the "antibureaucratic revolution."[27] According to the same estimate, 80 percent of all managers of state-owned companies were replaced, especially in the sectors of the oil industry, railways, and telecommunications.[28] Milošević's loyalists took over all positions of power, and by the middle of the following year, the *Gleichschaltung* in Vojvodina was completed. Vojvodina's constitution was overthrown, and provincial institutions destroyed or marginalized. This was Milošević's first attack on the federal order of communist Yugoslavia; in the words of Nenad Dimitrijević, the "'antibureaucratic revolution' was the final chapter in the history of the second Yugoslavia."[29] Twelve years minus one day before an angry mob in Belgrade swept his regime from power in much the same way, Milošević took control of Vojvodina, his first stop on a long and winding road of conquering and relinquishing various territories, murdering, exchanging and deporting various populations, all in an attempt to fit these geopolitical factors into his urge for personal political control.

Ethnic Minorities and Refugees in Vojvodina: Hrtkovci and Beyond

Vojvodina, as a region, is unique in Europe with its mix of ethnic groups. Apart from the Serbs, who constitute the ethnic majority in the province today, significant numbers of Hungarians, Croats, Slovaks, Romanians, Ruthenians, and members of other ethnic groups have been living in the region throughout its modern history. According to the census of 1991,

Vojvodina had 2,013,889 inhabitants, including 1,143,723 Serbs (56.79 percent), 339,491 Hungarians (16.85 percent), 174,295 declared Yugoslavs (8.65 percent), 74,808 Croats (3.71 percent), 63,545 Slovaks (3.15 percent), 44,838 Montenegrins (2.22 percent), 38,809 Romanians (1.92 percent), 24,366 Roma (1.20 percent), et al.[30] Although in the years after World War Two, various Yugoslav politicians (including Tito and Milošević, as well as the various political opposition leaders from Vojvodina and Serbia proper who ascended to power after 5 October 2000) have stressed that ethnic relations in Vojvodina have "traditionally" been good, this line of argument has been somewhat of an overstatement.[31] Genocides, massacres, population exchanges, and forcible confiscations of property (usually coinciding with ethnic divisions) have been no strangers to this "tradition." In the mayhem of World War Two, during which Vojvodina had been divided among Hungary (Bačka), the newly established Independent State of Croatia (Srem), and the German *Reich* (Banat), ethnic tensions exploded into the open and damaged the fragile history of ethnic coexistence. Periods of conflict in the history of Vojvodina have been rare and could be considered "aberrations" in a larger narrative of coexistence; the populations in the region, for the most part, have managed to live peacefully, to mix, and to maintain decent ethnic relations. However, the potential for division, distrust, and outright hatred seems to have been either forgotten or understressed by Vojvodinan and Serbian politicians.

Milošević's subjugation of Vojvodina, predictably, did not help ethnic relations. The wave of Serbian nationalism which had brought him to power, together with the proximity of ethnic warfare, and the influx of Serb refugees from Croatia, spurred currents of distrust and outright fear on the part of ethnic minorities in Vojvodina in the first years of the 1990s. Although nominally not nationalist, and recognizing the benefits of ethnic diversity in Vojvodina, the regime of Slobodan Milošević thoroughly alienated most non-Serb citizens (in addition to large numbers of their Serb compatriots). This was done directly or indirectly, by nonintervention as well as direct institutional and extra-institutional action. Today, after twelve years of Milošević's domination, ethnic relations in Vojvodina are very different from what they were in 1988. In the process of deterioration of these relations, the cases of two different ethnic minorities in Vojvodina—Hungarians and Croats—are paradigmatic.

With the dissolution of Yugoslavia and the creation of independent Croatia, the Croat minority in Vojvodina came into a peculiar position: as a constituent nation of federal communist Yugoslavia, it had not been guaranteed the minority rights that other major non-Yugoslav ethnic groups had been.[32] The status of the Croat ethnic group thus became difficult, as its minority status was not recognized on political grounds until 23 August 1996, the date of the official "normalization" of relations between Croatia and the Federal Republic of Yugoslavia.[33] As the war started in 1991, the Croats in Vojvodina suddenly became an "enemy" group, often accused of being a fifth column of the Croatian Democratic Union (HDZ),[34] the ruling party in Croatia headed by Franjo Tudjman, then the President of Croatia. The leading mouthpiece of such accusations and other instances of hate speech directed against the Croats in Vojvodina—which were later followed by concrete actions with disastrous consequences— was the leader of the outlawed Serbian Chetnik Movement, later the parliamentary Serbian Radical Party, Vojislav Šešelj.[35] The infamous case of Hrtkovci and some other villages with significant Croat populations in Srem is illustrative of the intimidation, threats, and expulsion to which numbers of Croats were subjected by Šešelj and his followers.[36]

After the war in Croatia began, some three hundred Serb refugees from Slavonia arrived in Hrtkovci, a small village in Srem, during the summer of 1991.[37] At that time, Hrtkovci had 2,684 inhabitants, of whom 1,080 declared themselves as Croats (40.23 percent), 550 as Serbs (20.49 percent), 515 as Hungarians (19.18 percent), and 445 as Yugoslavs (16.57 percent).[38] As the war intensified, some Croats left the village, although it seems that there was no organized pressure to do so.[39] This, however, changed when the local branch of the Serbian Radical Party was founded in the village on 6 May 1992. On that day, Vojislav Šešelj visited Hrtkovci and declared that "all Croats who have done wrong must leave," producing a list of seventeen local Croat villagers who had allegedly "done wrong."[40] Soon, all seventeen people from the list, together with their families, fled Hrtkovci, as their safety was no longer guaranteed. Soon thereafter, as it became obvious that no real law existed in Hrtkovci, and that, instead, it was up to Šešelj in Belgrade and his armed followers in Hrtkovci to determine what the law really was, pressures on the local Croats intensified. Groups of refugees, themselves forced from their homes in Croatia, frequently visited the houses of local Croats, urging them to leave, threatening and intimidating them. Instances of grenade throwing, forcible break-ins and even murder were not uncommon.[41]

In the early summer, Ostoja Sibinčić, a local thug and a member of the Serbian Radical Party, took over the municipal assembly by force and became the ruler of the village.[42] Local Croats found themselves being fired from their jobs, and the nonintervention of the Serbian authorities was taken to signify approval of this new reality.[43] On 13 July 1992, the new village authorities under the leadership of Sibinčić decided to rename the village; the new name was to be "Srbislavci," crudely asserting its "Serb" character over "Croat"-sounding Hrtkovci. Soon, road signs with "Srbislavci" were put up as well; they were removed by the police, but the old "Hrtkovci" signs were not returned.[44] By that point, some long-standing residents of Hrtkovci (Serbs, Croats, and Hungarians) appealed to Ruma county authorities to stop Sibinčić, claiming that by 1 July 1992, 186 Hrtkovci-Croat or ethnically mixed families had departed from the village; some of them had done so after direct threats and physical violence, some of them after being forced to sign documents which effectively meant giving up their property, and some of them had fled simply because of fear for their safety.[45] Federal authorities—then led by Prime Minister Milan Panić, who was increasingly becoming hostile to Milošević—reacted: Momčilo Grubač, the federal minister of justice, and Tibor Varadi, the federal minister for human and minority rights, received a delegation of Hrtkovci residents (10 August), and Varadi also received a delegation of prominent Belgrade intellectuals (15 July), who presented a well-documented case that the campaign of intimidation of Croats in Vojvodina was an organized one. By then, public opinion in Serbia had been informed of the situation in Hrtkovci through a series of articles in *Borba*.[46] However, the real power to stop the exodus was vested in Serbian, not federal, institutions; they acted too late, and not seriously enough. In August 1992, Sibinčić and four others were arrested; in November, they were released pending trial, and on 5 May 1993, Sibinčić received a suspended six-month sentence for disturbing the peace and illegal possession of firearms, while the four others were released.[47]

Unfortunately, the case of Hrtkovci was not unique. Similar instances of intimidation, physical violence, forced property exchange, and organized expulsion were recorded in other villages and towns with significant Croat populations: Golubinci, Bač, Šid, Kukujevci, Morović, and others.[48] Recognizable patterns of putting pressure on local Croats to leave and either slow or no reaction by the police made it plausible that there was an organized campaign aimed at changing the ethnic structure of those villages. As a result of this campaign, which was by no means restricted to the area of Srem, it has been estimated that around 70 percent of the local Croat population fled the counties of Apatin, Bač, and Šid beginning in 1991; around 60 percent the counties of Sremska Mitrovica, Ruma, and Stara Pazova; and around 40 percent the counties of Novi Sad, Sremski Karlovci, and Petrovaradin.[49] Different estimates place the proportion of Croats who have fled Vojvodina since 1991 at between 30 percent and 40 percent.[50] After the end of the wars in Croatia and Bosnia-Herzegovina, open intimidation seemed to subside, but the pressures on the Croats nevertheless continued.[51] Again, the name of Vojislav Šešelj comes up: after the Serbian Radical Party won the local elections in Zemun (a county technically in Vojvodina but incorporated into the municipality of Belgrade) in November 1996 and he became its mayor, instances of forcible breakins into the apartments of local Croats, as well as administrative procrastination by the local authorities in such cases, were recorded.[52] Only after the full figures of the 2002 census are published will it be possible—however incompletely—to grasp the consequences of this shameful campaign of constant low-level ethnic intimidation and violence against the Croats in Vojvodina.[53]

The situation with the Hungarians in Vojvodina has been different. Unlike the Croats, the Hungarians in Vojvodina were recognized as a minority with guaranteed minority rights by the 1974 federal constitution. This ethnic group, unlike the Croats, has been a "traditional" minority in Vojvodina and was not generally considered an "enemy" when ethnic tensions escalated into open warfare in 1991. Moreover, the Hungarians in Vojvodina, unlike the Croats, populate a relatively compact territory; 39.43 percent of Vojvodinan Hungarians live in seven counties along the Tisa in northern Bačka and Banat: Ada, Bačka Topola (Topolya), Bečej (Becse), Kanjiža (Kanizsa), Mali Idjoš (Kishegyes), Senta (Zenta), and Čoka (Csóka), in which they constitute an ethnic majority; in the city of Subotica (Szabadka), they constitute a plurality.[54] The rest of the Hungarian population in Vojvodina lives as a substantial minority dispersed across the province, but mostly in Bačka and Banat. All these factors contributed to the different situation in which this large minority found itself at the outbreak of the Yugoslav wars in 1991. Most importantly, the Hungarian ethnic minority in Vojvodina has been able to organize itself politically and influence political developments in Vojvodina and Serbia.

The Democratic Community of Vojvodina Hungarians (DCVH), the first political organization of the Hungarian minority in Vojvodina, was founded in January 1990; although originally not envisioned as a political party but rather as a "mechanism for the formation and expression of collective interests of the Hungarians in Vojvodina," with the formal establishment of the multiparty system in Serbia later that year, it turned into a regular political party.[55] Under the leadership of András Ágoston, the party participated in the first multiparty elections in Serbia in December 1990 and won eight seats (out of two hundred fifty) in the Serbian assembly in Belgrade. The party also won majorities in the local assemblies of the

seven counties in which Hungarians constituted an ethnic majority in
1991.[56] However, although in the first elections in 1990 the DCVH carried
the majority of the Hungarian vote in Vojvodina, soon different political
views and personal issues emerged within its leadership; the party was
officially divided in March 1994, when a splinter group under the leadership of József Kasza left the DCVH to form the Union of Vojvodina Hungarians (UVH).[57] Over the years, as its dynamic leader and the mayor of
Subotica led it skillfully through the minefield of Serbian political life, the
UVH became the most important party of the Vojvodinan Hungarians.
In the meantime, the political scene of Hungarians in Vojvodina became
ever more fragmented, with Sándor Pál taking over the DCVH from Ágoston (in 1997), who, in turn, went on to form the Democratic Party of Vojvodina Hungarians (DPVH).[58] Three other political organizations of
Hungarians in Vojvodina were formed as well, none of them ever emerging from the margins of political life.[59]

The Hungarians' geographic concentration, and the ability of their political representatives to govern their own affairs at the local level to at least
some extent, meant that the discrimination against this ethnic group—
which, as has already been pointed out, was not really considered an "enemy nation" in the Serbian nationalist rhetoric of the early 1990s—was
going to take guises that were different from the persecution and outright
organized expulsion of the Croats from Vojvodina. Indeed, there is no
Hungarian counterpart to Hrtkovci; this, however, does not mean that ethnic relations between the Serbs and the Hungarians did not deteriorate
during the 1990s. According to some estimates, between thirty-five thousand and thirty-eight thousand Hungarians (more than 10 percent,
according to the 1991 census) left Vojvodina in the period from 1991 to
2000, most of them because of fear of war and being drafted, for economic
reasons, or simply owing to the general feeling of insecurity.[60] This is
not to claim, of course, that only Hungarians, as an ethnic minority, felt
insecure or feared war, or that economic considerations did not play a role
in the process of emigration; the percentage of the total population of
Hungarians from Vojvodina who left in the course of these nine years,
however, is staggering.

The increasing marginalization of Hungarians in Vojvodina, as well as
the insensitive politics of their exclusion on the part of the regime, must
have contributed significantly to this feeling of insecurity and fear. Of the
already mentioned seven counties in which Hungarians constituted the
ethnic majority in 1991, Serbs came to occupy positions of the chief of
police or president of the district court (or both) in five; in Subotica,

where Hungarians constituted a plurality, the chief of police and the majority of police officers were Serbs, as were the presidents of the municipal and district courts.[61] This process was in part the result of the massive purge—the scale of which was outlined above—of all levels of administration in Vojvodina in the wake of the "antibureaucratic revolution." It is possible, of course, that at least some of those people were qualified individuals who were not guided by "ethnic" or party concerns in doing their jobs, although, toward the end of Milošević's regime, this situation was becoming increasingly difficult to imagine, especially when it came to the courts and police. But it is, at any rate, certain that such underrepresentation of Hungarians in these sensitive positions and in the areas where they lived as an overwhelming majority (in the county of Kanjiža, for example, where both the chief of police and the president of the local court were Serbs, Hungarians constituted 87.5 percent of the total population) did not advance their feeling of integration and ethnic equality in Vojvodina.[62] In addition, the rights guaranteed by the constitution, such as the right to the use of the Hungarian language in local administration, or the right to education in the mother tongue, were often observed only sporadically.[63]

Another right guaranteed by law—the right to education in a minority language (in this case, Hungarian)—has frequently been circumvented as well. Because of the high census of students necessary to form a class taught in a minority language, education in Hungarian has effectively been possible only in those areas where the Hungarians constitute a significant portion of the population (such as, for example, in northern Bačka). This also means that in the areas where there are relatively few Hungarians, classes in Hungarian would be taught in one or two schools that would have to cover a substantial geographic area; many parents would not be ready to have their children travel to another town to attend school. On a different level, history textbooks—to give just the most obvious example—for classes in Hungarian in elementary and high schools were mere translations of the (nationalist) Serbian history textbooks that paid little and often no attention to Hungarian history and culture; schools that taught classes in Hungarian were not allowed to use textbooks published in Hungary, even for "nonpolitical" courses such as physics or mathematics.[64] In general, curricula were tainted by "ethnocentrism, traditionalism and daily politics."[65]

The media in Hungarian were in a similar situation. The electronic media in particular served (like their government-controlled counterparts in Serbian) as mouthpieces of the regime. An important exception was the independent Novi Sad-based daily *Magyar szó,* which, however, had a relatively small circulation and was confined to a limited readership that did not pose a real threat to the stability of the regime.[66] Hungarian cultural institutions (such as, for example, the Ujvidéki színház in Novi Sad, or the Népszínház in Subotica) received most of their funding from the Vojvodinan budget, which, in times of general economic crisis and reduction of that budget, meant that they were severely impoverished.[67] As a result, their activities were visibly reduced, which certainly contributed further to the atmosphere of marginalization of Hungarian culture in Vojvodina.

Of course, the Croat and Hungarian ethnic minorities are not, as has already been pointed out, the only ethnic groups in Vojvodina. Nor is ethnic identification the only, or even primary, framework through which various individuals tended to perceive the situation in Vojvodina in the 1990s. However, as ethnic identification became increasingly important in Vojvodina from the late 1980s on, and as ethnic relations in the province deteriorated due to the proximity of ethnic warfare and the policies of the regime in the 1990s, an analytical framework which takes ethnicity into account is the most appropriate tool for understanding the history of the last decade in Vojvodina. This is not to claim that every individual thought of him- or herself primarily as a member of an ethnic group; this is to claim, however, that such concerns played a very prominent role in the everyday lives of many, even most, individuals. It is for this reason that much attention has been paid to the examination of the process of deterioration of ethnic relations in Vojvodina. Croat and Hungarian ethnic minorities have stood out because of their characteristic relationships with the majority ethnic group and the regime. Members of other major ethnic groups, such as Slovaks, Romanians, Ruthenes, and Roma, have also had their individual and collective experiences and perceptions of ethnic relations in the province. Some of those were specific, while others were similar to the ones of other ethnic groups, such as the Hungarians, for example. However, because of the limited space for this chapter, attention has been paid only to the two minorities whose different fates in the 1990s in Vojvodina have been illustrative of the larger process of deterioration of ethnic relations.[68]

Another major problem which affected all citizens of Vojvodina, ethnic minorities and Serbs alike, was the problem of refugees. Since the wars around Serbia started in 1991, large numbers of refugees had fled from the war areas in Croatia and Bosnia-Herzegovina to various parts of the former Yugoslavia and abroad; many ended up in Vojvodina. The largest wave of refugees arrived in August 1995, after the Croatian army's "Operation

Storm," which had retaken the UN-protected areas in Croatia, effectively driving the entire population of the so-called Republic of Serb Krajina out of the country. Most of the refugees arrived in Serbia, though some stayed in Serb-controlled areas of Bosnia-Herzegovina. In May 1996, after the end of the wars in Croatia and Bosnia-Herzegovina, the refugee agencies of the Serbian and Montenegrin governments and the office of UNHCR in Yugoslavia organized a census designed to establish the number of refugees in Yugoslavia. According to the results of that census, there were 646,066 "persons affected by war" in Yugoslavia, of whom 566,275 were refugees.[69] Of all these persons, Serbs constituted an overwhelming majority, at 89.4 percent. Most of the refugees, or 42 percent, settled in Vojvodina, which means that around 240,000 extra Serbs joined the population in the province between 1991 and 1996. Belgrade became home for 27 percent of the refugees during the same period, Serbia proper without Belgrade for a further 27 percent, while some 4 percent of refugees settled in Kosovo. Although it is unknown what the situation on the ground in Vojvodina is today, it is reasonable to assume that the ethnic composition of the province changed significantly as a result of the influx of a large number of Serb refugees.

The arrival of such large numbers of Serb refugees in Vojvodina was a fundamental problem which affected the whole society; by no means were the fragile ethnic relations in Vojvodina the only social sphere that would be affected in unforeseen ways as a result. The influx of refugees—especially after August 1995—contributed to the further disintegration of social cohesion in Vojvodina. Refugees were a heterogeneous group of individuals; however, they tended to be perceived as homogeneous by both the majority ethnic group (the Serbs) and the indigenous ethnic minorities.[70] The impoverishment of all segments of the population in Vojvodina, as well as the existing and probably prevalent feelings of insecurity and marginalization on the part of ethnic minorities in Vojvodina in the mid-1990s, contributed to the formation of mostly negative attitudes on the part of the local population toward refugees. Economic competition in the conditions of a grave economic crisis, high unemployment, and black marketeering played a role in creating an atmosphere of distrust toward the refugees on the part of the locals, regardless of their ethnic affiliation. On the other hand, ethnic tensions rose and ethnic distrust deepened as a result of the practice (deliberate or not on the part of the regime) of settling refugees in areas with significant Croat and Yugoslav populations—in ethnically mixed areas, in other words.[71] Thus, for example, disproportionate numbers of refugees were settled in the Srem counties of Indjija,

Šid, and Ruma, which had been the scenes of ethnic violence against the local Croats by Serb refugees and radical locals a few years before.[72]

One of the most persistent prejudices against refugees in Vojvodina has been the belief that they are privileged in economic and social terms.[73] However, this has not been the case; indeed, quite the opposite has been true. Of all the refugees in Vojvodina in 1996, fully two-thirds of those older than fifteen did not have a job.[74] This, of course, was in part due to the more systemic disability to which the refugees were subjected: until the very end of Milošević's regime, it was virtually impossible for refugees to regulate their legal status in Yugoslavia. It was impossible for a refugee to obtain Yugoslav citizenship or an ID card (unless s/he married a Yugoslav citizen, or one of his/her parents was a citizen); in the absence of either of these conditions, one could not be employed legally in Serbia. This meant in effect that refugees constituted a separate corpus of population, almost beyond the legal system: they did not have a right to work, they could not vote or run for office, and their refugee status could at any moment be revoked. Forced to take up jobs on the black market or work for private firms without contracts, social security, or any kind of insurance, the overwhelming majority of refugees were barely managing to survive; more than half of all refugees in Vojvodina in 1996 depended on humanitarian assistance for survival.[75]

All these factors—ethnic violence against the Croats in the early 1990s, the politics of marginalization and exclusion of the Hungarian ethnic minority (together with other ethnic minorities), the large and socially disruptive influx of refugees at the end of the summer of 1995, as well as the general economic crisis that had persisted throughout the decade—contributed to the creation in Vojvodina of a specific atmosphere of fear and distrust. Ethnic relations in the province, which have always been one of its defining factors and its most important legacies, were seriously shaken. It is not yet clear what kind of new ethnic situation has emerged in Vojvodina as a result of wars, repression by the regime, emigration, and refugee immigration, but it is reasonable to assume that the ethnic picture of Vojvodina has changed substantially. This change, with all the implications of forced migration, violence, disruption, and injustice, has been one of the key achievements of Milošević's regime in Vojvodina.

Opposition to Milošević and the Struggle for Autonomy

Together with the defining issue of ethnic diversity and the problem of ethnic relations, the question of the autonomy of Vojvodina has been one of the most important and most hotly debated issues in the history of the province. Ever since the royal proclamation of the "Serb Vojvodina" within the Habsburg monarchy in 1850, different people with different political agendas have debated what exactly Vojvodina was, and what prerogatives its institutions should have. The issue of autonomy was also at the heart of Milošević's plans for constitutional reform in the late 1980s, and has played an important role in the political life in the province since the 1990s.

The province of Vojvodina, as a political unit within federal Yugoslavia, was established by the communists after the end of World War Two. The dynamic struggle of competing factions of centralizers and decentralizers among the Yugoslav communists resulted in frequent constitutional changes, and the status of the province was modified with the inauguration of each new constitution, in 1953, 1963, and 1974. These were, in addition, thoroughly amended in 1967, 1968, 1971, 1981, and 1988.[76] The constitution of 1974 gave the provinces in the Yugoslav federation, Vojvodina and Kosovo, wide political jurisdictions. In effect, the constitution promulgated on 21 February 1974 fundamentally redefined the federation, as the provinces de facto became equals of the six republics in all but name. The document specified that the provinces were part of the Socialist Republic of Serbia, but no subordination of political institutions was mentioned. The provinces had a right to administer their own affairs, as well as to participate in federal affairs (most notably, by the right to veto legislation in the upper chamber of the federal parliament, a right which before 1974 had been reserved for republics), without interference from Serbia; at the same time, they could also choose not to participate in Serbian affairs, if they so wished.[77] Based on the new constitution, Vojvodina was able after 1974 to organize its own state institutions, such as the presidency, the executive council, the parliament, and the supreme court. De facto, Vojvodina (together with Kosovo) became a state, and Yugoslavia a confederation.

The bulk of the Serbian elite found such a state of affairs unsatisfactory. The concerns of Serbian party leaders, intellectuals, and various public figures had tended to focus on the seeming impotence of the Serbian institutions in the province of Kosovo, the increasing "Albanization," as the term went, of the province, and the "genocide" against the Serbs perpetrated by the Kosovo Albanians.[78] The intolerable situation in Kosovo dictated, in the minds of many Serbs (communist or not), that some kind of action be taken to change the situation; however, the problem was systemic, and if it was to be solved on the systemic (i.e., federal) level, Vojvodina was going to be affected as well. In October 1984, the Serbian party organization offered a "reform package," which, in effect, proposed a return to the status quo ante 1974 as far as the political status of the provinces went, in addition to a plan to strengthen federal institutions.[79] The leader of the Serbian communists, Ivan Stambolić, favored a "unified and strong Serbia," and bemoaned the "disintegration" of the republic under the existing legal order.[80]

It was, thus, the Serbian communists who proposed changes aimed at addressing the Serbian grievances, but they were by no means the only ones who grumbled about the situation. In the absence of an open and democratic public debate in Serbia about the status of Kosovo and Vojvodina in particular, and the state of affairs in the Yugoslav federation in general, an atmosphere started to emerge of an unchanneled dissatisfaction that affected different social groups in Serbia. By the mid-1980s, discourses of victimhood had emerged, disseminated by individuals, groups, institutions, and media that were traditionally "dissident," that had no direct connections to the party, and that were implicitly (and, later, explicitly) revisionist. Themes of economic exploitation of Serbia by its partners (who had increasingly tended to be perceived as enemies) in the federation, of deliberate weakening of Serbia by the federal institutions by granting substantial autonomy to Vojvodina and Kosovo and allowing the "Albanization" of the latter, of oppression of the Serbs in Yugoslavia and the imposed burden of historical guilt for the cultural, economic, and political imperialism of the Serb ruling elites in the first Yugoslav state, all started gaining currency and being discussed outside the party-controlled institutions.[81] The "protest evenings" at the Writers' Association of Serbia, petitions of Serbian intellectuals, the Memorandum of the Serbian Academy of Sciences and Arts, the yellow journalism of *Duga,* the pulp-fiction variations on national themes of Dobrica Ćosić and Vuk Drašković—all contributed, diverse and addressed to different audiences as they were, to the construction and legitimation of the theme of Serbian victimhood. It was in such an atmosphere of escalation of revisionist voices stressing Serbian grievances that Milošević emerged as the leader of Serbian communists after the 8th Session in the fall of 1987. He appealed to communists by his seeming success in co-opting these heterodox discourses and subjecting them to communist rhetoric, while the revisionist nationalists cheered his willingness to talk about issues which had, until then, been considered taboo.

The "public debate" about constitutional changes, the most important legal implications of which would be the change of status of autonomous provinces within Serbia, took place in this atmosphere of strong nationalist overtones. It turned out to be little more than a campaign run by the controlled Belgrade media against the "disintegration" of Serbia.[82] After a relatively short "debate," and with dissenting voices marginalized, the new constitution of Serbia was promulgated in March 1990; it radically limited (and practically abolished) the autonomy of Vojvodina and Kosovo.[83] The constitution of Vojvodina was reduced to a statute (adopted the following year); the executive and judicial powers were abolished, while legislative powers were reduced to meaningless phrases of "rights to suggest" legislation, "rights to implement" legislation enacted by the Serbian assembly, and "rights" to enact decisions—if they are in accordance with the constitution of Serbia—in the fields of "culture, education, official use of minority languages, public information, etc."[84] Vojvodina's budget was cut severely; in 1999, for example, a year before Milošević's regime collapsed, it was more or less equal to the municipal budget of the city of Subotica, and could barely cover the costs of administration.[85] Vojvodina was stripped of all of the important jurisdictions it had had according to the constitution of 1974, and became, in the words of the Novi Sad lawyer Slobodan Beljanski, "the autonomy without self-rule and the province without territory."[86] In two articles on the new statute of Vojvodina, Beljanski enumerated the rights that had been abolished by the statute, making it clear that Vojvodina had become an autonomous province just in name.[87]

If one takes into account the gaping abyss between the merciless and often absurd policy of centralization that the Serbian government undertook in the years following the abolition of autonomy of Vojvodina, and the substantial powers that the provincial institutions had had before that abolition, it does not come as a surprise that much of the political history of Vojvodina in the 1990s revolved around the question of its autonomy. While the anti-autonomist camp led by the regime and its satellite parties portrayed any proposal or political program that advocated genuine autonomy for Vojvodina as a treacherous project aimed at dismembering Serbia, the autonomist camp itself was divided over the question of autonomy. Not only did the question of autonomy become the key question in Vojvodina by the end of Milošević's regime, but the related question of just what kind of autonomy in Vojvodina became equally relevant and divisive. Political parties representing the interests of Hungarians had tended to favor a kind of autonomy based on ethnic principles, while the nonethnic autonomist parties focused their political programs on the redefinition of relations in Serbia, and the return of Vojvodina to the status

of 1974. The decade of the 1990s in Vojvodina was also a decade of the failure of these two political visions to combine into a viable autonomist alternative to Milošević's regime.

The first political party to openly criticize the new situation regarding
the abolition of autonomy was the League of Social Democrats of Vojvodina (LSV). The party was founded on 14 July 1990 in Novi Sad, by thirty-
year-old Nenad Čanak, a rock guitarist and an employee of the state-owned
Naftagas oil company. From the very first day of his political activity (he
had not been involved in politics before the summer of 1990), Čanak's
appeal had been rooted in his radicalism, which was, refreshingly, not ethnic. The crux of the program of the League was the advocacy of the autonomy of Vojvodina, and—should this political project fail to materialize
through dialogue with the Serbian institutions—a referendum for the
independence of the province. Not only was such a political project highly
unpopular in the nationalist atmosphere orchestrated by the regime in the
early 1990s, but it was also considered an antistate activity and was, as such,
an easy target for regime propaganda.[88]

Čanak's appearance, his uncompromising attitude, and his radical
stand won the LSV a small, but devoted, group of followers in Vojvodina. The leader of the small opposition party was shunned not only by the
regime but also by most opposition leaders as well; while some Belgrade-
based opposition parties, such as, to name just one, Vuk Drašković's Serbian Renewal Movement (SPO),[89] competed with Milošević in drawing
western Serbian borders and in their patriotic calls for the solution of the
"Serbian question," Čanak aggressively offered an alternative, nonethnic
political program of economic reform and political decentralization.
Moreover, his style was aimed at provoking his enemies as well as the general public: at the beginning of the presentation of his party program for
the first multiparty elections in Serbia in December 1990—every party that
was to take part in the elections was allotted one hour of time on state
TV—Čanak played footage of Adolf Hitler's speech about Germany and
Germans, stressing common points of Milošević's variations on the theme
and implying that Milošević, in fact, was just another Nazi thug. He did
not shy away from explicating this idea, either.[90] In 1991, during the fiercest
fighting between the emerging Croatian armed forces and the Yugoslav
People's Army around Vukovar, Čanak was "rewarded" by the regime for
the courage in promoting his political views: he was forcibly mobilized
and sent to the front line. He returned, alive and well, after a few months.

Two other important organizations were formed in the early 1990s that
were autonomist from the beginning and that were courageous enough

to oppose the regime (and many opposition parties as well) on the issue of the autonomy of Vojvodina. The Independent Society of Journalists of Vojvodina was formed by Miodrag Isakov on 17 January 1990. The Vojvodinan Club, a broad organization of intellectuals committed to changing the legal status of the province after the abolition of autonomy and the inauguration of the new statute, was founded by Stanimir Lazić and Veselin Lazić on 29 September 1992. However, in the atmosphere of ethnic radicalization, as well as the proximity of wars in Croatia and Bosnia and the struggle of the Serbs that the regime successfully asserted as more urgent problems, all these organizations remained marginal until the middle of the decade. In the early 1990s, they represented a few dissident voices against the abolition of autonomy and the increasing centralization of Serbia.

In contrast to the nonethnic concepts of autonomy based on the return to 1974, another vision of autonomy emerged in the early 1990s which was based exclusively on ethnic principles. On 25 April 1992, the General Assembly of the DCVH adopted the *Memorandum on the Self-Government of Hungarians in the Republic of Serbia*. The document envisioned the establishment of a three-level autonomy of the "Hungarian national community": personal autonomy, the establishment of "communities with special status," and the establishment of the so-called Hungarian Autonomous Area.[91] The level of personal autonomy would entail the creation of a parliament of the Hungarian ethnic group and a self-government council, which would regulate individual rights to the use of language, education, culture, etc. Municipalities in which the Hungarian population constitutes a majority would become "communities with special status" and would have a separate right to self-government. Finally, the contiguous communities with special status would constitute a Hungarian Autonomous Area with separate political institutions. This was the first proposal for autonomy by a party whose voter base came from the Hungarian ethnic minority in Vojvodina; the later proposals changed slightly, but the autonomy for which the so-called Hungarian political parties in Vojvodina fought was based on ethnic principles. A telling detail is the fact that the title of the memorandum does not mention Vojvodina, but "Hungarians in the Republic of Serbia." It was an indication that the DCVH was trying to deal directly with the regime in Belgrade and possibly win some concessions directly from Milošević. This was later the tactic of the UVH as well: in late 1997 and early 1998, József Kasza met with Milošević to discuss the problems of Hungarians in Serbia and propose changes along the lines of ethnic autonomy.[92]

That Milošević accepted such conversations at all suggested that he may have aspired to divide the autonomist camp in Vojvodina. Indeed, the history of Vojvodina in the 1990s is a history of a number of failed attempts of the autonomist parties in Vojvodina to form an anti-Milošević bloc which would, at the same time, have presented a genuine alternative to the Belgrade parties' notions about the right extent of autonomy for Vojvodina on the one hand, and include the so-called Hungarian parties on the other. On 17 September 1994, the Vojvodinan Club adopted the *Platform for Contemporary Autonomy of Vojvodina*.[93] The document stressed the "economic exploitation and political dependence" of Vojvodina, and argued that such a state of affairs was contrary to the needs of the citizens of Vojvodina and the Serbian national interest.[94] The focus of the platform was economic exploitation of Vojvodina, and indeed this theme became a rallying point of the autonomist parties in the following years. On 7 December 1995, a Manifest for the Autonomy of Vojvodina, based on the platform of the Vojvodinan Club, was signed by seventeen political parties and nongovernmental organizations.[95] It called for urgent constitutional change that would restore the autonomy of Vojvodina "within Serbia and Yugoslavia."[96]

The so-called Hungarian parties did not sign the document, and the rift between the political forces that advocated ethnic concepts of autonomy and those that stressed economic and political autonomy based on the 1974 constitution persisted. Simultaneously, most of the Belgrade-based political parties still showed no understanding of the problems of Vojvodina, and the opposition Zajedno coalition, which was to beat Milošević's Socialist Party of Serbia (SPS) in more than twenty municipalities (including all the major ones in Vojvodina) and lead successful street protests for the recognition of election results in the winter of 1996–97, was formed without the parties from Vojvodina. Formed just several weeks before the federal elections of November 1996, the new Vojvodina Coalition, comprised of Čanak 's LSV, the Reformists of Vojvodina of Miodrag Isakov, and the People's Peasant Party of Dragan Veselinov, was the big surprise of the elections, winning two seats in the federal parliament. The result was astonishing, considering the fact that there was virtually no election campaign and that the coalition was comprised of unlikely political partners.

The destructive potential of this latter fact was revealed after the poor showing of the coalition in the Serbian parliamentary elections of 1997. Now considered a major political bloc, the coalition was prevented from achieving better results (it won a mere five seats in the parliament) by extensive gerrymandering on the part of the regime and the concerted "antiseparatist" campaign of the regime and some Belgrade-based opposition parties.[97] Poor election results and personal hostilities between Čanak and Veselinov brought about the dissolution of the coalition soon after the elections.[98] Kasza's UVH won their guaranteed four seats in the predominantly Hungarian municipalities in the north. After 1996, when it became apparent that the autonomists were somehow coming back, the results of the 1997 election disappointed many followers of Čanak and other autonomist leaders. It seemed that in spite of the rise of autonomists' expectations, the political conditions in Serbia and in the province were not yet ripe for change. Another major factor which contributed to the seeming political impotence of the autonomists was the persistent rift between them and the UVH.

This, however, changed after the NATO intervention in Yugoslavia in the spring of 1999. After the military intervention, Milošević became vulnerable; the ever more nervous moves of the regime indicated that it was crumbling, and that—if the people in Serbia were presented with one united political group that would present a viable alternative to Milošević's regime—it would be possible to remove it from power in an election. In the summer of 2000, when the Yugoslav presidential election was announced for 24 September, the Democratic Opposition of Serbia (DOS) was founded in Belgrade as a united bloc of nineteen parties that would support a single candidate who would run against Milošević. The only significant party that stayed out of the bloc was Vuk Drašković's SPO; because of this strategic mistake, the party all but disappeared in post-October 2000 Serbia. All major autonomist leaders—Čanak, Isakov, Veselinov, and Kasza—joined the DOS, agreeing to put aside their differences until Milošević was gone. The DOS, in turn, claimed in its program that it was going to "return autonomy to Vojvodina" once it came to power. On 24 September 2000, in a presidential election that turned into a referendum on Milošević's rule, Vojislav Koštunica, the presidential candidate of the DOS, beat Milošević in the first round. After the regime's attempt to annul the election, a popular uprising brought it down on 5 October.

Epilogue: Koštunica, Djindjić, and Beyond

The fall of Milošević fundamentally changed the situation in Vojvodina, but some old tensions have persisted. The rift between the Vojvodinan and Belgrade-based parties, as well as among the Vojvodinan parties themselves, remains. Koštunica's party, in particular, has resisted the calls for the return of autonomy to Vojvodina and has diluted the issue by presenting vague proposals for the decentralization of Serbia. However, major breakthroughs have taken place since the end of the Milošević era. Emerging from the shadow of opposition in which they spent an entire decade, the leaders of the Vojvodinan parties have become members of the political establishment and have started pushing through an autonomist agenda from positions of political power. In the year 2002, Čanak was the president of the Vojvodinan assembly, Kasza and Isakov were vice presidents of the Serbian government, and Veselinov was the minister of agriculture.[99] Such developments would have been unimaginable under Milošević, and the very readiness of the DOS government to allow certified autonomists to share power and talk about autonomy from the position of power is a major change. On 4 February 2002, after a long discussion in the Serbian parliament, the so-called "Omnibus Law" was passed, which returned some of the previously abolished functions to the Vojvodinan institutions.[100] Some of the important functions still remained vested in the Serbian parliament and government, and the law was passed amidst loud grumbling of some of the members of the ruling coalition, but the fact is that the issue of the political autonomy of Vojvodina was debated in Serbian political institutions, after a decade of silence.

On the other hand, the flip side of the struggle for autonomy in Vojvodina has been the steady rise of firm support for Šešelj's Serbian Radical Party, which could now be said to have its base in the province. The Radicals have consistently argued against autonomy and have been true to their ideals of far-right Serbian nationalism. The "radicalization" of Vojvodina—in more senses than one—will be one of the lasting consequences of Milošević's rule. The pattern of various election returns in the province (parliamentary, presidential, provincial, local) indicates that the voters in Vojvodina are roughly divided into four camps: autonomist, "ethnic," broadly reformist, and Serbian nationalist. These camps are mobilized differently at different times, and it is difficult to trace their overlaps over extended periods of time. However, it seems that the question of Vojvodinan autonomy is fading out from the political agenda of the mainstream political parties in Serbia. Especially after the murder of Zoran Djindjić, and the disintegration of the DOS in its aftermath—even though the disintegration had been long in coming, and is not directly connected to the assassination of the skillful prime minister—the struggle against organized crime, privatization, and various other aspects of transition (however one understands it) have topped the agendas of political parties across the board. On the eve of the 2003 parliamentary elections in Serbia, which would bring substantial gains to rightist nationalists (including the Serbian Radical Party), it seemed that the Vojvodinan issues would again be put on the back burner.

What is certain, however, is that the regime of Slobodan Milošević has left a disastrous legacy in the area of ethnic relations. It will take long for trust and tolerance among different ethnic groups in Vojvodina to recuperate. It is only after the full official data of the 2002 census are published that we will be able to gauge the impact of war, economic crisis, intimidation, and forced migration on different ethnic groups in the province. Whatever the ethnic makeup in Vojvodina after Milošević ends up being, it will define the framework of politics in the province for years to come.

Notes

1. In the words of Slavoj Žižek: "The fragile equilibrium on which Yugoslavia rested was irreparably damaged . . . when Milošević stripped Kosovo and Vojvodina of autonomy by changing the Constitution. From that moment on, Yugoslavia lived only because it did not notice that it was already dead." Slavoj Žižek, "NATO, leva ruka Boga?" *Reč*, no. 56.2 (December 1999), p. 47.

2. On 24 April 1987, Slobodan Milošević visited Kosovo Polje, a predominantly Serb suburb of Priština, in order to talk to local leaders about the situation in the province. During the talks, a crowd of local Serbs gathered in front of the building where the communists from Belgrade were meeting their comrades from Kosovo, and tensions increased between the angry demonstrators and the local police. Milošević, disturbed by the noises coming from the outside, left the meeting and decided to see for himself what was going on in front of the building. The local Serbs started complaining about their difficult position in Kosovo, and how the local Albanians were allegedly raping and beating them and their children. "No one should dare beat you," Milošević uttered; this famous sentence, replayed time and again on Belgrade TV by his friends Ratomir Vico and Dušan Mitević, was one of the several important events that enthroned Milošević as the unofficial leader of all Serbs (and the future official leader of the Serbian communists, Republic of Serbia, and Federal Republic of Yugoslavia). See Laura Silber and Allan Little, *Yugoslavia: Death of a Nation* (New York and London: Penguin, 1997), pp. 37–39.

3. Dragiša Pavlović, the leader of the Belgrade communists, was the principal casualty of the 8th Session. However, his was not the only fall: a critical attitude toward Serbian and Albanian nationalism and responsible, cool-headed decision

making also went down the drain. For Pavlović's views of the 8th Session and the larger issues surrounding it, see Dragiša Pavlović, *Olako obećana brzina* (Zagreb: Globus, 1988). The title of the book refers to the "easily promised speed" of solving the problem in Kosovo, which was the backbone of Milošević's appeal and "political program."

4. *Dnevnik* (Novi Sad), 10 July 1988, p. 8.

5. Sava Kerčov, Jovo Radoš, and Aleksandar Raič, *Mitinzi u Vojvodini 1988 godine: Radjanje političkog pluralizma* (Novi Sad: Dnevnik, 1990), pp. 26–27.

6. *Dnevnik,* 10 July 1988, p. 8.

7. *Dnevnik,* 11 July 1988, pp. 1 and 4.

8. *Dnevnik,* 12 July 1988, p. 4.

9. *Dnevnik,* 13 July 1988, p. 5. "Pashalik" refers to an Ottoman-era administrative unit, implying subjection to the imperial order.

10. *Dnevnik,* 14 July 1988, p. 1.

11. Kerčov, Radoš, and Raič, *Mitinzi u Vojvodini,* p. 30.

12. Ibid., p. 59.

13. Dimitrije Boarov, *Politička istorija Vojvodine* (Novi Sad: Europanon Consulting, 2001), p. 184.

14. Ibid., pp. 182–84.

15. The "antibureaucratic revolution" was termed "the birth of political pluralism" in the subtitle of Kerčov, Radoš, and Raič, *Mitinzi u Vojvodini* [note 5].

16. Slobodan Milošević, "Oktobarska eskalacija bratstva, gneva i Jugoslovenstva," in *Godine raspleta,* ed. Slobodan Milošević (Belgrade: BIGZ, 1989), pp. 264–71.

17. Slogans at the rallies were diverse and colorful, and included numerous general ones like "Živela radnička klasa," "Za lepu i bolju budućnost," "Tata, ne daj da bude rata," "Dajte nam hleba," etc. However, the tone of the rallies was set by the more ominous ones, like "Slovenci, sram vas bilo," "Jože Smole, želimo ti sreću: Drven sanduk i najlepšu sveću," "Tovariš Smole, povučeš nas dole," "Kruniću pizdo, narod si izd'o," "Hoćemo oružje," "Smrt Šiptarima," "Ubićemo Azema," "Ubićemo Vlasija," "Ubićemo Fadilja," "Svi Albanci su krivi," "Ko nije s nama, taj je protiv nas," "Idemo na Kosovo," "Ubićemo, zaklaćemo, ko sa nama neće," "Nećemo se seliti, hoćemo se boriti," "Dole Šiptari." The songs included well-known Serbian nationalist classics like "Oj vojvodo, Sindjeliću," "Ko to kaže, ko to laže, Srbija je mala," "Igrale se delije nasred zemlje Srbije," "Srpska se truba s Kosova čuje," etc. *Dnevnik,* 13 July 1988, p. 5; Kerčov, Radoš, and Raič, *Mitinzi u Vojvodini,* pp. 120–21. For the perceptive descriptions of the atmosphere at the rallies, see Pavlović, *Olako obećana brzina,* pp. 171ff, and Slavoljub Djukić, *Izmedju slave i anateme: Politička biografija Slobodana Miloševića* (Belgrade: Filip Višnjić, 1994), pp. 78ff.

18. Djukić, *Izmedju slave i anateme,* p. 104; and Boarov, *Politička istorija Vojvodine,* p. 216. On the role of the Belgrade media in the "antibureaucratic revolution," see Aleksandar Nenadović, "'Politika' u nacionalističkoj oluji," p. 588, and Rade Veljanovski, "Zaokret elektronskih medija," p. 616, in *Srpska strana rata: Trauma i katarza u istorijskom pamćenju,* ed. Nebojša Popov (Belgrade: Republika, 1996). For a personal, quite unorthodox, but nevertheless insightful account of the ways in which political propaganda in *Politika* had been functioning (although in a later period), see Ivan Čolović, *Kad kažem novine* (Belgrade: Samizdat B-92, 1999).

19. *Dnevnik,* 3 October 1988, p. 6.

20. *Dnevnik,* 5 October 1988, p. 1, and *Dnevnik,* 6 October 1988, p. 1.

21. Djukić, *Izmedju slave i anateme,* p. 107.

22. Ibid., p. 108.

23. Ibid.

24. *Dnevnik,* 7 October 1988, p. 1.

25. Ibid.

26. At the already mentioned rally in Novi Sad on 5 October 1988, Kertes said: "Ako se ja kao Madjar ne plašim Srbije, zašto bi se Srbi plašili?" *Dnevnik,* 6 October 1988, p. 8.

27. Boarov, *Politička istorija Vojvodine,* p. 217.

28. Ibid.

29. Nenad Dimitrijević, *Slučaj Jugoslavija: Socijalizam, nacionalizam, posledice* (Belgrade: Samizdat B-92, 2001), p. 84.

30. *Popis stanovništva, domaćinstava, stanova i poljoprivrednih gazdinstava u 1991 godini* (Belgrade: Savezni zavod za statistiku, 1993).

31. Slobodan Milošević, whose regime has contributed significantly to the deterioration of ethnic relations in Vojvodina, for example, claimed, in January 1990, that the "unity in which the citizens of Vojvodina live can serve as an example to Yugoslavia." Slobodan Milošević, "Sloga u kojoj žive gradjani Vojvodine može da posluži kao primer Jugoslaviji," in *Godine raspleta* [note 16], pp. 321–25.

32. Sonja Biserko, ed., *Manjine u Srbiji* (Belgrade: Helsinški odbor za ljudska prava u Srbiji, 2000), p. 37.

33. Jan Briza, *Prava nacionalnih manjina u Jugoslaviji* (Subotica: Minority Rights Group International, 2000), p. 15; and Biserko, *Manjine u Srbiji,* p. 37.

34. From the Croatian *Hrvatska demokratska zajednica.*

35. Šešelj's paramilitaries became infamous for their participation in the war in Croatia, especially in eastern Slavonia, where much of the looting and crimes against Croat civilians has been ascribed to them and similar groups, such as Željko Ražnatović "Arkan's" "Tigers." On numerous occasions, including a speech in the Serbian parliament, Šešelj publicly threatened the Croats in Vojvodina with

expulsion and confiscation of property; he went on record saying that the Croats should be expelled because they are not loyal to Serbia, and because they are the fifth column that is coordinating destabilization of Serbia with the Zagreb regime. *Borba* (Belgrade), 3 April 1992, pp. 10–12; and *Borba,* 26 May 1992, p. 6.

36. On 14 February 2003, the International Criminal Tribunal for the Former Yugoslavia in The Hague released the indictment of Vojislav Šešelj, who was charged with crimes against humanity and violations of the laws or customs of war. Apart from the charges related to Šešelj's crimes in Croatia and Bosnia-Herzegovina, the indictment states that "[i]n public speeches [Šešelj] called for the expulsion of Croat civilians from parts of the Vojvodina region in Serbia and thus instigated his followers and the local authorities to engage in a persecution campaign against the local Croat population." The indictment is available online at www.un.org/icty/indictment/english/ses-ii030115e.htm.

37. Nataša Kandić, ed., *Human Rights, 1991–1995* (Belgrade: Humanitarian Law Center, 1997), p. 85. For the story of the events in Hrtkovci, I have relied on this excellent publication of the Humanitarian Law Center.

38. *Popis stanovništva* [note 30].

39. Kandić, *Human Rights,* p. 86.

40. Quoted in ibid.

41. Ibid.

42. Ibid., p. 87.

43. Ibid.

44. Ibid., p. 88.

45. Ibid., p. 87.

46. Ibid., pp. 87–88.

47. Ibid., p. 88.

48. Ibid., pp. 95–108.

49. Biserko, *Manjine u Srbiji,* pp. 47–48.

50. Ibid., p. 50; and Briza, *Prava nacionalnih manjina,* p. 15.

51. Biserko, *Manjine u Srbiji,* pp. 44–45.

52. Ibid., p. 49.

53. In a sense, even with the full census figures, it will be impossible to know the real situation on the ground, as the census figures would probably not reflect the full import of the demographic change in Vojvodina during the 1990s. It is reasonable to assume that the citizens of Serbia—Hungarians, Croats, Serbs, the undecided alike—who left the country for various reasons during this period kept their Serbian citizenship and never officially changed their place of residence in Serbia; they were counted—the author of this article included—as living in Serbia. One of the more formidable tasks of the Serbian reformists, if Serbia is ever to "go to Europe" (to use their dominant metaphor, whatever it means and what-

ever one might think of it), will be to finally write down (literally) who lives where and owns what.

54. *Popis stanovništva* [note 30].

55. Zoran Lutovac, "Političko organizovanje nacionalnih manjina u SRJ," in *Položaj manjina u Saveznoj Republici Jugoslaviji,* ed. Miloš Macura and Vojislav Stanovčić (Belgrade: Srpska akademija nauka i umetnosti, 1996), p. 206.

56. Miroslav Samardžić, *Položaj manjina u Vojvodini* (Belgrade: Centar za anti-ratnu akciju, 1999), p. 123. A good resource for election results in Vojvodina and Serbia is the Internet site of the independent election-monitoring agency, Centar za slobodne izbore i demokratiju (CeSID), at www.cesid.org. The site contains the complete results and statistical analyses for all elections that have taken place in Serbia since 1992.

57. Ibid., p. 125.

58. Biserko, *Manjine u Srbiji* [note 32], p. 25.

59. In 1994, József Berecz founded the Civic Movement of Vojvodina Hungar-ians; Ferencz Pap led the Christian-Democratic Movement of Vojvodina Hun-garians, while Gábor Tóth Horthy presided over the Christian-Democratic Bloc of Vojvodina Hungarians; ibid.

60. Ibid., p. 18. Of course, it was not only the Hungarians who were leaving Vojvodina in the 1990s. The general atmosphere of fear, distrust, and economic crisis took its toll, and the decade witnessed a massive exodus of mostly educated population of all ethnic backgrounds. It remains unknown how many people left Vojvodina and Serbia as a consequence of the decade of war and economic crisis.

61. Biserko, *Manjine u Srbiji,* pp. 32–34.

62. One general theoretical observation is in order at this point. I do not believe that ethnic identity is the primary framework through which individuals construct reality and which motivates their actions. My understanding of this problem is informed by a number of writings by authors who have put forth constructivist theories of nation, nationalism, and identity. That I am de facto appropriating the dominant discourse of Serbian politics in the 1990s—that is, counting "Serbs" and "Hungarians," and judging their ethnic identities by their names—is an ironic consequence of my determination to fully grasp a moment in history in which identities become fixed and seemingly permanent. To write about how these iden-tities were constructed, and under which social conditions they were fixed, would be to pose questions that, unfortunately, go beyond the scope of this chapter. For an excellent introduction to the history of theories of nation/alism and identity, see Geoff Eley and Ronald Grigor Suny, "From the Moment of Social History to the Work of Cultural Representation," the introduction to *Becoming National* (New York: Oxford University Press, 1996), which they edited.

63. According to the Law of Official Use of Language and Alphabet, counties

with significant portions of minority populations have the right to decide under which conditions minority languages can be officially used on the territory under their jurisdiction (*Službeni glasnik Republike Srbije*, no. 45/91). This provision is vague, and it is up to the goodwill of each local assembly to decide whether it wants to allow for an official use of a minority language or not; in Novi Sad, for example, the municipal assembly has tended to ignore the official use of Hungarian, even though it voted in favor of its official use. See *Informacija o sprovodjenju Zakona o službenoj upotrebi jezika i pisma u opštinama na teritoriji Vojvodine,* adopted at the 5 February 1997 session of the Executive Council of the Province of Vojvodina.

    64. Biserko, *Manjine u Srbiji,* p. 22.

    65. Samardžić, *Položaj manjina u Vojvodini,* p. 74. For a detailed analysis of elementary school textbooks, see Ružica Rosandić and Vesna Pešić, *Ratništvo, patriotizam, patrijarhalnost: Analiza udžbenika za osnovne škole* (Belgrade: Centar za antiratnu akciju, 1994).

    66. Biserko, *Manjine u Srbiji,* p. 30. For the case of *Borba,* see Eric D. Gordy, *The Culture of Power in Serbia: Nationalism and the Destruction of Alternatives* (University Park, Pa.: Penn State University Press, 1999), pp. 81–95.

    67. Biserko, *Manjine u Srbiji,* p. 30.

    68. The already extensively quoted book edited by Sonja Biserko and published by the Helsinki Committee for Human Rights in Serbia—*Manjine u Srbiji*—is a good source of information about specific problems of specific ethnic minorities.

    69. The remaining 79,791 persons were refugees that had managed to change their status to that equal to the citizens of the Federal Republic of Yugoslavia, and had thus lost their refugee status. The results of the census are quoted in Samardžić, *Položaj manjina u Vojvodini,* pp. 39–41. It is probable that the number of refugees is higher, as not all of them registered themselves during the census. Ibid., p. 40.

    70. Vladimir Ilić, *Manjine i izbeglice u Vojvodini* (Belgrade: Helsinški odbor za ljudska prava u Srbiji, 2001), pp. 82–90.

    71. In post-World War Two censuses in Yugoslavia, including the last one in 1991, citizens could identify "Yugoslav" as their ethnicity; this identification has usually meant (and, more importantly, has been widely perceived to mean) that these persons were of mixed ethnic origin.

    72. Samardžić, *Položaj manjina u Vojvodini,* pp. 41–42.

    73. Ilić, *Manjine i izbeglice u Vojvodini,* p. 83.

    74. Samardžić, *Položaj manjina u Vojvodini,* p. 41.

    75. Ibid.

    76. Vojin Dimitrijević, "The 1974 Constitution as a Factor in the Collapse of Yugoslavia, or as a Sign of Decaying Totalitarianism," in *The Road to War in Serbia: Trauma and Catharsis,* ed. Nebojša Popov (Budapest: Central European University Press, 2000), p. 399.

77. Ibid., p. 407.

78. See Branka Magaš, *The Destruction of Yugoslavia: Tracing the Breakup, 1980–1992* (London: Verso, 1993), pp. 49–73.

79. Sabrina P. Ramet, *Balkan Babel: The Disintegration of Yugoslavia from the Death of Tito to Ethnic War,* 2d ed. (Boulder, Colo.: Westview Press, 1996), p. 14.

80. Ivan Stambolić, *Rasprave o SR Srbiji, 1979–1987* (Zagreb: Globus, 1988), pp. 49, 62. After Slobodan Milošević, a comrade and a good friend of Stambolić's, ruthlessly replaced the latter as the leader of the Serbian communists in 1987, an image of Stambolić emerged among the intellectual circles opposed to Milošević that portrayed him as a moderate politician, prone to compromise and dialogue. Years later, Stambolić openly criticized Milošević; he might have considered running against his one-time friend in the crucial presidential elections of 24 September 2000, and this was probably the reason for his disappearance in August 2000. Vojislav Koštunica, who defeated Milošević in September, had not yet announced his candidacy at the time of Stambolić's disappearance. On 28 March 2003, at the time of the sweeping police operation during the state of emergency that followed the assassination of Zoran Djindjić, the Ministry of the Interior announced that it had solved the Stambolić case. Stambolić was kidnapped in Belgrade on 25 August 2000 and taken to an isolated location in the woods of Fruška Gora, where he was executed and buried. It is widely believed that either Milošević or his wife authorized the execution of their political opponent.

81. See Ljubomir Madžar, "Who Exploited Whom?" (pp. 160–88), Marina Blagojević, "The Migrations of Serbs from Kosovo during the 1970s and 1980s: Trauma and/or Catharsis" (pp. 212–43), Olivera Milosavljević, "The Abuse of the Authority of Science" (pp. 274–302), Drinka Gojković, "The Birth of Nationalism from the Spirit of Democracy" (pp. 327–50) in Popov, *The Road to War in Serbia.* For the "Serbian cultural backlash" in literature, see Andrew Wachtel, *Making a Nation, Breaking a Nation: Literature and Cultural Politics in Yugoslavia* (Stanford, Calif.: Stanford University Press, 1998), pp. 197–226.

82. The Belgrade-based media component of the "public debate" about constitutional changes could not pass unnoticed by the journalists from the media in Novi Sad (which were just as controlled). Nada Vujović of *Dnevnik,* for example, denounced tendentious reporting of Radio-Television Belgrade and *Politika,* as well as the general manipulation of the Belgrade media. *Dnevnik,* 12 July 1988, p. 5.

83. While in the case of Vojvodina the political institutions of the province were allowed to function even though they had no real power, the ones in Kosovo were practically abolished and never got to function, even nominally.

84. Tamás Korhecz, "Chances for Ethnic Autonomy in Vojvodina" (paper presented at the conference Minority Governance in Europe on the Threshold of the 21st Century, Bolazno, Italy, 5–9 October 2000), p. 5. The conference was organ-

ized by the European Center for Minority Issues, Flensburg, Germany. I would like to thank Mr. Korhecz, who was at the time this chapter was being written the minister for minority rights in the Vojvodinan provincial government, for allowing me to read and quote his paper.

85. Ibid.

86. *Novosadski glas* (Novi Sad), 8 March 1991, p. 12.

87. *Novosadski glas,* 22 February 1991, pp. 11–12, and *Novosadski glas,* 8 March 1991, p. 12.

88. Boarov, *Politička istorija Vojvodine*, p. 221.

89. From the Serbian *Srpski pokret obnove.*

90. See, for example, a collection of Čanak's articles (from November 1994 to February 1996) in *Nezavisni,* reprinted in Nenad Čanak, *Godina raspleta* (Novi Sad: Yu Top agencija, 1996), in which he referred to "fascism" and "Naziism" in Serbia.

91. See *Memorandum on the Self-Government of Hungarians in the Republic of Serbia* (Budapest: Foundation for Southland Hungarians, 1992).

92. *Vreme* (Belgrade), 24 January 1998, pp. 19–21.

93. For the text of the *Platform* (Platforma za savremenu autonomiju Vojvodine), see Slobodan Budakov, ed., *Knjiga o Vojvodini* (Novi Sad: Vojvodjanski klub, 1995), pp. 11–43.

94. Ibid., p. 14.

95. Boarov, *Politička istorija Vojvodine*, p. 228.

96. Quoted in ibid., p. 229.

97. For example, every elected member of parliament "cost" the Union of Vojvodina Hungarians (UVH) around 12,000 votes, Milošević's ruling coalition (SPS-JUL-ND [Nova demokratija, "New Democracy"]) around 14,000, Drašković's Serbian Renewal Movement (SPO) around 20,000, while Čanak, Isakov, and Veselinov had to "pay" around 30,000 votes for each elected representative. Boarov, *Politička istorija Vojvodine,* pp. 230–31.

98. *Vreme,* 2 October 1997, pp. 24–25, and *Vreme,* 9 May 1998, pp. 20–21.

99. On 29 May 2003, Veselinov resigned under strong pressure by the general public. In a traffic accident involving excessive speeding in the center of Belgrade, Veselinov's SUV killed a pedestrian. Veselinov's matter-of-fact attitude to the tragic event, the fact that the SUV was not his official vehicle, and the denial of responsibility by his driver—all led to public outrage and, ultimately, to his resignation.

100. *Danas* (Belgrade), 5 February 2002, available online at www.danas.co.yu.

14

THE YUGOSLAV ROMA UNDER
SLOBODAN MILOŠEVIĆ AND AFTER

DENNIS REINHARTZ

In the intricate history of Eastern and Central Europe since the Middle Ages, the Roma (Gypsies) repeatedly have been the oppressed "forgotten other." This congenital torment has also been aggravated periodically by war, as with the victimization of the Roma during the Holocaust of World War Two.[1] Since the beginning of the dissolution of Titoist Yugoslavia in 1989, the persecution of the Roma once again has gone largely unnoticed in the West and by the Western media. As a consequence of a combination of chronic historical intolerance and more current political and socioeconomic factors, during the wars of Yugoslav succession—the wars between the new Yugoslavia (Serbia and Montenegro) and Slovenia and Croatia, the Bosnian civil war, and the Kosovo crisis—the Roma were yet again severely maltreated.

Within the scope of this presentation, the roles of the historical issues, the current deteriorating conditions, and the apparent lack of Western attention to the situation of the Roma and their ongoing persecutions are assessed while at the same time discerning the specific localisms vis-à-vis the Gypsies of Slobodan Milošević's Serbia and Montenegro and the other pertinent Yugoslav successor states. The prospects for the former Yugoslav Roma in the shorter term are considered briefly as well.

From the End of the Pax Ottomanica
to the End of Titoist Yugoslavia

As throughout much of Eastern Europe, there has been a continuous Romany presence in the Yugoslav lands since at least the Middle Ages. Having perhaps come north from Thrace, the first Gypsies arrived among the South Slavs sometime in the middle of the thirteenth century. Their first documented appearance was in Macedonia in 1289.[2] Certainly, after the Turkish conquest of the Balkans in the fourteenth and fifteenth centuries, especially Muslim Roma were encouraged to settle in the Yugoslav lands beyond Macedonia among the Serbs of Kosovo (1348), the Sandžak, Bosnia, and elsewhere.[3] This kind of resettlement was in line with the long-standing Ottoman policies to transplant and thereby mix subjugated peoples to make them easier to control.[4]

Many of the Gypsies came to reside in the cities and towns.[5] With the gradual elimination of the Ottoman overlordship prior to World War One, the Roma largely remained to become a part of South Slav life. Gypsies were part of Karadjorje's rising against the Turks in 1803–04,[6] and by 1815, there were about ten thousand of them in the Ottoman Paşalik of Belgrade.[7] The majority were still Muslim, but a growing minority of them also were Serbian Orthodox.[8] Serbian state councilor Steven Petrović Kničanin's victorious army against the Hungarians in 1848–49 included a legendary "squadron of Gypsies."[9]

The sparse and largely anecdotal historical record of the Yugoslav Roma in the nineteenth and early twentieth centuries is marked by periodic discrimination, though on occasion favoritism as well.[10] A good number of them were illiterate, and to survive and even prosper, they also became very good at not being noticed by officialdom. In the newly expanded Serbia of Knez Miloš Obrenović of 1833–34, most towns had flourishing Gypsy quarters, where the traditional occupations of blacksmithing, horse-trading, bear leading, faith healing, tinkering, cobbling, textile and basket weaving, music, and begging were practiced.[11] Obrenović even had his own Gypsy orchestra.[12] In the first volume of his memoirs, Montenegrin writer and Yugoslav leader Milovan Djilas points out that the employment of Roma in occupations like blacksmithing and even grave digging was very necessary before World War One. The Gypsies, even Muslims, were therefore generally tolerated.[13] He also reflects that in his town the Gypsy houses were indistinguishable from those of Montenegrin peasants.[14] In Serbia, the Roma also were perhaps more tolerated because of Serbian Orthodoxy, whereas the Roman Catholicism of the Croats and Slovenes of the Austro-Hungarian Empire to the north may have been conducive to greater discrimination, as it also seems to have been toward the Jews.

The Roma managed much the same under the Kingdom of Serbs, Croats, and Slovenes, proclaimed by the Declaration of Corfu in 1917, and its successor, the Kingdom of Yugoslavia, declared in 1929 under the royal dictatorship of King Aleksandar. By 1941, there were more than three hundred thousand Gypsies in Yugoslavia, and most of them, with the exception of those in Montenegro, the Gurbeti, were permanently settled, many in ghettos in the larger cities like Belgrade, Skopje, and Sarajevo. Many of them also were well along on the road to assimilation. About three-fourths of the Roma were situated in Serbia and Macedonia.[15] During the first week of April 1941, the recently crowned King Peter II was forced to flee to London. As Yugoslavia fell to invasion, with the conquest came the fragmentation of the country and the genocide of the Roma in the Yugoslav lands, and because no real records of the Gypsy killings were kept, this genocide remains difficult to reconstruct specifically and for the most part unreported.[16]

Of the over three hundred thousand pre-war Yugoslav Gypsies, approximately two-thirds of them perished in the Holocaust. Despite their severe losses in Serbia and Croatia, the Romany populations of Yugoslavia rebounded. Today, there are perhaps as many as eight hundred thousand of them in the Yugoslav lands.[17]

The Milošević Era

A historic problem for the Roma that presently bears quite strongly on their circumstances in the Balkans and elsewhere is their failure to gain significant international recognition as a nation and national minority. A principal difficulty of course stems from the fact that national legitimacy (and therewith national self-determination) has been and still is linked primarily to territoriality, and the Roma make up a global diaspora that has not inhabited a specific territory since they vacated the borderlands of the Indian subcontinent more than a millennium ago. Today, Romany identity is maintained and furthered largely by the activism of its national organizations such as the International Romany Union. In this state of affairs, the Romany nation is not unique, the Kurds, Basques, Catalans, Mari, and Maasai being yet other examples, and the question of what is a nation is of growing concern to international bodies such as the United Nations and the European Union (EU). As a recognized nation internationally and national minority within other established nation-states, the Roma would better be able to work toward their national unity, self-preservation, and self-determination without a homeland, for as most Roma and their leaders agree, the state of "Romastan" is a state of mind.[18]

Only a few states such as the Czech Republic, Hungary, and Romania have officially accepted the Roma as a legitimate national minority.[19] Austria did so in 1995, but the European Union has not yet followed. There were nevertheless physical attacks by skinheads on Roma in Vienna around Adolf Hitler's birthday in 1996. Before its breakup in 1989–91, Titoist Yugoslavia was the first country to have extended, for their suffering and service against fascism in World War Two, such recognition to the Roma. And despite their often somewhat sizeable Roma minorities, none of the Yugoslav successor states except Macedonia and tiny Montenegro have followed suit. The state of affairs of the Macedonian Roma will be treated below in connection with the ongoing Kosovo crisis. In 1991, there were an estimated 20,000–28,000 Roma in Montenegro, out of a total population of 615,035, with about 7,000 of them located in and around the capital, Podgorica.

Yet while they have this status under the Montenegrin constitution, they are nevertheless regularly the targets of discrimination, and there is no similar identification to be found in the federal or Serbian constitutions.[20] Throughout the Milošević era and into the present, the Gypsies continue to be only an ethnic group rather than an ethnic minority. Roma leaders formally petitioned Yugoslavia for national minority status in 1998. To date, whether under the Milošević or the Koštunica government, there has been no action on this petition. Thus, for example, they are still officially prohibited from studying in their own language, and this has contributed greatly to their alienation in Yugoslavia and Serbia and Montenegro.[21]

Like the Roma of the rest of Europe, those in the Yugoslav successor states "face segregation in education and the military, discrimination in housing and employment and are routinely the target of police beatings. According to a report by the Commission on Security and Cooperation in Europe, the Roma 'constitute the poorest, least healthy, least educated and most discriminated sector of . . . society.' And democratic changes . . . have done little to improve their plight."[22] A significant obstacle in the education of Romany children across Eastern and Central Europe, for instance, is their almost routine placement in classes and schools for the mentally challenged. Due to their parents' and grandparents' social isolation and lack of basic education, these children's verbal and social skills may be subpar for their age group, and they may need extraordinary help, but they are not mentally retarded.[23] On top of this nearly universal European condition of the Roma, in the former Yugoslavia must be added the effects of the trauma of war.

During the Bosnian civil war, they were the most impacted group. In the countryside, Serbian and Croatian militants alike forcibly expelled Muslim and Christian Roma. In Sarajevo, the site of the largest Romany community in Bosnia-Herzegovina, they suffered equally and more with the other remaining residents from the near-constant Serbian and Croatian-Bosniak shelling and shooting and the other deprivations of war. Along with others, many Roma fled for safety beyond the city and the country, only to find, upon their return after the signing of the Dayton agreements, that many of their homes and other property had been confiscated and turned over to Bosnian Muslims loyal to the regime of President Alija Izetbegović and his Muslim Party for Democratic Action (SDA). These expropriations were in clear violation of the Dayton agreements. Again along with others, some of those Roma who remained found food, comfort, and other support from the long-established Jewish community of Bosnia-Herzegovina in Sarajevo.[24]

One of the places where the fleeing Bosnian Roma could not easily find sanctuary was in the Serbian lands of Yugoslavia. Although the Roma make up approximately 4 percent of the population of Yugoslavia and had for their own defense publicly supported Slobodan Milošević at the polls and on the bridges of Belgrade during the NATO air raids, for example, they remain a "definite segregated and unwanted underclass" in Serbia.[25] In Belgrade especially, there is a well-documented record of discrimination and violence against them. One of the most shocking instances was that of the atypically internationally publicized beating to death while on the job of a fourteen-year-old Roma pizza delivery boy, Dušan Jovanović, by Serbian skinheads in 1997.[26]

There are two weak and disorganized, semilegal Romany political parties in Yugoslavia—the Romany Democratic Political Party and the Yugoslav Democratic Party of Gypsies—that consistently fail to win any seats in parliament. Currently, there are only two Roma in leadership positions in the country. Dejan Marković is a member of the Belgrade city government, and Osman Balić is a member of the Niš city government.[27]

As elsewhere in Eastern and Central Europe, to escape identification and thereby discrimination, beginning in the early 1980s, primarily in Macedonia and Kosovo, some Yugoslav Roma declared themselves as "Egyptians" and formed "Egyptian societies." In many languages, "Gypsy" is derivative from "Egyptian." Having adopted the new national identity primarily as protection against the Albanians in these areas, the more than ten thousand Yugoslav, mostly Albanophone "Egyptians," now deny that they are Gypsies. These rather sad and transparent efforts have, however, not gained the backing of Egypt or any other members of the international community of nations.[28]

The increasingly anti-Yugoslav postures of the United Nations and European Union also hurt the Roma substantially. Located at the bottom of the economic ladder, the Roma suffered disproportionately as a result of the stresses put on Yugoslavia by the Western trade embargo and other punitive economic policies. Furthermore, in the months of NATO bombings during the Kosovo crisis, the Roma were particular victims due to the fact that many of them live in ghettos surrounding the rail yards, power plants, and factory zones of Yugoslavia's major cities that were the prime targets of air sorties and missile attacks. Understandably, given the over-all situation of the Yugoslav Roma, these bombed-out Roma could not easily "connect" with relatives or friends for relief.[29]

In addition to their historic problems with the Serbs, and since there has long been no love lost between Albanians and Roma, in the Kosovo crisis the Roma of the province fared far worse even than others of their people elsewhere in Yugoslavia. Accordingly, in Albania in 1996, there was a stepped-up campaign of discrimination initiated against the Roma, again based on accusations of their being kidnappers and child traffickers.[30] Since 1989, the conditions of the Roma in Kosovo have been deteriorating, and, under a government policy of divide and rule, they have been forced to assimilate both by the minority Serb community and by the majority Albanian community, hence finding themselves once again caught "between two fires."[31] Today, 60 percent of them live below the poverty line, mak-ing it even more difficult to make their unique voice heard.[32]

In the largely Albanian town of Obilić, twenty kilometers north of Priština, for example, even the Albanian-speaking Roma suffered severe vio-lence at the hands of their Albanian Kosovar neighbors. These Albanian-speaking Roma were set upon in part because of the collaborative acts with the Serbs carried out by other Roma (Serbian-speaking?) reported elsewhere in the province. Eventually, eight hundred fifty of the Obilić Roma were collected in a UN refugee camp outside the town and protected by KFOR (Kosovo International Security Force) Norwegian troops. Although the Roma have even regularly set up their encampments on or near SFOR (Sta-bilization Force) and KFOR garbage dumps from Vukovar to Sarajevo to the cities and towns of Kosovo, during the wars of Yugoslav succession, they generally had little faith in the West to guarantee their future.[33]

During the Kosovo crisis, significant numbers of Roma did side with the Serbs, most of them being Serbian speaking with Serbian surnames and of the Serbian Orthodox faith. But Duijzings also offers that even Mus-lim Gypsies, feeling at odds with the Albanian majority, might have iden-tified more with the Serbian minority in Kosovo.[34] They never had any real power, yet nevertheless also supported the Milošević government. Some did actual duty work for the Serbian paramilitary forces, ranging from digging graves and defensive trenches to destroying and pillaging Alba-nian property. On several occasions, Serbian paramilitaries reportedly em-ployed Romany children to set fire to still-occupied Albanian houses. Nat-urally, the verified Romany acts of mayhem as well as others that are only rumored to have occurred have contributed significantly to the continuing animosity between the Albanians and the Roma.[35]

As elsewhere, the Romany population figures for Kosovo are unclear. But before the crisis, the Roma in various stages of assimilation may have totaled up to twenty thousand, and over half of them reportedly became refugees. No Roma from the province have been allowed to enter Serbia. In fact, during the crisis, Roma on the Serbian side of the border were driven into Kosovo by the Serbs. Numbers of largely Muslim, Albanian-speaking Roma, however, have been accepted into Montenegro. Serbian-speaking and Albanian-speaking Roma (when detected) were prohibited from entering Albania by Albanian border guards.[36]

Most of the Roma who exited the province sought refuge across the eastern border in Macedonia, but were unwelcome there as well.[37] Traditionally, the Albanians and Roma have been greater and lesser national minorities, respectively, competing for jobs (e.g., taxicab drivers) at the lower end of the Macedonian economy. Consequently, not only did the Macedonian majority not want any more Roma or Albanians in their relatively new country, but also nor did the Albanian minority want any more Roma. The predicament of these Romany refugees in Macedonia has been aggravated because their plight has remained largely unidentified and uncovered in the Western media hype relating to the Albanian Kosovar refugees.[38]

By 1 October 1999, there were approximately twenty-nine hundred Romany refugees in three camps *(Romski kampi)* organized by the United Nations High Commissioner for Refugees (UNHCR)—Stenkovec II, Cegrane, and Neprosteno—in Macedonia. Uncounted others were living with Macedonian Roma host families, many in Suto Orizari, the major Romany suburb of Skopje, or in the cities of Kumanovo, Štip, Tetevo, and Gostivar. This is a relatively small group in comparison to the much larger number of Kosovar Albanian refugees in Macedonia or refugees in general resulting from the Yugoslav wars of succession, but the Roma are a comparatively small people.

The Roma often were without basic documentation, having lost or destroyed it in the chaos of the Kosovo crisis. Many Roma who identified themselves as Albanian, do not speak Romany, and/or are Islamic were counted as Albanians. Some of them were repatriated to Kosovo after the bombing only to be discriminated against yet again by the Albanians and Serbs of the province. Most of the Roma refugees who remain in Macedonia do not want to return to Kosovo or any other part of Yugoslavia. Nor do they want to stay in Macedonia. Rather, they hope that Macedonia will serve as a bridge to a third country somewhere, preferably in the West.[39]

The worsening state of the Roma of the former Yugoslavia therefore is based on a combination of historical and more contemporary factors. The historical discrimination against the Gypsies as "eternal outsiders" in the societies of Eastern and Central Europe continues relatively unabated into the present, and now this maltreatment is exacerbated by the tensions resulting from the transition out of communism (e.g., Titoism) and its related military conflicts in the region. Rehabilitated nationalism (e.g., Greater Serbianism) has led not merely to stepped-up social and economic isolation and discrimination that has rendered Roma even more politically impotent, but also to violent attacks against them by rabidly antialien, neofascist skinheads in periods of peace and by assorted military and paramilitary forces in the various theaters of the wars of Yugoslav succession.

Conclusion

The fall of Milošević has begun to usher in new policies toward national minorities. But while Belgrade moves nearer to the European Union, the Milošević inheritance lingers and incidents against the Gypsies persist. A number of such confrontations were reported during the 2001 Vareso aver (week of Romany culture) that was sponsored by the federal Ministry of National Minorities. Among other incidents reported were that radical Serb nationalist groups peppered Belgrade with anti-Roma graffiti, skinheads in Belgrade assaulted performers from the Romany theater, and in Vojvodina, a Gypsy was set upon for having a Serb girlfriend.[40]

At this moment, the Roma are a very vulnerable people. In the Balkans and especially Serbia and Montenegro, as the old Gypsy tale relates, they indeed are caught between at least two fires and in serious danger of being burned by one or more of them while not being able to secure warmth and comfort from any of them.

Notes

In addition to the contemporary scholarship and reporting of others, this essay is also based on the author's encounters with the Roma of the former Yugoslavia while working as a consultant to the United States Holocaust Memorial Museum since 1996. A portion of this chapter appeared recently in my article "The Roma and the Wars of Yugoslav Succession," *The South Slav Journal* 23, nos. 1–2 (Spring–Summer 2002), pp. 39–45.

1. See Dennis Reinhartz, "Unmarked Graves: The Destruction of the Yugoslav Roma in the Balkan Holocaust, 1941–1945," *The Journal of Genocide Research* 1 (March 1999), pp. 81–89, and idem, "Damnation of the Outsider: The Gypsies of Croatia and Serbia in the Balkan Holocaust, 1941–1945," in *The Gypsies of Eastern Europe*, ed. David Crowe and John Kolsti (Armonk, N.Y.: M. E. Sharpe, Inc., 1991), pp. 81–92.

2. Chris Hellier and Chris Walsh, "All Roads Lead to Roma," *Geographical Survey*, no. 72 (December 2000), p. 42.

3. Miranda Vickers, *Between Serb and Albanian: A History of Kosovo* (New York: Columbia University Press, 1998), p. 22.

4. For a good introduction to the Balkan Gypsies under Turkish rule, see Elena Marushiakova and Vesselin Popov, *Gypsies in the Ottoman Empire: A Contribution to the History of the Balkans* (Hertfordshire, U.K.: University of Hertfordshire Press, 2001).

5. Michael Boro Petrovich, *A History of Modern Serbia 1804–1918* (New York: Harcourt Brace Jovanovich, 1976), vol. 1, pp. 9–10.

6. Ibid., p. 34.

7. Ibid., p. 169.

8. Ibid., p. 175.

9. Ibid., p. 245.

10. Nebojša Bato Tomašević and Rajko Djurić, *Gypsies of the World: A Journey into the Hidden World of Gypsy Life and Culture* (New York: Henry Holt and Co., 1988), pp. 7–8.

11. Petrovich, *A History of Modern Serbia*, p. 175. Also see Noel Malcolm, *Kosovo: A Short History* (Washington Square, N.Y.: New York University Press, 1999), p. 207.

12. Petrovich, *A History of Modern Serbia*, p. 175.

13. Milovan Djilas, *Land without Justice* (New York: Harcourt Brace Jovanovich, 1958), pp. 149 and 195.

14. Ibid., p. 239.

15. Karola Fings, Cordula Lissner, and Frank Sparing, ". . . einziges Land in dem Judenfrage und Zigeunerfrage gelöst: *Die Verfolgung der Roma im faschistisch besetzten Jugoslawien 1941–1945*" (Cologne: Rom e.V. Köln, 1991), p. 7.

16. For example, see *New York Times*, 7 September 1986, p. A1. Among scholars, only Vladimir Dedijer, Antun Miletić, Milan Bulajić, and a few others are taking a deeper interest. Also see Dennis Reinhartz, "Damnation of the Outsider," pp. 81–92; and idem, "Unmarked Graves," pp. 81–89.

17. See Minton F. Goldman, *Russia, The Eurasian Republics, and Central/ Eastern Europe*, 7th ed. (Guilford, Conn.: Dushkin/McGraw Hill, 1999), pp. 171–89; Nebojša Bato Tomašević and Rajko Djurić, *Cigani Sveta* (Belgrade: Jugoslovenska

revija, 1988); "Roma in Montenegro," *Fact Sheets* 1, no. 3 (22 November 1999); online at www.org/publications/factsheets/Montenegro.shtml (accessed 19 December 1999); and "Romani Populations in Central and Eastern Europe," *Patrin* 1, no. 2; online at www.geocities.com/Paris/5121/romani-pop.html (accessed 19 December 1999).

18. See Cara Feys, "Towards a New Paradigm of the Nation: The Case of the Roma," *Patrin* 1, no. 15; online at www.geocities.com/Paris/5121/paradigm.htm (accessed 19 December 1999).

19. Vladimir Derić, "International Protection of Roma Rights," in *The Roma in Serbia,* ed. Goran Svilanović and Dobrivoje Radovanović (Belgrade: Centre for Anti-War Action, Institute for Criminological and Sociological Research, 1998), pp. 87–92.

20. Ibid. The Romany population estimates for the Yugoslav successor states in 1997 were (Roma/total population): Bosnia-Herzegovina, 35,000–80,000/3.3 million; Croatia, 180,000–300,000/4.7 million; Macedonia, 110,000–260,000/2 million; Slovenia, 7,000–10,000/2 million; Yugoslavia, 400,000–600,000/11.3 million. See the sources listed in note 18.

21. Dragan Ristić, "Fighting Tradition: The State of Roma Affairs in Yugoslavia," *Central Europe Review* 13, nos. 1–2 (21 May 2001); online at www.ce-review .org/01/18/ristic18.html (accessed 13 June 2002).

22. Tom Giles, "Gypsies: Tramps and Thieves?" *Patrin* 1, no. 4; online at www.columbia.edu/cu/sipa/PUBS/SLANT/SPRING/gypsies.html (accessed 10 February 2000).

23. Theresa Agovino, "Hungarian Educators Try to Get Gypsies into the Mainstream—and Into College: Centuries of Suspicion and Mistreatment Have Left the Ethnic Minority Largely Unschooled and Underemployed," *The Chronicle of Higher Education* (18 February 2000), p. A68; online at www.chronicle.com/weekly/ v46/i24/24a06801.htm (accessed 17 February 2000).

24. Dragica Levi, general secretary of the Jewish community of Bosnia and Herzegovina, interview by the author, Sarajevo, 21 May 1997.

25. See Mattijs van de Port, *Gypsies, Wars and Other Instances of the Wild: Civilization and Its Discontents in a Serbian Town* (Amsterdam: Amsterdam University Press, 1998); Miloš Macura, ed., *Razvitak Roma u Jugoslaviji: Problemi i tendencije* (Belgrade: Serbian Academy of Sciences and Arts, 1992); and Svilanović and Radovanović, *The Roma in Serbia* [note 19].

26. *New York Times,* 22 October 1997, p. A8.

27. Ristić, "Fighting Tradition" [note 21], p. 2.

28. Ger Duijzings, *Religion and the Politics of Identity in Kosovo* (New York: Columbia University Press, 2000), pp. 152–56.

29. Terrence Sheridan, "Gypsies in Belgrade—The Underclass of a City under

the Gun Somehow Manages to Keep Its Head," *JINN* 1, no. 4 (5 April 1999); online at www.pacificnews.org/jinn/stories/5.07/990405–belgrade.html (accessed 11 November 1999).

30. See *No Record of the Case: Roma in Albania,* Country Report Series, no. 5 (Budapest: European Roma Rights Center, June 1997).

31. Galjus Orhan, "Roma of Kosovo: The Forgotten Victims," *Patrin* 1, no. 8 (7 April 1999); online at www.geocities.com/Paris/5121/kosovo.htm (accessed 19 December 1999).

32. Nivedita P. Haran, "The Roma Population in Kosovo: A Search for Identity and Roots," *Newsletter of the Gypsy Lore Society* 25 (August 2002), p. 4.

33. Alexander Pooles, "The Roma of Oblic," Radio Free Europe/Radio Liberty, *Newsline* (14 December 1999); online at www.newsline@list.rferl.org (accessed 15 December 1999).

34. Duijzings, *Religion and the Politics of Identity,* p. 71.

35. Pooles Fisk and Robert Fisk, "Liberation of Kosovo: Gypsies Abandoning Kosovo, Taking Their Guilt with Them," *The Independent* 1, no. 2; online at www.zoran.net/afp/independent/gypsies_abandoning_kosovo.htm (accessed 11 November 1999).

36. Kate Carlisle, "Field Report: Romani Refugees from Kosovo in Albania," *Roma Rights* 2, nos. 1–15 (25 November 1999); online at errc.org/rr_nr2_1999/field1.shtnl (accessed 12 January 2000); and "Roma in Montenegro" [note 17].

37. See *A Pleasant Fiction: The Human Rights Situation of Roma in Macedonia,* Country Report Series, no. 7 (Budapest: European Roma Rights Center, July 1998).

38. For example, see "Four Years after Fleeing Kosovo, Gypsies Try in Vain to Return Home, AP, 30 May 2003," *Serbian Unity Congress,* Washington, D.C., 30 May 2003; online at news.serbianunity.net/by date/2003/May_30/9.html (accessed 17 September 2003); and "Police Stop Attempt by Gypsies Stranded at Border from Pushing into Greece, AP, July 18th 2003," *Serbian Unity Congress,* Washington, D.C., 18 July 2003; online at news.serbianunity.net/bydate/2002/July_18/8.html (accessed 17 September 2003).

39. "Boat Crowded with More Than 1,000 Yugoslav Gypsies Docks in Southern Italy," *Focus on Kosovo,* 1 August 1999; online at www.cnn.com/WORLD/europe/9908/01/italy.gypsies (accessed 1 May 2002); Elsie Dunin, "Kosovo Roma—The Forgotten Refugees," *Newsletter of the Gypsy Lore Society,* no. 22 (November 1999), pp. 1, 6–7; and Fisk and Fisk, "Liberation of Kosovo" [note 35], p. 1. Also see Lubica Stavrić, "Dani tugom rasplakani," *NIN,* no. 2675 (4 April 2002), pp. 32–33.

40. Ristić, "Fighting Tradition" [note 21], p. 1.

CONCLUSION

15

THE SIRENS AND THE GUSLAR:

AN AFTERWORD

SABRINA P. RAMET

I

The ancient Greek bard Homer recounts how Odysseus, the wily war hero winding his way home, wanted to hear the singing of the legendary Sirens, of whose powers he had been warned by Circe. According to legend, men who heard their songs became overwhelmed by the desire to be with them, swimming desperately to their isle and ending up as their victims. Odysseus was driven by curiosity. What was this song which could drive men to distraction? What was the secret of the Sirens' power? What were their charms? But Odysseus knew better than to expose himself to certain doom, and instructed his crew to plug their ears, and then to bind him firmly to the mast of their common vessel and not release him until the Sirens were far behind, no matter how persistently he might implore them or even command them.

If one might take one man to represent a certain number, then one might describe Dobrica Ćosić, the author of the novel *Vreme smrti* (A Time of Death), as a latter-day Serbian Siren. His novel painted nationalism as glorious, made the dream of national glory seem little short of celestial. The nation was important, was it not? What could be more important than the nation? What could be more worth dying for than one's nation? What could be more beautiful, more invigorating, more exhilarating, more noble than fighting for one's nation? To struggle, to fight, to risk all, to suffer, to endure, to win, to conquer, to achieve victory—surely that is the best that life has to offer.

There is, of course, a significant difference between the Sirens and Dobrica Ćosić, viz., that without the Sirens, there would have been no sweet melody luring sailors to their doom, whereas nationalism, including Serbian nationalism, has a life independent of the Serbian bard. On the other hand, the problem with nationalism is the same as that with the Sirens:

like them, the nationalist lures men to their doom. Moreover, when the air is thick with nationalism, few can escape its lures, its temptations, its illusions. Serbs, Croats, and Bosniaks, and later Kosovo's Albanians as well, all became infected with nationalism, and while there will always be those who believe that nationalism can be healthy and positive, it is clear that the nationalism which spread among the peoples of what was once socialist Yugoslavia was neither healthy nor positive. The nationalism which was stirred up by propaganda in order to mobilize the locals for war was, on the contrary, fueled by resentment of other groups[1] and characterized by chauvinism. Whether such "ethnic nationalism" is somehow related to civic-mindedness, as members of a common set, so that the latter might even be termed "civic nationalism"[2] is a question beyond the scope of this afterword, though if that were so, then it would seem that the word "nationalism" might be used to refer to any bonds which draw people together, whether or not they believe that they share a common ethnic and national identity. I shall not use the word in this way; on the contrary, in using the word "nationalism" I shall mean *that passion which preaches that the rights of the individuals of either one's own nation or of other nations count for less than the rights of one's own nation, that the rights and interests of other nations count for less than the rights and interests of one's own nation, that glory is a goal worth pursuing and consists in building up the power of one's own nation (possibly, but not necessarily, through territorial conquest), and that such universalist or cosmopolitan values as tolerance, fairness, human equality, and respect for the harm principle are delusions at best—and, potentially, delusions dangerous for the nation.* Such a definition does not prejudge what attitude one may take toward the phenomenon thus specified; Vojislav Šešelj, the neofascist leader of the Serbian Radical Party, has used the term in much the way in which I do, and yet he has considered it a badge of pride to call himself a "nationalist" and has even boasted of being "chauvinistic."

Thus defined, nationalism is rather obviously dangerous for those who lose in the ethnic wars it drives. But I would add that nationalism is not only destructive of those who lose at war. On the contrary, its venom debilitates all who succumb, regardless of the outcomes of the tides of war. Nationalism devalues activities unrelated to the national struggle, infiltrates and subverts culture, exploits and perverts religious institutions, marginalizes feminists, environmentalists, liberals fighting for various forms of tolerance, and above all pacifists. Nationalism can justify policies in which those with power become fabulously rich, while those without power become impoverished. Nationalism can drain the soul. Nationalism can reduce the individual to pure instrumentality. Nationalism can divide people and peoples whose friendship seemed undying and set them against each other. Nationalism can twist and warp the patterns of a society to such an extent that it requires decades to recover, changing some aspects of society permanently. Like the victims of rhinoceritis in Ionesco's play *Rhinoceros,* those who succumb to nationalism are changed, to the extent that their own past seems different, even incomprehensible or "wrong," to them.

Nationalism, as I have defined it, also debases politics by replacing the debate over alternative programs with the debate over alternative strategies for realizing the same program. Milošević and his cohorts stirred up nationalist resentments in order to mobilize Serbian society for war. The fundamental illegitimacy of the communist state made it vulnerable, as did economic deterioration, and the Belgrade regime took advantage of these factors to advance a program which took the country to war; nationalism was a key tool. In a society infected by nationalism, the liberal project is thrown on the defensive, if it is not trampled underfoot.

Nor is nationalism good for democracy. When all candidates must be nationalists in order to garner support and when none but nationalist media attain to a large audience, democracy suffers. Nationalism in its more extreme variants is, in short, the political equivalent of delusional hysteria or, better, it is a form of collective neurosis. A nationalistic society is, accordingly, a dysfunctional society; a national regime is both dysfunctional and debased (which is to say, illegitimate).

II

If one were to catalogue the outbreaks of nationalism and related phenomena around the world and over the centuries, one would, I suspect, end up with a very long list. Serbian nationalism is, thus, not unique. Even its pretensions to uniqueness (à la Tsar Lazar and his choice of the heavenly kingdom, the sufferings of the Serbs under the Ottomans and during World War Two, the victimization of Serbs, and in spite of it all, the Serbs' steadfast commitment to "safeguard" old Yugoslavia) are not unique. Indeed, part of the nationalist syndrome is precisely the pretension to uniqueness.

And yet, not all nationalisms are the same; and not all nationalisms have as intense a pretension to uniqueness. I have, elsewhere, endeavored to outline a typology of nationalisms, distinguishing among heroic nationalism and defiant nationalism, both of which have a triumphant recol-

lection of the past, defensive nationalism, muted nationalism, and entrepreneurial nationalism, all of which associate the past with uncertainty,
and messianic nationalism, problematic nationalism, and traumatic nationalism, all of which have a cataclysmic recollection of the past.[3] What
distinguishes the variations of nationalism at each of these three levels is
their perception of the world, with, for instance, messianic nationalism
having a "beckoning" image of the world, problematic nationalism having a mixed image of the world, and traumatic nationalism viewing the
world as threatening. Nationalisms having a cataclysmic view of the past
will have the strongest pretensions to uniqueness and greatness, with the
traumatic variant being, I would argue, the most volatile and the most
dangerous.

And then there is war, which, quite apart from those effects arising from
nationalism per se, has further effects on a society. These effects may touch
every aspect of society from the structure and ownership of the economy
to the prioritization of policy agendas to the behavior of clerics and prelates
to fashions and even cosmetics. On the latter point, one may recall the appearance of a Serbian perfume called "Miss 1389" on the six hundredth
anniversary of the Battle of Kosovo, and the appearance, four years later,
of a rival perfume marketed in a bottle the shape of a grenade. War is also
associated with a rise in domestic violence and may also be associated with
a proliferation of gun-related incidents, whether during the war itself or
after. War induces withdrawal in some people, neurosis and schizophrenia and paranoid-like responses in others. The stress associated with war
has also been known to cause premature aging and profound changes in
personality.

In the case of Serbia, the war, even though not fought on Serbian territory (until 1998), resulted in the glorification of pathological criminals
such as Vojislav Šešelj and Željko Ražnatović "Arkan," and even their election to the national assembly. This result is not unrelated to Serbia's
specifically traumatic nationalism, in which the society was invited to dwell
on past injuries and sufferings. Igor Krstić has called this "Serbia's wound
culture." But this experience of transcendent pain is adulterated, at the
same time, by the experience of a kind of pleasure. Indeed, as Krstić notes,
crediting Slavoj Žižek, nationalism may be understood as "the eruption
of enjoyment into the social field." Thus, as ethnic tensions escalate, the
community is retroflected back upon itself in a reaction which is experienced simultaneously as defensive and pleasurable.[4] But in a traumatic
wound culture, attacks on the national community are easily translated,
as they were in Serbia, into attacks on a community which is situated in

history. This is scarcely unusual: patriotic Americans are apt to summon the ghosts of Washington, Jefferson, and Lincoln, just as the French invoke the memories of Joan of Arc and Napoleon or the Germans, the spirits of Beethoven, Goethe, Hegel, and yes, Bismarck. That the Serbs should look back to St. Sava, Vuk Stefanović Karadžić, and Chetnik leader Draža Mihailović is nothing unusual; on the contrary, it is typical nationalist behavior. On the other hand, the "return of the living dead," as Žižek calls it— the phenomenon exemplified with the discovery of mass graves in parts of Croatia in 1989, in which Croats and Serbs reopened old quarrels, blaming each other as nations for those lost more than a generation earlier— figures as a symbol of unresolved historical traumas.[5]

Here is where the invocation of the spirits of the past assumes different forms. When American politicians invoke Washington and Lincoln, this is within the context of a society which does not understand itself as being in a traumatized state, let alone as a great historical victim. But when Serbian politicians in the 1980s and 1990s invoked the ghosts of St. Sava and Tsar Lazar, the context was collective fear being transformed into a state of collective paranoia.[6] Even as the perceived danger was enhanced in the Serbian media, so too was the sanctity of the Serbian cause, as repeatedly hammered home through allusions (for example, on the part of Patriarch Pavle) to "celestial Serbia." If, indeed, Tsar Lazar chose the eternal "heavenly kingdom," then was this not the inheritance of all Serbs forever? And, in that case, as Shakespeare put it in *King John,*

> . . . methinks, an angel spake:
> Look where the holy legate comes apace,
> To give us warrant from the hand of heaven
> And on our actions set the name of right
> With holy breath.[7]

Fired by self-righteousness, Serbs could disbelieve, disregard, or willfully deny the evidence of atrocities committed by their own side, because these atrocities were not, allegedly, of the essence. What was essential, from this point of view, was that Serbia was the victim and its cause was sanctioned by God.

The sweet melody of paranoid nationalism was as compelling as anything ever sung by the Sirens, and its fruit as bitter. Following Milošević and Karadžić and Mladić into battle did not usher Serbs into the company of angels, and Milošević's Serbia, with its corruption, cronyism, despoliation of the public, gangland killings, and subversion of the media,[8] could not be mistaken for the heavenly kingdom. But throughout the Milošević era, the bards of Serbian nationalism never tired of hearkening back to the past, and in this fixation on Serbia's past, the gusla, a one-stringed instrument associated with folk music traditions in Serbia, Macedonia, and Bulgaria, took on mythic proportions. It became a concrete, physical symbol of what was essentially Serbian, as opposed to Croatian or Bosniak, and the Serbian troops fighting in Croatia and Bosnia took along their guslas. "Whenever we are not shooting, we play the gusla," said one guslar.[9] Radovan Karadžić, it turned out, could play the gusla, and in film footage taken in the birth house of his namesake, Vuk Stefanović Karadžić, in 1992, the Bosnian Serb leader is shown strumming on a gusla. The gusla inevitably appeared in comic strips too; for example, in a *hajduk* comic strip from 1991, in which Serb insurgents in Knin are shown readying a fortress in anticipation of an attack by Croatian forces: at the center of the picture kneels a burly, mustachioed, middle-aged man playing the ubiquitous gusla.[10] The implied message seemed to be: wherever you find the gusla being played, there Serbs are safe.

III

After the outbreak of the war in 1991, the State Council of Education in Belgrade introduced new history textbooks in the elementary and secondary schools. As Dubravka Stojanović has shown, these textbooks cast Serbs as the perennial victims of their neighbors, and, using emotionally charged language in describing certain periods, offered pupils a picture of the world "brimming with xenophobic contempt and hatred for neighboring nations, [as well as for the] European and the world community."[11] In discussions of the Ottoman Empire, which ruled Serbia for roughly four centuries, the Christian subjects are described as "the enslaved peoples," with every lesson "followed by a short passage taken from historical sources in which those who commit the described actions (usually atrocities) are called Turks."[12] Needless to say, there is no mention of the fact that, for most of this period, the Ottomans were more tolerant of both confessional diversity and linguistic diversity than any other state in Europe, with the partial exception of Prussia.

But in turning to the discussion of the fortunes of Serbs under Bulgarian and German occupation during World War One, of the sufferings of the Serbs in the Independent State of Croatia during World War Two, and of the Serbian Insurrectionary War of 1991–95, the textbooks presented their accounts "in a brutal, almost morbid way."[13] The textbooks thus contributed to building up hatred for non-Serbs, on the part of Serb pupils, with this hatred being especially focused on Muslims (whether Turks, Albanians, or Bosniaks), Croats, and Germans. Based on a careful study of primary and secondary school textbooks, Stojanović concluded that they "offer[ed] a picture of an archaic, bellicose, antimodern society, that isolates itself from the world" and nurtures "anachronistic notions about itself and its historic mission."[14]

IV

It is customary in an afterword not only to evoke the spirit of the subject and to refer to such factors as may have been salient in the recent history of the subject—tasks which I have already undertaken—but also to take stock of what the various chapters in the book have argued, where they agree, and where there might be disagreement. It is to this task that I shall now turn.

This book takes its point of departure from 1989, the year in which Milošević suppressed the autonomy of the autonomous provinces and removed the duly elected leaders in Montenegro, replacing them with his own people—bringing the story up to the present. While Milošević had embraced the nationalist banner in 1987, it was only in 1989 that he could be said to have declared war, in a manner of speaking, on the federation. The year 1989 was also the year that relations between Slovenia and Serbia broke down, culminating in the Serbian boycott of Slovenian goods and services, declared at the end of the year. During the next eleven years, the Milošević regime survived on a diet of insurgencies and wars, using them to feed the nationalist paranoia which bound the Serbian people to Serbia's "first family." Serbs rallied in public places bearing aloft the portraits of St. Sava, Tsar Lazar, and Slobodan Milošević, chanting "Slobo, Slobo!" as if he were the fulfillment of age-old promises of the second coming; he was, many Serbs thought in the 1990s, the Serbian Savior, whose rule would fulfill the prophecies thought to have been implied in the epics about Tsar Lazar and in the poetry of Njegoš. And if Milošević was not a religious man, he would at least save Serbs from the Croats, Bosniaks, and Albanians, and fight off the Germans, the Vatican, and the Americans.

Milošević's speeches, especially in the early years, were riddled with references to Serbs being surrounded by enemies, about needing to fight, about Serbia never losing a war. When the Serbian Orthodox Church itself blessed the war, the violence could be seen as "holy violence." In this sense, Ibrahim Rugova, the literary scholar who established the League of

Democrats of Kosova and was later elected president of Kosova in 1992 and again in 2002, proved to be the perfect foil for Milošević. Where Milošević and his cronies had orchestrated a campaign of "holy violence" against non-Serbs, Rugova countered by calling upon Albanians to emulate Gandhi, evoking what one might call "holy nonviolence." Even if the Albanians eventually felt constrained, after the disappointment of being excluded from the Dayton settlement of 1995, to take up arms, their pacifism, maintained over the years 1990–95, made a decisive contribution toward legitimating their cause in the eyes of the world.

One cannot build a functional system on the basis of paranoid culture and an ethic of holy violence. Nor can one create patterns of legitimate politics in the context of official promotion of what Niyazi Kizilyurek has called "collective narcissism."[15] Some observers have mistaken the cause for the effect: it is not the wars which led to the dysfunctionality of the Serbian system, but rather it was its dysfunctionality which, insofar as it relied on an essentially unstable formula, kept stirring up fresh problems, not only outside the Republic of Serbia but also within it—in Vojvodina, in the Sandžak, and above all in Kosovo. Legitimacy does make a difference; indeed, it makes the crucial difference. But legitimacy should not be understood subjectively, as if all that was required for a "legitimate" system was that it enjoy the overt or tacit support of the majority of its citizens. On such an understanding of "legitimacy," the Third Reich would have to be seen as a "legitimate" system, and the term "legitimacy" will end up meaning only that the given regime has an effective propaganda apparatus. If, however, the term is understood to have an objective sense—with moral, political, and economic components of system legitimacy[16]—and a procedural sense—in which one may measure a system's conformity to its own supposed rules—then the term can have both explanatory and predictive power. On this understanding, illegitimate systems are fundamentally unstable and, like unstable chemical compounds, "yearn" to find a stable equilibrium; illegitimate systems may last for a decade or so, but, in the absence of war, will quickly look for ways to "reform," to "restructure," to "democratize," to "revive." All of these are but excuses for refusing to admit that the given system lacks legitimacy and is therefore dysfunctional. The characterization applies to Tito's Yugoslavia, and it applies also to Milošević's Serbia.

For post-Milošević Serbia, the great challenge is legitimation. Can Serbia's leaders create a legitimate and functional system, in which liberal values are fostered and in which a stable democracy is developed? This is the underlying theme in this book. Whether one looks at issues of remembrance (Eric Gordy's chapter) or the behavior of the Orthodox Church (my own chapter) or the fissiparous tendencies emerging in Kosovo and Montenegro (as described in the chapters by Frances Trix and Reneo Lukić), this is a theme which lurks in the background. The system's dysfunctionality is the most important reason for the separatist movements in Kosovo and Montenegro, and reflects syndromes tied to the denial of complicity[17] as well as to the specific character of Serbian Orthodox religiosity.

The chapters in this volume are divided into four parts: the center, with chapters on the politics of Serbia and relations between Serbia and Montenegro; the legacy of the war, with chapters devoted to the psychological aspects of Serbian wartime propaganda, to Serbian efforts to come to terms with the past, to the economy, and to the trial of Slobodan Milošević; culture and values, with chapters devoted to the Serbian Orthodox Church and to gender relations; and the periphery, with chapters devoted to Kosovo, Vojvodina, and the Roma of Serbia. The sundry strands in this book are tied together, finally, in an analytical introduction by Vjeran Pavlaković.

The chapters in part 1 paint the Milošević era in broad brush strokes, and also assess the major figures dominating Serbian (and Montenegrin) politics since the fall of Milošević. Pavlaković shows how the Milošević regime adopted the external trappings of democracy—not the first authoritarian regime to choose this strategy—and appropriated nationalist symbols to rouse people for war. But, Pavlaković warns, "the system that Milošević built for more than a decade cannot be expected to completely collapse with the removal of one man, regardless of how much power and responsibility he had." Pavlaković also notes the way in which the revival of Chetnik symbols and the rehabilitation of the Axis-collaborationist Chetnik movement stirred up and validated nationalist values and contributed to system dysfunction. Moreover, Pavlaković warns, Vojislav Koštunica, elected Yugoslav president in September 2000, showed himself to be "no less nationalistic than Milošević," while Djindjić appeared to be "more pro-Western and more inclined to push through reforms." Obrad Kesić documents the contestation between the political Right and the political Left over the nationalist legacy, with the former continuing to insist on the positive value of nationalism and its compatibility with democracy, and the latter insisting on the negative character of nationalism and denying its compatibility with democracy. Kesić and Reneo Lukić, like Pavlaković, see elements of dysfunctionality in the post-Milošević Yugoslav state; both of them see the legacy of the Milošević era at work, but where Lukić focuses on the structural dimensions of this dysfunctionality, Kesić emphasizes the personal rivalry between Koštunica and Djindjić in the first two years after Milošević, as well as the role of organized crime. This latter theme is picked up in the chapter written by Marko Attila Hoare and Maja Miljković (in part 2), who document cases of embezzlement by government ministers, show how political and criminal elites overlapped, and, in particular, show how the Red Berets, the Special Operations Units which "were deeply implicated in the crimes of the Milošević era," became a key pillar of the Koštunica regime. To put it succinctly, government ministers in the Milošević era promoted their own economic interests rather than the economic interests of the country as a whole. The result was that the Milošević regime "succeeded in transforming Serbia from one of the richest countries of communist Europe to one of the poorest of postcommunist Europe within the space of less than fifteen years."

Other chapters in part 2 throw light on other effects and legacies of the war. My own chapter on Serbian wartime propaganda examines the sundry themes which emerged with the nationalist tide in Serbia and which were systematically reinforced by Serbian propaganda. The effect was to distort the value system of Serbian society by inculcating fears, behaviors, and syndromes which are characteristic of neurosis, paranoia, and even psychosis. Since such fears and syndromes do not disappear overnight, Serbian society is still having to cope with this legacy of the war. In addition to the psychological impact of the war, there have also been social, political, and economic consequences for Serbia, as James Gow and Milena Michalski show in their chapter; among other things, they note the loss of jobs in the economic sector, the withering of investment and innovation, and the loss of traditional markets, at least in part as a consequence of the UN economic embargo—which, taken in combination, had a catastrophic effect on Serbian society. Kari Osland assesses the significance of the trial of Milošević both for Serbs and, one might say, for history. She cites opinion poll data from 2002 showing that while 83 percent of the residents of Kosovo approve of the International Criminal Tribunal in The Hague, only 7.6 percent of citizens of Serbia trust the tribunal. As she notes, some Serbs would have preferred to see Milošević stand trial in Belgrade rather than in The Hague—and on different charges! Finally, Eric Gordy's chapter takes up the theme of remembrance and responsibility. He cites Ljiljana Bačević of Belgrade's Institute for Social Sciences to the effect that about 75 percent of Serbs want to see indicted war criminals put on trial, and argues that complete denial of any Serb culpability in war crimes and atrocities is "a marginal position, restricted to exponents of the extreme right and people who have a material interest in denial." Be that as it may, the radical right Serbian Radical Party attracted some 27.7 percent of the vote in parliamentary elections on 28 December 2003, to emerge as the most powerful party in the newly elected parliament, well ahead of the second-place Democratic Party of Serbia (DSS)—Koštunica's party— which managed to win 18 percent of the vote.[18]

The chapters in part 3 on culture and values examine the role played by the Serbian Orthodox Church in the recent history of the region, and the relationship between the nationalist program in Serbia and rather obvious processes of "re-traditionalization" of gender roles promoted during Milošević's years in power. My own chapter on the Serbian Orthodox Church notes how Serbian Orthodox clergy see theirs as "a world apart, a better world, potentially even a celestial kingdom," and details the insensitive symbolic actions taken by the Serbian Orthodox Church in 1989–91, which contributed to the stoking of war fever, thereby catapulting the country into war. The chapter also discusses controversies concerning Kosovo, Montenegrin autocephalism, and the Macedonian schism, closing with a detailing of the Serbian Church's seven-point social agenda. Evidence is presented in this chapter that the Church is hostile to secularism, liberalism, homosexuality, and globalization, while championing nationalism in the sense in which I have defined it above.

Biljana Bijelić's chapter on gender relations closes part 3. Bijelić shows how the Milošević regime promoted a re-traditionalization of gender roles, manipulating notions of women's alleged political passivity and of "motherhood as the highest vocation for women." These themes resonate with radical right approaches to women's roles.

Finally, in part 4—devoted to the peripheries—there are chapters devoted to Kosovo/Kosova, Vojvodina, and the Roma. Dennis Reinhartz summarizes recent developments in the social and political life of the Roma of Serbia, while Frances Trix and Emil Kerenji show how Milošević's repressive policies transformed the situations in Kosovo and Vojvodina respectively and how his policies excited pressures for secession in Kosovo and autonomism in Vojvodina. Trix is critical of the international response, noting that "the main criticism of [the] international authorities . . . is that they still cannot bring themselves to acknowledge that Kosovar Albanians will not be governed by Belgrade." In her view, thus, any effort to keep Kosovo in political union with Serbia will only condemn the region to further instability, dysfunction, and violence. As for Vojvodina, Kerenji notes that since October 2000, Koštunica's party "has resisted the calls for the return of autonomy to Vojvodina, and has diluted the issue by presenting vague proposals for the decentralization of Serbia."

V

The contributors to this volume do not all share the same perspective on Serbia. They differ sharply, for example, on the relative merits of Zoran Djindjić and Vojislav Koštunica. Hoare, for example, considers it self-evident that Koštunica is a "nationalist," as does Trix, who calls the new Serbian prime minister "a traditional right-wing nationalist," citing his "connections with Serb paramilitary leaders" in Kosovo. Kesić dismisses such characterizations of the DSS leader, representing him rather as a champion of pluralist democracy who has had legitimate worries that other DOS leaders have continued to have a "community mentality." For Kesić, Koštunica is a legalistic "Girondin," while Djindjić behaved as a "Jacobin," ever ready to promote "rapid reforms by any means necessary, even if they were illegal, unconstitutional, or even unethical." For Lukić, by contrast, it is Koštunica who has proven to be the "Jacobin," while Gow and Michalski describe Djindjić as "the most able political figure on the [political] scene" and conclude that he was "undoubtedly on the side of the angels."

There are other differences as well. Kerenji, for example, writes that, as a result of the NATO campaign in spring 1999, Milošević became politically vulnerable, while Pavlaković asserts the very opposite, claiming that "the NATO bombing appeared only to strengthen Milošević," at least in the short run.

Tallying up the record of the years since 1989, however, the contributors to this volume reach a high degree of consensus, painting a bleak picture. Trix strikes a common chord in noting the persistence of destructive nationalism in Serbia. Again, Kerenji writes that the Milošević era "has left a disastrous legacy in the area of ethnic relations," while Gow and Michalski argue that Serbian society has been "debased and atomized" and that the war resulted in a collective "loss of integrity." Although the Serbian Orthodox patriarch has suggested that it would be possible for Serbs to regain a childlike innocence even after so much killing, Gordy argues that this may be more complicated—among other reasons, because of the damage to the collective psyche. This, in turn, is treated at greater length in my chapter, "Under the Holy Lime Tree," where I discuss the psychological dynamic associated with the war and suggest that "one may speak of Serbia having been sucked into a kind of collective psychosis."

Nor has the fall of Milošević opened up the gates of Elysium. As Miljković and Hoare note, "Serbia is still burdened by a criminal-bureaucratic infrastructure inherited from the Milošević regime," while Pavlaković writes that "the pace of change [after Milošević] has been exceptionally slow," with "[e]thnic and territorial issues continu[ing] to pose difficult challenges for Serbia."

The contributors to this volume, thus, find a considerable degree of consensus about "the big picture" and certainly agree on the dysfunctional character of the system as well as on the continued pervasiveness of an unhealthy strain of nationalism. Indeed, dysfunctionality and nationalism have figured as the twin themes of this volume. In Serbia, dysfunctionality has been manifested, among other things, in the fact that, throughout the period covered by this volume, the Albanians of Kosovo/a have rejected the framework of the Serbian state and have built up an alternative framework, at first informally, but beginning in 1992, also in formal terms. The Kosovo problem is sufficiently serious that that alone would be sufficient to define Serbia as a dysfunctional state. Moreover, in the wake of NATO's air campaign against the rump Yugoslav state in spring 1999, violence spread to southern Serbia, where local Albanians attempted to attach the districts of Preševo, Medvedja, and Bujanovac to Kosovo. At this point in time, the Albanians of Kosovo are fully committed to eventual independence, with a recently established guerrilla group, the Albanian National Army, already making a name for itself as a military resource in the event that negotiations should fail.[19] But Belgrade remains unreconciled to such an eventuality and, as recently as 27 August 2003, the Serbian parliament adopted a resolution (with 186 votes in favor, 23 abstentions, and 0 votes against) excluding independence for Kosovo and demanding that the international community enforce UN Security Council Resolution 1244, which recognized "Yugoslav" sovereignty over Kosovo.[20] The difficulty with applying this resolution is that, with the change in the name of the country in March 2003 to Serbia and Montenegro, there is no longer a "Yugoslavia" to which Kosovo has been guaranteed. By early March 2004, Vojislav Koštunica—Djindjić's old rival—had been sworn in as Serbia's prime minister. Even before the parliamentary vote which confirmed him in office, Koštunica announced his government's program, which included a proposal to extend "personal and cultural autonomy" to the Albanians of Kosovo within the context of a "cantonization" of the province, seen as a first step toward the eventual partition of Kosovo, a proposal which outraged Serbian Radicals and Albanians alike, though for opposite reasons.[21] Less than two weeks later, after the bodies of two young Albanians were discovered in the River Ibar, Kosovo was engulfed in violence once again, leaving thirty-one dead and about five hundred wounded by the evening of 18 March.[22] At least sixteen Orthodox churches were burned to the ground by Albanians, and scores of Serb homes were incinerated. The violence served as a reminder that the Albanians of Kosovo are determined to win their independence and that efforts by the international community to keep Kosovo within Serbia have only served and can only serve to prolong the political instability in the region. Koštunica's response, as Serbian prime minister, was to renew his demand for the cantonization of Kosovo at a meeting of the Contact Group in Kosovo; among other things, the cantonization scheme was intended to tie Serb-inhabited areas of Kosovo more closely to Serbia.[23]

But there have been other serious problems as well, quite apart from Kosovo. Certainly the fact that, by 1993, Serbia was fielding between 60,000 and 70,000 police, or 7 police officers for every 1,000 Serbian citizens, was a symptom of dysfunctionality. In Britain, there are 2 police for every 1,000 inhabitants, in Latin American and African countries, it is usual to have 4 policemen for every 1,000 inhabitants, and even among dictatorships, the ratio is rarely more than 5 police for every 1,000 people.[24] *Borba* interpreted this statistic as a sign that Milošević had lost confidence in the military. And, in conformity with the "praetorian" syndrome once described by Huntington,[25] there have been repeated incidents of murder of political opponents, both in the Milošević era and since (as, example, in the cases of the murder of former Serbian president Ivan Stambolić in 2000 and the assassination of Serbian prime minister Zoran Djindjić in 2003).

Moreover, Serbia has had to endure other problems as well, such as corruption in the judiciary,[26] widespread bribery with not only officials but police, teachers, customs officials, and even physicians said to be "on the take,"[27] money laundering,[28] the penetration of the so-called Red Berets by criminal elements and development of cooperative contacts between the regime and the criminal underground (detailed in Pavlaković's chapter as well as in the chapter by Hoare and Miljković), the rehabilitation of Axis collaborator Draža Mihailović (including the erection of a statue in front of the Ministry of Culture),[29] and the diversion of the savings accounts of private persons into the state treasury and of funds in the state treasury into the pockets of close collaborators of Milošević.[30] Even opposition figures such as Vuk Drašković and Zoran Djindjić became involved in illegal economic activities, growing very well-to-do as a result.[31] Moreover, the election law, requiring that at least 50 percent of the eligible electorate take part in presidential elections in order to elect a winner, proved dysfunctional, with presidential elections in 2002 and 2003 failing to elect a president, for lack of interest!

The record of the Milošević regime also demonstrated that repression can have unintended results. Quite apart from Kosovo, the repressive measures undertaken during the Milošević years in the Sandžak and Vojvodina[32] provoked autonomist resistance. Although ostensibly innocent, the call for dual citizenship with Hungary for Hungarians of Vojvodina, issued by the three leading political parties of Vojvodina's Hungarians in August 2003, came after the expulsion of tens of thousands of residents of Vojvodina and in the context of an unresolved dispute about Vojvodinan self-governance.[33]

A dysfunctional state goes together with a dysfunctional society; indeed, it usually is the main reason that a society becomes dysfunctional. What are the characteristics of a dysfunctional society? Here one may mention significant increases in domestic violence, suicide, and drug abuse. Where Serbia is concerned, suicide rates increased in the years that Milošević was in power and even in 2001, some 900 persons took their own lives in Belgrade alone.[34] Domestic abuse also increased during the war years. And in 2001, Serbs—who number about 7 million persons—swallowed 144 million pills of Diazepam and Bromazepam alone. Belgrade is thought to have at least 30,000 addicts (as of March 2003). By early 2003, the government had become sufficiently concerned about the growing problem of dependence on tranquilizers and ordered a crackdown on the illegal drug trade, stepping up security at pharmacies as well.[35]

In the years since Milošević fell from power, as Kesić notes, Serbs have seen their hopes for a better life dashed and have lapsed into despair. Although Djindjić, who promised extensive reforms, built up more power than Koštunica in the first two years after Milošević, it was Koštunica who emerged as simultaneously the most popular and the most controversial figure in the immediate transition.[36] Koštunica was heralded by his supporters and apologists as a "moderate nationalist," a constitutional lawyer with a detailed knowledge of constitutional law, and a legal literalist. His critics likened his thinking to that of neofascist Vojislav Šešelj,[37] and have characterized Koštunica as a dangerous nationalist,[38] raising suspicions of his intentions as regards Bosnia-Herzegovina. In at least one respect, ironically, Koštunica bears a certain comparison with Milošević, viz., in his efforts, especially in his first year in office, to argue that Yugoslavia's obligations under international law had to be subordinated to the specific stipulations of Yugoslav and Serbian law, in effect placing Serbia above international law. Hans Kelsen, the highly regarded scholar of international law, described this illusion in a 1948 article, noting,

> The view that international law is part of one's own national law is advocated by those who insist upon the sovereignty of their own state, and who take it for granted that legal interpretation of facts is identical with interpretation according to their national law, that is, the law of their own state. This juristic imperialism is usually not consistent enough to admit that by this interpretation the own state of the interpreter becomes the sole and absolute legal authority, the god in the world of law.[39]

For that matter, Kelsen argued elsewhere that notions of sovereignty which place the law of the nation higher than that of the international community are at best atavistic, at worst dangerous.[40] Serbia is no longer a danger to its neighbors, of course, but the dangerous ideas spawned in the past are still in circulation. The chapters in this book are, on the whole, inclined to deep pessimism about the prospects for Serbia to move toward liberal democracy and political stability. And yet, at the same time, they show what would be necessary to accomplish such a task—specifically, that it is not enough to change officeholders and laws, or even institutions, or even to combat crime; it is also necessary, if liberal democracy is the goal, to promote the ideals of liberalism and, to use the terminology associated with Gabriel Almond and Sidney Verba, to develop a "civic culture."

Notes

1. For discussion of the role of resentment in fueling chauvinistic nationalism, see Roger D. Petersen, *Understanding Ethnic Violence: Fear, Hatred, and Resentment in Twentieth-Century Eastern Europe* (Cambridge: Cambridge University Press, 2002), esp. "Introduction" (chap. 1).

2. Jack Snyder, *From Voting to Violence: Democratization and Nationalist Conflict* (New York: W. W. Norton, 2000), pp. 15–31, 39–42, 45ff. I have enormous respect for Snyder's argument, even though I disagree with his notion that ethnic chauvinism and civic-mindedness are somehow related, and would commend his book to anyone wishing to acquaint him- or herself with an alternative argument.

3. Sabrina Petra Ramet, "The Serbian Church and the Serbian Nation," in *Beyond Yugoslavia: Politics, Economics, and Culture in a Shattered Community*, ed.

Sabrina P. Ramet and Ljubiša S. Adamovich (Boulder, Colo.: Westview Press, 1995), pp. 101–5.

4. Igor Krstić, "Re-thinking Serbia: A Psychoanalytic Reading of Modern Serbian History and Identity through Popular Culture," *Other Voices* 2, no. 2 (March 2002), pp. 9, 11, online at www.othervoices.org/2.2/krstic/.

5. Ibid., pp. 8–9.

6. Danilo Kiš, "On Nationalism," *Performing Arts Journal* (1996), as cited in William W. Bostock, "South Africa's Language Policy: Controlled Status Enhancement and Reduction," *Mots pluriels*, no. 13 (April 2000), pp. 2–3, online at www.arts .uwa.edu.au/MotsPluriels/MP1300wban.html.

7. William Shakespeare, *King John*, V, ii.

8. See Sabrina P. Ramet, *Balkan Babel: The Disintegration of Yugoslavia from the Death of Tito to the Fall of Milošević*, 4th ed. (Boulder, Colo.: Westview Press, 2002), chap. 14 ("Serbia's Unending Crisis"); Dušan Pavlović, *Akteri i modeli: Ogledi o politici u Srbiji pod Miloševićem* (Belgrade: B92, 2001), pp. 124–52, 171–221.

9. Quoted in Ivo Žanić, *Prevarena povijest* (Zagreb: Durieux, 1998), p. 71.

10. The comic is reproduced in ibid., p. 386.

11. Dubravka Stojanović, "The Balkans, Wars, and Textbooks: The Case of Serbia," *Association for Social History* (2001), p. 10, online at www.udi.org.yu/Founders/ Stojanovic/textbooks.htm.

12. Srdjan Rajković and Dubravka Stojanović, "Yugoslavia," in Center for Democracy and Reconciliation in Southeast Europe, *Balkan Horizons* (Thessaloníki, 2001), p. 17, online at www.cdsee.org/book1.htm.

13. Stojanović, "The Balkans, Wars, and Textbooks," p. 2.

14. Ibid., p. 13. See also Christina Koulouri, ed., *Teaching the History of Southeastern Europe* (Thessaloníki: Center for Democracy and Reconciliation in Southeast Europe, 2001).

15. Niyazi Kizilyurek, "History Textbooks and Nationalism," in Koulouri, *Teaching the History of Southeastern Europe*, p. 71.

16. See the discussion in Sabrina P. Ramet, *Whose Democracy? Nationalism, Religion, and the Doctrine of Collective Rights in Post-1989 Eastern Europe* (Lanham, Md.: Rowman & Littlefield, 1997), introduction, chap. 3, conclusion.

17. See the discussion in Milan Šahović, "Individualna krivična odgovornost Slobodana Miloševića," *Republika* (Belgrade), no. 280 (1–15 March 2002), online at www.yurope.com/zines/republika/arhiva.

18. *Glas javnosti* (Belgrade), 29 December 2003, online at www.glas-javnosti .co.yu.

19. See, for example, Jeta Xharra, "Kosovo: ANA Menace Growing?" Institute for War and Peace Reporting (hereafter IWPR), *Balkan Crisis Report*, no. 430 (16 May 2003), online at www.iwpr.net.

20. Radio Free Europe/Radio Liberty, *Newsline,* 28 August 2003, online at www.rferl.org.

21. *The Independent* (London), 3 March 2004, online at www.news.independent .co.uk; and *The Economist* (London), 20 March 2004, p. 32. Regarding the Radicals, see *Glas javnosti,* 4 March 2004, online at www.glas-javnosti.co.yu. See also *Politika* (Belgrade), 4 March 2004, online at www.politika.co.yu.

22. *Vjesnik* (Zagreb), 19 March 2004, online at www.vjesnik.hr; and *Slobodna Dalmacija* (Split), 19 March 2004, online at www.slobodnadalmacija.hr.

23. As admitted at the time by Dušan Proroković, a DSS functionary. See *Glas javnosti,* 23 March 2004, online at www.glas-javnosti.co.yu.

24. *Borba* (Belgrade), 26–27 June 1993, p. 6, trans. in Foreign Broadcast Information Service (FBIS), *Daily Report* (Eastern Europe), 19 July 1993, p. 72.

25. Samuel P. Huntington, *Political Order in Changing Society* (New Haven, Conn.: Yale University Press, 1968), chap. 4, esp. pp. 195–97.

26. Vera Didanović, "Purges in the Serbian Judiciary," *AIM Press,* 27 November 2001, online at www.aimpress.ch.

27. Siniša Stanimirović, "Serbia: Corruption Clampdown," IWPR, *Balkan Crisis Report,* no. 315 (6 February 2002), online at www.iwpr.net.

28. Željko Cvijanović, "Serbia Rocked by Seychelles Affair," IWPR, *Balkan Crisis Report,* no. 448 (30 July 2003), online at www.iwpr.net.

29. See, for example, *Glas javnosti,* 29 April 2003, online at www.va.glas-javnosti .co.yu.

30. For further discussion, see Sabrina P. Ramet, *The Three Yugoslavias: The Dual Challenge of State-Building and Legitimation among the Yugoslavs, 1918–2004* (Indiana University Press and the Wilson Center Press, 2006), chap. 17.

31. For details, see Norbert Mappes-Niedliek, *Balkan-Mafia. Staaten in der Hand des Verbrechens—Eine Gefahr für Europa* (Berlin: Ch. Links, 2003).

32. For details, see Ramet, *Balkan Babel,* pp. 167–68, 347.

33. See Jan Briza, "Serbia: Hungarians Pressure Budapest," IWPR, *Balkan Crisis Report,* no. 450 (6 August 2003), online at www.iwpr.net.

34. Siniša Stanimirović, "Poverty and Upheaval Are Driving a Desperate Population Closer to the Edge," IWPR, *Balkan Crisis Report,* no. 344 (20 June 2002), online at www.reliefweb.int/rwb.nsf.

35. *The Independent,* 31 August 2002, online at news.independent.co.uk; and *The Scotsman,* 28 March 2003, online at www.scotsman.com.

36. See Sabrina P. Ramet and Philip W. Lyon, "Discord, Denial, Dysfunction: The Serbia-Montenegro-Kosovo Triangle," *Problems of Post-Communism* 49, no. 5 (September-October 2002), pp. 3–19.

37. See Norman Cigar, *Vojislav Koštunica and Serbia's Future* (London: Saqi Books, in association with the Bosnian Institute, 2001), pp. 10–11, 39, and passim.

38. See Sonja Biserko, "[The] New Serbian Nationalism," *Helsinki Committee for Human Rights in Serbia,* online at www.helsinki.org.yu/ hcs/HCSnewserbian.htm.

39. Hans Kelsen, "Absolutism and Relativism in Philosophy and Politics," *American Political Science Review* 42, no. 5 (October 1948), p. 910.

40. Hans Kelsen, "Sovereignty and International Law," *The Georgetown Law Journal* 48, no. 4 (Summer 1960), reprinted in W. J. Stankiewicz, ed., *In Defense of Sovereignty* (New York: Oxford University Press, 1969). See also W. Michael Riesman, "Sovereignty and Human Rights in Contemporary International Law," *American Journal of International Law* 84, no. 4 (October 1990), esp. pp. 869–70, 872; and W. J. Rees, "The Theory of Sovereignty Restated," in *Mind* 59, no. 236 (October 1950), pp. 495–521.

GLOSSARY

Badinter Commission. A commission appointed by the European Union in 1990 to make recommendations concerning the request for diplomatic recognition filed by Slovenia, Croatia, Bosnia-Herzegovina, and Macedonia and concerning the claim filed by the FRY for a revision of frontiers

BiH. Bosna i Hercegovina, Bosnia-Herzegovina

Borba. A daily newspaper published in Belgrade, Serbia

CEDEM. Center for Democracy and Human Rights, a Montenegrin nongovernmental organization

Chetniks. Serbian nationalist warriors, existing already in the nineteenth century, operating as an illegal paramilitary force tolerated by the Belgrade government during the years 1918–41 and as an anticommunist force during World War Two; resurrected during the War of Yugoslav Succession, 1991–95, to fight for a Greater Serbia

CSCE. Council for Security and Cooperation in Europe, later renamed the Organization for Security and Cooperation in Europe

DCVH. Democratic Community of Vojvodina Hungarians

DEPOS. Demokratski Pokret Srbije (the Democratic Movement of Serbia), an anti-Milošević opposition coalition

Der Spiegel. A weekly magazine published in Hamburg, Germany

DHSS. Demokratska Hrisćanska Stranka Srbije (the Democratic Christian Party of Serbia), a political party led by Vladan Batić

DOS. Demokratska Opozicija Srbije (Democratic Opposition of Serbia), the last of a number of anti-Milošević coalitions, which finally succeeded in taking power in 2000

DM. Deutschmark (German mark), the currency of the Federal Republic of Germany until the introduction of the euro as a common European currency in 2002

DPS. Demokratska Partija Socijalista (Democratic Party of Socialists), a political party led by Momir Bulatović, a prominent politician in Montenegro

DPVH. Democratic Party of Vojvodina Hungarians

DS. Demokratska Stranka (Democratic Party), the political party established and led by Zoran Djindjić, until his death in 2003

DSS. Demokratska Stranka Srbije (Democratic Party of Serbia), the political party established and led by Vojislav Koštunica

DZB. Da živimo bolje (That we might live better), a coalition formed by Milo Djukanović, a prominent politician in Montenegro, in 1998

EPS. Električno Preduzeće Srbije (Electric industry of Serbia)

EU. European Union, a confederal union of European states

FRY. Federal Republic of Yugoslavia, the union of Serbia and Montenegro, 1992–2003

GSS. Gradjanski Savez Srbije (the Civic Alliance of Serbia), a political party led by Vesna Pešić

HDZ. Hrvatska Demokratska Zajednica (Croatian Democratic Community), a Croatian political party established and led by Franjo Tudjman, who served as president of Croatia 1990–99

ICC. International Criminal Court

ICTR. International Criminal Tribunal for Rwanda (based in Arusha)

ICTY. International Criminal Tribunal for the former Yugoslavia (based in The Hague)

JAT. Jugoslovenski Aerotransport (Yugoslav Air Transport), the Yugoslav/Serbian airline

JNA. Jugoslovenska Narodna Armija (Yugoslav People's Army), the official name of the army of the SFRY

JSO. Jedinice za Specijalne Operacije (Units for Special Operations), militarized units tied to organized crime, known colloquially as the "Red Berets" and commanded by "Frenki" Simatović

JUL. Jugoslovenska Udružena Levica (the Yugoslav United Left), the political party led by Mirjana Marković, Slobodan Milošević's wife

KFOR. Kosovo International Security Force

KLA. Kosovo Liberation Army, the Albanian resistance force which fought the Belgrade regime during the years 1997–99

Krajina. Formerly Vojna Krajina; literally, "the Frontier" (formerly "Military Frontier"), the area of Croatia historically with a large Serbian population which claimed the right to self-rule in 1990

KVM. Kosovo Verification Mission, headed by William Walker

LCM. League of Communists of Montenegro

LCS. League of Communists of Serbia

LCY. League of Communists of Yugoslavia

LDK. Lidhja Demokratike e Kosovës (the Democratic League of Kosova), a political party established and led by Ibrahim Rugova

LSCG. Liberalna Stranka Crne Gore (the Liberal Party of Montenegro), a Montenegrin political party

LSV. League of Social-Democrats of Vojvodina

MUP. Ministarstvo Unutrašnjih Poslova (Ministry of Internal Affairs)

NATO. North Atlantic Treaty Organization

NGO. Nongovernmental organization, used to refer to charitable, human rights, environmental, and pacifist groups; not used to refer to such nongovernmental organizations as Churches or ethnic associations or labor unions

NIN. Nedjeljne informativne novine (Weekly Informational News), a weekly news magazine published in Belgrade, Serbia

NS. Narodna Stranka (People's Party), a Montenegrin political party led by Dragan Šoć

NS. Nova Srbija (New Serbia), a Serbian political party led by Velimir Ilić

NSS. Narodna Socijalistička Stranka (People's Socialist Party), a Montenegrin political party led by Božidar Bojović

NUNS. Nezavisno Udruženje Novinara Srbije (Independent Association of Journalists of Serbia)

ODIHR. Office for Democratic Institutions and Human Rights

OSCE. Organization for Security and Cooperation in Europe; formerly the Council for Security and Cooperation in Europe

OTP. Office of the Prosecutor

Otpor. Literally, "Resistance," a student opposition group that staged anti-Milošević demonstrations

Politika. A daily newspaper published in Belgrade, Serbia

Red Berets. *See* JSO

Republika Srpska (RS). Serbian Republic (the Serbian portion of post-Dayton Bosnia-Herzegovina, with its capital at Banja Luka, not to be confused with the Republic of Serbia, which has its capital in Belgrade)

RS. *See* Republika Srpska

RTS. Radio-Televizija Srbije (Radio-Television Serbia)

SAA. Stabilization and Association Agreement, an agreement between the European Union and the FRY

SANU. Srpska Akademija Nauka i Umetnosti (Serbian Academy of Sciences and Arts)

SDA. Stranka Demokratske Akcije (Party for Democratic Action), a Bosnian political party led by Alija Izetbegović

SDB. Služba Državne Bezbednosti (State Security Service), Belgrade's internal security police

SDP. Socijalna Demokratska Partija (Social Democratic Party), a Montenegrin political party

SFOR. Stabilization Force, the military detachment mandated by NATO to monitor compliance, within Bosnia-Herzegovina, with the terms of the Dayton Peace Accords

SFRY. Socialist Federated Republic of Yugoslavia, which died in 1991

SiCG. Srbija i Crna Gora (Serbia and Montenegro)

Skupština. Assembly or parliament

SNP. Socijalistička Narodna Partija (Socialist People's Party), a political party established by Momir Bulatović in 1998. *See also* DPS

SPO. Srpski Pokret Obnove (Serbian Renewal Movement), the political party led by Vuk Drašković

SPS. Socialistička Partija Srbije (Socialist Party of Serbia), the political party led by Slobodan Milošević

SRS. Srpska Radikalna Stranka (Serbian Radical Party), the political party led by Vojislav Šešelj until his remanding to The Hague, and since then by Tomislav Nikolić

SSJ. Stranka Srpskog Jedinstva (Party of Serbian Unity), the political party established and led by Zoran Ražnatović until his death, and since then by Borislav Pelević

TO. Teritorijalna Obrana (Territorial Defense), the official citizens' militia

UÇK. *See* KLA

UNMIK. United Nations Mission in Kosovo

UVH. Union of Vojvodina Hungarians

Večernje novosti. Literally, "The Evening News," a daily newspaper published in Belgrade, Serbia

Victory for Montenegro. A pro-independence coalition formed by Milo Djukanović, then president of Montenegro, in 2001

Vijesti. Literally, "The News," a daily newspaper published in Montenegro

VJ. Vojska Jugoslavije (the Army of Yugoslavia), the official name of the army of the FRY

Vreme. Literally, "Time," a weekly news magazine published in Belgrade, Serbia

Zajedno. Literally, "Together," an anti-Milošević opposition coalition

CONTRIBUTORS

BILJANA BIJELIĆ (born in Karlovac, Croatia) is an activist in several women's and human rights organizations in Croatia. Currently she is working toward her Ph.D. in history at the University of Toronto. In 2000, she was a recipient of a Ron Brown Fellowship sponsored by the U.S. Department of State.

ERIC D. GORDY was born in Seattle, Washington (U.S.A.). Since receiving his doctorate in sociology from the University of California, Berkeley, in 1997, he has been a member of the faculty of Clark University in Worcester, Massachusetts, where he is currently Associate Professor of Sociology. He is the author of *The Culture of Power in Serbia: Nationalism and the Destruction of Alternatives* (Penn State University Press, 1999), as well as a contributor to journals such as *Balkanologie, Problems of Post-Communism, Human Rights Review,* and *Southeast European Politics.*

JAMES GOW is Director of the International Peace and Security Programme at King's College London. He is the author of *Triumph of the Lack of Will: International Diplomacy and the Yugoslav War* (1997), *The Serbian Project and Its Adversaries: A Strategy of War Crimes* (2003), and other books, and coeditor of *Bosnia by Television* (1996). From 1994 to 1998, he was an expert adviser to the Office of the Prosecutor at the UN International Criminal Tribunal for the former Yugoslavia. He is currently researching war and war crimes, media, and security, and writing a book with Milena Michalski on viewing contemporary conflict.

MARKO ATTILA HOARE is a British Academy Research Fellow and member of the Faculty of History at the University of Cambridge. He was born in London and received his Ph.D. from Yale University in 2000. He has been studying the history of Yugoslavia and its successor states for the past ten years and has an intimate knowledge of Serbia and its people, having lived in Belgrade between 1998 and 2001. Following that, he worked as a Research Officer at the International Criminal Tribunal for the Former

Yugoslavia. His first book, *How Bosnia Armed* (London: Saqi, 2004), examines the birth of the Bosnian army and its political and structural evolution during the war in Bosnia-Herzegovina of 1992–95. He is currently working on two book projects: a history of the Partisan movement in Bosnia-Herzegovina during World War Two, and a study of the emergence of the Bosnian identity and its relationship to the Muslim, Serb, and Croat national movements. He is the author of numerous published academic articles which have appeared in such journals as *Journal of Genocide Research, Journal of Slavic Military Studies, Nationalism and Ethnic Politics,* and *East European Quarterly.* He is a regular contributor to the *South Slav Journal* and to *Bosnia Report.*

EMIL KERENJI (born in Novi Sad, Serbia) holds an M.A. in history from the Central European University, Budapest, and is currently a Ph.D. candidate in the Department of History, University of Michigan.

OBRAD KESIĆ (born in Smederevo, Serbia) is a senior partner with TSM Global Consultants LLC, a Washington, D.C., firm providing business consulting services and government affairs representation to American companies interested in doing business with Russia, Eastern Europe, and the Balkans. TSM also offers the same services to international companies interested in doing business with the United States. Kesić has enjoyed a successful and wide-ranging career in international relations. From 1991 to 1998, he worked with the International Research and Exchanges Board in Washington, D.C.; from 1998 to August 1999, he was the representative in Washington for the Alliance for Change, the largest democratic opposition coalition in Serbia; and in 1999 he traveled to Yugoslavia with Jesse Jackson's Rainbow Push Coalition to assist negotiations for the release of three U.S. prisoners of war held by the Yugoslav army. The group was successful in negotiating for their release, and Kesić received the Rainbow Coalition/Operation Push Peace Award for his assistance in this successful mission. Kesić earned a master's degree in international relations from Old Dominion University in Virginia, and contributed a chapter to *Gender Politics in the Western Balkans: Women and Society in Yugoslavia and the Yugoslav Successor States* (Penn State University Press, 1999), edited by Sabrina P. Ramet. His articles have appeared in *Problems of Post-Communism, Mediterranean Quarterly,* and other journals.

RENEO LUKIĆ (born in Požega, Croatia) is Professor of History at Laval University, Quebec, Canada. He is the author of *The Wars of South Slavic*

Succession: Yugoslavia 1991–1993 (Graduate Institute of International Affairs, Geneva, 1993) and *L'Agonie Yougoslave (1986–2003)* (Les Presses de l'Université Laval, 2003), and coauthor (with Allen Lynch) of *Europe from the Balkans to the Urals: The Disintegration of Yugoslavia and the Soviet Union* (Oxford University Press, 1996). He is also coeditor (with Michael Brint) of *Culture, Politics, and Nationalism in the Age of Globalization* (Ashgate, 2001), and has contributed articles to *Nationalities Papers, Acta Slavica Iaponica,* and other journals.

MILENA MICHALSKI teaches and researches Russian and Soviet film at University College London. She is the author of a number of articles on Russian literature. Michalski edited and translated *The Akhmatova Journals, 1938–1941* (1994) and is currently working on a study of the representation of young people in the Soviet films of the Stalin period. In addition to researching and writing on Russian and Soviet film, she has also published on Yugoslav film, and has worked for the British Film Institute, most recently researching and writing on TV news content for the *After September 11: TV News and Multicultural Audiences* study. She is currently collaborating with James Gow on viewing contemporary conflict.

MAJA MILJKOVIĆ (born in Belgrade, Yugoslavia) earned her B.A. in history at the University of Belgrade in 1994, with a dissertation on "The Newspaper *Politika* and South Serbia." Her main field of research is the social and cultural history of Europe, with a special focus on southeast Europe in nineteenth- and twentieth-century Europe. She has been Research Assistant at the Institute of Contemporary History since 1996 and member of the subcommittee and lecturer of the Centre for International Studies and the Faculty of History at the University of Cambridge since October 2002. She is coauthor of *Mostar* (Belgrade, 2001), which deals with the cultural and political history of Serbs in this old Bosnian town. Her articles have appeared in *Istorija 20 veka, South Slav Journal, Glasnik INI,* and elsewhere.

KARI M. OSLAND (born in Bergen, Norway) is a political scientist from the University of Bergen and has been working as a researcher at the Norwegian Institute of International Affairs (NUPI) since 1998. Osland is also head of the UN Programme at the Department of International Politics at NUPI. She is the author of *Genocide: A Process-Theoretical Approach Applied on the Cases of Bosnia and Hercegovina and Rwanda* (University of Bergen Press, 2000), and coauthor (with Tor T. Holm) of *Regional*

Civilian Police Training in South Eastern Europe: The Stability Pact (NUPI, 2000). She is also editor of *Sørpolitikkens plass i et utenrikspolitisk hel-hetsperspektiv* (NUPI, 2000), and has contributed articles to several journals and books, among them *En annerledes supermakt? Sikkerhets og forsavrspolitikken i EU*, edited by Pernille Rieker and Ståle Ulriksen (NUPI, 2003), and *Bridging the Accountability Gap in the EU*, edited by Ståle Ulriksen and Giovanna Bono (special issue of *The Journal of International Peacekeeping*, 2004).

VJERAN PAVLAKOVIĆ (born in Zagreb, Croatia) is a Ph.D. candidate in the Department of History, University of Washington. He is coauthor (with Sabrina Ramet and Philip Lyon) of *Sovereign Law vs. Sovereign Nation: The Cases of Kosovo and Montenegro* (a publication of The Trondheim Studies on East European Cultures & Societies, no. 11, Trondheim: PEECS, NTNU, October 2002). He is also editor of (and contributor to) *Nationalism, Culture, and Religion in Croatia since 1990* (a publication of The Donald W. Treadgold Papers in Russian, East European, and Central Asian Studies, no. 32, Seattle: The HMJ School of International Studies Russian and East European Studies Program, November 2001). His articles have also appeared in *Human Rights Review* and *Modern Greek Studies Yearbook*. During 2002–4, he was a Fulbright fellow at the University of Zagreb, Croatia, where he conducted research on Yugoslav volunteers in the Spanish Civil War.

SABRINA P. RAMET (born in London, England) is a Professor of Political Science at the Norwegian University of Science and Technology (NTNU), Trondheim, Norway, a member of the Royal Norwegian Society of Sciences and Letters, and a Research Associate of the Science and Research Center of the Republic of Slovenia, Koper. She is the author of seven books—among them, *Balkan Babel: The Disintegration of Yugoslavia from the Death of Tito to the Fall of Milošević*, 4th ed. (Westview Press, 2002)—and editor or coeditor of more than a dozen books. She studied philosophy at Stanford University and subsequently received her Ph.D. in political science from UCLA; she taught at the University of California at Santa Barbara, UCLA, the University of Washington, and Ritsumeikan University in Kyoto, Japan, before moving to Norway in 2001. Her book *Whose Democracy? Nationalism, Religion, and the Doctrine of Collective Rights in Post-1989 Eastern Europe* (Rowman and Littlefield, 1997), was named an Outstanding Academic Book by *Choice* magazine. Her articles have appeared in *Foreign Affairs, World Politics, Problems of Post-Communism,* and other journals.

DENNIS REINHARTZ was born in Irvington, New Jersey, and received his Ph.D. in history from New York University. He is Professor of History and Russian at the University of Texas at Arlington. He is the author of *Milovan Djilas: A Revolutionary as a Writer,* numerous book chapters, and articles appearing in *Journal of Genocide Research, Genocide Studies, The South Slav Journal,* and *Social Science Journal,* among others. He has been a consultant to the United States Departments of Justice and State, and the Commission of Enquiry into the Activities of Naziism in Argentina, and serves as a consultant to the United States Holocaust Memorial Museum. He is also the past president of the Western Social Science Association, Rocky Mountain Association for Slavic Studies, and the Southwestern Association for Slavic Studies.

FRANCES TRIX (born in Bellefont, Pennsylvania) is a linguistic anthropologist who received her doctorate in linguistics from the University of Michigan in 1988. She is currently an Associate Professor of Anthropology at Wayne State University in Detroit, Michigan. She is also a Research Associate at the Center for East European and Russian Studies at the University of Michigan. Her research has focused on discourse analysis of face-to-face interaction, with special interests in transmission of spiritual knowledge, Islam in the Balkans, gender in the workplace, and the place of religion in ethnic diaspora communities. Her books include *Spiritual Discourse: Learning with an Islamic Master* (University of Pennsylvania Press, 1993) and *Albanians in Michigan: A Proud People of Southeast Europe* (Michigan State University Press, 2001). She is currently working on a biography of Baba Rexheb, the major Bektashi leader of the twentieth century. She has also published articles in *American Anthropologist, Discourse & Society, Slavic and East European Information Resources, The International Journal of Middle Eastern Studies,* and other journals. Besides research on ethnic communities in the United States, Trix has had IREX fellowships for research in the former Yugoslavia and in Albania. She has an ongoing interest in discourse research in Turkish, Arabic, and Albanian. Recent awards include the President's Award for Excellence in Teaching and the Distinguished Faculty Honors Convocation Award.

INDEX